America Reflected:
Language, Satire, Film, and the National Mind

Also by New Academia Publishing

Cinema

MOSCOW BELIEVES IN TEARS: Russians and Their Movies, by Louis Menashe

SCIENCE FICTION EXPERIENCES, by Angela Ndalianis

HERETICAL EMPIRICISM, by Pier Paolo Pasolini

PIER PAOLO PASOLINI: In Living Memory, Ben Lawton and Maura Bergonzoni, eds.

EVERY STEP A STRUGGLE: Interviews with Seven Who Shaped the African-American Image in Movies, by Frank Manchel

IMAGING RUSSIA 2000: Film and Facts, by Anna Lawton

BEFORE THE FALL: Soviet Cinema in the Gorbachev Years, by Anna Lawton

Popular Culture/ Visual Culture

PASSION AND PERCEPTION : Essays in Russian Cullture, by Richard Stites

RUSSIAN FUTURISM: A History, by Vladimir Markov

WORDS IN REVOLUTION: Russian Futurist Manifestoes 1912-1928 A. Lawton and H. Eagle, eds., trs.

SHOPPING FOR JESUS: Faith in Marketing in the USA, Dominic Janes, ed.

SUPER/HEROES: From Hercules to Superman, Wendy Haslem, Angela Ndalianis, and Chris Mackie, eds.

WE'RE FROM JAZZ: Festschrift in Honor of Nicholas V. Galichenko, Megan Swift and Serhy Yekelchyk, eds.

TERROR ON THE SCREEN: Witnesses and the Reanimation of Terrorism as Image Event, Popular Culture and Pornography, by Luke Howie

REMEMBERING UTOPIA: The Culture of Everyday Life in Socialist Yugoslavia, Breda Luthar and Maruša Pušnik, eds.

VISUAL CULTURE IN SHANGHAI, 1850s-1930s, Jason Kuo, ed.

See excerpts at: www.newacademia.com

America Reflected:
Language, Satire, Film, and the National Mind

by Peter C. Rollins

New Academia Publishing
Washington, DC

Copyright © 2010 by Peter C. Rollins

New Academia Publishing, 2010

All rights reserved. No part of this book may be reproduced or transmitted in any form or by any means, electronic or mechanical, including photocopying, recording, or by any information storage and retrieval system.

Printed in the United States of America

Library of Congress Control Number: 2010930183
ISBN 978-0-9844062-5-8 paperback (alk. paper)
ISBN 978-0-9844062-6-5 hardcover (alk. paper)

New Academia Publishing, LLC
P.O. Box 27420
Washington, DC 20038-7420
www.newacademia.com - info@newacademia.com

*To Ray and Pat Browne,
who encouraged us to find
America and ourselves.*

Contents

Foreword   xi
Preface   xiii
Acknowledgments   xix

Introduction   1

Part I America Reflected in Language, Satire, and Film   25

Will Rogers' Popular Culture   27

1. The Evolving Persona of Will Rogers: Symbolic Man, Journalist, and Film Image   29
2. Will Rogers and *The Saturday Evening Post*: Kindred Spirits?   69
3. The Context and Rhetorical Strategy of Will Rogers' *Letters of a Self-Made Diplomat to His President* (1926)   87
4. Will Rogers on Aviation: A Means of Fostering Frontier Values in an Age of Machines and Bunk?   105
5. Regional Literature and Will Rogers: Film Redeems a Literary Form   125
6. The Making of *Will Rogers' 1920s: A Cowboy's Guide to the Times*: An Experiment in Historian Filmmaking   147

Benjamin Whorf on the Native American vs. Western Languages/Cultures   157

7. Benjamin Lee Whorf: Transcendental Linguist   159
8. The Sapir-Whorf Relationship Reconsidered   189
9. The Whorf Hypothesis as a Critique of Western Science and Technology   211

Part II   America's Wars: Film Images and Historical Realities   229

World War I   231

10. Memories of War: Was World War I a Heroic Crusade or a Traumatic Nightmare?   233
11. Parallels or Continuities in Two Historical Compilation Films: *Goodbye Billy* and *The Frozen War*   251

World War II   277

12. Frank Capra's *Why We Fight* Series and Our American Dream   279
13. Remembering D-Day: Perspective from the Fiftieth Anniversary   299
14. *Storm of Fire*: Reflections on Cadre Films and the Historian as Filmmaker   311

Cold War   325

15. *Victory at Sea*: Cold War Epic   327
16. *Nightmare in Red*: A Cold War View of the Communist Revolution   351

Vietnam   379

17. Using Popular Culture to Study the Vietnam War: Perils and Possibilities   381

18. *Television's Vietnam: The Impact of Visual Images*   407
19. Press History Repeating Itself as Farce?: Critical Responses to *Television's Vietnam: The Real Story* (1985)   435
20. Behind the Westmoreland Trial of 1984: What Was so Wrong with the CBS Program, *The Uncounted Enemy* (1982)   455
21. The Uncounted Expert: George Carver's Views on Intelligence "Deception" Reported by CBS in *The Uncounted Enemy: A Vietnam Deception* (1982)   487
22. Neil Sheehan's *Bright Shining Lie*: The Story of John Paul Vann or of America's New Media Elite?   511
23. *Dear America* (HBO 1988): Oral History as Interpretation of the Vietnam Experience?   543
24. Para dismentir "television's vietnam": Los motivos de un Documentarista   553
25. Teaching International Politics: What the Historian-Filmmaker Has to Offer   569

Part III American Cultural Figures, Movements, Classics   581

26. *Uncle Tom's Cabin* (1852): Harriet Beecher Stowe's Declaration of Independence from Calvinism   583
27. Frederick Henry Hedge: Brookline's Conservative Transcendentalist   619
28. Amy Lowell of Brookline: The Patterns of a Life   635
29. John James Audubon: The "American Woodsman"?   657
30. Ideology and Film Rhetoric: Three Documentaries of the New Deal Era (1936-1941)   679
31. *Tulsa* (1949) as an Oil Field Film: A Study of Ecological Ambivalence   699

Photo credits   713
Index   720

Foreword
by Michael T. Marsden

It is undeniable that popular culture has emerged world-wide as a legitimate field of study. But certainly that was not the case when I entered graduate school more than four decades ago. Nor was it so when Peter Rollins returned from the battleground of Vietnam to complete his graduate work.

This volume presents selections from a lifetime of Peter's work in the fields of Popular Culture and American Culture Studies. It clearly demonstrates the impressive scope of his scholarly embrace from Will Rogers and Benjamin Whorf to studies of the history of wars and their depictions on film from World War I to Vietnam. But Peter has also continued throughout his career to examine the cultural significance of major American personalities from Harriet Beecher Stowe to John James Audubon.

This volume, then, pays witness to an ever active mind searching through the artifacts of the American experience in order to make sense of them. The scholarly work that Peter has done in film and history is well known and well respected. With his dozens of books, hundreds of articles, films, television programs and CDs, Peter has reached out to the general public as well as to the scholarly community with his insights.

Very early in his career Peter was not content to work only within the confines of his classroom and study, or even only within his professional organizations for that matter. He chose instead to pursue the role of what we refer to as the "public intellectual," seeking every opportunity to bridge the academic world and the world of public discourse on topics of major importance. Whether it was a focus on the significance of Will Rogers or new insights into the Vietnam conflict, Peter sought to enlighten and inform. As a consequence of this reaching out, his scholarly work found audiences both within the academy and among the several publics who attend to media outlets such as Public Broadcasting, the Discovery Channel, and C-SPAN. For Peter there is no bridge too far, no matter what the effort, if the result is sharing new knowledge.

Peter's untiring work on behalf of the Popular Culture Association and the American Culture Association from their foundings to the present is noteworthy. Whether it was his organizational work for hosting the national PCA/ACA Meeting in Wichita, for the many Southwest Texas PCA/ACA Conferences, or for the PCA/ACA Meetings in Mexico, Peter's efforts were everywhere noted and appreciated. Peter was also the founder and co-moderator of the H-PCA/ACA internet discussion list at a point in the organizations' history when the transition to computer based communication was essential to the long term well being of the organizations. Peter was also there when the late Ray Browne and others wanted to start an endowment for the organizations, the results of which have subsequently supported many graduate students and young faculty members in their scholarly work.

On yet another level, Peter has been a gracious mentor to many young scholars across the country who have sought and received his wise counsel. A distinguished faculty member at Oklahoma State University, Peter has reached out to those who needed assistance from across the country in the same gracious manner and spirit exhibited to him and to me by the late Russel Nye and the late Ray Browne when Peter and I were finding our way in the scholarly world.

This volume is but a glimpse into the life's work of a scholar who may live and work in Oklahoma, but whose scholarly reach knows no state or national borders. Peter has received many awards and recognitions for his work over the years. But his real reward is to be found precisely where Russel Nye's and Ray Browne's rewards are to be found in the lives and work of the generations of young scholars they and he have encouraged and supported through the years.

Michael T. Marsden is Dean of the College and Academic Vice President and Professor of English, American Studies, and Media Studies at St. Norbert College. He is also Co-Executive Editor of the *Journal of Popular Film and Television*.

Preface

As one of my mentors, Alan Heimert, characterized the scholarly method, the goal was to determine not only what was *said* but what was *meant*. His understanding became part of my scholarly radar in the 1960s, and I have applied it ever since:

> To discover the meaning of an utterance demands what is in substance a continuing act of literary interpretation for the language with which an idea is presented, and the imaginative universe by which it is surrounded, often tells us more of the author's meaning and intention than his declarative propositions. An understanding of the significance of any idea, or of a constellation of ideas, requires an awareness of the context of institutions and events out of which thought emerged, and with which it strove to come to terms. But the full apprehension depends finally on reading, not between the lines but, as it were, through and beyond them. (Heimert 11)

Because the chapters of *America Reflected* involve so much personal interpretation, it seems desirable to assist the reader by offering some background information at the outset, giving some exposure to the mindset of this particular cultural historian.

The Brookline Influence

After service in World War II as a Marine officer, my father resumed participation in the political scene of Brookline, Massachusetts—an independent suburb of Boston since 1705—in the tradition of his father, who had been a judge in the municipal court for decades.

Captain Daniel G. Rollins, 1945

Grandfather, who was a Theodore Roosevelt Republican, iterated and reiterated to us the maxim of *mens sana in corpore sano*, echoing his political hero's belief in the necessity of a "strenuous life," while Father, by taking us to concerts at Boston's famous Symphony Hall, showed us that a real man also should be interested in the arts—even avant-gardism (which to him meant Stravinsky, Le Six, and early 20th-century composers of the French school). On the political front, Dad brought me along to multiple evenings of Brookline's town meetings where I observed him in a professional role: he led the singing of the national anthem at the opening of each evening session; as the Town Counsel (i.e., the municipal lawyer), he rendered real-time judgments on procedure and any legislative motions proposed by the assembled 100-plus elected representatives. These events—amplified by daily telephone calls from agencies and interested parties and occasional hand delivery of confidential documents by uniformed Brookline policemen—gave me an insider's perspective on governmental affairs. I learned that politics required decisive leadership, often by an elite with the best interests of the polity in mind. And certainly one of the fundamental lessons was that public servants more often attempt to do what is right than to garner benefits from the perquisites of office—although there were some lagniappes which were enjoyed. How decisions and political images played out in the press was a regular topic of discussion at home (see Chapter 24 and interview with Wilson of *Americana*).

In the process of preparing four book reports during the spring break of freshman year (1956) at Brookline High School, I discovered that intellectual pursuits propelled the mind across space and time, and that such explorations were enormously stimulating. Creative writing and the history classes at BHS opened up vistas of intellectual growth and *Atlantic Monthly* prizes for poetry and fiction reinforced the lessons of closely-supervised writing experiences.

The Dartmouth Opportunity

Then on to Dartmouth College in a Rollins tradition since the 1820s. Grandfather and father reflexively referred to "the sacred soil of Dartmouth College" and even casual visitors to the Dartmouth Green are impressed by The Rollins Chapel—a martial, Romanesque building designed in the 1880s style of H.H. Richardson, the architect of Boston's Trinity Church where father and the three Rollins brothers sang in the choir. Alas, as an English major at Dartmouth, I was very unhappy with the narrow perspective of

The Rollins Chapel: Vox Clamantis in Deserto

the "New Criticism" approach to literature embraced by many in the department and attempted to enrich literary studies with music and history classes—when not distracted by irksome "distribution courses." As I later learned from mentors who shared Alan Heimert's vision, New Criticism's emphasis on paying attention to the text alone impoverished and "dehumanized" that text by seeking to suppress the author who wrote it. At the end of the sophomore year, I found myself unmotivated to continue marching to the Big Green's drummer. During a student break, a Brookline High classmate who was studying at Harvard introduced me to the school's Widener Library, where he had his own carrel (shared with others, but still a carrel). He was effusive about his experiences in the History and Literature (honors) Program—which combined both disciplines in a way that linked art to life—and "made the sale." After much soul searching and hesitation about turning my back on the family alma mater, I transferred to the Cambridge, Massachusetts, school some five miles from Brookline and joined an interdisciplinary program started in 1906 by Barrett Wendell (1855-1921), biographer of the Rev. Cotton Mather (1663-1728).

The History and Literature Approach

The History and Literature Program's mission was to urge honors students to connect cultural/political texts to their contexts—from the Puritans to the (then present) Cold War. As an undergraduate in

Perry Miller, Model Scholar of "the American Mind"

the shadow of such teachers as Perry Miller (Puritans and romantics), Donald Fleming (intellectual history), Louis Hartz (political thought), Conrad Wright (religion), Alan Heimert (American culture) this pursuit was aerobic for mind and spirit. After earning my bachelor's degree and serving a challenging tour with the Marine Corps as an infantry officer (1963-66), I returned to Harvard to study for a Ph.D. in The History of American Civilization—what is called "American Studies" in schools where the programs were formed after World War II. In all phases of this scholarly training, I was prodded to interpret how works of nonfiction and fiction; paintings and architecture; and popular culture and motion pictures—either singly or in concert—reflected and impacted the America imago.

During the graduate years from 1966-1972, nearly everybody was reconsidering the meaning of America in an atmosphere which gave a special piquancy to the "continuing act of literary interpretation" urged by Heimert.

The Introduction which follows will bring this experience and method to bear on the chapters of *America Reflected: Language, Satire, Film, and the National Mind*.

Peter C. Rollins, Stillwater, Oklahoma

Works Cited

Heimert, Alan. *Religion and the American Mind: From the Great Awakening to the Revolution*. Cambridge, MA: Harvard UP, 1966.

Wilson, Leslie. "Conversations with Scholars of American Popular Culture: Featured Guest, Professor Peter C. Rollins." *Americana: The Journal of American Popular Culture, 1900 to Present. www.americanpopularculture.com/home.htm* and, in book form, as *14 Conversations with Scholars of American Popular Culture*. Los Angeles: Press Americana, 2006.

Acknowledgments

Oklahoma State University and its library provided me with an inspiring workbench. A series of supportive department heads held my reins loosely and supported nontraditional projects over a thirty-seven year career. I am particularly grateful for a succession of Humanities librarians who helped me and my students with an enthusiasm that made up for gaps in the collection. As one of them, Terry Basford, explained to a graduate class, the interlibrary loan service was like the Colt .45 for the cowboy West: it made everybody equal. The trick was to stay at the task and to be productive. Electronic developments have only made their tool box more comprehensive, but I still rely on the librarians themselves when I am stumped—which is often.

Ray and Pat Browne, founders of the Popular Press and devoted leaders of the popular culture movement, did all within their powers to advise and to exhort thousands of us to keep looking for America reflected in areas so often ignored by Academe prior to the 1960s—especially in media, popular fiction, and material culture.

The Will Rogers Memorial in Claremore has been a constant source of inspiration. From the first day I set foot on the property in 1972, I have received enthusiastic support. There are many more articles, books, and films to be written about Will Rogers and I hope others will tap this indispensable resource supported by the State of Oklahoma. Steve Gragert, the current director, is a knowledgeable guide to the collection and always has been ready to work with serious researchers.

In the late 1960s, Mrs. Celia Peckham Whorf invited me into her home on a number of occasions where she shared her personal knowledge of the more metaphysically ambitious half of the

"Sapir-Whorf hypothesis." No researcher could be more grateful for the generosity shown by Mrs. Whorf, especially her sharing of unpublished manuscripts.

Work in film was encouraged and fostered by John E. O'Connor of *Film & History: An Interdisciplinary Journal of Film and Television Studies*. The Vietnam era in academe was a frosty one for this veteran; although John as citizen was adamantly against the war, he welcomed my ideas, even when he disagreed with them. Over the years, I have striven to reciprocate his generosity.

It would be difficult to exaggerate the importance of my Marine Corps years. It was truly a "hands on" experience with the realities of history—or at least one set of them. While I was across the globe in a distant land, America fragmented. As a scholar, I have sought to gather the shards I found on my return, fusing together their slivered reflections of identities and ideologies into a picture that is richer and more meaningful than the whole of its sometimes jagged, diverse parts—a stained glass vision of hope and faith that echoes my admiration for the Oliver LaFarge windows at Boston's Trinity Church. In 2010, the Marine Corps Memorial and Museum in Quantico, Virginia, will include a brick in its Walk of Honor. Maneuvering within the terse limitations on text, the brick will read: "ROLLINS. Daniel G., Dan. Jr., Peter C. WWII, Korea, Vietnam" in a dedication which celebrates family, corps, and country.

It would be impossible to thank everyone who provided intellectual inspiration, but those teaching in the undergraduate History and Literature Program at Harvard and, later, in the History of American Civilization graduate program gave me inspired academic training. As for my awareness of standards, all graduates from the "Am. Civ." program in my era are constantly signaled by a "Perry Miller satellite" circling the earth in geosynchronous orbit, telling us to work harder, to work smarter, and to remember that Jonathan Edwards was the greatest mind America ever produced—despite his many detractors and misleading anthologizers. God bless Perry Miller and his industrious disciples who have studied the American Mind!

Beginning in 1997, Deborah Carmichael became a worthy colleague and friend. We toiled endless hours together. The professionalism she brought to the journal *Film & History* has carried over into her current performance as managing editor of *The Journal of Popular Culture*. In more recent days, this collection of essays was enhanced by the computer skills and dedication of Debbie Olson. Dr. Leslie Fife devoted considerable time and talent to shaping the text for publication. In all these instances, it has been a joy to see former students evolve into productive, scholarly peers.

Susan Rollins has been a steadfast companion and helper for the last two decades and, by her watchful supervision of the medical regimen, has kept me alive for the last eight of them. I am most grateful for her caring help and want to be one of the first to thank her for creating a cadre of docent "Ropers" at the Will Rogers Memorial. No one could have predicted such an important contribution to the cultural life of our State, but we are all grateful!

A number of these chapters first appeared in scholarly journals and general reader publications, only some of which are accessible — even in the day of the Internet. Ray Browne, as Editor of the *Journal of Popular Culture* and the *Journal of American Culture*, published early versions of Chapters 1, 7, 12, 16, 19. The *American Quarterly* graciously published Chapters 9, 18. Always supportive of Will Rogers and film scholarship, the *Chronicles of Oklahoma* published Chapters 2, 3, 4, 32. John O'Connor of *Film & History* cheerfully carried Chapters 6, 14, 31. *The World and I* commissioned journalistic efforts that were the starting points for Chapters 10, 13, 15. Chapter 5 first appeared in the *Literature/Film Quarterly*. Last, but not least, the *Proceedings of the Brookline Historical Society* carried early talking papers expanded into Chapters 28 and 29. Chapter 8 began as a slide show for the Mid-America Linguistics Association and was published in its *Proceedings*. Special issues of the *Journal of the Vietnam Veterans Institute* carried early versions of Chapters 21, 22, 23. Many thanks to these publications for the opportunity to put them under one editorial roof. John Deveny contributed his Spanish language expertise to Chapter 24.

Like the chapters of this collection, its photographs have accumulated over the last forty years after visits to the Library of Congress; the U.S. Archives; the Marine Corps Historical Center; the Sherman

Grinberg Film Libraries; the Houghton Library; the Academy of Motion Picture Arts and Sciences Library; the Museum of Broadcasting; the Vietnam Archive at Texas Tech University; the Vietnam Archive, LaSalle University; the UCLA Film and Television Archive; the archives of ABC, CBS, NBC, and PBS; the LBJ Presidential Library; the JFK Presidential Library; the Harry S. Truman Presidential Library; the Film Archive; the Bartlett Art Library; the Cadre Films Archive; the Center for the Study of Film and History Archive. Many thanks to these institutions for their support and encouragement.

Introduction

Peter C. Rollins

First as student and then as scholar, I found myself drawn to Orestes Brownson, Benjamin Lee Whorf, Will Rogers, and Hollywood's motion pictures. Does such a diverse list suggest a fickle heart? Before you draw that conclusion, let me tell what I have found them to have in common. All show an acute consciousness of American values, reflecting them in creative ways that can deepen our awareness of their times. Will Rogers did this in syndicated weekly and daily newspaper articles as well as in more than seventy motion pictures. Benjamin Whorf, whose "linguistic relativity hypothesis" stemmed from his studies of Native American languages, stepped outside his time, hoping to share an Emersonian vision of human harmony with self, society, and Nature. Audubon, Stowe, and Brownson all wrestled in unique ways with the political and spiritual aspirations of their day while Brookline's Frederick Henry Hedge and Amy Lowell evinced mind-sets cultivated by a privileged Boston suburb. And, of course, the movie culture has constantly influenced and reflected American values and visions—as much now as ever. Wars are constantly with us and so are war films, often shaping and reflecting national mood swings. These journalists, artists, philosophers, and genre influences are the focal points for *America Reflected: Language, Satire, Film, and the National Mind*, a selection of my scholarly efforts over the last forty years.

America Reflected: Beginning with Brownson

My initiation to cultural studies began with an undergraduate honors thesis devoted to Orestes Augustus Brownson (1803-1876). Brownson seemed like a productive choice because he had been committed to so many different movements and publications from

Orestes A. Brownson (1803-1876)

the 1820s through the 1870s: he was more than just a social activist and prominent democratic spokesman; he was also a philosopher for whom epistemology and faith were paramount. *Orestes A. Brownson: Epistemology of a Crucified Redeemer* explored the relationships among the following elements: political activism for a just society, epistemological investigation of *how* we know, and a search for faith in an era of "isms." Brownson sought salvation through service as a public intellectual. Like John Bunyan's allegorical Pilgrim, he trudged from movement to movement, ultimately losing faith in the *demos* after the "hard cider" presidential campaign of 1840 — it was won by the Whig, William Henry Harrison, rather than the incumbent democrat, Martin Van Buren. After a few years of wandering in a spiritual wasteland, Brownson embraced Catholicism — which he valued as a hierarchical faith privileging the intellectual elite, while *also* caring for the laboring classes. The lesson derived from a close study of the evolving perspective recorded in Brownson's *Boston Quarterly Review* (1838-1842) was that cultural historians must be simultaneously attentive to politics, and myth, as well as philosophical issues often overlooked by historians who can be myopic in their search for "cold, hard facts."

During my undergraduate years (1959-1963), students and teachers were excited by such books as *The Virgin Land* (1950) and *Andrew Jackson: Symbol for an Age* (1962)—both pioneering studies of America's popular myths and symbols. Henry Nash Smith, in his classic *Virgin Land: The American West as Symbol and Myth* (1950) traced America's proud celebration of its self image as "nature's nation." In his short, colorful book, John William Ward sketched the portrait of a hero who promised to bring the frontier's natural virtue and egalitarian spirit to Washington—it is a cliché, today, but was an innovative marketing concept in 1828. Ward documented Andrew Jackson's charismatic influence with news stories, cartoons, and popular songs like "The Hunters of Kentucky." Both books used the concept of "myth" to indicate a cluster of values combining intellectual content and emotional power. While not uncritical of potential excesses, both scholars presumed that human beings are myth-making creatures.

In the last years of graduate study, I attended meetings of the American Studies Association and the Popular Culture Association where senior scholars Daniel Boorstin, Russel Nye, and Ray Browne invited acolytes to march with them to the newest scholarly frontier, the study of popular culture. As I moved forward in trace of these pioneers, I retained the lesson from the Brownson project: studies of culture should bundle elements of politics, history, and epistemology. *America Reflected* maps the weigh stations along the trail of my own intellectual pilgrimage. Stopping points included Will Rogers, satirist; Benjamin Lee Whorf, anthropological linguist; America's wars and war eras; as well Harriet Beecher Stowe, novelist; Frederick Henry Hedge, Unitarian minister; Amy Lowell, poet; John James Audubon, naturalist; and a host of films and filmmakers—a diverse group of people and movements, but all touchstones of our national culture. Two—Lowell and Hedge—were from Brookline, Massachusetts and of special interest in my search for what we now call "roots."

Will Rogers in the 1920s and 1930s

As part of my duties at Oklahoma State University, some happy years were devoted to editing and interpreting the journalistic and film efforts of the state's favorite son. *The Writings of Will Rogers*

A Satirical Voice from America's Past

(21 vols.) revealed the enduring impact of the cowboy and frontier myths. Americans experienced ambivalence as they moved from "nature's nation" status to a more complex identity associated with machines, cities, and mass media. Rogers addressed the psychological tensions of this evolving national audience: his readers felt guilty about deserting their small town values, parents, and friends, even as they accepted the benefits of an industrial civilization. As a cowboy who rode a 20th-century bronco, the airplane, Will Rogers showed that the best of 19th-century culture could thrive in the era of mass production, mass marketing, and—alas—"bunk" (Chapter 4). That he should die in 1935 at the age of 55 in an airplane crash at Point Barrow, Alaska—the most northerly point of the American continent and the last genuine frontier—seemed as symbolically appropriate as it was poignant.

America Reflected begins by tracing the evolution of Will Rogers as a symbolic man, journalist, and film image (Chapter 1). He wrote "daily telegrams" from 1926 until his death; these insightful capsules were carried on the first page of newspapers across the land. Longer was his experience with weekly articles—which allowed him to study public persons and major issues of the day from 1922 to 1935. Beginning in 1920, the Newspaper Enterprise

Association engaged Rogers to report on the Republican and Democratic presidential nominating conventions. *The Saturday Evening Post* (hereafter *SEP*) dispatched Rogers on world tours to check out how ordinary people were faring in a troubled world. As part of a 1926 European jaunt, Rogers sent home humorous "open letters" to President Calvin Coolidge (Chapter 3). Showing a better sense of humor than what one might expect from a taciturn Vermonter, Coolidge returned the compliment by inviting Rogers to brief him at the White House upon the Oklahoman's return. Will Rogers was a favorite writer for the *SEP* because the editor, George Horace Lorimer, although a wealthy Philadelphian, shared many values with his Midwestern correspondent (Chapters 2 and 5). However, there were significant differences in their world views, differences which reveal Rogers' greater generosity of spirit. In silent and sound motion pictures based on regional novels—some which had been serialized in the *SEP* previous to book publication and then later screen adaptation—Will Rogers represented middle west values in action. The novels and scripts prepared for the films sometimes included Nativist animadversions against Irish and Italian immigrants, Jews, and African Americans, but, when the cameras started rolling, Rogers exercised his privilege as a star to deviate from these unworthy portrayals; indeed, he usually found a way to collaborate with the minority and underdog characters in the films to overcome the Establishment figures. This cooperation was especially noteworthy in the rural communities brought to life by such films as *Dr. Bull* (1933) and *In Old Kentucky* (1935)—two Twentieth Century-Fox productions which also reflected the world view of director John Ford.

As my interest in making motion pictures blossomed, opportunities emerged from regular research visits to the Will Rogers Memorial in Claremore, Oklahoma—where thousands of photographs, sound recordings, and paper documents boisterously invited visual treatment. With the help of Patrick Griffin and R.C. Raack, I produced an "historian-made film" for which all film archive research, interviews, and the editing were directed by trained scholars. Entitled *Will Rogers' 1920s: A Cowboy's Guide to the Times* (1976), the resulting historical compilation explored the ways in which the Oklahoman interpreted the major issues and personalities of the silent era (Chapter 6). One major goal was to replace overbearing and didactic narration with music and montage—in other words, to communicate cinematically rather than by an illustrated lecture. The film which resulted from this project won a host of awards and was shown on public television in Oklahoma as well as nationally on The Discovery Channel. Rather than dwell on the tragic 1935 demise of the cowboy philosopher, the film evoked his special place in the 1920s as both a spokesman and cultural symbol. The Council for International Exhibition (CINE) presented this study with a Golden Eagle, the highest award in the United States for a non-theatrical film. (It is currently shown daily at the Will Rogers Memorial and Museum.)

Benjamin Lee Whorf: Brownson Redux?

Benjamin Lee Whorf (1897-1941) is a prominent figure in the history of linguistics and communications; as English as a Second Language (ESL) becomes an established component of the university curriculum, Whorf has found a new academic niche. In 2009, two philosophers, writing in the journal *Philosophy Compass*, announced that recent empirical studies had brought Whorf back into focus in a virtual revival of linguistic relativity studies (Reines and Prinz). Like the Orestes Brownson of my senior thesis at Harvard, Whorf was fascinated with studies in perception. At the same time, he shared with Will Rogers concerns about industrial development; indeed, he admired the Native Americans of the Southwest for their cultural resistance to the technological thinking of the American mainstream. (Much has been written, by the way, about the Cherokee perspective which informed the satire of Will Rogers.)

Whorf Found Patternment Even in the Monosyllabic Word

A graduate of MIT (1918) in chemical engineering, Whorf was fascinated by the "new physics" of the day which he saw as releasing humanity from the positivism of the 19th century. He lamented the polemical conflict between soi-disant proponents of science and fundamentalist defenders of religion during the Scopes trial, interpreting the debate to be symptomatic of the broader unrest of the 1920s and 1930s and clear evidence of popular misunderstanding of the implications of the work of Max Planck and Albert Einstein (Chapter 7). (In this regard, he joined such British writers as Arthur Eddington (1882-1944) and Sir James Jeans (1877-1946) whose names appear on Whorf's reading lists for this period.) It is my contention that the consistent goal of his work in Native American studies was to prove the appropriateness of different ways of "knowing"—both the scientific method (dominant for Western languages) and the way of spiritual intuition (dominant for Native American tongues). During his mature years as a thinker, Whorf argued that a proper study of the linkages among language, mind, and reality would resolve apparent antinomies. In this approach, he was in the New England tradition of Emerson, Thoreau, and other Transcendentalists—including Orestes A. Brownson, at least in one phase of the mercurial reformer's epistemological pilgrimage toward Catholicism and conservatism.

Whorf's name is often associated with that of his teacher, linguist Edward Sapir—with whom he studied at Yale University and for whom he taught a class or two during his apprentice years. The basic differences behind their language studies are explored; while Whorf hungered for belief, Sapir was a modern humanist (Chapter 8). Previously unpublished papers by Whorf provided me with a new perspective on the religious concerns of Sapir's prize pupil. As a believer, Whorf saw the empirical validity of the doctrine of original sin in the world around him; he deplored the arms race of his day, and he predicted a future war from the air which would target civilian population centers. At the same time, he lamented the vulgarization of science by pundits such as H.L. Mencken—whom the New Englander hoped to challenge in public debate after publication of a potentially controversial novel entitled *The Ruler of the Universe* (1925). Alas, Whorf never enjoyed the public exposure he sought because no publisher would take up the manuscript.

But Whorf never lost interest in finding a place for faith in an age of science. This motivation suffused his language studies and is the major difference between the New Englander and his teacher. Sapir was a gifted anthropologist and linguist, but also a sophisticated modern who took joy in the arts—he was both a poet and a pianist—without the need to introduce the topic of religious faith. Drawing on the insights of Franz Boas, pioneer of American Indian studies at the Smithsonian, Sapir explored the unique formal characteristics and poetic qualities of the American Indian languages. The Yale professor was impressed by the spiritual richness of American Indian culture, but he did not detect a special gift in the Navaho and Hopi tongues to praise, nor a dangerous limitation in English to cause alarm. In contrast, a close reading of Whorf reveals that he discerned metaphysical promises in the pioneering work of both Boas and Sapir. The "linguistic relativity hypothesis" would be Whorf's special "spin" on this heritage with the goal of relieving the spiritual drought of a lost generation (Chapter 8).

Whorf offered the Native American world view as an alternative. In the late 1930s, his ideas burgeoned about the spiritual resources of Hopi and Navaho language and culture—in part because of his anthropological studies and in part as a result of exposure to the writings of French and German linguists. Both Antoine Fabre d'Olivet (1767-1825) and F. Max Müller (1823-1900) were visionaries who laced their linguistic studies with a soupçon of mysticism. Their books encouraged Whorf to postulate an antinomy between Indo-European languages (which he designated "Standard Average European" and abbreviated as SAE) and Amer-Indian tongues. The latter group—especially the Navaho and Hopi—communicated in languages more facile with the spiritual dimension of life while offering a more agile way of describing the world of energy and matter revealed by the "new physics." By doing so, they proved the insularity of SAE (Chapter 9). These findings clearly went beyond mere linguistic studies and provided the basis for a broad perspective on the putative "progress" of what we now call the "first world."

For Whorf, the continued use of military force was a sign that Western cultures were in much need of complementary perspectives.

America's Wars: Reflections in Film and Television

One of the career-changing decisions I made in the 1970s was to tap my experience as a Marine Corps officer (1963-1966). Academic studies of novels, films, and television documentaries revealed to me such basic ignorance of the tactics and equipment that the generalizations reached by such works lost credibility. With basic facts in error, how could the conclusions built upon them *not* be in error? For example, if you do not know the difference between an M-79 grenade launcher and a 3.5 rocket launcher, what else do you miss in studying America's infantry at war? What are the three basic types of ambush and what are the advantages of each? Why are the two most dangerous elements on the battlefield a Marine lieutenant and his map? For lack of understanding of similar details—or appreciation that the last query is a sardonic joke—it seemed obvious that academics were unable to differentiate the realities and images of war in personal narratives, novels, poems, and films. Having spent three years of my life on active duty (plus grueling boot camps during college summers), I decided that it would not be off target as a scholar to apply the cultural perspective to America's wars (see Preface and Chapter 24 for details about my military experiences).

Part 2 of *America Reflected* devotes attention to military images and realities for World War I, World War II, the Cold War, and

Lt. Rollins Aboard the USS Renville, 1964

Vietnam. Sixteen chapters interweave historical themes with readings of literature and motion pictures devoted to the conflicts; throughout, there is a pervasive concern about how perception and memory affect interpretation of these tragic historical crises.

World War I

World War I inflicted a trauma on Western civilization from which we are still attempting to recuperate. The leading academic study of World War I in our time has been Paul Fussell's *The Great War and Modern Memory*, a volume which has received much-deserved éclat. In *America Reflected*, "Memories of War" (Chapter 10) tries to give a balanced assessment of how WWI was remembered: Fussell has stimulating insights to offer about the disillusionment evidenced by prominent writers after the conflict, but—perhaps because of his own combat experiences and wounds during WWII—he overlooks the heroic version which was much more evident in popular poems, monuments, and statues such as E.M. Viquesney's "The Spirit of the American Doughboy" installed by the American Legion on hundreds of public squares and the lawns of public buildings across the land. While such powerful films as *All Quiet on the Western Front* (1930) perpetuated a memory of defeat and suffering, other motion pictures—such as *The Big Parade* (1925) and *Wings* (1927)—counterbalanced the pain and loss with national pride in the battlefield valor of America's fighting men. Disillusionment was prevalent during the decade following the war, but not dominant. As a second world war seemed to become inevitable, the heroic version of WWI emerged in such WWI films as *Sergeant York* (1941) and the documentary feature by the March of Time group entitled *The Ramparts We Watch* (1940).

Drawing on the work of Fussell, but also synthesizing research concerning the ripple effects of the war in linguistics and the arts, I address the Great War's legacy (Chapter 11). WWI is still with us and has defined, for example, the way in which the Vietnam conflict was interpreted by American culture—and its film culture. Two documentaries by the Cadre historian group are the focus of this exploration so that the study is at the same time a close reading of two award-winning short films, while having more general application to the experience of WWI. Americans lost a sense of innocence in WWI—a theme at the heart of both *Goodbye Billy* (1972) and *The Frozen War* (1973)— for the world-wide conflict marked the end of the "Whig interpretation of history" in which technological advancement was equated with moral progress. As a member of the post-war generation, this issue was a major concern of Benjamin Whorf in his novel, *The Ruler of the Universe*, but also an embedded theme of the Whorf hypothesis. The two documentaries under examination stressed the perspective that "war is the health of the state," another theme of importance to Whorf. Finally, the films demonstrate that language has been disjoined from truth after a "war to end all wars." In *The Meaning of Meaning* (1923) and a lifetime of scholarship and pedagogy, I. A. Richards pursued this theme as an influential scholar and teacher. Outside of Academe, post-war panaceas claimed to cure the breakdown of communication. In Esperanto, reformers attempted to create an international language, hoping that a shared means of communication would promote world peace. Others devised a General Semantics filter to restore trust in language. As earlier, the issue of how we know what we know (epistemology) shines through as relevant to WWI studies as the balance of power or the economic consequences of the war. The ripple effects continue into our own time and are a source of constant discussion on the Internet—as will become evident by an Internet search for "Whorf."

World War II and the Cold War via Compilation Documentaries

Before, during, and after World War II, the struggle against the Axis powers gave impetus to some of America's most ambitious films of persuasion. The academy award-winning director Frank Capra was a Sicilian immigrant who, at the age of six, came to the United States and embraced the American Dream. His Gary Cooper and James Stewart films about of the triumph of democracy inspired courage and hope for millions during the Great Depression. When war came to America in 1941, he was "drafted" by Chief of Staff General George C. Marshall to produce a series of orientation films for the U.S. Army (Chapter 12). These films were also distributed to commercial theatres—often after a White House premiere before the nation's leading film buff. Understanding that the mass of American soldiers—most of them drafted from a society that was largely isolationist—or had been isolationists until the Japanese "sneak attack," Capra set about the daunting task of justifying an aggressive internationalist agenda. In doing so, he tapped telluric cultural myths and revived their power. The seven hour-length documentaries of the *Why We Fight* series have been praised for their statement of America's war aims, but the series is equally important for its reification of the American Dream—which had been grievously eroded by nearly ten years of economic depression. By the end of the war, 54 million Americans had been instructed by Capra that their nation stood as a "lighthouse of freedom" for a fallen world, an image which harkened back to the Puritans (and forward to the Reagan years). In the 1950s, the lessons about compilation documentary were applied in such television series as NBC's *Victory at Sea* (26 episodes) and CBS' *Air Power* (16 episodes) (Chapter 15). The *Victory at Sea* style of historical filmmaking was later applied to the Cold War threat of the Soviet Union, tracing the dangers back to the reprehensible vision of Vladimir Illyich Lenin, leader of the 1917 communist revolution (Chapter 16). Later, the genre was inverted to condemn the American military in such exposé feature-length documentaries as *Hearts and Minds* (1974) and *Fahrenheit 9/11* (2004).

Decades later, Richard Raack's *Storm of Fire: World War II and the Destruction of Dresden* reconsidered the wisdom of wartime decisions—which may have been based on an excessive will to fight or even vindictiveness (Chapter 14). More recently, the anniversaries of the D-Day invasion have attracted the attention of political leaders, pundits, and filmmakers to the heroic invasion of Hitler's Fortress Europe; certainly, since the success of Steven Spielberg's *Saving Private Ryan* (1998), the sacrifice and bravery of those who fought to drive fascism from the continent have received respectful annual memorials (Chapter 13).

Vietnam

As a returning Vietnam veteran, it was my distinct displeasure to observe how both print and television media egregiously misreported the conflict—both in regard to policy, and also when depicting our servicemen. From 1980-1983, in collaboration with

Introduction 13

Television's Vietnam: Impact of Visual Images

David H. Culbert (Louisiana State U) and Townsend Ludington (U of North Carolina-Chapel Hill), I researched and directed a 2.5-hour documentary entitled *Television's Vietnam: Impact of Visual Images*. This longish historical compilation made maximum use of Marine Corps combat footage, reconstructed newsreels, television commercials of the day, popular tunes, and the testimonials of those involved—from the battlefield to the diplomatic and White House echelons of the struggle (Chapter 18). This "epic" production was edited down to an hour-length program and "bootlegged" without my knowledge; one of the recipients of the truncated version was Reed Irvine (d. 2001), Director of Accuracy in Media (Washington, DC), who telephoned me at my office in Morrill Hall, Oklahoma State U, to suggest a reworking of the program using additional archival footage and interviews. Together, we designed a major conference on the subject in Washington, DC and, with the help of additional interviews with media analysts, journalists, and diplomats, produced two hour-length programs: the first, *Television's Vietnam: The Real Story* (1985), was in rebuttal to the PBS series *Vietnam:*

A Television History (1983) with Charlton Heston as the narrator/host. Heston also hosted the second program, *Television's Vietnam: The Impact of Media* (1986), a documentary focusing on specific stories from the Tet offensive 1968. The reporting of Tet served as a microcosm of the errors committed by the press throughout the years of direct U.S. involvement in the Vietnam conflict (1965-1973). These programs were distilled from a considerable research base—about the existing fiction and nonfiction on Vietnam—established long before production (Chapter 17). In addition, as a veteran, I was highly motivated to balance the public record, albeit in my second language, Spanish, which allowed me to be more forthright on the personal motivations animating the film projects (Chapter 24). Over the years, I have been asked by teachers to recommend Vietnam documentaries for the classroom (Chapters 23 and 25), but the prolific—though delayed—production of Hollywood versions of Vietnam demanded analysis (Chapter 17). Despite these animadversions, to my surprise, I was asked to step in for Oliver Stone on a college campus after he reneged on his contract with the student speakers' forum. (He had been offered $30,000 to give an hour's presentation; my PowerPoint lecture with clips turned out to be yet another of my charitable contributions to the principle of "free speech.")

During production phase of these programs, some academic panels on which I appeared were picketed by protestors—most memorably by the Young Socialist League at a 1981 national Popular Culture Association meeting in Cincinnati. In the run up to broadcast of the programs on public television (PBS), the producer of the 23 episode WGBH series, Richard Ellison, warned the press about the—to his mind—egregious errors of our documentaries and predicted a "chilling effect" in the wake of their broadcasts by PBS. In the afterglow of an annual Phoenix, Arizona junket for television critics, most urban dailies in the US echoed Ellison's dire predictions, although the *New York Times* distinguished itself as a defender of the programs and their right to be aired (Chapter 19). Ellison ceased his harangues only after the President of WGBH told him, in a public forum, that he was out of line.

General William C. Westmoreland (1914-2005)

General Westmoreland and his Trials

During the Vietnam conflict, General William C. Westmoreland went from the elevated status of *Time* magazine's "Man of the Year" to its "Man on the Spot." Westmoreland was a well-intentioned and honorable man who became a scapegoat for America's Vietnam debacle. It was my pleasure to organize a conference in 1980 at which Westmoreland volunteered to share his views; the event was timely because his autobiography, *A Soldier Reports*, had just been published. He won over a full auditorium of initially unsympathetic students and faculty by his unpretentiousness sincerity and his passion to defend the legacy of Vietnam veterans. Throughout his retirement, he and wife "Kitsy" gave of their time and prestige for veterans events, seminars, television programs, hoping to lift the stigma borne by troops who came home to an indifferent—or, in some cases, hostile—nation.

In the same time frame as our Chapel Hill conference, Mike Wallace approached the General aboard a commercial airline—Wallace was seated in first class and came back to coach class to talk with the retired leader. The CBS television celebrity gave every impression that he was interested in pursuing the truth about the intelligence estimates of Vietcong and regular enemy units prior to the Tet offensive—and the contribution of those reports to the confusion and dismay resulting from the sudden Tet attacks at the end of January, 1968. Westmoreland agreed to fly to New York City for a filmed interview with Wallace and thus began work on a controversial documentary entitled *The Uncounted Enemy: A Vietnam Deception* (1982). The "Westmoreland trial" (*Westmoreland v. CBS*) which followed the broadcast of the exposé received banner headlines week after week especially after sources inside CBS headquarters leaked details about unfair questioning by Wallace and fraudulent editing by director George Crile (Chapter 20). Sometime after the trial, a cherry wood box of research materials from the trial was prepared for scholarly use by the Clearwater Publishing Company; it contained microfiche copies of the pre-trial depositions and other documents from the courtroom drama. This treasure trove of information was borrowed via interlibrary loan and I remember two chilly months during the winter of 1996 vetting the lengthy testimony of the CIA's George Carver deposed in preparation for the trial. Although a major player in the numbers debate, Carver was never interviewed by Director George Crile until the post-production phase of the project, most likely as a self-protective ploy. Carver's deposed testimony revealed that a legitimate debate among intelligence agencies had been transmuted by CBS into a nefarious plot—an error of conspiratorial interpretation of the kind frequently embraced by journalists and other amateur historians (Chapter 21).

But Westmoreland was not the only Vietnam-era scapegoat. The subtitle of journalist Neil Sheehan's *A Bright Shining Lie: John Paul Vann and America in Vietnam* indicated an exposé of a leading optimist about the war in Southeast Asia, a government official whom Peter Arnett, David Halberstam, and Neil Sheehan—at least in the early days of the conflict—relied upon for colorful inside stories (Chapter 22). Sheehan's epic "history" portrays a brilliant man fighting a bungled war; at a critical turn of his research, the investigative reporter even discovered a back story of perverted sex for his protagonist, a story introduced as a devastating *ad hominem* argument to discredit the war's most convincing proponent. The *New York Times* correspondent describes himself as "a newsman who got diverted into history"—and it shows. *A Bright Shining*

Lie is fascinating reading, but is guided by the same crusading journalistic perspective which led to much of the errant reporting of the era itself—rather than being a detached analysis written with the benefit of hindsight. In the Neil Sheehan version, the US military was blind to changing realities, especially in the Third World. General W.C. Westmoreland epitomized this myopia in his choice of a "big unit" strategy—rather than listening to the wisdom of Marine General Victor Krulak who advocated placing combined US and ARVN units in each threatened village. The book's message is that national leadership should be wrested from the hands of aging governmental and military elites. A new generation—for some unexplained reason, 100% of whom are Harvard graduates—has the public interest at heart with David Halberstam representing the reportorial side and Daniel Ellsberg standing out as the model policy analyst. Within the book, Ellsberg is lauded for being both a Harvard Fellow *and* a company commander in the Marine Reserves, the perfect balance of thought and action. Sheehan concludes that the press and geniuses like Ellsberg turned against America because they were forced to do so—not because they espoused a competing ideology.

During the summer of 1998, HBO broadcast its film adaptation of *A Bright Shining Lie*, with Bill Paxton playing John Paul Vann. If it is true that the WGBH series on Vietnam would have been a better work of history had it followed more faithfully the narrative of Stanley Karnow's companion history, it is equally true that the film version of Sheehan's epic would have been more worthwhile if the screenwriter and director, Terry George, had *read* the book. Instead, the film recycles familiar clichés of the war era—many of them either disproven or seriously revised since the 1975 American debacle. The film's treatment of the 1963 Buddhist immolations shows no historical perspective or interest in the many scholarly studies—to include Sheehan's nuanced version. The famous photograph of Kim Phuc burned by napalm and running toward the camera is presented as an atrocity by careless Americans in 1967 when it was an accident of war committed by South Vietnamese in 1972. Tet, in 1968, is presented using the standard misleading microcosms of the day. In all, HBO spent $13 million to revive the anti-Establishment "spin" of the 1960s reporting. Even putative friends of the project were revulsed. After reading the script, Daniel Ellsberg, who is vital to the narrative of both book and film, threatened a law suit, demanding that his character's name be changed. He concluded a stinging memo to director/writer Terry George with a coup de grace: "That [changing his name] would not solve all my troubling concerns about this script. What would go a long way in that direction would be to change two other real names in it, as well, to frankly fictional ones: 'John Paul Vann' and 'Vietnam'" (quoted in Chapter 22).

Of lesser intellectual content, but of greater public exposure was another HBO production entitled *Dear America: Letters Home from Vietnam* (1987). Ostensibly based on an eponymous anthology, director Bill Couturie tapped the power of music and montage to convey a message quite different from that of Bernard Edelman's anthology of letters from New York soldiers to their families. While the book emphasized themes of courage and suffering, the film evoked a Vietnam that was a brutal, demoralizing conflict of no redeeming value—one which demolished the country in which we fought while corrupting the young soldiers and marines sent to prosecute a misguided strategy (Chapter 23). For negativity, the program is exceeded only by Peter Davis' *Hearts and Minds,* an Academy-Award winning compilation film praised by the North Vietnam government in a telegram read by the film's producer at the 1974 Academy Award ceremony (Chapter 17). There are both ideological and formal (i.e., film as an art form) elements which "determined" a special formula for portraying the war and the veterans who survived it; discerning viewers need to anticipate this pattern. Chapter 17 outlines this formula and contrasts the results in film with a 1980 Harris poll of veteran attitudes. Most readers will be surprised to learn that over 80% of our troops believed, some five years after the fall of South Vietnam, that they had done the right thing by defending the South Vietnamese from Communist conquest. No credibility gap could be larger than the abyss between the Hollywood version and the experience and memories of American service men and women who served. For twenty years, I tried to uphold their perspective and memory, an effort not without difficulty in Academe.

Other Figures and National Myths and the Film Record

Part 3 of *America Reflected* focuses on selected figures and films—in two cases, fascinating people from my home town of Brookline, Massachusetts. Founded in 1705, Brookline is an independent suburb just west of Boston and contiguous with it. The town has nurtured writers, scholars, and filmmakers—from Amy Lowell (poet) to Mike Wallace (adversarial journalist) to Richard Goodwin (presidential speech writer) to Ellen Goodman (pundit) to the Albert and David Maysles (pioneers of direct documentary). Two chapters of local history are here devoted to leading hometown figures. Frederick Henry Hedge (1805-1890) was the only New England Transcendentalist fluent in German. (Many of Immanuel Kant's ideas were imported into New England by way of English translations or in French through the writings of Victor Cousin, a pen pal of Brownson.) Hedge, unlike other members of the "Hedge Club"— later called "the Transcendentalist Club"—remained within the Unitarian fold; his flirting with ideas about liberating the ego were counterpoised by a steadfast respect for tradition, a characteristic ambivalence for many nurtured in a protected and stable Boston suburb (Chapter 27). Also studied in detail is another denizen of Brookline, Amy Lowell (1874-1925), an iconoclastic member of a proud family whose childhood diaries disclose a youthful search for identity which flourished like the garden of "Patterns" in the poems of her maturity (Chapter 28). Her rootedness was such that her headstone (alas, in Cambridge) is satisfied to identify her simply as "Amy Lowell of Brookline." Although of the product of Calvinism and Connecticut, Harriet Beecher Stowe's (1811-1896) spiritual search connects with Lowell's theme of identity. Chapter 26 explores this theme as it surfaced in *Uncle Tom's Cabin* and the regional novels in which she nostalgically evoked the *weltanschauung* of early New England. With passage of the Fugitive Slave Law, the shame of slavery overwhelmed Stowe; her compulsion to write the anti-slavery tract stemmed from her conflicted sense of being a scion of Calvinism in an age of romantic optimism. She found self expression for her anguish by writing about the dilemma of slaves in the American South.

America's attitudes toward nature are central to our national identity, an historical principle recognized long before it was formally codified by Frederick Jackson Turner in his famous 1893 address, "The Significance of the Frontier in American History." It is a revealing reflection on our culture that John James Audubon (1785-1851) fervently shared the expansionist enthusiasms of his day; the "bird man" admired pioneer settlement, extractive industry, and the growth of cities—indeed, the full menu of Manifest Destiny—at the same time he recorded the disappearing aviary beauties of the wilderness (Chapter 29). The same kind of ambivalence about industrial development is reflected in the post-WWII motion picture, *Tulsa* (1949). Like Audubon, the makers of this crusading film were often more on the side of exploitation than their stated conservationist philosophy would seem to have justified (Chapter 31). Will Rogers understood these contrary feelings and, as a national spokesman for the 1920s and 1930s, repeatedly played to them in his daily and weekly articles. As part of his fascination with the Native American language and culture, Benjamin Whorf also shared in the dilemma; an offspring of his research as an anthropological linguist, he hoped, would be the lesson of cultural humility. His late articles call for an admission by Western civilization that technological advances need to be tempered by spiritual growth. Indeed, he saw himself as living proof that an MIT graduate could be a man of faith. In the film *Tulsa*, this search for balance is symbolized by the romantic choices for the protagonist, Cherokee Lansing (Susan Hayward). Initially, she is attracted to Bruce Tanner (Lloyd Gough), whose goal is to extract as much oil as possible in the most wasteful way; later in the film, she recognizes that the oil industry must respect the environment, leading her to turn to Brad Brady (Robert Preston), spokesman for New Deal-style planning.

The New Deal films of the Roosevelt Administration are recognized for their innovative work in social documentary, but they are rich texts for understanding the vision of FDR as he sought to heal the economy *and* the land. David Lilienthal's book, *TVA: Democracy in Action* (1944) is a classic book describing the environmental problems of the day and the presenting government planning as an ideal—on a regional basis subsuming many states. Two films by Pare Lorentz, *The Plow that Broke the Plains* and *The River*, synthesize government views about the careless treatment of the land which led to drought and floods, but are also successful works of art that stir the emotions as they weave together editing, music, and evocative narration. Made for theatrical distribution, these short films are worthy of perennial study by those seeking America reflected (Chapter 30).

Conclusion

The quest for *America Reflected* began with Brownson. His spiritual journey paralleled many of the twists and turns found in the lives of Amy Lowell, Harriet Beecher Stowe, and Frederick Henry Hedge. Along with some great living teachers, he instructed me that cultural studies should be guided by concerns which transcend the trendy and dodge the dogmatic—even when the results are unpopular. Will Rogers added a sense of humor and an understanding that each era needs its spokesmen—whose messages mean much to their times, even as their limitations become obvious to later generations. Benjamin Whorf carried the interest in epistemology to the margins of culture and understanding, questioning the entire Western tradition and calling for alternative spiritual resources to complement our limited *weltanschauung*. War experiences and activist work for veterans after the Vietnam conflict reminded me of the goodness of ordinary people who are willing to sacrifice their lives for a worthy cause—as they did in the previous national conflicts studied in this collection—WWI, WWII, and the Cold War. My own immersion in war as a small unit leader in a time of conflict and domestic debate endowed me with a perspective unusual for an academic. In particular, it gave me an apercu into the ideological blinders of the press—which is populated by an elite with as much pack subjectivity as any other elite in our culture. The Brookline background and the experience of leadership gave me tolerance for the errors of decision makers caught on the treadmill of history while constrained by the political forces and limited real-time information. But it all began with Brownson's insight that the cultural historian needs to consider modes of perception—even his own—as much as history and politics. If we do not strive for such a perspective, we will merely reflect the predilections of our class and place, thereby adding to the ambient noise of our time rather than contributing insight and wisdom.

Works Cited

Air Power. 16 episodes. CBS: 11 Nov 1956.
All Quiet on the Western Front. Dir. Lewis Milestone. Perf. Louis Wolheim, Lew Ayers. Universal Pictures, 1930.
Doctor Bull. Dir. John Ford. Perf. Will Rogers, Vera Allen. Fox Film, 1933.
Edelman, Bernard. *Dear America: Letters Home from Vietnam.* New York: Pocket Books, 1985.
Fahrenheit 9/11 Dir. Michael Moore. Lions Gate Films, 2004.
The Frozen War: America Intervenes in Russia, 1918-1920. Cadre Films, 1973.
Fussell, Paul. *The Great War and Modern Memory.* New York: Oxford UP, 1975.
Goodbye Billy: America Goes to War, 1917-18. Dirs. Richard C. Raack, William F. Malloch, and Patrick Griffin. Churchill Films, 1972.
Gragert, Steven K., and Judy G. Buckholz. *The Writings of Will Rogers.* Stillwater: Oklahoma State U, 1973-1983.
Hearts and Minds. Dir. Peter Davis. BBS productions, 1974.
H(ome) B(ox) O(ffice). *Dear America: Letters Home from Vietnam.* Dir. Bill Couturie, 1988.
In Old Kentucky. Dir. George Marshall. Perf. Will Rogers, Dorothy Wilson. Fox Film, 1935.
Ogden, C. K, and I. A. Richards, et al. *The Meaning of Meaning; A Study of the Influence of Language upon Thought and of the Science of Symbolism.* New York: Harcourt, Brace, 1923.
Reines, Maria Francisca, and Jesse Prinz. "Reviving Whorf: The Return of Linguistic Relativity." *Philosophy Compass* 4.6 (2009): 1022-1032.
Rogers, Will. *Will Rogers' Weekly Articles.* James Smallwood, and Steven K. Gragert, eds. Vols. 1-6. Stillwater: Oklahoma State UP, 1981.
Rollins, Peter C. "HBO's Version of Neil Sheehan's Epic: Old Wine in New Bottles?" *Perspectives* Film and Media Section. 37.4 April 1999. *Newsletter of the American Historical Association.* [online]
Rollins, Peter Cushing. *Orestes A. Brownson: Epistemology of a Crucified Redeemer.* Diss. Harvard U, 1963.
Sergeant York. Dir. Howard Hawks. Perf. Gary Cooper, Walter Brennan. Warner Bros., 1941.
Sheehan, Neil. *A Bright Shining Lie: John Paul Vann and America in Vietnam.* New York: Random House, 1988.
Smith, Henry Nash. *Virgin Land: The American West as Symbol and Myth.* Cambridge: Harvard UP, 1950.
Stowe, Harriet Beecher. *Uncle Tom's Cabin.* 1852. New York: Viking Press, 1982.
Television's Vietnam: The Impact of Media. Dir. Peter C. Rollins. SONY Video, 1986.

Television's Vietnam: The Real Story. Dir. Peter C. Rollins. SONY Video, 1985.
The Big Parade. Dir. King Vidor. Perf. John Gilbert, Renee Adoree. MGM, 1925.
The Ramparts We Watch. Dir. Louis De Rochemont. Perf. John Adair, John Summers. RKO, 1940.
"The Uncounted Enemy: A Vietnam Deception." *60 Minutes*. CBS, 23 Jan. 1982.
Tulsa. Dir. Stuart Heisler. Perf. Susan Heyward, Robert Preston. Walter Wanger Productions, 1949.
Victory at Sea. Dir. Henry Salomon. 26 episodes. NBC: 2 Aug. 1954.
Vietnam: A Television History. WGBH-PBS, 1983.
Ward, John William. *Andrew Jackson: Symbol for an Age*. New York: Oxford UP, 1955.
Whorf, Benjamin. *The Ruler of the Universe*. 1925. *Benjamin Lee Whorf Legacy CD ROM*. Ed. Peter C. Rollins. Cleveland, OK: Ridgemont Media, 2008.
Why We Fight. Dir. Frank Capra. U.S. War Dept. Twentieth Century Fox, 1943.
Will Rogers' 1920s: A Cowboy's Guide to the Times. Dir. Peter C. Rollins. Churchill Films, 1976.
Wings. Dir. William Wellman. Perf. Clara Bow, Charles Buddy Rogers. Paramount, 1927.

Part I

America Reflected in Satire, Language, and Film

Will Rogers' Popular Culture

1
The Evolving Persona of Will Rogers: Symbolic Man, Journalist, and Film Image

On August 15, 1935, Will Rogers and his pilot Wiley Post were killed in a plane crash at Point Barrow, Alaska. Exactly one week later, the offices of Twentieth Century-Fox and Universal Studios closed at noon so that office workers could attend a special memorial service at the Hollywood Bowl "where over twenty thousand gathered to pay tribute to the memory of the beloved humorist" (Stone no. 3). That evening, twelve thousand motion picture theaters across the country observed two minutes of respectful silence before beginning their evening programs.

Just before leaving for Alaska, Rogers had completed two films. At least previous to this tragedy, Hollywood had observed "an unwritten law forbidding the release of a picture after the death of a star" (Rogers, File box 14). But in the case of Will Rogers, there were obviously other factors to be considered. In fact, the rationale behind the release of *In Old Kentucky* and *Steamboat Round the Bend* in 1935 provides a glimpse of the special relationship between Will Rogers and his American audience. After a long conference, Joseph Schenck (Chairman of the Board of Directors) and Sidney R. Kent (President) of Twentieth Century-Fox determined that the distribution of these last two pictures would not have the same morbid overtones which might have accompanied a similar posthumous release of films by other actors: "Rogers was totally different from Valentino, Wallace Reid and Lon Chaney, where audiences appreciated their work. Rogers was loved as a man, as a national character, as the greatest of all home philosophers" (Rogers, File box 14).

Will Rogers: America's Conscience

Joseph Schenck was right about the unique place of Will Rogers in the hearts of Americans. Although he never held public office, the popularity of his daily syndicated columns, his weekly articles, his books, and finally his movies made him one of the most important influences on America's self-image from 1922 until his untimely death in 1935 at the age of 55. Will Rogers as public person, as journalist, and as film star confronted and subdued many of the pressures and anxieties of his time. A typical Will Rogers fan had very special ideas about Rogers' behavior as a private individual; and derived a special pleasure from the gentle satire of Rogers' journalism. With these elements in mind, Americans attended and surrendered to the seductive nostalgia of the avuncular Oklahoman's late films.

In the last stage of his Hollywood career, Rogers became the film industry's best paid ($225,000 per film) and most popular male movie attraction. From 1933 until 1935, Will Rogers portrayed a film character who deeply moved Americans during the Great Depression. If correctly interpreted, these nostalgic rural dramas are as relevant as documents of the gist of the 1930s as a book like *I'll Take My Stand* (1930). Like that famous protest against progress, the city, and declining estimate of man, the late films of Will Rogers imagine an alternative society where the traditional elements of the American national character have free play. Franklin Delano Roosevelt was not alone in concluding that the sanity of Americans in the turbulent early decades of the twentieth century had been preserved because of the sympathy and humor of this avuncular companion of the American people (Memorial no.14, 32). The films *Steamboat Round the Bend (1935)* and *In Old Kentucky* (1935), released after Rogers' tragic plane crash, are excellent depictions of a nostalgic, small-town America; in them, Rogers tapped memories of a harmonious rural past when people cared.

I. The 1920s: The Price of the New

Americans in the 1920s were excited by the rapid changes going on around them, yet at the same time they were uneasy, for assuming the new identity in the twentieth century entailed rejection of traditional values. The tension induced by these changes led some Americans to strike out at the new. The infamous Red Scare led by A. Mitchell Palmer sought to stamp out the threat of bolshevism. Gathering new members among native stock Americans, the Ku Klux Klan expanded its crusade against change. Its new enemies

Urban America in the Jazz Age

included "the city, sexual freedom, modern life...[and]...liquor" (Leuchtenberg 213). While militant fundamentalists in Tennessee brought John T. Scopes to trial, the Daughters of the American Revolution and others who feared the rising political power of the immigrant launched campaigns for 100% Americanism. The majority of Americans attempted to find a place for themselves in this new world, but unquestionably all Americans in the period were ambivalent about the juggernaut of progress—was it steaming toward a better society or away from it?

Industrialism had posed increasing challenges since the end of the Civil War. Those Americans who went to the city to profit from the new wealth and social mobility available there were rewarded handsomely. A ready supply of docile immigrant labor assured that quick-witted Americans could rise up the ladder of success. Yet for all their successes, these same newcomers to the good life of urban and industrial America experienced anxiety: "For millions of people torn from accustomed rural patterns of culture and thrust into a strange, urban environment, the meaning of industrialism lay in a feeling of uprootedness, in the disintegrations of old ways of life" (Hays 190). Many of those who remained behind in small towns believed they were left out, creating a paradoxical situation in which the liberated were anxious while the innocent were resentful.

The technique of mass production initiated what has been called a "second industrial revolution" (Leuchtenberg 178-203). The

Ford Innovations "Move" America

United States was transformed as this manufacturing technique was pressed into service to turn out large quantities of automobiles, radios, and other new inventions of the era. The advertising industry expanded its efforts to convince Americans that they required the massive number of goods which could now be produced. Americans were urged to consume, to buy on credit, to become part of this new economy of abundance. If they had money left when they finished shopping, Americans were advised to invest in the stock market. If they had no money left, they were assured that they could buy on the margin.

Parallel with these major changes in economic life, a "revolution in morals" was significantly altering the outlook of Americans. As the authority of religion declined, the gospel according to Sigmund Freud gained true believers. The family had already lost its economic role; its cohesion as an institution was further reduced by pleas for individual liberation. As a result, many observers were distressed because new guides of conduct were not being offered. Perhaps the greatest consternation arose when the new woman appeared. Rather than a socially constructive idealist, like Jane Addams, she turned out to be a flapper and a flirt!

The liberation of writers in elite culture yielded the creative literary work of Hemingway, Faulkner, and Fitzgerald. But in popular culture liberation appeared to have unstopped the bottle of cheap-and-nasty: popular songs on the radio were titled "Hot Lips," "I Need Lovin'," "Burning Kisses," while popular magazines such as *Paris Nights* and *Flapper Experiences* covered the newsstands. Hollywood concentrated all of these pyrotechnic changes into one half-baked city: Los Angeles, California. Advertisements for the "smart" and "sophisticated" films produced there promised "brilliant men, beautiful jazz babies, champagne baths, midnight revels, petting parties in the purple dawn, all ending in one terrific climax that makes you gasp" (qtd in Leuchtenberg 169).

According to Edward Sapir (a contemporary social scientist), industrialism, urbanism, advertising and the unreflective celebration of the individual all had worked to fragment the traditional culture of the West. Much like Will Rogers, Sapir was careful to explain that so-called "progress" in the early twentieth century was more a matter of material improvement than an advance in the quality of "genuine culture." Even the most well-adjusted twentieth-century American sensed a certain incompleteness in his life: "Even if he succeeds in making a fairly satisfactory compromise with his new environment, he is apt to retain an uneasy sense of the loss of some vague and great good, some state of mind that he would be hard put to it to define but which gave him a courage and joy that latter-day prosperity never quite seems to have regained for him. What has happened is that he has slipped out of the warm embrace of a culture into a cold air of fragmentary existence" (97). The price of material conquest of the environment had been paid for by an emotional tax on true happiness:

> Here lies the grimmest joke of our present American civilization. The vast majority of us, deprived of any but an insignificant and cruelly abortive share in the satisfaction of the immediate wants of mankind, are further deprived of both opportunity and stimulation to share in the production of non-utilitarian values. Part of the time we are dray horses; the rest of the time we are listless consumers of goods which have received no least impress of our personality. In other words, our spiritual selves go hungry, for the most part, pretty much all the time. (101)

From his elevated position as Professor of Anthropology at Yale University in New Haven, Connecticut, Edward Sapir could see the fragmentation of culture in a historical sweep that went back to the seventeenth century. (For more on Sapir, see Chapter 8.) On the level of popular culture, most Americans sensed the same inadequacies in their lives, but their frame of reference was considerably smaller. Many sought solace in thinking of the 1890s as a lost Eden from which the America of their own post-war era had departed. At least as nostalgically recalled by these unsettled people, that earlier America had been a face-to-face society, a comprehensible world painted in primary colors:

> By 1932, the prewar years had taken on a luminescence that they did not wholly have at the time. In retrospect, the years before World War I seemed like a lost Arcadia. Men remembered county fairs and church socials, spelling bees and

sleigh rides, the excitement of the circus train or the wild dash of firehorses from the station house, the cool smell of an ice cream parlor and the warm fragrance of roasted chestnuts.... They remembered people: the paper boy with his off-key whistle, the brawny iceman sauntering up the walk with his five-cent cake of ice, the Negro stable boys, the printers and devils in the newspaper offices. They recollected general stores: the bolts of calico and muslin, the jars of cinnamon and gunpowder tea, bins of dried peaches and cornmeal, kegs of mackerel, canisters of striped candy. From the vantage point of 1932, it seemed as though they had danced endlessly at tango teas and strummed mandolins every evening. (Leuchtenberg 4)

Not the realities of the 1890s, but the anxieties of the 1930s motivated Americans to long for that (apparently) simpler decade.

II. Will Rogers: Public Person and Public Spokesman

A. *Living a Life in Public View*

Will Rogers was important to Americans in the 1920s and 1930s because he addressed his humor to their basic sense of rootlessness and loss. As a cowboy version of Washington Irving's Rip Van Winkle, Rogers passed through this era of change, judging new developments by the standards of the 1890s. And despite the criticism he delivered, he somehow bridged the gap between the old and the new. Because he made the transition without losing his identity, his audience was intensely concerned with his highly publicized "private" life: in a world where divorces were increasing, Rogers remained happily monogamous; while his audience felt itself to be under constant pressure to perform, he seemed somehow to be unruffled. In an era of big government's delays, Will Rogers stood out as a symbol of ready sympathy and practical help for the distressed, for—unlike his uprooted audience—he was still in contact with "The Real Things of Life."

1. Love and Marriage

From the beginning, Will Rogers was admired as a man who was somehow able to remain simple and pure, even in an age of puffery and bunk. He seemed miraculously unaffected by the erosion of values. His good qualities were highlighted further by the Hollywood context:

> He became nonetheless dear to us because of the falsity of much that surrounded him: the spurious nature and illegitimacy of much of the screen threw him into relief as someone really genuine (Stone "Chatting"). Rogers' sexual purity was universally respected. Reviewers of early Rogers' films were surprised that he could succeed on the screen without pandering to the usual demands for sex appeal. One critic observed that he was unique as a male film star in "outwitting the sexy fellows (Sargent).

Many admired Will and Betty Rogers for holding their family together. One reporter, realizing how important this happily monogamous couple was to her audience, breathlessly told her readers the results of a telephone interview "over four thousand

Will Rogers and Family

miles with a model married man" (Peterson). The readers necessarily understood that Hollywood was the leading edge of sexual liberation, and thus a city where the family was most endangered. In this context of dizzy freedom, "Will Rogers and his wife have been married longer than some stars, several times divorced, have been alive" (Memorial no. 24, 35). Rogers himself encouraged the press to report this eccentricity. He proclaimed proudly (and often) that he was "the only motion picture star who has the same wife he originally started with." The result of all this interest and self-promotion was that the Rogers household was celebrated as "an ideal home" where (in contrast with many American homes) parents spent every free moment teaching the children or playing with them (Memorial "An Ideal Home").

A review of Rogers' first sound film, *They Had to See Paris* (1929), clearly shows how intensely concerned his film audience was with this reputation for cleanliness and fidelity. When Pike Peters (Will Rogers) and his wife (Irene Rich) reach Paris, Mrs. Peters immediately begins to dress in the styles of the beau monde. During a bedroom scene, Pike, pleased by the way his wife looks in her new fashions, gives her a very innocent kiss. Rogers' audience was so involved with their public man off the screen, that there was a very intense response to this act on camera: when "he blushingly kissed her, the audience broke into happy applause. They knew it was Will's first screen kiss, and they realized that he never would have done it had it not been for the years of devoted friendship that had grown up between them in their pilgrimage to the top of the screen ladder. Also knowing Will's domestic happiness, the roof went off when he admitted that his kiss was almost like 'infidelity'" (Memorial "The Movies"). The film audience admired the Rogers family for maintaining "a real house, even in Hollywood" because so many families in their own neighborhoods were disintegrating under the stress of change.

2. Transcending the Pressures of Middle-Class Life
Americans were fascinated by Will Rogers' ability to surmount the pressures of his busy life as an entertainer, journalist, and film star. As an admiring newspaperman reported: "Will Rogers probably is the only person alive who can face the Associated Press totally

unembarrassed. Big news is but the happenings of a small town to him. To him important personages are but fellers of his acquaintance" (Memorial no. 15, 62). Rogers himself delivers a line in *Life Begins at Forty* (1934) which summarizes the lesson which his viewers drew. Speaking of another character, he observes that: "he solved the problem which all the world has been looking for—how to relax. Just to look at him makes me feel better."

Rogers' freedom from pressure was communicated in numerous ways. When radio was a new invention which stymied a number of professional performers, Will Rogers made his broadcasts extemporaneously. He conveyed the impression that he was too secure in himself to be worried. As one commentator noted, Rogers was "the only guy in radio who dares to hem and haw away air time" (Memorial no. 24, 152). Rogers' motion picture fans were aware that he was equally blasé on the set. Part of the delight in viewing a Rogers movie was watching Rogers deviate from the script, and seeing the confusion which his improvisation caused for fellow actors. While this horseplay might have been a pleasure for an audience accustomed to being programmed during working hours, it caused some consternation at Twentieth Century-Fox. Rochelle Hudson (who played ingénues in *Doctor Bull, Mr. Skitch, Judge Priest,* and *Life Begins at Forty*) admitted that Rogers' liberties with the script caused her great distress, for she often missed her mark. As she recalled, Rogers' proclivity for improvisation left her "listening for cues that never came . . . had me ad libbing to myself in my sleep long before my first picture with Bill was finished" (Memorial no.1, 13). A young and ambitious director, John Ford (forewarned about the onset insouciance of Will Rogers and Irvin Cobb), began the filming of *Steamboat Round the Bend* (1935) with the simple but knowing question: "Does either of you two gentlemen have the faintest idea of what this story is about?" (Rogers "His Last").

Will Rogers' screen audiences were delighted by his improvisations, for his liberty even from the verbal restrictions of a script conveyed the impression that he was a man at ease with himself who (unlike his middle-class audience) was capable of transcending the petty demands of a busy life. One reviewer accurately spoke for millions when he said that "You feel, somehow, that he has captured the secret of being happy, and that if you watch the screen

The Evolving Persona of Will Rogers 39

Will Rogers as "Relief" During the Depression Years

carefully, this secret may be yours" (Memorial *Doctor Bull*). As with the other virtues described in this section, the audience believed that this secret applied to Rogers the man as well as to the Rogers screen persona.

3. The Sympathetic Spirit
Rogers' humanitarian activities were widely followed and admired. When an earthquake destroyed Managua, Nicaragua, in 1931, Will Rogers flew south to lend his name to fund raising efforts; after floods ripped through the lower Mississippi Valley in 1927, Will

Rogers was on the spot to entertain and to ease the pain of the dispossessed; when Oklahoma and surrounding states became a "dust bowl' during the famous drought of the 1930s, Rogers stumped Oklahoma, Arkansas, and Texas for the Red Cross. The itineraries of what were called his "tours of mercy" boggle the mind. His contemporaries found it difficult to believe that a man could do so much for so many without some kind of mission of love inspiring him. One contemporary went so far as to call these tours as representative of Will Rogers' "Christ-like spirit of giving." When they reported these tours, newsmen did not hesitate to contrast the personal concern demonstrated by Rogers with the foot-dragging and bureaucratic bungling of an inept and indifferent government. There is little doubt that, by circumventing the red tape and empty debates, Will Rogers gave many 'forgotten men' in the age of Coolidge and Hoover the sense that someone of national stature was personally concerned about their suffering.

A writer for Florida's *Jacksonville Journal* summed up the profound effect of Rogers' personal charity. Note the emphasis in this response upon Rogers' spiritual use of one of the principal symbols of the age of technology:

> Giving wings to most people does not add to their ability to be of benefit to the world...though it may increase their economic efficiency.... But when a genius such as Will Rogers 'got wings,' he becomes a sort of superman, not by reason of superiority of attitude, but by the multiplication of his contacts with human creatures who need a bit of cheer in their helplessness or weariness or misery. Like St. Francis, he is a lover not of mankind, at large, but men as individuals. St. Francis used the 'shabby expedient' of a rope to tie around his waist in his spiritual vocation; Will Rogers used it to humanize his philosophy. And the good he does in this world is increased by his mobility. (Stone "Simple Life")

As a representative person, Will Rogers embodied a ready sympathy, a freedom from the selfishness which seemed to be the guiding spirit of the materialistic American twenties. In a society where members of the same apartment building did not know each other, Will Rogers communicated the notion that cities and nations (through his example) could be linked by neighborly bonds of affection: "he comes nearer being a Jongleur de Dieu than any modern world personage—a jongleur and a troubadour in one—not for a single community, but for thousands of cities and for the remotest cabins. To have wings for such service is not merely to minister to more people directly; but is to carry them the human kindness of others and to bring these people into wider human relationships" (Stone "Simple Life").

4. "The Real Things of Life"
The news surrounding Will Rogers' response to his sister's death binds together many of the values and qualities which his audience identified with Will Rogers the "private" man. One report may stand as a representative of the whole: "The Real Things of Life" begins with an explanation of Rogers' wealth and popularity as an entertainer and journalist. The major point of the article (and a very important one for Rogers' followers) is that no matter how successful, how far on top of the heap, Will Rogers proudly kept his spiritual roots in the soil of Oklahoma (Memorial no. 25, 43).

The articles about the death of Rogers' sister and his response to it emphasize two incidents. The first occurs while Rogers is entertaining a convention hall filled with ministers. As he delivers his planned comic lines, Rogers is overwhelmed by the thought of his sister's suffering, and breaks into tears. With an immediate change of mood, the Oklahoman asked the assembled clergy to pray for his sister, Mrs. C. L. Lane. Far from ridiculing Rogers' display of emotion, an admiring reporter wrote: "He could not hide his sorrow, nor would it have been more manly in him to suppress his tears" (Memorial no. 25, 43).

The second incident involves Rogers' response to a newspaper story which he saw while returning to Claremore, Oklahoma, to attend his sister's funeral. Perusing a state newspaper, he noticed a headline calling his sister "Mrs. C. L. Lane, sister of famous comedian, Will Rogers." Rogers' response was noted well because it reaffirmed his respect for rural America, even though he was himself a success in the new world of the city. After seeing the headline, he attempted to correct what he saw as a very false impression. Reflecting about the reverent, mourning crowds of country people, he demonstrated his respect for "The Real Things of Life": "It's the other way around. I am the brother of Mrs. C. L. Lane, 'The Friend of Humanity.' And I want to tell you that as I saw all these people who were there to pay tribute to her memory, it was the proudest moment of my life that I was her brother. And all the honors that I could ever in my wildest dreams hope to reach, would never equal the honor paid on a little western hilltop among her people to Maude Lane. If they love me like that at the finish, my life will not have been in vain" (Memorial no. 25, 43).

Such a statement of respect for the values and judgment of small town America had broad resonances in 1925. The revolt from the village had long before become a trendy cause in popular and serious literature: Sinclair Lewis added the word "Babbitt" to the American language in 1922 in his searing portrait of a Middle Western businessman, soi-disant sophisticated readers of H. L. Mencken's *American Mercury* (1924-33) were learning to chortle over the strange and antiquated manners and morals of the "booboisie" of the American hinterland. This was indeed a period when "The Midwest stood for all that was tedious, humdrum, and false about human existence" (Leuchtenberg 156). Within this context of contempt for rural America, Rogers' newspaper audience took note of his emotional reaction to his sister's death. Unquestionably, Rogers' followers were probably reading at least some of the writings of Lewis and Mencken, but they were impressed (and perhaps reassured) by this incident. Clearly, Rogers had his feet in basic old American values even though he was living in California and earning one of the highest salaries in show business.

Members of his audience may have made the same rise, but they feared that they had left a society which could value people for non-economic virtues. In contrast, Will Rogers had made the same passage to the new without losing touch with the old. His ability to bridge the gap (and their capacity to admire him for doing it) salved their consciences. As one Hollywood acquaintance summed up Will Rogers' unusual capacity to keep his feet planted in both realms, "Bill is perhaps the world's most widely traveled citizen with the hometown feeling completely untouched" (Memorial no.1, 13). Thus, to a disturbingly mobile people, Will Rogers "represented something fundamentally honest in human nature, something which, in the hectic movement of the passing time, we seem to be in danger of forgetting and eventually losing" (Stone "Chatting").

B. Rogers the Journalist

Because Americans imputed so many anachronistic (yet estimable) characteristics to Will Rogers, they willingly turned in their confusion to his newspaper column every morning for a dose of common sense. Will Rogers seemed to be uncorrupted by the fads of the period, and this exemption convinced people that he (unlike them) could look straight at the new and see whether or not the Emperor had on a new set of clothes.

1. The Old (the Essential), the New (the Inessential), and the Crash (a Judgment)

While Will Rogers is remembered today as simply a "humorist," his contemporaries were very much interested in Rogers as a moralist. The moralism of his social commentary was rendered in his humor as much by a dramatic technique which runs through it as by the words employed. The basic inner technique of Rogers' humor is implicit in the relationship which he articulates between himself as an observer and the modern world, which he then reports for us. The

Rogers as Both Cowboy and Journalist

observer in Will Rogers' humorous journalism is always an "old boy" from Claremore, Oklahoma, who has been by-passed by the germs of fashion. We are always forced to assume that this speaker has some kind of contact with a core of uncorrupted, "natural" rural values. Because our speaker is pre-modern, pre-urban, he can see though many of the artificial problems which perplex urban man.

The society and leaders observed in Will Rogers' humorous journalism are usually associated with ideas, institutions, inventions, or problems which are new to the twentieth century. As Rogers' innocent eye scans the contemporary horizon, it focuses quickly on the exaggerated sense of self-importance which the urban man claims for himself. The lesson which Rogers tries to communicate is that men in cities, in corporations, at the head of big governments and major political parties may have convinced themselves that they are important to the world, but our rural commentator—who is closer to nature—knows better. Since men's pride is the subject of so much of Rogers' commentaries, it should be underscored that the insights which he presents are penetrating not because of his special intelligence, but by virtue of the perspective of the human comedy which his rural (and pleasantly backward) location gives him. Only in exceptional cases (the pilot Lindbergh is one) does a product of the twentieth century prove itself to be a match for a counterpart in the 1890s. We are told both explicitly (by argument) and implicitly (by metaphor) that people at the turn of the century knew who they were and what they wanted, but that twentieth-century American man (because he has lost his roots) is pursuing a set of hollow and trivial goals.

Rogers' device of speaking for an older value system is especially obvious in the following criticism of Nevada's infamous (and then shockingly new) divorce mill: "Lawyers meet the trains and line up and holler out the same as porters do down South at depots for Hotels. They got lawyers there that can get you loose from an Octopus. Lots of the women buy...cottages till their probation is over. Lots of them keep their houses there, and then use them when they come back on the next case. Some women have as many as four or five 'notches' on the same house, showing that they had got their man" (Day 146). The humor in this passage is created by the speaker's attitude: he is a curious innocent looking on in bewilderment. The moralistic judgment is implicit in the verbal pictures constructed, especially the metaphor of the female as gunslinger. A society which tolerates such role reversals is obviously decadent.

Surveying a modern civilization which produces so much that the institution of advertising has been needed to force people to consume, Rogers tartly observes that "One-third of the people in the United States promote, while the other two-thirds provide" (Day 85). The judgment in this remark stems from Rogers' adherence to the ethic of work and productivity rather than the goals of leisure and consumption so praised by the twentieth century, especially by the ubiquitous voice of advertising. To Rogers' mind, advertising was especially dangerous because it frequently convinced people to relinquish valid old truths that had been tested over years. Such a negative judgment is the buried irony of the famous phrase which became a sort of verbal signature for Rogers the journalist. While the phrase "All I know is what I read in the papers" led most of Rogers weekly articles, it did not mean what it literally said, but precisely the opposite. Rogers despaired that the average middle-class American in his audience swallowed the reports of the press and the claims of advertisers whole each morning along with their new vitamin pills. To his peril, it was the average American who knew only what he read in the papers. As a man who represented a fading value system, which had been forgotten by mass media, it was Rogers' purpose to hold the perspectives and information of these opinion-creating newspapers up to the light of his older, tested truths.

While Will Rogers the humanitarian certainly did not gloat over the stock market's resounding crash and the subsequent economic depression, he did believe that the depression validated the criticism which he had been delivering all through the twenties. Although the Oklahoma humorist expressed himself in homier language, his critique was not unlike that which voiced by the anthropologist, Edward Sapir. While Sapir, the academic, explained that Americans were living in a "spurious culture," Rogers summed up his criticism in the famous insight that "there ain't no civilization where there ain't no satisfaction, and that's what's the trouble now, nobody is satisfied" (Day 221). One quip by Rogers is particularly devastating: "Two hundred years from now, history will record: 'America, a nation that flourished from 1900 to 1942, conceived many odd inventions for getting somewhere, but could think of nothing to do when they got there'" (226). His very famous observation that "America is the only nation to go to the poorhouse in an automobile" is a compression of this ironic criticism of the mindless worship of technology. As the depression deepened, so did Rogers' vision grow darker, bordering on an uncharacteristic despair. Shortly before his death, he wrote that "Civilization is nothing but acquiring comforts for ourselves, when before civilization they were so hard they didn't need 'em. We will strive to put in another bath, when many of our neighbors can't even put in an extra loaf of bread" (365).

2. Let Me Play With Your Problems

Because Will Rogers had faith that men could survive both their problems and their leaders, he was fortunately spared the kind of despair which the last quotation seems to reflect. For although he was a political commentator for most of his adult life he believed that "history makes itself, and statesmen just drag along" (Day 323). For some men, such a conclusion could be fatalistic, but in Rogers the message which is hammered home repeatedly is that we should not take our politicians, intellectual systems, or ourselves as seriously as we do—life is more fun and less taxing when we learn to see that man is not at the center of the universe. Rogers could remain aloof even during the crucial presidential election of 1932. In response to the exaggerated predictions of gloom by both candidates, Rogers retorted that "This country is a thousand times bigger than any two men in it or any two parties in it. This country has gotten where it is in spite of politics, not by aid of it. That we have carried as political bunk as we have and still survived shows we are a super nation." Given this perspective, Rogers advised the candidates to take a rest and let the people make up their minds: "Get the world off your shoulders and go fishing. Then come back next Wednesday and we will let you know which one is the lesser of two evils of you" (Day 298).

In the "playful" (vs. the "moralistic") vein of his journalistic humor, Rogers seems to have appointed himself to be a translator of the new to the American people. In this role, he strove not so much to judge the new as to play with it as his audience looked on with admiration. On first inspection, many of these playful articles seem superficial. After all, they formulate no solutions for the problems which they discuss. Such an analysis misses the real point of these articles—in them, Rogers is not attempting to formulate answers so much as to give his audience a sense that the novelty discussed is not so awesomely complex and threatening as it might appear at first. His major goal in these articles is not to turn out stock answers to the daily headlines. He modestly wished to slow down their impact on the mind of his audience. If he could only juggle them long enough, the result would be that his audience could deal with them more sensibly.

Some small sampling of these playful articles is necessary to counterbalance the impression that Rogers was strictly a moralist. In the following daily telegram, Rogers sends President Coolidge a mock warning about the popular tune, "Valencia." It is on its way to deeply poison the public mind of America: "My dear Mr. President: There will be a song hitting you now if it hassent already hit you. Do what you can to keep people from going entirely cuckoo over it. It is in exchange for 'Yes, We Have No Bananas,' and is called 'Valencia.' It ain't the Piece—it's all right—it's the amount of times they will play it, Have Ear Muffs ready" (Day 128). This is the voice of a man who delights in the absurdities of popular culture!

Rogers' capacity to make his readers laugh at their own frenetic involvement in change must have released psychological tensions. In one telegram that became famous he observed: "Give an American a one-piece bathing suit, a hamburger, and five gallons of gas and they are just as tickled as a movie star with a new divorce" (Day 325). Here Rogers addresses himself directly to manifestations of the rapid changes in the moral, social, and physical environments: the one-piece bathing suit was considered to be a daring symbol of rebellion from Victorian prudery; the hamburger is the snack of a society which is in a hurry (and probably not exactly sure where it is going); the automobile is obviously a symbol of industrial civilization. The final, synthesizing line about the movie star with a divorce gives the description a special twist. The reader does feel guilty and confused about the rapidity with which his life is changing in all sectors, but he knows that he is not as fallen as the movie star. The inappropriate conjunction in this humorous comparison helps the reader to feel reassured that he has not yet gone off the deep end, for all his movement away from the certainties of the 1890s.

To the obvious delight of his audience, Rogers would "play" with the most unplayful of problems. The growing combativeness in Europe and Asia was no laughing matter to Americans in the 1920s and 1930s. The innocent provincial could not hold back, however, because he was driven to be the representative tester of the new: "Japan wants a 'Monroe Doctrine' with them playing the part of Monroe, 'doctoring' on China. Not only 'doctoring,' but operating" (Day 310). Here is a line directed at events which were in the papers of the previous day. What Rogers succeeds in doing here is subtle, but essential to understanding the appeal of his daily articles. In a short space, he has summarized the nature of the threat. He then exaggerates the justifications of the belligerent so that they appear ridiculous and self-criticizing. Finally, he provides a summary judgment of the problem. When a typical reader of Will Rogers' daily article put down the newspaper, the problem was no less real to him, but it was certainly psychologically more manageable. With numerous messages of violence, war, and depression pouring in from all points in the world, people needed to laugh so that they could function. Rogers' humorous treatment helped insulate them from the shocks. As one of the townspeople says in *The Will Rogers Story*, (1952, starring Will Rogers, Jr.): "You don't tell us much, Will, but you sure do keep us laughing."

Speaking in his moralistic voice, Rogers could conclude about the depression that it wasn't "Hoover, the Republicans, or even Russia that...[was] responsible. I think the Lord just looked us over and decided to set us back where we belonged" (Day 234). But for all his criticism, Rogers had a deep faith in the ability of the American people to adapt. To help them with their adjustment, Rogers undertook for himself the role of reducing massive, abstract threats in politics and society to manageable proportions. By making Americans laugh at Japan's Monroe Doctoring, he skillfully provided a catharsis for real and profound tensions. The common denominator which links Will Rogers' moralistic journalism to his playful journalism is his explicit and articulate discussion of the new and challenging in the contemporary setting.

Unlike his journalism, Will Rogers' films appear to have no relation at all to contemporary events and themes. We search these films in vain for the excoriator of advertising, or the debunker of disarmament conferences. We cannot even find the intransigent foe of the one-piece bathing suits. For this reason, the question immediately poses itself: Why is the *persona* which Rogers portrays in his films so out of touch with twentieth century America? Are these merely flimsy "entertainment films" which are intentionally irrelevant? Or is it possible that below the surface of Will Rogers' films there is a symbolism and a mood which spoke clearly to the millions who flocked to see them? Is it possible that the problems of the 1920s and 1930s which Rogers dealt with in his journalism are latent within the films in a coded form, waiting to be decoded by the historian who is both sensitive to the historical issues and the impact of film?

III. An Evolving Screen Persona: From Cowboy to Uncle Will

In a scene from the (now lost) film, *One Day in 365*, Rogers is sitting in the sunroom of his beautiful house in Santa Monica Canyon, reading the newspaper. The headline reads: "REGARDLESS OF DISARMAMENT PLANS, THERE ARE RUMBLINGS OF WAR." He looks up from his paper and says to Betty Rogers, "I guess the Republicans want another war, to show how much better they can run it than the Democrats." When he finishes reading the paper, he throws it down in disgust saying, "Same old junk—murder and divorce—the people who were divorced last year are being murdered this year" (Memorial no. 8). This scene is pertinent because its relevance to current events is *atypical*. Rogers played many parts on film, but the common characteristic of all of them was their *detachment from contemporary issues*. And the longer Rogers remained in Hollywood, the farther back his character moved into an Arcadian—and seemingly irrelevant—pre-industrial.

The Cowboy and Jubilo

Will Rogers made his first film, *Laughing Bill Hyde* (1918) while twirling his rope on the stage of Ziegfeld's *Follies*. He was cast as

Will Rogers in *Jubilo* (1919)

a cowboy in various melodramatic and comic roles and had real problems with his audience in the early films. New York critics who knew the Oklahoman from the *Follies* brought an understanding of his humor to the theatre. On the other hand, the general public was indifferent because it had not yet been properly exposed to this fresh breeze from the West. Although times were good during what we now call "the Jazz Age," records show that Samuel Goldwyn lost at least $40,000 on these early films ("Series R").

After a short time as a cowboy, Rogers developed a second film persona. Called "Jubilo," the figure is a rural clown, a perpetual loafer who floats through society getting himself into trouble and avoiding work whenever possible. Jubilo is an eccentric figure whom we love despite his numerous flaws. He is distinctly unlike the late, philosophical Rogers persona: Jubilo can fall in love, and even has a few (rather athletic) fist fights. The image was still evolving.

The Innocent Abroad

During Rogers' middle film period (1929-1932) he developed still another screen persona, one which would have been readily recognized by his daily readers. In these portraits of an "Innocent Abroad," he is a simple down-to-earth figure (usually from Claremore, Oklahoma) who is forced to travel outside his

As Innocent Abroad in *A Connecticut Yankee* (1931)

provincial world to Washington (*Going to Congress*), New Orleans (*Handy Andy*) or Europe (*They Had to See Paris*). The Innocent is usually escorted out of his normal environment by his wife, who aspires to be a sophisticated and "broad minded" citizen of the twentieth century. In a few instances, some local political faction accidentally elects the Innocent to Congress, assuming that he can be manipulated. The humor in all of these films about the Innocent Abroad derives from the interplay between the central character and the "sophisticated" people of the urban centers. In most cases, Will Rogers overwhelms the effete urbanites by the sheer force of his ebullient personality.

In playing these roles as the Innocent, Rogers began to show that he was more than merely a good actor. One reviewer discerned deeper themes. In speaking of Pike Peters (a character portrayed by Rogers in *They Had to See Paris*, 1929)—a reviewer noted that "Will Rogers has become a national character, infinitely more characteristic of America than the grotesque figure of Uncle Sam. It would be an artistic and patriotic crime to let such a film character [i.e., the Innocent Abroad] die" (Memorial no.8, 204). The reviewer and his public were not disappointed, for a sequel entitled *So This Is London* (1930) provided Rogers with a similar ironic contrast.

America's new place in the international world determined the strong response to Rogers in this role. While America had refused to enter the League of Nations, the facts of international life could not be denied—the United States was the most powerful nation in the world, but was still unsure of its place and its role. Rogers' Innocent Abroad films gave Americans a confident sense of poise in the international setting. The message of these films is always that older civilizations may have posted their claims to pre-eminence before the United States, but post-war realities obviously showed that the United States was the only country in the world whose spirit had not been broken by the experience of the Great War. As one discerning reviewer reported, Rogers not only gave Americans confidence inspiring self-image, he also conveyed a better picture of American character and values to the outside world:

> There was always the quiet homely voice and the loveable smile to keep us in touch with the things we knew and understood. He was a Westerner talking to Westerners in a language and with an awkward grace readily comprehended. He was the epitome of the spirit of the West: open-handed, free and easy, loquacious, oddly philosophical, genuinely sentimental with a smile ever within reach of one of the boys. And we liked to think that this was the picture of us that he carried to other and far corners of the world, where people, not knowing us too well, were apt to think of us as uncouth and six-shooting. (Stone "Chatting")

The advent of sound films effected a transformation in what Rogers could convey to his audience. Prior to sound, viewers missed much of his special brand of humor if they were not prepared by a night at the *Follies*, or had read a weekly or daily column. With sound, it was impossible to miss his radiating humanity. Speaking of this power to project personality, a reviewer of Rogers' first talkie, *They Had to See Paris*, noted that: "This picture changes all the difficulties of communication in the silent films. Rogers' shadow is almost a living thing. The wit is spontaneous and droll ... the disarming humanness of the man envelopes the screen, the orchestra and the auditorium with one surging feeling of brotherhood" (Stone *Beverly*).

Uncle Will

What was now needed in the era of sound was the proper screen "vehicle" and persona. Of importance in selecting that role was the awareness that the camera could supply much of the atmosphere, that Will Rogers in a film could say less and actually *personify* the values which had guided his "private" life and his journalistic commentary. In the late Will Rogers films (three of them with director John Ford) he is no longer the cowboy, the clown, the satirist—nor even the innocent abroad—but a very different symbol of a harmonious America before the turn of the century. He lives in the mythical world which Americans nostalgically projecting back into the 1890s.

Actually, Rogers had experimented with the small town role during the 1920s. One critic was extremely impressed by its possibilities. In a review of *Jes Call Me Jim* (1920), he noted that the kind of effects which would later be attributed to the Rogers of the later sound films—that he was not merely amusing his audience, but conveying a much needed message of brotherhood and a refreshingly positive perspective on human possibilities. In this way, the Rogers films were serving a social function: "Will Rogers'...good natured personality seems to spread throughout the world a sense of happiness and kindness. I suppose a man like this, acting as he does before almost countless millions, does more good to this old earth than scores of preachers and philanthropists; able to reach more hearts than can be reached through any other medium" (Memorial no.20, 37).

In *State Fair* (1933) Rogers came back to this role. Audiences, executives at Twentieth Century-Fox, and critics all recognized immediately that this was the ideal persona for Rogers because it placed him "in a day when American village life was far more isolated than it is today" (Croy no. 24, 90). Celebrating that "Will Rogers Restored Picture Themes to Provincial Subjects," a reviewer captured the national response: "*State Fair* taught Rogers his correct métier and it taught the industry that pictures concerning inland provincial characters were more appealing than penthouses and gun-spattered pavements." The reviewer concluded that these nostalgic pictures had tapped a "forgotten public" which "had lost interest in crime and so-called 'smart' films [and had] stayed away entirely from cinema" (Rosenfield).

At least in the beginning, both the film critics and this "forgotten public" shared a common enthusiasm. Some critics thought that they saw a "complete metamorphosis [in Rogers] from amusing philosopher into character actor" (Memorial no. 1, 46). Other critics saw that after being a cowboy, clown, and innocent abroad, Rogers had finally stumbled upon the right character for the screen. But after the formula was repeated a few times, critics tired of the rural Rogers "vehicle." Ironically, while the cinephiles stopped applauding Rogers' films, the American public swarmed to them in ever-increasing numbers, and film rentals for Fox averaged about $2.5 million per film. The irony of this disaffection of the critics was that Rogers had begun his career as a darling of the critics but a box-office failure; in these late films, Rogers was obviously appealing to real and profound popular emotions, emotions that could easily be overlooked by a critic interested in film as an art form. For the average viewer of these films did not buy a ticket to see art, but for psychological relief and fatherly support.

The world of the late Will Rogers films is purposefully insulated from contemporary strains and pressures. For this reason the psychological "payoff" from these rural dramas was the opportunity to temporarily escape from the world of ethical confusion, economic depression, and impending war. In *David Harum* (1934) this place is called "Homeville," a term which will used hereafter to describe the nostalgic, pre-industrial world of the late films. Economic breakdown, the separation of a democratic society into rigid classes, the professionalization of knowledge may exist in this world of the later films, but in a special form. In Homeville, all of these threats are reduced to human proportions; they may challenge Homeville's citizens, but they never seem to overwhelm the good denizens of this pre-1900 imaginary town.

Because the challenges to happiness and fulfillment have been reduced, the Will Rogers persona in Homeville can deal with them. (Rogers in these last films will hereafter be called "Uncle Will" because of his avuncular role.) In a few instances, Uncle Will enlists the aid of the threatened, but most often he is capable of solving the problems by himself—or with the help of servants, members of minorities and the working class. He is really more than just an inhabitant of Homeville: he is its superintending consciousness. Uncle Will has a special insight into the human heart. Because of this special power, and because every problem in Homeville has a human face, Uncle Will is a master of this world. The best metaphor for the perspective given the viewer of the late Rogers films is that of a reversed telescope. The result of scanning the world in this perspective is that everything appears smaller and therefore less challenging.

The remainder of this chapter will look closely at *David Harum* (1934) and *In Old Kentucky* (1935) to detail this miniaturizing process.

David Harum *(1934)*

The first scene of *David Harum* (1934) could not be more explicit about the nostalgic function of the late Rogers films. Will Rogers plays a rural banker who has come to New York City to visit General Woolsey, a Wall Street banker. The panic of 1893 has forced the General to close his doors and he is very curious to know how Uncle Will can remain open for business during times of "depression, unemployment, and starvation." What is the secret?

David Harum's answer is hardly an answer at all. Its dramatic purpose is to accentuate the differences between the two worlds which these men inhabit: the General lives in an American city which has proven itself to be out of balance; Uncle Will lives in the country where people may not be good, but the proximity of

Uncle Will at work (with Kent Taylor)

people to each other assures that they are always under control. Harum explains to the General: "Well, General, I go a long way on character, and after I've gone a long way on character, I check on collateral. Then I give 'em half of what they ask for."

This statement says something about the volume of business which Uncle Will does up in Homeville. He knows everybody in the small town, but he also realizes that it is "human nature" for borrowers to pad both their loan requests as well as to overestimate their ability to repay. Fully aware that even his best clients will cheat, Uncle Will gives them half of what they request—which, ironically, is probably what they really need! The point of all this dialogue is that the urban banker is a victim of impersonal economic forces which he cannot control. David Harum's Homeville, on the other hand, is never affected by anything as abstract as twenty-one year periodic economic cycles. As David explains, the people of Homeville are not dependent on a fickle outside market for their prosperity. Because they are closer to nature, they are self-sufficient and can therefore "roll their own" in hard times.

A young male figure enters *David Harum* with troubles not entirely foreign to a 1930s audience. John Lennox's father recently committed suicide because of his heavy losses on the stock market. To compound John's problems, his urban fiancée has closed out their engagement as she would a savings account—there is no more money in it. John has been searching for a job in a city that has none to offer. But because this is the panic of 1893 (and not the depression of the 1930s) John has recourse to the country to renew his chances for a good life. General Woolsey cannot help John personally, but he makes arrangements for David Harum to take John into the bank up in Homeville. When John leaves the befuddled city for the stable, self-sufficient countryside, he remarks pointedly: "Thanks, General—I want to get away from the city and get to work."

John Lennox (played by Kent Taylor as an urban man who must learn to get some roots back into "the real things in life") has severe initial difficulties with the primitive conditions of Homeville. On the stormy night of his arrival, he finds the kitchen of the local hotel closed, and learns that if he wants to use the tub, he must pay extra. Upstairs, he finds that the ceiling of his room leaks, and that a broken pane in his window is not interfering with the rain. The night clerk informs John that the town's only carpenter will fix the window when his rheumatism improves—which will probably be never. The purpose of piling up these details of backwardness and inefficiency is to communicate clearly that, in Homeville, work is not the most important part of life. As a result of not being obsessed by the Protestant ethic, Homevillers are happy—even if they are unwashed and a little behind on conveniences.

Uncle Will (as David Harum) personifies Homeville's indifference toward work and money. He is liberated from material concerns: in order of their priority, his worldly interests consist of horse trading; ring toss (played in his office with his pocket knife stabbed into the middle of his papers as a pole); and fishing. Uncle Will even has difficulty making it to his office at all on many days because of the chances for horse trades and conversation along the way.

If considered closely, the six horse trades in *David Harum* fit into the overall pattern of reduced threats that we find in Homeville. As explained by Uncle Will to his skeptical sister, the golden rule of the horse trade is "Do Unto Others What They Want to Do Unto You." Translated into the world of the 1920s and 1930s as a business ethic, this is precisely the doctrine which led to disaster. Yet in the setting of Homeville, the false representation and sharping of the horse trades seem quaint and entertaining, for what is destructive in Hooverville can be transformed into humor in Homeville.

David Harum's practices as a banker reflect his easygoing attitude, his charity, but also his power to see into the human heart. His opening lines about gouging a client taught that human beings are neither good nor bad, but a little of each. Because they can easily go astray, they cannot be completely trusted; but because they are not completely evil, there is no need for cynicism. The film also indicates that a small town is an ideal social unit because, in a small town, people have an opportunity to study one another over a long period of time. The small town is an ideal society, not because people act better there, but because, in a small town, a better watch can be kept over a wayward human nature.

Uncle Will's behavior as a banker reflects this basic philosophy. When an impoverished widow cannot keep up with her mortgage payments, Uncle Will discovers a "forgotten" bank account which clears her of debt. This tender act of charity is followed by an entirely different scene which demonstrates that—for all his sympathy—Uncle Will is no sentimentalist. Immediately after his scene with the widow, Uncle Will is confronted by a burly customer who arrogantly refuses to pay his loan on time, claiming that an improper signature of his co-signer makes him exempt from prosecution. Uncle Will looks out of the corner of his eye—he knew that this confrontation would come eventually—and slyly explains to the defaulter that he had obtained the proper signature months earlier in anticipation of this ploy. The note must be paid. This revelation leads to a fist fight; although no one is hurt in the uproar, a significant message comes through: if you are angry in Homeville, you can actually identify and take a swing at your oppressor. This personalized environment allows the individual to let off steam is in clear contrast with the frustratingly complex world of Muley Graves in Steinbeck's *Grapes of Wrath*. Unlike that impersonal setting of land companies, banks, and distant corporations, the forces that operate in Homeville always have a human face. As noted, the charitable spirit of Uncle Will controls Homeville because he has special powers to see into the human hearts of his small town.

Uncle Will's inveterate matchmaking in these last films tells much about his concern for particular human hearts. Reviewers tired rather quickly of the Kent Taylor/Evelyn Venable coupling that is repeated over and over again in the late films, but the mass audience kept coming back for more. To understand the full effect of these love-matches, we must realize that everyone in the audience understood that Rogers was in no way interested in the young girls he helps to find their man. One reviewer summarized the audience's sense that Rogers was a "sympathetic and comforting 'old man': If ever a man was a father, it's Will. When Ann comes up to Will's bedroom [at the opening of *David Harum*] while he is dressing, there is no embarrassment. With any other actor, the audience might smirk and think naughty thoughts. But with Will, he is so much the father type, naughtiness occurs to nobody" ("Daddy"). These romances are really of no interest in themselves, but they have a function in the late films. Just as marriages in nineteenth-century novels frequently have social and other significances, so the presence of separated young people in the late sound films is used to convey a deeper meaning. Simply, the young lovers exist in these films so that Uncle Will can have something loving to do.

It is not difficult to decode the appeal of this element of the late films. Rogers' audience was living in a world which was growing increasingly impersonal. Not only community feeling, but the small loyalty demanded by the nuclear family was becoming exhausted as the result of the intellectual and economic strains. The appeal may have been sentimental, but an image of such a man as Rogers was very much needed by his audience to counterbalance this drift toward depersonalization. In a treacherous world which seemed to be out of control, here stood a sympathetic personality, completely unselfish, concerned with warding off harm rather than amassing power. Viewers of the late films were shown lovers who were separated because of financial differences (*David Harum*); the law's delays (*Steamboat Round the Bend*); the dishonesty of a spoiled rich boy (*Life Begins at Forty*); the covetousness of city folk (*In Old Kentucky*). Fortunately for the young lovers, in all these cases, democratic Uncle Will is present to help. He manipulates the people of Homeville (and even the weather) so that these barriers can be surmounted. The result is that the young people finally recognize that they are just human beings, and that the differences which seemed so insuperable are really artificial and flimsy when weighed against the inner promptings of the heart. As a result of all this matchmaking, Rogers comes to represent a generous spirit of brotherhood. And while this message is transmitted in the later films through a flimsy set of conventions, the ultimate effect is to demonstrate that we Americans still have the capacity to transcend our materialism and our growing class barriers.

Our superintendent of hearts frequently calls into play some form of *deus ex machina* to extricate him and his friends from the predicaments in which they find themselves. The most absurd of them all (from *In Old Kentucky*) is worth relating for its unreality and its appeal. Grandfather hires a rainmaker to salt the clouds so that the track will be muddy during the climactic race. When the rainmaker's standard concoctions prove to be unsuccessful, he ties a bundle of dynamite to a cluster of balloons and hopes for the best. When the balloons fail to lift the dynamite, the bundle slams into a water tower near the finishing stretch, with the result of completely flooding the track. Because the track is flooded, the Martingale horse, Blueboy, comes from behind at the last moment to win the race. His victory ends all of the personal difficulties and family feuds which have caused so much division and unhappiness. Only in Homerville, the land of wish-fulfillment, can such *dei ex machinii* grind out their answers without complaints from the audience!

Here the theme of the use and abuse of power enters in a coded form. Always a critic of men who aspired to hold power, how does Rogers on the screen avoid the abuses which he found in others? Here the contrived conclusions of the films find their meaningful (and comforting) place. Certainly most of the films achieve their happy endings in this way: in *Judge Priest*, Uncle Will persuades his Southern jury to acquit his client by playing "Dixie" outside the courtroom window at just the right moment; in *Steamboat Round the Bend*, a race, which eventually joins the lovers and saves an innocent man's life, is won because an unexpected supply of patent medicine (with a high alcoholic content) is discovered at the last minute to be effective as a high energy fuel; *In Old Kentucky* ends with a horse race in which the track becomes providentially muddy. In every case cited, Uncle Will sees to it that all the love knots are tied, and that society's conflicts are resolved—but always without an overt display of power. Uncle Will always gives the impression that he has somehow transformed power into love. Unlike political and business leaders outside the theater, he has the gods on his side. In all of the late films, viewers are encouraged to identify with the young lovers, to experience their (temporary) sense of tension and unfulfillment, but then gradually to be rewarded by the tutelary deity of Homeville, Uncle Will. Those who succumbed to these love stories may have been guilty of taking an emotional holiday, but we can understand their deep need for such an escape from the world that awaited them outside the theater. In these hours of escape, viewers could smile at the pleasing notion that John Lennox and Ann Madison are married at the conclusion of *David Harum*. They could applaud John and Ann's decision to remain in Homeville rather than return to the city. Unfortunately, the viewers of *David Harum* could not lean on the comforting spirit of Uncle Will, nor could they stay in the protected landscape of Homeville; they had to go home when the lights went on.

Will Shows "Horse Sense"

In Old Kentucky *(1935)*

Much of what has been said about Homeville and Uncle Will applies to the Rogers figure and the community portrayed in one of his last two films, *In Old Kentucky* (1935). The story brings two very different families into conflict: the Martingales are an out-at-elbows rural family whose very special horse, Blueboy, is coveted by a neighboring gentleman farm and his daughter (the Shattocks). Somewhere in the past, a piece of property was added illegally to the Shattock farm, initiating a feud between the two families. Uncle Will in this setting plays a horse trainer, Steve Tapley, who is especially concerned about the boy and girl who have become separated because of the feud.

The style and behavior of the Shattocks show that the city is encroaching upon the countryside. Grandpa Martingale becomes the center of controversy, because he is still angry about his stolen piece of land. He aims his shotgun at the Shattock automobile whenever it passes the Martingale house. But Grandpa never fires. Viewers quickly learn that Grandpa is an eccentric old man who is really quite harmless. Nevertheless, because they are city people, the Shattocks know how to call the impersonal force of the law into play. They file a complaint against Grandpa, with the hope that legal pressure will force the Martingales to sell their horse, Blueboy.

As Steve Tapley, Uncle Will is hard pressed to avert a tragedy. After all, he is a mere horse trainer in this film, and therefore lacks the social leverage which was his when he was David Harum, Homeville's only banker. Nevertheless, Uncle Will lives up to the occasion because in Homeville (unlike Hooverville) character is the source of power, not money or social position. For this reason, a social inferior like Uncle Will can gain complete control. With his insight into the darker regions of the human heart, Uncle Will can anticipate the ploys of the Shattocks as they attempt to buy (or steal) Blueboy; with his more tender concern for individuals, Uncle Will can assure that Nancy Martingale and Lee Andrews are eventually matched. As in *David Harum*, so here, Homeville brings threats in manageable proportions. For example, the issue of class comes up quickly. The Shattocks exhibit the worst characteristics of the American rich: they dress according to the latest fashion; they speak with an affected accent; they have themselves chauffeured around Homeville in an enormous Packard touring car. In distinct contrast, the Martingales are unaffected citizens of Homeville: Grandpa still dresses like a farmer; young Nancy is always in a loose sweater and riding clothes; and, when the Martingales travel, they either bounce along on a buckboard or ride one of their fine horses. At their farm, the Shattocks have hordes of retainers, while the Martingales do their own work.

In Old Kentucky provides Will Rogers with an opportunity to comment on the new woman. Her superficiality and artificiality are contrasted with the virtues of Nancy Martingale (Dorothy Wilson), an ingénue of the fin de siecle style. While Ms. Shattock (Louise Henry) is identified quickly by her dress, her accent, her snobbery as the bitch that the new woman has become, Nancy Martingale shows herself to have feelings for animals (always a cardinal virtue in Homeville). Nancy also knows enough to rely on Steve because she seems to recognize in him both a confidant and guardian.

A scene in which Uncle Will visits a dress shop in the city most effectively contrasts the life styles of the urban Shattocks and the rural Martingales. A kick-off dance at the local country club has been planned for the night preceding the big race. Knowing that Nancy cannot afford a dress for herself, and aware that she must be at the dance to meet her young man, Uncle Will decides to take direct action. In this scene, Rogers dramatizes the distance between the sensibility of an older, rural America and the worldliness of the contemporary American mentality that is reflected in women's fashions. The store owner who greets Uncle Will speaks and acts more like the Madame of a bordello than a saleswoman. From the beginning, she and Uncle Will operate under a misconception: he wants a modest dress for his young employer; the manager of the dress shop thinks that he wants something spicy for a mistress. While Uncle Will is muttering to himself in a corner, the Madame parades out six or seven models who line up behind him half dressed (or half undressed) in diaphanous nightgowns and peignoirs. When Uncle Will turns around to see what has been brought out, he is shocked. Averting his eyes, he apologizes profusely for stumbling into the ladies dressing room! When the confusion is finally cleared up, Uncle Will buys a white, high necked, long-sleeved dress which is more consonant with his old-fashioned ideas about women. Predictably, on the night of the dance, Arlene Shattock is wearing one of the low-backed, clinging gowns which made Uncle Will blush. The lesson is obvious—in her covetousness and in her dress, Arlene has shown herself to be all that is misguided about the new woman.

In Old Kentucky miniaturizes the problem of the professionalization of knowledge, a twentieth-century development which Rogers wrote about frequently. Rogers was extremely suspicious of professional or school-trained experts, for he suspected that they frequently ascribed expertise to their work when none really existed. Whether bogus or not, the idea of the world becoming too complicated for the average man to understand was very much on the minds of Americans.

Dr. Lee Andrews (Russell Hardie) enters Homeville as a representative of professional learning. Whereas Uncle Will became a trainer by working with horses, Dr. Andrews has taken copious notes in the classrooms of Kentucky's new agricultural and mechanical college. Within the setting of Homeville, this symbol of complexity is quickly subdued by Uncle Will. Not only does Lee show complete respect for the old-fashioned trainer, the young doctor is entirely dependent upon Uncle Will in his love match.

In Old Kentucky thus presents (and reduces) the problems of a society breaking down into rigidly isolated classes; of a new morality and a new woman; of the professionalization of knowledge. Instead of being overwhelmed by these developments, our response (like our response to Will Rogers' "playful" journalism) is one of reassurance—Uncle Will's presence on the screen has lessened the impact. Throughout, the most important factor is that the environment and the people in Homeville are entirely malleable under the workings of the spirit of Uncle Will. Millions of Rogers' fans must have watched such resolutions of conflict with satisfaction. They must have been impressed by what one contemporary reviewer noted was Rogers' power "to set right all the troubles of the impulsive people around him" (Memorial no. 1, 31).

Conclusion

Given a sympathetic understanding of the forces affecting Americans in the 1920s and 1930s, it is difficult to vouchsafe them their inner need to love such a symbolic man. He meant so much to his people in a time of change and deprivation because he presented them with an image of what Americans had been told to believe was the best in their national character. In preserving this image of humanity and love, Rogers was making no small contribution to the sanity of Americans in a world rushing toward international violence. A reviewer of *In Old Kentucky* hit upon some of the essential positive factors of Rogers' contribution as man and as a film image. These late Homeville movies reassured Americans (especially frenzied New Yorkers) "about the solidity and innate common sense of this country." While the reviewer granted that Rogers was probably playing "himself," he felt compelled to add that as a representative figure, Rogers supplied welcome reassurance in an era of bad news: "Will Rogers has a curious national quality. He gives the impression somehow that this country is filled with such sages, wise with years, young in humor and life, shrewd, yet gentle." Most importantly for the reviewer, "He is what Americans think other Americans are like" (Rogers "Rev. of"). After the erosion of values in the 1920s, after the economic disaster of the 1930s, Americans were indeed fortunate to have such a public person to keep a hopeful image bright.

Discussion of the Literature about Will Rogers

Most biographers of Will Rogers claim that Rogers was a "failure"

"All I know is what I read in the papers."

in silent films, but a "success" once sound was introduced. In terms of box office receipts this is true, but Rogers' biographers also believe that he was a poor actor in the early films. *New York Times* reviews indicated that Rogers' silent films were much admired by those who understood Rogers' brand of humor. The real problem for Rogers was to make the nation aware of his personal style. This he did from 1922 onward as a public person, public speaker, and syndicated journalist. The thesis of this chapter is that Rogers became such a powerful film image precisely because of the associations which viewers—who understood his perspective—brought with them to the theater.

Rogers' "Jubilo" persona, the figure of the rural clown, can be found in such films as *Jubilo* (1919), *Honest Hutch* (1920), *Boys Will Be Boys* (1921), *The Headless Horseman*, *Fruits of Faith* (1922), *Too Busy for Work* (1923), *Jubilo, Jr.* and *Don't Park There* (1924). Some of Rogers' "Innocent Abroad" persona films include *Strolling Through Europe with Will Rogers* (episodes) (1926), *Going to Congress*, *A Truthful Liar* (1924), *A Texas Steer* (1927), *They Had to See Paris* (1929), *Lightnin'* (1930), *So This Is London*, *Young as You Feel*, *A Connecticut Yankee*, *Ambassador Bill* (1931), and *Business and Pleasure* (1932).

In Rogers' later film roles, he is neither the Jubilo, the Innocent Abroad, the Clown, nor the Cowboy, but is instead a symbol of the

1890s for depression America. In this final persona, Rogers plays a variety of small town figures: in *State Fair* (1933) he is a farmer anxious to see his pig take first prize; in *Doctor Bull* (1933) he is a small town doctor who is resistant to new-fangled ways; in *David Harum* (1934) he is a small town banker who is more interested in fishing and horse trading than gain; in *Handy Andy* (1934) he is a small town druggist who runs amuck when he tries to become part of the leisure class; in *Judge Priest* (1934) he is a small town judge in the post-Civil War South; in *County Chairman* (1935) he is a frontier politician in Wyoming about the time that Owen Wister's fictional hero, the Virginian, would have been settling down; in *Life Begins at Forty* (1935) he plays a small town newspaper editor with his hand on the pulse of the community; in *Steamboat Round the Bend* (1935) he is an avuncular captain of a renovated steamboat, the *Claremont Queen*; *In Old Kentucky* (1935) tells the story of the world of the Kentucky Derby before the syndicate moved in. This desire to look back at a simpler time is not new to the American Mind. In the 1970s people were learning to "groove" on the good-old fifties, forgetting in the process the atomic bomb, air raid drills, the Korean War, and the rampage of Senator Joseph McCarthy. In the 1860s and the 1870s Harriet Beecher Stowe held her inverted telescope up to the religious and social history of New England and discovered the nostalgic and peaceful towns she describes in *Oldtown Folks* (1869) and *Poganuc People* (1878). Still earlier, Royall Tyler wrote probably the first work of nostalgia in "The Contrast" (1787), a play about a country squire and his man who visit the corrupt city of New York.

Most of the contemporary responses to Rogers the man and film image in this paper have been taken from the numerous 2ft by 3ft scrapbooks collected by the Will Rogers Memorial and Museum. The Fred Stone, Memorial, and Homer Croy scrapbooks are held at the Will Rogers Memorial and Museum in Claremore, Oklahoma. All of the scrapbooks have been microfilmed and are on deposit at Oklahoma State University, Stillwater, Oklahoma.

Works Cited

Croy, Homer. Scrapbooks. Will Rogers Memorial and Museum. Claremore, OK.
Day, Donald, ed. *The Autobiography of Will Rogers*. Boston: Houghton Mifflin, 1949.
Hays, Samuel P. *The Response of Industrialism: 1885-1914*. Chicago: U of Chicago P, 1957.
Leuchtenberg, William E. *The Perils of Prosperity: 1914-1932*. Chicago: U of Chicago P, 1958.
Peterson, Ada. "Via Long Distance." Will Rogers Memorial and Museum. Claremore, OK. No. 15: 47.
Rogers, Will. File box 14. Will Rogers Memorial and Museum. Claremore, OK.
—. Rev. of *Life Begins at Forty*. *New York Sun*.
—. "His Last Precious Days with Will Rogers Recalled by Irvin Cobb."
Rosenfield, John, Jr. "Screen Loses Star at Peak of Influence." Will Rogers Memorial and Museum. Claremore, OK. No. 53: 27.
Rubin, Lewis P., ed. *I'll Take My Stand: The South and the Agrarian Tradition*. 1930. Rpt. 1978. Baton Rouge, LA: Louisiana State UP, 2006.
Sapir, Edward. "Culture, Genuine and Spurious." *Culture, Language, and Personality*. Ed. David G. Mandelbaum. Berkeley: U of California P, 1968. 305-331.
Sargent, Thornton. "Will Outwits the Sexy Fellows." Will Rogers Memorial and Museum. Claremore, OK. No 24: 152.
Scrapbooks. No.1, 8, 9, 14, 15, 20, 24, 25. Will Rogers Memorial and Museum. Claremore, OK.
—. "An Ideal Home." No. 20: 17.
—. "Daddy of us All." No. 24: 48.
—. "Doctor Bull." No. 1: 31.
—. "The Movies." *Beverly Hills Script*. No. 9: 204.
"Series R." Goldwyn Contracts. Dec. 29, 1923.
Stone, Fred. Scrapbook. Will Rogers Memorial and Museum. Claremore, OK.
—. *Beverly Hills Citizen*. No.11.
—. "Chatting with the Editor." No. 3.
—. "Simple Life and Kindly Manner Marked Life of Will Rogers." No.11.

2
Will Rogers and *The Saturday Evening Post*: Kindred Spirits?

Will Rogers often referred to George Horace Lorimer (1869-1937), editor of *The Saturday Evening Post* (*SEP*), as "the boss." Along with millions of American readers, Rogers greatly admired Lorimer for informing and entertaining the country with a weekly publication which had become a family institution by the 1920s—and continued to be so for the next thirty years. Rogers was forever plying "the boss" with ideas for future articles; conversely, Lorimer was not averse to assigning Rogers to serious topics needing the Oklahoman's light touch. Either way, the resulting articles for the *SEP*, whimsically illustrated by Herbert Johnson, were regular fare for the weekly.

Telegrams back and forth between Rogers and Lorimer reveal that "the boss" paid well. However, the relationship between writer and editor was more than financial; the tone of communications was always warm for, in many ways, Will Rogers and George Horace Lorimer were kindred spirits. Despite this close personal relationship, a study of the world view of *The Saturday Evening Post* reveals the similarities and differences between the political and social visions of Lorimer and his Oklahoma author. On key issues of domestic importance—especially as the boom era began to break up in the 1930s—the "boss" and Will Rogers disagreed on how to interpret America to itself. Lorimer lost his social vision; in contrast, Will Rogers was fascinated by change and dedicated to helping the nation fulfill its pluralistic potential.

Lorimer Was "The Boss"

Being an editor of a national magazine was more than just a job for George Horace Lorimer. As he explained to his publisher, Cyrus Curtis, his goal was nothing less than "to interpret America to itself, always readably, but constructively" (Wood 153). Lorimer assumed that most of his audience was tired of muckraking and the continuous harping upon political problems at home and abroad. It would not hurt to celebrate America's past nostalgically. In answer to this need, Lorimer commissioned covers with traditional icons such as Benjamin Franklin, George Washington, and Independence Hall. Famous covers by Norman Rockwell frequently celebrated the gemeinschaft of hometown America and its virtues. Fiction in *Post* carried readers back to the American Revolution or to antebellum Southern days before the issue of slavery tore that organic society apart. Through the 1920s, a number of writers such as Irvin Cobb and Ben Ames Williams celebrated America's rural past. Each American region was portrayed regularly by a "stable" of writers handpicked by Lorimer. Western tales contained stereotypes of effete dudes, virile cowboys, and sophisticated girls from the East whose hearts were won by unaffected manliness. Countless tales were written in this formula by Peter B. Kyne, Ben Ames Williams, Emerson Hough, and Edna Ferber. In fact, Ben Ames Williams supplied nothing but this genre from 1917 to 1919. Many of Will Rogers' silent films would be drawn from this pool of rustic stories.

The Middle West was evoked nostalgically by a number of regular *Post* writers. Booth Tarkington began his long financially-rewarding career with *SEP* in 1912 with the first of many stories about his fondly remembered Indiana. Tarkington was as aware as *Post* readers that the Indiana he recreated in his stories had vanished with the nineteenth century: "[T]hat small city, Indianapolis, where I was born, exists no more than Carthage existed after the Romans had driven the ploughs over the ground where it stood. Progress swept all the old life away" ("Booth"). In all of these Middle-West

Will Rogers Brought Will, Jr., on the 1926 Trip

fictions, a pre-industrial and pre-urban era was celebrated as a time of individualism and Anglo-Saxon hegemony. At every possible opportunity, Lorimer used his patronage to promote such nostalgia, a nostalgia that was basic to the literary style of Will Rogers.

Assigning Writers: Will Rogers Sails for Europe

Lorimer influenced *SEP* content through the selection of writers and Will Rogers was a representative example. Because the Oklahoman shared many of Lorimer's views, Will Rogers was frequently assigned to cover national and international stories.

In 1926 Lorimer saw a need for a trip by Rogers—this time to Europe. On April 15 Lorimer invited Will Rogers to lunch and asked the cowboy humorist if he could follow the format of Lorimer's own successful *Letters of a Self-Made Merchant to His Son* (1902), but taking a slightly different slant. In this case, Rogers would tour the European capitals and discuss a number of pressing foreign policy issues. The tone of the articles would be humorous, but with a serious undertone—something along the lines of Mark Twain's travelogue, *Innocents Abroad* (1879).

Rogers agreed to go on the junket and to adopt the epistolary technique. Some ten years earlier, Rogers had devised a comic style in which he kidded—in a manner which did not alienate the subject—famous men in office. During the Wilson years, this experiment had yielded excellent results. The President heartily responded to Rogers counsel, and frequently quoted the comedian to the press and to public audiences. President Harding had been another case, indeed. On one occasion, Harding even refused to attend the *Follies* because Rogers was on the program; Ziegfeld and Rogers received telephone calls from Harding's staff requesting that the Oklahoma humorist temper his comments about Harding's leisure time activities, especially his golf.

Calvin Coolidge was now the chief executive, and there was some question how the intimate style of the humorist would work with such a dour man. Rogers and Lorimer were satisfied that the series would not affront the president, and they carried through with the "Letters" format. There were significant literary advantages in writing letters rather than essays. Rogers could

Will's Pen Pal

employ an informal style, emphasizing personal observations and feelings rather than abstractions. Hundreds of books had been written by professors and pundits on the future of Europe; Will Rogers needed a literary vehicle which would allow him to emphasize the human dimensions. Why not a series of letters from one rural man to another? Coolidge was from Vermont and often posed with his father pitching hay at the family dairy farm.

On commission from *SEP*, Will Rogers visited London, Italy, France, and Ireland. Always a busy man, Rogers also made a number of short travel films in each country which stressed the awkwardness and confusion of a country-bred American abroad for the first time. Both the films and *SEP* articles discussed themes important to *SEP*. Whenever possible, Rogers celebrated the superiority of the American landscape. European painting might be excellent, but the untouched wilderness of America was still first in the heart of the Oklahoman. European history might be filled with great men and epic stories, but human nature, as Rogers observed it embodied in such dictators as Mussolini, had not been improved by environment. The Oklahoman questioned how Europe could have become involved in so many wars if it was such a superior continent. As he surveyed the continent, Rogers saw nations biding time until the next war.

Both Rogers and Lorimer agreed that the League of Nations was too weak to withstand the rising tide of bellicosity. Peace treaties were mere smokescreens behind which nations like Italy were constructing war machines. The scene was bleak:

> Russia hates everybody so bad it would take her a week to pick out the one she hates most. Poland is rarin' to fight somebody so bad that they just get up and punch themselves in the jaw. They can't make up their minds whether to jump on Russia, Germany, or go up and annex Lithuania. Turkey has been laying off three months now without war, and Peace is just killing them. You can't even pass out of the south of Russia into Romania. Bulgaria is feeding an Army and deriving no benefits from it whatever. (Stout and Rollins 106)

For both Rogers and Lorimer, the lesson was obvious. The United States would adhere to its "traditional" policy of isolation from European entanglements.

The Rogers series was published as *Letters of a Self-Made Diplomat to His President* and was a very humorous—yet deadly serious—serial for *SEP*. One reader in particular enjoyed the experiment: Calvin Coolidge was so pleased by the humorous ploy of addressing the letters to him that when Rogers returned, he was greeted at the dock by a professional limousine and driven to the White House.

There were a number of echoes to this reaction. The foreign policy series commissioned by Lorimer had reached millions of Americans and had reinforced a popular prejudice against European involvement; a humorous series had also moved a normally sober Calvin Coolidge to smile, thus enhancing the prestige of both the Oklahoma humorist and *SEP*. What seems most important is that the entire "pseudo-event" was tailored from the beginning by George Horace Lorimer. Will Rogers may have been contributing his own reflections, but the editor of *SEP* had known in advance what the basic orientation would be and how to

I didn't get a shave, figuring I might pass as a native.

Rogers 'Beards' the Soviet Union

shape a fundamental American self-perception—what we now call "isolationism."

Rogers to the Soviet Union and Mexico

There's Not a Bathing Suit in Russia (1927) was the result of another special assignment. First serialized in *SEP*, the articles were published separately as a volume—a customary practice for a popular *Post* series (Stout). Lorimer sent Rogers to Russia because he knew that the Oklahoman—unlike many American observers of the Russian Revolution—had no political axe to grind. Rogers' down-to-earth observations would enlighten *Post* readers about the enduring human problems of the revolution. Rogers' study of the Russian Revolution served to deflate much of the rhetoric about progress in an experimental society. Unlike so many others, the humorist was attuned to the power struggles and ageless abuses of power; for example, to those who sang of the industrial advances, Rogers pointed out that there was indeed not a single bathing suit in the new nation—meaning that consumers and their needs were not being served. A corollary related to this conclusion—one close to Lorimer's own prejudice—was that America's free enterprise system was superior to any radical experiments abroad. Americans should be happy with the status quo in a boom era.

In 1927 Lorimer asked Rogers to visit Mexico with the goodwill delegation sent by President Coolidge. In the company of Dwight Morrow (the American ambassador to Mexico), Charles Lindbergh (public hero since 1927), and other public figures, the Southwesterner turned his eye to the humorous clash of cultures—without forgetting the deeper significance of the mission as a peaceful gesture. As in his previous writings about diplomatic meetings, Rogers provided *Post* readers with a combination of Yankee wit and sympathy for the Mexican perspective. In one of his talks, he summarized his perspective: "I came down here to laugh with you and not at you." His personal presence at the talks and informal gatherings cleared the air for serious discussion; his five articles for *SEP* gave a sense of the flavor of the meeting. No mindless enthusiast for progress, Rogers reminded Americans to recall the exploitive attitudes which had caused the breakdown of trust between the two countries: "Up to now, our calling card to Mexico or Central America has been a gunboat or a bunch of violets shaped like Marines" (Day 173). The whimsical approach made the effort seem fraught with perils, but manageable when addressed by men like Morrow, Lindbergh, and Rogers.

...and the Far East

Later, as the Far East became a serious concern to Americans, Will

Rogers was dispatched to investigate. A six-article serial for *SEP* billed Rogers as a one-man "Hoover Commission for investigating all Depression West of the Pacific Ocean," but the mission was more political than economic (Gragert). Rogers consulted with the Japanese about Manchuria, but then went to China to see for himself. Throughout the tour, the Oklahoman brightened his reports of realpolitik with delightful comments about the clash of cultures. After a stop in the Philippines—where he identified American exploitative interests—Rogers returned to the United States. The Oklahoman predicted that political ideology and strong economic conflicts would lead to clashes in the region. As always, Rogers supported the desire of nations to have their own governments rather than the guidance of others: "[T]hey like to run their own business. Sure, Japan and America and England can run countries perhaps better than China, or Korea, or India, or the Philippines, but that don't mean they ought to" (132).

Whether touring Europe, Russia, Mexico, or the Far East, Will Rogers was in substantial harmony with the Lorimer view toward international politics: Leave other nations to build as they will or to fight if they must; we should remain too concerned about our own problems to have time for meddling in the affairs of other nations. Still, there was always a special Rogers twist. While Lorimer scorned the international chaos, Rogers tried to empathize. The Oklahoman's isolationism was more a product of respect for differences, a reluctance to impose American values on others.

Some Limitations of *The Saturday Evening Post* as a National Interpreter

Without question, George Horace Lorimer was a dedicated man who brought a mirror before Americans in the form of a weekly magazine; unfortunately, like many in his audience, Lorimer's vision of American life was ethnocentric, and therefore incomplete. *SEP* stories about rural life reflected a strong antipathy to inexorable contemporary developments. Speaking of the modern city, Emerson Hough expressed a profound discontent: "I wouldn't live in a little town which produced me a thousand dollars a week; at the same time I wouldn't poke fun at it for two thousand dollars a week;

I would for nothing a week take pleasure in flaying the absolute rottenness which is a part of this city life which some of us falsely think is a superior sort of thing" (Tebbel 140). Every Western story or antebellum Southern tale was a fantasy about a simpler society which better suited human needs. Such stories and such humorous insights entertained those unhappy with recent developments; on the other hand, it is also true that such nostalgic celebrations were not preparing readers to cope with contemporary realities.

At least part of the popularity of Will Rogers stemmed from this nostalgic impulse. The Oklahoman came from the last open frontier and spoke with a twang which was distinctively rural. His insights were based on a continuous contrast between things as they are as opposed to things as they were in the "good old days." But a close look at Rogers' coverage of contemporary domestic developments reveals a less condemnatory tone toward the present and no lack of criticism for the past.

The Saturday Evening Post and Will Rogers were at greatest distance in their view of the role of immigrants in American society. *SEP* smeared the labor movement by portraying it as a foreign experiment inappropriate to the American scene. In countless editorials and articles, America's favorite weekly followed the Lorimer line, vehemently condemning unionization. Some of the interactions between the readership and the staff are shocking. For example, in 1919 Emerson Hough received a letter dealing with unions. A xenophobic reader said of union organizers and followers: "They have no more idea of what the real people of this country are or what they will do if it comes down to cases, than so many animals. ...Every meeting of a labor union or labor council is the scene of a row nowadays, often of a free-for-all fight between radicals and conservatives. ...So keep a gun handy, for you may need it awful bad someday." Hough's response, rather than chiding the writer, actually indicated full agreement: "What you say about the lack of Americanism is too sadly true. There is trouble ahead in this country. I look for the old-time Americans to put it down, one way or another, with gentle or hard hand as the case may require. As for myself, I also keep a gun handy. ...I think I am able to entertain any really bloodthirsty Bolsheviks" (Tebbel 141). Hough's direct involvement in rooting out "foreign radicals" during the famous

An "Object Lesson" in the SEP Style

"Red Scare" era showed that these were not merely words. Editorials and feature stories reflected George Horace Lorimer's full sympathy for these nativist notions.

For a number of reasons, Will Rogers did not share the nativist perspective of *Post* staffers. There were simply too many similarities between the history of his family and region and the plight of immigrants. As a Cherokee Indian, he had seen the long-term impact of the infamous Trail of Tears migration from Georgia and Tennessee to Indian Territory. His father had fought in the Civil War with the Confederacy and had suffered both the shame and financial loss which defeat brought to the lost cause. Finally, as an Oklahoman, Rogers shared the real Westerner's notion that the New York and Washington sectors of society represented interest groups rather than the national will. In any case, Rogers' writings invoke the names of Jews, Italians, and other minorities as friends and colleagues for whom he felt esteem.

Minorities and Immigrants in the Sound Films of Will Rogers

The feature films of Will Rogers highlight his special way of looking at the immigrant in America. Since many of the late sound films from the Twentieth Century-Fox were adapted from works of *SEP* fiction, the adaptations are particularly revealing. *Doctor Bull* (1933) was drawn from a novel by James Gould Cozzens, a work in conformity with the *SEP* school of regional fiction. At one point in the novel, the main character accounts for the decline of Connecticut society in words which read like a vitriolic *SEP* editorial:

> Well, Connecticut's going to hell, that's about the size of it. ...If I were fixing it, I'd have things the way they were thirty years ago. New Winton was a place to live, then, not something a road went through. ...Look at the mills down at Sansbury and the Polacks! Time was when Sansbury was a white man's town. Look at the Roman Catholic convent there, or whatever they made of the Jenny place! What the hell are those monks and priors and novenas of the Little Flower doing in New England? Same with a lot of these Jewish artists, like Lincoln over in the Cobb place. Jumping Jesus, what's he mean by calling himself Lincoln? Early American house. Why doesn't he go restore himself a synagogue in Jerusalem? (Cozzens 30)

In his screenplay, Paul Green retained this invidious contrast between the established Yankee natives of New Winton and the foreign invaders. Stage directions for a scene in which Dr. Bull arrives to deliver an Italian baby describes Louie Papoliti, the father, as "a swarthy, fat jowled Italian about thirty." When Louie nervously comes for the doctor, Green has the Yankee greet the distraught foreigner with what must have struck Green as a clever

Will Rogers: A More Generous Approach

Rogersism. Instead of showing concern for the expectant father, the script's Dr. Bull flippantly quips to Louie: "You never know when another Washington is born—or an Al Capone." In Green's pseudo-Rogersism, Italians (and by inference, all foreign born) are portrayed as potentially irresponsible, criminal, and credulous (Green 33-34).

It is refreshing to note that Will Rogers and film director John Ford completely ignored the derogatory lines in Paul Green's film script. While Italians are portrayed as working class people, their vulnerability is used to highlight Dr. Bull's sympathy for all members of the community. When the film's Dr. Bull arrives, the Papoliti apartment is crowded with concerned members of the family and the community. The male members are clustered around a table, silently drinking red wine from large bottles. After Will Rogers delivers the baby boy, he comes back to the living room and surveys the quiet (and slightly tippled) crowd.

Instead of launching into a sermon about the evils of drink and the responsibilities of the working class, Rogers turns the situation entirely around. He uses this moment to extemporize about Anglo-Saxon repression. He is favorably impressed by the community involvement, and sees that the wine has acted both as an anodyne to calm the nerves. Pouring himself a tall glass of chianti, Rogers says: "I love to bring Italian babies into the world. If you go out to a farmer's place to deliver a baby, after it's all over all you get is a cup of coffee" (Green 34). Rogers obviously here implies that the "native" Americans who supported the Volstead Act of 1920 needed this infusion of new blood into their repressed culture. Thus, where *SEP* would have invoked some sort of slur about "Americanskis," Rogers implicitly supports a cosmopolitan acceptance.

There was no room in the films of Will Rogers for the backward-looking and dehumanizing messages found in *The Saturday Evening Post*. Rather than attempting to provide solace for those of "old stock," Rogers used his regional vehicles to convey messages concerning human brotherhood. To do this, he was often forced to deviate from the racist and politically conservative scripts that were prepared for him. In *State Fair* (1933) and *Doctor Bull* (1933), Rogers simply left out such lines. *David Harum* (1934) provided Rogers with an opportunity to utter an articulate defense of the goals of President Roosevelt's New Deal. Because Americans in his time needed these messages about social reconstruction and racial harmony more than they needed the nostalgia of *The Saturday Evening Post*'s regional fiction, Will Rogers' films constitute a significant case in which film redeems a literary form.

SEP and Rogers in the Crisis of the Great Depression

Lorimer and Rogers parted company over the New Deal. Lorimer despised the New Deal's use of executive power so much that his biographer describes the editor as visibly changed by the re-election of Franklin D. Roosevelt in 1936: "After Election Day, his family was shocked to see how suddenly old and bewildered he looked. He seemed to be casting about in his mind for a reasonable answer that would tell him why he had been so wrong in interpreting America, after three decades of near infallibility" (Tebbel 390-410). Lorimer's ties to an Anglo-Saxon, Republican past were so binding that he could not walk into the new era.

Will Rogers, on the other hand, supported the New Deal as the only way to effect peaceful change in America. As an act of charity, Rogers campaigned over the radio for specific New Deal programs.

His famous radio talk entitled "Bacon and Beans and Limousines" urged Americans—rich and poor—to support the organization on Unemployment Relief. As Rogers humorously reminded his fellow citizens, the country still had resources: "There's as much money in the country as there ever was. Only fewer people have it, but it's there" (Gragert 66). When pleas over the radio failed to move the nation, Rogers flew around the country on a "mission of mercy." In doing so, he boosted morale and gave Americans a sense that someone of national stature cared about them. Along with funds for the poor, Will Rogers contributed mightily to comic relief in a stressful time. Meanwhile, Lorimer grieved for things past.

Looking at *The Saturday Evening Post* of the Lorimer era (1898-1936), it is clear that a brilliant editor and a popular weekly magazine reflected the aspirations of a large body of Americans, most of whom were white, Anglo-Saxon Protestants. When those Americans and their magazine refused to adapt to a changing world, they were passed by. On the other hand, the nostalgia and humor of Will Rogers' writings and films reached a broad, popular audience which returned the Oklahoman's compassion with an unprecedented affection. Rogers' fans knew he was sincere when he

Rogers with the First Lady, 1933

said that he never met a man he didn't like; they could appreciate his acceptance of both the old and the new. In his writings, Rogers evinced a humane enthusiasm for progress and development—for all sectors of American society. Without question, he was fully in *SEP* camp when it came to foreign affairs. Isolationism made sense to both Lorimer and Rogers, albeit for slightly different reasons. On other key issues, however, Rogers and *SEP* drew apart when the twenties became the thirties. As an Indian, a Southerner, and an Oklahoman, Rogers saw through most of the trendy shibboleths of his time; most importantly, he was very alert to the sensitivities of minority groups. In sum, Rogers' natural love for change and his quick sympathies for people of other backgrounds made him a better interpreter of America than George Horace Lorimer, his "boss" at *The Saturday Evening Post*.

Discussion of Literature

The telegrams and correspondence between Will Rogers and George Horace Lorimer are available at the Will Rogers Memorial, Claremore, Oklahoma.

The best portrait of *SEP* editor, George Horace Lorimer, can be found in Tebbel. Gragert's volume contains the transcripts of twelve broadcasts Rogers made for E.R. Squibb and Sons in 1930 and sixteen of the fifty-three radio shows sponsored by Gulf Oil Company in 1933-1935. "Bacon and Beans and Limousines" (1931) was a charity broadcast.

Works Cited

"Booth Tarkington." *Twentieth-Century Authors: A Bibliographical Dictionary of Modern Literature.* Stanley Kunitz and Howard Haycraft, eds. New York: H.W. Wilson, Co., 1952. 1384.

Cozzens, James Gould. *The Last Adam.* New York: Harcourt, Brace, and World, 1933.

Day, Donald. ed. *The Autobiography of Will Rogers.* Boston: Houghton Mifflin Company, 1949.

Gragert, Steven K., ed. *More Letters of a Self-Made Diplomat.* Stillwater: Oklahoma State UP, 1982.

—, ed. *Radio Broadcasts of Will Rogers.* Stillwater: Oklahoma State UP, 1983.

Green, Paul. *Doctor Bull*. Screenplay. Will Rogers Memorial Filmscript Collection. Claremore, OK. 33-34.

Lorimer, George. *Letters of a Self-Made Merchant to His Son*. 1902. Washington, D.C.: Regnery Publishing. 1995.

Rollins, Peter C. *Will Rogers: A Bio-Bibliography.* Westport, CT: Greenwood Press, 1984.

Rogers, Will. *There's Not a Bathing Suit in Russia*. Eds. Joseph A. Stout, Jr., and Peter C. Rollins. Stillwater: Oklahoma State UP, 1977.

—. *Letters of a Self-Made Diplomat to His President.* 1926. Eds. Joseph A. Stout, Jr., and Peter C. Rollins. Stillwater: Oklahoma State UP, 1977.

Tebbel, John. *George Horace Lorimer and* The Saturday Evening Post. New York: Doubleday, 1948.

Wood, John Playsted. *Magazines in the United States*. 3rd ed. New York: The Roland Press, 1971.

3
The Context and Rhetorical Strategy of Will Rogers' *Letters of a Self-Made Diplomat to His President* (1926)

1926 was an exceedingly busy year for Will Rogers. He began a transcontinental United States speaking tour toward the end of February, and was in constant motion until his return from Europe in September. The pace of his American tour was staggering. Small cities kept him one night; larger ones demanded two evenings. On the average, the forty-six year old Oklahoman was seeing a different American city every day. But the rewards of touring were as great as the labors. Rogers enjoyed prowling about the country, for travel allowed him to plumb the mood of average Americans (whom he called "the regular birds") outside the political and commercial worlds of Washington and New York. He took advantage of this opportunity to feel the pulse of his audience. And the pay was excellent. Charles Wagner, manager of the tour, reported that Rogers and the DeReszke Singers had grossed over $82,000 in receipts during their eleven weeks on the road.

There were competing demands for Rogers' valuable time after the national tour. On April 2, he received a telegram from Florenz Ziegfeld pleading for help. Ziegfeld had heard that Rogers was thinking of sailing to Europe at the close of his transcontinental lecture series. Hoping that Rogers would instead join the *Follies* for the coming year, Ziegfeld advised against leaving the country: "decide to postpone visit to Europe. Rotten over there anyway." Ziegfeld was sanguine about the prospects for his show if Rogers would participate: "I could make the Twentieth Follies (and probably the

Will Rogers on Tour (with Newspaper)

last) the greatest of them all." On the telegram was a conspicuous blue stamp instructing the recipient that an immediate answer was expected by wire or phone. "Flo" got a negative response, for Rogers was determined to talk with "the Regular Birds" of Europe (Memorial Scrapbook).

Rogers had joked and written about European affairs in his book of 1919, *Rogers-isms: The Cowboy Philosopher on the Peace Conference,* but he had not visited the continent in twelve years. Americans were curious about how Europe was emerging from the wreckage of war; they were especially concerned about the international

Lorimer's Own Epistolary Effort

responsibilities in the postwar era, the war debt question, and the viability of the new League of Nations. Rogers was anxious to get a first-hand appraisal of these developments, and he had found a sponsor, *The Saturday Evening Post.*

On the fifteenth of April, Rogers had lunch with George Horace Lorimer, the famous editor of the *Post.* Early in his tenure, Lorimer authored *Letters of a Self-Made Merchant to His Son* (1902). Lorimer wondered if Rogers could write another special series of weekly articles which would take a similar approach to the pressing foreign policy issues confronting the nation in the wake of WWI, something along the lines of Mark Twain's famous travelogue, *Innocents Abroad* (1879).

As was always the case, Lorimer knew how to pick the appropriate writer for an assignment. The very basis for Rogers' humor was that of the stance of an Innocent Abroad: He assumed the persona of an Oklahoma cowboy thrown down in the middle of modern American and the appeal of his social commentary stemmed primarily from his ability to judge modern developments by the values of traditional American life. Most Americans in the Twenties were aware that their modern mores and values were moving away from a tested life style. They turned to Rogers for humor, but also for insights about which changes were beneficial and which were ephemeral or even harmful. Lorimer wanted to commission Rogers to pass through the European scene with such a perspective, judging recent political developments in his homespun way.

As a writer, Rogers had a literary problem to overcome. To whom would the letters of this self-made diplomat be sent? Fortunately, a comedic technique developed by Rogers in the *Follies* suggested itself. It was Rogers' habit in the *Midnight Frolic* to call celebrities in the audience up on the stage, or to address them as they sat with their friends. Always an energetic reader of newspapers, the budding journalist would refer to some business or political issue currently before the public, gently "roasting" the celebrity or giving "personal" advice on the issue—always with an eye toward entertaining the audience rather than embarrassing the butt of his humor. Playing the role of public confidant had proven popular at the *Follies*, but experiments in print had yielded only mixed results. President Woodrow Wilson heartily responded to Rogers' counsel, and frequently quoted the comedian to the press and to public audiences. Like a later President—Franklin Roosevelt—Wilson recognized that attention from Will Rogers could not hurt men in the public eye. Unfortunately, the imaginary advisory role had not been well received by Wilson's successor, Warren G. Harding. On one occasion Harding even refused to attend the *Follies* because Rogers was on the program; Ziegfeld and Rogers received telephone calls from Harding's staff requesting that the Oklahoma humorist temper his comments about Harding's leisure time activities, especially his golf.

Rogers knew that Calvin Coolidge was not as dour as the press portrayed him. He decided to make the President his pen pal. A cartoon advertisement for the *Post* series conveys the light tone of the letters. A slender man, who is obviously President Coolidge, faces away from us. Into his ear, Rogers is whispering sagely counsel about foreign affairs: "Now listen, Mr. Coolidge. This is between you and me…and the rest of the nation." The technique was simply a carry-over from Rogers' *Midnight Frolic* show except that now the audience numbered in the millions, for admission to this show cost only a nickel.

It should quickly be added that Rogers intended no disrespect toward the President from Vermont. On the contrary, he was a great admirer of Coolidge, whom he addressed as "a great politician. He looks further ahead than any of them." Choosing the letter format had more to do with literary considerations than political judgments. In writing letters rather than essays, Rogers could employ an informal and intimate style, emphasizing personal observations and feelings rather than abstractions. Hundreds of books had been written on the future of Europe by professors and pundits; Rogers needed a literary vehicle which would allow him to emphasize the human side of the story. Why not a series of letters from one rural man to another?

Overview of the Trip

Rogers' tour of Europe and Russia would have the same lively pace which characterized his early spring transcontinental speaking tour. There was no fixed itinerary. Rogers was simply to wander according to impulse, provided that he sent back colorful and instructive copy. While the title of the series had been conceived in jest, the role which Rogers was to play was ambassadorial in a serious sense: he was performing a special service for the nation. There had been so many variant reports, perplexed Americans looked forward to reading his down-to-earth findings.

At 12: 30am the morning of 1 May, the *Leviathan* backed out of its berth in New York harbor carrying among its passengers Will Rogers and his fifteen-year-old son, Will Jr. Six days later the modern liner was next to a dock in Southampton. After a week in London, father and son flew to Paris in a large new French airliner. It was a rough trip, and an air-sick-prone devotee of aviation experienced one of the negative effects of flight. The next day, the Americans were on a train bound for Rome. When they stopped *en route* to visit the disarmament proceedings in Geneva, business almost came to a halt. As the *Tulsa Daily World* proudly reported, "Will Rogers, American Lariat Artist and 'Wise Cracker' bobbed up in the League of Nations Disarmament Commission session in the afternoon and attracted more attention than many delegates."

Rogers Checked In with the Blustering Dictator

Dictator Benito Mussolini was the object of Rogers' trip to Rome. A "non-interview" between the representative from Claremore and Il Duce is one of the more enthusiastic moments of the *Letters of a Self-Made Diplomat,* for Rogers saw the early work of Mussolini as constructive and beneficial to Italy. (It should be noted that this evaluation preceded by four years the excesses of Mussolini's foreign policy, and that Rogers' views at this time were shared by many to include Franklin D. Roosevelt).

While in Rome Rogers was given an audience with the Pope. His letters give evidence that he saw many of Italy's masterpieces of architecture and painting while in the eternal city. From Italy, Rogers sailed to Spain for an interview with another dictator, Primo de Rivera. The American democrat took pleasure in the traditionalism which he encountered in this backward country.

Within two weeks, Rogers was back in London preparing for a flight into Russia. Permission to observe the communist experiment in social engineering had arrived while Rogers was in Italy. *The Saturday Evening Post* was as obliging in this case as it had been about the European tour, and for the same reason. Because there had been so many contradictory reports by commentators, the American people would take pleasure in a Rogers' treatment of the subject. The series was published independent of the European travelogue under a facetious title, *There's Not a Bathing Suit in Russia and Other Bare Facts.* Like the *Letters,* the series first appeared in the *Post* and was later published in book form.

By mid-July Rogers was back in London where he signed a much-publicized contract with British National Pictures. The British were hoping to break Hollywood's monopoly on film comedy. While in London, Rogers found other ways to communicate with the British while paying expenses. Almost as soon as he stepped off the plane from Moscow, he signed a contract with "Cochran's Revue," the British counterpart to Ziegfeld's *Follies*. In addition, he began to appear in a late night cabaret in a show similar to the *Midnight Frolic* which had made him so popular among New York's elite. Finally, the Oklahoman made quite a stir when he went on the air in August "for the largest fee ever paid to a radio talker in this country" and then donated the fat check to a London hospital.

Early September found Rogers in Ireland, delighting in the Irish landscape, but again taking time to do benefits for charity. A tragic fire in Drumcollogher had recently killed many and seriously injured scores. Rogers immediately volunteered to perform

Rogers Meets Europe in a Series of Short Films

at a theater in Dublin, with all proceeds to the sufferers. He raised $2,000 at the door, to which he added a contribution of $500. Rogers was fast transforming himself into an Ambassador of good will! (In 1927 President Coolidge capitalized on this humanitarian image by sending Rogers on a good will tour of Mexico with Dwight Morrow and Charles A. Lindbergh, see Chapters 2 and 3.)

Mrs. Rogers, daughter Mary, and younger son Jim joined the humorist in early August. Will Jr. was sent home; he had been away from his books long enough. After the comedian settled his family into comfortable quarters in Switzerland, he left for a hasty last reconnaissance, to include Greenland, Scotland, Wales, and Germany. On the 21st of September the entire family boarded the *Leviathan* for home.

As the *Leviathan* sailed back to the U.S., Rogers could total up a number of accomplishments: he had plumbed the motives of the intellectual and political leaders of the "new" Europe; his travels had allowed him the opportunity to talk with average citizens; and he now had first-hand information about basic foreign policy matters. It was no longer true—as it had been during the war—that all he knew was what he read in the papers. His horizons had enlarged, and his insights deepened; his observations in the future would be increasingly authoritative.

The Innocent Abroad

The distance between the country bumpkin and the city slicker seems always to have tickled the American funny bone from Royall Tyler's 18th-century play, *The Contrast,* to the continuing television sitcom, *The Beverly Hillbillies.* Rogers put himself in the role of innocent abroad for both comic and serious purposes. He was aiming strictly for comedy when he described the difficulties of gaining entrance to the House of Commons. According to his tall tale, all doors were suddenly opened when he announced that he was from Claremore, Oklahoma. The letter goes on to report that not only was he given a seat immediately, but that the English were very curious about Claremore's exemplary city government! Following Mark Twain's example in *Innocents Abroad* (1879) Rogers played upon the theme of the superiority of the American landscape. His disdainful comparison of the bay of Naples with American ports is only one example among many:

> Did you ever see the bay of Naples that you have heard and read so much about? Did you ever see the harbor in San Francisco? Well it makes the bay of Naples look like the Chicago drainage Canal, and I am from Los Angeles, too. When even the harbor of Los Angeles with its growing barley fields, and its thriving subdivisions, if it had any water in it would be better than Naples. Why Houston stole a better harbor from Galveston than Naples is. It hasn't got the blue water that Naples has, but it will float an old tug full of cotton. Why Miami Florida if they ever cleaned those gin bottles out of that harbor of theirs would lay it all over the Mediterranean. (55)

The obvious point made by the loyal provincial was clear: he loved his country and refused steadfastly to be hoodwinked by Europe's pretensions.

But Rogers used the device of American innocence for serious purposes, especially in Rome. He was irritated by the claim that living among historic monuments automatically made Europeans more cultured than Americans. As a dedicated observer of the Washington scene, Rogers could deny this environmentalism without much difficulty: "Men in Washington you know yourself, Calvin, live where Washington and Jefferson and Hamilton lived," but their actions had clearly shown that "association has nothing to do with culture" (73). The much vaunted grandeur of the Roman republic made little impression on this professional critic of senators and congressmen. Rogers was more alert to the brutality of the Roman games than the civic genius of the republic. Over the entire city, he sensed a dark cloud of accumulated sin, a history of human wrong which his own isolated, "innocent" nation had been exempted from experiencing: "Everything in Rome was stolen from somebody at some time. It's just a question of who's got it last" (80).Curiously, Nathaniel Hawthorne, a very different sort of American visitor to Rome, had come to the same conclusion some sixty-seven years earlier.

Another serious idea emerged during Rogers' light-headed discussion of American innocence. As he warned his President, Coolidge was "standing guard over the best little patch of ground in all the various Hemispheres" (81). The thought had broader meaning, to include a corollary that the United States should stay out of European affairs in order to maintain its innocence. Europe seemed destined to quarrel and fight. Our self-interest therefore dictated a healthy distrust of any entanglement with the fallen continent.

War Debts

As *The Letters of a Self-Made Diplomat to His President* revealed, the issue of war debts owed to the United States was hotly debated on both sides of the Atlantic. In fact, Rogers noted that Secretary Mellon was visiting Europe, consulting with the former allies about payment. There were two very different sides to the debt question. Most Europeans believed that they had paid an incalculable price on the battlefield. Many attributed the astronomical casualty figures to the United States for vacillating four years before joining the Allied cause. On the other hand, the average American saw the war debts as simply financial obligations to be honored by borrowers. As Rogers simplified the matter for his readers, it had come down to two plans: either the European Plan (no payments) or the American Plan (partial payment). Using rhetorical irony, Rogers' personal contempt for anything less than full payment was conveyed in the following description of the French response to a recent settlement: "It seems that there is just some little minor difference or defect in the agreement with America. The change don't mean anything, but they want to have it put just right before passing on it. There is just some three 000—naughts—on the end of some figures that they want to have erased. It was probably just a misprint, and taking off just those three little figures will of course make no material difference in the main settlement" (86).

As with other judgments in his writings, Rogers analyzed the issues in terms of individual morality. The French Deputies might wish to assume a *nonchalant* attitude, but from Rogers' old-fashioned perspective, a debt was a debt. For millions of his readers at home who were experiencing the pangs of post-war inflation, such thinking made good sense.

The League of Nations and Disarmament Prospects

President Woodrow Wilson had entered the Great War with an ideal, one which at first attracted considerable enthusiasm. The President hoped that out of the peace settlement would emerge a League of Nations which could place the international community under a new rule of law. Nations, the argument went, could disarm when both a World Court and a League of Nations supervised international relations.

Will Rogers was a sanguine supporter of preparedness. Germany's conduct in World War I had proven to the Oklahoman that the ability to hurt an opponent was much more persuasive than arguments on paper. The inefficacy of President Wilson's many notes and telegrams to the Kaiser just prior to America's entrance into the war seemed *prima facie* evidence that a nation best protected itself by supporting a powerful and mobile military establishment.

Rogers' European tour was only to confirm this prejudice. While aboard the *Leviathan* he chuckled over the absurdity of sending military men to negotiate a disarmament agreement: "Can you picture these Army and Navy fellows being enthusiastic for disarming? Can you see Andy and Hilary [Pollard Jones] voting a Battleship out from under themselves? It's a great move to pacify the pacifists, but these are pretty smart old Birds and they know when those boats will come in handy." Any concessions made would probably be limited to antiquated equipment and weapons: "General Nolan and Major Strong say if they give up anything it won't be anything more than their Spurs" (8). During their non-interview, Mussolini re-enforced Rogers' sense of the futility of disarmament schemes. The Oklahoman asked the Italian Premier about the prospects for the Geneva meeting. Mussolini first laughed, and then replied that "we disarm when England disarm on sea; when France in air and land. So you see we never do disarm" (68). Spain's ruler, Primo de Rivera, answered similarly. As Rogers reported to his friend Calvin, "I got the same laugh out of him I had out of Mussolini. He had the usual European reply: 'When everybody else disarms, I will disarm'" (93).

The dictators had very little good to say about the fledgling League of Nations. Mussolini hinted that the organization would be unable to cope with areal emergency. Primo de Rivera told Rogers about the ridiculous treatment of Spain by the Geneva Conference. Age-old national rivalries were heightened rather than restrained by the supposedly supranational organization: "Now, between you and I, Calvin, I have talked to everybody that I could possibly get to that I could understand in this whole trip, and they all feel the same about this League and Disarming and World Courts and all that stuff. They feel like England and France run the whole thing and they don't want anything to do with it" (93).

Will Rogers' Final Letter: An Ambassador's White Paper

The final letter of the *Post* series distilled the many lessons learned during the month fact-finding mission. The question of America's image abroad could now be settled. While it was obvious that part of the animosity toward America could be linked to the debt question, Rogers espied deeper roots: "We don't stand like a Horse Thief abroad. Whoever told you we did is flattering us. We don't stand as good as a Horse Thief. They know what you were sore at them for" (107). Europe's "regular bird" had disclosed a deeper motive than the recent money problem. The hate-America campaign was just a temporary fad, one that would disappear as soon as American aid was needed again. The truth was that Europe was an armed camp with every nation hating the others, and summoning up memories of past grievances if current ones were not bilious enough: "If you can find me one Nation in Europe that has a real down-to-earth, sincere regard for any other Nation, I will jump out of the top of the Washington Monument." The specificity of Rogers' itemized list of grievances shows how much he had learned from his European tour: "Russia hates everybody so bad it would take her a week to pick out the one she hates most. Poland is rarin' to fight somebody so bad that they just get up and punch themselves in the jaw. They can't make up their minds whether to jump on Russia, Germany, or go up and annex Lithuania. Turkey has been laying off three months now without any war, and Peace is just killing them. You can't even pass out of the south of Russia into Rumania. Bulgaria is feeding an Army and deriving no benefits from it whatever" (109).

Rogers blamed conditions rather than human nature for these portents of war. Principally he blamed geography and the spirit of nationalism. Pacifists were simply ignorant of these principles: "You let France change places with Cuba, and Japan with Hawaii, and you see if we would be so anxious to disarm." The fires of nationalism were so strong, Rogers saw little hope for the future: "Say, if I didn't have any more friends than some of these Nations have around them, I not only would not disarm, but I would get another Gun, and wouldn't only have a gun in each hand as I went to bed, I wouldn't go to bed; I would stay up and watch all night" (111). Americans had helped shape these fatal conditions. To Rogers' mind, President Wilson's principle of self-determination of nations had only added more fuel to the fires of nationalism. In a short time, the result of arbitrary nation building would lead to a "self-disintegration of small nations. You see, the more Nations you create, the more chances you have of war" (112).

The final letter of the *Post* series contained a number of serious recommendations for President Coolidge. Rogers was very pessimistic about the efficacy of any action by the United States. Every major power was tottering as a result of internal upheaval: strikes were plaguing the British while the French could not maintain a government in office for more than a few weeks, and often for only a few days. Many smaller powers were on the brink of revolution. The general tone of bellicosity on the continent simply increased Rogers' pessimism. World War I and other recent examples of American intervention had shown that we were often blamed even though our intentions were good: "All we have to do to get in bad is just start out on what we think is a good Samaritan mission, and we wind up in the Pesthouse" (114).

It is important that Rogers' isolationism was thoroughly consistent. He did not advise detachment from European affairs only. He counseled total aloofness and decried the brand of imperialism practiced during the 1920s by his good friend Calvin. Our hemispheric diplomacy must be guided by the same principle of non-involvement: "If Argentina, Brazil, Peru, Chile, or anyone else has any disputed territory, and they want to populate it why let them go ahead and do it. What business is that of ours?" Rogers told his President to concentrate on domestic inequities. America would attract the friends it deserved by setting an example to the rest of the world: "It will take America fifteen years steady taking care of our own business and letting everybody else's alone to get us back to where everybody speaks to us again" (115).

Until recently "isolationism" has been more of a smear word than a legitimate foreign policy position. But the term does accurately describe Rogers' outlook, if it is properly understood. After thousands of miles of travel and hundreds of hours of talk, he simply concluded that no one—not even a well-meaning United States— could significantly affect the European conditions described in the *Letters of a Self-Made Diplomat*. The air was charged with national rivalries. Even the small nations created after the recent war were enthusiastically training pilots for the next conflagration. The League of Nations had failed to exert the elevating effect upon the international community which President Wilson had promised. With two oceans serving as geographical barriers, Rogers recommended that the U.S. devote its energies to improving domestic conditions, an activity which would produce tangible results. In an interview for the film *Will Rogers' 1920s*, Will Rogers Jr. stressed that his father's position was positive, that it included a respect for the rights of other nations, a dimension of Rogers' isolationism which could be overlooked:

> I think that Dad represented what we think of as fundamentally American at that time. He wanted us to be the most powerful country in the world and he wanted us to have a big Army and Navy and later a big Air Force, but he didn't want us to use it. He didn't want to see America go into Nicaragua, for example. He didn't want us to send the Marines into China. ...He was very outspoken in that way. He was anti-imperialist; he didn't want us to interfere with other people's business. ...He said, "I saw an odd thing. I saw a Marine in Washington." He took a lot of cracks at our expansionism. (*Will Rogers' 1920s: A Cowboy's Guide to the Times*)

Certainly Rogers was no xenophobe. The Oklahoman kept an open mind, recognizing that differing cultures should expect to see the world differently: "I am not the fellow to go to a Country and start criticizing it from our angle at home. You have to look at a thing through their eyes to be fair." Rogers made an effort to apply this principle of cultural relativity in his analysis of Mussolini. He knew that the typical American view of the Italian was simplistic: "Well, you got to be in Italy to really understand this fellow. Now to us he looks like he was the Tyrant and the Dictator, and that he was always posing like Napoleon, and that he was going to get his Country into war any minute. Now that's our angle on him" (65). But in context, Mussolini was only adapting to Italian conditions. In fact, Rogers tried to show that while Coolidge and Mussolini appeared to be very different kinds of political leaders, in many ways both were working for the same ends, but within very different constitutional conditions:

> He gets up in Public and tells Austria and Germany what to do. You have Kellogg send Mexico a note telling them what time to quit work that day. He comes into the House of Deputies over there and tells them the measures that shall be put through. You have five or six Senators for breakfast and the same thing happens.
>
> You see, everyone of us in the world have our audience to play to; we study them and we try to do it so it will appeal to what we think is the great majority. Now Italy likes everything put on like a Drama; they like a show, they like to have their patriotism appealed to and spoke about. ...Mussolini says a lot of things publicly that sound like boasting, but they are only meant for Home consumption. (65)

It would be hard to imagine Will Rogers as a devotee of the Communist system, but he was willing to see the world through the eyes of the Russian intellectual, Trotsky, if only for a short time. Unfortunately, Trotsky was going out of favor and Rogers was not allowed to speak with him. Responding to cancellation of an appointment, Rogers reflected: "If I had met him and had a chat with him, I would have found him a very interesting and human fellow, for *I have never yet met a man I didn't like.* When you meet people, no matter what opinion you might have formed about them beforehand, why, after you meet them and see their angle and their personality, why you can see a lot of good in all of them" (52).

Appearing in the slender volume entitled *There's Not a Bathing Suit in Russia* (1927), this was the first public formulation of a phrase for which Rogers would be long remembered, "I never met a man I didn't like." The statement in its full meaning should be seen as a counterbalance to the theme of isolationism which runs through Rogers' advice to President Coolidge. Will Rogers was certainly no mindless nationalist who supported his country right or wrong; nor did he ever adopt an irresponsible attitude toward the world community. Finally, Rogers was never misanthropic; his writings abound with humor about the joys of being a social human being. The aphorism which is now inscribed at the base of his statues in Claremore, Oklahoma, and Washington, D.C., was internationalist in the best sense. It meant that below nationality, class, sex, religion, or politics there is a basic humanity which we must honor. Respect for this common humanity could serve as a foundation for a peaceful world community.

Such was Rogers' hope. But he was also keenly aware that men had great difficulty detaching themselves from their roles and the influence of ideologies. As he sailed back from Europe in 1926, he felt that the barriers of class and nationality had been constructed to insuperable heights. Thus, while Will Rogers hoped for mutual respect among nations, his *Letters of a Self-Made Diplomat* focused upon the actual state of affairs in Europe. Instability characterized both internal and external politics. Governments were toppling; the masses were turning to dictators to restore order. Rogers advised his President to cast his influence where it would do palpable good, in settling the America's farm problem, in bringing a new tone to our nation's politics, in confronting honestly that legislative fluke, Prohibition. In the 21st century, many Americans are again advocating that internal rejuvenation should be given priority over our bumbling attempts to shape the destinies of distant nations.

But it was not necessary to share all of Will Rogers' conclusions to enjoy his articles for the *Saturday Evening Post*. Franklin D. Roosevelt was as internationalist as any American politician, but he could savor the combination of drollery and insight of which he found in the *Letters:* "In addition to my deep appreciation of his humor, the first time I fully realized Will Rogers' exceptional and deep understanding of political and social problems was when he came home from his European trip in 1926. While I discussed European matters with many others, both American and foreign, Will Rogers' analysis of affairs abroad was not only more interesting but proved to be more accurate than any other I had heard" (Memorial 32). Whether Calvin Coolidge agreed with all that his Ambassador had to say was not as important as the President's much-publicized response when Rogers returned home. An official car was sent to bring the literary Ambassador to the White House for an "official" report. Rogers was asked by the Coolidges to spend the night at their House. A literary device had become a reality! But there was more than poetic justice involved; it was only right that the pen pals should meet.

Information for this survey of Rogers' movements was culled from the numerous chronologies, datebooks, and scrapbooks in the vault of the Will Rogers Memorial, Claremore, Oklahoma. Newspaper review and responses are preserved in a number of scrapbooks at the Memorial.

Works Cited

Rogers, Will. *Letters of a Self-Made Diplomat to His President*. 1926. *Writings of Will Rogers*. Joseph A. Stout, Jr., and Peter C. Rollins, eds. 6. Stillwater: Oklahoma State UP, 1977.
—. *Rogers-isms: The Cowboy Philosopher on the Peace Conference*. *Writings of Will Rogers*. Joseph A. Stout, Jr., and Peter C. Rollins, eds. 4. Stillwater, OK: Oklahoma State UP, 1976.
Letters of a Self-Made Diplomat to His President. 1926. *Writings of Will Rogers*. Joseph A. Stout, Jr., and Peter C. Rollins, eds. 6. Stillwater: Oklahoma State UP, 1977.
—. *There's Not a Bathing Suit in Russia and Other Bare Facts*. *Writings of Will Rogers*. Joseph A. Stout, Jr., and Peter C. Rollins, eds. 2. Stillwater, OK: Oklahoma State UP, 1976.
—. Memorial Scrapbook No. 14, Will Rogers Memorial and Museum. Claremore, OK. 32.
Rollins, Peter C. Dir. *Will Rogers' 1920s: A Cowboy's Guide to the Times*. Los Angeles: Churchill Films, 1976.

4
Will Rogers on Aviation: A Means of Fostering Frontier Values in an Age of Machines and Bunk?

Sometime during 1920, while working on a film in Hollywood, Will Rogers was offered a ride in a studio airplane. Former Army Ace, G. B. Manly, made the short trip as exciting as possible with the hope of flustering the cowboy actor. As the pilot later recalled, Rogers "looked out over the edge of the careening cockpit and chewed his gum a little faster. When we came down, Will shifted his gum to the other cheek and remarked dryly: 'Try anything once. Try some things oftener. When you goin' again?'" (Rogers 41). Will Rogers had been bitten by an aviation bug. From that time on, the Oklahoma humorist jumped at every opportunity to fly. General James ("Jimmy") Doolittle believes that Rogers was characteristically excited by this new gadget: "I don't remember him refusing my call [to fly] if he didn't have anything else to do" (*Videotaped*). During the post WWI years, Rogers decided that the flying machines were more than novelties. They were needed for national defense to be sure, but they could serve a higher purpose: the challenges of flight could foster frontier values in an age of machines and "bunk."

The 1920s: A Decade of Bunk

What most disturbed Will Rogers about American life in the 1920s can be summarized by an all-inclusive neologism of the period, "bunk." Mass production was turning out consumer goods, but did Americans know how to use them to improve the quality of their lives? Urban growth provided the opportunity for social mobility, but what were the costs of denying one's roots? If the new lifestyle of a "boom" era helped young people, why was the fiction of the new generation strewn with sterile heroes, automobile accidents, and suicides?

Industrialism required a greater centralization of production and the Great War (1914-1918) had allowed big government to take on many new powers. Rogers feared the rise of bureaucratic structures because he distrusted managers and plans. His writings constantly pointed out the natural tendency of bureaucrats to serve their own interests rather than the needs of their clients, whose ordinary language they abandoned in favor of what we now call "newspeak." Producers communicated with consumers through a form of bunk called advertising, and government spokesmen seemed more concerned with staying in office than providing leadership. Frontier values such as individualism, flexibility, and neighborliness were endangered. In 1928, *Life* magazine and Rogers became so frustrated by political bunk that they founded an "anti-bunk" party, with Will Rogers a mock Presidential candidate. He campaigned in jest, but voiced serious complaints. Prosperity could be a threat to values by removing Americans from the real things in life:

> Our children are delivered to the schools in automobiles, but whether that adds to their grades is doubtful. There hasn't been a Thomas Jefferson produced in this country since we formed our first Trust. Rail splitting produced an immortal President in Abraham Lincoln; but Golf, 29,000 courses, hasn't produced even a good A-Number-1 Congressman... . Suppose Teddy had took up putting instead of horseback riding. (Day 173-4)

A flood of manufactured goods could not foster leaders, but it could affect the nation's sense of priorities. Especially after 1929, Rogers was impressed that consumer acquisitiveness had supplanted other values. Somehow Americans had forgotten that material advances were not an infallible index to meaningful cultural progress: "Civilization is nothing but acquired comforts for ourselves, when in those days [i.e., frontier times] they were so hard they didn't need 'em. We will strive to put in another bath, when

Technology, Luxury, and Values

maybe our neighbors can't even put in an extra loaf of bread" (Day 354-5). The perils of prosperity were not solely economic: as a contemporary social scientist, Edward Sapir, observed of the typical American in the 1920s:

> Even if he succeeds in making a fairly satisfactory compromise with his environment, he is apt to retain an uneasy sense of the loss of some vague and great good, some state of mind that he would be hard put to it to define, but which gave him a courage and joy that latter-day prosperity never quite seems to have regained for him. What has happened is that he has slipped out of the warm existence of a culture into a cold air of fragmentary existence. ("Culture" 97)

Material success had clouded the American dream and led to anomie.

Will Rogers spoke for the values of frontier America to Americans troubled by an erosion of moral standards: as a cowboy version of Rip Van Winkle, Rogers passed through this era of change judging new developments by frontier standards. In an era of sexual liberation, his highly-publicized family life was traditionally monogamous, so much so that his first kiss on the screen was a subject for much newspaper discussion. Although Rogers lived a faster-paced and more mobile life than his urban readers, he retained his spiritual roots. His syndicated daily and weekly articles exploited this traditional perspective, and Rogers' famous lead sentence, "All I know is what I read in the papers," meant exactly the opposite. To his peril, the average American knew only what he "learned" from journalists, radio commentators, and motion pictures—many of them purveyors of bunk.

As spokesman for a point of view forgotten by mass media, Will Rogers tested current fads, personalities, and events by frontier standards. The airplane clearly symbolized the new era of machines, but the inveterate passenger admired the life-and-death struggles of pilots with elements of wind, fog, and darkness or such geographical barriers as oceans and mountains. In fact, Rogers believed that the ocean of air above the American continent could serve as an inexhaustible testing ground for America' youth. He hoped that the airplane might constitute a new kind of transportation revolution, helping Americans to fly into the twentieth century without abandoning values of the nineteenth-century experience; perhaps this product of technology could foster frontier values in an age of bunk.

The Frontiersmen of the Air

Will Rogers responded hastily to the March, 1928, decision to display Samuel Langley's flying machine at the Smithsonian Institution. The announced exhibit sounded like Washington bunk. Rogers admired the Wright Brothers as individualists who succeeded against great odds in heavier-than-air flight. Yet he believed Langley was to receive special recognition simply because he was an administrator at the Smithsonian: "Just read the Smithsonian

General Mitchell's Bona Fides

Institution's explanation about the Wright flying machine. They say the trustees decided Langley's machine could have flown first but didn't. I could have flown to France ahead of Lindbergh, but I just neglected doing it. I had a lot of other things on my mind at the time" ("Will Rogers Criticizes" *Daily Telegrams* 186-7; hereafter, *DT*). Bureaucratic back-scratching appeared to be winning out over honest merit.

The William ("Billy") Mitchell controversy was the quintessence of bunk. Rogers followed the developments closely, both because of his personal friendship with Mitchell and because he feared that federal bunk might endanger national defense. On December 11, 1925, Rogers rode a train from Baltimore to Washington to attend the Mitchell court martial. The journalist's presence caused a stir; the presiding officer, General Howze, called a brief recess to receive Rogers, after which the commentator took a seat among the attorneys. (This kind of research enabled Rogers to know more than what he "read in the papers.")

Articles on the Mitchell affair stress the bunk of officials devoted to punishing a subordinate who had caused them public embarrassment. In an especially clever weekly article, Rogers invented a dialog between the Secretary of the Army and one of his advisors. In this imaginary discussion, the underling suggests that a civilian jury be appointed to the Mitchell case in order to lift the onus of prosecution from government shoulders. Being a master of bunk, Rogers' Secretary of the Army retorts: "That is all right, but suppose the jury takes Mitchell's part? Where will we be? They are liable to take aviation away from the army and navy and put it into the hands of a separate department. We must never let it get away from us, no matter how bad it gets" ("Mitchell's Back " 370-71). It would have been difficult to fashion a more persuasive parody of governmental officiousness and the valuing of "turf" over mission.

Early in the Mitchell debate, Rogers flew over the nation's capital with Brigadier General Mitchell. In a short article describing the sightseeing tour, Rogers evoked an American hero who would not truckle with bunk. The aviator faced the risks of flight with equanimity. Prior to takeoff, Mitchell asked Rogers if he used cotton to keep out engine noise, one of the hazards of flight; finding a bunk-related contrast, Rogers replied: "No, I only use cotton in my ears when I visit the Senate Gallery" (Day 113).

After the trip, Mitchell shared some shocking news with his passenger. For his outspoken stand on air power, Mitchell was soon to be demoted to Colonel and transferred to a minor airfield in Texas. Rogers was sad for both personal and political reasons. The article concluded with a popular cultural parable against bunk: "We had just flown over Washington's home, the Father of our country, whose first claim to Fame was telling the truth about a Cherry Tree! But George wasn't in the Army then, and the cherry Tree had nothing to do with our National Defense" (113-14). Obviously, Mitchell was a nonconformist willing to sacrifice personal advancement for *res publica*.

Had Mitchell's aerial battles with storms and mountains given him such strength? Certainly Rogers described pilots as the last individualists in an era of conformity, prohibition, and consumerism. These ex-army and navy officers were intelligent and tested professionals. Rogers admired the autonomy of the machine-mounted heroes: "They don't have to take off unless they want to. It's up to them. They are the last word. The company knows they will go if it's physically possible, and they let them decide" (Clancy 285). Rogers envied such independence in an era of assembly lines.

Lindbergh and Friend

Lindbergh's flight blew a breath of fresh air into an era of bunk. The story of a "tall, bashful, smiling American boy" taking on the Atlantic Ocean alone, a frontier "where no lone human being has ever ventured before," seemed to give hope that America was still producing heroes ("No Jokes" *DT* 90). A month after the "lone eagle's" flight, Rogers tried to identify the source of public excitement stirred by Lindbergh: "The reason that people have eaten it up all this time is because it's the only thing that has been in the papers in years that was clean, and no dirt connected with it in any way. People hadn't read clean stuff in so long that they just went crazy over this" ("Let's Keep Lindbergh" 1). Perhaps young Americans could do more than play golf, drink gin, and drive recklessly.

Rogers promoted Lindbergh as a living embodiment of traditional values. An age of bunk needed such role models: "This lad is our biggest national asset. He is our Prince and President combined. We only get one of these in a lifetime" ("How to Reward" *DT* 91). Journalistic use of the name "Lucky Lindy" irritated Rogers because it detracted from the young hero's accomplishments ("Calling Lindbergh" *DT* 96). In 1929, Rogers made his strongest criticism of the press: after their wedding, Charles and Anne Morrow Lindbergh eluded reporters. Disappointed newsmen accused Lindbergh of ingratitude; after all, they felt they had created the popular hero. Rogers reprehended: this hero "was made by just two things—the Lord and a Wright whirlwind motor. Newspapers couldn't have flew him from one side of a razor blade to another" ("Press is Told" *WA* 96; hereafter, *WA*). *Any* other explanation was bunk.

Rogers often described pilots as machine age cowboys. During a trip through Russia in 1926, the traveling Oklahoman met a Bolshevik with a trusty mechanical steed, "the funniest looking old chucklehead, shave-haired Russian boy that didn't look like he was over twenty. But say, Bob, that clown could sure rein that thing around and make it say uncle and play dead and roll over. He was an aviator" (25). The Fokker aircraft which ferried Rogers through Russia was personified as a skittish mount needing constant guidance from a skilled horseman: "This little plane seemed mighty small and jumpy to me, but this old Russian boy pulled the slack out of his reins, kinder clucked to her, and I want to tell you she left there right now... He just give her her head, and didn't seem to pull up for rivers, railroad crossings, or mountains" (Stout 26). While the image of a Bolshevik cowboy taming a mechanical Pegasus made amusing copy, the idea behind the comic image was serious: given youths like this pilot, men—rather than machines and bunk—could ride in the saddle.

Rogers employed equine imagery frequently. On his way to the Republican national convention in 1928, America's "anti-bunk" candidate suffered two accidents. While Rogers was landing in Las Vegas, a wheel fell off and the plane turned over; some hours later, the landing mechanism of a second plane broke during a landing in Wyoming. The Oklahoman could relate to the experience, even though machines seemed to buck very hard: "Once in a while, I've had a horse throw me where I've been underneath him and him top most, but I've never been thrown like I was today. They're getting easier, however. The first spill wasn't so bad, and the second was almost a pleasure" (Clancy 284). As always, such real, physical dangers contrasted with pitfalls back in the world of bunk. Of the Las Vegas crackup, Rogers reflected: "Wheel broke when she came down and turned over and lit on her back. I am the first candidate to land on his head, and being a candidate, it didn't hurt the head" ("Will Roger's Own Version" *DT* 230).

When Lindbergh began to take senators and congressmen for short flights to win them over to aviation, Rogers congratulated the young hero for getting them "air broke" ("Rogers Glad" *DT* 191). Lindbergh married Anne Morrow in 1929 and then began a cross-country flight with his new wife. Rogers was pleased to see the couple as pioneers: "See the Lindberghs are flying West. They have their camping outfit with 'em. If somebody lands in your back yard and you smell bacon frying, it won't be a soul but Annie and Charley. He is the first aviator to carry his own cook" ("Will Rogers Compliments" *DT* 43).

Despite the fact that this aviation couple traveled by machine, they appreciated the simple things in life. They obviously enjoyed getting away from the press and doffing their celebrity status: "You have never seen him at his best till you sit out in the pilot's seat by his side. When he has a plane in his hands, there is no careworn or worried look. That's when he is in his glory" ("Will Rogers Takes a Flight" *DT* 130). Once airborne, Lindbergh could forget the pressures of a bunk society.

Rogers especially admired the pioneering qualities of America's airmail pilots. These young men summoned the courage to confront elements of earth (mountains) and wind (storms) for a socially constructive purpose—their dangerous work brought Americans closer together. Rogers admonished his readers to be grateful for the sacrifice: "When you get an air mail letter...you just ought to stop and think what a chance a half-dozen fine young men have taken with their lives to get that letter there one or two days earlier" ("Airplanes" *WA* 183). Rogers could not understate his admiration for these trail makers of the air: "Boy, what pilots these air mail babies are. Lindbergh came from a great school" ("Will Rogers Chases Wolves" *DT* 140). As a contrast to this professionalism, elected officials in Washington—who should have provided living examples of civic heroism—were generating hot air, and this could be a problem: "They say hot air rises. And I guess it does. An airplane flying over the Capital the other day caught fire from outside sources" ("Weekly Exposure" *WA* 186). Though Lindbergh and many clean young heroes had been disciplined by flight experience, the society of bunk was still dominant.

Aviation and the Brotherhood of Man

The airplane could bring societies closer together and promote better feelings among nations. Through personal example, Will Rogers taught this lesson, especially during his mercy tours when he rode to the rescue of troubled Americans. Floods ripped through the Mississippi Valley in 1927, dispossessing thousands of farmers and covering many rural towns. Rogers wrote about the problem regularly. Even in the famous telegram which saluted Lindbergh, the Oklahoman added a charitable suggestion about America's flood victims: "What could be better to celebrate his arrival than another donation to 600,000 of our very own, that are not even fortunate enough to be flying over water, but have to stand huddled upon the banks and look into it as it washes away their lifetime's work" ("No Jokes" *DT* 90). In one highly publicized trip, Rogers flew to Louisiana to survey the damage. He asked the governor of Louisiana to put a plane at his disposal: "I want to get a look at first hand so when I speak on the flood, I can talk with authority" (Memorial Scrapbook 15: 80). (When Congress later convened a committee to study flood control, the airborne humorist was called to testify.) Rogers played a number of benefit performances to raise money for flood victims. A special trip to Mexico with Lindbergh during the same year demonstrated that the airplane could help nations feel more neighborly.

When drought destroyed the crops of the Southwest, turning the region into a Dust Bowl, Will Rogers showed that the airplane

Frank Hawks Piloted the Mercy Flights

could speed up missionary procedures and allow one neighbor to help another. President Hoover would not commit public funds to alleviate the suffering because of his belief in free enterprise. Rogers refused to stand by; people were in trouble and immediate action—not more bunk—was needed. Rogers persuaded a Texas company to supply him with a plane along with a famed former ace, Frank Hawks. Mounted aboard the loaned craft, the humanitarian galloped from state to state on his mission of mercy: he visited ten cities in Texas; he made at least eighteen stops in Oklahoma; he stopped at five locations in Arkansas. All proceeds from his performances were donated to the Red Cross; half could be used by the city in which he raised the money, while the other half was to be shared with impoverished rural communities.

Rogers dramatized his efforts in daily telegrams and weekly articles, stressing the contribution of both pilot and plane to the tours of mercy. Both the 1927 and 1931 trips made an indelible impression on his contemporaries. In a representative response, an editorial of the *Jacksonville Journal* (Jacksonville, Florida) tried to express the admiration of Americans for the symbolic actions of the Oklahoma humorist:

> Giving wings to most people does not add to their ability to be of benefit to the world...though it may increase their economic efficiency... But when a genius such as Will Rogers got wings, he becomes a sort of superman, not by reason of superiority of attitude, but by the multiplication of his contracts with human creatures who need a bit of cheer in their helplessness or weariness or misery. Like St. Francis, he is a lover not of mankind, at large, but men as individuals. St. Francis used the 'shabby expedient' of a rope to tie around his waist in his spiritual vocation; Will Rogers used it to humanize his philosophy. And the good he does in this world is increased by his mobility. ("Simple Life")

In a society where members of the same apartment building did not know each other, Will Rogers seemed to convey the idea that cities and nations (through his example) could be linked by neighborly bonds of affection: "He comes nearer being *a Jongleur de*

Dieu than any modern world personage—a jongleur and a troubadour in one—not for a single community, but for thousands of cities and for the remotest cabins. To have wings for such a service is not merely to minister them to more people directly; but is to carry them the human kindness of others and to bring these people into wider human relationships" ("Simple Life"). This was more than a boost for aviation—it was a tribute to Rogers' living lesson that machines could serve human purposes.

The Joys of Flight

Will Rogers regularly tried to portray the pure fun of flying, cowboy-style, across the aerial frontier: "it's like sitting astride a lively cloud and sailing over the earth with a marvelous, ever-changing mountain-top view beneath you." The American continent revealed special beauties to those aloft: "In the east, you get the colorful panoramas of spring's tender greens and autumn's gorgeous foliage. Out west, you soar over magnificent painted deserts lonesome as the moon... Then you strike a valley with pretty little ranches all along the edges, and feel as if you were back on earth again" (Clancy 285). In an article touting the pioneer efforts of Western Air Express, Rogers celebrated the sense of open land which air flight conveyed: "Brigham Young might have seen more women than I have, but I have seen more of Utah today than he ever saw. Who said this country was all settled up?" ("Will Rogers Chases Wolves" *DT* 140). Flying provided so many different perspectives that the beauty of the land seemed inexhaustible: "Even if you go over a country one way and come back by the very same route, the whole thing looks different to you. It's because you're seeing it from exactly the opposite angle. You will swear you didn't come that way before." Such variety inspired awe. Night runs were even more exhilarating than day flights. Although danger increased, an inexpressible feeling of transcendence offered more than sufficient reward, "especially the thrill of sailing over a big lighted city at night. Below, you see hundreds of lighted rows of streets running in every direction, the dark outlines of the rivers and lakes, and the thousands of automobile headlights that dart around like bugs." Above every city—no matter how crowded—was a frontier ocean of air where young men and women could test their mettle, gain a sense of the power for good available in the machine age, yet return to an orderly society once the experience of flight was over. Americans needed both the challenge offered by the ocean of air as well as the orderly world created by technology: "when you swoop down out of the darkness into all this flood of light and efficiency—well, you'll just have to experience the sensation yourself, that's all" (Clancy 285).

The Frontier and American Character

In a weekly article written during the summer of 1929, Rogers described an endurance flight being conducted over a Los Angeles suburb. The article is worth close examination because it indirectly addressed a broader issue: what kind of testing ground was the ocean of air and how were America's young people rising to the challenge?

Rogers began by describing the location of the test, Culver City, California. Although little known, it was an influential community:

Hope for the Youth of America

"all over the world, you hear about Hollywood, and hear of it as the home of all the films, when as a matter of fact there are more pictures made in Culver City than in all Hollywood. This Culver landed some of the biggest studios three years ago and they have grown bigger ever since" (Staying Up" *WA* 45). As a representative American city, the previously open land of Culver was becoming crowded with studios, homes, and golf courses.

The endurance pilots were sons of local leaders: Paul Whittier was "a mighty fine young Pilot, son of a very wealthy family out there who were the founders of Beverly Hills"; one of the sponsors was "Young McAdoo, W. G.'s oldest boy." The entire Culver Field team consisted of young men accepting the challenges of a grueling endurance flight even though they lived in one of the wealthiest and most protected communities in the United States.

Rogers detailed the dangers braved by the young men. Simply refueling the circling "Curtiss Pigeon with an old Liberty motor" was fraught with peril. Passing the refueling hose between ships put the men on both crafts in danger: "If at any time during all these contacts it had ever touched the propeller it would have been all off." Other hazards made the endurance flight as much a test of character as of equipment: on one occasion, the refueling ship could not fly and improvised means had to be devised to keep the ship afloat; at another time, when thick fog prevented the planes from finding each other, in a daring maneuver, they linked up under the low ceiling seconds before the endurance ship ran dry. These unexpected moments of difficulty forced the young pilots to draw upon resources of courage and flexibility; they were measuring up to the challenges of a frontier.

Living in an endurance plane was not unlike earlier forms of roughing it. Air sickness proved a debilitating factor, but "as time went along, they got stronger and more cheerful every day." The heat was so intense that "they didn't wear their clothes just run the ship in their underwear, with all the windows open." Sleep was allowed only briefly on an improvised inflatable air mattress. The conditions could not have been more primitive. Given Will Rogers' concern about American youth and frontier values, the endurance flight heartened him: "it was a real kick to stand on that field and see them at the very moments that they were breaking the record, the longest any humans had ever stayed up." The rich boys had extended a frontier: with the assistance of their machines, they had stayed up even longer than "birds and fowl." Their accomplishment was a tribute both to character and to engineering.

The pilots over Culver Field were not unique. Young aviators in Dallas, Cleveland, and other American cities were testing their powers on the ocean of air. As a result, Rogers could be confident that leaders were being molded, leaders who could master machines and employ executive skills to explore: "There is a whole lot more to this than just saying I will go up and break a record. It takes a lot of cooperation and work and much planning ahead." Those tested in the air could assume leadership roles in the technological society below. Fortunately, aviation assured that the age of bunk could still produce heroes: these men had the qualities of frontiersmen, but they were also skilled in making machines and organizations work toward constructive ends.

As machines became more sophisticated, more distant frontiers could be explored. Rogers envisioned American youths eventually mounting their mechanical steeds and riding off into outer space. Lindbergh had crossed the Atlantic; these future Lindberghs would conquer even greater obstacles: "Round June 22, 1950, here is what will be headlined in the planet Mars morning papers: 'A young man from a place called Earth flew in here yesterday. He had been in the air continuously for two months. He had some letters of introduction from the Chamber of Commerce from a place called Englewood, New Jersey. He asked to have his ship refueled as he is taking off for Venus in the morning'" ("Mr. Rogers Peers" *DT* 182).

Conclusions

Will Rogers' fantasy was prescient. Ten years after the predicted date of 1950, John F. Kennedy called for Americans to dream of a "New Frontier." Like the 1920s, the 1950s had been an era of conformity and stagnation: post-war prosperity encouraged Americans to become soft. The American space program was launched on the premise that Americans needed to recapture the thrill of pushing back frontiers. In 1979, Tom Wolfe found heroic qualities—what he called "the right stuff"—in our astronauts. Wolfe's celebration of

The Concern about American Character Continues

space exploration, *The Right Stuff*, became a bestseller because contemporary American readers shared Will Rogers' concerns about the deleterious effects of a closed society. In the 21st century, we hope that young Americans will show the courage and resourcefulness Will Rogers saw exhibited over Culver City, California, in 1929. Yet our dilemma seems so much more grave: our dependence upon machines has increased and the forces of bunk seem so much stronger.

Discussion of Literature

According to *Webster's Third New International Dictionary of the English Language* the origin of the word "Bunk" can be found in "a remark made by Felix Walker, c.1820, U.S. Representative of North Carolina from the Congressional district that included the county of Buncombe." In trying to explain a seemingly irrelevant speech in Congress he stated that he was "speaking to Buncombe." In a number of variants, the word has since been applied to "insincere public talk or action" (297). Henry Ford, H. L. Mencken, and Will Rogers gave the term new currency in the 1920s.

When Will Rogers accepted the Presidential nomination of the Anti-Bunk Party in 1928, he clarified the word: advertising, party platforms, committee reports, prohibition, all seemed variants of bunk. Any duplicitous statement designed to advance a spokesman, rather than to provide insight, was bunk. When Coolidge explained that he "did not choose to run"—thus leaving open a chance to be drafted by his party—he was peddling bunk. Although Rogers admired Herbert Hoover in 1928, he predicted that as a politician, the Great Engineer would eventually succumb to bunk: "Herbert Hoover is a fine man and would make an excellent President. To do this, however, he must first be nominated, and to be nominated, he must first kneel down and do obeisance at the shrine of the Great God Bunk, foreswearing all irreverent or independent thoughts" ("I Accept"). The editors at *Life* picked Rogers "as a bunkless candidate, who will run for President on an honest, courageous, and reasonably intelligent platform" (17 May 1928: 1). Like Rogers, *Life* vowed "to fight bunk in all its forms" (24 May 1928: 1).

For a discussion of the Langley machine as experimental craft and tourist attraction, see Black. Rogers' response to the Smithsonian's decision to display the Langley flying machine was characteristic, although his facts were wrong. The Langley machine *was* placed on exhibit; however, no one—least of all Samuel Langley—was attempting to obscure the accomplishments of the Wright brothers.

For a more detailed documentary film study of Will Rogers, see Rollins' *Will Rogers: A Bibliography* and *Will Rogers' 1920s: A Cowboy's Guide to the Times* (1976). For another discussion of the Presidential Candidacy phase of Will Rogers' career see Ketchum.

A daily account of the life of Will Rogers can be found in the *Will Rogers Chronologies*, Will Rogers Memorial, Claremore, Oklahoma. Since 1938 details about Rogers' day-to-day activities have been accumulated and recorded in this fascinating and invaluable resource.

Works Cited

Black, Archibald. *The Story of Flying*. New York: McGraw-Hill, 1940.
Clancy, Stearns. "Aviation's Patron Saint." *Scientific American* Oct.1929: 285.
"Culture: Genuine and Spurious." *Culture, Language and Personality*. Ed. David G. Mandelbaum. Berkeley: U of California P, 1968. 97-126.
Day, Donald. ed. *The Autobiography of Will Rogers*. New York: Avon Books, 1975.
Grave, P.B. ed. *Webster's Third New International Dictionary of the English Language Unabridged*. Springfield, MA: G&C Meriam Co., 1966.
"I Accept the Nomination." *Life Magazine*, 31 May 1928: 2.
Ketchum, Richard M. *Will Rogers: The Man and His Times*. New York: Simon and Schuster, 1973.
"Let's Keep Lindbergh Out of Vaudeville." 9 June 1927. The Will Rogers Publication Project, Stillwater, OK: Oklahoma State University.
Rogers, Will, James Smallwood, and Steven K. Gragert, eds. *Daily Telegrams of Will Rogers*. Vols. 1-4. Stillwater: Oklahoma State UP, 1978.
—. "Calling Lindbergh 'Lucky' Arouses Will Rogers' Ire." Vol. 1: 96.
—. "How to Reward Lindbergh: Ideas From Will Rogers." Vol. 1: 91.
—. "Mr. Rogers Peers into the Future and Sees Inter-Planet Flier." Vol. 1: 182.
—. "No Jokes From Rogers Till Lindbergh Arrives." Vol. 1: 90.
—. "Rogers Glad That Lindbergh Took Prize From the Marines." Vol. 1: 191.
—. "Will Rogers Chases Wolves on His Flight Back Home." Vol. 1: 140.
—. "Will Rogers Compliments Lindbergh and Fletcher." Vol. 2: 43.
—. "Will Rogers Criticizes Smithsonian Airship Stand." Vol. 1: 186-7.
—. "Will Rogers' Own Version of the Airplane Accident." Vol. 1: 230.
—. "Will Rogers Takes a Flight with Lindbergh as his Pilot." Vol. 1: 130.
Rogers, Will, James Smallwood, and Steven K. Gragert, eds. *Will Rogers' Weekly Articles*. Vols. 1-6. Stillwater: Oklahoma State UP, 1981.
—. "Airplanes, Ladies, and Politics." Vol. 4: 183.
—. "Mitchell's Back and Coolidge Is Letting Nature Take Its Course." Vol. 1: 370-71.
—. "Press is Told to Hold its Tongue." Vol. 4: 342.
—. "Staying Up in the Air: Aviators Have Got the Birds beat for Endurance." Vol. 4: 45.
—. "Weekly Exposure Dishes up the News." Vol. 1: 186.
Rogers, Will. Memorial Scrapbook Nos. 15, 24. Will Rogers Memorial and Museum. Claremore, OK.
Rollins, Peter C. *Will Rogers: A Bio-Bibliography*. Westport, CT: Greenwood Press, 1984.
"Simple Life and Kindly Manner Marked Life of Will Rogers." Fred Stone Scrapbook, No. 11. Will Rogers Memorial and Museum. Claremore, OK.
Stout, Joseph A., Jr., ed. *There's Not a Bathing Suit in Russia and Other Bare*

Facts. Rpt. Stillwater, OK: Oklahoma State UP, 1973.
Videotaped Interview with General James Doolittle. ABC. KTUL,Tulsa. 5 Nov. 1979.
Will Rogers Memorial and Museum. Claremore, OK.
Will Rogers' 1920s: A Cowboy's Guide to the Times. Dir. Peter C. Rollins. Churchill Films, 1976.
Wolfe, Tom. *The Right Stuff.* New York: Farrar, Straus, and Giroux, 1979.

5
Regional Literature and Will Rogers: Film Redeems a Literary Form

Will Rogers is not usually associated with questions of literary form or literary consciousness, yet his relationship as a humorist to American regional literature poses some interesting questions for students of film and literature because almost all of Rogers' films were adapted from works of the regional genre. The first section of this chapter will explore the "mind" of *The Saturday Evening Post* in order to determine why regional literature remained a staple for this popular weekly as late as the 1920s and 1930s—long after it had been deserted by serious American writers. The findings are based on a close reading of the regional novels, the *Post* regional stories, and the screenplays written from these literary sources. The Rogers films based on these fictions have been examined closely—with heartening results. Much of the basic setting, plot, and dialogue for Will Rogers' films were borrowed without modification from literary sources. These portraits of American life were nostalgic and showed a yearning for simpler times. Alas, many included derogatory stereotypes of racial minorities. Yet when Rogers appeared on the set, he injected into these films messages about American life which were more relevant and humane than those to be found in either the original stories or the final shooting scripts. It is often said that Will Rogers paid little attention to the scripts for his films.

It is more likely that he dropped lines out of his prepared parts and improvised from his journalism while the cameras rolled because he found the official lines to be repugnant. Whatever the

SEP and the 'Old West' of Emerson Hough, 1923

reasons for changing the lines and developing scenes to suit his own taste, the result of Rogers' extemporaneous editing was to break the restrictive mold prepared for him by his Hollywood minders. For this reason, rather than being forced to relate the process by which literary classics have been vitiated by Hollywood, the second section of this chapter will describe an unusual case in which film redeems a literary form.

The "Mind" of *The Saturday Evening Post* and the *Post* School of Regional Fiction

When Cyrus Curtis purchased *The Saturday Evening Post* in 1899, he installed an ambitious editor who vowed "to interpret America to itself" (Wood 153). Indeed, from 1899 to 1936 George Horace Lorimer developed a magazine which one historian has said "had more influence on the cultural life of America" than any other periodical (Mott 716). Yet for all its claims to being "the dominant and representative American publication" of the 1920's and 1930s, the *Post* contained a highly selective portrait of American life (Lorimer qtd in Wood 158). Most significantly, big business, big labor, and the immigrant were perceived by the *Post* as threats to "native" middle-class Americans whose roots were (supposedly) deeply planted in genuine cultural soil (Hofstadter 132).

The *Post* was especially reactionary on the immigration issue for Lorimer was a firm believer in the pseudo-scientific racial theories popularized during the twenties by Theodore Lothrop Stoddard, Madison Grant, and Max Nordau (Higham 131). For Lorimer, these proponents of Nordic superiority had supplied Americans with "a trustworthy key and codebook to the underlying mysteries of bolshevism, syndicalism, the Age of Jazz, the silly season of politics and the devastating epidemic of fool ideas" which had swept America after the European war (Lorimer 22). In Lorimer's eyes, only a few, select races could live up to the high standards of American citizenship. Through editorials and non-fiction articles, Lorimer's *Post* helped to sway public opinion in favor of the restrictive Immigration Act of 1924, a law which remained in force until the son of immigrants became President in 1961.

The *Post* worked hard to fight one ineluctable tide of political change. In May, 1936, Lorimer announced to his readers that "There is one issue and only one issue before the country today -the New Deal and all its works, public and private, and its threat to the fundamentals of government and society" (Tebbel 139). Without encouragement from the candidate, the *Post* voluntarily mounted a campaign for the cause of Alf Landon. When Roosevelt won a landslide victory at the polls, Lorimer was stricken with a bout of depression, for the American public had repudiated the social attitudes and cultural values for which the *Post* had spoken during Lorimer's thirty-seven-year reign as editor (208).

The regional stories and novels in the fiction section of the *Post* played a part in Lorimer's campaign against social and political change. With a seemingly tireless repetition, these *Post* stories celebrated the peaceful life of small-town America before that way of life was disrupted by the industrial and transportation revolutions. It appears that these idylls allowed the *Post's* "native" American

Hough's *The Covered Wagon* Adapted to Film, 1923

readers to sense an imaginary link with their roots: a pre-urban, pre-industrial, pre-immigrant America.

The West of the untamed cowboy and the rugged pioneer was represented in romances by Peter B. Kyne, Ben Ames Williams, Emerson Hough, and Edna Ferber. Ben Ames Williams supplied the *Post* with nothing but this type of story from 1917-1919. In 1922 the editor of the *Post's* "Out of Doors" section serialized an immensely popular novel in this vein, *The Covered Wagon*. This "epic" quickly became a Book-of-the-Month-Club selection, a Pulitzer Prize winner, and a landmark silent film. Middle-class Americans in the age of flappers and flirts obviously enjoyed being reassured that ideals such as pioneer courage and self-sacrifice were still a living part of their heritage.

Although Booth Tarkington earned a handsome living by supplying the *Post* with nostalgic stories about Indiana, he was as aware as his readers were that "the small city, Indianapolis, where I was born, exists no more than Carthage existed after the Romans had driven ploughs over the ground where it stood. Progress swept all the old life away" (Kunitz 1384). Clarence B. Kelland contributed a number of crackerbox philosophers in his stories of Vermont and New Hampshire. In all cases, a pre-industrial and pre-urban America was pictured as a high moment in American history when rugged individualists of Protestant extraction and their values were dominant. In this light, it was no matter of chance that J. P. Marquand's *The Late George Apley* (1937) was first serialized in the *Post.*

It was also no matter of chance that *Post* regional stories abound with derogatory stereotypes of Black Americans and immigrants. Irvin S. Cobb and Octavus Roy Cohen developed a specialty in the area of stories about the stupidity and dishonesty of the Negro race. For many regular readers of Lorimer's racist editorials, these stories must have provided an opportunity to look down the racial ladder at an irresponsible and immoral under-class. (The Black stereotypes designed by script writers for Will Rogers' films were drawn from these *Post* stories.) In 1911, *The Saturday Evening Post* published "Words and Music," the first of what would eventually amount to some seventy tales about a rural southern lawyer and social symbol, Judge Priest. These Judge Priest tales were filled with a host of Black stereotypes. It is instructive, however, to note that Cobb not only fabricated his characters for profit—he believed in them. The following "humorous" description of one of his "sources" reveals the strength of Cobb's racism:

> To support Judge Priest in his fictional aspects, I drew heavily on the actual personalities in the Paducah I had known as a cub reporter. For my choruses, for the bit players, I grazed through the Negro community and there found fallow fields rich in types and topics. There is Connie Lee, still the town's leading chiropodist and the only survivor of all the individuals white or black who marched across my manuscripts. He was the original of Judge Priest's private retainer, the one called "Jeff Poindexter." It was Connie, who, seeing his first passenger plane come zooming across the Ohio River southward bound, remarked that so far as his race was concerned, he didn't believe it ever would be necessary to put on a Jim Crow section. (Cobb 348)

The atmosphere of the Judge Priest tales is harmonious: since everyone has a clearly defined place, everyone is happy. If the South pictured was out of step with the realities of contemporary American life, this did not therefore mean that *Post* readers did not enjoy a weekly view of such a stable world.

Hugh Wiley and Octavus Roy Cohen also contributed stories with demeaning Black stereotypes. As the commanding officer of a Black Labor Battalion during World War 1, Wiley had supposedly gained an ear for the excited chatter of Blacks at play. The sheer volume of Wiley stories indicates that *Post* readers never tired of these "unique" transcriptions of back-alley jive talk, for while the plots of Wiley's tales may have varied, they inevitably led to a crap game. Two students of contemporary literature have observed that "For a time, an issue of the *Saturday Evening Post* without an Octavus Roy Cohen serial or short story was hardly thinkable" (Kunitz 29). Cohen created a favorite *Post* character, Florian Slappy, a "radiant dresser" with an eye for women and a disdain for work. Lorimer even allowed Cohen a special leeway on sexual matters so that his white readers could vicariously experience the abandon of a class which appeared to be exempt from the anxieties which accompany social ambition and responsibility.

The racial stereotypes in *Post* fiction were reinforced on the advertising pages. One glaring example will stand for many. A Cream of Wheat ad fills the entire second page of the December 17, 1921 issue. Dominating the page is "Rastus," a black cook dressed in a white chef's hat and smiling at the viewer:

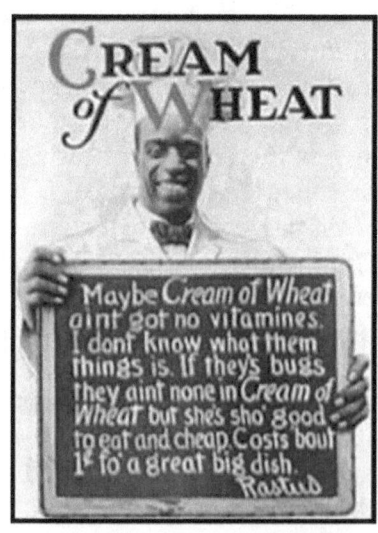

The *Post*'s Racial Stereotyping

The humor of this advertisement stems from Rastus' illiteracy. He violates every rule of Standard English, and in addition shows that he is ignorant of the importance of vitamins, which he associates with bugs. "Rastus" is obviously a character straight out of an Irvin S. Cobb story, ready to do the bidding of his Judge Priest.

The nostalgia and racial distortions which characterize "the *Post* School of Fiction" were chosen and sustained by the weekly's editor, George Horace Lorimer. The implicit message of these regional tales was that *Post* readers could congratulate themselves for having roots in the traditions of Anglo-Saxon, small-town America, roots which were too deep to be affected by war, the boom of the 'twenties or the bust of the 'thirties. With such reassurances about their lineage, *Post* readers could press on up the ladder of success. When fatigued by their climb, they could relax with a humorous story about carefree Blacks. It is unquestionable that executives at Twentieth Century-Fox wished to capitalize on the success of these *Post* stories in the films tailored for Will Rogers. What Rogers felt about regional fiction and how he broke the narrow mold created for him in these films will be considered in the next section of this paper.

Literature to Film: Will Rogers Redeems the Regional Form

Unlike the authors of the *Post's* school of fiction, Will Rogers believed that the regional genre was a resource for live metaphors which he could use to provide insight into contemporary life. Rogers' ability to use regional diction and metaphors for constructive rather than nostalgic purposes applied directly to his work in film.

The Silent Era: Some Regional Clichés Satirized

Many of Will Rogers' first films were either adapted from works of regional literature or from *Post* stories of the regional type. The most meaningful film for our purposes is *Two Wagons—Both Covered* (1924). We have already indicated the circumstances which inspired Emerson Hough to write his "American epic," *The Covered Wagon* (1922). Shortly after the novel was selected by the Book-of-the-Month Club, James Cruze began working on what is still judged to be one of the classics of the silent film era. As the son of a pioneer, Rogers did not put much stock in the glorifications selling so well to film and *Post* audiences (Day 31).

Two Wagons—Both Covered (1924) is a point-for-point satire of the sententiousness of the literary and film "classics" of Emerson Hough and James Cruze. In the opening scene, the title is suddenly made surprisingly clear—there are in fact only two wagons and about five cows involved in this "epic." Later when the two small wagons stop for the night, we discover that in circus fashion, each of the wagons contains about one hundred passengers! The comedy of *Two Wagons* continues in this burlesque fashion, running through a host of clichés from Western fiction and films. Are trappers and guides gifted with special powers of perception? Rogers as Joe Jackson shows that he can identify the Mississippi River by its taste! Are Natty Bumppo and his literary and film grandchildren always portrayed as unmarried, solitary figures? Jim Badger, trapper, is shown with his two wives and thirty children. His family is so large that Rogers as Joe Jackson concedes, in admiration, "Jim, you're not only a scout, but a man!" Does an epic of migration require fording scenes in which property, cattle and families are hazarded? In *Two Wagons,* furniture is floated across, and the cattle are equipped with water-wings. The effect is to mock-heroically destroy the seriousness of the works of Hough and Cruze. Having played with some of the conventions of Western romances, Rogers' satire comes to an abrupt close. The last scene fades out with a shot of Joe Jackson trying to drown one of the stragglers left behind by the "Escrow Indians" (Los Angeles realtors in modern dress).

Regional Adaptations in the Sound Era

State Fair (1933): **The Power of Sympathy**

In Phil Stong's *State Fair,* (Book-of-the-Month Club selection for 1932) an Iowa farmer and his family travel to a state fair where their rural values are put to a test. Their ideas about the magnitude of their achievements at the fair are humorously portrayed: Abel Frake, the *paterfamilias,* is concerned only with the health of his competition boar named Blue Boy; Mrs. Frake has concocted a recipe for mince meat which she hopes will strike the fancy of the drinkers among the judges. Wayne Frake has been practicing ring-toss for the last year in preparation for revenge against a carnival sideshow which took his money the preceding year. Finally, Margie

Uncle Will at Work

is in search of a substitute for her Homeville suitor, an awkward dairy farmer named Harry.

The Frake children find more than they anticipated. Wayne not only embarrasses the ring-toss barker, he walks away from the concession with a girl named Emily who is an expert in Hotel Hospitality. Wayne is shocked that this city girl will not return to Homeville with him after their intimacy. Meanwhile, Margie strikes up an acquaintance with a Chicago journalist named Pat Gilbert. At first, she surrenders to him with "anguish and delight" (Stong 167). After their moment of passion, however, she realizes that she belongs back in Homeville, where her socio-sexual role is clearly defined for her. As a country girl, she fears the anonymity of the big City.

Script and Film
The authors of the screenplay develop Abel Frake into a conservative Republican critic of the Roosevelt Administration. Their Abel is not impressed by the New Deal or Farm Relief: "Yes, we've heard four years of his [i.e. Roosevelt's] talk. But so far I haven't seen any relief" (Josephson). Instead of supplying his own alternative views about the New Deal, Will Rogers as Abel Frake simply ignored these political remarks. Rogers instead concentrated on being a symbol of personal concern. This is especially effective in his interaction with his daughter, Margie. Uncle Will understands her post-adolescent yearnings and takes her on his knee. There is no such scene in the script, but the impression is conveyed in the film that this is a true and concerned father. He is not interested in the abstractions of politics, but rather with individual people and their problems. *State Fair* was the first sound film in which Rogers was cast as a small-town character. One reviewer expressed the hope that the Oklahoman would appeal in similar rural roles for a large segment of potential filmgoers who were remaining at home because they were uninterested in "penthouses and gun-spattered pavements" (Rosenfield). The remaining films examined in this section are all of this rural genre.

Doctor Bull (1933): The Passing of a Great Race
Like Phil Stong's *State Fair* (1933). James Gould Cozzens' *The Last Adam* (1933) was a novel which conformed to the rules for *Post* regional fiction. Certainly Harcourt, Brace, and Company, publisher of this Book-of-the-Month Club selection, stressed the regional emphasis in its advertising. In his *New York Times* review of the book, John Chamberlain expressed his pleasure that the fading New England type was being commemorated in print: "For better or worse, the urbanization of the United States and the spread of tabloid culture and moral attitudes are leveling the races and putting salty individuals like the 'old horse doctor' out of the running" (Chamberlain 6).

The decay of New England's Yankee culture is implied by the title of John Gould Cozzens' novel, *The Last Adam*. To account for this decline of New Winton's society, many "native" Americans utter racist lines which sound as though they have been lifted *verbatim* from a *Post* editorial. George Bull in Cozzens' novel is not untainted by this search for a scapegoat to explain his loss of status over the last fifty years:

> Well, Connecticut's going to hell, that's about the size of it... If I were fixing it, I'd have things the way they were thirty years ago...New Winton was a place to live then, not something a road went through...look at the mills down at Sansbury and the Polacks! Time was when Sansbury was a white man's town. Look at the Roman Catholic convent there, or whatever they made of the Jenny place! What the hell are those monks and priors and novenas of the little Flower doing In New England? Same with a lot of these Jew artists, like Lincoln over in the Cobb place. Jumping Jesus, what's he mean by calling himself Lincoln? Early American house. Why doesn't he go restore himself a synagogue in Jerusalem? (Cozzens 110)

The Script
In his screenplay, Paul Green retained this invidious contrast between the established Yankee natives of New Winton and the foreign invaders. Stage directions for a scene in which Dr. Bull arrives to deliver an Italian baby describes Louie Papoliti, the father, as "a swarthy, fat, jowled Italian about thirty" (Green 33). When Louie nervously comes for the doctor, Green has the old Yankee greet the distraught foreigner with what must have struck Green as a clever Rogersism. Instead of showing concern for the expectant father, the script's Dr. Bull flippantly quips to Louie, "You never know when another Washington is born or an Al Capone" (34). In Green's pseudo-Rogersism, Italians (and by inference, all foreign born) are portrayed as potentially irresponsible, criminal, and credulous.

The Film
It is refreshing to note that Will Rogers and John Ford completely ignored the derogatory lines in Paul Green's film script. While the Italians are portrayed as working class people, their vulnerability is used to highlight Dr. Bull's sympathy for all members of the community. When the film's Dr. Bull arrives, the Papoliti apartment is crowded with concerned members of the family and community.

The male members are clustered around a table, silently drinking red wine from large bottles. After Will Rogers delivers a baby boy, he comes back to this living room and surveys the quiet (and slightly tippled) crowd.

Instead of launching into a sermon about the evils of drink and the responsibilities of the working class, Rogers turns the situation entirely around. He uses this moment to extemporize about Anglo-Saxon repression. He is favorably impressed by the community involvement, and sees that the wine has acted both as a social cement and an anodyne to calm the nerves. Pouring himself a tall glass of chianti, Rogers says: "I love to bring Italian babies into the world. If you go out to a farmer's place to deliver a baby, after it's all over, all you get is a cup of coffee." Rogers obviously here implies that the "native" Americans who supported the Volstead Act need this Infusion of new blood into their repressed culture. Thus, where the *Post* would have invoked some sort of slur about "Americanskis," Rogers implicitly supports a cosmopolitan outlook.

David Harum (1934): The "Real Things in Life"

Edward Noyes Wescott's regional novel *David Harum: A Story of American Life* (1898) is drenched with a nostalgia for the "happy days" before America became entirely overrun by big business, big labor, and "foreign" ideas. Within its own literary context, *David Harum* received a mixed response not unlike that accorded Will Rogers' late films: the critics rejected the book, but the public made it a best seller. Contemporary critics were correct in calling *David Harum* an anomalous book. While muckraking journalists and young writers of fiction were involving themselves with the problems of American life in relation to science, the city, and industrialism, Wescott's novel seemed to be looking back to an earlier and personal America. This retrospective glance accounts for the novel's popularity. In filling out his portrait of Homeville, Freeland County, New York, Wescott mustered a host of representative village types. The central character, David Harum, represents the inner spirit of Homeville's way of life. While his business is ostensibly banking, his real passion in life is horse trading. David's slow pace gives him plenty of time to moralize about people and to keep a concerned eye on those in Homeville who are in trouble.

To involve the reader in the exploration of these rural values, Wescott introduces an urban young man named John Lenox. As a result of the panic of 1893, John is hard pressed to find gainful employment. His father's business was destroyed by the panic. To preserve John from some of the economic consequences, John's stoical father killed himself. After this calamitous opening, the bulk of the novel involves John's learning the values and emulating the integrity of his adopted spiritual father, David Harum. Every experience for John at Homeville works to teach the young man of the city a new orientation toward life. Endurance comes first. During his first morning at David Harum's rural bank, John must help subdue an angry customer who resorts to fisticuffs after being out-witted by David Harum. Honesty comes next: David Harum tests John's mettle by ordering him to shuffle some counterfeit bills (discovered in the daily cash) in with money for the next day's disbursements. John immediately burns the fake bills, a significant gesture in an era which was suffering the inevitable results of over speculation. David also teaches John the meaning of Charity when he invents a reason for paying off the Widow Collom's mortgage.

That Wescott was forced to direct his attention back in time and away from the city to find the proper teacher may be an indication of a second layer of meaning in *David Harum*. As with the regional fiction of *The Saturday Evening Post* it may be that a fascination with a simpler, uncomplicated past is more an index of unhappiness with the present than a sign of optimism for the future.

The Script
The screenplay for *David Harum* is concerned about the destructive effects of the 1893 depression, but its focus is more on how the slump hurts the business class than on what happens to the little man. The script by Walter Woods contains an executive who is angry about the cause of the decline in profits and blames the "radical administration of Cleveland for his woes." When John asks his father to explain the cause of the panic, the elder Lenox explains: "Cleveland with his socialistic equality program. A policy of soaking the rich. It doesn't matter how—just soaking 'em" (Woods 9). (Throughout *David Harum*, "Cleveland" is a code name for Roosevelt.) In his screenplay, Woods was attempting to emphasize that the middle-class suffered as much as the wage earners.

The Film

A formal dinner party scene early in the film gave Will Rogers an opportunity to present an entirely different perspective of the Great Depression and the New Deal. When asked about the Depression in the film, Will Rogers supplied a monologue of his own. Rogers must have recognized that this was a perfect opportunity for him to speak as a representative of the old values, but also to inspire his viewers with enough courage to help them through the hard times. Sitting at a table in an uncomfortable tuxedo, Rogers makes a bold statement in favor of the economic policies of his friend, President Franklin Roosevelt: "A panic is just like a war. You can talk yourself into one but you have to fight yourself out." When a wealthy businessman condescendingly remarks that "A panic is a condition of the mind," Rogers quickly answers: "A panic is a condition of the pocket book. When money ain't moving and it's all blocked up. A technical name would be a congestion of the purse or a torpid checkbook. And the only thing that'll cure it is a good dose of spending. And the government's got to spend some, too."

At this moment, one of the dinner guests predicts with exasperation: "Cleveland (i.e., Roosevelt) will ruin this country with his newfangled ideas." This line was perfectly suited to elicit a statement of Rogers' own philosophy, the famous extemporizer was obliging. Not a line of the following quote is in the conservative script prepared by Walter Woods: "No. This country is bigger than any man or any party. They couldn't ruin it even if they tried. Bet you this feller's gonna pull us through and we'll live to see the day when there is a hundred million people in this country and we'll have trouble remembering the day and the year that this panic was in." The qualified optimism of this statement is an excellent example of what Rogers projected through the conservative regional vehicles provided him by the Fox studios. The bulk of the film *David Harum* is a story of how the American Everyman will find a resolution for his problems in bad times and not (as in the novel or screenplay) an exploration of the fall and rise of a special American group.

As we have already noted, the *Post* stories from which many Will Rogers films were taken contained a number of degrading Black stereotypes. It is not surprising therefore that similar parts for

Blacks were written into the screenplays for *Judge Priest* (1934), *The County Chairman* (1935), *Steamboat Round the Bend* (1935) and *In Old Kentucky* (1935). Yet while it must be granted that Will Rogers was not a civil rights crusader, a close look at his films indicates that he participated in a silent conspiracy with his fellow black actors to modify the stereotype in such a way as to allow blacks to display their skills as actors.

Anyone who will take the time to actually watch Rogers' films will recognize the close relationship he established with Black actors. An excellent courtroom scene involving Rogers and Stepin Fetchit (Theodore Lincoln Perry) exemplifies the manner in which bigoted screenplays were transformed into something human. Jeff Poindexter is before the Judge for stealing chickens. This is obviously a stereotypical crime, and the script directs that Poindexter conform to the *Post* image –he is told to cringe before the judge and act "very scared." In the film version of this scene, Will Rogers and Stepin Fetchit as two accomplished actors work out an entirely different relationship than that of White Power sternly curbing the spread of Black Criminality. As the prosecutor drawls on in a seemingly endless presentation, Judge Priest is very alert—to the racing results in his newspaper. In the docket is Stepin Fetchit who is neither rolling his eyes nor shivering with fear—he is peacefully asleep. When the prosecutor finally completes his vacuous presentation, Judge Priest lowers his paper and asks the bailiff to awaken the accused. Rogers and Fetchit then conduct an intense conference. As they talk, they become sidetracked on the subject of fishing –a recreation they share in common. Poindexter mentions that he has discovered an excellent stream for perch. To satisfy the forms of justice, Rogers declares Poindexter to be in his "protective custody." As soon as the absurd trial is declared adjourned, they leave side by side to try their luck at the new fishing grounds! It appears that Rogers and Fetchit are in conspiracy together against society's demands—demands which include regulations about actors learning bigoted lines!

The theme of co-operation is evident in a 1935 Will Rogers release, *In Old Kentucky*. Here, the famed tap dancer Bill "Bo Jangles" Robinson joins forces with Will Rogers to subvert the Blue Grass Establishment. Throughout the film, "Bo Jangles" is asked to dance for curious Whites. In the early segments of the film, he is more than willing to click his heels, for he and Rogers are working together to distract the attention of the local sheriff and his rich patrons from the misdeeds of Grandpa Martingale. Later, Bo Jangles performs before the Country Club set in top hat and tails. It is important to note that Robinson's dancing ability is appreciated as a skill. To underscore this message, Rogers pretends to imitate Robinson's act. After shuffling for a few moments, he loses control and falls in slapstick fashion off camera. The implication of the entire scene is that Robinson's act looks easy because he is such an accomplished professional.

Stepin Fetchit has always admitted that he played a stereotypical role, but unlike his critics, he claims that he made a significant contribution toward modifying previous and more degrading images of Blacks on film. He summarizes his role in the following way: "I wiped away the image of rapist from the Negro, and made him a household word, somebody it was all right to be associated with. Look back in my old pictures; you'll never see me showing my teeth, lazy, stupid, eye-rolling—all those things. That was my imitators. I gave hope and opportunity to those that didn't have no skills and education. I was proof that all men are created equal" ("What Ever Happened"). Fetchit and Rogers acted out their scenes so that the underdog could either show a supreme contempt for authority, or profit from the system that proclaimed him an inferior. Many scenes in the Rogers-Fetchit films obviously indicate that a bright stereotyped man can take advantage of the ignorance of his oppressors.

Lincoln T. Perry

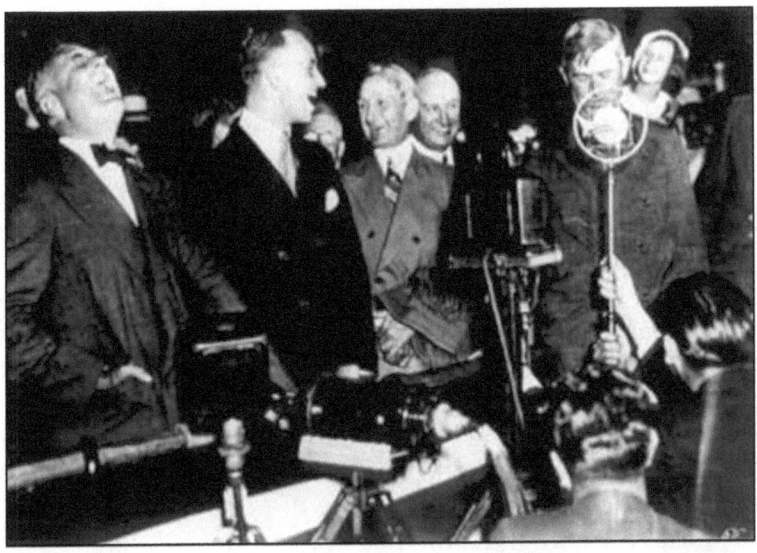

Will Rogers Campaigns with FDR, 1932

In summary, there was no room in the films of Will Rogers for the backward-looking and dehumanizing messages we have found in *The Saturday Evening Post*. Rather than attempting to provide solace for those of "old stock," Rogers used his regional vehicles to convey messages concerning human brotherhood. To do this, he was often forced to deviate from the racist and politically conservative scripts that were prepared for him. In *State Fair* (1933) and *Doctor Bull* (1933), Rogers simply left out such lines. *David Harum (1934)* provided Rogers with an opportunity to utter an articulate defense of the goals of President Roosevelt's New Deal. Because Americans in his time needed these messages about social reconstruction and racial harmony more than they needed the nostalgia of *The Saturday Evening Post's* regional fiction, Will Rogers' films constitute a significant case in which film redeems a literary form.

Discussion of Literature

For a detailed account concerning Will Rogers' popularity as public person in the eras of boom and bust (1920-35), see Rollins. Ben Ames Williams' serialized short novel, *Jubilo* (1917), was the first piece of *Post* fiction adapted to a film for Will Rogers. Rogers portrayed this lazy rustic clown in a number of films for Samuel Goldwyn and Max Sennett. It should be noted that the story "Words and Music," *Saturday Evening Post.* 28 Oct. 1911, provided the working text from which Will Rogers' film *Judge Priest* (1934) was constructed.

The origin of Hough's *The Covered Wagon* provides an insight into Lorimer's work as a "creative" editor. Emerson Hough was feeling despondent about his talent as a writer and decided to bring his problems to his boss. Lorimer convinced Hough that the Oregon Trail theme—which Hough had recently covered in a series of non-fiction articles for the *Post*—could be rendered into immensely popular fiction. As was so often the case, Lorimer proved that he knew both his writers and the *Post* audience.

Some of the "amusing" chatter of the crap games in the Hugh Wiley and Octavus Roy Cohen stories deserves to be quoted since otherwise the contemporary reader will not believe how abusive these stories actually were. In "Red Tape Cutter" (*Saturday Evening Post.* 6 March 1922: 37) there is a representative example of this chatter. Wildcat, the criminal central figure of the story, sings the "Finance Blues" as he rolls the dice: "Shoots a dallah: / Fade me quick / Look for a seven / When the gallopers click / Wham! I see / De specks shut pay! / Fo' on' three / I lets it lay. / Bones get right! / On yo' way. / Read 'Leven / Lets It lay." A representative of Cohen's popular Florian Slappy stories is "Presto Changer," (*Saturday Evening Post* 6 March 1922: 12-20). Slappy and a friend named Percy cruise around town in search of women. During this joy ride they are almost wiped out by hoodlums, for, unknown to them, their car was lost in a poker game by Percy's unlucky business partner. As so often in stories by Cohen, the sloth, irresponsibility, and impecunity of blacks is underscored.

For an account of the popularity of the notorious racial theorists after World War One, see Higham. Kenneth Roberts began his long and lucrative career with the *Post* as Lorimer's bulldog on the Immigrant Issue. Roberts was dispatched to Europe on a number of stories, all of them designed in advance to prove the hopelessness of attempting to integrate inferior racial stock into the American family.

Rogers' audience seemed to believe that Will Rogers from the Oklahoma territories was immune to the fads of the period. He appeared to be a curious innocent looking on in amusement and judgment at the confusion of modern civilization. Here is an example of such a posture. Surveying a society which was becoming increasingly bureaucratic, Rogers tartly observed that "One-third of the people in the United States promote while the other two-thirds provide." The judgment in this remark stems from Rogers' adherence to the older ethic of work and productivity rather than the goals of leisure and consumption so praised by the twentieth century. The insights of an older system of values are here used to evaluate current behavior.

Rogers' more sophisticated silent films deal ironically with regional stereotypes and their exploitation by Hollywood. *Doubling for Romeo* (1921) spoofs the swashbuckling films of Douglas Fairbanks. Sr., but it also shows how vast the distance is between a real cowboy and the Hollywood imitation. *The Ropin' Fool* (1922) ridicules Hollywood's demand for an up-beat ending to every film. Western or otherwise, *Almost a Husband* (1919) was a humorous adaptation of *Post* author Opie Read's story, *Old Ebenezer*. *Jubilo* (1919) was taken from a Ben Ames Williams *Post* serialized story by the same title. *Cupid, the Cowpuncher* (1920) was drawn from a comic ranch story by Eleanor Gates. Garret Smith, a *Post* regular, wrote the basic story from which *Honest Hutch* (1920) was taken. *Boys Will Be Boys* (1921) was taken from a story by Irvin S. Cobb. And, of course, *The Headless Horseman* (1922) is taken from perhaps the first American regional tale.

During the sound era, the *Post* supplied Rogers with a great number of literary vehicles for his films. Homer Croy, scriptwriter for *They Had to See Paris* (1929), *So This Is London* (1930), and *Down to Earth* (1932), learned the writing trade at the *Post*. In addition, Rogers' films such as *David Harum* (1934), *State Fair* (1933), and *Doctor Bull* (1933) were drawn from rural novels which conformed to the nostalgic style of the *Post's* regional stories. For instance, the Museum of Modern Art's film catalog describes *The Covered Wagon* as "one of the first Western spectacles." While conceding that a love story slows the pace, MOMA claims that there are some impressive Indian attacks, and a fording sequence or two which help the film to retain "its magic sweep." As Rogers jokingly relates, his people took the wrong turn in their movement West: " My father was Clem V. Rogers, a part Cherokee Indian, who was a Captain under Stand

Watie during the Civil War . . . *The Covered Wagon* went West and got into pictures. We went South. If he had gone West instead of South, he might have got into *The Covered Wagon* or maybe the *Ten Commandments*" (Day 31).

It should be noted that in his journalistic role Rogers took a part in making the plight of Black Americans visible. For example, in a nationally syndicated daily article he displayed public compassion for Black victims of the massive 1927 Mississippi flood: "Then when you talk about poor people that have been hit by this flood, look at the thousands and thousands of Negroes that never did have much, but now it's washed away. You don't want to forget that water is just as high up on them as it is if they were white. The Lord so constructed everybody that no matter what color you are you require about the same amount of nourishment" (Day 149).

Works Cited

Chamberlain, John. Rev. of *Doctor Bull*. by John Gould Cozzens. *New York Times* 8 Jan. 1933.

Cobb, Irvin S. "Gold Is Where You Find It." *Exit Laughing*. New York: Garden City Pub Co., 1942.

Cozzens, John Gould. *The Last Adam*. New York: Harcourt, Brace and World, 1933.

Croy, Homer. *Our Will Rogers*. New York: Duell, Sloan, and Pearce, 1953.

Day, Donald. *Will Rogers: A Biography*. New York: David McKay, 1962.

Green, Paul. *Doctor Bull*. Screenplay. Will Rogers Memorial Filmscipt Collection. Claremore, OK.

Higham, John. *Strangers in the Land: Patterns of American Nativism 1860-1925*. New Brunswick, NJ: Rutgers UP, 1955.

Josephson, Julian and Phil Stong. *State Fair*. Screenplay. Will Rogers Memorial Filmscript Collection. Claremore, OK.

Kumitz, Stanley and Howard Haycraft. eds. *Twentieth-Century Authors: A Biographical Dictionary of Modern Literature*. New York: H. W. Wilson Co., 1952.

Lorimer, George Horace. "Who Does Your Thinking For You?" *Saturday Evening Post* 4 Nov. 1922: 22.

"Presto Changer." *Saturday Evening Post* 6 Mar. 1922: 12.

"Red Tape Cutter." *Saturday Evening Post* 6 Mar. 1922: 37.

Rollins, Peter C. "Will Rogers' Symbolic Man and Film Image." *Journal of Popular Film* 2.4 (1973): 323-52.

Rosenfield, John, Jr. "Screen Loses Star at Peak of Influence." *Dallas Texas News* 17 Aug. 1935.
Stong, Phil. *State Fair.* New York: The Century Co., 1932.
Tebbel, John. *George Horace Lorimer and the Saturday Evening Post.* New York: Doubleday, 1948.
"What Ever Happened to Stepin Fetchit (Theodore Lincoln Perry)?" *Ebony* Nov. 1971.
Woods, Walter. *David Harum.* Screenplay. Will Rogers Memorial Filmscript Collection. Claremore, OK.
"Words and Music." *Saturday Evening Post.* 28 Oct. 1911.

6
The Making of *Will Rogers' 1920s:* *A Cowboy's Guide to the Times*: An Experiment in Historian Filmmaking

It is obvious that Will Rogers spoke for and to his times. As a syndicated journalist, radio voice, and film image, he utilized all of the new mass media to communicate his special brand of humor and wisdom to millions of Americans. An ardent Will Rogers fan, Franklin Delano Roosevelt, summarized the meaning of the Oklahoman's contribution to national morale: "There was something infectious about his humor. His appeal went straight to the heart of the nation. Above all things, in a time grown too solemn and somber, he brought his countrymen back to a sense of proportion." The collaborators proposed a film project on Rogers to the National Endowment for the Humanities, believing that Americans in the Seventies needed a renewed "sense of proportion" about their national identity. In a world increasingly polarized by divisions of race, sex, and class, we hoped that Americans could profit from re-exposure to a humorist who could honestly say, "I never met a man I didn't like."

From the beginning, a fortunate conjunction of events made the project especially favored. As part of his duties at Oklahoma State U, Peter Rollins had become immersed in a rich collection of materials at the Will Rogers Memorial and Museum, Claremore, Oklahoma. Manuscript editing activities for Oklahoma State University's Will Rogers Publication Project had also demanded close readings of daily and weekly articles, radio broadcasts, and presidential convention reports by the great Oklahoman. At the same time, members of Cadre Films (R. C. Raack, Patrick Griffin,

The Will Rogers Memorial, Claremore, Oklahoma

and William Malloch) were refining their cinematic skills. (For an overview of the Cadre methods and style, see Chapters 6 and 14). The group had been organized in the late Sixties. Cadre's first film *Goodbye Billy America Goes to War, 1917-18*, was screened before the American Historical Association in 1971. Later that year, the film received the audience prize at Ann Arbor Film Festival, and the Chris Award for Excellence. After completing a second film, *The Frozen War: America Intervenes in Russia, 1918-20* (1973), the Cadre team invited Rollins to help prepare a workbook stressing Cadre's introduction of film language to spark a sense of both historical experience and historical inquiry. The workbook project proved to be a rewarding initiation into the research methods and cinematic style of the historian-filmmakers.

Gathering the Fragments for an Historical Film

The actual making of *Will Rogers' 1920s* began at the 1975 meeting of the Popular Culture Association in St. Louis. A screen treatment of the film was discussed by a panel entitled "Will Rogers in Print and Film." Patrick Griffin and R. C. Raack devoted special

Rogers a Radio Presence

attention to methods by which sight and sound could be related to build levels of meaning to the proposed cinematic experience. Lessons from two previous attempts at compilation filmmaking here proved valuable in counteracting the abstractness of the screen treatment prepared by Rollins. Observations from attending popular culturists attuned members of the film team to future audience expectations. The historian-filmmakers left the session convinced that a final script should not be written until after a full exploration of archival sources.

The Will Rogers Memorial and Museum in Claremore, Oklahoma, contained most of the sources, which displayed Rogers on screen or before microphones. Since 1938, the Commission and Staff of the Memorial have diligently accumulated aluminum discs, phonograph records, tapes, as well as the prints of approximately seventy-four fiction films, which Will Rogers made between 1919 and 1935. The fiction films of the silent era were readily available. Will Rogers' voice was a bit more difficult to lasso, for only a few of his radio programs were recorded and only some of those had found their way to the Memorial's fireproof vault. The limitations of available sound had a direct—and unanticipated—impact upon scripting. (This problem with sound was exacerbated by the discovery that no Movietone newsreels would be available for our use due to high costs of archival footage from that commercial resource.)

The authenticity of commentative music has always been of great importance to the Cadre filmmakers. In *Will Rogers' 1920s* there are many moments when music subtly evokes meaning. A representative example comes very early in the film. We were attempting to evoke the abrupt changes experienced as America became an industrial nation. Very important to our film was the notion that Will Rogers was evolving in a parallel fashion: he had been simply a Wild West cowboy; he was trying to become a wry commentator on public affairs. William Malloch found two recordings which evoked these changes while, at the same time, belonging to the relevant period, 1905-08. As in other sections of the film, music, and sound were thus served, at the same time, as historical documents of the 1920s and as vehicles for interpreting history through documentary filmmaking.

During the late spring and early summer of 1975, the collaborators spent two weeks at public and commercial film archives. William T. Murphy, Chief of the Motion Picture Section, U.S. Archives, suggested that the Ford Motor Company collection housed in Washington might be of special help in evoking the theme of industrialization. R. C. Raack's familiarity with the Ford materials accelerated the search through this massive visual record. Footage from the Ford collection was especially attractive because it had not been employed previously by documentarians. It could therefore provide visual information as fresh and pertinent as the aural materials from the Memorial's collection of tapes and records.

The archive search was time consuming. Often, footage was in negative form, or otherwise too delicate to be threaded with the sprockets of standard Steenbeck viewing machines. But painstaking efforts were not without their rewards. Some details about a two-minute segment early in the film are here supplied because they are representative of the problems and opportunities of the entire research and production effort.

Recreating a Critical Career Moment in Image and Sound

First, some thematic information. In 1916, the *Ziegfeld Follies* traveled to Baltimore for a short stay. One evening, President Woodrow Wilson decided to attend the show. The President had recently ordered Brigadier General John Pershing to launch a punitive raid into Mexico in retaliation for Pancho Villa's attack on Columbus, New Mexico. The military foray was a complete failure, revealing much about American attitudes toward Southern neighbors, and inadvertently exposing more about Wilson's attitudes toward war and political power than contemporaries recognized at the time. Will Rogers worried over the topic as he prepared for the *Follies* performance: should a comedian joke about such matters before a President? With some trepidation, Rogers decided to experiment and, to the delight of the Oklahoman and his audience, the President joined in the laughter. From that time forward, Will Rogers felt invited to serve as a humorous gadfly for men and women in public view—to the delight of both his audience and those who were the objects for his gentle satire.

Our cinematic problem was as simple to define as it was difficult to solve: how could the liveliness of this important confrontation

Rogers' Humor Tickled President Wilson

between jester and politician be evoked? A series of archival discoveries led to an answer. First, a few short subjects by Rogers were found in the U.S. Archives. Entitled *The Illiterate Digest*, these films intercut brief scenes of Rogers on stage with titles about topics in the news. They had long been considered lost. But these films proved to be more than an historical "find"; their discovery was extremely important for cinematic purposes. The early Rogers of the Ziegfeld period, dressed in chaps and twirling a rope, could be authentically established with motion picture footage. Cartoons about the confrontation were available in the Will Rogers Memorial and Museum. Camera movements could be executed over them to evoke the tension of this pivotal moment in the humorist's career. As Rogers finished his lines, the camera could pan across the page from humorist to President—to discover a smiling Chief Executive. Other footage in the U.S. Archives helped bring this scene to life. Because Army Signal Corps photographers had accompanied American troops into Mexico, actuality footage of the 1916 event was available. In a two-minute segment, the historian-filmmakers were able to weave all of these disparate cinematic and aural fragments into an effective experience which combined the telling of history with an analysis of the event by way of montage. This transition established Rogers, within the film, as crossing a Red River from regional humorist to national pundit.

The notion of "an effective experience for the viewer" deserves amplification. There was an imaginary audience for *Will Rogers' 1920s* looking over the Cadre group's shoulders in the archives and in the editing room. Let me describe this audience: it consisted of high school and college students weaned on television and film, but needing special motivation to turn to books. As they vehemently debated about the film essay and its impact, they shared a common objective. They were convinced that a sophisticated production could "switch on" the historical imaginations of media-oriented students, and that savvy teachers could then lead these aroused students to amplifying print sources.

Rollins completed a script in late August, 1975, based upon detailed notes taken at the archives. With this script in hand, Griffin began assembling segments of the film as it issued from the laboratories of the National Archives in Washington, the

Will Rogers, Jr., and James Rogers

Will Rogers Memorial in Oklahoma, and a newsreel library in Los Angeles. During these activities, something unexpected happened—the filmmakers encountered people who had gone through the 'Twenties with Will Rogers, and the film was affected in ways which could not have been planned.

The Impact of Interviews on the Production

Will Rogers, Jr., and James Rogers were interviewed at the Will Rogers State Park in Santa Monica—previously the Rogers family home. While they provided colorful details about family life on the suburban ranch, they were also anxious to comment on the meaning of their father's career. Mrs. Evelyn Venable Mohr had performed in an ingénue role in such Rogers films as *David Harum* (1934) and *County Chairman* (1935). At the time of the interview, she was professor of Classical Literature and agreed to be interviewed near her office at UCLA. She provided insights about how Rogers mixed his movie acting with work on daily articles; she also contributed important general statements about Rogers' public role in the 1920s. Back in Oklahoma, Dr. Reba Collins, Curator of the Will Rogers Memorial and Museum, added her findings about Rogers' journalism and American values. Both the content and feeling of the interviews began to permeate the film. The need for an omniscient commentator gradually diminished. A natural rhythm between present and past began to emerge in the editing sessions. We were becoming oral historians by day, editors of related images and sounds at night. The film began to take on a life and growth of its own.

Revising the Production and a Workbook

Late in the spring of 1976, a fine cut of *Will Rogers' 1920s* was brought to a Los Angeles studio for a final mix of sight and sound. The resulting print was tested with high school and college audiences. The narrator's voice proved to be ineffective, and the narration often poorly timed in relation to images and other sound elements, especially the music. Transitions which seemed effective on paper were patently inadequate, leaving students confused about the film's message and direction. One section was potentially explosive: Rogers appeared to be cruelly laughing at the subjects of his humor—Dust Bowl victims—rather than attempting to supply them with a sympathetic ray of comic relief. The sound of the film was remixed with a new voice reading narration written to respond to student criticisms. In one case, where there was a patent error in editing, narration seemed to make sense out of the mistake—proving an old lesson that a narrator can make an audience see what filmmakers want it so see.

Meanwhile, during the winter and spring of 1976, Arthur Peterson of the San Francisco School System developed materials for a workbook to accompany *Will Rogers' 1920s*. The finished spiral binder contained information designed to prepare students for the film, to test their abilities on viewing and recall, and, finally, to send them to other verbal and visual sources. The most significant test of the film and workbook has taken place in classrooms and libraries around the country. The filmmaking efforts were justified because *Will Rogers' 1920s* rewards a number of viewings and the workbook has sparked fruitful research activities. Experimental screenings to teacher and student audiences convinced the Cadre group that this interpretive essay in celluloid has both entertained and informed. It is a historically valid portrait of the man and his times which, unlike commercial productions, has respected the visual and aural sources employed. For these reasons, *Will Rogers' 1920s* has accomplished the basic objectives, which were set for the project by the historian-filmmakers. Unlike most historical essays, it will reach our students—and, perhaps, give them a sense of the vitality of historical studies.

The Historian as Filmmaker Legacy Continues

In 1977, *Will Rogers' 1920s* won a CINE Golden Eagle, the highest award for a non-theatrical documentary. Churchill Films, the distributor for years, sold hundreds of copies in 16mm format to public school and university audiovisual centers. (The profits were plowed back into paying back the National Endowment for the Humanities for its contribution to the budget and remaining profits were used by Oklahoma State University to promote visual literacy.) It is gratifying to know that this film is still being shown on a daily basis at the Will Rogers Memorial and Museum in Claremore. It carries on as a living example of historian filmmaking and offers a standard which has been met by few contemporary productions for network and cable television; alas, the historical methods and cinematic principles of the Cadre group have not "trickled down" to the mass media—which still believes in the "quick and dirty" methods of traditional television and scoffs at the notion that a film should be seen more than once to be fully appreciated.

Benjamin Whorf on the Native American vs. Western Languages/Cultures

7
Benjamin Lee Whorf: Transcendental Linguist

Whorf from the Current Perspective

Benjamin Lee Whorf earned his living as an industrial fire insurance inspector for the Hartford Insurance Company; he began working for Hartford immediately after graduating from the Massachusetts Institute of Technology in 1918, and reached the vice presidential level in the company shortly before his death in 1941. History has not recorded much about his achievements in this role, although television advertisements for Hartford over the years have capitalized on their use of a preventive inspection protocol devised by Whorf.

Benjamin Lee Whorf, to those who are familiar with his name, is an idea rather than a person. The "Whorf hypothesis" or "Sapir-Whorf hypothesis" is usually considered by introductory courses to linguistics and anthropology. In a famous quotation from his article, "Science and Linguistics," Whorf stated this position succinctly:

> We dissect nature along lines laid down by our native languages. The categories and types that we isolate from the world of phenomena we do not find there because they stare every observer in the face; on the contrary, the world is presented in a kaleidoscopic flux of impressions which has to be organized by our minds—and this means largely by the linguistic systems in our minds. We cut nature up, organize

B. L. Whorf: Engineer, Linguist, Visionary

it into concepts, and ascribe significances as we do, largely because we are parties to an agreement to organize it in this way—an agreement that holds throughout our speech community and is codified in the patterns of our language. The agreement is, of course, an implicit and unstated one, BUT ITS TERMS ARE ABSOLUTELY OBLIGATORY; we cannot talk at all except by subscribing to the organization and classification of data which the agreement decrees. (214)

In another article, "Linguistics as an Exact Science," Whorf capsulized this view in a single sentence:

What I have called the 'linguistic relativity principle,' means...that users of markedly different grammars are pointed by their grammars toward different evaluations of externally similar acts of observation, and hence are not equivalent as observers but must arrive at somewhat different views of the world. (221)

Whorf's untimely death at the age of forty-four in 1941 prevented him from fully embellishing his provocative speculations. His reputation and interest in the principle of linguistic relativity grew through the instrumentality of others. For example, in 1941, S. I. Hayakawa printed excerpts from Whorf in the appendix of *Language in Action*, a Book-of-the-Month Club selection.

In 1952, some of Whorf's provocative late essays were published for the first time in a single volume by the Foreign Service Institute of the State Department. With America a world power hastily in search for ways to communicate effectively with vastly different cultures, Whorf's statement of the principle of linguistic relativity seemed to provide just the right kind of warning about cultural differences.

In the same year, a conference of anthropologists, linguists, philosophers, and psychologists was held at the University of Chicago. A preliminary statement proclaimed that the academics had assembled "to define, as clearly as possible, the problems raised by the attempt to interrelate language and other aspects of culture, particularly in reference to the hypothesis suggested in Benjamin

Whorf's Major Articles Republished and Reconsidered

L. Whorf's *Collected Papers on Metalinguistics*" (Hoijer vii). The impression that Whorf was a seminal figure, without whom such a conference would never have been held, is incorrect. Actually, the then recent state department collection provided the academics with an *occasion* rather than an inspiration for meeting. Furthermore, the transcript of the conference reveals how pessimistic linguists were about the famous amateur's methods. The final consensus about Whorf's work was so unrelieved by praise that John Carroll, when he edited a larger collection of Whorf's papers in 1956, found it necessary "to counteract the essentially negative, pessimistic tone which pervaded this conference" (*Language, Thought, and Reality* 29).

Whorf's standing among linguists in the 1960s is perhaps best represented by Max Black's description of the Whorf hypothesis in Black's popular survey, *The Labyrinth of Language*. Black was blatantly sarcastic, rejecting Whorf's perception of facts, Whorf's developed picture of the Hopi world-view, and, finally, the general predilection of anthropologists to exaggerate cultural immersion and cultural differences. Black superciliously observed that Whorf derived a considerable amount of his data from a Hopi resident of New York City, and dismissed as mere "curiosa" what little evidence was presented by Whorf's supporters at the Chicago gathering. With tongue in cheek, he concluded that the Whorf hypothesis would not be a useful tool for social science "until some other 'near genius,' with a talent for exact thought, succeeds in deriving some reasonably precise hypothesis" (95).

It is my contention that Whorf's three famous articles for MIT's *Technology Review*, plus his last major article, "Language, Mind, and Reality," have aroused such consternation among professional linguists because they have not been read correctly. Rather than dispassionate inquiries into the structure of language and its relationship to the human mind, these articles are efforts in persuasion. Their polemical thrust is directed against the West's slavish surrender to the pretensions of science. The gentler arts of persuasion are invoked by Whorf to convince his readers that unpopular religious ways of knowing have been given a new dispensation because of recent discoveries. An examination of the ends which Whorf had for his unpublished novel, *The Ruler of the Universe*, provides a first step toward a more contextualized reading of Whorf's famous later work. It will also explain why his writings should be embraced by historians of American culture.

The Ruler of the Universe (1925): A Novel of Ideas

Benjamin Lee Whorf was twenty-eight when he began in 1924 to compose *The Ruler of the Universe*. He had been raised in the Methodist church, but also trained as a chemist at the Massachusetts Institute of Technology. These two factors, plus his native genius, made him eminently qualified to speak out on the conflict between science and religion which was soon to reach a journalistic climax in the "Monkey Trial" of John T. Scopes.

Whorf's novel was an epic of the fear, disgust, and piety of a large group of educated Americans in the post World War I era. The sad irony of the story of its failure to reach a reading public revolves around Whorf's ambition to supplant William Jennings Bryan as the spokesman for orthodoxy—an ambition which was soundly thwarted and had profound effects upon Whorf's later intellectual development.

The aspiring disputant submitted the manuscript of *The Ruler of the Universe* to no less than six publishers, all of whom refused to undertake it. Whorf's letters to these potential publishers give an excellent picture of the motives which lie behind the novel. The major import of the letters is that the novel was directed toward a large audience which Whorf suspected was ready to rise in wrath against the apparent popularity of science, technology, and secular values. In writing to G. P. Putnam's Sons, the fifth publisher solicited, Whorf was particularly clear that he considered that "The...work contains the elements of what might be the most hotly-contested literary discussion of recent times" (Letter to Putnam Sons).

In his quiver, Whorf had stocked a host of special theories concerning biology, physics, and the history of science. He hoped that the novel would attract irate criticism from pundits like H.L. Mencken, because such attacks would immediately elevate him and his defense of orthodoxy to a national platform:

> To a certain group of critics the ideas of this book will be anathema. The book should be allowed to come at once

before their attention in a challenging manner and receive a full broadside, the more vitriolic the better...I myself will reply to each and several of the critics in no milk-and-water fashion. (Letter to Putnam Sons)

Whorf was extremely bitter about the blind worship of science, technology, and secular values which seemed to preoccupy the popular mind of America in the 1920s. He claimed to discern that a great number of Americans shared his disgust. Furthermore, he believed that simple anti-evolutionism was not only intellectually inadequate to combat the assaults of science and secularism, but that such a simplistic argument, based on an anachronistic reading of the Bible, did a positive disservice to the Christianity it sought to defend.

While Whorf was aware of the efforts of religious modernists like Shailer Matthews, he believed that he could defend a traditional God who would be more acceptable to the orthodox. In writing *The Ruler of the Universe*, Whorf was attempting, on the one hand, to utilize the kind of scientific awareness that was part of the "modernist" position of men like Matthews, while, on the other hand, he hoped to revive belief in the mysterious God Americans were accustomed to finding in their Bibles. He described this ambitious mediating role at the conclusion of one of his letters:

> Heretofore a religious book written from an intellectual and scientific standpoint has been filled with the error of trying to get rid of supernaturalism. No wonder the people do not care much for such books. The prevailing Christianity of the American people has a deep and essential element of supernaturalism. The people love their faith and object, rightly I believe, to the removal of its supernatural, miraculous, and Providential elements, all of which they, and I, hold to be Divinely revealed. You know this. Whoever champions the Bible and the popular religion against intellectual free-thinking is sure of a hearing from them, and though he may call forth diatribes from the intelligentsia, you know that the people cheer him to the echo...
> Here is a book written by a layman of scientific training

(Bachelor of Science, chemistry and chemical engineering, including physics, Mass. Inst. Tech.) that comes out boldly for flat supernaturalism and the supernatural truth of the Bible. To the people it will appear that an intellectual in bringing science, logic, and rationalism to the defense of their faith is challenging the other intellectuals and offering to beat them at their own game. (Letter to Putnam Sons)

None of the publishers was sufficiently convinced about the commercial prospects for *The Ruler of the Universe*. Without ceremony or *éclat*, even before it started, a phase in the intellectual career of Benjamin Lee Whorf came to an end as the fuse on Whorf's bomb beneath the fundamentalist controversy fizzled, smoked, and finally went out.

Whorf's decision to use a fictional mode is important, and was not simply a device adopted to attract the attention of an easily distracted audience. In one of his letters to prospective publishers, the author justified the more literary approach:

> [The novel]...clothes the scientific skeleton in imaginative and allegorical flesh, so that it becomes story-like and readable; and so that two parallel meanings run in it, one addressing itself to the reason, one to the poetic instinct, one grasped by anyone who knows anything of science or philosophy, while the other can be followed by anybody, although its inner meaning is quite the same as that of the science and philosophy. (Letter to George H. Doran Company)

Whorf expanded on his intentions in the introduction to the novel, to the point of celebrating the intuitive powers of the common man—powers which he believed were more than adequate enough to discern the basic truths of the physical and moral systems:

> The work which is to declare the universal and immortal truths that are approaching the fullness of their time for

manifestation cannot do justice to its mission if it is a book for scholars only...it ought to be such as to merit the attention of scholars, but it should especially endeavor to make some appeal to the thoughtful ones who are not scholars in a form out of which they can extract truths according to their own gifts of understanding. For ordinary people who are not scholars often have gifts of understanding which are not to be despised. (*Ruler* i)

The implications of this democratic vision lead to a more interesting reason for Whorf's using a genre which allowed him to express himself in metaphors, dreams, and symbols. Benjamin Lee Whorf, whether by cultural immersion or specific inspiration, was a man who, like Ralph Waldo Emerson (1803-1882), looked at nature and civilization with an instinct to adore and venerate the creator of the continuous pattern underlying them. As a latter-day Transcendentalist, Whorf believed that communion with such a pattern could not be achieved merely by the intellect, but required the activity of the whole personality. To make this communion an experience, Whorf relied upon the total exposure of intellect and emotion which fiction can accomplish. Thus, in a deeper sense, Whorf is not simply attempting to force his arguments upon his readers; he is also trying to guide them to their own authentic realization of them. To an age befuddled by intellectualism, Whorf claims to employ "those qualities that we refer to in the words sublime and beautiful," through his role as a poet of the "ineffable realities":

Eternal realities are ineffable, but the poet and he who perceives the sublime, the beautiful and even the harsh and terrible in Nature, in the universe, and in human character, comes near to them in a fashion which the scientist, the philosopher, the abstract reasoner and systematizer can hardly surpass for excellence of understanding. That is why such a work as this should not be a work solely for scholars, and those well versed in metaphysical and philosophic terminology, when perhaps one of the humblest of my readers has heard secrets in the evening winds such as a scholar might well pawn his library to know. I have tried to clothe

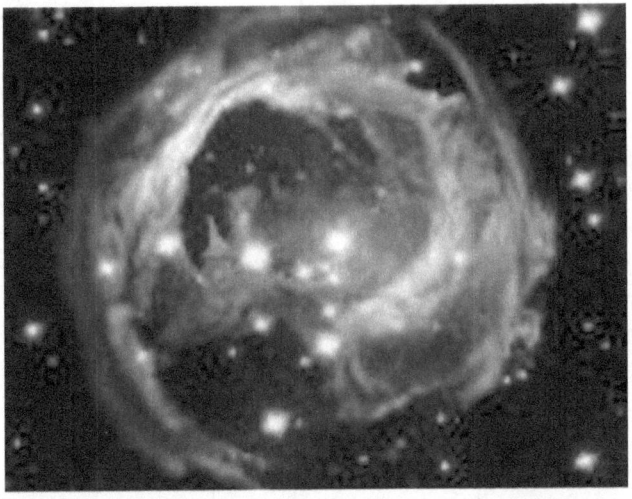

Hubble Images Renew a Sense of Cosmic Beauty

the dry skeleton of dialectic in flesh of concrete imagery, in pictures and symbols from the outer world, to suggest as much as to explain, and especially to arouse that spirit of wonder toward this universe, toward man, and toward Divine Revelation (for these three wonders are all connected) the lack of which constitutes the most conspicuous failure of science in furthering wisdom. (*Ruler* iii)

The complexity of Whorf's metaphysics, more than any other single factor, accounts for why all six publishers rejected *The Ruler of the Universe*. Despite this stumbling block for the popular audience, his vision of the natural continuity between the physical and the moral worlds supports his searing condemnation of the modern era. To respond properly to the latter, we must first explore the former.

A New Approach to "Let there be light!"
To some observers (Whorf among them) the recent speculations of quantum mechanics and relativity physics had called into question accepted Newtonian concepts of space, matter, time, and light. The Michelson-Morley experiment, followed by Einstein's various

theories, had even seemed to prove that there was a mysterious interdependence among the natural phenomena described by these concepts. We know from his unpublished reading lists that Whorf was an avid follower of the speculations of Sir Arthur Eddington and Sir James Jeans, both of whom wrote and spoke at length to popular audiences about philosophical and spiritual implications of the new discoveries. As John Landon, the protagonist of *The Ruler of the Universe* announces, quantum mechanics and relativity physics had broken down the corpuscular matter, the uniformitarian time, and the extensional space of Newton's picture of the natural world. Indeed, the modern mind had been reset to the kind of mysterious relationship with reality which the author of Genesis had felt as he described the creation:

> We live in an unknown universe. How vast, how dark are the abysses around the little circle of knowledge that is lit by the light of the lamp of science...that circle of light was much narrower forty years ago, and the things that could be seen within it then were less amazing, less mystifying, than can be seen within it now. The universe seen within that lesser circle seemed simpler and more tightly regulated, and that more restricted but clear-cut prospect was more comfortable and more calculated to induce the cocksure attitude than are the dim outlines of immense and unknown country that appear beyond the lighted circle today. Mysteries of space, mysteries of time, mysteries of gravitation, mysteries of light, of electricity, of radioactivity, mysteries of the constitution of the elements, mysteries of life, mysteries of heredity, mysteries of species-formation, of psychology, of personality, of the so-called telepathic and psychic and super-psychical. How little do we know of what this universe contains! (*Ruler* 24)

Drawing out what he saw to be the consequences of the "new physics," Whorf claimed that Light, the mysterious constant of Einstein's famous $E=MC^2$, was an underlying force which served as God's building block for all levels of existence. Matter was constructed of light energy compressed into a definite form by the

Sir Arthur Eddington, Scientist and Quaker

deity. Living beings used the elements of the second level, Matter, according to divinely implanted habitual patterns. They also possessed the mysterious capacity to repair themselves, to maintain body integrity, and to reproduce forms like themselves. Man stood as the highest link of Whorf's 20th-century version of "the great chain of being." Unlike other creatures, Man was not restricted to instinctual activities, because he is graced with the possession of mind. Man alone was free to manipulate and control all the other forms in nature: "Mind was not...restricted; it could explore the whole range of possible forms" (*Ruler* 94).

One of the corollaries that he drew from this hierarchical scheme was that *science* should be focused on the investigation of Light, Matter, and Life, while *religion* was more appropriate for the study of Mind. Man, as a form-using animal, is by definition a "scientific" creature; but man has proven that his "natural" proclivity has been to use these God-given forms for evil purposes—hence man is a scientific animal who has shown his immersion in sin. In addition, because Whorf considered the human race to be a single "form," he proved (to his own satisfaction) that the descendants of the first sinners have passed on their fallen condition, and thus that the traditional conception of original sin was still valid. The ugliness and putrefaction of man's sinfulness is manifested to John Landon by a fungus growth which he observes on one of his walks. It is a representative instance of Whorf's impulse to derive spiritual meaning from natural structures:

> The voluntary fall of that free creature and its consequences...the involvement in a struggle for sin similar to their struggle for existence; the practical loss of freedom in the shacklement of that ever-ramifying destructive growth that sprang from the roots of original sin and pervaded the human race as the mycelia of the fungi pervaded the rotting wood of the old factory. For John knew that the puffballs and warty shapes and long danglers that extruded from the wood were not the real fungi but only the fructifications of the real fungi, the mycelia so-called—ever growing networks of corps eating living tissue that devoured and rioted among the dead cells of that wood which was the inner substance of the building. So was it with the edifice of humanity! (Ruler 160)

The Father, Son, and Holy Ghost of the Trinity all cooperate to elevate man. Indeed, the Trinity was a powerful force for illumination:

> Modern people have thought it odd that in other days men of giant intellects should have been content to spend them on pursuing with logic and dialectic the metaphysical ramifications of this system, to engage those intellects in a task that could yield no practical return nor discover any basic principle, but could only explore the inexhaustible *rapport* of the system and delight in the unlimited harmonious expansibility of its Divine laws. But if this be odd, a much odder phenomenon is observable at the present day. It is the spectacle of men with great intellects using them to develop a *rapport* of music, than which anything more tenuous or abstruse could hardly be imagined, not only void of practical application, or discovery of new principles, but casting no light on life, on Man or on the Deity, sharpening no logical faculties, evoking no majesties of reason or intensities of faith; mental, yet framed out of vague sensation rather than cognition...

But the system and rapport of principles and consequences flowing from the appearance of Christ on earth is immeasurably grander than the grandest symphony ever conceived by genius. How much more amazing, elevating, and awesome is its harmony than any music! Though at once far more complex, divaricated, structural, and far more simple, organic, and unified than any symphony, it composes itself mentally not of feeling, but of knowing, not of diffuse sensibilities and appetencies, but of the most luminous concepts and of the emotions most potent to regenerate the world—a *rapport* which extends its consequences from the mental into the physical, wherein it begins to develop man's yet underdeveloped might. (*Ruler* 227-28)

The coming of God's Kingdom will permit the unimpeded manifestation of the positive energy latent in the universe. Whorf's picture of this transformation was intensely mystical:

When this world of space and time, vast, yet finite in susceptibility of being known by Mind, shall be all known by created human Mind, then a great stage or arrival-place in the workings of God will be reached. It will be the fullness of the Kingdom of Heaven, whether on earth or in heaven will then be indistinguishable, immaterial. Earth will be added to Heaven as conquered territory; Heaven will expand to take in Earth; the two shall be one Kingdom. Then the Creation of this realm of space and time, and of its interpreting human soul, will have reached its full development, will have perfected its maturity, and will stand at the beginning of the great end for which it was made. Then will be seen the full meaning of Completion, of Consummation, and of Perfection. (*Ruler* 234)

After the thousand year reign of Christ, man's limited three-dimensional world will merge into the undifferentiated oneness of God. The Bible describes this step cryptically in the declaration, "Before Abraham was, I AM"; Whorf attempts to state this prophecy in contemporary scientific terms:

> The return of the full glory of Creation's bright dawn, the return of Space and Time to their common reality, the consummation of all forces, the manifestation of all latencies, the revelation of all pre-existences, the final assimilation of the subjective and the objective. (*Ruler* 247)

By "natural," then, Whorf meant the tendency of all forms along his hierarchical chain to lapse into formlessness. (He here was applying the second law of thermodynamics to moral phenomena.) By "supernatural" Whorf meant any forced *formfulness* which resisted this latent "natural" tendency of forms to lapse unsubstantial. The reader will recognize immediately that the usefulness of this dichotomy comes in its power to unite Whorf's physics and his metaphysics: in both the physical and moral realms, whoever or whatever works to further the creative manipulation of the "forms" is thereby furthering the movement of the world toward the Kingdom of God; whoever or whatever acts in a contrary manner, wrenching forms from their rightful course, is delaying that development, and thereby is tempting the Creator to abandon his creation. For it is only the continuous impress of the "supernatural" which maintains each link in the chain and sustains the chain as a whole. According to Whorf, the grim condition in which modern man found himself was due to this very misuse (because of original sin) of nature's inherently good forms. The powers of human destructiveness had actually been enormously multiplied because scientific man had devised ways to make his "natural" powers work in concert with nature's "natural" proclivities toward disintegration (*Ruler* 107-120).

Whorf assembled his physics and his metaphysics to refute certain reigning scientific generalizations which he considered to be antipathetic to belief. Among these threats to traditional piety were geology's assumption of uniform time, and Darwin's theory of evolution.

Genesis vs. Geology
The protagonist of *The Ruler of the Universe* visits an Episcopal minister in his town, hoping to reconcile his need for faith with the apparently unscientific absurdities of the account of creation given in

Genesis. John just happens to be a member of "The International Science Club," an association to which curious laymen are encouraged to write for expert advice about scientific topics. John hits upon the happy idea of writing to a physicist named Doctor Murchison, "an expert on time," rather than a geologist, to settle the sticky question of the nature of time and the age of the rocks. Dr. Murchison, we are told, is the author of a number of volumes whose titles resemble Sir Arthur Eddington's publications in the 1920s. Some of the works of this fictional "expert on time" include *Time, Velocity and Acceleration; Translation in Time; Properties of Motions, Time;* and *Velocity of Light*.

Dr. Murchison's response letter effectively negates the uniformitarian conception of time. Geologists, according to Dr. Murchison,

> may know all about the physical conformation of rocks and fossils as they are found by geology to be disposed in the three dimensions of space, but the time-dimension which they supply from their imagination is from the physical standpoint erroneously conceived. I may say that they conceive Time as a flowing sheet or ribbon, something like a seismograph ribbon or ticker tape, which is driven at a perfectly constant speed by a mechanism the regularity of which they are absolutely certain. (*Ruler* 55)

The uniformitarian hypothesis was proposed in the eighteenth century by James Hutton. It was an operating assumption for Darwin's theory of evolution. Dr. Murchison explains that this is most definitely *not* the only kind of time currently accepted by the scientific community. It is "between you and me and the gatepost, a geologically convenient symbol and nothing more" (*Ruler* 56). Bringing his arguments to bear on the supposed conflict between Genesis and Geology, Murchison concludes that, in using the word "day" as the unit of time, the author of Genesis may well have been linking the concept of time to that mysterious entity, light, and not to the revolution of the planet earth:

> A day is not only a unit of time, but a description in terms of light. Light is not bound up in Motion as Time is. It would be nearer the truth to say that Motion and Time are bound

up in the mystery of light. Light appears to be a very primal thing, lying back of matter and electricity...Hence my final answer is that an absolute description of Creation or earth-formation could speak of it as a thing of Days in a far more accurate sense than it could speak of it in terms of any other time-unit. (*Ruler* 57)

The Mystery of Evolution

The investigations of post-Darwinian biologists, especially Hugo DeVries, convinced Whorf that mutations were a form of divine "mystery." As we have already mentioned, the ability of living things to retain their body integrity and to reproduce was in itself evidence of the presence of a "supernatural" force at work. Whorf goes one step further in the following description of an Agave plant. The reader is forced to feel the presence of a divine symphonic conductor who is carefully regulating the tempo of his creation:

> Plant the seed of an Agave and there comes up a rosette of fleshy blue-green spine-toothed leaves. The plant grows through the years till the rosette of enormous leaves would more than cover this table. Many years pass, and then the plant seems to hear a mysterious mandate, '*Let that form that is hidden in you and was hidden in your ancestors be brought forth.*' From the center of the plant there arises a stem like a pole which proceeds to shoot up at a prodigious rate. In a month or so it towers forty feet high and extending many horizontal branches assuming the shape of a pine tree. Meanwhile the big fleshy leaves below shrivel and collapse, for their substance is being used to clothe and manifest the new form. Then the branches become covered, not with leaves, but with golden bells, each a perfect flower. Striking as this instance is because of the great size of the plant, it is really no different from what happens when a violet flowers, or for that matter when any plant flowers, be it rose, clover or orchid. (*Ruler* 73)

After admiring the sublime complexity of this hereditary information, Allen Chase, the Episcopal minister to whom John Landon has turned, sweeps aside Darwin's gradualism. Chase's argument from design rests on his own theory that mutations are not products of the chance crossing of genes; instead, they are the manifestations of hereditary data which lies dormant until it is summoned by the "mysterious mandate" of the ruler of the universe.

At the end of the discussion, he proves to his own satisfaction that neither the uniformitarian theory of Hutton, nor Darwin's gradualist evolution is valid in the light of contemporary breakthroughs. Both time and genetic development have become mysterious, again, to the modern who perceives them through the light of recent theory—as mysterious as they were to the author of Genesis and his audience, and perhaps as accurately described by the ancient prophet's poetry as by any scientific treatise.

Attack on the "Lost Generation"

After establishing an intellectually formidable base, Whorf launched out on what is probably the most interesting foray of *The Ruler of the Universe*. He contends that happiness about the success of science and secularism is possible only for those who are blind to the moral ugliness of the modern condition. Because the modern mind is so blind to the problem of evil, Whorf proclaims that the defense of original sin is "the only warfare that... [means] anything...the only issue worth taking sides on..." (*Ruler* 142). John Landon's description of his desire to save the world of believers from this pseudo-sophistication reveals Whorf's intentions at the age of twenty-eight in writing *The Ruler of the Universe*: "He wanted to tell them to rise in revolt against their false priesthood, to assert themselves, and discover triumphantly that nothing at all worth being afraid of hindered them from going the very opposite way if they chose" (*Ruler* 185).

As Whorf assays the current alternatives to Christian morality, they either point the individual toward a hedonism and mindless consumerism, or they encourage an uncritical acceptance of inhumane efficiency programs and covertly oppressive bureaucratic organizations. Viewing these contemporary choices, Whorf predicts catastrophe for the modern world. The one way out is for his audience to assert its democratic weight against the patently evil "pseudo-intellectuals," "experts," and all others who conceal perennial the age old will-to-power behind the smiling mask of modernity.

But fallen man cannot help himself up by his bootstraps.

The Leopold and Loeb Case: Original Sin in the Jazz Age

Education, sophistication, even the social sciences will only provide more intricate channels for man's expression of his fallen nature. The much-publicized, premeditated murder of 14-year-old Bobby Franks in 1924 by Nathan Leopold and Richard Loeb—two young men with all the benefits of urban and industrial life— had proven the ineffectiveness of the liberal panacea, education. The willingness of Germany's social scientists to embrace racial theories during World War I proved the inefficacy of even the most sophisticated forms of organized knowledge. Whorf's ironic (and bold) conclusion was that the doctrine of original sin, rather than belonging to the never-never land of religious superstition, was actually a viable intellectual generalization proven by the daily headlines:

> Considered as a doctrine of religion, this doctrine of the Fall of Man was probably the least mystical and the most matter-of-fact truth in religion. Although to call any aspect of religion scientific was not really to praise it but merely to confuse it with a quite different sphere of intellect, yet it could quite legitimately be said, if any wished to say it, that the doctrine of the Fall of Man was scientific. It

could be derived directly, like gravitation, from the closest familiarities of experience, and quite agreed with scientific method in its manner of compression of a world of facts into a compact generalization. (*Ruler* 130)

The Military-Industrial Complex
Whorf's keenest criticisms were directed at the developing symbiotic relationship between science and war. War research and war strategy were the most representative activities of modern, liberal man: once man has new instruments to control natural forms and forces at his disposal, he inevitably turns these tools against his fellow man. In the following picture of a munitions plant, Whorf pulls out all the stops of both his metaphysics *and* his moral outrage. Note the passion for scientific detail as well as the admiration for the orderly structure of the material world. There is also in this description a sublime picture of man's capacity to draw benefit from the reservoir of nature. In this case, the pall of original sin has led man to pervert his power. But this element of original sin, rather than darkening the picture completely, actually illuminates it with a lurid, demonic light:

> Consider the gigantic manufacturing plant that was reared in the land of Tennessee in the year 1918; its great quarries and coke ovens and lime kilns, its miles of railroad track, its fleets of freight cars and tank cars, its enormous buildings, its batteries of mighty turbines and dynamos, its banks of rock crushers, its rows of electrical furnaces wherein dazzling blue and violet and orange fires continually transformed lime and carbon into a queer substance unknown in nature, its mazes of moving machinery and crisscross pipes wherein air was condensed to a simmering liquid or scalding coldness, its ranks of huge stills and retorts and pulverizing mills, and all these miles of paraphernalia and prodigies of heat and cold to accomplish that which a little bacterium cell, microscopic and unorganized, could do quietly and invisibly at ordinary temperature—the bringing of nitrogen from the air into chemical combustion—consider this and reflect that the purpose of all this vast-scaled chemistry

was to make uncounted ton after ton of explosives with which to blast human beings into bits of decaying slime. Was it not extraordinary? Was it not especially remarkable and evidential of original sin that such giant co-ordination and harmony of chemical, electrical, physical, mechanical, economic sciences should be possible only for a destructive purpose, and that such delving among mysteries and miracles of intensest heat and cold and most marvelous fusion and crystallization should require the stimulus of animosity and await the day of hate and perversion for its full fashioning?

'Hast thou entered into the treasures of the snow? Or hast thou seen the treasures of the hail? Which I have reserved against the time of trouble, against the day of battle and war ?' Not until the day of Science had Man appeared to reply to that Divine and now ominous-seeming question. Science was beginning to reply with the roar of munitions mills wherein was heard the beat of great refrigerating engines cooling nitrates and diazoting vats and long storehouses of explosives, with the continuous gurgle of icy liquid chlorine and phosgene down frosty pipes to the nozzles where the flat-cars of empty gas-shells came increasingly to be filled, and with battalions of researchers doing their bit as they ransacked the treasures of God-created substance for new agencies of suffering that could be made to do worse things to living flesh than ever had been done to it before. (*Ruler* 155)

War and the World

In this novel of 1924, John Landon has a prophetic nightmare in which he sees the world destroyed by the kind of nuclear catastrophe which has haunted mankind since August, 1945. Because the peoples and the leaders of the world have lost the insights of Christianity, they are pulled along by the destructive drift of events. An arms race eventually explodes into a final war of all against all. In the wars of the future, Whorf explains, the combat soldiers will become as antiquated as cross bows. Instead, the credit for our final destruction will be shared between the scientists who create, and the pilots who deliver, the new weapons—weapons targeted not at the opponent's armies, but at population centers:

> John, who had a little knowledge of chemistry, perceived that the advance in science of that day...was especially notable in chemistry, where again it was most conspicuous in the skilled use of catalytic agents. With this superior chemical skill and the lean toward chemical warfare that even in 1917 was apparent, it was not surprising that the outset of the war brought forth a host of poison gases, flesh-corroding liquids, and similar agents of affliction and misery...the powerful toxins which sprang into attention in 1917 and 1918, such as mustard gas and lewisite, were thrown into the shade by these new inventions. The terrible liquid known as cacodyl could now be stabilized by catalytic agents to the extent of overcoming the danger of explosion, and was used in large bombs or spread by shells similar to shrapnel or played in streams from nozzles on small fast flying machines. Spontaneously inflammable, it flared up wherever it fell, causing horrible burns that produced eventual death from the intense arsenical poison they carried into the system; it also filled the air with deadly fumes...When a city was being bombed from the air with phosphorous, thermite, and high explosives, the poor fleeing people choking the roads to the country would be pursued by low flying aviators spraying cacodyl until the ground was heaped with the smouldering cadavers. (*Ruler* 192)

Because he is a Christian believer, John Landon can see through the machinations of politics and the sublimations of science to the psychological essence of hatred and self-destructiveness which lie below them:

> John saw flying in the clouds of heaven an aircraft that had just dropped many bombs of bend gas and other torture gases on a city, a city that wailed like a person in the throes of its doom. He saw something go wrong with the aircraft high in the ethereal dome; he saw it cant over and go sliding

down through space, and then saw two other aircraft come wheeling into view and go rushing for the falling one, spurting fire and hurling detonations at it. A change seemed to come over things in the vision, and the falling aircraft became a falling man, none other than he who had doomed the city. Down he falls into a deep pool of liquid among mighty rocks; up he comes to the surface again and begins to swim for the nearest of the rocks. There arise from the depths of the pool two huge heads and make for him. They are partly like globular fish of the skate type, partly like half-human heads expressive of malice and pleasure. The swimmer sees them, turns white as paper, tries desperately to reach the rocks, but the heads, grinning and licking their chops, make a rush for him; the first one bites him right in two, the other seizes a half of him and thrashes it about; the water turns dark red; the heads disport themselves most furiously, they rip the body to pieces, they scatter the entrails, they shred the flesh from the bones and crack the bones and spew them up into the air—and then the monsters become two aircraft gliding away while the scattered wreckage of a third goes downward through space. (*Ruler* 200)

John's dream reveals to him how the escalation of weaponry leads to the ultimate destruction of mankind. All nations devote their resources toward the development of a doomsday weapon. Following a familiar logic, it is reasoned that such a super weapon will be so horrible that war will cease to be an extension of politics. John Landon's perception of the processes used to develop these weapons (which in the first stages are chemical) emphasizes both Whorf's sense of the potential natural harmony in the universe as well as the distance which fallen man has traveled from it:

Researches in toxicity...were prosecuted with unparalleled vigor and at enormous expense. Never for the sake of obtaining dyes or medicines were the effects of the organic radicals in combination so carefully studied or such a great number of new and very complex compounds synthesized as in this search for poisons and the production of pain. The mercaptans, the thio-ethers, the nitriles, the phosphines and arsines and metal-alkyls, were linked together and built up into heavy molecules like no molecules ever found in God-created Nature, that seemed almost to feel an enmity for living tissue and to bite into the nerve cells like infinitesimal bulldogs. All the chemical properties that God had combined with such infinite skill into the wonderful myriad intertwining rapport of Nature, wherein by a miracle of harmonious ordination none became noxious save for some protective purpose, seemed to have been taken apart and then jumbled together into wild, grotesque, and monstrous man- made forms to constitute these wines of horror. (*Ruler* 197)

The promised super weapons emerge from an arms race. The promised super weapons are not more effective forms of older explosive devices, but are designed to facilitate the "natural" forces toward disintegration. Near the end, scientists succeed in tapping the "natural" forces of the atom itself. From modern man's point of view, the nuclear device appears to be precisely that weapon which will make future wars unthinkable. In fact, the development of an atomic weapon at first appears to be nothing other than a final triumph for science. Whorf's perspective yields him an entirely different conclusion. While fallen man may think himself to be at the height of his petty glory, what is *really* happening is that God is allowing his coercive, form-sustaining, "supernatural" force to loosen. As John intuits this situation in his dream, a discouraged God is withdrawing from his creatures and their three-dimensional world:

It seemed to John that God was withdrawing Himself and His divine light from the world, withdrawing Himself to far universes unrelated to this universe, and leaving the world in the fading twilight of that light's departure to the pleasure of a grim and unholy monster until world and monster alike should be dissolved in the ever-encroaching, compressing, grinding, all-disintegrating Darkness. (*Ruler* 200)

Thus, it is not the supreme glory of science which should be heralded as the first successful fission process started in a weapons laboratory somewhere in the Rockies, nor is this discovery a harbinger of the promised era of peace. As John's dream unfolds, we witness the beginning of a runaway nuclear chain reaction. The scientist who initiates the chain reaction panics and throws the glowing radioactive material down a well outside the weapons laboratory, unintentionally initiating what would later be called the "China syndrome":

> Before long steam was rising from the mouth of the well. The investigator gathered his assistants and they all ran down the mountain. The next day steam was rising all over the mountain from a thousand fumaroles, and all the springs on the mountain were boiling hot springs. The men then knew despair: they realized that they were seeing the sky for the last time, and that it would not avail them to fly to the uttermost parts of the sea...The next day there was a terrific earthquake, the mountainside caved into a white-hot inferno, and a great torrent of incandescent lava, seething, boiling, and effervescing with helium gas, poured down the valley. And that lava never cooled, but on the contrary got constantly hotter and hotter! As it got hotter it melted down into the earth and made canyons that grew rapidly deeper, with fiercely red-glowing sides that grew more and more brightly. (*Ruler* 204)

As the forms in our three-dimensional world are finally burst asunder in this chain-reaction, God's creation returns to the original building block of the universe, light. The apocalypse recapitulates, in reverse order, the stages by which God created the world out of formlessness:

> That degeneration of matter which he had seen begun was cumulative, like water rushing through a dike or a snowball rolling down a snowy mountain...The earth would spout lava from 10,000 volcanoes; the earth's green coat of vegetation would char, smoke, and blaze; the earth would become

red hot, orange hot, golden hot, white hot, blue hot; liquefy, gasifying, expanding with the rush of broth boiling over; now an enlarging sun bigger and hotter than the old sun, now enveloping that sun and its planets. The nebula explodes; all its energy becomes rectilinear; it flashes into pure light. When that mighty blast of energy reaches the nearest stars they likewise expand and explode; the disturbance is propagated from star to star to the farthest outposts of the universe, and bodiless light is all that remains. (*Ruler* 205)

The Ruler of the Universe, Benjamin Lee Whorf's defense of religion, and his attack on the complaisance of modern man closes with a vision of the beautiful universe which God created—but man perverted—devolving to its preformed state of chaos.

Implications for Whorf's Famous Final Articles

The elements for Whorf's theory of linguistic relativity are present in the works of the linguists who introduced him to the study of language. Antoine Fabre d'Olivet (1767-1825) and F. Max Müller (1823-1900) invited Whorf to see language as a medium which influenced perception. Franz Boas, through his written works, and Edward Sapir as a classroom teacher, helped to cultivate Whorf's keen interest in the languages of the American Indians.

Boas and Sapir provided Whorf with a special approach to the American languages. The uniqueness of the structure of the American languages seemed to set them and their cultures outside of the evolutionary metaphor which was popular among anthropologists before Boas. Because they emphasized the uniqueness and the distinct complexity of the American languages, Boas and Sapir laid the groundwork for an entirely different interpretation of the development of human civilizations. In the place of the self-congratulatory image of a mountain at the top of which rested Western culture—a view popularized by the British anthropologist E. B. Tylor—the new perspective of "the American school" of anthropology postulated that all cultures were complex, but that special forces of history and certain accidents of location had allowed a few to develop a thinking class, whose speculations were wrongly identified with "culture." According to the scheme of the American School of Boas and Sapir, *all* cultures were potentially capable of sophisticated intellectual and technological innovation and development, given the proper material and historical conditions (see more on Sapir in Chapter 8).

There is a third element in this preparation of Whorf's mind for the formation of his linguistic relativity principle. As he had so passionately asserted in *The Ruler of the Universe,* the discoveries and theories surrounding relativity physics and quantum mechanics had not only precipitated a "crisis in modern physics." These breakthroughs had also betokened the beginning of a creative era for the spirit. The mind yearning to believe could once more, after a long exile during the reign of Newton, return to a religious sense of relatedness to the mysterious and beautiful physical and psychical systems surrounding it.

Whorf's assumption about the revolutionary nature of the new physics becomes the linchpin of his theory of linguistic relativity. If there is a structured psycho-physical continuum; if different

New Perspectives from Ancient Cultures/Languages

languages have different structured ways of attempting to link-up with the structure of the physical world; and, if the new physics has revealed that Western science has been entirely misled about such basic concepts as "time," "space," and "matter," then profound reconsiderations should to follow for the West.

We need to re-examine the structure of our Indo-European languages, initially because of their poverty of terms for dealing with the revelations of the new physics, but also in a historical way. It is possible that misleading patterns have been built into these languages. All such *impedimenta* must be surgically removed. Finally, languages exotic to the Indo-European experience may actually render a more accurate picture of reality as the new physics has unveiled it than does our own language. Whorf's conclusion was that such languages do in fact exist, and that the Hopi Indians speak one of them.

The Hopi *Weltanschauung* described in Whorf's famous articles is no less than his picture of an ideal religious consciousness in accord with the universe with an enviably spiritual intensity. Seen in this light, Whorf's final articles must be interpreted as polemical documents in which the limitations of the Western mind, its structured matrix, language, and its product, science, are unfavorably contrasted with the spiritually superior and (potentially) scientifically more accurate mind, language, and world-view of the Hopi culture. In these contrastive studies, Whorf hammers the Western perspective. His ultimate conclusion is that the West must reorganize its method of relating to the world by drawing on the spiritual insights of the so-called "primitive" peoples of the world. Thus, in his last articles, Whorf restated the theme of his novel, *The Ruler of the Universe*, although through a different intellectual matrix. In the novel, he based his arguments on the prestige of the new physics, whereas in the last articles he draws upon a more refined epistemology. Despite the differences in the means used, the end toward which both the novel and the last articles were directed remained the same: to prove that the most sophisticated science could be reconciled with the deepest yearnings of the religious affections.

Notes on a New Resource

During the late 1960s, Mrs. Celia Peckham Whorf allowed me to Xerox hundreds of unpublished pages of material she had held back from previous researchers. These documents were initially published as an appendix to my 1972 Harvard University dissertation on Whorf and much later collected on a CD-ROM for researchers and libraries. *The Benjamin Lee Whorf Legacy CD-ROM* (2008) contains the following unpublished items *by Whorf*: the novel discussed in this chapter, *The Ruler of the Universe*; an archive of seven documents concerning the history of linguistics, some handwritten; fourteen documents concerning the conflict of science and religion; a list of books read by Whorf, 1924-1928. The CD-ROM also contains the following *items by Peter Rollins*: the full text of my 1972 Harvard dissertation; a book-length intellectual biography of Whorf written in 1980; three journal articles about Whorf. For details, see www.petercrollins.com (Also, see Ray Browne's review of the CD-ROM).

Works Cited

Black, Max. *The Labyrinth of Language*. New York: Frederick A. Praeger, 1968.

Boas, Franz. *The Mind of Primitive Man*. Rev. ed. New York: Macmillan, 1938.

Browne, Ray B. Rev. of *The Benjamin Lee Whorf Legacy*. Ed. Peter C. Rollins. *Journal of American Culture* 32.2 (2009): 182-183.

Carroll, John. "Introduction." *Language, Thought, and Reality: Selected Writings of Benjamin Lee Whorf*. 5th ed. Cambridge, MA: MIT Press, 1970. 1-34.

Hoijer, Harry, ed. "Introduction." *Language in Culture: Conference on the Interrelations of Language and Other Aspects of Culture*. U of Chicago P, 1954.

Rollins, Peter C., ed. *The Benjamin Lee Whorf Legacy CD-ROM*. Cleveland, OK: Ridgemont Media Productions, 2008.

Sapir, Edward. *Language*. New York: Harcourt, Brace, 1920.

Schultz, Emily Ann. *Dialogue at the Margins: Whorf, Bakhtin, and Linguistic Relativity*. U of Wisconsin P, 1990.

Whorf, Benjamin Lee. *Collected Papers on Metalinguistics*. Foreign Service Institute. Dept. of State, Washington, D.C.: GPO, 1952.

—. *Language, Thought, and Reality: Selected Writings of Benjamin Lee Whorf.* Ed. John Carroll. 5th ed. Cambridge, MA: MIT Press, 1970.
—. Letter to George H. Doran Company. November 12, 1925. In Rollins.
—. Letter to Putnam's Sons. September 8, 1925. In Rollins.
—. "Linguistics as an Exact Science." *Language, Thought, and Reality.* 220-232.
—. "Science and Linguistics." *Language, Thought, and Reality.* 207-219.
—. *The Ruler of the Universe.* In Rollins.

8
The Sapir-Whorf Relationship Reconsidered

The "Sapir-Whorf Hypothesis" has been discussed a good number of times over the last forty years, and it is not without a certain sense of guilt that I throw another log on the fire. My only excuse for adding to a substantial body of literature is that access to unpublished manuscript materials by Whorf has yielded a perspective of his views on language which is significantly different from that which can be found in currently published accounts. My exposure to these unpublished Whorf manuscripts has also encouraged me to take a fresh look at pertinent articles by Whorf's friend and mentor, Edward Sapir. The result has been a perspective which emphasizes the differences between these two students of language—differences of temperament, of aspiration, of theoretical formulation—which are clouded over when we call the hypothesis of linguistic relativity the "Sapir-Whorf Hypothesis."

While taking note of the many "promises" which Edward Sapir seems to tender at buoyant moments, this chapter will try to show that Whorf invested Sapir's ideas with a pregnancy of possibility not intended for them by their author. The final portion of the essay will seek to show that Sapir himself departed from his early sanguine attitude, turning to more modest objectives for linguistics as a social science.

Acoma Pueblo, New Mexico

The Sapir-Whorf Relationship Reconsidered 191

Franz Boas and the American School of Anthropology

It is impossible to discuss the influence of Whorf's teacher, Edward Sapir, upon Whorf's linguistic studies without at least mentioning the significant work of Franz Boas, founder of what has been called the "American School" of anthropology. It is no less demanded by the fact that Boas was a mentor to Sapir, whom Boas "discovered" as a promising young undergraduate at Columbia. The essence of Boas' teaching (and the distinguishing feature of the American School's approach to the study of primitive peoples) was that all Western theories concerning non-Western societies had been premised on the unwarranted assumption that material complexity was an infallible index of cultural complexity. To this Boas objected: if we properly view the development of world civilization on an extended time scale, the advantage currently held by the West will be seen to be the product of historical circumstances, and not the superiority of the culture itself (19-34).

The respect which Boas (and later, Sapir) showed for primitive cultures had profound effects on Whorf's orientation. For if the notion of a hierarchy of cultures is abolished, it is possible that other cultures not only see the same objective reality from a slightly different angle. It might be that non-Western cultures—because of the structure of their languages—actually see a different world. Such was the conclusion which Whorf recorded in an unpublished

Boas: Father of the American School

"Outline of the Historical Development of Linguistic Theory," where he *incorrectly* claimed that Boas was responsible for the "recognition that American [i.e., American Indian] and other exotic languages exemplify different kinds of thinking." Whorf was here creatively misreading Boas—as he would Sapir. Boas believed that language structure and intellectual content, rather than being inextricably intertwined, actually moved further apart from one another over the passage of time. In fact, Boas saw the "deep structure" of language to be useful to the student of culture precisely because it was so well insulated from cultural change. It could serve the anthropologist not as a key to unlock the *Weltanschauung* of a culture (as Whorf would later claim), but as a form of carbon-14 to help the anthropologist to measure the vicissitudes of cultural change over long periods (Sapir, "Time Perspectives" 389). Both Boas and Sapir held that while languages may lack certain ideas, they are creative systems which can be manipulated by native speakers to generate such concepts: "all languages are set to do all the symbolic and expressive work that language is good for, either actually or potentially" (Sapir, "The Grammarian" 155). If Kant's *Critique of Pure Reason* would be difficult to translate into primitive languages, the fault did not lie with the languages as systems: "If these languages have not the requisite Kantian vocabulary, it is not the languages that are to blame, but the Eskimo and the Hottentots themselves. The languages as such are quite hospitable to the addition of a philosophic load to their stock-in-trade" (154). In sum, every language may have its unique manner of manipulating its phonetic sound symbols, but all have the potential to describe every facet of the world known by man.

Edward Sapir

Any scholar might envy Edward Sapir's intellectual and aesthetic versatility. His bibliography lists over 100 poems, some of which appeared in *The Nation* and *Poetry*. Harriet Monroe often called upon Sapir to review contemporary verse for *Poetry*. Yet Sapir the linguist and anthropologist also found time to write about music and the arts for *The Dial* and the *Music Quarterly*. Sapir did more than merely write about art—he was an accomplished classical pianist. Knowing this, it is not surprising to hear Sapir described as "an intoxicating man." As a teacher, his exciting and versatile

Sapir: Disciple of Boas, Mentor to Whorf

manner seems faithfully recorded in one student's memory that "Listening to him could be a lucid adventure in the field of ideas" (Mandelbaum ix).

Language as Structured

Sapir was both intellectually and aesthetically fascinated by the ways in which languages evolve into independent symbol systems, detached from the specific facts of environment (Sapir, *Language* 11-12). Sapir likened this ever greater autonomy to a pyramid "called civilization." The pyramid of civilization was distinctly separate from raw experience. Carrying out the implications of this metaphor of civilization as a man-made monument, Sapir noted with some pride that "in this structure, very few bricks touch the ground" ("Sound" 44). Sapir's fascination with man's involvement in the symbolic labyrinth of language went beyond a mere special emphasis of a portion of Boas' doctrine. At least at one point in his career, Sapir seems to have experimented with the notion that the detailed study of the phoneme as a meaningful, patterned unit of sound could possibly lead to a new and profound science of man. It was to this prospect of linguistics as a new, synthetic science of man that Whorf enthusiastically responded.

Whorf must have been aroused by Sapir's call for linguists to probe for the depths of mind below the sound features of language. Whereas Leonard Bloomfield was interested only in the overt situations and responses to speech acts, Sapir invited the researcher to explore the intuitive "feel" of language in its operation. As Boas had taught, so Sapir believed that this "feel" for linguistic form was below the level of conscious awareness of the normal native speaker. If this were so, the lessons learned in the study of language seemed inevitably to be useful in future studies of other patterned cultural forms. Sapir seemed to promise that the anthropological linguist could go beyond mere external observation to develop a kind of *verstehende Psychologie*.

Sapir undeniably expended a considerable amount of time in his works exploring the unconscious "feel" which native speakers display in their use of the complicated mechanisms of language. He frequently celebrated this behavior as comparable to an aesthetic act. But if we consider these passages closely, we find that Sapir adduces precious little evidence to support his claims. Instead of hard data, we find a recurrent expression of hope that someone will eventually discover a way to muster the lessons about form which have been acquired during the study of language, and apply these lessons to the study of man (Sapir, *Language* iii).

In "The Status of Linguistics as a Science," an article which has become the *locus classicus* for demonstrating the connection between Sapir and Whorf, Sapir again announced his hopes for a future science of the mind which will unfold as linguists and psychologists learn to combine their artificially separated studies of man. Sapir hoped that psychologists would jettison their behavioral and physiological prejudices and eventually come to see man as a symbolic animal. Once man is recognized to be an *animal symbolicum*, psychologists will inevitably feel the need to turn to the most disciplined science of human symbolism, linguistics. At the same time, Sapir proposed that the detachment counseled by Bloomfield was ultimately sterile. Linguistics would grow as a science only if it could develop a broader vocabulary which would bridge the gap between its polished studies of linguistic forms and the minds of men who use those forms. Under these optimum (future) conditions, language could be a "symbolic guide to culture" (Sapir, "The Status" 162).

Coming to Sapir as Whorf did, he must have been immensely stimulated by the prospects offered by Sapir's psychologically oriented linguistics. As Whorf later reflected about his teacher's contribution to modern linguistics, "Sapir attempted to put meaning and thought back into linguistics or to see them as linguistic problems" ("Outline"). Whorf's reading of the metaphysical implications of Sapir's unsubstantiated promises about the science of language must have been something like the following: although the connection has not yet been discovered, there are links between the structure of mind, the structure of language, and the structure of nature. For some reason, man has yet been unable to connect himself properly with these interrelated structures. Given Whorf's misinterpretation of Boas' ideas about the impact of differing linguistic patterns on perception and expression, it probably was not too great an intellectual leap to the conclusion that man has been cheated of his proper, harmonious place in the form-filled world because of misleading structures in his language.

Whorf enthusiastically recorded that Sapir had taught that "linguistics was fundamental to the theory of thinking and in the last analysis to ALL HUMAN SCIENCES" (*Language* 78). In his unpublished "Outline of the History of Linguistics," Whorf notes that Sapir's "untimely death in 1939 prevented his making the direct and overwhelming integrated statement that would have eventually come." Clearly, Benjamin Whorf believed that his linguistic relativity principle was a very close approximation of what Sapir's "overwhelming integrated statement" would have been.

Sapir and the Whorf Hypothesis

Edward Sapir was very suspicious of the kind of correlations between language and culture which Benjamin Whorf would make. Sapir shared Boas' belief that, when languages lacked certain terms to describe the world, the problem was conceptual and lexical rather than structural.

In Sapir's view, the "culture" of a socially definable group at any given moment is the sum of the group's conceptual inventory of experience. This culture is separable—in fact, it does historically separate itself—from language, the medium of expression. If environmental and intellectual states are in flux, cultural change may be extremely rapid. This volatile cultural change, however, does not affect the deeper layers of language. Sapir, like Boas before him, is ready to allow that the vocabulary of a language will change rapidly in response to the needs of the users, but he cautions that "this superficial and extraneous kind of parallelism is of no real interest to the linguist... [For]...the linguistic student should never make the mistake of identifying a language with its dictionary" (*Language* 7).

"The Status of Linguistics as a Science," the article in which Sapir promises that language will serve as *"the symbolic guide to culture"* (163), can be reappraised by the light of this discussion. Whorf's interpretation was that linguistic analysis would in many cases supplant other disciplines concerned with the analysis of the human mind and culture. Sapir, on the other hand, was merely suggesting that language analysis would prove to be a very useful device for sociologists and psychologists as something to be added to the conceptual equipment they currently had at their disposal. It may be helpful to take a look at Sapir's statements about the power of language to determine perception. Probably the strongest form of such an assertion appears in *Language*:

> Language is...unreasonable and stubborn about its classifications. It must have its perfectly exclusive pigeonholes and will tolerate no flying vagrants. Any concept that asks for expression must submit to the classificatory rules of the game, just as there are statistical surveys in which even the most convinced atheist must perforce be labeled Catholic, Protestant, or Jew or get no hearing....It is almost as though at some period in the past the unconscious mind of the race had made a hasty inventory of experience, committed itself to a premature classification that allowed no revision, and saddled the inheritors of its language with a science that they no longer quite believed in nor had the strength to overthrow... . Linguistic categories make up a system of surviving dogma—dogma of the unconscious.

They are often but half real as concepts; their life tends ever to languish away into form for form's sake. (*Language* 104-5)

Sapir admonished his readers that they can and should "fight" the restrictions imposed by language. At any given moment, a new word can be a key, but over a period of time, "it may also be a fetter" (14). But even at this moment, when he is ever so close to a statement of linguistic relativity, Sapir did not support Whorf's ideas about language as a medium whose shape determined the message, but instead supported Boas' view of language (at least as related to culture) as a reservoir of concepts.

Sapir's position on the viability of an international auxiliary language instructively revealed his tendency to avoid imputation of special powers of linguistic determinism. Whorf rejected "Basic English" because its proponents were oblivious to the subtle forces below the surface of language. Sapir joined Whorf in ridiculing the provincial notion of forcing English on the world—English was "simple" and "basic" only to native speakers of English. At this point, Sapir and Whorf part company. Whorf believed that ultimately the science of language would be capable of formulating a truly "basic" language which would be consonant with the most fundamental structure of the human mind. Such a language would emerge from a global survey of all of man's languages, and its creation would yield unprecedented social and even spiritual results.

Sapir made no such metaphysical claims. The purpose of an auxiliary language was to facilitate communication and mutual understanding in the jungle of national rivalries. Basic English was no solution to the problem because it was the national language of one of the more successful predators. Esperanto or any other fashioned international language would succeed, not because it has tapped mysterious resources of patternment in language, but because it would be an artificial, supra-national product. The language would work precisely because it is artificially and self-consciously acquired: "only that can be freely accepted which is in some sense a creation of all. A common creature demands a common sacrifice, and perhaps not the least potent argument in favor of a constructed international language is the fact that it is equally foreign, or apparently so, to the traditions of all nationalities" (Sapir, "The Function" 112). To Sapir, man's limitedness as a perceiver and as a social being was an outgrowth of more traditional flaws and conflicts, and not the result of a lack of harmony that could be attributed to the structure of language.

If there is any form of linguistic relativity to be found in Sapir's writings, it appears in his discussion of the "style." Unlike Whorf, who believed that the concepts of science were taken from the compulsory forms imbedded within language, Sapir asserted that a "scientific truth is impersonal; in its essence it is untinctured by the particular linguistic medium in which it finds expression. It can as readily deliver its message in Chinese as in English" (*Language* 238). In contrast, the style of language, the life blood of literature, was dictated to the artist by the language itself: "The major characteristics of style, in so far as style is a technical matter of building and placing words, are given by the language itself, quite as inescapably...as the general acoustic effort of verse is given by the sounds and natural accents of the language" (242). Sapir's contemporary, Ezra Pound, was holding up Chinese poetry to the Western literary world for stylistic emulation. To Sapir such an endeavor was useless, for it ignored the relativity of linguistic style: "We must not envy Chinese its terseness unduly. Our more sprawling mode of expression is capable of its own beauties, and the more compact luxuriance of Latin Style has its loveliness, too. There are almost as many natural ideals of literary style as there are languages" (243).

My conclusion must be that, in the study of Edward Sapir's works, it has been exceedingly difficult to discover the egg which Benjamin Whorf supposedly hatched. The remainder of this chapter will explore themes in Sapir's writings which point to the differences in temperament between the two men who are associated with the Sapir-Whorf hypothesis of linguistic relativity.

Sapir on the Modern Condition

We know that Edward Sapir's father was a cantor in a New York City synagogue, and that this son of German Jewish immigrants put his childhood faith behind him as he moved into manhood. A student of Whorf's development will be disappointed, however, if he seeks for the same passion to reconcile science with religion that is found in *The Ruler of the Universe*. While Sapir was never contemptuous of religious faith, he himself was what we would probably call a "sensitive modern."

He was tentative in his intellectual formulations, humanistic in his sense of the personal dimension of experience that is neglected by intellectual abstractions. While capable of admitting that he paid a price for his intellectual and emotional sophistication in the form of the insecurity which accompanies choice and freedom, he was consistently a defender of the modern spirit of rational inquiry. Intellect was the only force to save man from his lesser self in an international setting where the fruits of science are in the hands of self-interested nations motivated by primitive group passions. Surveying the drift of modern history, Sapir saw the fabric of customary society (to include his orthodox family) being disentangled into isolated threads by a combination of intellectual and economic forces. Whether for good or for ill, the division of labor, rationalism, internationalism, and celebration of the rights of the individual were working in concert to sever man from social traditions, leaving him to his own resources: "The ideal which is latent in the modern mind would seem to be to break up custom into the two poles of individually determined habit, on the one hand, and of large scale institutional planning for the major enterprise of mankind on the other" ("Custom" 371). Separated from tradition, modern man was faced with the perilous task of maintaining without help his intellectual and emotional equilibrium.

If Sapir was committed to modernism, he was so with an admitted sense of the price that must be paid for self-consciousness. He understood that men have deep and demanding emotional needs, which, ironically, primitive cultures were often far more sophisticated in satisfying than modern civilization had proved itself to be. America in the Jazz Age seemed to epitomize modern man's failure to integrate the intellectual and emotional elements of his nature in a cultural way. With more than a little bitterness, Sapir called this failure of integration the grimmest joke of our present American civilization:

> The vast majority of us, deprived of any but an insignificant and culturally abortive share in the satisfaction of the immediate wants of mankind, are further deprived of both opportunity and stimulation to share in the production of

non-utilitarian values. Part of the time we are dray horses; the rest of the time we are listless consumers of goods which have received no least impress of our personality. In other words, our spiritual selves go hungry for the most part, pretty much all of the time. ("Culture" 321)

Here we begin to see a fundamental tension which permeates Sapir's discussions of language and culture. Separation of means from ends, of the individual from customary society, of intellect from emotion, of science from art are all inevitable consequences of modernity. Recognizing this condition, Sapir continually explored means by which modern man could somehow self-consciously rejoin aesthetically what had been separated by intellectual and economic forces. Throughout his investigations, Sapir was always painfully aware that the "native" of an integrated culture could have the unconscious joy of pure function, not just at the rare aesthetic moments allowed modern man, but as an ordinary daily experience. Thus, for all his defense of modern self-consciousness, Sapir often conveyed the impression that man was mentally healthiest when he was fully and unselfconsciously immersed in the forms of his culture ("Unconscious Patterning" 544). Those who have read Chapters 1-6 of *America Reflected* will recognize that Will Rogers shared this perception and used it as a basis for social satire and comic "relief."

The Resulting Themes

The Conflict Between Intellect and Emotion
Central to all of Sapir's discussions of the place of intellect and emotion in human thought and behavior was his underlying assumption that the modern mind must have a versatility which allows it to use intelligence in different ways at different times. The picture which emerged is one of the human mind resting on a sliding scale between intellect and emotion. Each had an appropriate proportion of influence in man's activities, depending upon what is desired from the process of thought.

A scientific statement, for example, should strive for the greatest possible use of the intellectual "pattern of reference" within language. This objective, intellectual language of science is capable at its best moments of being "impersonal, in its essence... untinctured by the particular linguistic medium in which it finds expression" (*Language* 238). As we have already noted, Sapir was well aware of man's deep need for more than an objective statement about external relations. Once his scientific and intellectual curiosity had been satisfied, man must also be given room for expression of his wide range of feelings toward the persons and things in the world which surrounds him: "The feeling-tone of words are of no use, strictly speaking to science; the philosopher, if he desires to arrive at truth rather than merely to persuade, finds them his most insidious enemies. But man is rarely engaged in pure science, in solid thinking. Generally his mental activities are bathed in a warm current of feeling and he seizes upon the feeling-tones of words as gentle aids to the desired excitation. They are naturally of great value to the literary artist" (*Language* 42).

A significant difference between Whorf and Sapir can now be distinguished. In Whorf's analysis of the modern condition, the forces of intellect were identified with science and technology; the holistic needs of the individual to integrate his experience were identified with the religious affections. The resulting conflict between science and religion was thus perceived by Whorf as irreconcilable. Sapir's analysis was quite different: as a sensitive modern, he saw the conflict as taking place within each individual, and celebrated what modest aesthetic pleasure the modern could experience in his secular world. For our convenience, Sapir himself distinguished between the aesthetic and religious temperaments in terms which can accurately be applied to the difference between himself and Whorf. Sapir sought some kind of balance between intellect and emotion, while a religious mind like Whorf's was in search of perceptions of the ultimate structure of the universe:

> Religion seeks neither the objective enlightenment of science nor the strange equilibrium, the sensuous harmony, or aesthetic experience. It aims at nothing more or less than the impulsive conquest of reality, and it can use science and art as little more than stepping stones toward the attainment of its own serenity.... The serenity of art seems of an utterly

different nature from that of religion. Art creates a feeling of wholeness precipitating the flux of things into tangible forms, beautiful and sufficient to themselves; religion gathers up all the threads and meaninglessnesses of life into a wholeness that is not manifest and can only be experienced in the form of a passionate desire...the religious spirit is antithetical to that of art for religion is essentially ultimate and irreconcilable. Art forgives because it values as an ultimate good a here and now, religion forgives because the here and now are somehow irrelevant to a desire that drives for ultimate solutions. (Sapir "The Meaning" 348)

Although Sapir disavowed connection with the religious attitudes and goals of men like Whorf, his particular interest in man's need for aesthetic satisfaction did affect his discussion of language. And it is here that I suspect Whorf was most attentive to his teacher. It appears that the high value which Sapir recurrently placed on the "intuitive" and "form-feeling" dimension of language was put to use by Whorf for his more ambitious purposes. We know that Boas was the first to draw attention to the fact that the overall pattern of any language is never perceived by the ordinary native speaker. We also know that Sapir's concern with language as a psychological system caused him to linger over this unconscious, yet intelligent form-following behavior. Man's ability to blithely juggle the complex forms of language without dropping pieces of meaning must have seemed to Sapir to be a token of the aesthetic dimension of man's nature. Man communicated with his fellow creatures not by conscious plodding, not by piling concept upon concept, but by the free, unconscious flow of his acculturated mind along the courses established by language. On the level of high culture, formalized art achieved this same reunification of experience. What Sapir conveyed to his reader was that man as an "intuitive" language animal was in a small way actually an unacknowledged artist in his daily life.

Whorf later added a few elements of his own to this picture. He injected the notion of linguistic "crypotypes" buried in languages which established patterns echoed throughout the culture. What for Sapir was a nostalgic fancy for immersion in aesthetically sensed patterns, in Whorf is transformed into a mold which shaped the individual consciousness into a rigid form. Obviously, Whorf's conclusions were of a different order. Sapir saw the relationship of language to culture to be extremely complicated and increasingly distant with the passage of time. If Whorf's hypothesis means anything at all, it is that there is a one-to-one relationship between the two. In addition, while Sapir's sense of modern man's loss of intuitively felt patterns was evident in his writings, his belief that art could be a compensatory form of expression restrained him from making extravagant claims about the implications of the form-feeling quality of man's ability to handle language. Without question, Whorf was the kind of religious mentality we have seen described by Sapir. A moderately balanced life in a world in which God was dead could not satisfy Whorf's emotional needs for connection. For this reason, he took up Sapir's promises about the possibilities of a psychology of unconscious social patterns guided by linguistics and loaded those promises with the maximum metaphysical freight that they could carry.

Cultural Patterns and Individual Personalities

Sapir's celebration of the intuitive quality of man's use of language may have provided grist for Whorf's mill, but another prominent theme in Sapir's writings clearly set him apart from his inspired student. I have noted that Sapir adduced precious little evidence to support his assertions about the intuitive dimensions of language as a sound system. My feeling is that at some point he decided that such speculations were fruitless. His attention instead became drawn to problems related to ways in which individual personalities learn to adapt to the cultural patterns presented to them by their societies. While this theme is not exactly an outgrowth of Sapir's sense of the different purposes of intellect and emotion, the continuity between these two themes deserves mention. All intellectual systems constructed by man (i.e., not the systems which like language are unconscious) take on a suprapersonal status as they attempt to attain an objectivity of description. Just as the exclusive use of the intellect deprived man of the needed satisfaction of his emotional nature, so the goals of science frequently ignored the individual's experience. For example, in anthropology a concept like "culture" was extremely useful to the investigator, but it became a handicap when it was taken as a final statement rather than a stimulus for research. If we are to learn about the actual operations of culture, the macrocosmic perspective of anthropology must be counterpoised by psychiatry's concept of "personality." Only then will we see in specific, measurable ways how the gross forces described by social science actually affect individuals.

Sapir believed that he could distinguish between the underlying motivation of students of culture and students of personality. In doing so, he accurately described the tensions within his own personality which were responsible for his binocular approach to social science: "The study of culture...has a deep and unacknowledged root in the desire to lose oneself safely in the historically determined patterns of behavior. The study of personality...proceeds from the necessity which the ego feels to assert itself significantly" ("The Emergence" 592). This statement helps us to see another difference between Sapir and Whorf. To arrive at his principle of linguistic relativity, Whorf applied a typological interpretation to cultures taken as wholes. Whorf believed he had found patterns which had a uniform effect upon the entire populations of the cultures whose languages he studied. The drift of Sapir's later thought was in an entirely different direction. Sapir grew increasingly suspicious of the notion that "a completely impersonal anthropological description and analysis of custom in terms which tacitly assume the unimportance of individual needs and preferences... [was]... possible for a social discipline" ("Why" 570).

Sapir hoped to see a different science of man come to fruition. This science, while unique in its sensitivity to the complexity of human experience, would not have to be built upon entirely new foundations: "The anthropologist...needs only to trespass a little on the untilled acres of psychology, the psychiatrist to poach a few of the uneaten apples of anthropology's Golden Bough" ("Psychiatric" 585). Rather than being satisfied with glowing generalizations which tend to gain a life of their own, this new science would be attentive to the unique ways in which individuals give their own special shape to the cultural configurations which affect them: "We can postpone this psychiatric analysis indefinitely, but we cannot theoretically eliminate it. With the modern growth of interest in the study of personality and the growing conviction of the enormous flexibility of personality adjustment to one's fellow men, it is difficult to see how one's intellectual curiosity about the problems of human intercourse can be forever satisfied by schematic statements about society and its stock of cultural patterns" (Sapir, "Why" 575).

The inability of the social sciences to comprehend the human tragedy of the economic depression of the 1930s had a significant impact on Sapir. As he had assailed Bloomfield's methodological detachment, so he railed against the lack of imaginative sympathy of his fellow social scientists. Social scientists were proving themselves to be more loyal to the corpus of their disciplines than the human beings whose thought and action they were designed to describe: "It is not really difficult to see why anyone brought up on the austerities of a well-defined science of man must, if he is to maintain his symbolic self-respect, become more and more estranged from man himself....Fantasied universes of self-contained meaning are the very finest and noblest substitutes we can ever devise for that precise and loving insight into the nooks and crannies of the real that must be forever denied us" ("Psychiatric" 580). Epistemologically and morally, Sapir's critique of his fellow social scientists' insensitivity to individuals (whom he calls "the nuclei of consciousness" [581]) closely resembles Noam Chomsky's criticism in the 1970s of the symbiotic relationship between academics and the military-industrial complex. Both our contemporary, Chomsky, and Whorf's teacher, Sapir, believe that social thought will remain humane only so long as it keeps within its purview the flesh-and-blood human beings it is designed to understand and serve:

> We must not reverse the arrow of experience and claim for experience's imaginative condensations the primacy in an appeal to our loyalty, which properly belongs to our perceptions of men and women as the ultimate units of value in our day-to-day view of the world. If we do not thus value the nuclei of consciousness from which all science, all art, all history, all culture, have flowed as symbolic by-products in the humble but intensely urgent business of establishing meaningful relationships between actual human beings, we commit personal suicide....Not for one single moment can we allow ourselves to forget the experienced unity of the individual. (Sapir, "Psychiatric" 581)

By shifting his focus away from larger patterns to the process of individual socialization, Sapir had divorced himself from his early hopes of formulating an "overwhelming integrated statement" which Whorf attempted with his linguistic relativity principle. The underlying psychological reasons for this final difference seem clear: Sapir had no faith that a commanding synthesis could liberate the individual from the tension of his identity as both a culturally immersed and culturally transcendent being. While Sapir recognized that the primitive mind had experienced a more intensive and culturally unified existence, he did not (as Whorf appears to have done) consider the mind of primitive man to be a model for an alternative way of apprehending reality. Instead, Sapir held himself delicately poised between science and art, culture and the individual, in the belief that if the modern condition required unprecedented exertion by the individual to keep himself afloat. Flight from complexities did not constitute a solution. Within Sapir's scheme, this flight from reality could be in either the direction of the intellect or the emotions: hermetically insulated social scientists had demonstrated that the intellect frequently rested satisfied after attaining conceptual consistency rather than significant truths. At the opposite end of the intellectual-emotional spectrum, the pseudo-solutions of nationalism and religion had proved themselves equally incompetent to master the complexities of the modern condition. Some kind of compromise was the only solution: man must allot a place in his life for both intellectual analysis as well as gratification of the needs of the whole person. If he can succeed in learning how to use each as a counterpoise for the other, he will become a fully developed human personality. Modern man can be whole only if he is both scientist and artist. The kind of mystical synthesis which Whorf was pursuing was no longer possible, for modern man was cut off from the animistic universe and superintending deity which his fathers had worshiped.

What can man do under these conditions? Through his art, through his humane personal and institutional relations, he can at least be committed to the material and spiritual elevation of his community and himself as an individual. Science, the product of his intellect, can satisfy his craving for abstract understanding. If properly used, applied science can improve his material environment. Art, the record of his holistic reactions to the entire range of his experience, should contribute to the integration of his internal environment. While it may be true that man can no longer link-up with the ruler of the universe, "the self...[can]...set itself at a point where it can if not embrace the whole spiritual life of its group, at least catch enough of its rays to burst into light and flame" ("Culture" 326). Through art we "relate *our* lives, *our* intuitions, *our* passing moods to forms of expression that carry conviction to others and make us live again in those others." This aesthetic communion, Sapir believed, would help man to achieve "the highest spiritual satisfaction we know of, the highest wedding of one's individuality with the spirit of his civilization" (327).

Sapir on the Uses of Language Study
A final evaluation of Sapir's hopes for language study can now be made. Because Whorf identified man's needs for emotional expression with his own need for religious beliefs, he was tempted to carry his critique of science into a cross-cultural contrast between the mind shaped by our Western scientific culture and the counterpart evolved in the world of the Hopi Indians. Whorf concluded his studies with the judgment that the Hopi language had helped its primitive speakers to retain a special spiritual connection with the mysterious forces of the universe. Sapir saw the problem differently: a viable course was present within the context of modern Western civilization, but it required a delicate science which would take into account both the systematic relationships in a society (which the budding social sciences were attempting to describe) while simultaneously keeping within its purview the complex ways in which unique individuals integrate these forms. Sapir's sense of the inviolable quality of any individual's system of adaptation (vs. any given standard type in a society) is revealed in his warning to psychiatry. While he preached that it was essential for students of society acquire psychiatry's sensitivity to the individual's development, he joined many of his contemporaries in deprecating psychiatry's rigid concept of "normality." In doing so, Sapir stood at his furthest remove from Whorf's desire for a commanding synthesis, for Sapir was aware that even man's most individually attuned social science was constricted by a rigid, standardized intellectual

scheme: "Modern psychiatrists should be tolerant not only of varying personalities, but of the different types of values which personality variations imply. Psychiatrists who are tolerant only in the sense that they refrain from criticizing anybody who is subjected to their care and who do their best to guide them back to the renewed performance of society's rituals may be good practical surgeons of the psyche. They are not necessarily the profoundly sympathetic students of the mind who respect the fundamental intent and direction of every personality organization" ("Cultural" 521).

Anthropology's concept, "culture," or Freud's standard, "normality," as abstractions, could be useful first level of inquiry guides for social scientists. Similarly, the unique structure of language could be a starting point for the investigation of the symbolic and communicative dimensions of social life. In all of these cases, however, the social scientist must penetrate beneath the larger patterns until he reaches the individual: "The true locus of culture is in the interactions of specific individuals and, on the subjective side, in the world of meanings which each one of these individuals may unconsciously abstract for himself. Every individual is, then, in a very real sense, a representative of at least one sub-culture of the group of which he is a member. It is not the concept of culture which is subtly misleading, but the metaphysical locus to which culture is generally assigned" ("Cultural" 515). Using Sapir's terms, we may say that Whorf's linguistic relativity principle was guilty of claiming too large a "metaphysical locus" for the impact of language. In contrast, Sapir's late writings indicate that he was becoming ever more sensitive to the nuance, the play, the multiple uses which a single linguistic form might have when used by different speakers, or by the same speaker in different contexts. Speech became important to Sapir not so much as a key to a new psychology nor as a cryptotype which would reveal the hidden assumptions of a *Weltanschauung*, but as "a personality trait." Through the analysis of the intonation, rhythm, pronunciation, vocabulary, and general style of the individual's voice, much of his personality and his place within his society could be discerned:

> In spite of the fact that language acts as a socializing and uniformizing force, it is at the same time the most potent

single known factor for the growth of individuality. The fundamental quality of one's voice, the phonetic patterns of speech, the speed and relative smoothness of articulation, the length and build of sentences, the character and range of vocabulary, the scholastic consistency of the words used, the readiness with which words respond to the requirements of the social environment—in particular the suitability of one's language to the language habits of the persons addressed—all these are so many complex indicators of personality. ("Language" 17)

At the end of his career, Edward Sapir was exploring the kind of approach to culture associated with Erik Erikson (1902-1994) and explored in Erikson's *Young Man Luther: A Study in Psychoanalysis and History* (1958). Both the larger intellectual and cultural patterns as well as the personal experience of particular individuals are taken into account. The validity of the investigator's analysis will greatly depend on his capacity to listen sensitively to the delicate interplay between the symbolic patterns of culture and the often devious reactions of man, the symbolic animal. Whorf made a daring application of Boas' and Sapir's suggestions about the systematic and unconscious nature of language. Edward Sapir, a sensitive modern, followed a different route toward understanding: he moved steadily away from all encompassing generalizations to an ever more detailed study of the modern world's social unit—the individual, whom Sapir treasured beyond all systems as a mysterious and irreducible "nucleus of consciousness." Language study

Whorf Saw (Mystical) Patternment in the Permutations for a Monosyllabic Word in English would not release the individual from the problem of his relationship to society and reality; it could only illuminate the complexity of that relationship. Understanding, not revelation, was the fruit of study.

Works Cited

Boas, Franz. *The Mind of Primitive Man*. Rev. ed. New York: MacMillan, 1938.
Hymes, Dell. "Linguistic Method in Ethnography: Its Development in the United States." *Method and Theory in Linguistics*. Ed. Paul L. Garvin. The Hague: Mouton Press, 1971.
Mandelbaum, David G. Introduction. In Sapir, *Selected Writings*. i-xii.
Rollins, Peter C., ed. *The Benjamin Lee Whorf Legacy CD-ROM*. Cleveland, OK: Ridgemont Media Productions, 2008.
Sapir, Edward. "A Study in Phonetic Symbolism." *Selected Writings of Edward Sapir on Language, Culture, and Personality*. Ed. David Mandelbaum. Berkeley: U of California P, 1968. 61-72.
—. "Cultural Anthropology and Psychiatry." *Selected Writings*. 509-21.
—. "Culture, Genuine and Spurious." *Selected Writings*. 308-31.
—. "Custom." *Selected Writings*. 365-72.
—. "Language." *Selected Writings*. 7-32.
—. *Language: An Introduction to the Study of Speech*. New York: Harcourt, Brace, 1921.
—. "Psychiatric and Cultural Pitfalls in the Business of Getting a Living." *Selected Writings*. 578-89.
—. "Sound Patterns in Language." *Selected Writings*. 33-45.
—. "The Emergence of the Concept of Personality in a Study of Cultures." *Selected Writings*. 590-97.
—. "The Function of an International Auxiliary Language." *Selected Writings*. 110-21.
—. "The Grammarian and his Language." *Selected Writings*. 150-59.
—. "The Meaning of Religion." *Selected Writings*. 346-56.
—. "The Status of Linguistics as a Science." *Selected Writings*. 160-66.
—. "The Unconscious Patterning of Behavior in Society." *Selected Writings*. 544-59.
—. "Time Perspective in Aboriginal American Culture: A Study in Method." *Selected Writings*. 389-462.
—. "Why Cultural Anthropology Needs a Psychiatrist." *Selected Writings*. 569-77.
Whorf, Benjamin Lee. *Language, Thought, and Reality: Selected Writings of Benjamin Lee Whorf*. Ed. John B. Carroll. Cambridge, MA: MIT Press, 1956.
—. "Outline of the History of Linguistics." Appendix B, document 1, Rollins CD-ROM.

9
The Whorf Hypothesis as a Critique of Western Science and Technology

> We dissect nature along lines laid down by our native languages. The categories and types that we isolate from the world of phenomena we do not find there because they stare every observer in the face; on the contrary, the world is presented in a kaleidoscopic flux of impressions which has to be organized by our minds—and this means largely by the linguistic systems in our minds. We cut nature up, organize it into concepts, and ascribe significances as we do, largely because we are parties to an agreement to organize it in this way—an agreement that holds throughout our speech community and is codified in the patterns of our language. The agreement is, of course, an implicit and unstated one, BUT ITS TERMS ARE ABSOLUTELY OBLIGATORY; we cannot talk at all except by subscribing to the organization and classification of data which the agreement decrees.
>
> B. L. Whorf, *Science and Linguistics*

Theosophical Influences of Early Readings

Benjamin Lee Whorf's first exposure to the study of language came through the works of an early 19th-century French Theosophist, Antoine Fabre d'Olivet. Fabre d'Olivet's hieratic use of linguistics to "translate" the biblical account of creation attracted Whorf. Many have discussed this response to Fabre d'Olivet the linguist, but little

Müller as Gifford Lecturer: Both Linguist and Believer

has been said to date about Whorf's interest in Theosophy. Theosophy attracted Whorf because it promised to help him throw off the doctrine of original sin which had been so central to his novel and its critique of modernity. (For a full discussion of the novel, see Chapter 7). At the same time, it allowed him to sustain the reconciliation of science with religion for which he had argued in *The Ruler of the Universe*: Theosophy seemed to offer a nondenominational affirmation of the powers of religious perception. In addition, Theosophy seemed to be up-to-date in its reading of the physical and psychological sciences, without losing the ability to integrate these new insights with the aspirations of the soul. (When I visited Mrs. Whorf in the late 1960s, she was still a great admirer of Theosophy.)

The works of Frederick Max Müller broadened and refined the interest in language which Fabre d'Olivet had excited. Müller's writings are also full of defenses of religion—to include Theosophy. Müller's *Science and Thought* (1887) explains that, in the discussion of language, all roads lead back to the controversy between Locke and Kant: "Locke's work, in spite of all its imperfections is, as Lange in his *History of Materialism* perceived, a 'Critique of Language' and together with Kant's *Critique of Reason* it forms the true starting point of modern philosophy" (Müller *Science* 295). Like Fabre d'Olivet and the later Whorf, Max Müller intensely resented Locke's dissection of the perceptual process and Müller refused to grant that man's linguistic formulas can be surgically detached from the so-called "things" perceived. According to Müller's alternative model, "sensations" cause men to have "perceptions" which in turn give rise to "concepts" which are given "names." This entire process, from the initial "sensations" to the final "concepts" must be considered as an organic unit. (In Locke's model, a name is a convenient symbol arbitrarily affixed to a sublinguistic idea.) Müller admired Kant for combating Locke's pernicious sensationalism; indeed, in "a world-wide struggle...for...primacy between mind and matter...Kant stood forth to stem and turn the tide" (134).

Like Fabre d'Olivet, Müller was contemptuous of the approach to man taken by empirical science. The coldness of such an intellectually detached method caused it to tear at the living body of experience. The science of language, as *the* science of man, would not be so insensitive. On the other hand, the science of language would be "scientific" in a sense in which Kant's work never was. (Distinguishing the methodology of the linguist from the approach of a traditional philosopher like Kant was indeed one of the major purposes of *The Science of Thought*.) Kant's basic position, that man perceived the world only through (and never around) the basic categories of his consciousness, was not rejected. Müller tried to build a basis for an objective science of consciousness upon this fundamental insight. Whereas Kant postulated the existence of vehicles of mental organization such as the concepts of time, space, and the idea of cause, Müller thought he could develop an objective science by restricting his focus to the external cultural data provided by the elements of language: "Without these categories man would indeed be ἄλογος that is, not only speechless, but mad." The difference between Kant's view of the categories and my own is that Kant takes them as the *sine qua non* of thought in the abstract, while I take them as the *sine qua non* of thought, as embodied in language" (*Science* 476-77).

Whorf's progression from Fabre d'Olivet to Max Müller was assisted by more than the similarities between the linguistic theories of these two Europeans. F. Max Müller, it should be remembered, was as concerned with the evolution of the religions of the world as he was with the science of language. In fact, after Müller delivered the Gifford lectures on mysticism at the University of Glasgow in 1892, he gave the resulting volume the provocative title, *Theosophy: or, Psychological Religion*. *Theosophy* must have intensified Whorf's interest in mysticism, especially Indian mysticism. As Müller explained, the philosophy of India bypassed Western Christianity's obstacles of sin and conversion, teaching rather "that beatitude requires no bridges, it requires knowledge only, knowledge of the necessary unity of what is divine in man with what is divine in God. The Brahmans call it self-knowledge, that is to say, the knowledge that our true self, if it is anything, can only be that self which is All in All and beside which there is nothing else" (Müller, *Theosophy* 93). To an anguished modern believer like Whorf, these must have been comforting words!

Unlike Fabre d'Olivet, however, Müller never "bends the knee" in his studies of religion. No single tradition seemed broad enough for modern man. Instead, the highest form of spiritual contemplation was attained by the intellectual historian who could vicariously identify with the achievements of religious spirits, without becoming committed to the specific tenets of any particular sect. Thus, for Whorf, the rewards of anthropology were added to the appeal of linguistics. In both cases, the investigator was not merely promised that his scientific curiosity would be enlivened; in addition, he could expect an intensification of his own personal spiritual awareness. With the insights of Fabre d'Olivet and F. Max Müller behind him, Whorf was to be an unusually well-prepared student for Edward Sapir when this eminent representative of what has been called the "American School" of anthropology moved from the University of Chicago to Yale in 1931. (For details on the American School, to include the impact of Franz Boas and Edward Sapir, see Chapter 8.)

Hopi Observers, 1906

The American School of Anthropology

Franz Boas (as interpreted by Whorf) and Edward Sapir (at least in one phase of his career) had taught Whorf that study of patterns in language could produce keys to larger patterns in any given culture. Boas and Sapir considered language to be especially useful in this search for patterns because, of all cultural phenomena available to the anthropologist, the deep structure of language was least subject to self-conscious analysis by normal, native speakers. It was thus part of the "background material of culture" (Boas 209). By uncovering these patterns (which Whorf calls either "cryptotypes" or "covert categories") Whorf believed that he could unveil the hidden assumptions and subliminal associations built into the "habitual thought of a culture" (Carroll 147). Because Whorf conceived of human thought as a product of the interplay between the great minds of a culture and the cryptotypical categories embedded in the structure of language, his studies of the contrast between the world view of the Hopi Indians and the world view developed by the West inevitably amount to an unearthing of the cryptotypes hidden in each language system. The character of Whorf's famous articles comes from the elements which he selectively excavated from each system to prove that "the Hopi observer conceives events in a different manner from one whose native language is English."

Limitations of the Western Mind

Whorf tried to show that Western man was a prisoner of the overt and covert categories imposed upon him by the structure of the Indo-European language. In the process of his explanation, Whorf adopted a clever and effective stylistic device. He lumped all of the Western languages into an acronym, "SAE," which he employed throughout his discussion to represent the general characteristics of the "Standard Average European" languages. At first, such a ploy may seem to be no more than a space-saving convention, but the rhetorical effectiveness of the acronym soon becomes apparent. At every stage of the discussion, the Hopi tongue is depicted as superior to its competitor, "SAE." Within the confines of Whorf's discussion, the acronym effectively stripped the honorific associations which would otherwise prevent the reader from accepting Whorf's claims for the language of a small, primitive culture. By stealing from the reader his casual sense of superiority over the backward peoples of the American continent, Whorf persuaded the reader that those who have lived within the mental boundaries defined by the structure of SAE have seen only a fraction of the mysteries of the universe. The reader, I believe, is far more ready to accept Whorf's argument about the narrowness of the West's view of nature when it is described as belonging to those who speak "SAE." "SAE" looks and sounds colorless, devoid of depth and vitality, while "Hopi" conveys rich and rather romantic associations.

The cryptotypical pattern which has for so long provided the guiding light for the habitual thought and the science of the West is described by Whorf as a "binomial formula." This binomial formula not only guides the creation of individual sentences; it also provides the basis for analogous integrations of experience. Ever since Aristotle codified the use of subject and verb, the Western mind has been obliged to divide reality into an agent-acting, and a thing acted upon. Whorf's criticism here is that, because we are compelled to segment nature's (or our own) behavior into these categories, we are forced to arrive at certain conclusions about the operation of nature which are not given by nature herself: "The SAE microcosm has analyzed reality largely in terms of what it calls 'things' (bodies and quasibodies) plus modes of extensional but formless existence that it calls 'substances' or 'matter.' It tends to see existence through a binomial formula that expresses any existent as a spatial form plus a special formless continuum related to the form as the content is related to the outlines of its container. Nonspatial existents are imaginatively spatialized and charged with special implications of form and continuum" (Carroll 147).

At this point, some translation of Whorf's idea of the binomial formula may be in order. In his analysis of the Western manner of dealing with the concept of time, Whorf contended that the structure of SAE was such that it violated the scheme of nature. SAE was prone to "objectify" or "reify" what in the case of "time" is a flowing reality, a sense of "getting later." For example, when I say "I have been working on *America Reflected* for ten months," I have created false "metaphorical aggregates." As Whorf explained the situation, our actual perception of the passage of time involves in part the direct, present experience, and, in part, the memory of past experiences, but it never involves "ten months." This latter expression, according to Whorf, "Must be [regarded]...as an imaginary mentally constructed group" (Carroll 139). Westerners make this artificial analysis of nature, because they use "perceptible spatial aggregates" (for example, "ten men over there") and extend them to cover the verbalization of "metaphorical aggregates" (as in my example, "ten months"). The result was that "A length of time is envisioned as a row of similar units, like a row of bottles" (140).

The linguistic patterns of SAE led the Western mind to misconceive another significant category of physics. Physical "matter" or "substance" becomes a part of our background assumptions because of the manner in which we manipulate mass nouns. Because our mass nouns are so unwieldy, we are led to a hypostatization similar to that which was made with respect to the crucial concept, "TIME" (Carroll 141). Whorf ridicules "our whole scheme of OBJECTIFYING imaginatively spatializing qualities and potentials that are quite nonspatial" in a razor-sharp *reductio ad absurdum*: "I 'grasp' the 'thread' of another's arguments, but if its 'level' is 'over my head' my attention may 'wander' and 'lose touch' with the 'drift' of it, so that when he 'comes' to his 'point' we differ 'widely,' our views' being indeed so 'far apart' that the 'things' he says 'appear' 'much' too arbitrary, or even 'a lot' of nonsense!" (146). This impulse to push the Western mind off its pedestal was not peripheral to Whorf's concerns, as any reader of *The Ruler of the Universe* will know. His argument gradually works its way to a protest against the constricting bonds that have been imposed on consciousness by the Western cryptotype of binomialism and the resulting objectification. The intuitive wisdom of the ages (religious wisdom, of course, figuring large in this inheritance) has been ignored by the West because of built-in linguistic resistances. The "revelations" of relativity physics have called the omniscience of the Newtonian system into question, and a reassessment of the basic concepts of the Western mind is in order:

> Monistic, holistic, and relativistic views of reality appeal to philosophers and some scientists, but they are badly handicapped in appealing to the "common sense" of the Western average man—not because nature herself refutes them (if she did philosophers could have discovered this much), but because they must be talked about in what amounts to a new language. "Common sense" as its name shows, and "practicality" as its name does not show, are largely matters of talking so that one is readily understood. It is sometimes stated that Newtonian space, time, and matter are sensed by everyone intuitively, whereupon relativity is cited as showing how mathematical analysis can prove intuition wrong. This...laying the blame upon intuition for our slowness in discovering mysteries of the Cosmos, such as relativity, is... wrong....The answer is: Newtonian space, time, and matter are not intuitions. They are recepts from culture and language. That is where Newton got them. (152-53)

Given his dual insights into the related issues of linguistic structure and physics, Whorf's conclusion is that the Western mind must seek new means of articulation: "But what lies outside this spiral? Science is beginning to find that there is something in the Cosmos that is not in accord with the concepts we have formed in mounting

The Whorf Hypothesis

the spiral. It is trying to frame a NEW LANGUAGE by which to adjust itself to a wider audience" (154).

Before we can adequately understand the qualities which make Hopi a superior language to SAE, we must recall Whorf's fascination with the implications of the so-called "crisis of modern physics." Viewing the breakthrough which precipitated the "crisis of modern physics" as a linguist rather than as a chemist or physicist, Whorf was more impressed by the importance of linguistic factors than with the accumulation of new facts: "the new facts themselves of course have been many and weighty; but, more important still, the realms of research where they appear...have been marked to an unprecedented degree by radically new concepts, by a failure to fit the world view that passed unchallenged in the great classical period of science" (Carroll 220). Whorf concluded that the breakthroughs in modern physics should help us to understand that the West's way of describing the universe was only one among many equally valid modes: "Just as it is possible to have any number of geometries other than the Euclidean which give an equally perfect account of space configurations, so it is possible to have descriptions of the universe, all equally valid, that do not contain our familiar contrasts of time and space. The relativity viewpoint of modern physics is one such view, conceived in mathematical terms, and the Hopi *weltanschauung* is another and quite different one, nonmathematical and linguistic" (58). The assumption which holds Whorf's theoretical scheme together is that "language does

Hopi Kachinas

in a cruder but also in a broader and more versatile way the same thing that science does" (55). Such a statement of the parity of language and science as organizers of experience leads back to the importance of the covert categories deeply embedded in language.

What the Hopi See and Feel

It is properly at this moment that we can commence our explanation of the means by which the language of the Hopi Indians assisted them in achieving a clearer perception of those basic concepts "time," "matter" and "space," which had been so recently clarified for Westerners by the new physics. The Hopi language was far less prone than SAE to violate the wholeness and energism of the physical world as revealed by the new physics. Rather than wrenching the universe into substances and actors, the Hopi language brought into play subtle mechanisms such as "tensors," "aspects" and "validity forms." In addition to avoiding this pitfall on the physical plane, Hopi had a uniquely accurate way of dealing both with "time," and the mind's subjective relationship with the world—means from which the Western mind was totally debarred in an age when science had arrogated to itself the right to be the only legitimate form of knowledge.

Unlike the Western mind, the Hopi mind could commune with the pervasive forces of the universe in an enviably poetic way. It is not surprising, considering Whorf's ever present concern with the new physics, that he speaks of the process as one of "Events (or better, eventing)" and described objects as "manifesting" themselves. This is the language of the new physics, with its focus upon the quantum renewal of physically stable objects and its interest in the atom as an electrical energy unit: "The Hopi microcosm seems to have analyzed reality largely in terms of EVENTS (or better, eventing) referred to in two ways, objective and subjective. Objectively, and only if perceptible physical experience, events are expressed mainly as outlines, colors, movements, and other perceptible reports. Subjectively, for both physical and nonphysical events are considered the expression of invisible intensity factors, on which depend their stability and persistence, or their fugitiveness and proclivities" (Carroll 147).

Because SAE objectified "time" into units "like bottles in a row," it was amenable to a system of three tenses: past, present and future. The Hopi speakers were more fortunate: "The duties of our three-tense system and its tripartite linear objectified 'time' are distributed among various verb categories, all different from our tenses; and there is no more basis for an objectified time in Hopi verbs than in other Hopi patterns; although this does not in the least hinder the verb forms and other patterns from being closely adjusted to the pertinent realities of actual situations" (Carroll 147).

In dealing with another crucial category, "matter," or "substance," Hopi was free from the tortuous linguistic structure which in SAE was created by the existence of "a binomial that splits the reference into a formless item plus a form" (141). As with the concept of "time," the special manner with which the Hopi language organized the concept of "matter" fit directly into Whorf's persistent contrast between the old and new physics. While the "aspects," "voices" and "tensors" had the negative virtue of avoiding the suggestion of analogies for an imaginary space in which objects sit, they also had the positive ability to convey properly the energetic qualities of firm objects which quantum mechanics had so recently discovered. In fact, the Hopi seem to speak of the primary physical world in the language of Planck and Schrödinger: "our 'matter' is the physical subtype of 'substance' or 'stuff' which is conceived as the formless extensional item that must be joined with form before there can be real existence. In Hopi there seems to be nothing corresponding to it; there are no formless extensional items; existence may or may not have form, but what it also has, with or without form, is intensity and duration, these being nonextensional and at bottom the same" (Carroll 158).

The facility of Hopi for dealing with emotional and spiritual factors seemed to attract Whorf even more than did its nimbleness in handling the vibratile phenomena of the new physics. Here we begin to see how Whorf wed his scientific to his religious thinking. Not only did Hopi operate in its "objective" plane to describe physical occurrences without interjecting linguistic categories, but it also freed the wellsprings of the human soul to rush forth and mix with the larger forces in the universe. In his description of the development of the "subjective" element in the Hopi language,

Whorf, a scientific linguist, was providing a structured route for the traditional oceanic feelings of mysticism. The "subjective" or "manifesting" dimension of the Hopi language not only related to our concepts of "time" and "matter," it bound the human spirit within the circle of these aspects of reality, and thus reunites spirit and matter which are isolated in separate categories by the Western mind: "The subjective or manifesting comprises all that we call the future, BUT NOT MERELY THIS: it includes equally and indistinguishably all that we call mental-everything that appears or exists in the mind, or, as the Hopi would prefer to say, in the HEART, not only the heart of man, but the heart of animals, plants, and things, and behind and within all the forms and appearances of nature, in the heart of nature, and by an implication and extension which has been felt by more than one anthropologist, yet would hardly ever be spoken of by a Hopi himself, so charged is the idea with religious and magical awesomeness, in the very heart of the Cosmos itself" (Carroll 59).

We know how impressed D. H. Lawrence was by the subjective richness of the Hopi culture. Lawrence saw in the Hopi religion an emblem of his own drive toward unification of the blood with matter, a unification which eliminated the intellectual self-consciousness nurtured by Western culture. Whorf's interpretation, growing as it did out of his Christian background, plus certain Theosophical accretions, was closer to what we would call "prayer." In Whorf's eyes, what for the modern man was a private state of impotent urgency was converted by the religious Hopi into a transcendental unification of the private spirit with forces of the universe. Whorf's explanation of the centrality of this spiritual impulse of the Hopi culture was all the more revealing in the light of those characteristics which he singled out as imperfections of the Western world view. Where Lawrence used the Hopi in his war against the intellect, it is obvious that Whorf was using the emotive intensity of the Hopi culture to combat a cultural manifestation of intellect, science: "Every language contains terms that have come to attain cosmic scope of reference, that crystallize in themselves the basic postulates of an unformulated philosophy, in which is couched the thought of a people, a culture, a civilization, even of an era. Such are our words 'reality,' 'substance,' 'matter,' 'cause' such a term in Hopi is the word most often translated *'hope' tunatya*. It refers to the state of the subjective, unmanifest, vital and causal aspect of the Cosmos, and the fermenting activity toward fruition and manifestation with which it seethes—an action of HOPING; i.e. mental-causal activity, which is forever pressing upon and into the manifested realm" (Carroll 61-62).

Especially after his exposure to Theosophy (as explained by Max Müller), Whorf was fascinated by the Hopi linkage between man's emotions with the physical universe. At times, he was so fascinated that he made an outright defense of such Hopi schemes, not merely as justifiable within the Hopi world view, but as legitimate in an objective sense. Because they believed in the power of Hope, the Hopi stress "inner preparing" which "is use of prayer and meditation, and at lesser intensity good wishes and good will, to further desired results. Hopi attitudes stress the power of desire and thought....Moreover, to the Hopi, one's desires and thoughts influence not only his own actions, but all nature's as well" (149). Up to this point in the passage, Whorf was speaking as a subtle and discerning anthropological linguist. However, he then went on to make certain generalizations which (as in his earlier reflections of "time") seem to link Whorf with the Hopi on the ultimate philosophical issue involved:

> This is wholly natural. Consciousness itself is aware of work, of the feel of effort and energy, in desire and thinking. Experience more basic than language tells us that, if energy is expended, efforts are produced. We tend to believe that our bodies can stop up this energy, prevent it from affecting other things until we will our BODIES to overt action. But this may be so only because we have our own linguistic basis for a theory that formless items like "matter" are things in themselves malleable only by similar things, by more matter, and hence insulated from the powers of life and thought. It is no more unnatural to think that thought contacts everything and pervades the universe than to think, as we all do, that light kindled outdoors does this. And it is not unnatural to suppose that thought, like any other force, leaves everywhere traces of effect. (Carroll 149)

After demonstrating in specific terms Hopi's superiority as both a scientific and religious language, Whorf stepped back to generalize about the resulting attitude of the Hopi civilization toward the mysteries of the universe. *The Ruler of the Universe* (his unsuccessful novel discussed in Chapter 7) had described with lurid detail how the Western mind had perverted the active forces in nature. In the novel, however, man's immersion in original sin had been seen as the root cause of his perversity. In these later articles on language, Whorf's critique of SAE forms a basis for a somewhat different criticism: the "binomialism" which has shaped Western conceptions of "matter" and "time" has also inured Western man to the depths of mystery which surround him. Using field reports from his casebook as an industrial fire insurance inspector, Whorf sought to prove how insensitive Western man had become. Our rigid language structure has helped us to establish a sense of "routine" and has blinded us to the vast mysteries of time and space. Our language has also given us an inordinate capacity to manipulate intellectual concepts and material objects. But the West has been forced to pay a high price for its special powers in the form of emotional poverty and an almost complete loss of a poetic-religious sense of wonder.

In contrast, the Hopi culture has preserved a relationship between man and nature (as well as between man and man) which serves as a pointed contrast to society described by *The Ruler of the Universe:*

> In Hopi history...we...find a different type of language and a different set of cultural and environmental influences working together. A peaceful agricultural society isolated by geographic features and nomad enemies in a land of scanty rainfall, arid agriculture that could be made successful only by the utmost perseverance (hence the value of persistence and repetition), necessity for collaborations (hence emphasis on the psychology of teamwork and on mental factors in general), corn and rain as primary criteria of value, need of extensive PREPARATIONS and precautions to assure crops in the poor soil and precarious climate, keen realization of dependence upon nature favoring prayer and a religious

attitude toward the forces of nature, especially prayer and religion directed toward the ever-needed blessing, rain—these things interact with Hopi linguistic patterns to mold them, to be molded again by them, and so little by little to shape the Hopi world-outlook. (Carroll 157)

The Hopi *Weltanschauung* which Whorf described certainly contrasted vividly with that determined by the language and culture of the West. The Hopi was always in contact with the primary processes of nature, and was thus not capable of the brutalization which Western man has repeatedly displayed in his use of science and technology to find ever more efficient weapons. The Hopi language's strong subjective dimension (which, significantly, does not interfere with Hopi "science") seemed to provide a channel through which the social and transcendental affections could flow without the kind of conflicts which constantly confront the believer and the poet in an age of science.

Benjamin Lee Whorf: Engineer, Linguist, and Visionary

In his last four famous articles, Whorf mustered his contrastive studies to condemn the poverty of the Western spirit, and to link that poverty to the tyranny of science. In the first three articles ("Science and Linguistics," "Linguistics as an Exact Science," "Languages and Logic") he assembled the various critiques which we have discussed. In addition to attacking science, Whorf emphasized the leadership role which linguists must assume for Western science to progress. Given our understanding of Whorf's preoccupation with the conflict between science and religion, we can see the rhetorical significance of the corollary which Whorf drew from his linguistic relativity hypothesis. This corollary is that "From each unformulated and naive world view an explicit scientific world view may arise by a higher specialization of the same basic grammatical patterns that fathered the naive and implicit view. The world view of modern science arises by higher specialization of the basic grammar of the Western Indo-European language." Whorf argued that really significant breakthroughs of the foreseeable future would depend upon our capacity to create new languages with which to think and say new things about the external world (Carroll 220).

Whorf believed that the Western mind could not increase its perceptual capacities by sharpening and polishing its traditional logic. Instead, it must reach out (as it were, paradoxically, *around* the principle of linguistic relativity) for the exotic means of organizing experience which have been developed by non-Western peoples: "Western culture has made, through language, a provisional analysis of reality, and, without correctives, holds resolutely to that analysis as final. The *only* correctives lie in all those other tongues which by eons of independent evolution have arrived at different, but equally logical, provisional analyses" (Carroll 336).

The nature of Whorf's scientifically trained audience in the *Technology Review* series forced him to follow a tack which was tight and close to the prevailing wind of scientific opinion. In his final article, "Language, Mind, and Reality," the engineer/linguist/visionary made it clear that his new audience, because it consisted of Theosophists, invited him to open his imaginative sails to run free on a breezy spiritualist course. In this final article, the modern-day Transcendentalist united his religious and scientific passions in a sophisticated and culminative way. (For discussion of Transcendentalism, see Chapter 27.) Gone were the apocalyptic visions of retribution wrought upon the world by a vindictive God. In their place was a vision which provided for balancing intellect with emotion, science with piety — what an earlier New Englander who despaired of such a balance symbolized in a contrast between the Dynamo and the Virgin. Shortly before his untimely death at the age of 44, Benjamin Lee Whorf resolved the pressing demands of these contrary forces. In doing so, we might note, he speaks more like the Transcendentalist Emerson than the representative modern, Henry Adams:

> Yoga is defined by Patanjali as the complete cessation of the activity of the versatile psychic nature. We have seen that this activity consists largely of personal-social reactions along unperceived tracks of pattern laid down from the *Arupa* level functioning above or behind the focus of personal consciousness. The reason why the *Arupa* level is beyond the ken of consciousness is not because it is essentially

different (as it were *e.g.,* a passive network) but because the personality does focus, from evolution and habit, upon the aforesaid versatile activity. The stilling of this activity and the coming to rest of this focus, though difficult and requiring prolonged training, is by reliable accounts from widely diverse sources, both Eastern and Western, a tremendous expansion, brightening, and clarifying of consciousness, in which the intellect functions with undreamed-of rapidity and sureness. The scientific study of languages and linguistic principles is at least a partial raising of the intellect toward this level. (Carroll 268-69)

Discussion of Literature

Whorf's interest in the occult as a substitute for traditional Christianity was not as insular as it might at first appear. For an autobiography describing such a conversion to Theosophy by a man who (conveniently) was a spiritual mentor to Whorf, see Bragdon. For a discussion of the attractions and beliefs of occultism in an age of science, see Galbreath.

Readers familiar with discussions of the Sapir-Whorf relationship will recognize that my conclusion that Sapir became ever more suspicious of the kind of typological analysis of cultures that we find in Whorf's last articles is at variance with most of the literature on the subject. For an extended attempt to explain why Sapir turned away from broad cultural configurations to focus upon individual perceivers, see Chapter 8. For Sapir's discussion of how individual personalities learn to adapt to the cultural patterns presented to them by their societies, and the problems associated with such an investigation, see "The Emergence of the Concept of Personality in a Study of Cultures," "Why Cultural Anthropology Needs the Psychiatrist," "Psychiatric and Cultural Pitfalls in the Business of Getting a Living," "Culture, Genuine and Spurious" in Mandelbaum.

Finally, in Whorf's day, the *Technology Review* aspired to be an intellectual clearinghouse as well as M.I.T.'s alumni magazine. Whorf's last famous article, "Language, Mind, and Reality," was first printed in the *Theosophist*, the official journal of the Theosophical Society, Madras, India. His arguments in his *Technology Review* series ("Science and Linguistics," "Linguistics as an Exact Science," "Languages and Logic") and in "Language, Mind, and Reality" follow the same lines, but the difference in audiences invited a different rhetorical approach. In the *Theosophist*, Whorf was free to speak his mind.

Works Cited

Boas, Franz. *The Mind of Primitive Man*. 1911. New York: MacMillan, 1938.
Bragdon, Claude. *More Lives Than One*. New York: Knopf, 1938.
Carroll, John B., ed. *Language, Thought, and Reality: Selected Writings of Benjamin Lee Whorf*. Cambridge: MIT Press, 1964.
Galbreath, Robert, ed. *The Occult: Studies and Evaluations*. Bowling Green, Ohio: Bowling Green UP, 1972.
Hoijer, Harry, ed. *Language in Culture: Conference on the Interrelations of Language and Other Aspects of Culture*. Chicago: U of Chicago P, 1954.
Hymes, Dell. "Linguistic Method in Ethonography: Its Development in the United States." *Method and Theory in Linguistics* Ed. Paul Harvin. The Hague: Mouton, 1970. 250-325.
Mandelbaum, David G. *Selected Writings of Edward Sapir on Language, Culture, and Personality*. Berkeley: U of California P, 1968.
Müller, F. Max. *The Science of Thought*. London: Longmans Green and Co., 1887.
—. *Theosophy: or, Psychological Religion*. London: Longmans Green and Co., 1893.
Whorf, Benjamin Lee. *Collected Papers on Metalinquistics*. Foreign Service Institute. Dept. of State, Washington, D.C.: GPO, 1952.
—. *The Ruler of the Universe. The Benjamin Lee Whorf Legacy CD-ROM*. Ed. Peter C. Rollins. Cleveland, OK: Ridgemont Media Productions, 2008.

Part II

America's Wars: Film Images and Historical Realities

World War I

10
Memories of War: Was World War I a Heroic Crusade or a Traumatic Nightmare?

On August 30, 1993, a number of the nearly 48,000 living American veterans of World War I convened near Chicago to reflect on their experiences and heritage. Most stand in awe of the changes accelerated by the Great War. Winston Roche, a 94-year-old citizen of Dallas, reflected on the panorama: "We made America a world power. We saw America from the days of horses and mules, handguns, a few machine guns, and a few outdated field-pieces, all the way to jet fighters and the moon landing. We have lived in a wonderful generation of American history" (Rollins "Memories" 221).

The experience of battle gave many a new perspective on life. Speaking for many veterans from the Civil War to Vietnam, 93-year-old Orville Rummell observed, "It put a different value on what you did, how you did it, how you enjoyed what you got, how you lived each day" (Rollins "Memories" 221). But not every veteran emerged from the war in philosophical calm. An Oklahoma veteran spoke to me about his sense of long-term guilt. As a machine gunner, he had killed hundreds of young German soldiers. Speaking in faltering tones as if the experience had happened yesterday, this veteran sat on the edge of his bed, crying throughout our interview. On the eve of the seventy-fifth anniversary of the Armistice, he was worried about the fate of his eternal soul.

Among the literature, films, and war memorials connected with World War I, there are two contradictory ways of remembering the Great War. Veterans, monuments, and movies have promoted the heroic version and have celebrated the unselfish service of our

Movement to Contact in *The Big Parade* (1925)

fighting men; in contrast, some veterans, artists, writers, and filmmakers have argued that the war needlessly sacrificed the youth of a generation. Even today, both angles of vision survive.

"He Fights for You"

In the 1920s, Hollywood contributed to the heroic image. King Vidor's *The Big Parade* (1925) was the first financially successful film about the conflict. The famous battle scenes reenacted 1918 American actions in the Meuse-Argonne forests. The title does not refer to a military ceremony, but to the ineluctable march of America's troops to victory on the Western Front. When the doughboys fight and die in this film, they do so as democratic heroes for their nation's cause.

In *Wings* (1927), William Wellman followed the evolution of two aviators from their first days of flight training. Wellman had been a pilot in the war and sought to make the Army Air Corps look every bit as romantic as the Army infantry had in *The Big Parade*. The War Department provided a cast of thousands for a film that, even with government help, cost over $2 million. No expense was spared; for example, the reenactment of the 1918 St. Mihiel offensive cost Paramount over $250,000. All aerial duels were filmed aloft with cameras mounted on the planes.

Distributed soon after Charles Lindbergh crossed the Atlantic, *Wings* exploited America's fascination with aviation. Indeed, Lindbergh, through written titles, dedicated the film "to those young warriors of the sky whose wings are folded about them forever." America's young pilots could have had no memorial more heroic than this monument in celluloid. It should come as no surprise that *Wings* still rents well in video stores across the nation.

A week after the WWI Armistice was signed, the service newspaper *Stars and Stripes* carried a poem titled "Your Soldier," which prefigured the heroic themes of *The Big Parade* and *Wings*:

> It is for you.
> > Through endless nights
> > Of mud and rain he stubbornly
> > Plods on, head down, back bent beneath
> > His pack—on towards the shell-streaked sky
> > And maddening roar where truth and lies
> > And love and hate and life and death
> > All meet in war, red war! He loves
> > And hates, and so he fights. To all
> > His love be true. Guard well your heart
> > And keep the faith. He fights for you!

The anonymous author captured the proud spirit of the warrior's self-image.

Welcome Home, Unknown Soldier

A year after the May 1919 signing of the Versailles Treaty, the English buried their unknown soldier in Westminster Abbey and the French buried theirs beneath the *Arc de Triomphe*. On November 11, 1921, then known as Armistice Day, America's Unknown Soldier was buried with elaborate ceremony on the highest knoll of the Arlington National Cemetery. In one of the first nationwide radio broadcasts, President Harding tried to focus America's thoughts on current issues of war and peace. (The ceremony was taking place one day before the Washington Arms Limitation Conference.) At Arlington, however, the retrospective view prevailed. Secretary of

War Newton Baker emphasized the symbolic importance of the tomb in terms of national memory: "In the long run of history the names of individuals fade, but the great movements which have been inspired and defended by the mass of virtue, which we call the national spirit, remain as solid achievements and mark the advance which civilization attains." (Later, author John Dos Passos would draw different lessons from the ceremonies associated with the tomb.)

The tomb of 1921 has since become the tombs: here rest the Unknown Soldier of World War I, the Unknown American Serviceman of World War II, the Unknown Serviceman of the Korean War, and the Unknown Serviceman of the Vietnam era. Located on a plaza down the steps from the Arlington Memorial amphitheater, this hallowed place is guarded twenty-four hours a day by members of the First Battalion, Third Infantry, U.S. Army. On Memorial Day, 1993, President Bill Clinton spoke at the ceremonies in an attempt to render a former antiwar protester's gesture of respect to the mar-

Tomb of the Unknown

tial spirit. On the Inauguration morning in 2009, Barack Obama, the president elect and his vice president, Joe Biden, placed a wreath at the tomb in anticipation of decisions about troop commitments in Iraq and Afghanistan.

"The Spirit of the American Doughboy" (1920)

Popular outside of Washington has been a heroic statue called "The Spirit of the American Doughboy." Designed by Ernest Viquesney of Indiana and copyrighted in 1920, the metal statue depicts an American infantryman in the act of crossing no-man's-land (evidenced by tree stumps and some barbed wire at his feet). Ready for battle, the doughboy holds in his left had his trusty Springfield rifle, its characteristically long bayonet parallel to the ground. His right hand is aloft in the act of throwing a hand grenade in the direction of the German trenches. He wears a full cartridge belt around his waist; a gas mask pouch hangs from his neck. This heroic representation seems to have been inspired by a statue of Mercury by

The Heroic Version of WWI

Giovanni Bologna, now in the Louvre. (Mercury's hands are doing similar things; all that is needed is a set of fatigues, a gas mask, and a slightly more martial stride.) T. Perry Wesley, editor emeritus of Spencer, Indiana's local paper, is the world's expert on the Doughboy; he estimates that there are at least 150 such statues scattered around the country in at least thirty-two states.

To promote the statue, Viquesney sent out twelve-inch models to commanders of Legion posts: "In the early days, the copper sheet statue was about $1,000 whereas cast versions would be in the $9,000-11,000 range. Ground preparations, base, plaques, of course, would be additional." Clearly, Viquesney's Doughboy touched the American imagination at a mythic level, updating Mercury as a heroic Everyman. Yet, old-fashioned salesmanship may have contributed to the wide distribution of the statue. Wesley humorously observes that Viquesney "must have been a man who had the talent to sell bikinis in Alaska."

Americans were looking ahead in the 1920s, so the record of memorialization can be summed up by the Tomb of the Unknown Soldier at Arlington Cemetery and the many Doughboy statues across the nation. Perhaps there would have been a broader interest in memorials if there had not been a powerful, competing vision of the war.

World War I as a Meaningless Slaughter

The statistics from the Great War would give anyone nightmares: the Allies (France, England, the United States) reported a total of 2.3 million battle deaths; the Central Powers (Germany, Austria-Hungary) lost some 2.7 million. The machine gun, the tank, poison gas, the airplane, barbed wire, and the submarine thrust mechanization into a horse-and-buggy era. The dimensions of the nightmare were registered as early as the Battle of the Somme in 1916, a six-month struggle described by S. L. A. Marshall as "the most soulless battle in British annals.... It was a battle not so much of attrition as of mutual destruction" (260). A feature-length documentary called *The Battle of the Somme* was released in late summer of 1916. According to Paul Fussell, by this time the war had become "a hideous embarrassment to the prevailing Meliorist myth which had dominated the public consciousness for a century. It reversed the Idea of Progress"(8).

A "Lost Generation" and Its Memory of War

After Versailles, a host of exposés convinced many Americans that their country had been pulled into a European conflict that was not their business. George Creel described his role retrospectively in *How We Advertised America* (1920). Creel had been America's chief propagandist and a bit too gleefully explained how carefully orchestrated media blitzes had mobilized public support. Walter Lippmann's *Public Opinion* (1922) voiced a more sardonic evaluation of what he called "the myth of the omnicompetent citizen." Lippmann advised the nation to give up its traditional notion of democracy, believing America would be better served by a government of expert-professionals who were not susceptible to the wiles of propaganda. Within this context, Erich Maria Remarque's *All Quiet on the Western Front* (1929) crystallized an existing disillusionment. The protagonist, Paul Baumer, enters the struggle as an idealist, but months of shelling and death convince him that "when it comes to dying for your country, it is better not to die at all"(122). Some critics scrutinized Remarque's war record in an attempt to challenge the book's authenticity, but no one could deny that the German author had captured the mood of a "lost generation."

Fussell claims that the imagery of postwar writing came directly from the battlefront: "The rats' alleys, dull canals, and dead men who have lost their bones of T.S. Eliot's *Waste Land* and the "Valley of Ashes" in *The Great Gatsby* are only a few images that would spring to consciousness after the war to represent not just the war, but the postwar world"(22). Hemingway protagonist Frederic Henry spoke for late-twenties Americans when he rejected wartime shibboleths in *A Farewell to Arms*: "I was always embarrassed by the words sacred, glorious, and sacrifice and the expression in vain.... I had seen nothing sacred, and the things that were glorious had no glory and the sacrifices were like the stockyards in Chicago if nothing was done with the meat except to bury it" (66).

Hemingway would turn this kind of alienation into a stoic "code," a pose after which Americans—including a fictional detective named Sam Spade—would model themselves.

Lewis Milestone's screen adaptation of *All Quiet on the Western Front* (1930) shared the nightmare vision with mass audiences across the globe. During a famous battle segment, Paul Baumer

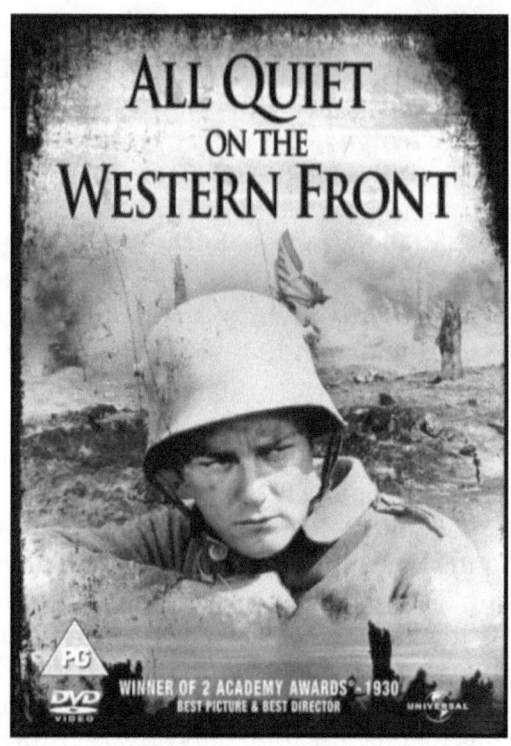

Nightmare on the Western Front

finds himself trapped overnight in a muddy shell crater with a dead French soldier. As a result, Baumer—and presumably the audience—come to realize that the world's little people are victims of bureaucracy, the nation-state, industrialism, and "progress." The fact that the film won Academy awards for Best Picture and Best Director was a sign that the nightmare vision was (temporarily) *au courant* in Hollywood. In Germany, Nazis under Joseph Goebbels first disrupted screenings of the "American propaganda" and then found legislative methods to prevent distribution. By 1933, Remarque's antiheroic books were being burned by the Third Reich.

In volume two of his epic work of fiction, *USA,* John Dos Passos addressed the meaning of World War I in terms of the burial ceremony for the Unknown Soldier. "The Body of an American" can serve as an example of the dark retrospection:

In the tarpaper morgue at Chalons-sur-Marne in the reek of chloride of lime and the dead, they picked out the pine box that held all that was left of

    enie menie minie mo plenty other pine boxes stacked up there containing what they'd scraped up of Richard Roe

    and other person or persons unknown...

    ...and Mr. Harding prayed to God and the diplomats and the generals and the admirals and the brasshats and the politicians and the handsomely dressed ladies out of the society column of the *Washington Post* stood up solemn

    and thought how beautiful sad Old Glory God's Country it was to have the bugler play taps and the three volleys made their ears ring.

    ...Woodrow Wilson brought a bouquet of poppies. (462-463)

Dos Passos had been to the war. As he looked back from the vantage point of 1932, he saw—in the symbolic return of America's first Unknown Soldier in 1921—only pain and political manipulation.

The Utopianism of *The Grand Illusion* (1939)

The Grand Illusion, directed by Jean Renoir and released just before Germany's 1939 attack on Poland, ranks with *All Quiet on the Western Front* as one of the most prominent antiwar films of the decade. As the story unfolds in a World War I prisoner of war camp, it argues that the nation-state has become an archaic institution that creates more problems than it solves; indeed, the film teaches that patriotism is a "grand illusion" plaguing society. As one major character exclaims, "Nature all looks alike. Frontiers are an invention of man!"

At the end of the film, two prisoners—now comrades in search of a brave new world—escape from the prison camp. Unfortunately, Renoir gives no specific idea about what kind of alternative society will be found on the other side of the mountains. Like Mark Twain's *Adventures of Huckleberry Finn* (1884), *The Grand Illusion* is better at decrying existing conditions than exploring realistic alternatives.

The Heroic Version of WWI Returns—In the Nick of Time

The cynical version of World War I was wheeled off the set as World War II approached. Louis de Rochemont produced a feature-length docudrama titled *The Ramparts We Watch* in 1940. A plea for military preparedness, the film tried to establish parallels between World War I and the coming conflict. Fast-moving events in Poland and France reinforced lessons about unpreparedness. Through the expert, *March of Time*-style use of newsreel footage, de Rochemont espoused the view that Americans needed to stop watching from their protected ramparts and should start building their own war machine so they would not be caught off guard again.

In 1941, Warner Bros. came forward with *Sergeant York*, the landmark picture for a new American mood. Alvin York was a Tennessee boy who killed twenty-five Germans at Argonne and captured another 132—a spectacular feat on any battlefield. For these exploits, York was awarded a host of medals including the Congressional Medal of Honor. Director Howard Hawks took this story about a man of natural virtue and exploited it to expose the flaws of isolationism. York's "conversion" scene (York was drafted

The Conversion of Alvin York

after being denied status as a conscientious objector) was aimed directly at those who said we should remain out of the fray. (As late as July 1941, polls showed that this meant 70 percent of Americans.) Here was a spin on the war that flashed back to 1917, when President Woodrow Wilson spoke idealistically about "a war to make the world safe for democracy."

Sometime near the premier of the film, the real Sergeant York—who joined FDR and Warner Bros. in endorsing the film's message about preparedness—called for aid to Britain. As concerned Citizen York, the nation's poster hero explained that Americans must stand up for democracy; if they did not, "then we owe the memory of George Washington an apology, for if we have stopped, then he wasted his time at Valley Forge." In a speech to the Veterans of Foreign Wars, York noted that the last war had been fought to make the world safe for democracy "and it did—for a while." With this statement, the memory of World War I had returned to the heroic stance embodied by Viquesney's "Spirit of the American Doughboy."

Rediscovering the Great War

The 1993 reunion of World War I vets took place near Robert McCormick's estate, Cantigny, under the upbeat rubric or slogan "A Grateful Nation DOES Remember." As a member of General Pershing's staff, McCormick was with the First Army Division in the battle of Cantigny (May 28-29, 1918). The untested American unit lost a thousand soldiers in the attack, but it took and held the objective in the face of counterattacks by some of Germany's most seasoned troops. The outcome was both a moral and military victory for the American doughboys. When McCormick returned to Chicago, he renamed his grandfather's estate in honor of America's first victory in World War I.

For the 1993 event, the McCormick Foundation created a commemorative medal based on the World War I Victory Medal given after the war to every soldier, sailor, and marine. On the front of the medal is a drawing of Nike, the classical Greek messenger of victory. The reverse side of the medal carries an epic inscription borrowed from a battlefield memorial in France: "They Came on the Wings of Eagles." All World War I vets were eligible for the medal, a gesture praised by veterans of World War I in light of this

244 *America Reflected*

The Original Victory Medal, 1919

nation's failure to commemorate the seventy-fifth anniversary of the outbreak of the "war to end all wars." Whether or not they attended the meeting, all World War I vets are entitled to the free medal distributed at Cantigny. (I had the honor of presenting them to three veterans in my home state of Oklahoma.)

Despite this positive gesture, the slogan of the event gives some hint of the dilemma, as it implies that the nation has pretty much forgotten. Yet a world conference on "Film and the First World War," held at the University of Amsterdam in the Netherlands just a month before the Cantigny reunion, revealed that scholars from many disciplines—history, English, communications, film, television, sociology—are just now rediscovering the war as a subject for study. Most scholars agree that World War I marked the end of one vision of the world and the beginning of something new. Although everyone applauds the stamina and vitality of World War I's living veterans, scholars are reconsidering basic interpretations of the events of 1914-18. Was World War I a heroic crusade, or was it a traumatic nightmare? We are beginning to discern that it was both—and more.

CODA: Memories of Other American Conflicts

Korea (1950-1953): Remembering the "Forgotten War"

Directly across the Reflecting Pool from the Vietnam Veterans Memorial is an area called the Ash Woods. There, on July 27, 1995—in conjunction with the forty-second anniversary of the Korean armistice—the Korean War Veterans Memorial will be dedicated, and America will remember its "forgotten war."

Korea will always be America's "coldest war." Through three brutal winters, U.S. troops fought shoulder to shoulder with soldiers from fifteen other members of the United Nations to contain communism. More than 34,000 Americans gave their lives, and more than 100,000 were wounded. During Senate hearings in 1985, Sen. John Glenn (D-Ohio), a former Marine pilot, spoke of his own "mental memorial" to one such soldier, a friend who died trying to direct air support to a target at Chosin Reservoir: "For me, the memorial of remembrance is enough. But I think for others it's not," said Glenn. Despite such personal sacrifices, the postwar reception of veterans was less than heroic. As Sen. William Armstrong (R-Colorado) observed, "When the war was over...there was nothing really in the way of a national time of recognition of the valor and sacrifice of these Americans." (Vietnam veterans justified building the Wall in almost identical language.)

Korean Patrol: "Freedom is not free"

In the design, nineteen freestanding statues are in a double-column formation. Ahead of them up a grassy slope, at the apex of the V-shaped memorial, the American flag waves aloft. Along a walkway a 164-foot etched mural wall will honor the quiet heroism of all support personnel, including nurses, crew chiefs, mechanics, cooks, helmsmen, pilots, tankers, and artillerymen. A special closed area of the Ash Woods behind the flag is designed to remember the nightmarish experience of POW/MIAs, which made brainwashing a household word during the Cold War. A quiet reflecting pool will honor the dead while providing the memorial with a symbol of life and renewal.

Vietnam (1959-1975): The Vietnam Veterans Memorial ("The Wall")

One evening in March 1979, Jan Scruggs went to see *The Deer Hunter*. In one memorable scene, a Vietnam veteran (played by Robert De Niro) lingers on the periphery of his hometown like a stranger, poignantly calling attention to the difficulty facing returning vets. After seeing the film, Scruggs says, he began to dream: "I'm going to build a memorial to all the guys who served in Vietnam. It'll have the names of everyone killed."

The Vietnam Veterans Memorial Fund started to work on a project to honor the 58,000 men and women who died in the first war America has ever lost. Money was raised with the help of Bob Hope and Ross Perot. In the meantime, a competition was launched focusing on the concept of names. The eventual winner, Maya Ying Lin, visited the designated site and was inspired to dig into the land. "It was as if the black-brown earth were polished

Memory on the National Mall

A Poignant Addition to the Memory

and made into an interface between the sunny world and the quiet, dark world beyond that we can't enter," she recalls. Her V-shaped, two-wall design was angled so the west wall pointed toward the Lincoln Memorial and the east wall pointed toward the Washington Monument—as if to tap the geomantic power of these two patriotic landmarks.

Some admired the winning design; others complained that the black marble "gash in the earth" lacked patriotic fervor. After much controversy, a statue by Frederick Hart titled "Three Fighting Men" was added to the site along with a pole from which an American flag flies twenty-four hours a day. The Wall and its additions have become very popular. Using pencils and paper provided on site, visitors make rubbings of cherished names. Although many visitors shed tears at the Wall, most describe their experiences as cathartic. Even President Clinton's controversial visit in June 1993 inspired beneficial discussions; for some, there was a sense that intergenerational antagonisms might be over.

The Vietnam Women's Memorial Project
November 11, 1993, is unveiling day for a trio of bronze figures commemorating the national service of some 11,000 women in

Vietnam. Some 8 military women and an estimated 37 civilian women were killed during the conflict.

Started in 1984, the Vietnam Women's Memorial Project was initially opposed by the Vietnam Veterans Memorial Fund because the Wall had been constructed to "honor the men and women of the armed forces of the United States who served in the Vietnam War." Organizers of the Wall had just recovered from a bitter debate over whether a statue and flagpole should be added to the site; after approval of these final additions, Congress had promised, in law, not to add further embellishments. In 1987, the Fine Arts Commission (the body responsible for the National Mall) voted 4-1 against the project. In 1988, Maya Ying Lin, the young Yale student who designed the Wall, added her testimony. She believed that this would be only the first in a series of proposals by individual units and special branches of the service for literal representation at a monument represented symbolically. (Dead and missing women's names appear on the Wall with the names of servicemen.)

After hearings were held by the Senate in 1988 and powerful appeals had been made by congressmen, senators, and interested parties, the bill to allow this additional—and, once again, final—memorial was approved by the Senate in a vote of 96-1. Supporters of the project argued successfully that "female medical workers in Vietnam bore the intensity and carnage of the war. Thousands died with a nurse beside them—she was the last person many of them saw." The vital role of women simply needed this kind of foregrounding. On November 15, 1989, President Ronald Reagan signed the bill authorizing the Vietnam Women's Memorial.

A design by Glenna Goodacre of Santa Fe, New Mexico, was approved in fall 1991. A concerned nurse tries to comfort a wounded GI in a pose reminiscent of Michelangelo's *Pietà*. Behind them, a standing nurse looks up—perhaps for incoming Hueys bringing more wounded from the battlefield. A third figure kneels as she gathers up the warrior's helmet and gear as part of standard triage procedure. All of the figures are connected in some way to a bronze facsimile of a sandbagged bunker. In contrast with Frederick Hart's approach in *Three Fighting Men*, Goodacre has striven less for realism and more for a pervasive mood of caring.

Works Cited

Dos Passos, John. *Nineteen Nineteen.* New York: Charles Scribner's Sons, 1932.
Fussell, Paul. *The Great War in Modern Memory.* New York: Oxford UP, 1975.
Hemingway, Ernest. *A Farewell to Arms.* 1929. New York: Charles Scribner's Sons, 2003.
Marshall, S.L.A. *World War I.* Boston: Houghton Mifflin, 1964.
Rollins, Peter C. "Memories of War." *The World and I.* 11 Nov 1993: 221-225.

11
Parallels or Continuities in Two Historical Compilation Films: *Goodbye Billy* and *The Frozen War*

> I am saying that there seems to be one dominating form of modern understanding: that it is essentially ironic; that it originates largely in the application of mind and memory to the events of the Great War.
>
> Paul Fussell, *The Great War and Modem Memory*

World War I and Vietnam: Beguiling Parallels or Telluric Continuities?

The most important contribution of Paul Fussell's *The Great War and Modern Memory* (1975) was to identify World War I as a continuing presence in contemporary consciousness. By examining both the belles lettres and popular literature produced by the war-serious poetry and prose of Siegfried Sassoon, Edmund Blunden, and Robert Graves, as well as popular poems, wartime rumors, and trench folklore—Fussell unearthed fundamental notions that originated in the Great War and continue in our time—what I call telluric continuities. Some of these ideas include our loss of innocent faith in establishment culture and politics; our sense that we are victims of history rather than its heroic shapers; our perception that machines and technology do not guarantee progress for the whole of humanity; our frustration that language has been disjoined from truth; and, finally, our reluctant acknowledgement that war is the quintessential expression of twentieth-century civic culture.

Rupert Brooke, "A dust whom England bore"

Certainly Fussell is correct in arguing that the differences between the work of an early war poet such Rupert Brooke (d. 1915) and a surviving postwar poet such as Siegfried Sassoon (d. 1967) register a loss of innocence as do the endless ruminations since World War I about "the future of tragedy."[1] Complaints about the disjuncture of language from thought and from reality were epitomized for the 1920s by Ogden and Richards in *The Meaning of Meaning*.[2] Three generations of readers and two generations of moviegoers know Ernest Hemingway's protagonist in *A Farewell to Arms* (1929), Lieutenant Frederic Henry, learned that "abstract words such as glory, honor, courage or hallow were obscene" while retreating from Caporetto in 1917.[3] Any number of historians would endorse Fussell's conclusion that the Victorian faith in Progress was nullified when the First Battle of the Somme (June-November, 1916) resulted in 1,265,000 casualties.[4] Yet readers of *The Great War and Modern Memory* often miss Fussell's fundamental point: the mental shelling from Flanders Fields to the Italian Alps was not restricted to the immediate postwar era, wounding the spiritual life of a single lost generation. The battlefield traumas and resulting modes of thought still affect us.

Charlie Sheen as Taylor in *Platoon*

Even casual digging for similarities between World War I and Vietnam unearths matching shell fragments. The loss of innocence by American boys in Vietnam is the central theme for most of the novels, personal narratives, and films from the war.[5] From the perspective of popular culture, the loss of innocence was driven home by a hit song, "19"—the title refers to the average age of the combat soldier in Vietnam. The perversity of language was a constant issue in the 1960s. Cynicism about official pronouncements was revealed in flipflop expressions such as "the Saigon Follies" (used sarcastically to describe daily press briefings in Saigon); "hearts and minds" (used by President Johnson in a serious way, but in 1974 reinterpreted by filmmaker Peter Davis to mean America's insensitivity to Vietnamese culture); "free fire zone" (used by the Army to describe an area clear of civilians, but perversely transformed by antiwar activists to [falsely] describe how American troops shot anybody anywhere). Nearly 40 percent of Noam Chomsky's *American Power and the New Mandarins* (1969) is devoted to debunking the language of social scientists who thrived on war-related projects—further evidence to support Fussell's concerns about the duplicities of language in our time. Junior officer Philip Caputo, in *A Rumor of War* (1977), repeatedly cites Wilfred Owen and Siegfried Sassoon in comradely homage to the Great War's trench poets. In Vietnam, devotees of President Kennedy's "New Frontier" found themselves bogged down in a noxious quagmire, sinking deep into what Pete Seeger satirized in song as "The Great Muddy."

With all of these thematic parallels between World War I and Vietnam, how could Cadre Films conduct their historical reconnaissance without wandering along some well-trodden paths? In Fussell's own language, the cinematic exploration of World War I brought the makers of *Goodbye Billy: America Goes to War, 1917-18* (1971) and *The Frozen War: America Intervenes in Russia, 1918-20* (1973) into contact with at least five major themes of "our own buried lives" (335).[6] What they explored were more than beguiling parallels with their own times, the 1960s; they dramatized themes with telluric continuities reaching back to the Battle of the Somme in 1916.

Capturing the "Lost Generation" Mood: *Goodbye Billy: America Goes to War, 1917-18*

Goodbye Billy's title gives some idea of the duality of this historical compilation film's approach. The second half of the title refers to the way in which the film focuses on the moods of the American nation as it evolved through three discernible emotional stages

Birth of a Lost Generation

during the Great War. In the opening ten minutes, *Goodbye Billy* evokes the innocent spirit of American enthusiasm as the country prepares to fight another "splendid little war." During the second third of the film, the experience becomes more complex: aural and visual elements are juxtaposed to reflect the confusion Americans felt once they confronted the realities of war. The final segment of *Goodbye Billy* further exploits the tool of cinematic irony to conjure up the post-war *angst* of a lost generation.[7]

To convey these three phases of the national mood, Cadre Films avoids using a didactic narrative and instead creates rapid juxtapositions of images and sounds, employing what Sergei Eisenstein called collision montage. Early in part one, sheep graze on the White House lawn; this shot from archival footage is followed by a shot of Woodrow Wilson looking out a window. Later, in part two of the film, the same shot of Wilson is juxtaposed with a shot of troops climbing out of trenches and trudging off into no man's land like "lambs to the slaughter." Halfway into part one, there is a particularly clever use of sight-sound irony. Charles W. Eliot, president emeritus of Harvard University, condemns German militarism aurally; the juxtaposed visuals contradict the statement by showing an American patriotic society (the Knights Templar) in elaborate military regalia as they parade along New York City's Central Park West. In the final segment of the film, the New York Philharmonic Orchestra plays Charles Ives haunting "Unanswered Question" while two portions in the soundtrack vie for attention. In the aural foreground, a young voice reads from the last chapter of John Dos Passos's novel *1919*, a chapter entitled "The Body of an American." In the background is President Warren G. Harding speaking at the grave of the Unknown Soldier. The implication is that a generation gap has opened. Young people, divested of faith, must now make their way through a cynical, postwar world.

While the nation passes through moods of optimism, confusion, and despair, the representative soldier, Billy, has his own story. He has a caring mother, a proud father, and a fiancée who becomes increasingly anxious he will be gone "for a long, long time." At the opening of the war, Billy shares in the war fever, but the reality of battle alters his view. While the protected civilians back home are still beating the drums of war with blind enthusiasm, he witnesses the horrendous impact of technology. Despite his efforts to maintain morale through horseplay and desperate, black humor, his spirits decline as the war "progresses"; finally, after he is slaughtered like an animal, he is brought back to become the nation's Unknown Soldier. While his family and fiancée mourn for Billy, politicians use him—even in death—as a symbol to justify their war. Like Billy Pilgrim of George Roy Hill's film, *Slaughterhouse Five* (1972), the protagonist of *Goodbye Billy* is the consummate victim of the war machine.[8]

Vietnam on the White Sea: *The Frozen War: America Intervenes in Russia*, 1918-20

As the last American combat troops were leaving the Republic of South Vietnam, Cadre Films came forward with a follow-up to *Goodbye Billy*. In 1918, an American Expeditionary Force (AEF) was ordered to land at Vladivostok, Russia. Concurrently, a second force was dispatched to the Russian city of Archangel, another major Russian port on the White Sea, and some six thousand miles away from Vladivostok. Some said the ten thousand troops were there to protect American civilians and property; more zealous "frozen warriors" claimed the challenge to America posed by the Bolsheviks must be met early, lest the contagion spread. In the end, American presence in a foreign land fostered conditions which increased, rather than attenuated, human suffering.

Luckily, Cadre filmmakers found a veteran from the Expedition. With his wonderfully expressive voice, Lynn McQuiddy is a more effective historical witness than the implied hero of *Goodbye Billy*. The challenge for the new film became how to convey the shock for a young American entangled in such an imbroglio.

To convey this theme as a film experience, *The Frozen War* used anti-Bolshevik cartoons, newsreels of Attorney General A. Mitchell Palmer's famous "Red Scare" raids, and films of the Expeditionary Force from the Army Signal Corps collection at the U.S. Archives. By juxtaposing popular songs of the 1920s against Russian religious and concert music, the filmmakers evoked the clash between Western and Eastern cultures. But the real challenge of this picture involved using the archival footage to communicate the sense of

Parallels or Continuities 257

alienation and repulsion of the protagonist, Lynn McQuiddy. Like Billy on the western front, McQuiddy is on the cutting edge of foreign policy where he can gauge the distance between official rhetoric and the painful consequences of misguided policy.

Themes Common to World War I and Vietnam in *Goodbye Billy* and *The Frozen War*

1. Loss of Innocent Faith in Establishment Culture and Politics

Early in *The Great War and Modern Memory*, Paul Fussell describes the citizens of England during World War I as "those sweet, generous people who pressed forward and all but solicited their own destruction" (19). Fussell admires Philip Larkin's elegiac poem "MCMXIV," a work that concludes there never will be "such innocence again." This same "loss of innocence" theme pervades novels and films about Vietnam. Typically, the American GI leaves a placid, civilian environment to fight in a war that leaves him emotionally spent. Ron Kovic's *Born on the Fourth of July* (1976) is a representative text. The media shape young Kovic's attitudes toward war; after high school, the Marine Corps adds its corrupting influence. When the stress of combat further degrades his spirit, Kovic reaches a dead low: he kills a friend by accident and participates in the accidental shooting of Vietnamese children. His spinal wound comes as a blessing of sorts; through it he learns to fight back against the

Tom Cruise as Ron Kovic

official authorities. Caputo's *A Rumor of War* follows a similar spiritual devolution in its effort to exculpate a young lieutenant from the guilt of his war crimes. At the climax of *Vietnam-Perkasie*, another tale of disillusionment, W. D. Ehrhart participates in the battle for Hue with demented fury:

> I fought back passionately, in blind rage and pain, without remorse, conscience or deliberation. I fought back...at the Pentagon Generals and the Congress of the United States, and the *New York Times;* at the draft-card burners, and the Daughters of the American Revolution...at the teachers who taught me that America always had God on our side and always wore white hats and always won; at the Memorial Day parades and the daily Pledge of Allegiance...at the movies of John Wayne and Audie Murphy, and the solemn statements of Dean Rusk and Robert McNamara. (246-47)

From the opening scene of Oliver Stone's *Platoon* to the closing scene of Stanley Kubrick's *Full Metal Jacket,* the motif of corrupted innocence is shared by nearly all major books and films that deal with Vietnam.

In the first third of *Goodbye Billy*, the filmmakers use symbolism to establish America's naïveté. U.S. Signal Corps footage of troops aboard ship is edited with a rousing pro-war ditty entitled "The Yanks Are At It Again" As the soundtrack tells of how "Kaiser Bill will surely get/His due before we're through," young soldiers aboard ship participate in a childish pillow fight. The event is clearly part of a "field day" exercise to keep the soldiers busy, but Cadre has transformed the images into a developed symbol for the lack of understanding on the part of the young Americans. In a montage described earlier, sheep—traditional symbols of Arcadian innocence—are shown on the White House lawn with footage taken by the Signal Corps to show that even the White House was conserving vital resources. When edited with a picture of Wilson looking out over them, the collision montage becomes more negative: America's soldiers are indeed mindless sheep being sent to the slaughter by a well-intentioned, but naively idealistic leader. These fascinating moments in *Goodbye Billy* resonate with meaning for both World War I and Vietnam.

In *The Frozen War*, McQuiddy admits he participated in the Vladivostok expedition with youthful enthusiasm. He speaks of being in "an adventurous mood." However, second thoughts quickly develop. McQuiddy discovers that America's intervention exacerbates the agony of a society that will inevitably go through many painful transformations. As an eyewitness, he is able to attest to the failure and irrelevance of the incursion. We may laugh with McQuiddy when he remembers the inadequacy of supplies or complains about not taking a proper shower for three months, but we are deeply moved as he amasses details about human suffering. His reports about disease, hunger, dislocation, and simple cruelty—intensified and amplified by archival footage—inculcate a profound loathing of the rhetoric used to justify U.S. intervention.

Woodrow Wilson, "the Peacemaker," may have sent us in to protect American property, but in the process of saving a few flivvers, thousands of Russian civilians died of disease or met more violent ends. The American ambassador to Moscow may intone that "we are not at war with the Bolsheviks," but McQuiddy has fought them and even taken some as prisoners. This might not be war on the ambassadorial level, but it is war enough for any participant with a life to lose. The word "innocence" in this context has a very negative connotation; it applies to the blundering efforts of a State Department whose misdirected policies will result in murder, rape, and starvation. Viewed from the Vietnam era, contemporary parallels must have been hard to avoid for Cadre in 1972; there certainly are reverberations for Bosnia in the 1990s.

2. We Are the Victims of History

The Great War and Modern Memory focuses upon this theme as perhaps the most important factor in modem consciousness. Fussell argues the Western world moved from a heroic self-image to one involving what literary scholars call "dramatic irony." (In a situation characterized by dramatic irony, the protagonist is unaware of his fate while the audience is painfully conscious of the incongruity between the individual's hopes and his certain defeat.) Such a world allows no heroes, only victims.[9]

Fussell compiles convincing evidence about how such a world view took shape during the slaughter. German troops did so "well"

Battle of the Somme

in their aggressive—but costly—assaults that their casualties quickly depleted the army of its finest junior officers and senior noncommissioned officers. Along the 400 miles of trenches on the western front, "the main business of the soldier was to exercise self-control while being shelled" (46). Through black humor, the troops tried to endure the war of attrition, but their sense of "bondage, frustration [and] absurdity" produced a new image of man in modem literature: "A standard character is the man whom things are done to. He is Prufrock, Jake Barnes, Charlie Chaplin" (313). Fussell makes a great number of comparisons between the sensibility produced on the western front (1914-18) and the world of Yossarian (1943-45), protagonist of Joseph Heller's *Catch-22* (1961). It is a world in which nature and society seem bent on destroying an individual who is spiritually—and sometimes even physically—naked. Interestingly, *Catch-22* is referred to more frequently by Fussell than is the poetry of Rupert Brooke—a revealing imbalance. Fussell's point is that the connections go deeper than parallelism. In fact, even Yossarian's "primal scene" with the wounded gunner, Snowden, was culled from the writings of R. C. Sherriff retaining "all its Great War [dramatic] irony" (34). The primal scene "embodies the contemporary equivalent of the experience offered by the first day on the Somme, and, like that archetypal original, it can stand as a virtual allegory of political and social cognition in our own time" (35). This is not a matter of mere likeness; it is continuity. Finally, *Catch-22* is considered by many to be the quintessential Vietnam War novel—despite the fact that it was written four years before American troops landed in Southeast Asia and despite its World War II setting. Fussell's argument that the ironic vision stems from the Great War helps to explain the confusing discrepancies.[10]

Dramatic irony suffuses the last two-thirds of *Goodbye Billy*, frequently in the form of music hall patter. During the opening third, the humor is light and irreverent. Pat asks Mike about the "story about the wooden man who swallowed the whistle." Mike doesn't understand at first; Pat explains the result: "He wouldn't (wooden) whistle." In part two, the humor darkens. Pat has been hit. Mike tells us the "humorous" result: first, he "wooden whistle," and now "he can't stir!" Vietnam veterans will savor the special irony in an exchange about tours of duty: Pat asks Mike how long he will be fighting the war. Mike answers that he enlisted for seven years. Pat responds, "Aw gee, you're lucky. I'm for the duration." Men as inanimate objects and victims, men in uniform forever—these notions are part of the legacy of World War I and the subsequent regimentation of society.[11]

The futility of America's intervention is questioned many times during *The Frozen War*. The film makes much out of the postwar industrial boom stimulated by the automobile. In two critical moments, Ford Motor Company footage and cartoons are edited to imply Americans see political problems as flat tires requiring patching. *The Frozen War* argues that nations are not so easily repaired and steered along the turnpike of history. When it comes to a Model T, we can "patch it up with anything, chewing gum or a ball of string and the little Ford will travel right along." Much to their chagrin, Americans should have learned after World War I that the world was not as susceptible to amateur tinkering.

The Frozen War concludes with a winter scene of Vladivostok harbor held in freeze frame. Large chunks of ice have halted boat traffic while fog drifts over the frigid waters. Through these images, the filmmakers attempt to relay a message about intervention. McQuiddy states with some exasperation, "I have had to wait for fifty years to tell this story. Anything that doesn't have a future to it...What the hell good is it?" Not only was the water at Vladivostok "frozen" in the sense of taking place in Eastern Siberia some hundred miles north of Korea; in addition, the policy of intervention was "frozen" in the sense of being inflexible to the complex realities of civil war.

Even the issue of the neglected Vietnam veteran is discernable in *The Frozen War*. One of the final shots looks down a railroad track at a minuscule figure. The music and his gait suggest a contemporary comic whose reputation grew in stature as film comedy evolved beyond slapstick. The link to Fussell's notion of victimization seems clear: this is a cinematic allusion to Charlie Chaplin. The men of the American Expeditionary Force were doing their job, but like "the little tramp," they were forgotten by the folks back home. (Consumer fixations of civilians are satirized in a song entitled "The Harem.") Like the Vietnam vets, the AEF troops have been left out in a "frozen war." The accumulating ice and snow symbolize the fruitlessness of the entire effort.

3. Machines and Technology Do Not Guarantee Progress

The introduction of technological innovations to the battlefield in World War I could hardly have been seen as "progress." The machine gun, the tank, poison gas, the airplane, barbed wire, and the submarine thrust mechanization into a horse-and-buggy context. With the introduction of "indirect fire" techniques, artillery made great "advances" so that weapons could be hidden deep behind friendly lines; from these protected gun positions, they could lob shells upon the enemy. Using aiming stakes, maps, and forward observers connected to the batteries by radio or wire, shells weighing up to a ton could be dropped on targets as far away as fifty miles. (Germany's so-called Paris gun was mounted on railroad cars and lobbed shells into the French capital from a range of seventy-five miles.) This unequal clash between machines and flesh amplified existing questions about the benefits of industrialism. Observers began to speak of a "war of attrition" (Fussell 9); whatever their speculations, Fussell says the war became "a hideous embarrassment to the prevailing Meliorist myth which had dominated the public consciousness for a century. It reversed the Idea of Progress" (8).

The Tank Brings Technology to War

In an effort to show progress in Vietnam, the government (and, echoing them, the press) made much of "body counts." Without definite front lines to measure progress, this cruel offspring of attrition tactics seemed to help provide "light at the end of the tunnel." An HBO Special entitled *Dear America: Letters Home from Vietnam* (1988) introduces body counts as a motif to convey the sense of mounting human tragedy in Vietnam—as opposed to hailing progress through such figures. Vietnam veteran and Desert Storm commander General Norman Schwarzkopf carefully avoided the progress-through-numbers approach during the Gulf War despite continual requests by the press that he somehow quantify the American victory.

Fussell observes that World War I writers often develop dramatic contrasts between a pastoral prewar life style and the meat grinding efficiency of the war machine; these same kinds of contrasts enhance the power of Vietnam films and books. Many reviewers were frustrated by the long homefront segment of *The Deer Hunter* where filmmaker Michael Cimino lavished detailed attention upon the intricate patterns of life and love among second-generation immigrant steel workers. What reviewers neglected to appreciate was that Cimino was imitating the rhetorical success of D.W. Griffith in his epic feature, *The Birth of a Nation* (1914). Both Griffith and

Cimino understood that audiences could not properly respond to the disruption caused by war if they were not fully apprised of the harmonies of antebellum life. On the literary front, the very title of Ehrhart's *Vietnam-Perkasie* highlights the clash of the warfront/homefront values. The infamous Russian roulette scenes from *The Deer Hunter* have been interpreted in many ways, but one valid interpretation is that they are microcosms of victimization. Francis Ford Coppola's *Apocalypse Now* (1979) hypes more obvious symbols of American machines in the Vietnam garden. Helicopter assaults to the strains of Wagner's "Ride of the Valkyrie" suggest all kinds of ironies about technological "progress."

Goodbye Billy addresses the issue of technology. During the optimistic opening section of the film, Samuel Gompers, president of the American Federation of Labor, proclaims, "The final outcome will be determined in the factories, the mills, the shops, the mines, the farms." In other words, industrial and technological potency will prevail. During this preparedness speech, images of ships, tanks, and troops fill the screen. Musically, a somewhat sinister industrial leitmotiv is introduced, although, at this point, it appears to be assertive rather than threatening. Sections two and three define the limits of technology. Pictorially, the film shows a team of horses attempting to extricate an Army truck from a sodden field; reintroduction of the industrial leitmotiv over these pictures defines an America bogged down in its first "Big Muddy." At the close of part two, the industrial leitmotiv is again-introduced over-pictures of massive urban destruction, conveying the notion that potentially constructive industrial might can quickly be retooled for war.

In *The Frozen War*, footage of Americans awkwardly training for ski-borne operations in Russia is used to portray American interventionists as inept Keystone Cops. The clear message is that America cannot play the European game of power politics without suffering a number of diplomatic pratfalls. In a dejected moment, the narrator of *The Frozen War* describes our efforts as "burlesque antics in fantastic side shows."

4. Language Has Been Disjoined from Truth

There were many recriminations after World War I, but certainly one of the major concerns of the 1920s was that propaganda misled decent people on both sides. Fussell speaks of a new distrust for language stemming from the "collision...between events and the public language used for a century to celebrate the idea of progress" (169). Early in *The Great War and Modern Memory*, he provides a list of terms that became "casualties of the war" (22). Prior to the trauma of 1916, soldiers did not enlist, they "joined the colors"; rather than dying, they "perished"; soldier's were "warriors"; and, rather than bleed, they lost "the red/Sweet wine of youth" (21-22). Post-war cynicism had not set in:

> Indeed, the literary scene is hard to imagine. There was no *Waste Land*, with its rats' alleys, dull canals, and dead men who have lost their bones: it would take four years of trench warfare to bring these to consciousness.... There was no "Valley of Ashes" in *The Great Gatsby*. One read Hardy and Kipling and Conrad and frequented worlds of traditional moral action in traditional moral language. (23)

Postwar consciousness would focus on the need for a new language to describe a new world. As I.A. Richards and C.K. Ogden would explain in their *Meaning of Meaning* (1923), "Words were

I.A. Richards Inherits the Meaninglessness of Meaning

never a more common means than they are today of concealing ignorance and persuading even ourselves we possess opinions when we are merely vibrating with verbal reverberations" (262).

The Vietnam record shows concerns about the dangers of euphemism and doublespeak. On the positive side, servicemen devised an entire vocabulary of black humor to distance themselves from the deadly facts of life. The Pentagon in Washington, where plans and programs were concocted, was "Disneyland East." Saigon-based tacticians were called "chairborne commandoes" or "REMFs" (Rear Echelon, etc.). Up North, in the I Corps Area, the Demilitarized Zone (DMZ) became known to local infantryman as the "Dead Marine Zone." After My Lai, the inept American Division gained a reputation for being "the butcher brigade." (The American Division was quietly disbanded after the war.) Lonelier than astronauts in outer space, young Americans counted every day in the 365 days of their tour until they "derosed" (Date of Expected Return from Over Seas or DEROS) back to "the world" (home).

Noam Chomsky attempted to demystify pseudoscientific jargon in his critique of Pentagon-supported social scientists. According to the feisty MIT linguistics professor, much of the work by people like Samuel Huntington, Daniel Bell, and Ithiel Pool was not true social science. Thus Chomsky argued that so-called pacification was really a matter of starving uncooperative villagers and forcibly removing troublesome leaders (37). "Modernization" in this context meant tearing apart the fabric of a traditional society which had expressed no desire for change (57). "Nation building" meant imposing America's political institutions on others (59). Chomsky explained the purpose of such language was not to deal with human problems, but to legitimize the work of "experts" who could wield social science "as a new coercive ideology with a faintly scientific tone" (58). In the title sequence of his novel, Joseph Heller explored the gap between language and reality with devastating wit, capturing the notion of Everyman as a prisoner of language. Having succeeded in the West, Chomsky saw America's "liberal technocrats" attempting to impose their linguistic bureaucratese on the Third World.[12]

Like those who speculated about the deviousness of language in the 1920s, *Goodbye Billy* takes a harsh look at the gap between the rhetoric of propaganda and battlefront realities. Part two of the film culminates with a scene in which visuals and sound embellish this theme. As the orchestra plays "The Washington Post March" out of tune, we see visuals of a destroyed Zeppelin. Under the defining influence of music, the image becomes a developed symbol: the gas of propaganda has been released and the vaporousness of its promises revealed. A pan of a cemetery tallies the deaths caused by the manipulation of patriotic symbols, a tragic result further dramatized by solarized shots of after-action rubble at Ypres (a Belgium transportation hub of some 20,000 citizens totally destroyed in late 1914). Although the war was sold as a crusade "to make the world safe for democracy," in the end, *Goodbye Billy* concludes that it was just another war smelling of "pukey dirt-stench." In its most powerful segment, the closing minutes of *Goodbye Billy* juxtaposes President Warren Harding's official dedication at the Tomb of the Unknown Soldier with the "real" version from John Dos Passos.[13]

McQuiddy constantly questions Washington-based policies in *The Frozen War*. In the opening montage, Ambassador Francis expresses his own exasperation: "Cable indicates State Department has heard that Soviet leaders acting under direction of German general staff. Regard suggestion of German control of Soviet government as absurd and impossible. If Washington credits this contention, why are we wasting time representing U.S. here in Moscow?" Shortly thereafter, the film shows American troops disembarking at Vladivostok, a screen action edited to coincide with President Wilson's saying that the "United States could not enter." In these opening minutes, we begin to sense that, just as Wilson falsely proclaimed he was "too proud to fight" prior to 1917, so with the Russian incursion, he will be dragged into some form of military involvement. (Viewers have noted parallels here to the 1965 Gulf of Tonkin incident and the escalation that followed.)

If Noam Chomsky had possessed a better grasp of American cultural history, he might have observed that his quarrel with social science and with the misuses of language had roots in the years immediately following World War I. Walter Lippmann's *Public Opinion* (1922) and George Creel's *How We Advertised America* (1920) share Chomsky's insights into the ways in which governments manipulate their citizens. The telluric continuities from Lippmann to Chomsky are implicit in an expression that came to symbolize our failed crusade in Vietnam, the famous statement "We had to destroy the village in order to save it." Probably invented by Associated Press correspondent Peter Arnett, the paradoxical explanation took hold and decades later is reiterated on TV talk shows as the quintessential sound bite for Vietnam. At first, the statement looks original in its mordancy, but the black humor involved clearly stems from the ironic mode which entered our culture after 1916. It is obvious that Australian Peter Arnett formulated the statement to reflect his repugnance at the nation-wide damage of the 1968 Tet Offensive; yet, in shaping this cynical aphorism, could his "modern memory" have been reaching back to the military reversal suffered by Australian troops fifty-three years earlier at Gallipoli?

5. War Is Health for the Twentieth-Century State

Fussell believes the current regimentation of society began with the World War I draft. He describes the Military Service Act in Britain as "an event which could be said to mark the beginning of the modern world" (11). Such a perception would make sense in the 1960s when the director of the Selective Service, General Louis Hershey, was threatening to draft anyone reported burning his draft card. In

Hair Meets the Draft

Hair (play 1968, film 1979), an innocent Oklahoman named Claude (John Savage of *The Deer Hunter*) dies in Vietnam not long after being drafted. Brutally torn from the "Age of Aquarius," he is the ultimate soldier/victim.

Goodbye Billy devotes a number of scenes to the draft. In part one of the film, the selection of names and the processing of recruits goes smoothly, but part two stresses the cruelty of chance and resentment against "the system." Samuel Gompers' comments on industrial might are visually supported by images of young men performing calisthenics. The implication is that youths are just more fuel for the War Machine. In *The Frozen War*, McQuiddy is cannon fodder but, fortunately for him and for us, he has survived to share his version of the fiasco with us.

Fussell believes militarism has dulled our moral sensibility. Citizens now passively accept the repression needed to keep the war-machine operating: "[T]he war would literally never end and would become the permanent condition of mankind. The stalemate and attrition would go on indefinitely, becoming, like the telephone and the internal combustion engine, a part of accepted atmosphere of the modern experience" (71). During the Vietnam era, the movie *M*A*S*H* (1970) (as well as the TV series to follow) screened a powerful metaphor of modern humanity caught in such a catch-22. Indeed, the enduring appeal of the series can be accounted for by its success in shaping such a lively metaphor for our world. In *Going after Cacciato*, Tim O'Brien carried the Vietnam patrol metaphor all the way to the streets of Paris, thereby acknowledging the accuracy of Fussell's insight. While Oliver Stone's *Platoon* revealed a counterculture making headway (viz. Sergeant Elias and his squad), his *JFK* illuminated the deadly commercial imperative of a military-industrial complex.

Goodbye Billy contains a number of montage sequences that focus on advertising. Cigarette and automobile manufacturers—even the makers of Pepto Bismol—try to tap patriotic emotions. The film's message seems to be that war helps those who help themselves. In the most ironic commercial appeal, a newspaper ad pitches dynamite as "the builder of Civilization." Within the montage of *Goodbye Billy*, the slogan is a powerful exposé quotation. *The Frozen War* explores how exaggerated Red Scare propaganda short-circuits

America's ability to understand the aspirations of revolutionary societies.

From Fussell's point of view, the result has been a general moral disenfranchisement: "Thus the drift of modern history domesticates the fantastic and normalizes the unspeakable...the catastrophe that begins it is the Great War" (74). The immediate occasion for this observation was a 1972 headline from the *New York Times* reading, "U.S. Aides in Vietnam See an Unending War." Fussell believes such reflections link Saigon to the Somme. These are not beguiling parallels or superficial similarities, but telluric continuities connecting the static defense at Khe Sanh to the trenches in Flanders' Fields. They explain how *Goodbye Billy* and *The Frozen War* explore both their ostensible subjects—World War I and America's thwarted attempts to bring a liberal consensus to Europe and Asia—and the concerns of America during the Vietnam era. Indeed, to explore these two films in the light of Fussell's categories may be the first step toward reinterpreting the last seventy-five years of our cultural life.

Notes

1. The loss of innocence, from the point of view of someone who lived through the period, is explored by Joseph Wood Krutch in *The Modern Temper: A Study and a Confession* (1929). Krutch observes that moderns can no longer see themselves in a tragic mode because "Tragedy arises when...a people fully aware of the calamities of life is nevertheless serenely confident of the greatness of man, whose mighty passions and supreme fortitude are revealed when one of these calamities overtakes him" (84). Faith in the greatness of man had been blown up on the Western Front. Fussell's ideas about the damage will be explored in this essay. In his assessment of *The Modern Temper*, Krutch could only predict "progressive [spiritual] enfeeblement" (159).

2. I. A. Richards spent an entire career exploring the postwar problems of communication, with special interest in the function of artistic language in a scientific age. In a chapter entitled "Linguistic Abuse and Linguistic Reform," Max Black's *The Labyrinth of Language* (1968) gives a brief overview of some of the panaceas offered after World War I: the General Semantics Movement, the nostrums of Ogden and Richards, as well as other linguistic reforms/reformers of the period.

3. For Hemingway's views on language and style, especially in regard to his skepticism about Victorian ideals, see Harry Levin's article. In

A Farewell to Arms, Frederic Henry discovers that life is really controlled by chaos, a force which he cannot even describe in English; he resorts instead to the Spanish word for nothingness, "*Nada*" (249, 327-28). He goes on in the famous quoted passage to observe, "I was always embarrassed by the words sacred, glorious, and sacrifice and the expression in vain...I had seen nothing sacred and the things that were glorious had no glory and the sacrifices were like the stockyards at Chicago if nothing was done with the meat except to bury it. There were many words that you could not stand to hear and finally only the names of places had dignity. Certain numbers were the same way and certain dates and these with the names of the places were all you could say and have them mean anything" (184-85).

4. S. L. A. Marshall's World War I describes the first battle of the Somme as "the most soulless battle in British annals. It was a battle not so much of attrition as of mutual destruction" (180). Siegfried Sassoon observed the battle from a distance, finding it "a sunlit picture of Hell" (Marshall 196). British losses for the entire campaign were 420,000. The French sector lost 195,000. In the meantime, the Germans lost some 650,000 soldiers, to include most of their best frontline leaders. Ironically, the Germans lost most of their troops during heroic—and "successful"—counterattacks. As a result, according to R. Ernest Dupuy, the German army "would never be the same again" (1053). Such experiences cut deep into the patina of Victorian optimism.

On August 21, 1916, a British documentary entitled *Battle of the Somme* opened at thirty-four London theaters. Public interest in the film was keen, perhaps because the authenticity of the production had been attested to by the king. In any case, Samuel Hynes believes that the widely seen film imparted a new image of war: "In this film, war is not a matter of voluntary acts, but of masses of men and materials, moving randomly through a dead, ruined world towards no identifiable objective; it is aimless violence and passive suffering, without either a beginning or an end not a crusade, but a terrible destiny" (125). All of these details support Fussell's contention that the Battle of the Somme—as fact and as film made an indelible impression on Western culture.

5. See my Chapter 18 for details about this motif in Vietnam books and films. At critical points in American cultural history, the notion has been celebrated and attacked and, sometimes, such as in the 1840s and 1850s, both celebrated (Emerson) and attacked (Hawthorne). *The American Adam* by R.W.B. Lewis is a *locus classicus* for discussion of this offspring of American Romanticism. Looking at the 1960s in *Gates of Eden*, Morris Dickstein believes that by translating "the Edenic impulse...into political terms...[the youth movement stressed] man's right to happiness in the

here-and-now" (viii-ix). Vietnam would become the nemesis for this revival of the Adamic spirit.

6. Prior to moving into description and detail of the two films, I wish to stress that I am *not* arguing that the filmmakers were shaped by 1960s issues to interpret the war as they did. I *do* wish to push Fussell's argument to its limits, asserting with him that the Great War shaped the structure of modern memory. The Cadre Filmmakers and their contemporaries interpreted *both* World War I *and* Vietnam the way they did because of the categories built into modern sensibility *by* World War I. This notion is a radical one with implications only partially explored by Fussell in *The Great War and Modern Memory*.

7. Scholars wishing assistance in dissecting this fine short film should consult the text by Harris J. Elder. It contains a detailed outline of the film and useful descriptive detail. In addition, Raack and Malloch made an extended radio documentary which was recorded on a two-sided long-playing record. *The Stars and Stripes and You* is sold with the complete lyrics and narration for the documentary, 80% of which were used in *Goodbye Billy*. In writing this paper, I was particularly aided by the record's printed transcript. (The record itself is a fascinating item and deserves its own critique.)

8. The film version of *Slaughterhouse Five* is an adaptation of Kurt Vonnegut's novel of the same title. Within the context of this discussion, it is important to note that the film leaves out the Vonnegut-as-historian character who constantly reflects on the story as it develops. This persona allowed the author to explore the actual processes of "modern memory." The five themes explored in this paper could be fruitfully applied to the novel and film versions of *Slaughterhouse Five*, perhaps revealing that Vonnegut is a victim of time-tripping, but not the futuristic type he celebrates in his novel. Actually, Billy's experience and the author's acts of memory are emotional regressions shaped by the legacy of the Great War.

9. The word "irony" is used many times in this article. Most historians probably consider irony to be identical with sarcasm which is often the case. On the other hand, film scholars know that *film irony* or *cinematic irony* refers to situations in film in which the visual track and the sound track conflict with each other. Sergei Eisenstein was an early proponent of this device to disorient viewers and to make them think. (Both *Goodbye Billy* and *The Frozen War* frequently use this cinematic technique.)

Fussell and literary scholars explore other possibilities for the term "irony." When we use *rhetorical irony*, we mean the opposite of what we say. Fussell most often uses the word to mean *dramatic irony*: individuals may think that they are important and that the universe heeds their aspirations; unfortunately, World War I bombed that idea. In the new world of the lost generation, human beings are pathetic victims who are no longer in charge of their own destiny.

Again, *The Modern Temper* by J. W. Krutch is a *locus classicus* for this postwar confession of powerlessness.

10. Black humor pervades literature and entertainment during the 1960s from the Jewish-American commentary of Mort Sahl and Lenny Bruce to the literary perspectives of Philip Roth, Woody Allen, and, of course, Joseph Heller and Kurt Vonnegut. In his important study of the 1960s, Morris Dickstein comes to the conclusion that "[o]ne effect of Vietnam and Watergate was that the official organs of our society lost much of the respect and credence they had commanded. Even middle-Americans began to live with less of a mystified and paternalistic sense of Authority. The disillusionment, and ruthless skepticism really spoiled idealism of *Catch-22* outlived the sixties to become a pervasive national mood" (118). It is Fussell's purpose in *The Great War and Modern Memory* to show that the roots of this skepticism go back farther in time.

11. As a volunteer in the Italian ambulance service, Ernest Hemingway, like the protagonist of *A Farewell to Arms*, was wounded by incoming fire. The trauma became a symbol to Hemingway of the wound borne by all postwar humanity and recurs as a motif in his short fictions and novels. Readers will recall that, in the words of *Goodbye Billy*, Jake Barnes of *The Sun Also Rises* (1924) suffers from "the worst wound of all." For more on the "symbolic wound" in Hemingway, see Hoffman's *The Twenties*.

12. During the 1960s, academics drew parallels between Chomsky's combined moral and philosophical critique with a very similar debate during World War I between Randolph Bourne (1886-1918) and John Dewey (1859-1952). (Christopher Lasch has written an excellent description and analysis of the latter collision.) Dewey, as the leading spokesman for pragmatism, argued that his followers in the managerial class should support the war effort in order to reform American society from within. War powers in their hands could yield long-term improvements for the nation. Bourne, previously a disciple of Dewey, opposed his mentor on very pre-pragmatic moral grounds. In a manner anticipating Chomsky's reproof of his peers, Bourne also warned American intellectuals about the pitfalls of courting governmental influence. Jane Addams (1860-1935) would also take Dewey to task with similar arguments, predicting that politicians would use experts as smokescreens for policies conceived without their help.

13. While the interactions of music, voices, and images in this section are extremely effective, literary scholars will notice that the "script" is implicit in the chapter from Dos Passos' novel *1919* (462-27). The theme of doughboy-as-victim is clearly the message of the chapter and the film.

In some respects, *Goodbye Billy* makes the point with less anger and more subtlety than its literary original.

Works Cited

Black, Max. *The Labyrinth of Language*. New York: New American Library, 1968.

Caputo, Philip. *A Rumor of War*. New York: Holt, 1977.

Chomsky, Noam. *American Power and the New Mandarins*. New York: Random House, 1967.

Cimino, Michael, dir. and writer. *The Deer Hunter*. Columbia, 1978.

Coppola, Francis Ford, dir. *Apocalypse Now*. United Artists, 1979.

Creel, George. *How We Advertised America; The First Telling of the Amazing Story of the Committee on Public Information that Carried the Gospel of Americanism to Every Corner of the Globe*. New York: Harper, 1920.

Dear America: Letters Home from Vietnam. Dir. Bill Couturie. HBO, 1988.

Dickstein, Morris. *The Gates of Eden: American Culture in the Sixties*. NewYork: Basic, 1977.

Dos Passos, John. *1919*. 1932. New York: Signet Classics, 1969.

Dupuy, R. Ernest, and Trevor N. Dupoy. *The Harper Encyclopedia of Military History*. 4th ed. New York: HarperCollins, 1993.

Ehrhart, W. D. *Vietnam-Perkasie: A Combat Marine Memoir*. Jefferson, NC: McFarland, 1985.

Elder, Harris J. *Writing About Film*. Dubuque: Kendall/Hunt, 1977.

Full Metal Jacket. Dir. Stanley Kubrick. Warner Bros., 1987.

Fussell, Paul. *The Great War and Modern Memory*. New York: Oxford UP, 1975.

Griffin, Patrick. "Film, Document, and the Historian." *Film & History* 2.2 (1972): 1-5.

—. "The Making of *Goodbye Billy*." *Film & History* 2.2 (1972): 6-10.

—. "Perspectives: Media in *The History Teacher*" *The History Teacher* 6 (1972): 107-8.

Heller, Joseph. *Catch-22*. New York: Simon and Schuster, 1961.

Hemingway, Ernest. *A Farewell to Arms*. New York: Scribner, 1929.

—. *The Sun Also Rises*. New York: Scribner, 1926.

Hoffman, Frederick J. *The Twenties: American Writing in the Postwar Decade*. Rev. ed. New York: Free Press, 1962.

Hynes, Samuel. *A War Imagined: The First World War and English Culture*. New York: Atheneum, 1991.

JFK. Dir. Oliver Stone. Warner Bros., 1991.

Kovic, Ron. *Born on the Fourth of July*. New York: McGraw-Hill, 1976.

Krutch, Joseph Wood. *The Modern Temper: A Study and a Confession.* New York: Harcourt, 1929.
Lasch, Christopher. *The New Radicalism in America, 1889-1916: The Intellectual as a Social Type.* New York: Knopf, 1965.
Levin, Harry. "Observations on the Style of Ernest Hemingway." *Kenyon Review* 13.4 (1951): 589-603.
Lippmann, Walter. *Public Opinion.* New York: Macmillan, 1922.
Marshall, S. L. A. *World War I.* Boston: Houghton Mifflin, 1964.
Marx, Leo. *The Machine in the Garden; Technology and the Pastoral Ideal in America.* New York: Oxford UP, 1964.
O'Brien, Tim. *Going after Cacciato.* New York: Dell, 1979.
Platoon. Dir. Oliver Stone. Orion, 1986.
Raack, R. C. "Clio's Dark Mirror: The Documentary Film in History." *The History Teacher* 6 (1973): 109-17.
Raack, R. C., Patrick Griffin, and William Malloch. *The Frozen War: America Intervenes in Russia, 1918-20.* San Francisco: Cadre Films, 1973.
—. *Goodbye Billy: America Goes to War, 1917-18.* Los Angeles: Churchill Media, 1971.
—. *The Stars and Stripes and You, 1917-1918.* San Francisco: Pox Productions, 1971.
Richards, I. A., and C. K. Ogden. *The Meaning of Meaning: A Study of the Influence of Language Upon Thought and of the Science of Symbolism.* 1923. New York: Harcourt, 1968.
Rollins, Peter C. "The Historian-Filmmaker's Contribution to the Study of Foreign Affairs." *Teaching International Politics in High School.* Ed. Raymond English. Lanham, MD: UP of America, 1989. 73-90.
—. "Teaching International Politics: What the Historian-Filmmaker Has to Offer." *Film and History* 19.1 (1989): 2-14.
—. "The Historian as Filmmaker: The Use of Visual Language." *The Frozen War* (1973). Booklet distributed with *The Frozen War.*
—. "*Storm of Fire* (1978): Reflections of Cadre Films and the Historian as Filmmaker." *The History Teacher* 12.4 (1979): 539-48.
Slaughterhouse Five. Dir. George Roy Hill. Universal Pictures, 1972.
Vonnegut, Kurt. *Slaughterhouse Five; or, The Children's Crusade, a Duty Dance with Death.* New York: Delacorte, 1969.

World War II

12
Frank Capra's *Why We Fight* Series and Our American Dream

Why We Fight Taught Courage in a Darkening World

General George C. Marshall, President Roosevelt's trusted Chief of Staff, knew a good show when he saw one, and he liked the movies of Frank Capra. Indeed, Frank Capra was Hollywood's champion of "the forgotten man"—the little fellow in the American crowd often referred to by President Roosevelt during his fireside chats. Passing over award-winning documentary filmmakers of the time, Marshall asked the leading Hollywood director to speak for the John Does and Mr. Smiths of America in a time of crisis.

The seven feature-length films of the *Why We Fight* series would be Capra's most important artistic contribution to his adopted country, a paean to democracy and a powerful indictment of oppression. David Culbert has praised the series as "the most comprehensive set of war aims released by the U.S. government *in any medium* during WWII" (187; emphasis supplied). Certainly, the programs aroused wartime audiences, but they continue to inspire today as statements of America's mission in a violent world.

Frank Capra and the American Dream

Frank Capra was living evidence of the American Dream. His impoverished family moved from Sicily to California in 1903 where the three-year-old Frank was placed at the bottom rung of the ladder of success. Through intelligence and hard work, Capra worked

Why We Fight Logo

his way through college and then into the movie industry, beginning as a technician in a developing house. At the next rung of the ladder, he worked at an editing table. True to the Horatio Alger formula, a benefactor came along in the person of Will Rogers. Rogers boosted Capra up the next few rungs; the clever young man began writing gags and scripts for Harry Langdon and then directing films at Columbia Pictures. By the 1930s, Frank Capra was Columbia's—and Hollywood's—leading director.

Released in 1935, Capra's comedy entitled *It Happened One Night* (starring Clark Gable and Claudette Colbert) won five Academy Awards in 1935. During a famous scene aboard a bus bound from Florida to New York City, the passengers (symbolizing American Society) joined in a group-singing of "The Daring Young Man on the Flying Trapeze." This scene—indeed the entire film—sent viewers home reassured that the search for individual fulfillment did not contravene America's sense of community. Capra's gift as a filmmaker was to evoke this serious idea within the context of dramatic conflict leavened by humor.

Capra had a strange reaction to the unprecedented critical and box office success of *It Happened One Night*. He feigned illness to avoid the resulting publicity. (Evidently, the top rung of the success ladder was a dizzy place.) After a few days, his imaginary sickness turned real, developing into a debilitating fever. Now stricken and lying in a hospital, Capra claims that he was visited by a little man

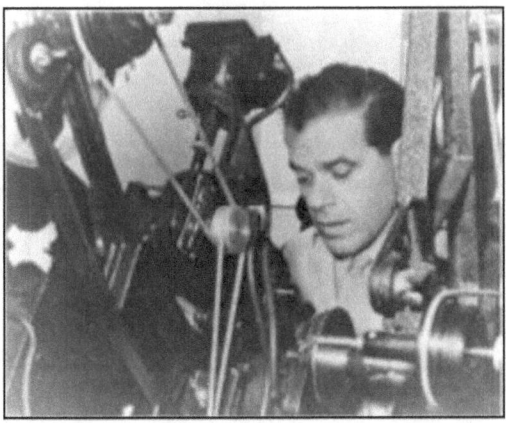

Frank Capra: American Dreamer and Master Editor

who will remind readers/viewers of Clarence, the novice Angel in *It's A Wonderful Life:*

> With the radio tuned in to a Hitler speech, the man castigated me for my selfishness. An evil man like Hitler could reach fifteen million people for twenty minutes, he argued, but a movie director like me could communicate with hundreds of millions for two hours. I was wasting my god-given talents, making me an offense not only to God, but to humanity. (176)

After his chastisement, Capra sought higher meaning for his work: "I knew that down to my dying day, down to my last feeble talent, I would be committed. Beginning with *Mr. Deeds Goes to Town*, my films had to say something." Whether an actual experience or a histrionic bit of "Capracorn," the result was the same: Frank Capra became a spokesman for democracy. His next few message films would serve as basic training for *Why We Fight*.

Mr. Deeds (1936) places a rural naif, Longfellow Deeds of Mandrake Falls, in conflict with the "fallen" values of the Gotham. Deeds triumphs in the end, but along the way he communicates an important message for Depression America. Our heritage offers many uplifting role models, and we could be inspired by them

Hitler Arouses Masses

if we took the time to reflect. To convey this message, Capra has Longfellow Deeds (played by Gary Cooper) visit Grant's Tomb during a tour of New York City. His guide, a cynical reporter named Babe Bennett (played by Jean Arthur), looks at the grim edifice and observes that most New Yorkers think of it as a "disappointment, a washout." Longfellow Deeds sees something quite different; indeed, he is genuinely moved by the sight:

> It's wonderful. I see a small, Ohio farm boy becoming a great soldier. I see thousands of marching men. I see General Lee, with a broken heart, surrendering. And I can see the beginning of a new nation, like Abraham Lincoln said. And I can see that Ohio boy being inaugurated President. Things like that can only happen in America.

Like Mr. Deeds, committed immigrant Frank Capra appreciated the heritage which Native-born Americans of the 1920s and 1930s had forgotten in their race toward modernism.

To prepare for his film *Mr. Smith Goes to Washington* (1939), Capra took the advice of the title and traveled to the nation's capital in October 1938. In Europe, Germany was absorbing five million Czechs as a part of the Munich Agreement while, at the opposite side of the globe, the Japanese air force was bombing Canton into submission in a cruel campaign that would be vividly detailed by *Why We Fight*. In America, the New Deal was stalled as a new business recession brought sharp declines to an already bearish stock market. Fully aware of these developments, Frank Capra made his pilgrimage to the Lincoln Memorial, leaving the building with an ebullient feeling that "the more uncertain are the people of the world, the more their freedoms are scattered and lost in the winds of change, the more they need a ringing statement of America's democratic ideals" (260).

As soon as Jefferson Smith gets off the train, he jumps aboard a similar tour. In a montage full of images to resurface in the *Why We Fight* series, the new Senator touches base with icons of America's heritage: the classicism of the Supreme Court building reminds him that America guarantees Equal Justice for All while the White House and the Capitol building depict the other two branches of government created by the authors of our Constitution to assure checks and balances. Statuary hall honors Jefferson Smith's noble

Lincoln's Message of Freedom

namesake; indeed, the quill in Thomas Jefferson's hand signifies the eloquence of the Declaration of Independence and its noble phrase "life, liberty, and the pursuit of happiness." The National Archives building displays the sacred texts of government and the resulting idea of liberty summons up bells and a reverential look at President George Washington's giant obelisk on the National Mall. Washington's face dissolves into a rampant Eagle which further dissolves into waving stars and stripes. This sequence then cuts to the Tomb of the Unknown Soldier, a solemn reminder of the spirit of resolve and community that led the nation through the Civil War and WWI.

Like Capra, Jefferson Smith ends up at the Lincoln Memorial, which an inscription above Lincoln's head reminds us is a temple of memory. Here Lincoln speaks of lack of malice, of reverence for sacrifice. The Gettysburg Address assures all that America's soldiers do not die in vain and silently admonishes Americans for neglecting to appreciate their hard-won freedoms. The montage closes with a ringing Liberty Bell imposed over the Great Emancipator's face. The lesson is clear. America's principles are vivid, transcendent, but require sacrifice. Such reflections were perfect classroom preparations for a film lecture on American fundamentals. When General Marshall called, Frank Capra was ready!

Getting Started: Learning from the Nazis

To prepare for his didactic responsibilities, Capra decided to check out the competition, in this case Leni Riefenstahl's *Triumph of the Will* (1935; hereafter *TOW*). *TOW* opens in billowing cumulus clouds above Germany as Adolph Hitler flies to the 1934 Nazi rallies in Nuremberg. From these opening moments of the film, the Fascist leader is depicted as a national savior who comes from on high to redeem Germany's John Does from the discomforts of individualism and the frustration of disunity. As the Fuehrer, Hitler embodies the national will and brings meaning and identity to a nation shamed by defeat in WWI and the vindictive Versailles Treaty of 1919. Through the deft use of moving camera, traditional and developed symbols, editing, and music, Riefenstahl crafted a cinematic paean to a national hero.

Frank Capra's *Why We Fight* Series

Frank Capra was shocked by the power of *Triumph of the Will* and made two decisions immediately. First, he would use the footage to condemn the mob psychology so blatant in *TOW*'s rally scenes, parades, and tableaux. Second, the Hollywood director believed that the documentaries of the series could equal—if not surpass—Riefenstahl's accomplishments. Ten years earlier, John Grierson had defined documentary as "the creative treatment of actuality." Although he would be working with actuality material, Capra knew that he could manipulate images and sound to prove that there were fundamental American reasons for joining the European struggle. Granted, the democracies had vacillated, but they could confront a demonic enemy and thereby experience their own "triumph of the will."

The Lessons to be Learned from *Why We Fight*

In its seven programs (*P-1* through *P-7*), *Why We Fight* (WWF) planned to cover the globe and centuries of history. Frank Capra was new to documentaries, but he was gifted in producing stories with dramatic villains and unimpeachable heroes. *Why We Fight* would shock, cajole, flatter, and uplift America; using every gimmick in Hollywood's sales kit, it would blend the dark necessity of military service into a theatrical epic. After the Jazz Age and the Depression, Americans were receptive to a melodrama which cast them as heroes riding to the rescue of a continent in distress.

1. The Folly of Isolationism and the Need for Collective Security

Prelude to War (*P-1*) explained the difficulties of selling the idea of collective security after WWI. Aggression in China, Europe, and Africa may have been a reality, but "it was impossible to convince a farm boy in Iowa, a driver of a bus in London, or a waiter in a Paris cafe that he should go to war because of a mud hut in Manchuria." Indeed, during the 1920s, Americans had been told that they were working for peace by destroying the weapons of war.

The Roosevelt Administration had decided to win in Europe first and only then to devote full resources to the Pacific campaign. For this reason, Pearl Harbor is mentioned only briefly at the opening of *P-1* and at the close of *War Comes to America* (*P-7*). Capra tried to exhibit what we now call "linkage," that the aggressive activities at various quarters of the globe were matters of a comprehensive Axis policy. In *The Nazis Strike* (P-2), the invasion of Poland is described as the logical outgrowth of events: "The fire that had begun in Manchuria and spread to China, Ethiopia, and Spain would now blaze around the world." Indeed, our isolationism and neutrality, our unwillingness to confront force with force, "gave the green light to the aggressors." The perfidy of Pearl Harbor was but one element of the enemy plan.

2. *The Slave World of the Axis Powers*
Led by gangsters comparable to John Dillinger—who is shown on an autopsy table in *Divide and Conquer* (P-3)—the Axis nations have quashed human liberty and snuffed out the human spirit. In Germany, the Nazi party has attacked religion. In a studio scene, a brick smashes through a stained-glass window of a church, shattering its portrait of Christ and revealing a poster of Hitler on a building across an alley. One of Hitler's spokesmen boasts that "it is only on one or two exceptional points that Christ and Hitler stand comparison, for Hitler is far too big a man to be compared with one so petty" (P-1). Interestingly, the anti-Semitism of Nazi Germany is soft-peddled; indeed, there are a few scenes which appear to have been shot in a studio to forcefully convey the notion but have voice-over narration which diverts attention to other forms of repression (P-1). (It is likely that the series chose to downplay any implication that FDR cared more about European minorities than American boys.)

Office of War Information guidelines required filmmakers to focus blame on the political elites in the Axis countries, so Hitler, Mussolini, and Tojo are constantly vilified. But *WWF* went beyond that narrow critique to blame the peoples. The masses have become "hopped up" with the propaganda about racial superiority and have surrendered their dignity and individuality: "'Stop thinking and follow me', cried Hitler. 'I will make you masters of the world.' And they answered 'Heil, Heil'" (P-1). In a characterization which raises eyebrows today, *WWF* explains that the Germans have been so easily misled by tyrants because they have "an inborn love of regimentation and harsh discipline" (P-1). The Italians and the Japanese have been similarly misled by their own charlatans and "gangsters." (Until FDR stepped in to demand a clearance for *WWF*, the Office of War Information imposed a ban on domestic distribution of the series because of these slurs, warning that fostering national stereotypes would, in the long run, cause more long-term harm than good.)

The Axis powers are acting on a plan for world conquest. In Berlin, the Germans have created a Center for Geopolitics to develop an inventory of the world's economic and human resources—a first step toward world enslavement. According to *The Battle of China* (*P-6*), the Japanese have followed their own plan to dominate the Pacific Rim. These aggressors will not stop voluntarily. As the narrator explains, "We lose the war and we lose everything: our honor, the jobs we work at, the books we read, the very food we eat, the hopes we have for our kids, the kids themselves" (*P-1*).

3. The Free World: Democracies as Reluctant Warriors

The democracies of the world believe in "government of the people, by the people, and for the people"—in essence, the lessons of Senator Jefferson Smith's tour early in Capra's award-winning feature of 1935. Moses, Christ, Confucius, and Thomas Jefferson passed these ideas along to us (*P-1*). When countries succumb to totalitarian regimes, it is usually the result of betrayal by key individuals rather than an error by the people: in Norway, it was Quisling; in France it was Maginot. In addition to being supportive of individual rights, democracies are inherently religious and their religions teach that "in the sight of God, all men are equal" (*P-7*). Recognizing this cultural and spiritual tradition as a threat, the Axis powers launched a *Kulturkampf* long before military actions.

Democracies crave peace. In fact, their naive adherence to disarmament treaties has proved their undoing in recent decades. The Washington Disarmament Conference and the Kellogg-Briand Pact were the kinds of agreements that democracies supported; in response, Germany and Japan built up, in secret, large cadres of officers who could assume command of instant armies. Devoted to peace, the Allies were caught flat-footed by the Axis powers in the late 1930s.

But the Allies will win because of their values. In the United

States, cultural diversity provides the basis for a composite national identity that is all the stronger for its many racial and national roots. Even assimilated Germans ("with their technical skills") have a place in this identity (P-7). The first test was the Battle of Britain and the Germans lost for lack of cultural flexibility: "A regimented people met an equally determined free people and the regimented people quit cold" (P-4). After the bombing of London, St. Paul's Cathedral survived as "a Christian monument defying barbarism" (P-4). The British found in WWF are of the middle class, the kind of endearing, peace-loving people found in Mrs. Miniver (1942), a film by Frank Capra's good friend, William Wyler. The Russians are proclaimed as "free people" who love their land and their God (P-5). Indeed, it is the Russians who prove the dictum that "generals may win campaigns, but people win wars" (P-5). In building the Burma Road in record time, our Chinese allies have proven they are living "the new spirit of the new China" (P-6).

The contrasts between the Slave World and the Free World are made most emphatically in connection with the treatment of children. *War Comes to America* opens with children of various ages and races reciting the pledge of allegiance; their protected status is immediately contrasted with the dangers and sacrifice—for them—on the battle front. America's children are indulged; on the other hand, their German and Japanese counterparts are shown practicing fire and maneuver with wooden weapons while wearing gas masks. Frightened, wounded, or dead children are displayed to elicit our pity and anger—pity for the helpless victims and anger at the Axis aggressors. All propagandists know the power of suffering children to pull at the heart strings and Capra gives a tug in every episode.

The Impact of *Why We Fight*

Over the years, there has been considerable debate about the impact of *Why We Fight*. After seeing *Prelude to War* in 1942, President Roosevelt told subordinates that "every American should see these films." When his Office of War Information opposed distribution to theaters across America because the films violated guidelines for treatment of enemy populations—for example, calling the Japanese "buck-toothed friends" of the Germans—Roosevelt simply countermanded the restraint order. Roosevelt wanted Americans to see and hear forceful arguments against isolationism; in addition, he was not averse to their experiencing an in-your-face statement of Germany's global designs.

By the end of the war, some 54 million Americans had seen the series. In those adolescent years of the social sciences, a special psychological unit was assigned to pre-test and post-test some 2000 soldiers who viewed the series. The results were published after the war, and there has been much debate about the findings. A famous historian of film, Paul Rotha, who lived through the war and was acutely concerned with impact of documentary as a genre, remembered the special power of *WWF*:

> Recent and familiar as were the events, it was nevertheless startling and often dismaying to have them so bleakly and lucidly set freshly forth as in this film; it is difficult even to describe the impact with which, to take an instance or two, seeing scrap metal being shipped to Japan, seeing and hearing President Roosevelt or Lindbergh or Willie in one of their historic speeches, now struck home. The facts were there in all their calamitous force but with hindsight added. It is impossible to deny the persuasiveness of such films but shocking, too, that they could, simply be presenting known facts, have so strong and startling an effect—the measure of the observer's forgetfulness, apathy, or unawareness. (350)

With all the action and excitement of Hollywood feature films, *WWF* crystallized the meaning of American life while sounding a bugle call to action.

The Secret Appeal of *Why We Fight* Yesterday and Today

But it did something more. And here we find the profound the appeal of the *WWF* series. Much of the literature of the post-WWI era expressed fears that the democracies had lost their values and "gone soft." Certainly, Nazi propaganda exploited this theme, but so did some of the most important American books and films between 1920-1940. Here are some authors for whom the "decline of the West" was an obsession: Ernest Hemingway, T.S. Eliot, and F. Scott Fitzgerald—indeed the entire "lost generation." Just prior to

Gary Cooper and Barbara Stanwyck in *Meet John Doe*

the sneak attack on Pearl Harbor, Orson Welles' *Citizen Kane* (1941) explored the emptiness of Horatio Alger's promise for American life. Charles Foster Kane rose from rags to riches, but found that success did not guarantee happiness. The opening moments of the classic film explore the grounds of Xanadu, an estate that symbolizes the dark side of a failed American Dream. Frank Capra's own *Meet John Doe* (1941) ends positively, but most critics have criticized the ending as a *deus ex machina*. The body of the film conveys all too persuasively that the John Does and John Q. Publics of this world can be hoodwinked by media moguls. The most convincing messages of *Meet John Doe* are that citizens in the modern world have lost control of their politics, their happiness—indeed, their very sense of reality. Despite the Christmas Eve setting for the finale, God seems absent.

Why We Fight Taught Courage in a Darkening World

The *Why We Fight* project may have come at the right time for Frank Capra as much as for America. Yes, we had gone soft, but Capra's generation could show that, like previous generations, it could live up to the historic mission of democracy. Many have noted that the war ended the Depression, thereby solving major economic challenges of the New Deal. Few have considered that the war came just in time to cure the nation's spiritual malaise. By rallying to the colors, by fighting for democracy and equality, Americans could renew their faith in themselves and the nation—as they had during the Civil War and during the early days of the 'War to End all Wars.' *Why We Fight* is thus not only an answer to the international challenges of fascism, but a rallying cry for Americans to ring the Liberty Bell, to rediscover the nation's mission as "a lighthouse of freedom"—perhaps even to reappreciate the aura of Grant's Tomb and the Lincoln Memorial. Decades later, from the vantage point of the 21st century, the *Why We Fight* series challenges us to address our current crises of values and violence, of jobs and justice, with the same sense of community and democratic populism Frank Capra invoked against global fascism.

An Overview: The Seven Films of the *Why We Fight* Series

1. *Prelude to War* (1942) (P-1)

By allowing the fascist aggressors to gain their objectives, isolationist America destroyed collective security. Appeasement culminated in the debacle at Munich. The Axis Powers have gained momentum and we are now in a struggle for our national existence: "the chips are down; it's us or them."

2. *The Nazis Strike* (1943) (P-2)

The Germans have a "passion for conquest." In the mid-1930s, Hitler quietly prepared his war machine in defiance of the Treaty of Versailles. Germans were told by the Fuehrer, "We have a sacred mission. Today we rule Germany, tomorrow the world." First, the Sudetenland land was absorbed, but then—in violation of the Munich Agreement—the remainder of Czechoslovakia was taken. Next came the invasion of Poland. Despite these setbacks, Winston Churchill predicts victory for democracy: "Lift up your hearts; all will come right. Out of the depths of sorrow and of sacrifice will be born again the glory of mankind."

3. *Divide and Conquer* (1943) (P-3)
Conquest of France, Denmark, Norway, Belgium, Holland. On October 6, 1939, Hitler promised to live in harmony with these nations. Contrary to his promises, he invaded, terrorized, and enslaved the peoples of the continent, showing himself to be little more than a gangster: "Society had a police force to deal with gangster Dillinger, but it had none to deal with gangster Hitler."

4. *The Battle of Britain* (1943) (P-4)
Attack from the air. On August 8, 1940, the battle begins with the RAF performing bravely. In September, serious bombing begins; in October, the Germans drop incendiary materials on London as part of a campaign of terror. Christmas Eve sees the most intensive bombing and the most destructive fires in London's history. Eventually, 40,000 people die, but no German troops set foot on British soil. Despite the tragic loss of life, there is good news: the Battle of Britain marks the end of the German invincibility myth. "For the first time, it was the Germans who ate the bitter dirt of defeat."

5. *The Battle of Russia* (1944) (P-5)
Using reenactments from a feature film, *Alexander Nevsky* (1938; Dir. Sergei Eisenstein), *TBR* drives home the message that the Germans have always been militarists and invaders. Realistic footage of the 1941 invasion of Russia shows that the Teutonic tradition of the black knights continues into the era of tanks and planes. Emphasis is lavished on aspects of Russian culture to which Americans can relate; for example, the music of Tchaikovsky interprets the images extensively. On the political front, the "C word" (Communism) is never mentioned during the entire 80-minute production! The Russian folk arise to defend the motherland, proving that "Generals win battles, but peoples win wars." (This episode was distributed within the Soviet Union.)

6. *The Battle of China* (1944) (P-6)
As with the other ally films (4&5), the goal of this production is to promote empathy for a friend in trouble. China's democratic movement was begun by Sun Yat Sen in 1911 and passed along to Chiang Kai-Shek. As denizens of "the Good Earth," China's people are

long-suffering and peaceful; indeed, "in 4000 years of continuous history, the Chinese have never waged a war of conquest. They are that sort of people."

The Japanese have launched an imperial offensive to steal raw materials and to enslave Chinese labor. In Nanking, "the Japanese outdid themselves in barbarism. Those who lived might better have died, for the horror of their bodies was worse than death." No mention is made of the Communist revolution or the competition it posed for Chiang Kai-Shek.

7. *War Comes to America* (1945) (P-7)

We are a nation of immigrants, but America's melting pot has given us one national identity associated with the ideas of freedom and equality. Indeed, "Without the idea, the country would have remained a wilderness; without the country, the idea may have remained only a dream." We were in error to practice isolationism after WWI, but, once war came, we lived up to our international responsibilities. Victory is assured because America's strength stems from our multicultural past.

Coda: The Historical Compilation Film: Capra to Burns

After the war, *Why We Fight* would become a staple for ROTC classes across the nation, perpetuating the Capra vision for another generation of American military leaders. But the films also became a model for programming on a new, smaller screen called television.

Television Recycles the Capra Success

NBC

Why We Fight fostered an appetite for compilation films—or so argued Henry Salomon to his Harvard classmate, Robert Sarnoff of NBC. As an assistant to Admiral Samuel Eliot Morrison, Salomon had helped to write the history of U.S. naval operations in World War II. With the help of the copious film archives becoming available, Salomon proposed to take a cue from Capra and depict the spectacle of war on screen. Yet the resulting series, *Victory at Sea*, did more; it echoed Capra's theme that America was a flawless bastion of freedom in a darkening world.

Many historians at the time, and later, were calling for more complex visions of the postwar world. *Victory at Sea* was a pat on the back to the victors of World War II—minus the vitriol of *Why We Fight* and with all the confidence of the Eisenhower era. The 26 half-hour episodes have been aired on PBS during the last year; in some major markets, the series has been on the air almost continuously since its first national broadcast in 1952. (See Chapter 16)

CBS

The CBS counterattack, *Air Power* (narrated by Walter Cronkite), would follow *Victory at Sea* in style, viewing the war from the air, accompanied by the music of Norman Dello Joio. Still later, *Twentieth Century*, under the leadership of Isaac Kleinerman (who had been the chief editor for *Victory at Sea*), carried CBS efforts at compilation to new heights, as did the Project XX series at NBC under Donald Hyatt (who had been Salomon's assistant for the *Victory at Sea* project).

Both *Victory at Sea* and *Air Power* would continue some of the dubious practices of *Why We Fight*. The use of fiction footage and reenactment belongs at the top of the list of flaws. Indeed, the "Battle of Leyte Gulf," the nineteenth episode of *Victory at Sea*, was constructed entirely from a mixture of training films, films from other battles, and feature materials. In addition, the television children of *Why We Fight* would imitate their documentary parent in using actuality footage out of geographical context or out of chronological order, following the still-honored principle that an entertainment medium should exploit "anything that works." Assuming that viewers were visually illiterate—and hoping that they remained so—the filmmakers felt little compunction about throwing in visuals for impact. When such scholar-filmmakers as Richard Raack and I railed against such practices, both the profession of history and the general public remained glued to the tube.

Vietnam Era: Hawks and Doves Compile Celluloid Arguments

The Vietnam era produced a curious information environment. President Lyndon Johnson was wed to his Great Society and considered Vietnam a distraction. For this reason, he and Dean Rusk agreed not to produce either a propaganda campaign or a film series like *Why We Fight*. They feared that the American public, once aroused, would demand that its leaders devote full resources to victory—thereby pulling the plug on the Great Society. The only counterparts to *Why We Fight*, then, are such films as *Why Vietnam* (1965).

Although *Why Vietnam* was shown to servicemen either prior to their assignment to Vietnam or during required orientation sessions after they arrived, it is nearly impossible to find anyone who remembers it. The reason for this failure to communicate was clear even in World War II: *Why We Fight* or any film of that kind cannot work without a supporting informational context. Theorists of persuasion tell us that it takes three acts of communication to "sell" an idea; the Johnson administration, with its "guns and butter" approach to Vietnam and the Great Society, simply did not provide the additional support (not to mention what was coming to the young by way of protest music in the 1960s).

Instead, the compilation documentary technique was exploited by those who opposed the war. In 1974, Peter Davis released *Hearts and Minds*, a two-hour exposé of America's Vietnam debacle. When the film won the award for best documentary on Oscar night, Producer Bert Schneider read a letter of gratitude from the Vietcong. Some 20 years later, a teacher at the University of Massachusetts described the film as "a stunning portrayal of the horrors of the Vietnam war," adding that "if my students are at all typical, it has the power to move people today."

Others were less impressed by this countercultural offspring of *Why We Fight*. When *Hearts and Minds* came out, Joseph Sobran of the *National Review* worried over the reverse Manicheanism of the film, where everything communist was praised and everything American was damned:

> I think the reviewers are afraid to say anything that sounds anti-Communist. It is not respectable. You don't keep writing for *The New Yorker* or even *Time*, if you use phrases as passé as "Communist tyranny." You have to be delicate. No matter if hundreds of thousands of people hastily leave their homes forever to fight their way onto departing ships bound for unknown lands, even paddle out to sea in tiny boats: We still do not denounce Communism. (621)

Hearts and Minds is still used today in classrooms with the approval of the history profession; on the other hand, if *Why Vietnam* is shown by teachers, it is with derision—rather than to promote an understanding of the film as a document of its time.

Vietnam: A Television History (1983; WGBH/PBS) continued the adversarial approach to Vietnam through the compilation medium. Ostensibly a balanced approach to the war—during the grant-seeking phase and in the book by Stanley Karnow—the series by WGBH-Boston was attacked by veterans, refugees, and some scholars for its skewed interpretations. While Ho Chi Minh was presented as a Jeffersonian democrat ready to effect agrarian reforms, America and its allies were depicted as exploiters and moral troglodytes. Neither a full-length book critique entitled *Losers Are Pirates* nor a series of films entitled *Television's Vietnam* (AIM, 1985-6) could do much to stop the PBS juggernaut (after three national broadcasts of all thirteen episodes) from finding its place in America's living rooms, universities, and film libraries (see Chapters 19, 20). Even to question the series exposed critics to personal attack from the media grandchildren of Frank Capra, descendants who now viewed America as the enemy of progressive global reform.

Return to Reaffirmation

In the 1990s, the compilation film returned to a Capraesque faith in populism and American strength through the films of Ken Burns. His *Civil War* series, first broadcast in 1990, was watched by 40 million Americans and received over 40 major film awards. Unlike ideologue Peter Davis and the moralists of *Vietnam: A Television History*, Burns seems to be more in the Capra tradition of dramatizing the virtues in the American legacy. The *Civil War* programs were evocative and poetic; like the *Why We Fight* series, they tapped something deep in the American spirit.

The success of Burns' films assures us that the historical compilation film is still a thriving genre. If the Capra practices of using footage for dramatic purposes as opposed to the dictates of authenticity still prevail, it is because they "work" and because qualified historian filmmakers—such as Richard Raack—have been ignored. Just as the Office of War Information inveighed uselessly against Capra's excesses, so the critics of *Vietnam: A Television History* and

Burns' films waste their time. Frank Capra launched the genre with all its excitement and its defects. Until historians and citizens are visually literate, we will still be in the thrall of the entertainers who strive—as Capra did—to "make the best damned documentary films ever made."

In retrospect, we can see that the *Why We Fight* project came at the right time for the United States. Much of the literature of the post-World War I era expressed fears that the democracies had lost their values and "gone soft." Certainly Nazi propaganda exploited the theme, but so did some of the most important American books and films between 1920 and 1940. Many have noted that the war ended the Depression, resolving major economic problems. Few have considered that the war came just in time to cure the nation's spiritual malaise. By rallying to the colors, by fighting for democracy and equality, Americans could renew their faith in themselves and the nation. *Why We Fight* was a catalyst in this renewal, for the series was not only an answer to the international threat of fascism but a rallying cry for Americans to rediscover the nation's mission as "a lighthouse of freedom." Fifty years later, from the safe vantage of this World War II anniversary year, *Why We Fight* challenges us to address our current crises of values and violence, of jobs and justice, with the same sense of community and democratic populism Frank Capra invoked against global fascism.

Note

This chapter, written in a journalistic style, revisits some of the same territory explored in Chapter 12. It has the virtue of giving a broader context for understanding the popularity and problems of compilation as a genre. Some of Capra's short cuts and showmanship in his work as a pioneer still restrains the compilation genre from becoming a genuine vehicle for interpreting history. (For a different approach by historians who make films, see Chapters 4, 6, 14, 25.)

Works Cited

Bohn, Thomas W. *An Historical and Descriptive Analysis of the "Why We Fight" Series.* New York: Arno Press, 1977.

Capra, Frank. *The Name Above the Title*. New York: Macmillan, 1971.
Culbert, David. "'Why We Fight': Social Engineering for a Democratic Society at War." *Film & Radio Propaganda in World War I*. Ed. K.R.M. Short. Knoxville: U of Tenn. P, 1983.
Maland, Charles. *Frank Capra*. Boston: Twayne, 1980.
OAH Newsletter. OAH.org. 1994.
Rotha, Paul. *Documentary Film*. London: Faber & Faber, 1952.
Sobran, Joseph. "Heartless and Mindless." *National Review* 27 (21): 621. EBSCO.

13
Remembering D-Day: Perspective from the Fiftieth Anniversary

Throughout the summer of 1994, fifty years after D-Day, American tourists will be walking the beaches and hinterlands of Normandy, France, in search of memories. In fact, to help manage this tourist invasion, the Pentagon has begun issuing priority passes to veterans, giving them VIP admission to events, buildings, monuments, and cemeteries.

One group of veterans getting ready for the big trip is from Stillwater, Oklahoma. The tour guide is Walter Price, a retired Army colonel who narrowly missed service in World War II due to his tender age but fully participated in the Korean and Vietnam conflicts. Price loves people, and this is a very people-oriented trip. "It's all about nostalgia for most of my travelers," says Price, "By the time you're my age, you have forgotten the bad things and only the positive and significant things remain. You even find positive things about negative people, even though some who were obnoxious long ago are still obnoxious. The thing to remember is that it was a war that had the total support of the people. There were hazards, there were dangers, but it was more than the right thing to do: It was the only thing to do!"

Price's participants in the fourteen-day tour will follow what he calls the "way of liberty." In London, they will visit Churchill's War Room and the Imperial War Museum. After busing to the seaside embarkation point of Portsmouth, they will inspect Southwick House, General Eisenhower's operational headquarters. A Hovercraft will

Omaha Beach Fallen

take them from Dover across the English Channel to Benouville and Caen, where they are scheduled to stop at the Museum of Airborne Troops and other memorial sites.

As they cross the French countryside, the participants will view military cemeteries from both world wars. The museums they will visit focus on a variety of subjects: the German capitulation of May 7, 1945; the heroic airborne defense of Bastogne (where Gen. Anthony McAuliffe made history by answering a request for surrender with his defiant monosyllabic response: "Nuts!"); the Battle of the Ardennes (popularly known as the Battle of the Bulge); and heroic Arnhem, where British and Polish airborne troops heroically—albeit unsuccessfully—tried to secure the Rhine bridges in September 1944. Veterans in Price's party anticipate a moving experience from visits to these scenes of past sacrifice and victory.

But retired Army Col. LeRoy Stanley of Stillwater, who considered the tour, would rather visit European battle sites privately: "I was one of those replacements—you know, a euphemism for a person to step in for somebody who got shot," he explains. "I'm not sure that I am enamored with the tour approach: I've seen enough cemeteries to last me a lifetime." Stanley was severely wounded during the July 1944 attack on St.-Lo. (In later chapters of his career, Stanley would help extend the "way of liberty" to Korea and Vietnam.)

June 6, 1944: Operation Overlord

At the Trident Conference held in Washington in May 1943, President Franklin Roosevelt and Prime Minister Winston Churchill reaffirmed their plan to invade Europe within a year. In February 1944, Gen. Dwight Eisenhower was designated commander of SHAEF (Supreme Headquarters Allied Expeditionary Forces). His career as a strategic planner had prepared him for this immense undertaking; as far back as 1942, he had drafted a rough sketch for just such an invasion. Yet, as plans moved closer to action, he was humbled by the imponderables; after all, as a recently reissued documentary about the Normandy invasion observes, the coast had been fortified by "a solid wall of steel, iron, and guns." Eisenhower's message to the troops was full of exclamations, but, not long after producing the official exhortation, he wrote this preliminary statement for transmission should the landings fail: "If any blame or fault attaches to this attempt, it is mine alone."

During the evening of June 5, thousands of paratroopers of the 82nd and 101st Airborne were dropped behind the coastal defenses —

Assaulting Fortress Europe

in some cases directly into the sights of German antiaircraft units. Not long afterward, silent gliders full of troops skidded to their landings, some into withering German cross fire. The 82nd Airborne's commander, General Gavin, is reputed to have shared a prescient—and chilling—prediction with his troops: "When you land in Normandy, you will have only one friend: God."

With the dawn of June 6, 1944, six hundred ships blasted the coastal revetments and guns of Hitler's "Atlantic Wall." Nearly ten thousand Allied airplanes filled the skies, preventing the Germans from reinforcing the beachheads. In the meantime, artificial harbors (called Mulberries), troops, ammunition, and fuel sailed from the English southern embarkation points of Dartmouth, Portland, and Portsmouth. As the four thousand troopships crossed the English Channel toward Normandy's Cotentin Peninsula, the reality of this long-promised assault on Hitler's "Fortress Europe" sank in. These soldiers were part of the mightiest armada in history! LeRoy Stanley, then a young platoon commander, remembers his trip across shortly after D-Day: "The weather was cold, there were rough seas. One of my friends and I were seasick, while another lieutenant was comfortable as could be. You would have thought that he was on a South Sea cruise!" Stanley's unit landed just behind an invasion force of one million.

At dawn, shipboard troops heard a fateful command: "Land the landing force." Heavily loaded soldiers clambered down rope nets into bobbing landing craft, carefully holding the vertical ropes to avoid having their hands stepped on by those above. Looking toward the hostile shore from the Channel, the Americans were on the right, under General Bradley, landing at Utah and Omaha beaches. To their left, the British and Canadians, under General Dempsey, landed at Sword, Juno, and Gold beaches. The Americans landed in heavy surf, always a dangerous proposition for the plywood troop carriers. One soldier recalled, "It seemed that we were slamming into waves with enough impact to start any rivet ever set." Once down the ramp, many soldiers, burdened with gear, found themselves in shoulder-deep surf. Tragically, the combined challenges of nature and man led to three thousand deaths and nine thousand casualties on this longest of days.

The entire front for the invasion was just over sixty miles wide. Thanks to Hitler's fixation on Pas de Calais as the allied landing site—plus the German command's belief that the weather was too rough for any sensible commander to order an amphibious assault—Allied invaders were spared the full fury of Rommel's pre-planned counter-attacks.

By June 12, the Allies had moved ten miles inland. Twelve days later, they "owned" almost all of the Cotentin Peninsula and were at the gate of St.-Lo. During preparatory bombing for the assault on St.-Lo, over five hundred American troops were killed by "friendly fire," a tragic opening to what became a successful advance to Avranches. (It was at St.-Lo that LeRoy Stanley was severely wounded by a mine.) But by the end of the first week of July, George Patton and his armor had taken the offensive. As a documentary film made of the event observed, "It was a display of mobility and power by men who had always understood the use of machines—whether for war or for peace." Paris was free by the end of August; indeed, the assault phase of the campaign to liberate Hitler's Fortress Europe was over by September 1944.

Remembering D-Day Here and Abroad

A number of memorial events are planned in the United States. During May, the Eisenhower Presidential Library in Abilene, Kansas, will unveil a new permanent exhibit called "D-Day, the Soldier's Story." A brand-new National D-Day Museum in New Orleans will sponsor a symposium at the end of May under the direction of Stephen Ambrose, the distinguished Eisenhower biographer. Chicago will sponsor a D-Day Commencement Weekend early in June. That same weekend of June 1, the Masterworks Chorus and Orchestra will present a concert titled "In Search of Peace" at Washington's National Cathedral. Over the next week, Virginia Beach will host parades, equipment displays, and a reenactment of the amphibious landing on its beautiful beaches. June 2-8 has been dubbed Fleet Week by New York City's Intrepid Sea Air Space Museum. On June 6, the Hotel Sontifel and "the French people" will serve a gourmet meal concurrently in Chicago, Houston, Los Angeles, Miami, Minneapolis, San Francisco, and Washington. Bangor, Maine, will host a free luncheon for veterans on that day.

On June 6, the Holocaust Museum in Washington, D.C., will dedicate its Eisenhower Plaza (on the west side of the building) to the American crusader whose condemnation of prejudice is impressed upon visitors as they exit the building. Other special events will take place at Fort Dix, New Jersey; the University of Utah; suburban Washington's Wolf Trap outdoor music theater; and aboard the battleship USS *Texas* in La Porte, Texas.

Those who travel to Normandy will find a number of events at different points of the former battlefield. (President Bill Clinton plans to attend one of them.) A sunrise memorial service will consign a memorial wreath to the sea from America's newest carrier, the USS *George Washington*. Around midday, there will be ceremonies for the Ranger Assault group at the famous vertical cliffs at Pointe-du-Hoc. Near midday, there will be joint U.S. and French services at Utah and Omaha beaches. As the day wanes, solemn ceremonies will be held at the Normandy Cemetery near Colleville sur Mer, where nearly ten thousand soldiers are interred and fifteen hundred of those missing in action are commemorated. The Department of Defense is issuing special veterans passes that will guarantee priority seating at these ceremonies, or, if the president is attending, admission to a closed event.

A Moment to Remember

Not everyone will travel to Normandy by boat or car. Ed Manley, 72, of Florida, has been practicing with friends to make a memorial jump, reenacting the night airdrop he made with members of the 81st, the 101st, and the 502nd Airborne. Also preparing for the highly publicized jump are Jack Dunn, 68, of Brookfield, Wisconsin; Ken Shaker, 78, of San Diego; Rene Dussaq, 83, a Frenchman who now lives in San Diego; and Richard Mandich, 69, of San Diego, organizer of a media-magnet group called the Return to Normandy Association. The French government has agreed to permit the jump if the veterans make three successful drops prior to June 6.

The U.S. government is still considering the problems of logistics (the area will be packed with veterans) and legal liability. After D-Day, these veterans became policemen, engineers, and scientists; this summer, they will be reliving—under relatively controlled conditions—a momentous challenge of their youth. Of course, the worst part of the 1944 airdrops was not the parachute ride to the ground but the murderous greeting by German armored units parked in a few of the landing zones. The only vehicular hazards to the 1994 descent will come from the protruding satellite dishes of remote TV trucks and vans waiting to film this pseudo-event. Nevertheless, Stanley, who has made many a jump, predicts that "a lot of brittle, old bones will be shattered."

The Legacy of D-Day: *Civitas* and its Values

Leo Elwell was a major with the 4th Armored Division. He went back to Normandy in 1983, rented a car, and then drove along the shore in an easterly direction from Utah Beach, past Omaha, and then by Gold, Juno, and Sword. Elwell felt a deep curiosity about the place: "You live on memories.... You're curious what it looks like without the noise, shelling, and gasoline problems; inland, I wondered what it would look like in the hedgerow country without the dead horses lying around. And then there were the guys: I'm so glad that I visited the cemetery near our beachhead to see the graves of those wonderful captains. They worried so little about their own lives; they knew the percentages, but they wanted to do their job right."

Describing his trip, Elwell spoke in halting phrases, pausing to catch his breath as memories tugged at his emotions. He suspects that officers fared better during and after D-Day because they had an overall picture of events, whereas enlisted men were immersed in the battle. Now 80, Elwell is still concerned about the troops, reminding me that "people were hurt mentally as well as physically by this longest of days."

For many Americans like Elwell, the fiftieth anniversary of D-Day will provide an opportunity to reflect on the many lessons of a struggle in which the invasion was a crucial turning point. Looking ahead, tour leader Walter Price anticipates a variety of responses: "Some will cry on Omaha Beach, remembering the pain of loss and the buddies who were shot away; some wives and kids will be wandering around, throwing trash on the ground and wondering what all the fuss was about; most will be silent and reflective, fitting this retrospective moment."

Certainly, the trip will be an opportunity to gain perspective on indelible memories of a day when individual lives meshed with history. In a decade seeking common values, the memory of D-Day can be important. Cemeteries are not simply places where men are buried; they are grounds of glory and sacrifice. These soldiers put society ahead of self and gave up their lives for their friends. In doing so, they displayed the spirit of *civitas*, which America's Founding Fathers believed was essential for preservation of liberty. Charles Cathon remembers D-Day with a sense of pride and loss: "Together we had been through months and years of wartime discomforts and strain; marched countless tedious miles; lived in mud and dust, heat and cold. The battalion dominated our time and efforts. Then it all came down to this brief first day of battle, and for them it all ended, and for the rest of us I believe that what has been since has not been exactly the same."

Revisionist Histories: No Friends of Vets

In the 1990s, some in academe have fabricated a dark spin on World War II, judging it to have been an amoral power play of a seriously flawed society. In *Wartime* (1990), Paul Fussell argues, "It was a war and nothing else...stupid and sadistic, a war...of which we are all ashamed...a war which lowers the standard of thinking and feeling" (142). Fussell declares that the war required leaders with

Remembering D-Day 307

"cynicism, efficiency, brutality, and blood-mindedness" (7). People in the 1940s and later missed these valuable insights, he opines, because they lacked "the Higher Skepticism...fueled by the assassinations of the Kennedys and Martin Luther King and the others and by the Vietnam war and by Watergate and by John Mitchell and Spiro Agnew and by Irangate" (167). When serving as a panelist at a World War II conference held in Denton, Texas, in 1991, Fussell ridiculed a presentation of wartime ballads and scoffed at its "sentimentalism." Critics charge Fussell's Olympian views lack the human touch.

Michael Adams' *The Best War Ever* seems to be a Fussell by-product. In his view, Americans spun a self-glorifying myth to ennoble their struggle:

> The war years have come to seem a golden age, an idyllic period when everything was simpler and a can-do generation of Americans solved the world's problems. In this mythic time of the Good War, everyone was united: there were no racial or gender tensions, no class conflicts. Things worked better, from kitchen gadgets to public schools. Fam-

A Revisionist Perspective

ilies were well adjusted, kids read a lot and respected their elders; parents didn't get divorced. (xiii)

Readers do not need a doctorate to predict the ripple effects of such condescension. Not surprisingly, Adams later argued that America's unwillingness to perceive the newly illuminated, nihilistic truths about World War II blinded leaders like John F. Kennedy, leading them to blunder into Vietnam.

Fussell and Adams hold to a chic version of isolationism that will be endorsed, or even understood, by few veterans. According to this "new school," the pride veterans feel is really a form of myopic moral smugness. Veterans will ignore these books, but they should be warned that these fatuous nostrums may someday become our history if we do not contradict them with the living truths of the war generation's experience. Ambrose has said that D-Day "was a pivot point in twentieth-century history." I sincerely hope his National D-Day Museum will preserve materials that will eventually yield a more humanistic and balanced historical understanding. Despite the confusion and loss in the heat of battle, veterans will remember that they did the right thing, the only thing Americans could do when their country called them to travel along their generation's portion of the way of liberty.

Notes

This article was written in the present tense for a journalistic audience, but has elements worth preserving for the record, especially the quotes and observations by veterans who were interviewed. Researchers with an interest in the human touch are urged to consult the archive of interviews on deposit at the Special Collections Section, Edmon Low Library, Oklahoma State U. (There are nearly 200 interviews from WWI on up the line.)

Additional Reading

Adams, Michael C.C. *The Best War Ever: America and World War II.* Johns Hopkins UP, 1994.
Ambrose, Stephen. *The Supreme Commander: The War Years of General Dwight D. Eisenhower.* New York: Doubleday, 1970.

Cathon, Charles. "On Omaha Beach." *American Heritage: World War II Chronicles* 1.1 (1992).
Eisenhower, Dwight D. *Crusade in Europe*. 1948. New York: Da Capo Press: 1988.
Fussell, Paul. *Wartime: Understanding and Behavior in the Second World War*. New York: Oxford UP, 1989.
Hart, B.H. Liddell. *History of the Second World War*. New York: G.P. Putnam's Sons, 1982.

14

Storm of Fire: Reflections on Cadre Films and the Historian as Filmmaker

In the early 1970s, Patrick Griffin (California State University, Long Beach), Richard Raack (California State University, Hayward), and William Malloch (KPFK, Los Angeles) formed Cadre Films and began to confront, in a constructive way, the challenge of educational media. Their first historical documentary, *Goodbye Billy: America Goes to War, 1917-18*, was screened at the 1971 meeting of the American Historical Association. The next year production began on a second historical compilation, *The Frozen War: America Intervenes in Russia, 1918-20*, which was shown at the 1973 biennial meeting of the American Studies Association. *Will Rogers' 1920s: A Cowboy's Guide to the Times* premiered at the 1976 meeting of the American Historical Association. Two of the Cadre Films productions received awards: *Goodbye Billy* received the Audience Prize at the Ann Arbor Film Festival; *Will Rogers' 1920s* was awarded a CINE Golden Eagle, the highest award in the United States for a nontheatrical film. This chapter will outline the working assumptions and early work of the Cadre group; how these ideas were utilized in *Storm of Fire* will then be examined.

Cadre Films and the Historian as Filmmaker

Teachers must use media if they are to compete successfully for the attention of their students. Unfortunately, most of the films available for classroom use are produced by those with training in photojournalism rather than history. As a result, the films on hand

Dresden on Fire

are either unbearably didactic or are organized around historical models that are no longer accepted by trained historians. Deficient in content and in style, these films "are designed, like the newscast, to provide information, predigested and summarized, as if the great issues of history might be purveyed with finality in neat packages fitting an allotted time slot" (Raack "Clio's" 110).

Elective media requires an inventive use of film language that stresses the complexities of the past. Unfortunately, teachers have not been shown how to select and use films intelligently. Upon becoming media editor of *The History Teacher* in 1972, Patrick Griffin observed, "There is a need for the teaching historian to become familiar with the 'language' of media, which includes not only its terminology, but more importantly, the logic of the visual process" (Griffin "Perspectives" 107). Under Griffin's editorship, media reviews for *The History Teacher* became as attentive to the uses of film language as to historical content, and that approach has continued in an important periodical concerned with classroom strategies.

In this writer's view, Cadre's assumption that visual language can be a potent device for teaching history is unchallengeable. The first Cadre production, *Goodbye Billy*, proved that rich cinematic texts reward repeated viewing. Whether or not print-oriented teachers learn with their media-oriented students to be attentive to elements of film language has yet to be proved; however, the commercial success of Cadre Productions *Goodbye Billy* and *Will Rogers' 1920s* seemed to augur well for the historian as filmmaker as the "movement" left the starting blocks.

Cadre films require active participation in the film experience. *Goodbye Billy* certainly demands agility. Because it has no narration, viewers must form their own interpretations of the film experience. The first third of the film evokes the enthusiasm of Americans as they prepared for another "splendid little war." Next, through the intellectual montage, film irony, and the selective editing, the film creates a dizzying sense of disorientation as a chauvinistic dream of glory collides with an obdurate reality. The concluding segment of *Goodbye Billy* explores the disillusionment of what became known as "the lost generation" (see Chapters 10, 11).

The Frozen War, Cadre's second production, mixes oral history interviews, archival footage, and still materials to evoke and criticize America's 1918-1919 intervention into Russian affairs during the early days of the Communist revolution. As in *Goodbye Billy*, stills, cartoons, popular songs, and slogans of the period are juxtaposed in a non-didactic manner. Carefully selected images, the constantly changing editing pace, meaningful transitions, and deliberate juxtapositions of sound challenge even the most sophisticated viewer. Unfortunately, lack of funds and the death of the principal oral history source left this film somewhat weakened, although it is a favorite for many.

Will Rogers' 1920s: A Cowboy's Guide to the Times is the most structured Cadre film, perhaps because it focuses on the evolving career of a single person. Yet the film is relatively free of didacticism. The segment dealing with Prohibition draws from a Universal newsreel to give information about enforcement raids, but the fact that the entire "news event" shown was acted for the benefit of Universal's cameras should lead to discussion about the newsreel—and today's television news--as genre. The section on disarmament poses a number of political and foreign policy questions about the "roaring Twenties" which are notably absent from nostalgic histories of the Jazz Age. Questions about the impact of screen images on American values are evoked in the portion dealing with Hollywood. The entire production demands close attention to imagery, editing, and the relationship between sound and image even though it has much in common with conventional biographical films.

We are dependent upon television and film for so many of our perceptions of "reality" that the Cadre Films demand for active viewing has more than academic importance. Close reading of complex films should foster critical skills which can be transferred to other viewing experiences. Students in our film classes at Oklahoma State University have complained regularly that we have "ruined" television for them; as teachers dedicated to a broad notion of literacy, we have been gratified by this reluctant and unintended tribute.

Cadre films engage the historian-filmmaker in significant research and writing. Patrick Griffin has described his research goal as an attempt to adapt the historical vocabulary to "the very contours of reality" (Griffin "Perspectives" 108). According to Griffin, film can help the historian to recapture the pace, motion, and rhythms of the past which elude the pen ("Film" 6). Indeed, the era of film itself may best be explored and analyzed through film. Commenting on *Goodbye Billy* at the 1971 meeting of the American Historical Association, Warren Sussman (d. 1985) noted that a trial screening of the film at Rutgers University had led him to a new respect for such experiments in historical "writing":

> The extraordinary nature of discussion and debate that can be raised, even questions about the use of evidence and what constitutes historical evidence, questions about the interpretation of the period, questions about point of view, indicate the enormous fruitfulness of the kind of activity the makers have undertaken.... We will only achieve the level of understanding and the true utilization of resources which are available to us when we go beyond what we have seen today and begin to accept something like *Goodbye, Billy* as the equivalent of a kind of historical study in its own right. This is something that was put together with care, work, and energy that goes way beyond many works of scholarship. (Raack "Clio's" 117-18)

Dresden in Ruins

Workshops from Oklahoma to Washington, D. C., have shown that there is growing fascination among historians about what can be done with the cine-pen.

Storm of Fire (1978): Another Cadre Essay in Celluloid

Storm of Fire: World War II and the Destruction of Dresden (1978) is sure to raise the same kind of questions about the use of evidence, the exercise of a point of view, and the nature of "historical writing" in film which greeted earlier Cadre productions. The plot of the film can be briefly stated: during the 1930s, Adolph Hitler mesmerized the German people into committing crimes against humanity. Although endangered countries at first looked on in disbelief, the German juggernaut eventually convinced the nations of the world that they must organize a resistance. The tension escalated: in his rise to power, Adolph Hitler—remembering the ignominy of World War I—promised to "repay bomb with bomb"; Winston Churchill retorted that the Allies would mete out reprisals on Germany in "the measure and more than the measure" (*Storm*). Eventually, the tide of war shifted and Germans learned "to endure the horrors of war they had worked upon others."

Storm of Fire's latter segments explore the sufferings of retreating Germans: tired emigrants catching rides in ox carts; children crying in their confusion; entire nurseries evacuated to the interior. While we are told that Hitler continued to "announce grand schemes," we see that the only Germans left to take up arms are either beyond retirement age or too young to fully realize that they were not participating in a macabre endgame. Though the war was actually over, many would die before hostilities were officially concluded.

The February 13, 1945, the firebombing of Dresden killed somewhere between 35,000 and 135,000 human beings. In the final moments of *Storm of Fire,* bells ring in memory for those who died at Dresden. Classes using this film will argue hard and long over who was to blame for the horrors seen and heard.

Cinematic Elements in *Storm of Fire*

1. Close Ups in Historical Films.
As early as their first project, the Cadre filmmakers discovered that official footage is deficient for close-ups; yet this type of shot is indispensable for compilation films which wish to register human reactions and promote historical empathy. To capture the human element in the *Goodbye Billy* project, Cadre members edited in close-ups from wartime posters and photographs. Raw materials for *The Frozen War* were also deficient in close-ups; some photographs owned by the oral history source, Lynn McQuiddy, added a much-needed personal touch. (Because *Will Rogers' 1920s* drew upon filmed interviews and feature films, there was no problem finding in-close camera perceptions.)

Close-ups in *Storm of Fire* help in two ways. One is to sense the human impact of events: when Hitler enters the Sudetenland (Czechoslovakia), close ups convey the elation of the moment for local ethnic Germans; in the fall of France we see the tears of women in the streets. During the latter portions of the film, close-ups convey a feel for the disorientation of those uprooted by war. Scenes which show the enlistment of teenagers are particularly effective both because of their subject matter and because they reveal how genuine youthful idealism can be misdirected by desperate national leaders.

Close-ups in *Storm of Fire* are also used to raise details of the environment to the level of symbolic significance. As the Nazis come to power, attention is riveted on drums and banners to evoke the primitive emotions induced by Nazi music and pageantry. When the war turns against the Nazis, an extreme close-up of a swastika ring on the hand of a dead tank crewman symbolizes that dreams of conquest have reached a dead end; in another, the inexorable force of Allied retaliation is symbolized by a close-up montage of bullets being sheathed into machine gun belts.

2. The Power of Montage to Communicate Historical Messages.

Sergei Eisenstein and other early Soviet filmmakers were among the first to explore the impact of juxtaposed images. One of the major criticisms the Cadre filmmakers have made of existing historical films is that they ignore the educational potential of montage. Perhaps as a reaction to the current state of the art, *Goodbye Billy* is one continuous montage. Although much of *The Frozen War* is edited to illustrate a personal narrative, "ReVue of the News" segments introduce intellectual montage to explore the paradoxes of America's intervention. The opening segment of *Will Rogers' 1920s* tries to compress the story of the Oklahoma commentator into forty-five seconds of rapidly changing images. The filmmakers have assumed that all such montage segments will be discussed in class on a shot-by-shot basis after an initial viewing of the films, applying a critical eye for imagery, editing—and the resulting historical interpretation.

An intellectual montage late in *Storm of Fire* accentuates the cultural heritage of Dresden. We scan the city at the very opening of the film before this architectural Eden was poisoned by Nazism. Music from Mozart is heard because it was a house rule of Dresden's Zwinger Palace that only Mozart's music could be played. Looking up from low angle, the screen is filled with picturesque pillars, domes, statues, and the fountains.

The camera swings past some of Dresden's castles, panning formal gardens and courtyards. Near the end of the montage, a series of close-ups is introduced: naked nymphs and satyrs are intercut to suggest a playful sensuousness. The final shot of the montage is ominous: it gazes down into a courtyard in which people appear extremely small and unimportant, the high angle shot providing a transition to a "newsreel" about the inhumane destruction to follow.

The Dresden montage helps the instructor explain why the city was such a hub of culture. Students can be asked to speculate about why the filmmaker has used a travelogue film at several points. The interpretive function of the poses of statues might be discussed. Is there an attempt to develop a notion of fertility mentioned in the travelogue? Why are there facial expressions of tension and fear toward the end of the montage?

3. Sound and Image Relationships.
When sound became an option for filmmakers, Sergei Eisenstein discovered that music *inappropriate* to a scene could prod thinking. Cadre films are replete with such cinematic irony. *Goodbye Billy* employs it often: as artillery shells explode among American troops in No Man's Land, Enrico Caruso entertains with strains of "Over There." Gruesome shots of dead and wounded are counterpointed by readings of vacuous patriotic poems by Edgar Guest. In *The Frozen War*, to show that the average American consumer was losing interest in foreign affairs, the filmmakers introduce popular songs about civilian issues and fads such as Prohibition and the newfangled Model T. The visual track shows American soldiers, with symbolic awkwardness, attempting to conduct military maneuvers in deep Siberian snow. Disagreement between sight and sound is important to the disarmament segment of *Will Rogers' 1920s*: General Billy Mitchell's bombers demonstrate that battleships are vulnerable from the air while angelic music supplies a religious atmosphere and Will Rogers talks about the Ten Commandments. Such non-narrative cinematic irony forces attentive viewers to reach their own conclusions. *Goodbye Billy* and *The Frozen War* developed insights about homefront versus battlefront perceptions of war. In its section on disarmament negotiations and weapons development, *Will Rogers' 1920s* demands reflection on the moral evil of war.

In what can be called the "ice follies" section of *Storm of Fire*, cinematic irony provides a sense of impending tragedy. Image and sound relationships are disorienting: a chorus line of skaters performs while the narrator intones, "Long before the atomic bombs fell on Japanese *cities*, the techniques of conventional bombing had so far advanced that Air Force leaders could plan the creation of storms of fire in which those inhabitants who escaped the bomb shock and destruction were baked in cellars and smoked and incinerated in other places of refuge. Whole cities were destroyed in one raid." These words describe the conflagration that came to Dresden, yet the images reflect an entirely different subject: we see that the inhabitants of the doomed city are ordinary people attempting to eke out a few joys, even among the ruins. Low-angle shots and close-ups of the "ice follies" audience further promote empathy and involvement.

To add tension to this sequence, the filmmaker intercut brief flashes of conventional battles raging not far from the city. Just after women applaud the skaters, there is a cut to Russians advancing on horseback; following a spin by the skaters, another quick cut reveals the smoldering body of a helmeted German; a second coordinated move by the performers is interrupted by shots of troops advancing under the covering fire of a flamethrower tank. Such intercutting undermines hopes for the inhabitants of Dresden; the recurring images of fire are portentous.

A second ironic segment further develops sympathy for the people of Dresden. Aerial acrobats of the Sarassani Circus display grace and timing. The cheerful music seems to support the flight of those who mock the dangers of fire and gravity, but the musical passage is actually an allusion to the same Shostakovich symphony that, within *Storm of Fire*, supplies a *leitmotiv* for the wanton destruction of total war. As in the "ice follies" segment, close-ups stress the humanity of the audience: these are people who can be better identified as parents and children than by any wartime stereotype or political label.

4. The Power of Music to Shape and Interpret History.

Commentative music has been essential to the film of ideas since *Potemkin* (1925). (That film on revolution made such effective use of music that a number of European countries permitted its showing only with the stipulation that the score *not* be used.) Some television compilations, such as *Victory at Sea* (1952), are virtually carried by their commentative music (see Chapter 16). The popular songs of the World War I era in *Goodbye Billy* are arranged and cut in such a way as to interpret events. *The Frozen War* uses a combination of Russian folk and symphonic music to communicate a sense of a foreign culture. Many segments of *Will Rogers' 1920s* simply would not communicate their meaning without musical support. William Malloch (d. 1996) deserves the credit for Cadre's unique integration of music and image and those who worked with him were constantly impressed by both his musical erudition and ability to connect ideas with appropriate musical evocations and leitmotivs.

Musical allusion is employed throughout *Storm of Fire* to dramatize Nazi aggression, but also to remind the viewer that the Nazis exploited the music of Wagner and others to promote themselves as heroes of mythical dimensions. Tunes from *Triumph of the Will* (1936) may stimulate discussion of Goebbels' faith in the power of propaganda. German assault on Russia is supported by "Les Preludes" by Liszt, a musical piece frequently inserted as a rousing finale for wartime newsreels in Nazi Germany. Of course, only an active viewer will savor these musical allusions, and even the sophisticated viewer will need to watch *Storm* of *Fire* more than once to understand them all.

Shades of feeling are conveyed by music. At the opening of *Storm of Fire* we see/hear a travel film which describes Dresden as an idyllic city; however, as we cut to the city itself, we see that buildings are clothed in Nazi banners. The musical change coinciding with the visual cut leads the viewer to sense that culture in "the very fertile valley" has gone sour. Later the *Eighth Symphony* of Shostakovich is introduced to comment on Allied advances, leaving the impression that total war corrupts all participants.

Music also establishes connections among disparate shots and scenes. In the opening montage of *Storm of Fire,* Wagnerian music joins shots of Nazi parades with images of ruin. The filmmaker seems to imply that some "twilight of the gods" may have been part of the Nazi dream from the beginning. Music from *Triumph of the Will* supports images of the German people hailing their victorious Fuehrer. But the same music accompanies Churchill's promise to "mete out on the Germans the measure and more than the measure of what they have meted out on us." The implication seems to be that the passion for revenge corrupts even the most righteous cause. A *leitmotiv* from Shostakovich returns insistently to remind us of the horrors of total war.

Some history teachers will resent being asked to listen so attentively to the musical elements of a documentary film. But like all good documentary filmmakers, the Cadre group assumes that music is not mere filler, but a significant part of the cinematic vocabulary.

5. *Propaganda vs. Interpretation.*
Cadre filmmakers have always been wary of archival and news films. Patrick Griffin has noted that "much of the footage of the twentieth century is staged, whether it be actuality footage produced during the war years for home-front consumption or the slick editing associated with the newsreel compilations of the interwar years" (Griffin "Film" 5). Richard Raack has obviously introduced the newsreel *Dresden Blasted* into *Storm of Fire* to provide teachers with an opportunity for propaganda analysis.

The narrator of *Dresden Blasted* speaks with conviction – too much conviction. He claims that the bombing of Dresden is essential to support Russian attackers seventy miles to the East. Much emphasis is placed on the sacrifice made by British and American flyers for their Russian buddies on the ground. As background, the narrator explains that this air attack is especially dangerous because the Germans are employing a new anti-aircraft weapon. *Dresden Blasted*

The Inner City is the 'Target for Tonight'

concludes with confident music backing a stentorian explanation that this was a stinging blow to the Germans.

Storm of Fire has prepared the active viewer to distrust *Dresden Blasted*. Footage has shown that the war is practically over. An intellectual montage has invested our sympathies in the cultural history of Dresden and film irony has excited our concern for the inhabitants of the Saxon capital. Narrative information has revealed that there was an "unspoken goal" to exact revenge for German bombings of London and Coventry. Classes using this film should evaluate every assertion in the newsreel. My own brief examination of David Irving's study, *The Destruction of Dresden*, reveals that *Dresden Blasted* is little more than a whitewash for an atrocity.

Conclusions

A close look at *Dresden Blasted* and *Storm of Fire* suggests that films always reflect a point of view and are colored by the period in which they are made. Cadre productions certainly show a discernible bias. *Goodbye Billy* reflects the anti-war feelings of the Vietnam era and received much kudos for doing so. *The Frozen War* makes overt comments about the fruitlessness of American interventionism. *Will Rogers' 1920s* over-plays the sardonic side of the Oklahoman's humor, especially in relation to national politics.

All Cadre productions treasure individuals over groups and group slogans. In *Goodbye Billy*, the Yanks may be out to prove American invincibility, but we are worried about what happens to Billy. In *The Frozen War*, the voice of Lynn McQuiddy provides a personal perspective on events which contradicts rationalizations used to justify our intervention into Russian politics. The common sense individualism of *Will Rogers' 1920s* exposes the pretensions of parties and national leaders. *Storm of Fire* shows solicitude for individuals caught in the crush between contending armies.

Cadre productions remind us that our stock of armaments makes total war so easy to initiate. *Storm of Fire* thus focuses upon an issue in history that has contemporary importance. Sensitivity to film language will help teachers and students obtain the maximum classroom benefits from this sophisticated essay in celluloid.

Discussion of Literature

Raack's "Clio's Dark Mirror" is a *locus classicus* for complaints about the shortcomings of existing historical films. Raack takes a more positive approach toward extant materials in his article, "The Documentary Film in History Teaching." O'Connor and Jackson's *Teaching History With Film*, attempts to show teachers how to "read" films for their point of view and ideology. Smith's *The Historian and Film* makes similar efforts. O'Connor synthesized his work in this area in his *Image as Artifact*.

Every semester during the late 1970s and early 1980s, 800 freshmen at Oklahoma State University elected a composition module with a film emphasis. The text for this course was Elder's *Writing About Film*. Chapter 3 of the Elder text concentrates on the film language employed by *Goodbye Billy*. Students watched the film twice, wrote a 750-word composition and were then led through the film shot-by-shot, using stop-action equipment. *Goodbye Billy* has proven to be an excellent primer for any visual literacy program. Griffin describes assumptions about the audience for *Goodbye Billy* in "Film." In "The Making of *Goodbye Billy*," Griffin also discusses the educational potential of montage in the film, as well as the many challenges faced by the filmmakers.

For the special challenges faced by the filmmakers of *Will Rogers' 1920s*, see Chapter 6.

Works Cited

Elder, Harris J. *Writing About Film*. Dubuque, IA: Kendall/Hunt Publishing, 1977.
Goodbye Billy: America Goes to War, 1917-18. Dir. Richard C. Raack, William F. Malloch, and Patrick Griffin. Churchill Films, 1972.
Griffin, Patrick. "Perspectives: Media in *The History Teacher*." *The History Teacher* 6.1 (1972): 107.
—. "Film, Document, and the Historian," *Film and History* 2.2 (1972): 1-6.
—. "The Making of *Goodbye, Billy*." *Film and History* 2.2 (1972): 6-10.
Irving, David. *The Destruction of Dresden*. New York: Holt, Rinehart, and Winston, 1963.
O'Connor, John E. *Image as Artifact: The Historical Analysis of Film and Television*. Malabar, FL: Robert E. Krieger Publishing, 1990.

O'Connor, John E., and Martin A. Jackson, *Teaching History With Film.* Washington, D.C.: American Historical Association, 1974.

Raack, R. C. "Clio's Dark Mirror: The Documentary Film in History." *The History Teacher* 6.1 (1972): 110.

—. "The Documentary Film in History Teaching: An Experimental Course." *The History Teacher* 6.2 (1973): 281-94.

Rollins, Peter C. "The Making of *Will Rogers' 1920s.*" *Film & History* 7.1 (1977): 1-5.

Smith, Paul. ed. *The Historian and Film.* Cambridge, England: Cambridge UP, 1976.

Storm of Fire: World War II and the Destruction of Dresden. Dir. Richard Raack. Churchill Films, 1978.

The Frozen War: America Intervenes in Russia, 1918-20. Prod. Richard Raack. Cadre Films, 1973.

Will Rogers' 1920s: A Cowboy's Guide to the Times. Cadre Films, 1976.

Cold War

15
Victory at Sea: Cold War Epic

> I have told my sons that they are not under any circumstances to take part in massacres, and that the news of massacres of enemies is not to fill them with satisfaction or glee.
>
> Kurt Vonnegut, Jr., *Slaughterhouse Five*

A television series like *Victory at Sea* may seem trivial as "history" when compared with the scholarly, fifteen-volume dreadnaught by Admiral Samuel Eliot Morison (on which it was based), but this academic judgment may miss the most important point for a media age. *Victory at Sea* received practically every major television award for which it was eligible: it won the Freedom Foundation's George Washington Medal; it was awarded an "Emmy" from the Academy of Television Arts and Sciences; it received "best documentary" awards from five major trade magazines, and a host of "outstanding achievement" awards. Its unforgettable, interpretive score by Robert Russell Bennett (based on tunes by Richard Rodgers), rendered by the NBC orchestra, became RCA's best-selling Gold Seal Album and is still available on CD. The series has become a permanent part of America's popular culture.

Furthermore, the series has had an enduring popularity since it was first broadcast in 1952. As of 2000, *Victory at Sea* had been shown in excess of fourteen times in New York, twelve times in Los Angeles, and nine times in Milwaukee. This record is especially impressive, since the series consists of twenty-six half-hour programs.

History with a Cinematic Pen

In 1961, when a ninety-minute version of the series was shown on television, Bob Williams of the *Philadelphia Bulletin* proclaimed that "*Victory at Sea* is television's most prodigious achievement, and this distinction has not been surrendered." An advertising pamphlet, with an eye on the bottom line, underscored this eminence in terms of dollars and cents: "*Victory at Sea* has knocked *The Untouchables* off its perch as the hottest network show of the season." The research department of NBC (the original broadcast owner of the series) reported that "*Victory at Sea* is a powerful attraction for men, women, and younger people in urban, suburban, and rural areas—in short, of every segment of the country's population." During the 1995 celebrations of the allied victory in WWII, the series was rebroadcast on the Public Broadcasting Service (PBS) and made available for sale through PBS. Such an offer seemed calculated to attract older viewers during the annual fund-raising drive. Later, Amazon.com advertised the entire series for sale at less than $100. Unlike Admiral Morison's official, multivolume history of naval operations during WWII, the series has never to be relegated to the mothball fleet of history.

Any serious student of American culture in the twentieth century must wonder what makes *Victory at Sea* such an entertaining spectacle. Could it be that the series not only recorded the history of naval operations in World War II on film, but also supplied a convincing interpretation of the larger significance of the war?

Admiral Morison's naval history may ultimately be the real history, but the reel messages of *Victory at Sea* continue to affect attitudes held by millions of Americans toward the character and utility of war, the place of the military in our society, and America's international mission.

Yet there are limitations to the image of war presented by *Victory at Sea*. The series certainly exhibited cinematic inventiveness and the many awards were deserved by the creators Henry Salomon (Producer), M. Clay Adams (Director), Richard Rodgers (12 musical themes), Robert Russell Bennett (musical score and direction), and Isaac Kleinerman (film editing). In 1953, when the U.S. Navy awarded Distinguished Service Medals to Henry Salomon, Richard Rodgers, and Robert W. Sarnoff, it was not because these men deserved to be rewarded for a successful publicity campaign. Such a construal of their efforts would be unimaginative and cynical. There is a more useful way to approach the limitations of this series: it can be examined as an historical document shaped by the currents of opinion in the era in which it was conceived and produced. From the distance of the 21st century, we see things differently because we are outside the dark penumbra that passed over the American landscape in the 1950s. What seemed so right then now strikes us as dangerously—even fatally—narrow. Yet while today educators are trying to wipe the slate clean, a popular series like *Victory at Sea* continues to inscribe on the popular mind perspectives which most informed Americans are trying hard to forget. Indeed, we need to *unlearn* some of the lessons taught by *Victory at Sea*, a dangerously seductive epic of the Cold War era.

Production History

Henry Salomon, the originator of *Victory at Sea*, devoted much of his time as an undergraduate at Harvard to the dramatic arts. After graduating, he went to work for NBC's script division. When the war came, Salomon enlisted in the Navy, where he was assigned to the public relations division where one of his tasks was to produce a radio series entitled *The Victory Hour*.

In 1942, President Roosevelt commissioned Salomon's former tutor at Harvard, Samuel Eliot Morison, to commence work on a living history of naval operations and Morison selected Salomon as his assistant. Roosevelt wanted his historians to be present while history was actually being made. He envisaged their "writing current history on the scene while events were happening for the first time since Thucydides accompanied troops in the Peloponnesian War." To carry out this Presidential mandate, Salomon landed in six major Pacific invasions, where his only task was to observe history. After the war, he was dispatched by Naval Intelligence to Tokyo to interrogate Japanese naval leaders and to study their side of the conflict.

From 1945-1948, Salomon continued to help with the fifteen-volume historical juggernaut. After leaving the Navy in 1948, he approached Robert W. Sarnoff (a Harvard classmate) with the idea of a television series based on the research. Sarnoff was enthusiastic about the project. The general concept for the series was straightforward enough. On hand, due to Salomon's close contacts with the military, were nearly twelve hundred miles of film covering nearly every aspect of the most massive war the world had ever known. The propaganda films of Frank Capra's *Why We Fight* series (see Chapter 12) had tapped only a few drops of this reservoir of film, and, for obvious reasons, none of the wartime films had attempted a grand, sweeping panoramic perspective of the entire global struggle from *both sides* of the conflict.

As historian and dramatist, Salomon was bold enough to propose such an epical treatment. Furthermore, with the war over, Salomon believed that he was free to concentrate on the pure human drama of the epic conflict. The raw footage available could be used to portray the preparations, plans, and finally, the collisions of the antagonists. Here indeed was a marvelous opportunity to recreate, in the words of the NBC Press Kit, "the drama that's packed into history."

Critical Reception

Two weeks into the twenty-six week series, *Time Magazine* enthusiastically proclaimed that the technique of depicting both sides of the action gave the new television series a "breathless" pace. The first episode ("Design for War") had successfully evoked the dangers of an Atlantic passage: "It leaps breathlessly back and forth between

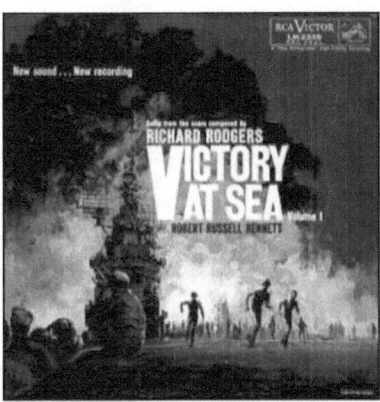

RCA Gold Seal Album

British film and captured German footage. The effect is to personalize the battle. The war becomes a stirring conflict between a Nazi submarine captain, gloating over a new kill as he downs periscope, and a half-drowned British mariner, hauled oil-covered from the wreckage of his torpedoed tanker"(105). The reviewer emphasized, quite accurately, that this would be a continuing technique of the series, one which distinguished it from its documentary predecessors. His sense of involvement in the drama of the action singles out the compelling quality of the series—its capacity to drag the viewer willy-nilly into the fighting spirit of the struggle: "This Week, *Victory's* second chapter, "The Pacific Boils Over," had TV critics cheering again: "The Pearl Harbor attack is pictured, from a conference of Japanese naval brass all the way through the fateful Sunday morning when the carrier-based Japanese squadrons flew in low over Oahu's mountains. Televiewers are able to watch from enemy planes, as the bombs are released. Then, from harbor vantage points, the film recreates the American feeling of dazed disbelief as the U.S. Fleet is crippled"(105). It is significant that the reviewer stressed the power of the music to draw viewers into the "mood" of the scene: "The entire sequence runs without spoken narration or sound effects; the Rodgers score comments on the situation far more effectively than the words could"(105). (We will return to the importance of music for the series later in this chapter.)

Like Arthur Knight of the *Saturday Review*, many found the

series "a stirring and dramatic demonstration of the power of the film medium to mold raw fact into artistic, meaningful, even memorable statement." All of the reviewers agreed that *"Victory at Sea* is supposed to stir up the emotions, and it does" (26). In many ways, the success of the series was harbinger of the popularity of compilation documentary as a genre for television. (See Chapter 14.) Unfortunately, none of the contemporary reviewers found it necessary to define precisely *what* emotions were excited or toward what end. The creators of *Victory at Sea* wished to involve their television audience in the drama of war. They were successful in arousing their audience—perhaps too successful. *Scholastic Magazine* interviewed Henry Salomon shortly after *Victory at Sea* first appeared on television. The reporter concluded that Salomon was a teacher of history with a very special student body: "Salomon's classes will be conducted not at the school blackboard, but right in the family parlor"(4). Clearly, the impact of such "teaching" could be as problematic as it seemed exciting.

Lessons for the Young

Many friends have recounted their childhood memories of the hushed atmosphere of these parlor-classrooms: no laughing, no random noises were allowed on those somber Sunday afternoons during the fall and spring of 1952-53. Even Bernard DeVoto (who was editor of *Harper's*) confessed proudly that his house was a tightly rigged ship when *Victory at Sea* was on the air: "For twenty-six Sundays last year neither the telephone nor the doorbell was answered at my house between 3 and 3:30 p.m."(8). As mainland China and Russian-occupied territories of Eastern Europe were being swallowed by the Communist behemoth, what DeVoto saw on these reverential Sunday afternoons provided him with consolation and inspiration about the role of America in international affairs.

As a result of his involvement in *Victory at Sea's* theme of liberation (including, it should be noted, the liberation of French Colonialists in North Africa), DeVoto arrived at a conclusion which is consonant with the message of the series. Americans have a duty to carry forward the spirit of Liberty: "We forget too easily; everyone should see the whole series every year. It will be all right with me if Congress sees it twice a year"(8).

Other journalists recognized that the organizing theme of the series was "the preservation of freedom and the overthrow of despotism," and quoted approvingly DeVoto's remarks about "liberation." But some critics, who were closer to their TV audience than the prestigious editor of *Harper's*, saw a more relevant contemporary application for these lessons. As Jack O'Brien concluded (not without a little chauvinism), the series proved that it wasn't "ever safe to push the U.S. too far. It might even be a good idea to show *Victory at Sea* to Nikita Khrushchev. A very good idea." Here was a viewer who had learned his lessons well!

Indeed, it would be extremely difficult not to sympathize with the allied cause in *Victory at Sea*. "Japs" may want rubber, oil, copper and other strategic goods. On the other side of the globe, German "hordes" may swarm into defenseless nations for purposes of exploiting resources and enslaving populations, but the Allies are above such worldly interests. The series elevates the argument above the level of power politics to the ethereal regions of "moralism" and "legalism" from where it makes many such ideological points, with the unfortunate effect of driving home into the consciousness of the audience precisely what George Kennan in his *American Diplomacy, 1900-1950,* had warned must be *unlearned* by Americans in the 1950s. In the Pacific, for example, we are not inching toward a military objective. Our efforts have a more transcendental meaning: "From island to island, continent to continent, the children of free peoples move the forces of tyranny from the face of the earth...it is, it will be so, until the forces of tyranny are no more." As a viewer absorbs this rhetoric of liberation, he is forced to survey the wreckage of machines and men. How will the viewer act on some future occasion because he has internalized such a summation of the war experience? If he has been totally uncritical, he will believe that it was not only the stern duty, but the quasi-religious honor of our military men to fight and die on the Pacific beachheads. Because they were strong men in battle then, we must be so in the future when our turn comes to defend the cause of freedom. Thus, while scholars in the 1950s were attempting to show that the myth of American innocence was a real obstacle to creative thinking, *Victory at Sea* was exploiting the myth for all the rhetorical freight it could carry.

A Consensus View of History

According to *Victory at Sea* America has no pressing social problems, and thus no real need for internal politics. The madness of political zealots and bigots is strictly a European and Japanese specialty. As an innocent nation, we are coerced into the global war by these greedy and rapacious antagonists. (Not a word is mentioned about America's desire for "normalcy" in the 1920s, or that our isolated innocence may have been purchased at the price of a second, larger war.) As an "arsenal of democracy," America manufactures arms, bandages, ships, and disciplined men. Since an isolated, innocent nation cannot assist unless its "goods" are delivered to the front, the U.S. Navy enters the story not so much as an arm of the military machine designed to kill but as a guardian for the conveyors of goods.

A person who holds to an ideal of political consensus will inevitably interpret dissent as an alien intrusion. At the time that *Victory at Sea* was being broadcast, such people were the willing tools of demagogues like Joseph McCarthy. The prescription for dissent in such a perspective is that we must cauterize the body politic of its unhealthy elements. The makers of *Victory at Sea* would reprehend such paranoia, yet their celebration of America's innocence provided fuel for such a crusade.

In addition to reconsidering the myth of national innocence, Americans in the 1950s should have been reassessing the uniqueness of America's revolutionary experience. *Victory at Sea's* lesson on our role as a democracy is as anachronistic as its statement about American innocence. We are told that the American experience has created a free society which is different in degree from other societies, but that our highly developed, free enterprise, capitalist nation is in no way different in kind. We may be freer, happier, richer than the rest of the world, but this is not because we have been so lavished with special privileges; as a result, it is our mission to transform the rest of the world into our image. If we become frustrated in our attempts, we are justified in using any power necessary, for we represent the cause of freedom.

Pearl Harbor pushed the United States into the global struggle. We certainly would not have gone to war to preserve the British Empire. Yet, in the Mediterranean episode of *Victory at Sea*, the

Victory at Sea: Cold War Epic 335

British naval campaign to keep the lifelines of empire open is reported with reverence and enthusiasm. Great Britain was fighting desperately to retain its colonies; yet many Americans at the time, including F.D.R., believed that the British had no right to an Empire. The episode titled "Mare Nostrum" does not allow time to make such cynical judgments. The orchestra interweaves the storm theme with the victory theme. Spectators become too emotionally involved to do anything more than absorb the spectacle and admire the courage of the British Navy. Other imperial designs are not so sympathetically treated. *Victory at Sea's* contempt for Italy's relatively smaller (although more recent) efforts in the colonial field provides a good contrast. During the March on Rome by the US Army, Leonard Graves explains that Italy is receiving (as Germany and Japan will eventually receive) a deserved punishment for toying with dreams of Empire.

Episode number seventeen ("The Turkey Shoot") conveys a similar judgment. The program first shows how the Japanese forcibly established themselves on Guam, which, since the Versailles Treaty of 1919, had been an American protectorate. The Japanese cruelly impose their language and customs upon the inhabitants. Next comes a savage battle to retake Guam. Finally, the program elicits admiration as the Americans develop the island as an *entrepot* for U.S. Pacific operations. Once the benevolent Americans have regained control from the Japanese, it seems only proper to teach the natives English in the public schools, and that George Washington's birthday should become an obligatory island festival. After all, we represent Liberty, not strategic self-interest. Our customs will enlighten and liberate whereas Japanese customs have been designed only to enslave. (In the 21st century, Guam has become even more crucial strategic site for U.S. Naval and Air Force bases.)

The unselfconscious acceptance of "the white man's burden" approach to Empire is best captured in a single image in episode number eight, "Mare Nostrum." A heavily clad Arab barely moves ahead of his obstinate donkey in the foreground of this visual portrait. Towering over him in the background is a sleek but threatening British cruiser which is gliding through the Suez Canal. The implicit message here is that Western man's technical superiority justifies control of strategic isthmuses and natural resources.

Film Language: Framing the Violence of War

Victory at Sea has very little insight into the individual participant's perspective of war. The screen is flooded with sublime scenes of machines in action: flaming broadsides are fired at enemy shorelines; the sky is filled with squadrons of fighters; hundreds of bombs fall in retribution toward enemy cities. Because it is infatuated with these technological elements, the series neglects to report as dramatically on the human costs. The reality of this human dimension—which might elicit sympathy or fear—is muffled by a number of framing devices.

Superior editing provides the most significant framing device. For example, the military operations in *Victory at Sea* are always perfectly planned and conducted. In the first stage of any operation, planners are working at their desks, or sitting (in dress uniform) around a large table knowledgeably discussing "the big picture"; this is the "think tank" from which plans trickle down to lower echelons. While NBC orchestra plays the "communications theme," a clear and precise attack order is sent by wireless to ships on station in the high seas.

At this stage appears a close-up of the admiral or general officer in command of the operation. The impression given is very important—the sequence of images and sounds conveys the message that

Film Rhetoric Recycled on DVD

battle orders are not impersonal, not based on scanty information, but are as clear and precise as the chain of command traced by the montage. We are certainly *not* living in the world of alienation and depersonalization which Joseph Heller explored in *Catch-22*. In *Victory at Sea* the chain of command always has a human face and always cares.

The preparations for battle are followed by undeniably "dramatic" battle scenes. Yet here again the camera is more interested in the machines of war and the visual excitement of the scene than with the less photogenic effects upon human beings. The series does not attempt to portray the individual's frustration, his sense of being an expendable cog in the gigantic machine of war—even under the best conditions. The mix of narration and music promotes deep involvement with the scene, assuring viewers that the great naval juggernaut has a broader purpose—with the implication that the participant in the actual battle is as conscious of this mission as the television viewer.

Some distinctions seem necessary at this point. Someone immersed as a living (and potentially dead) human being in an actual battle is a "participant." Those watching a film about a battle on a movie or television screen, and caught up in the emotional drama may be called "participant-observers." Finally, those who study the overall causes and cost of war are "observers." A "participant" in battle is concerned first and foremost with one thing—staying alive. Obviously, at least while he is firing his rifle, he is not in the mood to watch a TV documentary about war. On the other hand, the "observer" does not want to surrender critical faculties to the seductive drama of the media: sources of information should speak to real and pressing questions, deliver hard data rather than nostalgia or vicarious excitement. *Victory at Sea* has little to say to either the "participant" or the "observer."

Viewers as Participant Observers

The real target for *Victory at Sea* drama of battle is the "participant-observer." For the participant-observer, World War II becomes a masculine conflict unlike the Super Bowl only in the sense that historical relevance has been added to the contest. The ambiguous aspect of the participant-observer's relationship to the drama is that he often thinks of himself as an actual participant, when the only combat he has seen has taken place within the confines of his television screen. Even if he has once been a "participant" in the battles portrayed by the series, he will most likely jettison what terror and distress have clung to his memories in favor of the more reassuring "top brass" perspective which *Victory at Sea* gives him as a "participant-observer." The danger, therefore, of Isaac Kleinerman's superb film editing and the arousing orchestrations by Robert Russell Bennett is that they will convince even the combat veteran that the war was not an unmitigated horror.

The experience of death in combat is always framed; in addition, death in *Victory at Sea* is always public and dramatic. Men do not appear to die accidentally or senselessly—for example, we never see an infantryman blown up by a land mine, or a flight deck crewman of an aircraft carrier sliced in two by a propeller or a resting soldier accidentally shot by his foxhole buddy. These were common events in World War II, but they have no place in an epic. With whole armadas of ships and planes cruising on toward Victory, it is distracting to stop for consideration of individual casualties.

The music supplies a unifying emotion which makes the disparate parts of the scene cohere for the participant-observer. Even if the series does not show sailors or marines "wasted" *en route* toward the objective, the music communicates that something larger than individual lives is succeeding—indeed, living. Narrator Leonard Graves intones that what lives on is the spirit of freedom, but what appears on screen is the survival of naval vessels, planes, and tanks.

The music has other important molding influences on the participant-observer. The battle scenes always call for the most strenuous efforts of the orchestra. Yet an approach less fascinated with machines might pay more attention to the pain inflicted by the participants upon one another. For a participant, the sinking of a single ship (if he is on it) the wounds of a solitary individual (if they be his wounds); the loss of a single loved one (a husband or father) *could* be the climax of not only a single battle, but the entire war.

Narrator commentary prevents full recognition of the merciless beating imposed upon the First Marine Division in "Guadalcanal." Musical and editing effects are also used in the

Guadalcanal episode to frame the true violence of war experienced by a participant. First, the orchestra introduces the "Guadalcanal March," a melody around which editing orders visual perceptions. The fighting on Guadalcanal is going badly for the Americans, but with this rousing tune, the participant-observer is flown back to the states for a heartening tour of domestic mobilization and weapons production. The theme grows louder, and is developed by a rich orchestration during a montage showing America beginning to flex its massive industrial muscles. As the episode progresses through a number of impressive production sequences—steel mills flaming in the night, riveters and welders by the dozen putting the finishing touches on planes, tanks, and ships—the participant-observer grows increasingly confident that, however poor America's showing may be in the early rounds of the war, it will eventually drown the enemy in a torrent of productivity. With confidence thus fortified, the episode returns to Guadalcanal. The impression upon the participant-observer is one of immediate danger—but of long-term reassurance. While it may in fact be true that the "nation" as an abstraction, the "campaign" as a large-scale effort over a number of years here started on an upward climb, it is also important to note that viewers are relieved of the responsibility of absorbing the full intensity of the terror and pain incurred in this particular battle by the Marines of the First Division. As a result of his protected position, the participant-observer carries away a pseudo-realistic rather than a true picture of what war has been—and, therefore, what will be.

In episode number fifteen ("D-Day") there is an interesting twist. Narrator Graves muses over the confusions and miscalculations which characterized the invasion of Europe: "Few casualties occur where expected...Sometimes no casualties occur where the most are expected...but all men are doomed to experience their own end." There is an admirable candor in this description, but it is *not* reinforced by visual or musical materials. Such an examination of the confusion and chaos of war would detract from the impression of the inexorable momentum of the allied assault on Fortress Europe.

Because *Victory at Sea* is organized around an official perspective of the war, it has neither the time nor the desire to tell of the

Marines Swarm an Objective on Tarawa

human cost of advancing the struggle. The result is indeed paradoxical: although the series is composed almost entirely of "actuality footage," it does not give a truly realistic picture of battle. Through superior editing, through the reassurances provided by music and narration, the viewer as participant-observer is kept far enough away from the heart of darkness to see its lights and shades as romantic and alluring.

Neither the thoughts nor the voices of participants are allowed to thrust their way into our midst. Early in the *Victory at Sea* project, Henry Salomon established a rule that actual sounds should be used as little as possible. Instead of the actual voices of participants, the series employs the authoritative voice of Leonard Graves speaking about broad-sweeping generalizations such as "freedom" and "democracy." Rather than the actual sounds of supporting guns and exploding shells, or even the high whine of a ship's engine, there is the evocative orchestration of Robert Russell Bennett. Because these effects establish a distance between viewers and the visual images, no one is forced to confront the face of war.

Some Especially Egregious Scenes

There are a few moments—unforgivable moments—in *Victory at Sea* which deserve special attention, since they exhibit a lapse of taste which could have passed unnoticed only in an atmosphere like that provided by the Cold War.

We have talked about the sequence showing domestic mobilization in the "Guadalcanal" episode. One portion of this sequence shows African Americans bent over cotton rows, contributing to the national effort. The war was in part a tragedy because it diverted America's attention from needed domestic reforms. The use of this particular footage of cotton pickers is doubly ironic because it was lifted from a crusading *March of Time* documentary on the plight of tenant farmers in the South. One wonders what the responsible individual—probably Kleinerman—thought about as he extracted shots for this sequence. In a wartime documentary, we might be more tolerant of such insensitivity, but in a documentary assembled in 1952, this editing constitutes the callous misuse of archival footage just because it was available—alas a practice which has become a media tradition.

In episode number eight ("Mare Nostrum") the ear is caressed by a romantic lullaby as an Italian cruiser plunges to the bottom of the Mediterranean. In episode number nine ("Sand and Sea") the camera, accompanied by the peppy strains of a Broadway finale, flies over the captured enemies in the POW camp below. The music and the triumph raise the spirits—after all, the Allies won the battle for North Africa and the thirty thousand German prisoners seen stumbling along on the desert below deserve their humiliation. Even a tendentious German propaganda film such as *Baptism of Fire* (1940) never goes so far as to ridicule an enemy who has suffered an ignominious defeat.

Episode number eleven ("Magnetic North") offers perhaps one of the truly unforgivable sequences of the series. In its dramatization of the allied effort to convoy goods through the North Sea, a number of merchant marine vessels are sunk. In one case, after a ship goes down, the camera suddenly closes in on a dory filled with survivors where the camera explores the strained faces of the six crewmen who are rowing the lifeboat. At the helm is an elderly, bearded man, obviously the venerable captain. The captain looks up, and as he does so, the camera traces his line of sight to a German light bomber flying overhead. (By this time, we realize that we are not watching actuality footage at all, but a slice of venom from a wartime feature film.) The camera closes to within a yard of the cockpit, revealing the diabolical gleam in the eye of the flying Hun. He pushes the stick forward, and begins strafing, moving his shot pattern on line with the lifeboat, cutting into flesh and wood as the mechanically perfect pinpoints of fifty caliber bullets sweep across their target. After the plane passes over, the camera returns again to the lifeboat—it is now sinking and most of the crew is now dead. Those who are still living are wounded so badly that they probably will not be able to keep themselves afloat for very long.

Such sequences would be understandable in wartime propaganda films, but they are inexcusable in a documentary production in 1952. Why personalize the hatred of Germans seven years after the war? The historically useful emotion to encourage in 1952 was a hatred of war itself.

The two worst cases of *Victory at Sea* moral lapses are both in episode number thirteen ("Melanesian Nightmare"). The first involves a desperate, last-ditch attempt by the Japanese to reinforce their flagging defense of Rabaul, Papua New Guinea. The scene itself is dismal—the Japanese hoped that they could race an unprotected troop transport loaded with three thousand infantrymen across the Bismarck Sea without being discovered. Unfortunately for the three thousand troops on that ill-fated ship, an American observer plane spotted the lumbering transport.

For some reason, the creators felt that this was an exciting moment worthy of dramatic reconstruction. In this segment there is the same ironic contrast between the pathos of the situation and the exultation of the hunt that we saw in the episode ("The Killers and the Killed") which reported the capture of a German submarine. First, an observer plane spots the Japanese ship. The pilot radios his information back to an operations center where the course of the enemy transport is plotted. Then pilots are briefed and bombers loaded with their deadly cargo. (Most of the footage for these reconstructed stages of preparation was lifted from Navy training films.) As the planes make an initial pass over their defenseless target, the music reaches a heroic crescendo. Finally, the bombs and torpedoes do their work. No one would question the necessity of the participants to go through with their bloody drama, but in 1952 why give the whole performance an air of sport?

A second tasteless scene from "Melanesian Nightmare" explains that the significance of death depends upon whether or not you are on the winning side. For the dead Americans, there is a promise of afterlife and a deep tenderness in the voice of Leonard Graves as he reflects over the coffins: "Death...these brave men know thy sting...God grant they know thy victory." The death of Christ is subtly identified with the death of American soldiers for their nation's cause. In isolation, such a statement would be harmless, but clear contrasts are established with the fate of our Japanese adversary.

Japanese servicemen do not die with the same prospects before them, because their personal sacrifice has been for a *losing* cause. Footage from Japanese films shows grief-stricken families claiming urns filled with ashes of their sons, fathers, husbands. The narrator explains that there is little consolation for the survivors, and absolutely no spiritual reward to be expected by the men who sacrificed their lives. Speaking in ironic cadences, Leonard Graves addresses the dead Japanese: "Welcome home, young man.... . You are home, but you will never know anything but a long, endless night." This moral is reinforced by the visual contrast of American dead being shipped back home in full-sized coffins *versus* the Japanese delivery of ashes in little metal tubs. These images, plus the narrator's sarcasm about the Buddhist denial of an afterlife are perniciously effective. They communicate a message that American deaths are better, more glorious deaths than Japanese deaths.

This kind of moralist is dangerous. Winning the contest should not be a payoff for the deaths of our friends and loved ones. Death strikes us all as human beings, not as members of nations. If in no other way, recognition of the democracy of death could be the beginning of an insight into the democracy of the living. We have a duty to respect men above and beyond their group association or intellectual beliefs. To lose this universal perspective, to be thrilled by the bombing of a helpless target or to mock the tragic loss of husbands and sons, is to degrade both the series and our own humanity.

The purpose of *Victory at Sea* was to bring back into focus what was gradually slipping out of memory. But there are dangers of remembering the so-called "lessons of history" too well: a drama of commemoration may possess a dangerous beauty. As the thirteen-hour series progresses, it becomes ever more deeply involved with the military tactics and machines which are needed for the crusade to liberate enslaved peoples. The cause is just because America has been designated by nature as a land of liberty and plenty. By the time the entire twenty-six week cycle has come to a close, viewers are inextricably entangled in a psychology of self-righteous moralism—what some have called "the Cold War mentality." A *Victory at Sea* viewer is encouraged to associate any sympathy for fallen peoples with a military response and believes that it is useless for an individual to oppose this militaristic reflex. In short, the *Victory at Sea* graduate becomes trapped by reverence for World War II as a crusade for freedom. As George Kennan and others were trying to explain in the 1950s, Americans should have been learning entirely new lessons. But *Victory at Sea* did not foster a perspective characterized by complexity or irony. Instead, by exploiting the myths of American innocence, and the ideology of freedom, it impeded a fresh look at the America's global situation.

An Alternative Approach: Leo Hurwitz's *Strange Victory* (1948)

There were other cinematic ways to interpret the raw stuff of World War II history. *Strange Victory*, an excellent documentary made in the 1940's by Leo Hurwitz, used one of these alternative approaches. It serves as an excellent foil to *Victory at Sea* because it was released at about the same time *Victory at Sea* began its first run on television. It is also a fascinating contrast because, unlike the TV epic, *Strange Victory* was almost entirely ignored.

Strange Victory is as concerned with remembrance as *Victory at Sea* but there is a vast disagreement in these films about what is commemorated: *Victory at Sea* celebrates the efforts of "men called 'sailors,' 'marines,' 'soldiers.'" The 1948 Hurwitz film also does justice to the national war effort, but *not* as a good in itself. The nation's unity in time of war is considered in terms of our ability *after* the war to live up to the principles so self-righteously packed aboard our America's naval vessels. Hurwitz, in effect, reversed the dramatic perspective of *Victory at Sea*: rather than emphasizing what happened when America throws off "the lethargies of peace," Hurwitz explores the tragedy of her inability to throw off the habits of war; he is especially disappointed by the inability to make the Four Freedoms a domestic reality. Looking abroad, he drives home the irony of the nation's self-sacrifice in the allied cooperative effort to destroy the enemy as it contrasts with America's pettiness when similar occasions arise for unified action at home. The titles of both films proclaim their different perspectives: *Victory at Sea* creates an epic experience of war. By the end of the series, the impression is given that most of the work to establish a just society has already been accomplished. After all, America had no internal problems to begin with, and, since it has established democratic governments ("men, not dictators; men, not generals") in Japan and Germany, future harmony and freedom are guaranteed. Hurwitz's *Strange Victory* takes precisely the opposite approach. After it critically examines the moralism of our wartime rhetoric, it asks with embarrassing plainness: if the country was so idealistic in its aims, why is there inequality and racial prejudice once the war is over? Combat footage is used, but not to celebrate the drama of war. These scenes of battle serve as reference points for the ironic question: if we could mete out such brutal punishment on the Axis powers for their violation of freedom, how can we tolerate assaults upon freedom at home? Hurwitz shows men by the hundreds diving out of planes, or advancing by fire and maneuver. The narrator demands a special response to these scenes: "This was yesterday; this was how it was, remember? This is what Joe has put away in the album...pictures...momentos... . We paid, everybody paid... . This country fought for the four freedoms, world unity—remember? In the name of the four freedoms, we unleashed more force that has ever been seen before."

The film then presents a series of contrasts between sacrifices during the war in the name of the ideology of free peoples, followed by a return to the post-war America where indifference is allowing the country to fall back into acceptance of inequalities based on race, origin, religion. The narrator muses over these ironic contrasts: "Strange Victory indeed—the values of the defeated being adopted by the victors."

Rather than dramatizing the excitement of war, Hurwitz gives the center stage to the promise of a fulfilling life for the individual under ideal social conditions. In one scene, a pregnant woman day-dreams about the future of her child. The film then cuts to newborn infants in a hospital nursery. The camera closes in on the first prehensile movement of a hand. Hurwitz then expands the meaning of this first distinctly human act—the child's grasp, after all is an earnest of his tool-using ability. A long segment on tools and industrial production follows. It serves as a fitting contrast to the production and mobilization sequence in the "Guadalcanal" episode of *Victory at Sea*. The images commence with the simplest tools, and then progress to the most intricate electronic equipment of the day. The film then flashes back to a child taking his first steps, from which the ideal of physical dexterity is expanded by images until we see a high jumper clearing a bar at six feet. The hunger of a child for the breast is articulated as a metaphor of nourishment which includes the need to absorb culture. Creativity is the mark of the entire sequence. The child is shown as having an infinite set of possibilities: throughout these sequences the machines do not dominate man, they are never pointed toward his destruction; all of the forms at man's disposal in the arts and sciences are seen as means toward his self-expression.

Having given hope for the creative use of the tools and forms of the world, *Strange Victory* then steps back to the moment of the child's birth. As a newborn infant is delivered, whispers of "Nigger, Kike, Greaser," intrude onto the sound track, violating the sense of wonder and life. With the shock effect still lingering, the film returns to the battle scenes and a discussion of the mass movements at the roots of the world war. The goal is to suggest how easily societies (including American society) are brought to treat men as things.

In sum, *Strange Victory* agrees with *Victory at Sea* that the experience of the war may be slipping out of focus, but it disagrees about the significance of the "experience of war." By his visual presentation, Hurwitz has demonstrated the pain and brutality of combat, but he has continuously related the experience to pressing contemporary issues. War is to be remembered not for itself, not for the drama and excitement of the battle, not for the epic moments when intelligent armies collided. Instead, to invoke the title of Frank Capra's series of films, American's need to remember *why* they fought and to commemorate the price paid by our soldiers, sailors, and marines by carrying those idealistic principles into the present. Surveying contemporary America, *Strange Victory* is not optimistic about the prospects of renewed dedication: "Nobody seems to know where the victory is—lost, strayed, stolen—it isn't here. If we won [i.e., our value system triumphed with the armies and navies] why does it look as if we lost?" *Strange Victory* concludes with the moving explanation: "If we want Victory, we'll still have to get it." The point is telling: it cannot be assumed that America's efforts in the war against an outside enemy have solved the problems within. Hurwitz's cinematic essay may be faulted for over personalizing the forces of racism in America, but ultimately, his cinematic essay fulfills a powerful documentary function. He helps us to understand and feel intensely about real problems in our own time, problems which carry on their virulent life below the official rhetoric of freedom and self-righteousness which *Victory at Sea* is only too willing to accept at face value.

Conclusions

Ultimately, *Victory at Sea* failed as a documentary because it succeeded as a television spectacle. The filmmakers were too absorbed in the war experience for its own sake. They surrendered their true documentary role of informing and moving their audience to humane social action. The war may have had its drama, but "observers" betray their real duty to the men who died by allowing the causes of war to remain unexamined and uncondemned—especially if one of the causes of war is tacit public acceptance of military action as dangerous, but thrilling, manly sport. *Victory at Sea* draws attention away from reality, it bestows a national pat on the back; but it does not deliver what was really needed in 1952 and what is needed all the more, today—an insight into our real duties as Americans and as human beings in a world of supra-personal organizations, monstrous weapons, and a penchant for violence.

Discussion of Literature

Most of the encomia about the series can be found in the standard Press Kit distributed by NBC to prospective clients for *Victory at Sea*. This collection of reviews, statistics, and plot summaries will be quoted but not cited. Devotees can find it in Special Collections of the Edmon Low Library at Oklahoma State University.

A cluster of books were being written as *Victory at Sea* was being produced and broadcast, all of them directed toward a reconsideration of such important issues as American innocence, American uniqueness, and the American mission. None of these fine works—or their precursors in journals in magazines—was consulted as were none of the suggestions by George Kennan. Kennan's famous diatribe against "legalism" and "moralism" in the history of American foreign policy became standard reading for college students in the 1950's and 1960's, although it seems clear that Kennan's views were not shared with the makers of the NBC series—indeed, Salomon and his writers pushed "legalism" and "moralism" as far as they could for dramatic purposes.

The Virgin Land: The American West as Symbol and Myth by Henry Nash Smith provided an entirely new spin on the limitations of America's self-identification as Nature's nation, a land absolved from the evils of European politics and conflict. Two other works to achieve universal recognition—if not agreement—in academic circles attempted to redefine and to reinterpret the origin and significance of American political ideas. Daniel Boorstin's *The Genius of American Politics* concluded that the United States is actually a conservative country in the tradition of Edmund Burke, despite our claims about a "revolutionary" heritage. *The Liberal Tradition in America* by Louis Hartz examined the "irrational Lockeanism" of American political thought and further redefined our *soi-disant* revolutionary origins. For related analyses see Matthiesen.

Works Cited

Boorstin, Daniel. *The Genius of American Politics*. Chicago: U of Chicago P, 1953.
DeVoto, Bernard. "The Easy Chair." *Harper's* Jan. 1954: 8.
Hartz, Louis. *The Liberal Tradition in America*. New York: Harcourt, Brace, and World, 1955.
Kennan, George. *American Diplomacy: 1900-1950*. Chicago: U of Chicago P, 1951.
Knight, Arthur. "Victory at Sea." *Saturday Review*. 10 July 1954: 26.
Matthiesen, Donald J. "Persuasive History: A Critical Comparison of

Television's *Victory at Sea* and *The World at War*." *The History Teacher.* 25.2 (1992): 240-252.

O'Brian, Jack. "TV's 'Victory at Sea' Might be Shown to Mr. K." *Victory at Sea* Press Kit.

Sims, Larry. "History is Fun – on TV." *Scholastic Magazine* Aug. 1952: 4.

Smith, Henry Nash. *The Virgin Land: The American West as Symbol and Myth.* New York: Vintage Books, 1950.

Strange Victory. Dir. Leo Hurwitz. Frontier Films, 1948. Purchase: Museum of Modern Art.

Victory at Sea. Prod. Henry Salomon. NBC, 1952. Purchase: www.amazon.com.

Victory at Sea Press Kit. Special Collections, Edmon Low Library, Oklahoma State U.

"Victory by Installments." *Time Magazine* 19 Nov. 1952: 105.

Vonnegut, Kurt. *Slaughterhouse Five; or The Children's Crusade.* New York: Delacorte Press, 1969.

16
Nightmare in Red: A Cold War View of the Communist Revolution

As a public service in the fall of 1952, the National Broadcasting Company began to air a half-hour series entitled *Victory at Sea*. The twenty-six episode documentary drew a large audience including highbrows like Bernard DeVoto as well as people in the street. Reviewers lauded the artistry of these compilation films dealing with U.S. naval operations in World War II, but, as one member of the production team has recalled, *Victory at Sea* was one of the rare public-affairs programs that "could consider itself a barroom success." Thorough research in the world's film archives, masterful editing, rich musical orchestration, and an eloquent script convinced network executives that documentaries for television could be both artistic and popular, could both inform and make a profit—perhaps even in prime time (see Chapters 12, 15).

In 1953, the *Victory at Sea* production team became NBC's *Project 20* group, hoping to continue the momentum of the World War II success. Henry Salomon was the group's senior producer, but significant creative contributions were made by Donald Hyatt (assistant producer), Richard Hanser (writer), Daniel Jones (film researcher), and Robert Russell Bennett (orchestrator). Until his death in 1958, Henry Salomon's historical vision dominated *Project 20's* studies on contemporary issues; after 1958, Donald Hyatt's interest in Americana and historical paintings pointed *Project 20* in a nostalgic direction. *Nightmare in Red* is a classic early Salomon production; paradoxically, the Salomon vision and showmanship—which made *Nightmare in Red* a success scheduled against *The $64,000 Question* in 1955—seriously compromised the program's historical value. In its confusion between the attractions of drama and information, nonfiction television remains a genre in search of an aesthetic. The promises and problems of nonfiction programming can be traced back to the pioneer in network documentary, *Project 20*.

Victory at Sea was based on Admiral Samuel Eliot Morison's history of U.S. naval operations during World War II, an enormous project that Salomon, a former student of Morison's at Harvard, helped to research and to write. With the enthusiastic support of Harvard classmate Robert W. Sarnoff—who would remain a constant protector of *Project 20* within the NBC bureaucracy—Salomon brought the epic story to television.

Victory at Sea was an instant hit. Like many thousands of loyal *Victory at Sea* viewers, Bernard DeVoto, editor of *Harper's*, dropped everything to watch each new episode: "For twenty-six Sundays last year, neither the telephone nor the doorbell was answered at my house between 3: 00 and 3: 30 P.M." (DeVoto 8). *The New Yorker* hailed the series as "certainly one of the most ambitious and successful ventures in the history of television." The series won practically every major award for which it was eligible, including the Freedom Foundation's George Washington Medal, an Emmy from the Academy of Television Arts and Sciences, and the best documentary award from five major trade magazines, along with a host of outstanding achievement awards.

Henry Salomon's vision of history appealed to a Cold War television audience. The program lauded America's role as an international warrior in a global crusade for freedom; it taught that the United States was a nation which, innocent of geopolitical designs, could be brought into world struggles only when its cause was moral. Bernard DeVoto warmed to the Salomon vision: "The word 'liberation' has lost the face it had ten years ago, but gets it back when you look at *Victory at Sea*...repeatedly, you see tears of ecstasy of people greeting their deliverance...they are ravished by the fulfillment of hope." DeVoto suggested that postwar Americans were in need of the message *Victory at Sea* offered: "We forget too easily; everyone should see the whole series every year. It will be all right with me if Congress sees it twice a year" (DeVoto 8).

The Theme of Freedom

Indeed, most *Project 20* films of the Salomon era are parables of freedom. In *Victory at Sea* (1952), the allies are "free men [who] have given free men a chance to be free." During the Pacific campaign, "the children of free peoples move the forces of tyranny from the face of the earth—it is, it will be so, until the forces of tyranny are no more" (*Project 20*). Throughout *Nightmare in Red* (1955), the words of the poet-prophet Alexander Pushkin remind the Russian people (and American television viewers) that, despite eras of oppression, "the heavy hanging chains will fall, the walls will crumble at a word, and Freedom greet you in the light, and brothers give you back the sword." *The Twisted Cross* (1956) traced the eventual triumph of freedom over Hitler's totalitarian regime. *Call to Freedom* (1957), an ambitious program about Austria's postwar liberation, intercut excerpts from Beethoven's *Fidelio*—a paean to freedom— with its documentary report. Shortly before his death in 1958, Salomon announced that he would explore the theme in depth through "a new series of television programs dealing with the conflict between democracy and Communism in the middle of the present century" ("Henry Salomon" 86).

The theme of freedom was personally important to *Project 20* staffers. Richard Hanser remembers the outlook as "an American viewpoint, the freedom and unfettering of humanity." As a photojournalist in 1948, Hanser, a veteran of World War II, returned to Europe to cover the Berlin Airlift. On one memorable occasion he was allowed to steer an airlift plane en route to the embattled German capital. In a newsreel entitled "Berlin Powderkeg," scriptwriter Hanser depicted the courage and ingenuity of free peoples locked in conflict with totalitarianism. Freedom was no mere abstraction.

Donald Hyatt shared with me a similar memory about the *Project 20* team's interest in freedom as a theme: "We had just come through the war. We were sensitive people seeking out of those war themes that we wanted to do over again, themes of freedom, themes of brotherhood." While Hyatt readily admits that some will find such feelings "simplistic" and "corny," he was still proud of the common sense of "dedication, a patriotic spirit" among the *Project 20* members: "Even our Assistant Editor had been in the Battle of the Bulge." In the thirteen hours of images, narration, and music that was *Victory at Sea*, Salomon, Hanser, and Hyatt eloquently celebrated their chosen theme (Hyatt).

Victory at Sea's success convinced NBC that there was an audience for historical compilation films. The staff was asked to remain together under the designation *Project 20*, a name emblematic of the ambitions that Salomon had for the series: "This title derives from the 20th century and our aim to dramatize its major themes with a blending of film, music, and spoken narration"(Mannes 38). Privately, Salomon stressed to his team that "we are not documentarians, we are dramatists, we are playwrights." The next challenge was to find a worthy encore for *Victory at Sea* (Hyatt).

The study of modern totalitarianism seemed promising, and research began on a general approach to both fascism and communism. As Donald Hyatt remembers, "There was a change in the subject from *Victory at Sea*, but not a change in theme" (Hyatt). Once film research began, the discovery of numerous caches of hitherto unseen footage suggested a division of the study into two separate programs. The rise of Soviet communism would be studied in an hour-long program, which Salomon initially wished to call *Red Tide*, but finally renamed *Nightmare in Red*. A second program, eventually entitled *The Twisted Cross*, would exploit the rich film resources captured from the Germans and conveniently located in the Washington, D.C., area (Hanser). Common to both programs would be two general themes: the nobility of the human spirit—despite political oppression—and the eventual liberation of humankind from its oppressors (Hyatt).

Both films would aim at the timeless core of each experience, with each ending on a philosophical note, "a reflection on knowing ourselves better as a result of the particular experience explored by the film"(Hyatt). While the rise and fall of Nazism might be effectively explored in such general terms, would such a moralistic vision be supple enough to explain Soviet history and the appeal of world communism to Third-World peoples? Could an American drama about liberation provide sophisticated international insights?

The Six Segments of *Nightmare in Red*

Borrowing extensively from the Russian fiction film, *Potemkin* (1925), the opening moments of *Nightmare in Red* explode visually and musically. Shots of a shipboard mutiny are followed by scenes of street riots, culminating with the famous *tour de force* of dynamic montage, the Odessa Steps massacre. Juxtaposed with this uproar is a quiet aftermath: static shots of empty streets and men in chains are supported by discordant musical pulses that are barely audible. This alternation between unstable revolution and autocratic counterrevolution succinctly summarizes *Nightmare in Red*'s interpretation of Russian history: repressive regimes (first Czarist, then Communist) may enjoy years of success, but the Russian peasants periodically arise to throw off their chains. Unfortunately, the average Russian is so politically inept that schemers inevitably return to power. The pendulum of Soviet history swings regularly from one extreme to the other without resting at a liberal center.

Two Russian writers provide insight into the tragedy of Russian history. In a quote read by narrator Alexander Scourby, Leo Tolstoy explains to his people the fruitlessness of their unconstructive rages: "Change must come to Russia...but every revolution by force only puts more violent means of enslavement in the hands of those in power." Scourby then reads the previously given quote from Alexander Pushkin, who offers solace for those yearning to breathe free. There is always hope that the next liberation will succeed in bringing to birth a viable, liberal society. Such was the dream in 1917 and, according to *Nightmare in Red*, such was still the hope of the ordinary Soviet citizen in 1955. The remaining forty-four minutes of *Nightmare in Red* explore the details of this thesis.

Segment one examines the Romanoff dynasty, using recently discovered court footage to exploit the pathos of a doomed kingdom. Czar Nicholas II is described as an ineffectual ruler who would rather fiddle with his cameras or vacation in the Crimea than fulfill the responsibilities of office. The czarina is no happier with the family's lack of privacy, but is more autocratic. Neither the royal family nor the aristocracy will admit the existence of "a specter of revolution...behind the marble pillars and splendid villas." The closing minutes of this portrait of Russia's *ancien régime* are a masterpiece of showmanship. Hollywood filmmakers have often employed dress balls to dramatize the twilight of aristocracy. As early as 1914, D. W. Griffith's *The Birth of a Nation* evoked the poignant demise of the Confederacy through such a scene. Twenty-five years later, David O. Selznick's *Gone with the Wind* followed suit. Using fiction footage from *The Anna Cross* (1954), *Nightmare in Red* attempts to evoke a similar mood of dramatic irony. The narrator explains that "in the Crimea, in the capital of St. Petersburg, at the country seats of the great landowners, the privileged few dance away the ominous years of fancy dress…in heart-breaking ignorance." Dancers in *The Anna Cross* are shown in close-up, including shots of faces, feet, and swirling dresses. After a waltz, a serpentine line of dancers tries to keep up with an intoxicating musical tempo. At dawn, tipsy aristocrats depart, crowded into open carriages. They ride past a municipal employee extinguishing street lamps. Using a visual pun, the narrator cites Lord Raglan: "'The dancing years are ending, the party is over. The lamps are going out all over Europe. We shall not see them lit again in our lifetime.'" Maximum pathos of the final days is evoked by the skillful weaving together of music and fiction footage (Hyatt "Nightmare").

Segment two traces Lenin's rise to power. While the Czarist regime crumbles during World War I, Lenin enters the picture, a

V. I. Lenin Ignites the Flame

tool of the German high command: "We send Lenin into Russia just as we send shells and poison gas against an enemy." Visual and aural elements support this interpretation. Shots of Lenin are intercut with dynamic shots of railroad cars, engine stokers, tracks, all images dramatizing the sponsored arrival of the "brilliant, bitter, dedicated man." Certainly German assistance cannot be denied, but the implied conclusion offered by *Nightmare in Red* is obviously incorrect. Historians Palmer and Colton more aptly explain: "Lenin and the Bolsheviks did not bring about the Russian revolution. They captured it after it had begun. They boarded the ship in midstream" (723). A long battle scene from the Russian fiction film *Ten Days That Shook the World* (1928) is used to communicate a sense of the puissance of Lenin's revolutionary leadership.

Once in power, Lenin reveals the realpolitik behind his promises. In signing a treaty with the Germans, Lenin is accused of forsaking allies "who are still fighting to the death in France." No mention is made of Lenin's assumption that the world war was a product of the inner contradictions of capitalism. Domestic events are shown in an equally nightmarish light. Lenin declares that his government "seeks the frank liquidation of the idea of democracy by the idea of dictatorship." As a supporter of "rabid terrorism," he murders the royal family, an event presented with pathetic music and tender phrasing by narrator Alexander Scourby, along with a teary dissolve. Lenin's portrait could hardly be more negative.

Lenin's regime, although it promised to uplift society, was little more than a new chapter in Russia's tradition of repression. **Segment three** of *Nightmare in Red* provides disturbing details to drive this message home. Images of starving children, some of them eating the lice that infect their ragged clothing, are shown while the narrator makes the film's first reference to nightmares: "'Equality!' cried the Communists, and there comes the equality of the slaughterhouse and the democracy of the cemetery. The dream of a brave new world, of a new heaven and a new earth, develops into *a nightmare* of starvation and economic collapse" [emphasis supplied]. An Allied blockade of Russia during this period goes without notice, but not the privations it caused—those are Lenin's fault. When Lenin resorts to the New Economic Policy (1921-1927), which allowed private enterprise to function as a stopgap measure, playful street pictures and jolly music join narrator Scourby in ridiculing the failure of Communist dogma.

Segment four tracks Stalin's bloody footsteps. When Stalin attempts to foster bootstrap industrial growth, he is condemned for personal cruelty. The first five-year plan "makes enormous strides at enormous human costs. But the workers who survive cannot eat heavy industry, cannot wear it, cannot live in it." *Nightmare in Red* does not mention that the Soviet Union was forced to industrialize without the help of outside capital, yet—despite the obstacles—industrial production increased by 236 percent during the first five-year plan. By 1938, the Soviet Union had become the world's foremost producer of tractors and locomotives. *Nightmare in Red* neglects to evoke the excitement with which these heroic efforts at economic development were greeted by the Russian people:

> ...the feeling that everybody was busily toiling and struggling to create a socialist fatherland was perhaps the most distinctive achievement of the new system. Workers had a real belief that the new industrial wonders were their own. The sense of participation, of belonging, which democracy had given to the average man in the West in political matters, was widely felt in the USSR in economic matters also. People rejoiced at every new advance as a personal triumph. It became a national pastime to watch the mounting statistics, the fulfilling of quotas or hitting of "targets." (Palmer and Colton 721)

Quoting the Grand Inquisitor from Fyodor Dostoevsky's novel *The Brothers Karamazov* (1880), *Nightmare in Red* discounts the popularity of Stalin's programs: "the mass surrender of personal will and freedom—once Nicholas, now Stalin." Stalin signs of every description—Stalin rugs, Stalin commemorative bowls, and, as a climax of film rhetoric, a balloon-hoisted Stalin pennant—are briskly edited in a montage designed to prove that the Russian people are being brainwashed. Much screen time for section four is expended on the purge trials of 1936-1938. No historian would want to defend the trials, but the emphasis devoted to them by *Nightmare in Red* is excessive.

When World War II arrives in **segment five**, *Nightmare in Red* shows that Russians fight for "Mother Russia." Just as Lenin did in 1918, Stalin in 1939 signed a disastrous treaty with the Germans. *Nightmare in Red* blames Stalin for the horrible war to follow: "It is time for fear when tyrants seem to kiss." Stalin's comrade Molotov, and Hitler's, von Ribbentrop, sign their so-called "friendship pact" in the Kremlin. Hitler has his green light for World War II. Stalin has switched it on. Later, the two dictatorships share their common interest in booty, "this time over the corpse of Poland, the corpse of peace." They are birds of a feather.

Eventually, Germany violates the pact. Handsome, bareheaded German soldiers are welcomed by civilians somewhere in the Soviet Union, proving the spiritual bankruptcy of the Communist regime: "The myth of the people's devotion to Communism in the land of workers and peasants explodes as the workers and peasants greet the Germans as liberators." Staged scenes from German propaganda films are introduced to support this argument. Civilians greet German troops with flowers and hand salutes and tear down pictures and statues of Stalin, replacing these graven images with portraits of "Uncle Adolf." A montage of Georgians, Armenians, and Mongols in German uniforms stresses how many nationalities fought Stalin's regime under the German flag. For musical support of this counterrevolution, a tune in a minor mode is introduced in counterpoint with the revolutionary leitmotif. The World War is finally won by the "Russian soldier who fights not for Marx or Lenin or Stalin, but for one another—for Mother Russia." Stalin promised, as the film explains, that the effort was "part of a struggle of the peoples of Europe and America for their independence and democratic freedoms." The postwar period brings no such freedoms to Russia.

Segment six of *Nightmare in Red* treats the Cold War. Mounted guards outside the Kremlin remind the viewer of previous agents of repression who quelled the 1905 revolution. Moscow is described as a "symbol and magnetic core of an empire more powerful, more vast than any dream of any czar." The new empire is ruled by the Party, which has "unbridled sway" over the people who constitute 97 percent of the nation's population. The new aristocracy rules from the Kremlin "as master and warden casting a lengthening

Stalin Brings 1984

shadow." Section one of *Nightmare in Red* concluded with a dress ball. By introducing a cocktail party for Russia's technocrats at this point, *Nightmare in Red* asserts that there are historical parallels. Tables are crowded with liquor, fancy hors d'oeuvres, and bowls of fruit; a rumba accentuates the sybaritic tone of the visuals. The rumba is allowed to overlap shots of urban slums, accenting an ironic contrast between the life-style of workers and the luxuries enjoyed by Soviet officials. Stalin is quoted to justify the inequities.

Despite the tyranny of the czars, despite the repression of Lenin and Stalin, "the people and their faith endure." Surely the average Russian has been severely tested: "The state, knowing no creed but blind obedience, demands a captive mind, a captive spirit, a captive body. It must forever barricade its borders against the infection of freedom from without, against the escape to freedom from within." The final minutes of section six provide the title material for *Nightmare in Red*. The film moves to dungeons below ground. Using fiction footage illuminated by high-contrast lighting, the camera pans victims in overcrowded cells, men and women herded together. The camera follows a simulated flashlight, which blinds the prisoners. A montage designed to evoke the idea of oppression follows: after a number of shots of individual faces, a tracking shot moves through a crowded cell holding nearly one hundred prisoners. As the nightmare continues, prisoners are herded onto flatbed trucks where they are netted down like cargo. Trains then take them in crowded freight cars to Siberia where they dismount in snow at gunpoint. The final shots of *Nightmare in Red* concentrate on the corner of a barbed-wire stockade, shot from a low angle. The NBC logo is imposed over this last image.

Commentary for these concluding moments plays on verbal connotations, sounds, and allusions. While we look at suffering innocents in underground cells, the narrator intones:

> First the Cheka, with its motto: "The Cheka does not judge, it strikes." Then came the NKVD, and the MVD, then came the KGB, ever changing ominous initials which all mean secret police, which mean terror conscious and subconscious, which mean the power of reality, a *Nightmare in Red*: "My father chastised you with whips, but I will chastise you with scorpions." An ancient prophecy comes true.

The verbal rhetoric reinforces the sense of confinement and oppression provided by the visuals.

The only hope for the Russian people is an ancient one—revolution. Continued repression will eventually lead to a new outburst, recalling the dream of liberation announced by Pushkin in the early moments of the program: "Deep in Siberian mine, keep your faces proud; the bitter toil shall not be lost, the rebel thought unbowed. The heavy-hanging chains will fall, the walls will crumble at a word, and Freedom greets you in the light, and brothers give you back the sword." The Manichean conflict between liberty and tyranny could not be more dramatically rendered as barbed-wire images close the film.

Post-Production Issues

Nightmare in Red surprised the *Project 20* team by creating sponsor problems. Initially scheduled for broadcast on November 13, 1955, the program was delayed when Pontiac withdrew its support. Donald Hyatt remembers: "Salomon was livid over it and said it was typical of sponsor thinking." Since *Nightmare in Red* was the series premiere, the entire *Project 20* effort seemed to be in jeopardy (Hyatt).

Only fragments of the story exist, and few of those fragments are on paper. Donald Hyatt has reflected: "No one in this part of the world works on paper; they use the telephone" (Hyatt). There were many who could have made such telephone calls; pre-screenings of the program to at least twenty-three advertising agencies and corporations were only part of an aggressive NBC promotional campaign. A host of corporate executives, political figures, and reviewers had screened *Nightmare in Red* by the end of July 1955. Although a number of alternate sponsors were enthusiastic, Pontiac began to ease up on the accelerator (*Project 20*).

Sometime during the summer pre-screenings, Pontiac's advertising staff began to worry about *Nightmare in Red*'s bleak anti-Communist closing. In addition, members of the Soviet delegation in Washington, who attended a prescreening, launched a protest. Both negative responses eventually reached the desk of Charles E. Wilson, Secretary of Defense and former chairman of the board of General Motors. All sources agree that Wilson was responsible for withdrawing Pontiac support. Pontiac's reasons for not sponsoring an anti-Communist film throw light on the complex relationship between American history and American television (Hyatt).

Some members of the Eisenhower administration (1952-1960) were sincere in their efforts to chip away at the Cold War glacier. In mid-July 1955, President Eisenhower traveled to Geneva to attend a summit conference with the Soviet Union's new heads of state, Nikita Khrushchev and Nikolai Bulganin, the first such meeting in ten years. After a subsequent foreign ministers' conference in October 1955, many world citizens began to have some hopes that a "spirit of Geneva" would improve East-West relations. Although mistrust continued after the meetings, gestures were made by both sides to improve mutual understanding and trade. American businessmen were especially interested in "alleviating difficulties in performing usual business and maintenance services within the USSR," but the Russians were deaf to most American suggestions ("East-West Contacts" 375). Secretary Wilson was particularly interested in demonstrating that American corporations could do business without becoming bogged down in political rhetoric. Sponsoring a program like *Nightmare in Red* in the face of Soviet complaints was simply impolitic, a gesture that would stir up trouble; hence the phone call.

In a front-page story in mid-October, *Variety* validated the commercial motivation: "General Motors is adopting discretion as the better part of democratic valor and future trade. ...General Motors is a world-trading outfit and has been in the forefront for over 30 years of efforts to reduce barriers to business among nations. In coming face to face with the political embarrassment of *Nightmare in Red*, General Motors was completely consistent" ("Television's Nightmare" 1). By mid-November, *Variety* reported that Armstrong Cork had picked up the program and would be scheduling it for late December, preempting its Circle Theater program, but with Circle Theater host John Cameron Swayze introducing and closing the program. If Pontiac had been concerned about Soviet feelings, reviewer reactions clearly indicate that the automobile manufacturer had shifted into reverse at just the right time.

Reviewers accepted *Nightmare in Red* as a factual, objective study of the Russian revolution and its contemporary implications. In his introduction, host John Cameron Swayze encouraged such responses by explaining, "The film is real, and through the knowledge it imparts, perhaps people can prevent getting caught in a *Nightmare in Red*." Since Swayze's *Camel News Caravan* was one of the leading evening network news programs, such a statement firmly stamped the program with an imprimatur of fact. A closing by Swayze completed the nonfiction frame (Salomon program cards).

Sid Shalit of the *New York Daily News* was representative in his responses to *Nightmare in Red*. The film was factual: "There's no fiction or editorializing. ...None was needed. The story is told by authentic, sometimes blood-curdling newsreel shots, some of them never shown publicly." The film was a patriotic lesson: "America's Red Quislings wouldn't enjoy *Nightmare in Red*. ...Even the dumbest Commie stooge might begin to suspect that documentary films like these—ninety percent of them Russian made—can't be faked." For Mr. Shalit, *Nightmare in Red* was not an interpretation at all, but an object lesson, "a chunk of history-in-the-raw which every free citizen in the world should try to see, and remember" (Shalit).

One reviewer boiled the lesson down to a homily: "Over here, when there's a knock on the door at night, it is simply a neighbor borrowing a cup of sugar or collecting for a worthwhile charity... not the secret police inviting you to your own funeral" (Hanser). Although not usually known for critical insights about film and television, the Honorable John W. McCormack of Massachusetts took time to speak for the program two days after its second broadcast. Congressman McCormack was especially pleased by what he considered to be the program's objectivity, its use of "thousands of feet of factual, unembellished motion picture film," its cool appeal to the intellect: "In presenting the world menace that is Communism, this film is a true public service" (Hanser). The conservative *National Review* felt that the program's insights would be especially instructive during a dangerous post-Geneva thaw in the Cold War: "It should be shown throughout the world, often, and particularly in those countries recently and noisily visited by Bulganin and Khrushchev" ("*Nightmare in Red*"). All such reviewers reminded their readers of the contrasting blessings of the American way.

At the opposite extreme of the political spectrum, *The Daily Worker* launched a diatribe against "NBC-TV's orgy of hatred." The Communist newspaper resented the use of Nazi propaganda films and decried the cynical treatment of Communist objectives: "If an ignorant cop or a stoolie were to write the history of the Soviet Union, it would be something like NBC's nightmare." The reviewer noted than an Irving R. Levine-narrated program for NBC, *Look at Russia*, had been more balanced, stressing "what Americans and Russians have in common." The Levine presentation, according to *The Daily Worker*, provided insight, revealing that the Soviet Union was "hardly the gigantic prison the USSR is made out to be in the nightmares" (*Daily Worker* 6).

Somewhere between the saber rattlings of Congressman McCormack and the righteous indignation of *The Daily Worker* were some thoughtful responses about *Nightmare in Red* as an interpretation—rather than a mere presentation—of history. Marya Mannes came away from a preview impressed with the power of documentary for television: people in the industry were beginning to recognize the power of "facts, used as the instrument of art." She hoped that "this growing and infinitely useful form of art— the documentary in depth—becomes part of the American diet, so deficient in the vitamins of thought." Ms. Mannes was somewhat troubled, however, by potential misuses of such programs. Given the combined power of images, words, and music, the genre could be dangerous in the wrong hands: "Another team could have made a different picture from frames on the cutting room floor" (Mannes 38).

In a review for *Senior Scholastic*, Patrick Hazard recommended the program to teachers because of its point of view: students could develop critical viewing skills by dissecting the program. Hazard recommended that teachers assign student teams to critique such elements of cinematic rhetoric as editing ("Ask them if a single execution would have given the intended effect"), music ("Ask your students to feel how music reinforces mood"), and point of view ("The problem of editorializing in a documentary must be stressed") (Hazard 34). Hazard undercut claims to objectivity by suggesting that Soviet filmmakers could turn the tables on *Project 20* with an anti-American film entitled "*Nightmare in Red, White, and Blue*, in which racial discrimination, waterfront racketeering, juvenile delinquency and comic books are shown as the essence of American life" (Hazard 53). Hazard's observations about the plasticity of the compilation medium—as well as his classroom suggestions—are still valid.

The passage of time provides some perspective on *Nightmare in Red* as a documentary that may—or may not—have performed a service for its Cold-War audience. Two fundamental questions need to be asked, questions readers are urged to ask of any documentary broadcast over the commercial medium of television: first, did *Nightmare in Red* provide new insights, or did it cater to existing prejudices? Second, were the resources of visual language employed for the purposes of drama at the expense of information?

1. Did *Nightmare in Red* Provide New Insights?

Americans were intensely disturbed by the aftermath of their second world war 'to end all wars,' and the threat of world communism—sometimes called "Godless communism"—was at the heart of their anxiety. For a short time Senator Joseph McCarthy convinced a troubled public that its new problems were somehow linked to betrayal of public trust by officials and intellectuals. The

Berlin crisis, the Korean War, and the fear of subversion were all part of America's Cold-War nightmare.

A number of prominent historians in the 1950s warned that Americans needed to understand how their "revolutionary" heritage differed from the revolutionary developments in Russia, Asia, and South America. Daniel Boorstin exhorted Americans to appreciate their unique political experience: "We must refuse to become crusaders for liberalism, in order to remain liberals" (188). Harvard professor Louis Hartz suggested that the question for Americans in the 1950s was a rephrasing of a conundrum articulated in the nineteenth century by Alexis de Tocqueville: "Can a people 'born free' ever understand peoples elsewhere that have become so?" (Hartz 25). Especially in the case of Russia, George Kennan's *American Diplomacy: 1900-1950* argued for a detached approach that ruled out both the option of intervention and the hope for internal revolution. The Soviets needed time to evolve toward Western institutions and values: "Let them be Russians; let them work at their internal problems in their own manner" (Kennan 136-137).

Nightmare in Red, rather than tapping these new perspectives, succeeded as drama—but failed as history—in its unremitting attack on every Soviet motive, goal, and achievement. In the cause of drama, the czar's fall is treated with, great pathos, stressing the victimization of a trapped family rather than providing insight into the cruel necessity behind the execution. Lenin and Stalin make domestic and foreign policy decisions strictly to retain power, and neither allies nor Russia's peasants are spared in such selfish designs. As a result, according to *Nightmare in Red*, the basically religious and apolitical Russian masses yearn for liberation. When the expected revolution occurs, the Russian people will espouse liberal democracy, their "true" political heritage.

Using the phrasing of Tocqueville questions, *Nightmare in Red* had the responsibility to help those born free (Americans) understand peoples elsewhere who were supposedly struggling to become so (Russians). Revolutionary violence and bloodshed, extensively shown and discussed by the documentary, have always been an unavoidable, tragic experience when entrenched interests have resisted change, but typically present, too, have been noble ideals and dreams of a better life—the very fuel of revolutions. Instead of balancing its portrait, *Nightmare in Red* imputed the worst motives, introduced the most lurid anecdotes, and discounted Communist ideology as a verbal smokescreen concocted to sway public opinion. The revolution itself is reduced to a bloody and cynical game of musical chairs in which one self-interested elite replaces another. Rendering dramatically the theme of oppression invited the filmmakers to paint too many shadows; conversely, efforts to predict a liberating rebellion unrealistically prevented the would-be historian filmmakers from exercising even a modicum of empathy. In short, the complexity of history was sacrificed to fit a narrow, predetermined theme. One historian who uses *Nightmare in Red* in classes dealing with American perceptions of Russia has observed: "Sometimes I think it's merely that everything Russian is evil...the film does not inform nearly so much as it preaches. This is what I find so objectionable" (Waltz).

At a time when such theatrical films as *My Son John* (1952) and television fiction programming such as *I Led Three Lives* were manipulating viewer fears and prejudices about communism, the massmedia list of nightmares was long enough. In not fighting against the tide of xenophobia, *Nightmare in Red* failed to fulfill its responsibilities as a documentary. Marya Mannes, an otherwise friendly critic of Salomon's efforts, found *Nightmare in Red* lacking in this regard, failing to show "what went on in Russian minds and hearts during those convulsive years and what it is that has kept Communism alive and strong" (Mannes 38). Although Third World films such as *The Battle of Algiers* (1966) later made impressive attempts to show the appeal of revolutionary ideology, it is safe to say that Americans still need documentaries to illuminate this insight.

2. Which Was More Important, Drama or Information?

Henry Salomon, Richard Hanser, and others frequently referred to a quotation from Walt Whitman to explain their combined aesthetic and historical objectives: "I seek less to display any theme or thought and more to bring you into the atmosphere of the theme or thought—there to pursue your own flight." Most scholars who have studied *Project 20* concur that the series dealt "more with feelings than with facts."

Newsreels present pictures of events, but only documentaries that strive toward art take the care to match and weave compositional textures. *Nightmare in Red*, like other *Project 20* programs, was skillfully edited to yield the maximum feeling from compositional elements of archival footage. For example, it is no accident that *Nightmare in Red* finds Leo Tolstoy in a garden where he warns about the excesses of revolution; nor it is fortuitous that the film associates Lenin with an impact montage involving a train racing across the countryside. In both cases, compositional elements help to interpret the historical figures: Tolstoy shows the repose of reason while Lenin is a man of violence. Inclusion of Lenin's wife—who was afflicted by exophthalmoses ("pop-eyes")—adds a scurrilous piece of negative imagery to further undercut Lenin's image as a leader. In practically every scene, *Nightmare in Red* reflects a similar careful crafting of form to content; as a result, viewer feelings are masterfully orchestrated.

If a compilation film is a study of history, then its credibility is jeopardized every time dramatic considerations tempt the filmmaker to include visually exciting—but historically anachronistic—pictures. Despite their technical excellence, *Project 20* films during the Salomon period must be criticized for their cavalier attitude toward the historical authenticity of cinematic materials. Jay Leyda has warned compilation filmmakers that "As little as five fictional feet in an otherwise scrupulous compilation can shake the spectator's belief in the whole film, *including its ideas*. Even though he does not identify a shot as false, merely to sense that something is wrong, to get a whiff of arrangement can poison for him the whole setting of the tiny falsehood" (Leyda 130). No one on the *Nightmare in Red* project seemed to be concerned with such niceties, for a combination of faked nonfiction footage plus fiction materials crowd some twenty minutes of the fifty-four-minute program.

In segment five, *Nightmare in Red* dramatizes the disaffection of nationalities who greeted invading German troops as liberators. Although no one would deny that Mongols, Armenians, and other groups did indeed fight briefly against the Red army, the documentary's method of telling the story is extremely problematic. Without indicating its source, *Nightmare in Red* employs extensive footage from Nazi propaganda films. The section includes scenes staged

Sergei Eisenstein's *October*: A Major Source of "Reality" Footage

for Nazi cameras, and many anti-Communist moments in this section use whole, unaltered sequences from such Nazi propaganda. In 1942, these scenes must have been effective proof to native Germans that their expansive war was just, but incorporating such materials whole-cloth into a historical film some thirteen years later is clearly a showman's choice, presenting history that was crafted into drama rather than illuminating the drama in history. The materials here—and elsewhere—were chosen for their emotional impact, not for their veracity. The ploy is comparable to quoting without citation from a John Birch Society pamphlet in a serious essay opposed to fluoridation. Distortions in the quoted material would discredit the essay for discerning readers.

Fiction materials are generously included in *Nightmare in Red* to achieve maximum emotional effect. The chaotic nature of periodic outbursts of revolution in Russian history is supported visually by little else: the 1905 revolution is seen through Eisenstein's *Potemkin*, with segments selected to underscore *Nightmare in Red*'s theme of senseless violence rather than Eisenstein's theme of revolution for a good cause; the last flickering moments for aristocracy are played upon extensively through the use of a lavish studio production, *The*

Anna Cross, a Russian film that had nothing whatsoever to do with the revolution; the dynamic 1917 Communist takeover is excitingly communicated by long sections from the film *Ten Days That Shook the World* (1928) and other fiction sources. Last but not least, the final scenes—which caused so much consternation at the Russian Embassy, the Department of Defense, and Pontiac's ad agency— were totally fictional. They were used because they were, from an editor's perspective, enormously compelling pictures (Hyatt *Nightmare*).

It is silly to criticize a compilation film for being an interpretation of reality. As CBS documentary producer Burton Benjamin has observed, "If the compilation film is just a collection of 'newsreel clips,' then a history book is 'just a collection of library clips' and no history makes sense" (301-306). The basic problem with *Nightmare in Red*'s use of fiction materials had two components. First, from a production standpoint, it seems clear that fiction materials were selected because they dramatically conveyed a predetermined slant, not because of the novel pictorial or documentary insight they supplied. The polite name for such filmmaking is "persuasion"; an unfriendly label is "propaganda." A second aspect relates to the television audience: were 1955 viewers capable of joining *Project 20* filmmakers in the search for inner truths through fiction? Turning back to the often cited remark of Walt Whitman, once brought into the "atmosphere of the theme or thought," would audiences know in what direction to "pursue [their] own flight?" When asked this question by a Macon, Georgia, history teacher, film researcher Daniel Jones responded, "The huge American television audience, besides being intelligent, is sophisticated enough to realize these passages are re-enactments and introduced because of their effectiveness, to tell the story better" (Abady 63). An extensive survey of reviews indicates that only one newspaper columnist, Ethel Daccardo of the *Chicago Daily News*, even noticed the fictional materials (39). Staged scenes, fiction footage, and *Nightmare in Red*'s thesis were accepted without much critical reflection, presumably on the premise that pictures don't lie, especially pictures introduced by John Cameron Swayze. Then and now, the temptation to use whatever "works" visually is always present in the editing room, leading network documentarians in the direction of drama for drama's

Nightmare in Red 371

sake rather than toward Salomon's stated objective-drama as a device to discover the inner meaning of history. This problem is part of the baggage from the Capra tradition for compilation filmmaking (see Chapter 12).

Television Documentary in the Decade after *Nightmare in Red*

For *Project 20*, the Pontiac incident was a small bump in the road, not a serious collision. Within NBC, patrons like Robert W. Sarnoff and Sylvester "Pat" Weaver assured that nervous programmers could not interfere: "The network could never have applied pressure; that would have got their neck in a noose." (At that same time, however, sponsor pressures were placing such controversial CBS programs as Edward R. Murrow's *See It Now* [Alcoa Aluminum] in jeopardy.) The Salomon team was ensconced in a very privileged corporate suite: "Had we been outsiders, we would have been decimated...the Sarnoff power gave us freedom" (Hyatt).

Viewer interest helped to vindicate *Nightmare in Red* and the series of programs to follow. When broadcast two days after Christmas 1955, *Nightmare in Red* received a Nielsen rating of 23.9 (or approximately 9,420,000 homes), the best rating ever achieved in a difficult spot opposite CBS's *$64,000 Question*; the second broadcast on January 24 resulted in an equally impressive audience draw (Hanser papers). The advertising manager for Armstrong Cork, Pontiac's replacement, was elated: "In the history of this company, no effort of ours has ever provoked so much favorable response from so many people" (Salomon 32). Subsequent *Project 20* programs would receive even higher ratings. As *Playboy* later marveled, *Project 20* served to "enable the Sarnoffs, the sponsors, and the FCC—and even the public—to have its cultural cake and eat it, too" ("On the Scene" 103).

Avoidance of controversy also helped the series after 1955: *The Twisted Cross* (March 24, 1955; 32.4 Nielsen rating) assailed a long-since-toppled totalitarian regime; *The Great War* (October 16, 1956; 20.8 Nielsen rating) exploited the drama of a "singing war"; *The Jazz Age* (December 6, 1957; 35.2 Nielsen rating) played on nostalgic emotions; the turbulent era before 1900 was brought to the screen in a deceptively blithe program entitled *The Innocent*

Years (November 21, 1957; 27.0 Nielsen rating). The only Salomon program after *Nightmare in Red* to address contemporary issues was *Call to Freedom* (January 1, 1957; 27.2 Nielsen rating). Reviews were not enthusiastic about *Call to Freedom*'s mixture of the oil of opera with the water of documentary. Donald Hyatt remembers that the program lacked the compelling force of *Nightmare in Red*: "Yes, Austria has its freedom and its opera open, but there is nothing deep to reflect on. ...In the sense of drama, it doesn't work" (Hyatt). It may also be true that the theme of liberation, dramatic to a 1955 audience, was no longer so gripping in 1957. The one potentially controversial project, *That War in Korea*, was left on the shelf until the Kennedy years (November 20, 1963). In 1965, even a friendly observer of *Project 20*'s work had to admit that few programs "have taken a position contrary to the collective viewpoint" (Abady 88).

When Henry Salomon suddenly died in January 1958, at the age of 40, Donald Hyatt's tastes and interest led *Project 20* still further from controversy. Hyatt's debut as producer was *Meet Mr. Lincoln* (February 11, 1959; 26.6 Nielsen rating), a program that both justified continued support of *Project 20* and established a new style. Hyatt employed "stills-in-motion" techniques over Matthew Brady photographs to bring the Civil War years to life. The dignity of human beings was still an important theme, but it was focused more toward cultural expressions than politics and power. Enduring programs such as *The Real West* (March 29, 1961) and moving religious evocations such as *The Coming of Christ* (December 21, 1961) or *He Is Risen* (April 15, 1962) further explored spiritual themes while refining a stills-in-motion style. By 1967, *Project 20* had produced over twenty-five major documentaries for television.

It is difficult to overestimate the importance of *Project 20* to the history of television documentary. As *Variety* noted in its obituary for Henry Salomon, "The *Project 20* series was given prime evening time and not restricted to the Sunday afternoon 'intellectual ghetto' of public affairs programming" ("Death" 32). With sponsorship from Prudential Insurance, NBC's competitor, CBS, used *Victory at Sea* techniques to assemble *Air Power* (1956), narrated by Walter Cronkite and organized into the same twenty-six-episode format as its seaborne predecessor. Between 1957 and 1961, another CBS series entitled *The Twentieth Century* churned out 104 compilations.

Under the direction of Burton Benjamin, *The Twentieth Century* hoped to evoke in film "the smaller story which did not dominate history's headlines" (Jacobs 169). Controversy was successfully avoided in such programs as *Paris in the Twenties*, *The Movies Learn to Talk*, and other evocative historical compilations. Not to be outdone, ABC—the little fellow among the big three—came out in 1960 with a twenty-six-episode series on World War II entitled *Winston Churchill: The Valiant Years*. Eyewitnesses to history, on-camera narrators, and new footage at historic sites enriched both the CBS and ABC descendants of *Project 20*. Not only the techniques of *Project 20*, but its personnel circulated among the networks: editor Isaac Kleinerman moved to CBS, where he became an award-winning producer on *The Twentieth Century*; after working as a researcher for *Victory at Sea* and *Nightmare in Red*, Mel Stuart took his archival lessons to CBS and then on to David Wolper Productions.

The major networks began to lose interest in the compilation genre sometime in the early 1960s. Many producers—quite incorrectly—assumed that the world's archives had been fully exploited, forgetting that what made compilations interesting were the historical visions guiding them, *not* simply old pictures strung together with narration. Of greater significance was the appearance of new technologies, to include light cameras, "fast" film, and excellent portable tape recorders. Investigative reporting—once the monopoly of print journalism—was now possible for television. Compilations left the television screen, although they continued to be a classroom staple.

The birth of cable television seemed to have renewed an interest in compilation as a genre. In 1981, Home Box Office (HBO) aired a compilation series entitled *Remember When*. Not even the presence of Dick Cavett—entering and exiting the actuality footage by means of a special effect called "ultramat"—could hide the flaws of productions marred by dated historical interpretations, anachronistic film materials, and redundant narration. Rather than picking up where *Project 20* left off, *Remember When* seemed to be produced in total ignorance of the NBC legacy.

The compilation film has great potential for the exploration of history, only some of which was tapped by *Project 20*. As audiences become more visually literate, we must ask compilation filmmakers to tell us who we were on the condition that they relate that information—vividly, but honestly—to whom we are and who we need to become. Henry Salomon's promise for *Project 20*—to use archival films to explore the past for the benefit of the present—still awaits fulfillment.

Discussion of Literature

A number of public documents have been useful to this *Project 20* study. An early analysis which, while friendly, was not devoid of criticism is Albert J. Abady, "Project 20: An NBC Television Network Series" (Master's thesis, Pennsylvania State University, 1965). Very useful for those interested in *Project 20* after Henry Salomon's death is Philip J. Lane, Jr., "NBC-TV's *Project 20*: An Analysis of the Art of the Still-in-Motion Film in Television" (Ph.D. diss., Northwestern University, 1969). The only book to devote attention to *Project 20* is A. William Bluem, *Documentary in American Television: Form, Function, Method* (New York: Hastings House, 1965). I concur with Bluem's perception that there was a Salomon era (1951-1958) and then a Hyatt era (1958ff.) for *Project 20*. This chapter is restricted to the political and aesthetic visions of *Project 20* during the Salomon years, for which *Nightmare in Red* stands as a representative program. Those interested in a still narrower and earlier focus are invited to see Chapter 15. The delightful quotation about *Project 20*'s "barroom success" is from Richard F. Shephard, "Fact plus Flourish: *Project 20* Combines Two Elements on TV," *New York Times*, 25 December 1966, p. 2: 15.

The importance of Robert Sarnoff's concern for Salomon's projects cannot be overemphasized. Artistic liberties allowed stemmed from the Sarnoff connection, one Harvard man helping another against the Lilliputians at Rockefeller Center. As Richard Hanser told me, "It was one case in which nepotism worked out well." Richard Hanser and Donald Hyatt graciously shared their opinions, clippings, and precious time with me during interviews conducted in fall, 1981. I wish to thank them for all their courtesies.

The best study of compilation film history and aesthetics is Jay Leyda, *Film Begets Film: A Study of the Compilation Film* (New York: Hill & Wang, 1964). Leyda spends considerable time examining the successes and failures of the genre, 1898-1963. *Project 20* productions are briefly discussed in a chapter entitled "Smaller Screen–Larger Audience," pp. 97-100.

Although ideas of the "consensus historians" here cited are now considered passé by many, their challenges to existing formulations represented, at least for the 1950s, new strategies for understanding the American liberal tradition in an international context. As interpretative historians, the *Project 20* team should have been aware of the writings of Boorstin, Hartz, and Kennan; a new documentary should always consult the most recent studies available.

Leyda's *Film Begets Film* is an indispensable starting point. Ultimately, the ideal compilation filmmaker will have the cinematic eyes of a Hyatt, the historical vision of a Salomon, the verbal gifts of a Hanser, and the musical ear of a Bennett. Perhaps this is too much to expect of an individual; unfortunately, it is also doubtful that such a talented group will ever be assembled again. As a result, our classrooms will suffer from inferior productions unable to balance the demands of history and art.

History teachers have begun to make their own compilations for the classroom, a development made difficult by the high cost of film and television production. British aspirations and achievements are discussed in Paul Smith, ed., *The Historian and Film* (Cambridge: Cambridge University Press, 1976), pp. 121-85. American developments are evaluated in Chapter 14. Readers might wish to remind the author that The History Channel and PBS have produced works of merit into the 21st century. Alas, many of these productions recapitulate the historical and methodological errors of the Project XX group. (For further discussion of the flawed methodology, see Chapters 14, 15.)

Daccardo reviewed *Nightmare in Red* in the *Chicago Daily News* ("Russ TV Gives Grim Picture," 29 December 1955, p. 39) and just prior to the second broadcast ("Red Film Is 95 Pct. Newsreels," 24 January 1956, p. 35). Daccardo's misuse of the word "newsreel" is characteristic of the primitive state of television criticism and indicative of the vulnerability of audiences. There are very few "newsreel" materials in *Nightmare in Red*, although footage from documentaries, propaganda films, and actualities are abundant. No one seemed to know what to call the new programs. At various points in research for this article, the following terms were employed by producers and critics: telementaries, think films, films of life, nonfiction programming, docudramas, fact dramas, actuality dramas with a hard spine.

Works Cited

Abady, Albert J. "*Project 20*: An NBC Television Network Series." MA Thesis. Pennsylvania State University, 1965.
Boorstin, Daniel. *The Genius of American Politics.* Chicago: U of Chicago P, 1953.
Burton, Benjamin. "The Documentary Heritage." *The Documentary Tradition: From Nanook to Woodstock.* Ed. Lewis Jacobs. 2nd ed. New York: W.W. Norton, 1979: 301-306.
Daccardo, Ethel. "Russ TV Gives Grim Picture." *Chicago Daily News* 29 Dec. 1955: 39.
Daily Worker. 30 Dec. 1956: 6.
"Death of Salomon at 40 Cuts Short One of TV's Most Promising Careers." *Variety* 2 Feb. 1958: 32.
DeVoto, Bernard. "The Easy Chair." *Harper's* Jan. 1954: 8.
"East-West Contacts Stalled." *Facts on File 1955.* New York: Facts on File, Inc., 1956: 375.
Hamburger, Philip. "Far-off Places: TV's *Victory at Sea.*" *The New Yorker* 1 Apr. 1953: 79.
Hanser, Richard. Interview. 1981.
—. Papers. 1981.
Hanser, Richard and Henry Salomon, prods."*Nightmare in Red.*" Project XX. NBC. 27 Dec.1955.
Hartz, Louis. *The Liberal Tradition in America: An Interpretation of American Political Thought Since the Revolution.* New York: Harcourt, Brace, 1955.
Hazard, Patrick. "*Nightmare in Red.*" *Senior Scholastic* 6 Oct. 1955: 34, 53.
"Henry Salomon, TV Official, Dead." *New York Times.* 2 Feb. 1958: 86.
Hyatt, Donald. Interview. 1981.
—. Papers. 1981.
—. "*Nightmare in Red*-Legal." Personal papers.
Jacobs, Lewis. *The Documentary Tradition: From Nanook to Woodstock.* 2nd ed. New York: W.W. Norton, 1979.
Kennan, George. *American Diplomacy: 1900-1950.* Chicago: U of Chicago P, 1951.
Leyda, Jay. *Film Begets Film: A Study of the Compilation Film.* New York: Hill & Wang, 1964.

Mannes, Myrna. "Channels: The Hot Documentary." *The Reporter* 17 Nov. 1955: 38.

"*Nightmare in Red*." *The National Review* 18 Apr. 1956: 6.

"On the Scene: Donald Hyatt, A Way Out of the Vast Wasteland." *Playboy* April 1962: 103.

Palmer, R.R. and Joel Colton. *A History of the Modern World.* New York: Knopf, 1965.

Salomon, Henry, prod. *Project XX [20].* NBC. 13 Sept. 1954.

—. Papers and notes. Wisconsin Center for Film and Theater Research, Madison, Wis.

—. Program cards. Program analysis division, NBC.

—. "Timidity Will Get You Nowhere," *Variety* 25 July 1956: 32.

Shalit, Sid. *New York Daily News* 27 Dec. 1955.

"Television's *Nightmare in Red*: Pontiac Exits 'Hot' Programs." *Variety* 19 Oct. 1955: 1.

Waltz, John. Letter to Peter C. Rollins. 20 Feb. 1982.

Vietnam

17
Using Popular Culture to Study the Vietnam War: Perils and Possibilities

The Vietnam War is not over for the United States. It is still being fought in our popular culture, and the struggle provides rich opportunities for researchers and teachers of contemporary literature, mass media, and culture. The secret for exploiting this opportunity has less to do with identifying the kinds of materials than it does in defining the right approach to them, for, while there are possibilities, there are also perils. Existing Vietnam texts are short on hard, irreducible facts and long on bias; as a result, historians should look upon popular culture as a subjective prism of intense feeling rather than as Clio's reliable mirror.

Disagreements about interpreting Vietnam can lead to heated debates which echo the confrontations of the 1960s. For example, James Webb stepped on a rhetorical land mine at a 1985 conference on "The Vietnam Experience in American Literature" when he defiantly questioned the willingness of assembled academics to consider perspectives on the legacy other than those which portrayed America as exploiter, manipulator, and villain. As a highly decorated Marine combat veteran who felt that our cause in Vietnam was not only just, but vindicated by the post-1975 experience of the "killing fields" and the boat people, Webb deplored the uniformity of perspective along Academe's post-war paper trail: Webb's position is overstated—he is well known for his combativeness—but it bears consideration, especially his complaint about what he called the influence' of an "academic-intellectual complex":

Danang Landing, March 8, 1965

In media and publishing circles, supporting government policy of almost any sort becomes akin to selling out. Such a writer is quite often viewed by his peers and by critics to be either stupid or a pawn. Awards are lavished on those who discover new ways to question or attack government policy. Sometimes it takes more courage to confront the hostility of one's peers than it does to attack that amorphous dragon called government policy. (Lomperis 18-9)

Many present at the conference complained that Webb's remarks were not helpful, although a few of the assembled authors confirmed Webb's charges by recounting their own problems with publishers who rejected manuscripts by veterans which "did not exhibit enough guilt" (Lomperis 22). Scholars of my acquaintance who have taken an empathetic stand toward government policies or who have defended figures such as General Westmoreland against attacks by programs such as *The Uncounted Enemy: A Vietnam Deception* (1984) have been picketed at conferences and blackballed from speaking engagements. One veteran I know was refused employment and called "war criminal" for serving in the armed forces during the Vietnam conflict. Thus, while James Webb's statement oversimplifies, it points to a real question; in publishing, on television, and in the classroom, have Americans been exposed to a full spectrum of perspectives on our tragic experience in Vietnam?

Using Popular Culture to Study the Vietnam War

I think not. The purpose of this chapter is to briefly limn the problems of using existing histories, fictions, films, and television programs to study Vietnam. I do not wish to argue that the materials not be used—indeed, I feel that the opposite is the case, that they provide excellent teaching instruments. What I do offer is that there are wonderful possibilities in using existing texts, but there are also perils. The opportunity exists for showing that our study of Vietnam—like virtually every other period—is rich with differing perspectives and redolent with many "truths." The danger lies in accepting the report of any one document as the total picture. The first half of this chapter will survey the various documents and attempt to indicate potential pitfalls in using them; the second half will try to account for the biased consensus of approach to Vietnam. Along the way, I will speculate about the possible impact of two Gulf Wars on our retrospective image of Vietnam.

A Number of Popular Culture Genres Interpret Vietnam

Novels and Autobiographical Fictions

Vietnam fictions are so charged with feeling because veteran authors strive to dramatize the trauma inflicted upon them and their friends. Shortly after graduating (with me) from the Marine Corps' Basic School for officers at Quantico, Virginia, Philip Caputo found himself in Vietnam as an infantry Platoon commander; his *A Rumor of War* (1977) is an elaborate novelistic effort to depict himself as a youthful victim of war. W.D. Ehrhart's *Vietnam-Perkasie: A Combat Marine Memoir* (1983) similarly traces the frontline devolution of a young boy fresh from the backwoods town of Perkasie, Pennsylvania. James Webb's *Fields of Fire* (1978) traces the combat experience of officers and men in a tightly knit Marine infantry platoon; in an unusual coda for this literary genre, the narrative follows one of the protagonists back to a university campus. There the main character rebukes the college peace movement for taking the easy way out. Personal narratives like Michael Herr's *Dispatches* (1977) promote empathy for the pain and death which Herr witnessed during his psychedelic tour as a "new journalist" for *Esquire*. Each of these writers faithfully recounts his personal story; however, in addition, each comments implicitly and explicitly on the "big picture." Webb

A Marine Junior Officer's Personal Narrative

and Herr create an intense identification with their subjects—whom we gradually see as the victims of an inept, but dangerous, killing machine, the hateful war itself.

Caputo's work is more narrowly autobiographical; much of the novel tries to explain how the Marine Corps and America have brought young Philip to commit murder and perjury. These infantry fictions are colorful evocations of Vietnam; what makes them perilous as documents is that the authors ask us to accept their personal tales as reliable microcosms. Most of these "corruption of innocence" books draw heavily upon the American Adam motif, a topic to be discussed near the conclusion of this chapter. The motif has deep roots in our Romantic culture, but clearly skews interpretations toward a melodramatic mode of good versus evil rather than promoting a wiser tragic sense of life. Historians have long understood that a participant in an historical event may lack the perspective needed to identify larger patterns of meaning. War viewed from a foxhole will show vivid pyrotechnics, but the outlook is often as narrow as it is intense.

Letters, Diaries, and Oral Histories

Likewise, anthologies of letters, diary entries, and collected oral histories from Vietnam have their perils. Although such collections are promoted as argument-free, their editors inevitably shape the presentations. Stanley Beesley's *Vietnam: The Heartland Remembers* (1987) is a case in point. Beesley's own tour in Vietnam came during the later years of the war. He believes—with many others—that the Vietnam War had two phases for the ordinary fighting man: during the first phase (1965-69), units were committed to the field after training together; in the second phase (1969-73) replacements were inserted as individuals among complete strangers. As a result, according to this interpretation, the "second phase" was characterized by a breakdown of discipline, and a precipitous decline in morale. According to Beesley, second phase Army units refused to go out on combat operations; furthermore, such insubordination did not lead to disciplinary action. *Vietnam: The Heartland Remembers* appears to be merely a collection of oral history statements from veterans across the state of Oklahoma, but the evocative anthology misleads the reader by painting the *entire* war with "second phase" colors.

The New York State Vietnam Veterans Association collected a similar volume of letters entitled *Dear America: Letters Home From Vietnam* (1985). Interestingly, the book does *not* try to pour

NYC Vietnam Veterans' Memorial with Pool and Glass Wall

the experience into a preconstructed mold; instead, the anthology clusters letters around such topics as arrival in country, the experience of battle, what it means to be "short" on time, and other "generic" experiences for our boys in Vietnam.

In 1988, Cable TV's HBO came forward with a special program (very) loosely based on the anthology. This program could be used as a textbook in media manipulation. The visual rendering of *Dear America* places over 70% of the anthology's letters out of chronological order to support the "two phase" thesis. Filmmaker Bill Couturie, with the help of actors like Charlie Sheen, Matt Dillon, and others, transformed an act of devotion into a diatribe. HBO's *Dear America* was circulated theatrically in 1989 so that it could be considered for an Academy Award (see Chapter 23).

The lesson from these experiments is that oral histories and anthologies of personal documents are indeed perilous if approached as mere stores of "fact." When the subject is Vietnam, many anthologists find it hard to avoid shaping the raw materials into their own messages about the evils of a purposeless war.

Vietnam on Television

Our students are visually oriented, if not visually literate: some brag that they have seen major Vietnam movies more than once; others own large off-air collections of Vietnam documentaries. Yet the visual route can be the most perilous of all, because teachers are often as ill prepared as their students to analyze the visual rhetoric which the media giants of both coasts, and places in between, so effectively master.

There are a number of prominent documentaries which purport to probe Vietnam issues. As late as 1983, the Organization of American Historians Newsletter recommended *Hearts and Minds* (1975) by Peter Davis as a perfect companion to *Vietnam: A Television History*, a series purveyed by WGBH-TV (Boston)—one of the major centers for educational television in this country. The reviewer's suggestion was right, but not in the positive way it was intended. In an early review, even *Time Magazine* noticed that the historical interpretation of the Davis' *Hearts and Minds* was simplistic, that its rhetoric was strident. By 1977, April Orcutt had laboriously dissected the propagandist techniques of Peter Davis' *Hearts and Minds* in an excellent M.A. Thesis at Cal-State, Fullerton.

That much touted, prize-winning WGBH-TV series has not lacked its informed critics. *Vietnam: A Television History* was first broadcast in the fall of 1983. Shortly after the third episode was aired, demonstrations by Vietnamese refugees incensed by the programs occurred in Paris, London, Washington, D.C., New Orleans, Houston, and Los Angeles. The grievances against the series were consolidated by James Banerian in a book entitled *Losers Are Pirates* (1985), a volume which analyzed flaws of the series, episode by episode. Accusations of bias are substantiated in prolix detail. Editor Banerian and his staff also took Stanley Karnow's best-selling companion volume to task. Of *Vietnam: A History*, the critics asked rhetorically; "Has history come to this?" (36) Academic historians joined the criticism. Writing for the *Newsletter of the Organization of American Historians* in 1984, R.C. Raack said that the series "developed no sufficient methodology [...] and seemed to be unaware of the nagging problems deriving from missing as well as mendacious documentation." As a result, Raack concluded, "They failed to confront the 'television war' and made up their own television war" (8). Despite such criticism, the WGBH series won numerous awards and was purchased for instructional purposes by countless school systems and universities.

In 1984, Accuracy in Media (AIM), a Washington-based public interest group, received a controversial $30,000 grant from the National Endowment for the Humanities to produce a video critique of *Vietnam: A Television History*. (NEH had previously awarded WGBH over $1 million in a non-controversial grant to produce the series.) Two programs emerged from a Washington D.C. conference called by AIM to examine the PBS series. *Television's Vietnam: The Real Story* (1985) spelled out some of the points made by Banerian in his book-length critique. Some of the WGBH-TV's own consultants appeared on the answer program to voice objections to the Boston station's historiography. As Banerian observed, WGBH saw Vietnam as "America's war. America's mistake. America's responsibility" (28). With Banerian, AIM's conference faulted WGBH for not only showing bias in favor of the Communists, but, as well, for an unremitting—an almost racist—view of our allies, not to mention the terrible portrayal of America's fighting men as drug addicts and war criminals. AIM's video critique was itself

Rebuttal to the PBS Series and Other Journalistic "Histories"

criticized (and its major arguments found accurate) by an *Inside Story Special* broadcast by PBS in the fall of 1985. *The Real Story* has received a number of awards from Vietnamese groups worldwide for setting the record straight (from their point of view). It was favorably reviewed by *The New York Times* and *TV Guide*. Amazon.com now offers the AIM critique to customers interested in *Vietnam: A Television History*; in addition, a number of PBS stations broadcast the rebuttal as a fourteenth episode when they reran the WGBH series in 1985 and 1986. (Also available at aim.org.)

A second program from Accuracy in Media, entitled *Television's Vietnam: The Impact of Media* (1986), focused on the Tet offensive of 1968, comparing news reports with contrasting versions of the same stories by diplomats and soldiers involved in the action (see Chapter 18). Drawing heavily upon Peter Braestrup's *Big Story* (2 vols, 1977), *Impact of Media* dramatized the now widely accepted notion that the Tet offensive was so misreported by our media that a North Vietnamese military defeat in Vietnam was transformed electronically into a psychological victory in the United States. To

Using Popular Culture to Study the Vietnam War

General William C. Westmoreland, the Ground Commander, 1964-68

support its thesis, the program examined three microcosmic stories of Tet: the Saigon Embassy Incident, the Battle of Khe Sanh, and the Colonel Loan Photograph. In each case, the media image is contrasted with what actually happened. While *Impact of Media* does not eschew point of view in its presentation, it states its bias up front rather than smuggling it into the work *sub rosa*. Because the AIM shows are so candid about their point of view, Dr. Marvin Medhurst has described them as "bad" propaganda—as opposed to the WGBH shows which he ironically praises as "good" propaganda (30). It would seem that there are many perils for students and teachers when they approach "good" propaganda programs in search of truth.

The publication of a book entitled *Fair Play: CBS, General Westmoreland, and How a Television Documentary Went Wrong* (1988) revived interest in a CBS Special Report entitled *The Uncounted Enemy: A Vietnam Deception* (1982). The show promised to reveal "shocking decisions made at the highest level of military intelligence to suppress and alter critical information on the number and replacement of enemy troops in Vietnam." General William C. Westmoreland was the villain of the CBS melodrama. A long and inconclusive libel trial resulted from the show. Subsequently, books such as Don

Kowet's *A Matter of Honor* (1984) have alleged that Producer George Crile and media star Mike Wallace cooked up their own brew of deception in *The Uncounted Enemy*.

In addition, a CBS internal report by Burton Benjamin was published after it was "leaked" to the press by in-house sources who felt that the General was being treated unfairly. (This "source" was subsequently identified and fired by CBS.) Perils indeed seem to lie ahead for those who put their trust in this and other network exposés (see Chapter 20).

Vietnam from Hollywood

Hollywood's Vietnam has also been laden with tendentious metaphors and allegories. *Coming Home* (1978) is the story of a paraplegic veteran who makes a successful adjustment to civilian life and love. The film teaches that individuals should avoid military service because there is no moral basis for our involvement in a far-off land. In addition, we are asked to believe that anti-war activists have better sex than those who serve. That same year, *The Deer Hunter* attempted a mythopoetic approach to Vietnam as it followed the tour of duty of steel workers from Pennsylvania who are physically or emotionally crippled by a repulsive Asian war. In *Apocalypse Now* (1979), the American presence in Vietnam is depicted as an unmitigated evil which deserves the purging incineration it receives at the end of the film.

Within a twelve-month period, in 1986-7, five films saturated the Vietnam target. Viewers of Oliver Stone's *Platoon* are led to believe that American troops regularly shot civilians, that our field commanders used troops as "bait," and that our servicemen were so undisciplined that they spent more time "fragging" each other than fighting an elusive enemy. *Platoon*'s Hollywood *auteur* comments broadly about American history when the most sympathetic father figure in the film, Sergeant Elias, explains, "We've [the U.S.] been kicking ass for so long, it's about time we had ours kicked." Stanley Kubrick's *Full-Metal Jacket* looks back on the Marines: the first half of the film shows how basic training perversely redirected the natural energies of young men from love to war; the second half of the film traces the degradation which occurs in combat to the point where the narrator, "Joker," reflects that "I am in a world of shit, but I am alive and I am not afraid." Such is the result—Hollywood's Kubrick, looking backward, asserts—of Marine Corps brainwashing and Vietnam service. In *Good Morning, Vietnam*, Robin Williams is given his best screen opportunity for non-stop hilarity. Between riffs, the film stresses that the United States is fulfilling a French imperialist design—although the notion itself goes unexplored. Looking within the American "Establishment," we see that those who plan American policy are hypocritical, manipulative, and—like the top brass in *Platoon*—willing to endanger uselessly the lives of our young men. These messages are particularly memorable because Williams, himself, is genuinely funny. (The *real* Adrian Cronauer currently tours the country lecturing on the differences between his personal Vietnam experience and that portrayed by *Good Morning, Vietnam*.)

Two films stand out from the 1987-8 pack. *Hanoi Hilton* (1987) tells the story of American pilots held captive in the Hoa Lo Prison in Hanoi, 1964-73. Director Lionel Chetwyn's film is unlike its contemporaries because it portrays our servicemen as dedicated professionals whose military training gave them inner strength and discipline. The North Vietnamese, in contrast, are shown as cruel and manipulative captors. Finally, the American peace movement is criticized for naiveté. For taking such unorthodox positions, *Hanoi Hilton* was condemned by the Hollywood community and major critics. David Denby of *New York Magazine* challenged the research behind the film, decried its treatment of Jane Fonda, and concluded by describing the "tedious" production as suffering from "the grinding vindictiveness of an old Patrick Buchanan column" (91). Stanley Kauffman of *The New Republic* dismissed *Hanoi Hilton* as "filth" (26). In response to critical denunciations, Canon Films withdrew the offending film from circulation soon after its release, followed by a mini-revival of interest when veterans groups—including the POWS depicted— protested to local distributors.

A combat film entitled *Hamburger Hill* can be viewed as a cinematic rebuttal to *Platoon*. The film shows troops working together cohesively, respecting military discipline, and fighting courageously to complete their assigned mission, despite occasional friction within the unit. Like *Hanoi Hilton*, *Hamburger Hill* quickly disappeared from the theaters. As Harry Summers of *U.S. News and World*

Report observed in an early review, critics "will reject it as they rejected *Hanoi Hilton*, because it recalls shameful [wartime] events that they would rather not remember." Former Colonel Summers was right about the rejection, but his attempt to identify its motivation needs further thought. More recently, *We Were Soldiers* (2002) has stood out as a combat film which valorized both soldiers and their commanders—even a dedicated enemy.

Based on an eponymous 1992 non-fiction best-seller by Lt. General Harold G. Moore and journalist Joseph L. Galloway, and starring Mel Gibson, this film has benefited from the distance of time, but is not without its own historical inaccuracies. With *Hamburger Hill*, it is a powerful answer to *Platoon* because it shows the strong bond between officers and their troops, a bond which carried over into civilian life and inspired the two authors to collaborate on the memorializing project.

Understanding the Various Frames of Interpretation Ideological Elements

Objections by Those Who Served: Can They Be Ignored?

A cursory study of statistics from a Louis Harris poll of 1980 shows some glaring contradictions between the depressing portrait of the American fighting man in Vietnam novels, documentaries, and feature films when compared with the self-image of large numbers of

Mel Gibson, as Lt. Col. Moore, Promises to Be the First into Battle

veterans who are not part of the literary and movie communities. The executive summary brings the following disturbing conclusions to light (28-33):
- 90% of those polled were happy to have served
- 54% of those polled enjoyed their experience
- 79% denied that the U.S. had taken advantage of them

The Harris and later pollsters also found that Vietnam veterans were more likely to have gone to college and to purchase a home than others of their age; they were also more likely to have a better income than their peers. Syndicated editorialist Tom Tiede responded to these and other "surprising" statistics with the following observations:

> Ticking bombs? The people who were on duty in Vietnam are nothing of the kind. And they did not kill babies in the war. Rare exceptions to the contrary, the American troops were good, moralistic, and compassionate, and those are the principal characteristics for which they should be remembered.
>
> But they probably won't. The ugly image of the Americans in Vietnam may be permanent. It was a war in which slander became a national obsession, in which Jane Fonda is remembered while the heroes are forgotten, and in which we didn't have the determination to win or the good sense to abandon before losing. (Tiede 1)

Mr. Tiede's statement underscores the frustration which veterans (and some veteran correspondents) have when they see the negative images of the American fighting man in popular culture (see special note, below, on the Harris poll.)

The Wish to "Freeze" History?
During the Vietnam conflict, opponents of the war depicted America's presence in Southeast Asia as the cause of regional suffering. However, when the United States withdrew in 1975, the predicted era of peace and tranquility did not come to pass; instead, we saw "killing fields" in Cambodia and "reeducation" camps in South Vietnam. Some two million Cambodians lost their lives during the

murderous reign of Pol Pot. In 1993, we knew from headlines that Vietnam still held political dissidents in prison because American Congressmen had been barred from speaking with them about POW conditions. A number of Vietnamese-American students on my campus have told me that their fathers died from malnutrition or from unattended health problems while in Communist gulags; these wonderful kids strive for perfect academic records as a tribute to their lost fathers. Protests against political oppression in Vietnam continue into the 21st century, even as U.S.-Vietnam relations evolve toward "normality."

The revelation of these cruelties should have cast a new light on the meaning of the American struggle in Vietnam. For many it did. There was a "Second Thoughts" movement led by Peter Collier and David Horowitz, two former editors of *Ramparts Magazine* who were shocked by the unwillingness of colleagues on the American Left to criticize the post-war outrages in Vietnam:

> No matter that our old allies the National Liberation Front were among the first to be crushed; no matter that South Vietnam was conquered by the North; no matter that the Khmer Rouge, which we had supported with great enthusiasm had embarked on a policy of genocide. There were no enemies on the Left. (Collier 19)

Collier and Horowitz claimed that they were forced to reconsider their anti-war positions because of world developments, after 1975, including the reluctance of the American Left to criticize Communist excesses. These "lefties for Reagan" began to realize that "the Communists were every bit as bad as American supporters of the war said they would be" (26). For rethinking their historical commitments, former members of the new left were ostracized by their erstwhile comrades. Jeffrey Herf, once a leader of the Students for a Democratic Society (SDS) reports that "to take such a political position was just more than a number of old friends on the left could stomach. At their initiative, old friendships ended or cooled" (30).

The list of those who have changed their minds is formidable. Lloyd Billingsley was a leader of the anti-war movement; Peter

Collier cut his teeth on the Free Speech Movement at Berkeley and went on to become an editor of *Ramparts*, the mass distribution journal of the New Left; Jeff Herf was in SDS; David Horowitz wrote an excellent book about the student movement at Berkeley and went on to *Ramparts*; David Ifshin received quite a bit of media attention as Michael Dukakis' transition team leader due to his willingness, in student days, to broadcast over Hanoi Radio; Michael Medved went on in the 1980s to become co-host of the PBS version of *Sneak Previews* and then in the 2000s to be a conservative, syndicated talk show host, but, in the 1960s, he was Chairman of the Vietnam Moratorium in Connecticut. That student group succeeded in forcing ROTC off the Yale University campus. Stephen Schwartz, once a leading Trotskyite during the 1960s, now works with a conservative think tank in San Francisco. The list of those who have had second thoughts is long (Collier and Horowitz 263-7).

However long the list, the majority of those who participated in the anti-war movement—including those who were eligible for the draft, but found a way to avoid it—have a vested interest in "freezing history" circa 1968. By retaining the United States as the international villain, their opposition to the war during the 1960s continues to be vindicated. Unwillingness to serve their country in the war goes unquestioned. Even Johnny Carson could observe that *Platoon* was a movie which reflected well upon the draft dodger; what sensible person would serve in such an army? And if they served, how could they have emerged as anything but desperately wounded—psychically, if not physically. As one indignant reviewer of *Platoon* observed, "Needless to say, there are many people who think this movie is a tribute to those Americans who died in Vietnam. Needless to say, people who think so never knew anybody who went anywhere near Vietnam—Canada, yes, and Sweden, but not Vietnam" (Podhoretz). More research needs to probe how and why Vietnam stories (and some popular histories) are designed to retrospectively vindicate the judgments of those who opposed the war. Why are *auteurs* not now willing to reevaluate their position in the light of subsequent developments in Southeast Asia, Africa, and Afghanistan? Do they truly believe that the "radical chic" of yore caught correctly the real nature of events?

Radical Chic in Hollywood: From Spain to Vietnam to Nicaragua
Traditionally, a segment of artistic people in Hollywood and the media in general have been attracted to utopian radicalism. In the 1930s and 1940s, John Howard Lawson, Dalton Trumbo, Lillian Hellman and others clung overlong to the dream of a "Soviet America." In the 1960s, the Beverly Hills and New York radicals returned their political antennae to Fidel Castro of Cuba and then switched channels to Vietnam's Ho Chi Minh. Chairman Ho was portrayed as a Jeffersonian democrat who reluctantly turned to Communism when we rejected him, a preposterous view reiterated by George McGovern at an Air Force Academy Military History Symposium in 1990.

Many of these creative people still share the desire of the Left to cling to 1960s myths about Vietnam despite the tragic repression in Cambodia and in Vietnam following the 1975 debacle. For some, it would be spiritually disastrous to admit that support for the NVA brought about the deaths of millions and the misery of the thousands of "boat people," some 300,000 of whom died gruesomely at sea.

Central America was *chic* in the late 1980s. To many media celebrities, Daniel Ortega looked like a Jeffersonian democrat while Mrs. Ortega became a special darling of the "cocktails for Nicaragua" crowd in Beverly Hills. TV star Edward Asner established a nonprofit organization which has financed aid to rebels in El Salvador,

Vietnam's Boat People Experience the Agony of Exodus, 1975

some of whom have been identified as terrorists. The election of Violeta Chamorro to the Presidency of Nicaragua came as a big surprise and disappointment to the American intelligentsia—if not to ordinary Nicaraguans who exultantly exercised their franchise. For many American observers, Central America is Vietnam *redivivus*. The alleged Vietnam analogy to events down South was invoked constantly in Congress; even Richard Nixon is the author of a book entitled *No More Vietnams* (1985). But the Vietnam analogy is a two-edged sword: for the neo-isolationists, it means that we should never intervene because Vietnam proved that our meddling inevitably leads to tragedy; on the other hand, Richard Nixon and others deduced that it meant that we should intervene decisively when it is in our national interest—a policy which became known as "the Powell Doctrine." Shortly after our one-hundred-day victory in Operation Desert Storm, President George Bush visited the White House Press Room to announce that, as of March 1, 1991, "the Vietnam Syndrome is over." In many ways, he was describing, rather than shaping, a euphoric national mood of support for our actions in the Persian Gulf—a mood that had the potential to reorient entirely our retrospective interpretations of the Vietnam War.

Hollywood has not been passive in the Vietnam analogy debate: Oliver Stone's historical drama, *Platoon*, reached theaters during the same month that his *Salvador* went into distribution. Other films such as *The Mission* (1986) and *Walker* (1988) further drive home the Vietnam message, although *Walker* so overstated the lesson as to draw critical guffaws. In the penultimate scene, as Walker's pre-Civil War Nicaraguan empire crumbles, an American helicopter lands near his palace. Out springs a U.S. State Department official who explains that he is authorized to remove all U.S. citizens. This tendentious anachronism, a heavy-handed parallel to the 1975 evacuation of our embassy in Saigon, has actually been praised by some reviewers. More sensible critics have described the scene as silly at best.

We can look forward to future invocations of the Vietnam analogy in Hollywood films if recent examples are any guide to the future. After the success of Operation Desert Storm in 1991, however, the analogy will not have the impact it enjoyed prior to the triumph of our military efforts in the Persian Gulf. The second Gulf War in 2003 vindicated the Powell Doctrine and, at least in the early months of the military conflict, embedded journalists celebrated the courage and bravery of American troops; in contrast, drawing on the Vietnam legacy, as Michael Moore's tendentious documentary, *Fahrenheit 9/11* (2004), recapitulated the formula of Peter Davis' *Hearts and Minds* (1973) while features such as Brian DePalma's *Redacted* (2007) awkwardly rewound and replayed the flawed *Casualties of War* (1989). Video efforts by soldiers provided powerful rebuttals to such exposés (see Chown for an overview). One grass roots production, *Combat Diary: The Marines of Lima Company*, reached a large Arts and Entertainment (A&E) audience on Veterans' Day, 2006. The Home Box Office (HBO) feature with Kevin Bacon, *Taking Chance* (2008), projected an honorific attitude toward the American fighting man—a decided contrast to such portraits as *Coming Home* (1978).

Formal Factors

The Premise of a Lost War

James Banerian drew upon a Vietnamese proverb to title his book *Losers Are Pirates*. In thinking about popular culture in relation to Vietnam, the proverb provides valuable insight. People naturally want to join a victory bandwagon. In relation to the WGBH-TV history of the war, Banerian saw two related trends: on the one hand, the Boston-based producers—none of whom had substantial historical training—wanted to produce empathy for the then current regime in Vietnam so that wartime enmities could be transcended; as a dramatic byproduct, the "losers" in the war—the South Vietnamese and their American ally—had to occupy unsympathetic roles in the story.

The same perspective could be easily applied to other renderings of the Vietnam experience. Consider your own situation if you were involved in writing a novel or a screenplay or assembling an anthology; how would you conduct yourself if your basic premise was that we were the losers and moral reprobates to boot? First, you would have to explain how the most technologically advanced and mobile armed force in world history was defeated by an agrarian, Third World nation. Second, your task with respect to individual motivation would be to somehow explain how good American boys could be involved in such a dirty and disgusting foray. If possible, you would try to link these two themes.

Let us consider some eligible (and ineligible) themes. *Prohibited would be the following*: any intelligent defense of the concept of Containment by sympathetic characters (only "lifers" would swallow such claptrap); good relations between American fighting men and local civilians (strictly for rebels against a callous Establishment); concern for innocent human life or the destruction of civilian property (all Vietnam as a free-fire zone); racial harmony and teamwork on the front lines (racism rampant); mutual trust between officers and men (frequent fraggings); religious faith by fighting men (spiritual alienation only); intelligent conversation by officers or troops (f-words ad nauseam). At no time should commanders above the squad level be concerned about troop morale and safety. Whenever possible, include Lyndon Johnson's picture in frame with the face of a high-ranking villain. Never show that leadership experience can help a young person to grow in confidence of his powers so that he will make a contribution to his society on his return to the United States. Vietnam stories are stories of losers who return to our country as pathetic remnants, "walking wounded." Years after they return, TV can sponsor programs for them like the PBS special *For Vietnam Veterans* and *Others Who Should Care* (SONY Home Video). During such "happenings" we are urged to commiserate with the poor dupes. These are some of the spin-offs of the ubiquitous "Lost War" premise, results demanded by the artistic form more than the actual experience of veterans. (See special note on Harris poll results.)

The American Adam Motif

Concomitant with the "losers" premise is the American Adam Motif. The novels by Caputo, Ehrhart, as well as personal narratives by Herr and Beesley's collection of letters—but *not* Webb's *Fields of Fire*—draw upon this familiar American literary motif. Dark romantics like Hawthorne, Melville, and Poe ridiculed the motif's limitations when it became popular in the early nineteenth century, but the scheme is extremely useful in the Vietnam context where the purpose is to condemn the nation while forgiving the soldiers.

Our American Adam leaves a placid, civilian environment to become immersed in a war that leaves him devastated. Ron Kovic's *Born on the Fourth of July* (1976) is a model text. Films and television shape young Kovic's attitudes toward war; after high school, the Marine Corps adds its perverting influence. When combat experiences further erode his spirit, Kovic reaches a dead low: he kills a friend by accident and participates in the accidental shooting of Vietnamese children. His spinal wound comes as a blessing of sorts—through it, he learns to fight back against the official authorities—"Them." Caputo's *A Rumor of War* follows a similar outline in its effort to exculpate young Philip from his war crimes. At the climax of *Vietnam-Perkasie*, another tale of disillusionment, W.D. Ehrhart participates in the battle for Hue with demented fury:

> I fought back passionately, in blind rage and pain, without remorse, conscience or deliberation. I fought back [...] at the Pentagon Generals and the Congress of the United States, and the *New York Times*; at the draft card burners, and the Daughters of the American Revolution [...] at the teachers who taught me that America always had God on our side and always wore white hats and always won; at the Memorial Day parades and the daily Pledge of Allegiance [...] at the movies of John Wayne and Audie Murphy, and the solemn statements of Dean Rusk and Robert McNamara. (246-7)

In literary terms, the corrupted innocent is always pathetic, never heroic. From the opening scene of Oliver Stone's *Platoon* to the closing scene of Stanley Kubrick's *Full-Metal Jacket*, the motif presents viewers with American boys who merit our pity—never our admiration. We feel compelled to honor their broken and faltering requests for forgiveness. Big-heartedly, we welcome them home to whatever redemption a misdirected nation can offer them.

The lost war premise and the American Adam motif work together. Even the *Rambo* fantasies tap them. John Rambo (Sylvester Stallone) is an alienated vet; when society pushes him too far, he erupts into violence. In *Rambo II*, he asks an oft-quoted question; "Do we get to win this time?" Thus Rambo is an angry American Adam, flailing against "Them" as well as the evil enemy, rather than being an alternative heroic figure. Most critics have missed this important likeness between the maligned Rambo figure and his much-praised Adamic cousins in literature and film.

Search for a New Genre: The Vietnam Film

John Wayne's *Green Berets* (1968) was really a World War II film which conformed to well-established genre conventions; it cannot really be counted as an attempt to break ground for a new Vietnam-based genre. In subsequent efforts such as *The Deer Hunter* and *Apocalypse Now*, filmmakers groped early on towards the right metaphors and the proper formula to cope with the complexities of a limited war which America could not win. Robert Baird has argued that *Platoon* was such a box office success because it included good and evil characters in a way which allowed the protagonist (and the audience) to be exposed to the purported horrors of Vietnam without being fully corrupted. Chris Taylor (Charles Sheen) never suffers the full disillusionment of the American Adam. Audiences scratched their heads over *The Deer Hunter* and blew their minds over *Apocalypse Now*, but *Platoon* worked so well as a cathartic fiction that a now hip *Time Magazine* (which long since abandoned the cold warrior stance of its original publisher, Henry Luce) joined legions of reviewers in a cover story which (incorrectly) honored *Platoon* for portraying "Viet Nam, the way it really was." Baird's thesis seems more convincing: *Platoon* was so powerful as a metaphor for Vietnam because it seemed real as a war *film*, conforming to key elements of the genre while cleverly modifying factors to suit a new setting and special tensions. *Casualties of War* (1989) was an unsuccessful bid to repeat *Platoon*'s generic success. Not even Michael J. Fox could save Brian De Palma's jejune, sadopornographic attempt to decry America's "rape" of Vietnam.

Visual Language: Learning to "Read" Television and Film

For years, journals like *The History Teacher* have been exhorting historians to learn the language of film and television. Without such preparation, they are at a disadvantage— one which media producers cherish for the license it gives them—when they approach Vietnam productions. Here are a few obvious examples of distortion:

- In *Hearts and Minds,* General William C. Westmoreland says something along the lines that "the oriental doesn't value human life the way we do." Filmmaker Peter Davis then cuts to a graveyard in Vietnam where the wife of a Vietnamese soldier grieves for her husband; she becomes so over-wrought with anguish that she jumps into the grave! It is a heart-rending, "documentary" contradiction of the American general's apparently heartless observation.

  What really happened? General Westmoreland told Davis that, in *Korea,* the Chinese routinely anticipated high casualties for attacks, casualty counts inconceivable for American commanders who wanted to retain command. That experience, Westmoreland said, taught him that oriental commanders do not place the same value we do on individual human life. Davis extracted Westmoreland's observation and recontextualized it with the graveyard material to make the good general look callous, even racist. (The M.A. thesis by Orcutt identifies other such editing tricks in *Hearts and Minds*.)

- Westmoreland was bushwhacked again in the CBS documentary, *The Uncounted Enemy,* where responses to very different questions were edited to appear as answers to the *same* question. This is a notorious trick of the trade, something which was expressly prohibited by CBS News Guidelines at the time the show was broadcast, although that did not deter CBS's producers in their zeal to prove the malicious and untrue thesis of the program—that General Westmoreland hid intelligence information from Lyndon Johnson and the American people.

- *Vietnam: A Television History* employed Ngo Vinh Long as its translator, yet Mr. Long has been exposed in public court as a paid employee of Hanoi. Banerian's *Losers Are Pirates* documents numerous critical translation errors in the series, all of which point to a consistent intent to hide Communist rhetoric.

- Montage is a basic technique in all films, but *Good Morning, Vietnam* has a particularly significant example during the section in which Louis Armstrong sings "What A Wonderful World." Ostensibly, this is a laid-back segment, but a close reading of the shot sequence, as well as the interaction between pictures and words ("film irony") reveals a very serious message. Simply stated, the message is that Americans like Lieutenant Hauk (pronounced "Hawk") are inflicting pain on a placid and peaceful nation; Communist aggression is the natural response of a wronged people to the violence perpetrated by us and our ally. As the aggressors, we have taken a lovely and wonderful world and transformed it into a bloody battlefield.

Producers will be forever grateful to historians and teachers who ignore the place of visual language. They know that their messages are more readily absorbed by the visually illiterate and that they will remain society's true teachers with "mass-pop" as content.

IV. Conclusions

If popular culture novels, personal narratives, anthologies, and visual media dealing with Vietnam pose so many perils, why should we study them? The answer seems clear: our students, like us, are significantly influenced by the popular culture around them. We can let them make up their own minds about Vietnam, but we need to give them the tools to identify opinion and point of view as they consider the meaning of our longest war. We can make our students sensitive to the contexts from which novels and films are produced; we can prepare them with some notion of the formal and artistic elements which make "the medium the message." As we do so, we will be giving them analytical skills they can apply to other issues where the emotional stakes are high. It is conceivable that the sea change in our national mood following Operation Desert Storm and Operation Iraqi Freedom will help us to gain perspective and understanding of both the Vietnam experience and the differing artistic renderings of it. When we attain the proper distance, "the Vietnam Syndrome" will truly be exorcised; the perils of using popular culture to study Vietnam will be less dangerous and the possibilities brighter.

Special Note on the Louis Harris Poll of 1980

The executive summary contains some interesting findings in response to questions put to veterans:

1. "Looking back, I am glad I served my country."
Agree: 90%
2. "The United States took unfair advantage of me."
Disagree: 79%
3. "The Country owes me a great deal more in return for my military service than I've gotten."
Disagree: 75%
4. "If I were asked to serve again, I would refuse."
Disagree: 67%
5. "I enjoyed my time in the service."
Agree: 54%

Students are shocked by these statistics for obvious reasons; almost everything they have seen in the media is contradicted by the figures. (This Harris poll should be in most libraries and will definitely be in any library designated a "Federal Repository." As a commissioned work for the Veterans Administration, it is a government publication, VA study 792801, and contains both statistics and analysis.)

Works Cited

Baird, Robert. "*Platoon* and Truth: 'Art is Politics' – 'History is Lie'." M.A. Thesis. Oklahoma State U, 1989.

Banerian, James. *Losers Are Pirates: A Close Look at the PBS Series* Vietnam: A Television History. Phoenix, AZ: Tieng Me Publications, 1984.

Beesley, Stanley. *Vietnam: The Heartland Remembers*. Norman: U of Oklahoma P, 1987.

Benjamin, Burton. *The CBS Benjamin Report*. Intro. by Robert Goralski. Washington, D.C.: The Media Institute, 1984.

—. *Fair Play: CBS, General Westmoreland, and How a Documentary Went Wrong*. New York: Harper and Row, 1988.

Caputo, Philip. *A Rumor of War*. New York: Holt Rinehart, and Winston, 1977.

Chown, Jeffrey. "Documentary and the Iraq War: A New Genre for New Realities." In *Why We Fought: America's Wars as Film and History*. Lexington: UP of Kentucky, 2008. 458-487.

Collier, Peter, and David Horowitz, eds. *Second Thoughts*. Lanham, MD: Madison Books, 1989.

Culbert, David. "Television's Vietnam and Historical Revisionism in the United States." *Historical Journal of Film, Radio, and Television* 8.3 (1988): 253-67.
Denby, David. "Movies: Flea-bagged." *New York Magazine* 13 Apr. 1987: 90-91.
Edelman, Bernard. *Dear America: Letters Home From Vietnam.* New York: Pocket Books, 1985.
Ehrhart, W. D. *Vietnam-Perkasie: A Combat Marine Memoir.* New York: Zebra Books, 1983.
Harris, Louis and Associates, Inc. *Myths and Realities: A Study of Attitudes Toward Vietnam Era Veterans.* The Veteran's Administration. Washington, D.C.: GPO, 1980.
Herr, Michael. *Dispatches.* New York: Alfred Knopf, 1977.
Kamow, Stanley. *Vietnam: A History.* New York: Viking, 1983.
Kauffman, Stanley. "Hanoi and Elsewhere." *The New Republic* 27 Apr. 1987: 26-7.
Lomperis, Timothy. *"Reading the Wind": The Literature of the Vietnam War – An Interpretive Critique.* Durham, NC: Duke UP, 1987.
Medhurst, Martin J. "Propaganda Techniques in Documentary Film: *Vietnam: A Television History* vs. *Television's Vietnam: The Real Story.*" *Television Studies: Textual Analysis.* Ed. Gary Burns and Robert J. Thompson. New York: Praeger, 1989. 183-205.
Nixon, Richard. *No More Vietnams.* New York: Arbor House, 1985.
Orcutt, April Coleen. "An Eisensteinian Analysis of the Documentary Film *Hearts and Minds.*" Unpublished M.A. Thesis. California State U, Fullerton, 1977.
Podhoretz, John. "*Platoon*: Painful, Brutal, Much-Praised Movie on Vietnam Dishonors Veterans of America's Longest War." *Washington Times* 30 June 1986: IB, 6B.
Raack, R.C. "Vietnam: A Television History: Yet Another Vietnam Debacle? Caveat Spectator." *Newsletter of the Organization of American Historians* Feb. 1984: 8-10.
Rollins, Peter C., dir. *Television's Vietnam: The Real Story.* SONY Video, 1985.
—, dir. *Television's Vietnam: The Impact of Media.* SONY Video, 1986.
Tiede, Tom. "Writer Knows Vietnam First Hand." *Stillwater NewsPress*, OK. 10 Feb 1987.
Webb, James. *Fields of Fire.* Englewood Cliffs, NY: Prentice-Hall, 1978.

18
Television's Vietnam: The Impact of Visual Images

Three Icons: The Tet Offensive and Television News (January-March,1968)

There were three major stories from Vietnam during the Tet Offensive of 1968, and each provided a fragment for a composite picture of American confusion and defeat. Not only the matter reported, but the manner in which stories were conveyed contributed to this portrait. This chapter will discuss some television news techniques and then explore the application of these standard practices to three major stories of Tet: first, the attack on the U.S. Embassy in Saigon by "a squad of "sappers"; second, the execution of a suspected Viet Cong officer on the streets of Saigon by Colonel Nguyen Ngoc Loan, Chief of South Vietnam's national police force; finally, the defense of an airstrip at Khe Sanh by a Marine regiment against a surrounding force of more than two divisions of North Vietnam's Army regulars. In each case, dramatic Tet events were interpreted to be emblematic of the broader meanings.

The Art of Television News Is the Art of Selection
During early May 1975, I attended the annual TV Newsfilm Workshop of the National Press Photographers Association. For the fifteenth consecutive year, cameramen from local stations across the country came to the University of Oklahoma campus in Norman to learn the art of television news. Network professionals and award-winning news cameramen lectured, displayed their work, and

evaluated student pictorial assignments. Full editing and developing services were provided by Kodak.

In addition to information about film stock, lighting and equipment, there were aesthetic discussions. The professionals stressed that a television news story is a "story" in a literary sense, a form which has a beginning, middle and an end. For this reason, one of the most significant tasks of a camera operator is to decide what the real "story" at a given event is; only after making what professionals call a "commitment" does he then begin to collect shots. Later editing should follow the inherent visual logic of materials gathered. Even the shortest film stories are attempts to interpret; they are essays written with a cine-pen.

A second major precept was that a television account must tell its story visually. Cameramen should strive to give their stories visual integrity; any words later supplied will amplify the visual narrative. As a result, news stories are eligible for the same kind of detailed analysis which we customarily apply to documentary and fiction films: there is a reason for each shot; there is a viewpoint behind every edited assemblage of shots. The finished product tells a story from a particular point of view.

And there are stories within stories, "microcosms." Recognizing that the camera sees only externals, a news cameraman looks for surfaces and textures which reflect an understanding of the inner "meaning" of an event. Consider approaches to reporting a fire. Our teachers stressed that long shots of burning buildings and crowds of tenants were ineffective. We were instructed to uncover an "inner story" before shooting. In the case of a fire, an astute cameraman will follow the travails of a tenant, reporting the traumatic effect of this disaster with close-ups of facial expressions and of those few objects saved from the blaze. Once moved to emphasize with the suffering of a particular victim, viewers can then extrapolate to the broader story, microcosm will be related to macrocosm. As with other forms of communication, it is proper to assume that not only do practitioners hold to this doctrine of microcosms, but that audiences look for microcosms as a part of induced media expectations.

The three actual events during Tet were interpreted by correspondents in the field and by network anchors in New

York as representative microcosms and became so implanted in the American imagination that they could not be modified by subsequent reports: redolent with drama, they supplied a series of icons to which information would later cling. The putative "penetration" of the U.S. Embassy in Saigon, General Loan's "gratuitous" execution of a Viet Cong suspect, and the "hopeless" battle at Khe Sanh seemed to summarize both the meaning of the Tet Offensive and the significance of America's entire effort in the Republic of South Vietnam.

Invasion of the U.S. Embassy
One criterion of "news" is that something important is said or done by or to a person in the public eye. It is news when a politician, opinion maker, or media personality does something unusual or has something unusual done to him/her. Yet such an assumption can be misapplied; a whole publishing industry exploits the general public's curiosity about the goings and comings of celebrities. During Tet, 1968, a reinforced squad of Viet Cong blew a hole in a wall surrounding the U.S. Embassy, and then *unsuccessfully* attempted to storm the Embassy building.

The Embassy story was given saturation coverage partly because reporters were nearby. Press centers for a number of American networks, weeklies, and wire services were within a short walk or cab ride from the Embassy. A more important reason for coverage was the inherent visual symbolism of the event. Reporters arrived on the scene totally shocked by the urban fighting. As they assessed their "commitment" for reporting the Embassy battle, the symbolism must have been obvious: American diplomats had been caught by surprise, and could be extricated from their entrapment only with great difficulty, a predicament which seemed to summarize the war situation. Members of the Johnson administration had attempted to woo public opinion into support of the war with a recent campaign of good news. Tet attacks across the country seemed to expose the official stories as pure propaganda. While shutters clicked, there may have been some satisfaction in observing the discomfort of the embattled government position.

News footage for the Embassy story communicated a number of significant messages were conveyed by means of visual language.

410   *America Reflected*

Viet Cong Attack: Success or Failure?

Just before the dawn attack began, military policemen driving by were gunned down by those about to blow a passage into the Embassy compound. The jeep and its dead occupants crashed into a tree across from the main gate. Opening shots of Embassy stories lingered over the jeep and the twisted bodies of its dead occupants to convey that this was obviously a symbolic "crack-up" for Americans in Vietnam.

An unexpected deviation from news format further accentuated the sense of American unpreparedness. On the night of January 31, footage was sent via satellite from Tokyo. Because of haste, the footage was run unedited; as a result, TV viewers were treated to a rare experience of network news reported in the style of cinema verite. An NBC cameraman positioned himself behind a military policeman who was participating in a fire fight inside the Embassy compound. The M.P. is lying behind a column; in an over-the-shoulder shot, we experience with him the dangers of combat. At a distance, we see other soldiers attempting to throw a pistol to Ambassador George Jacobson who is at a second floor window of his bungalow. The long shot is unclear; as the camera continues to run, we sense the cameraman's attempts to find a proper focus. Because footage is unedited, we have a sense of participating in this awkward and dangerous scene. Later, we learn that the Ambassador caught the pistol just in time to shoot a Viet Cong soldier coming up the stairs.

Viewers accustomed to edited war reports must have taken pause over this footage. Combat in built-up areas is slow and difficult, because the "terrain" under such circumstances always works in favor of the defender. Viewers were not instructed in such subtleties; rather, the impression given was that our troops could not rout the invaders. Viewers were also told that the Viet Cong had entered the Embassy building, and that this penetration was of great "symbolic" and "psychological" importance. In fact, fighting had taken place in the courtyard only, but retractions and corrections were never supplied. As a result, the Embassy story provided the first of three powerful (and misleading) icons of the Tet offensive.

Colonel Loan's "Summary Justice on a Saigon Street"

Probably the most memorable visual story from the Tet Offensive—seen countless times in newspapers, magazines, posters—was that of Col. Nguyen Ngoc Loan executing a Viet Cong officer on the streets of Saigon. Heavy fighting was taking place near the race track in the Northeast section of Saigon, especially around a Buddhist temple which had been a hotbed of anti-government activity. From the street fighting, a man in ragged clothing was brought to before Loan. The uniformed captors carried a pistol which belonged to the Viet Cong suspect. As the suspect came before him, Loan unsnapped his holster, drew his pistol and put a bullet through the right temple of the victim.

Col. Loan Shoots Viet Cong Lieutenant

Eddie Adams of the Associated Press caught a still photograph just as the bullet entered the victim's head. NBC's cameraman caught most of the scene; fearing reprisal from Loan, the Vietnamese cameraman for ABC refused to film the shot itself. Both stories concluded with high angle, close-up zooms of the Viet Cong's head spurting blood over a foot in the air. The NBC footage was in living color. As he walked away from the scene, General Loan spoke to Howard Tuckner. Tucker quoted these reflections in a concluding statement for his NBC story. The still photograph and the motion picture footage provided a startling, barbaric portrait—and, apparently, an obvious one.

It also seemed to be a microcosm. For years the U.S. Government had attempted to impose democratic reforms upon the South Vietnamese government. In our public statements we had stressed that our aims were not simply geopolitical: we hoped that this oriental nation could learn to value democratic forms and liberties. We certainly claimed to be supporting a government which had rid itself of colonial-style abuses of power.

The photograph of Col. Loan seemed to contradict official rhetoric about democratic government. Sensing this meaning in the NBC footage, Frank McGee used it in a later report along with the following commentary: "South Vietnam's national police chief had killed a man who had been captured carrying a pistol. This was taken as sufficient evidence that he was a Vietcong officer, so the police chief put a bullet in his brain. He's still the police chief." McGee's narration was written after the event by those not present on the scene and unaware of the details of the events reported (qtd. in Bailey and Lichty 276). The remarks, however, are an accurate rendering of the drama implicit in the images: on the left, is a typically corrupt oriental official who obviously has neither concern for human life nor respect for public opinion. On the right of the frame is a man dressed in civilian clothes who stands defenseless before a representative of government authority. Compositional elements reinforce this contrast: the Chief is dressed in a protective flak jacket supplied by the U.S. Army; the suspect is clad only in a "Woody Allen" flannel shirt and shorts. General Loan is free to move as he unbuckles his holster, draws his pistol and fires; the prisoner is bound and totally passive. The Colonel fires the deadly shot from frame left; the victim moves in a paroxysm from frame right down to lower-right corner of the frame: in the Tokyo relay, as the prisoner falls, the camera zooms to his head, from which spurts a great volume of blood. In the interests of "taste," NBC showed the prisoner fall, after which the screen went black for three seconds. Ironically, editing out the geyser of blood may have intensified the visual experience, for cutting to black is a cinematic convention frequently employed to dramatize the finality of personal extinction. In this case, a cut to black gave viewers a sense of what it is like to be executed. In any case, the horrible moment of "rough justice" became a part of world consciousness.

Although Col. Loan's indiscretion was an important Tet story, it was not necessarily a representative microcosm. Editing supplied new ingredients or removed essential ones. The story began with "establishing shots" of street fighting, but in truth the shots had been taken after the execution. Because reporters arrived on the scene just prior to the big moment. Omission of such opening visuals might have indicated to viewers that reporters had not been present during the preceding street fighting and thus were not aware of the pitch of emotions for both slayer and slain. More significantly, Howard Tuckner's "stand-upper" after the execution was removed. Ron Steinman, NBC's Saigon Bureau Chief, believed that such verbiage would be "anticlimactic" (Bailey and Lichty 269).

Tuckner's comments would have placed the act in a human context. Loan was indeed the national police chief, a significant fact in relation to recent events: his capital city had become a maelstrom of fighting—passions were intense, revenge for the assassination of police force families was on the minds of those fighting in the streets. Within this context, Loan's cryptic comments to the foreign correspondent Tuckner were not irrelevant. As Loan reholstered his pistol, he observed: "Many Americans have been killed these last few days and many of my best Vietnamese friends. Now do you understand? Buddha will understand" (Bailey and Lichty 269). While not excusing the act, inclusion of such a statement (or indication that it had been made) would have changed the "picture," made it more complex.

It would also have changed the microcosm. As projected by print and visual media, the Loan execution told Americans that the

Saigon government was nothing but a continuation of an ancien regime. To this end, the picture seemed to be worth ten thousand words. But the picture's message might have been different had it been framed by additional commentary: atrocities had been committed recently against the wives and children of government officials; a fire fight was raging down the street. Within this context, General Loan committed an inexcusable act. No one noted at the time—and few noted later—that, at the very moment General Loan was shooting a single ununiformed soldier, North Vietnamese soldiers were systematically executing over 2800 South Vietnamese civilian government employees and public school teachers outside the city of Hue (Oberdorfer 202).

The shot looked familiar, very much like an earlier microcosm, the 1963 image of "Bull" Connor of Birmingham, Alabama, unleashing dogs to attack Civil Rights protestors. For Americans in 1963, Connor's photograph spoke volumes about the backwardness and misuse of power in the South, abuses which demanded federal intervention. Whereas the 1962 image catalyzed a nation's sympathies to effect significant changes in federal law, Col. Loan's indiscretion affected foreign policy. Reproduced on posters, T-shirts, banners, this icon symbolized the futility—indeed, the active stupidity—of our support of the Saigon regime. The archetypal power was recognized by the Vietnam Veterans Against the War: when that protest group selected its logo, it decided upon the Loan photo, although in a modified form. The image was stylized to a simple solid print of the figures against a lighter background. By that time, details of the image had been so implanted in the American mind that its message needed only to be triggered by suggestion. All knew its meaning.

Khe Sanh: A Microcosm of Military Stupidity. Or a Chance to Deal a Killing Blow?

To the chagrin of the Communists, none of the military objectives of the Tet Offensive were attained: The Army of the Republic of Vietnam (ARVN) fought bravely, the Saigon government maintained a semblance of authority, and, most significantly, civilians refused to rally to the Viet Cong cause. As dust settled in Saigon, the mood shifted from initial shock to qualified optimism. At Khe Sanh, dust

Was Khe Sanh Hell in a Very Small Place?

was still in the air and there was room for speculation: no one could divine the enemy's intention or strength; as facts increasingly contradicted prophesies of doom elsewhere, Khe Sanh was still offered a picture of the allies off balance.

For many observers, Bernard Fall's popular book, *Hell in a Very Small Place* seemed to suggest a compelling analogy between Dien Bien Phu and the battle developing at Khe Sanh:

> as the first Marine briefings on Khe Sanh took place in Marine Headquarters at Da Nang or Dong Ha, the name Dien Bien Phu insinuated itself like some tasteless ghost hawking bad news.
>
> Marines who had to talk to the press found references to the old French disaster irritating and even insulting. Most were not interested in fielding questions about it, and the rest were unequipped. The more irritated they became, the more the press would flaunt the irritant. For a while it looked like nothing that had happened on the ground during those weeks seemed as thrilling and sinister as the recollection of Dien Bien Phu. And it had to be admitted the parallels with Khe Sanh were irresistible." (Herr 99-100)

A corollary of the Dien Bien Phu analogy was that American military leaders were ignorant of the parallels and therefore walking blindly into a trap. Correspondents visiting Khe Sanh attempted to probe Colonel David Lownds (Commander of Regimental Landing Team 26) about the parallels, but with little success. Because Lownds was taciturn, reporters assumed that the battlefield commander was therefore as unaware of the obvious perils of his position as the nincompoops who ordered him to defend such a precarious outpost. Even Walter Cronkite, on the evening news of January 26, stood before a display comparing Khe Sanh with Dien Bien Phu and assured his audience that the prima facie likenesses between the two battles were "plain for all to see."

Few correspondents listened closely to what Colonel Lownds, General R.E. Cushman, and General W.C. Westmoreland said about differences to be noticed. General Westmoreland had ordered a staff study of Dien Bien Phu; he had even talked with one of the French commanders. These studies convinced Westmoreland that American advantages in artillery and air support more than compensated for differences in troop strength (Westmoreland 337-8). Even if the NVA were estimated to have two and one-half divisions in the Khe Sanh area, superiority of supporting arms gave the six thousand Marines of RLT-26 a considerable tactical advantage. Despite these assurances, they saw the battle through Dien Bien Phu colored glasses. That the fourteenth anniversary of the great battle would be in March did not help to clear the airwaves.

President Johnson Follows Khe Sanh Closely

Lyndon Johnson was also obsessed by the Dien Bien Phu analogy. To keep up with developments at Khe Sanh, the President had a three-dimensional replica of the battleground made in a 1/15,000 scale, a more detailed map scale than that available to troops in the field. Whenever the President visited the White House War Room during Tet, he inspected the Khe Sanh mock-up (Schandler 69). As Doris Kearns has noted, such objects as the relief map gave Johnson a sense of control when he felt challenged by intractable problems (286). A nervous President sought other assurances that Khe Sanh could be held: in an unprecedented move, Johnson forced the Joint Chiefs to sign a written guarantee. That President Johnson should go to such extremes over a single battle was less an index of his distrust of the military than an indication of the power of historical analogies on both actors and observers (Westmoreland 335-6).

The press was not alone in declaiming the obvious "stupidity" of the military's decision to fight at Khe Sanh. Scholarly observers joined in the clamor. Arthur Schlesinger, Jr., pleaded that "a humane or intelligent leadership would have arranged for the immediate evacuation" of the outnumbered Marines at the isolated air strip. Schlesinger saw the decision to fight at Khe Sanh as a result of poor planning rather than as a clever ploy on General Westmoreland's part. According to the CUNY professor, Westmoreland had been so discredited by the Tet Offensive that he hung on to Khe Sanh for lack of any more effective strategy. The inaction was leading to useless casualties: "We stay because Khe Sanh is the bastion, not of the American military position, but of General Westmorland's military strategy—his 'war of attrition' which has been so tragic and spectacular a failure." The academic saw a streak of orneriness running from Khe Sanh, through the chain of command, all the way up to the Presidency. "President Johnson likes to compare himself with Lincoln—'sad but steady'—but he lacks one prime Lincolnian quality: that is, the courage to fire generals when they have shown they do not know how to win wars. Lincoln ran through a long string of generals before he got to Grant. It is not likely that he would have suffered Westmoreland three months" (qtd. in Westmoreland 335-6). The echoes of Dien Bien Phu were reverberating everywhere but on the battlefield: press, President, and pundits were obsessed by an historical analogy.

With Dien Bien Phu precedents in mind, reporters who visited Khe Sanh spoke as if they were under a dark cloud of disaster. In a report for the evening of January 24, Don Webster asked troops within the Khe Sanh perimeter how they felt about the way the battle was shaping up. Troopers and officers evinced optimism, but Webster chose to conclude the story on an ominous note: somewhere out in the hills were adversaries in sufficient strength to overrun the doomed base. Comment by Walter Cronkite immediately following the Webster report explained that Khe Sanh was a "miniature Dien Bien Phu" and that wily General Giap was once again directing the attack.

Ed Needham of NBC covered the evacuation of Khe Sanh village on January 24. Military commanders had decided that a major battle could be better conducted if civilians were out of the Khe Sanh area. Rather than interpret the evacuation as a result of humanitarian concern, Needham explained that the North Vietnamese had won an initial victory: we were too weak to fight. Clips of frightened refugees entering the Khe Sanh perimeter seemed to corroborate Needham's claims. While refugees awaited helicopters, some incoming rounds hit the base. The resulting panic was filmed and aired; not so the orderly helilift of civilians from the battlefield.

Two days later, Ron Nessen of NBC reported that Marines could not leave the airfield's perimeter because they were so greatly outnumbered. While Nessen noted that Marines joked about comparisons with Dien Bien Phu, his report concluded with serious doubts about the high spirits: morale of the Marines was ebullient "despite their position." In a CBS report for January 26, Igor Ogennessof stressed the hazards of flying fixed-wing aircraft to and from the encircled airstrip. (Ogennessof said nothing about the availability of airdrops.) Hazards to troops at Khe Sanh were further underscored when program format was unintentionally disrupted: during his "stand-upper," Ogennessof was seriously wounded by fragments from an incoming mortar round. At the moment of impact, the reporter was standing beside the ramp of a C-130 being loaded with the day's dead and wounded. Commentator Walter Cronkite then came on to fill in details: Ogennessof had been operated on at Khe Sanh and was recuperating at a Danang hospital. In this Khe Sanh story, as at the Embassy, the medium supplied a significant part of the message: the vertiginous camera, the loss of perspective, the need for an outside commentator to intervene during a film report all added visual and aural confirmation to explicit statements about men in jeopardy.

In a particularly tendentious report for January 29, Don Webster of CBS interviewed troops along Khe Sanh's perimeter in an obvious attempt to coax complaints. Some of the questions asked were: "Why don't you have enough protection?" "Does lack of overhead in the bunkers make you scared?" "How did you Marines ever get into this fix?" All the Marines interviewed shrugged off these invitations to grouse. Their commander, Colonel Lownds, refused to talk about Dien Bien Phu. The closing scene of Webster's report was taken at a familiar spot, the ramp of a C-130 into which the bodies of dead and wounded were being loaded. As the correspondent intoned, "There will be more such cargo if the battle joins," the implication was clear: every day Marines were dying unnecessarily and their commanders were uninterested in mitigating the dangers.

Murray Frompson contributed to the gloom on January 15. At the conclusion of his Khe Sanh story, he surmised that "the North Vietnamese determine who lives and who dies at Khe Sanh." Even David Douglas Duncan succumbed to pessimism in a montage of stills for the *ABC Evening News* of February 23. Duncan suggested that camaraderie, humor and heroism were all part of the Khe Sanh experience, but he added his mite to the theme of vulnerability. Duncan knew that only four major aircraft had been shot down at the air strip; yet, speaking to his photos of a burning C-130, he observed: "sometimes they make it, sometimes they don't." This stress upon the tenuousness of supply lines to Khe Sanh further validated the Dien Bien Phu analogy.

Television is a visual medium which thrives on interesting and representative pictures. Every photojournalist attempts to find those physical details and actions which reveal the inner meaning of events. For the Embassy story and the execution by General Loan, "startling stuff" was exploited. In both cases, it seems clear that drama won out over intelligent discussion so that false (Embassy story) or distorted (Loan execution) impressions of the broader meaning of Tet were conveyed.

Television's Vietnam: The Real Story (1985) and *Television's Vietnam: The Impact of Media* (1986) reconstruct some of the unreported microcosms at Khe Sanh, with an eye toward stressing the intelligent planning and instances of active heroism which brought victory to the outnumbered Marines. Some of the television reports already described are contrasted with our reconstruction of the battle.

II: The Battle of Khe Sanh: Unreported Microcosms

The wisdom in defending Khe Sanh is still under debate: some observers feel that it was merely a feint by the NVA to draw troops away from urban areas; a few believe that it was initially scheduled to be a major confrontation, but that plans were changed (personal interview). General Westmoreland and the Marine Corps maintain that Khe Sanh was a major allied victory because of the massive employment of supporting arms (personal interview). Whatever the larger importance of Khe Sanh, it is certainly true that positive microcosms of the battle were either unperceived or ignored.

The Battle of Khe Sanh Takes Shape

On the evening of January 2, 1968 a Marine listening post outside the western perimeter of Khe Sanh observed a small squad of intruders heading for the base. When challenges were not answered, Marine automatic weapons stopped six of the figures. A search of the bodies revealed some startling intelligence information: the North Vietnamese soldiers killed were all high-ranking officers and their presence on a reconnaissance patrol seemed a harbinger of a major operation.

Over the next few days, the Twenty-Sixth Marine Regiment at Khe Sanh was reinforced: the perimeter of Khe Sanh base was strengthened; selected battalions were helilifted to dominant terrain features. Although hilltop battles were seldom reported, they were integral to the Khe Sanh defense. As the official Marine historian for the battle has noted, commanders "were well aware of what had happened at Dien Bien Phu when the Viet Minh owned the mountains and the French owned the valley" (Shore 31). In addition to dispelling the Dien Bien Phu analogy, media attention to hilltop battles would have depicted Marines in a posture more traditionally associated with the Corps. Although repeated confrontations between infantry units forced the young Americans to display

Marines Take the High Ground

their mettle, it would seem that only Department of the Navy records remember the heroic hilltop struggles. (In 2006, this imbalance was rectified by the National Museum of the Marine Corps when it created a special modular experience for Hill 881S. Visitors exit a mock-up of a CH-46 helicopter into a "hot landing zone" atop this important terrain feature; the experience is "hot" because there are sounds of battle and because the module provides a combination of elevated heat and humidity of Vietnam.)

Hill 881N (January 20, 1968)

On January 17, a Marine reconnaissance team was ambushed by North Vietnamese Regulars southwest of Hill 881N. Two days later, India Company of the Third Battalion moved out through thick morning fog to engage any enemy still in the ambush area. As the fog began to lift, advancing Marines were caught in a deadly crossfire: within seconds, twenty Marines were out of action. Forward observers called in artillery support from the valley. The effectiveness of the 155mm howitzers was so great that the third platoon could resume its advance. Second Lieutenant Thomas Brindley, the third platoon's commander, urged his men forward, and took the lead as they advanced over the objective. Unfortunately, enemy defensive fires were deadly: as the platoon moved into position, the Lieutenant and all squad leaders were killed. Responding to this emergency, a ranking corporal assumed command of the platoon and supervised consolidation of the defense.

During the battle the Marines showed concern for their friends. When Second Lieutenant Michael Thomas learned that one of his squads was in jeopardy somewhere forward of his position, he instinctively rose to lend assistance. About ten yards from the platoon command post, the Lieutenant was stopped by a mortal head wound. But the Lieutenant's example inspired action: led by Sergeant David Jessup, men of the platoon fought their way to the injured squad and brought the wounded back to safety.

An hour before sundown, India Company was ordered to return to its original position on Hill 881N to prepare for a major night assault by the North Vietnamese. As they moved back to their foxholes, members of the company could take pride in their dangerous work: while seven of the attacking Marines had been killed and some thirty-five wounded during the day, the North Vietnamese had lost over one hundred infantrymen. A day of violence and sacrifice, this "microcosm" never reached American living rooms.

Hill 861 (January 21, 1968)

During India Company's assault, a North Vietnamese officer surrendered to Khe Sanh base. The prisoner revealed that a major attack was planned for that evening, and it was this news which prompted RLT-26 Commander Colonel David Lownds to pull back India Company to a defensive position. Shortly after midnight on January 21, the defector's prediction materialized: after thirty minutes of preparatory fires, a company-sized attack was launched against Hill 861. Enemy demolitions experts led the way, exploding pathways through the Marine protective wire. Behind followed assault troops in sufficient numbers to penetrate the company perimeter. This incursion was countered by a Marine assault from both sides of the penetration: fighting broke down into hand-to-hand struggles. A body count at dawn revealed that only four Marines had been killed while the ground was strewn with forty-seven NVA attackers.

A number of Marines showed their mettle during the evening. During the preparatory fires, the company command post was hit directly by a mortar round: the company commander was taken out of action by three shrapnel wounds; the company gunnery sergeant was killed instantly; the first sergeant was bleeding profusely from a pierced jugular vein. Although completely blinded by powder burns, the company's radio operator continued to conduct necessary communications. A battalion level officer who received these messages later commented that the radioman was "as cool, calm, and collected as a telephone operator In New York City" (Shore 41).

Marines on Hill 861 found ways to express their cool under fire which no Hollywood director would dare invent for a fiction film. Somewhat dazed by his wounds, and attempting to stem the flow of blood spurting from his neck, the first sergeant trooped the line and stumbled upon a strange scene. Somewhere near the mortar pits, the sergeant heard the sound of music. A veteran of twenty-two years, imagine his incredulity as he looked down into a gun pit to find mortar men singing as they fed their tubes. Red-hot mortars provided the beat, but the voices were a cappella. The song had been taught to the men in boot camp—it was the Marine Corps Hymn!

Khe Sanh Base (January 21, 1968)

The shelling of Khe Sanh base began just after the fight for Hill 861. A little before sunrise, the base received incoming enemy artillery, mortars and rockets and many of the rounds were on target. In fact, just about everything above ground was hit: tents were destroyed; helicopters caught fire; both a fuel storage area and the largest ammunition dump went up in flames, providing a dramatic pyrotechnic display for the next forty-eight hours. As if to add insult to injury, an enemy shell landed amidst a cache of tear gas canisters; the resulting fumes and vapors spread throughout the base.

Like their fellows on the hilltops, Marines in the valley showed grace under pressure. Even though the First Battalion's trench line ran within thirty meters of the burning ammunition dump, Marines remained at their posts: duds nearly fell into their pockets; scalding particles of metal from antipersonnel grenades burned unprotected flesh. Support troops within the perimeter were equally ready to court danger: truck drivers rushed to their vehicles and drove them to protective cover; artillerymen operated their guns, supplying protective fires for the hills and hitting suspected enemy gun emplacements with counter battery fire. As duds landed

Khe Sanh Resupply Without Landing

among artillery pieces, Marines in volunteer parties of two lifted the hot rounds and carried them to a disposal pit some fifty meters away. Nearly one hundred of these uninvited guests were ushered away during the evening.

After sunrise, Khe Sanh village was attacked by a battalion-sized force of North Vietnamese Regulars. A combination of artillery fire from Khe Sanh Base (conducted as hot rounds continued to drop among the guns) and close air support helped to stop over one hundred enemy before they penetrated the defensive wire. Both a concern for civilian lives and for an economical defense prompted Colonel Lownds to evacuate Khe Sanh village. ARVN troops were reassigned responsibilities at the base perimeter; civilians were flown to the safety of Dong Ha and Da Nang. While it is unquestionable that civilians were forcibly removed, the alternative to displacement was not very attractive. An enemy probe after sunset confirmed the decision to clear fully all fields of fire.

The Marines of RLT-26 had been tested: the tactically important hilltops had been protected from enemy assault; while an embarrassing amount of material had been wasted in the valley, the defensive positions at Khe Sanh were undamaged. With the civilians of Khe Sanh village evacuated, there were no restrictions on fire missions. News reports did not reflect these developments. Television stories focused on the evacuation of body bags and wounded rather than on the active events of the day. Yet the high morale should not have been difficult to explain: Marines had repelled the first attempts to wrest Khe Sanh and had inflicted significant casualties. Confidence was further bolstered when more troops were flown in on January 22. With these factors in mind, it is not surprising; that the enlisted men interviewed were reluctant to grouse before cameras.

Hill 861 (February 5, 1968)
At three in the morning, preparatory fires began to hit Hill 861 were followed by an enemy penetration of Echo Commander's perimeter. Captain Earl Breeding led a counterattack:

> Because the darkness and ground fog drastically reduced visibility, hand-to-hand combat was a necessity.... Captain Breeding, a veteran of the Korean conflict who had worked his way up through the ranks, admitted that, at first, he was concerned over how his younger inexperienced Marines would react in their first fight. As it turned out, they were magnificent... Since the fighting was at such close quarters, both sides used hand grenades at extremely close range. The Marines had the advantage because of their armored vests, and they would throw a grenade, then turn away from the blast, hunch up, and absorb the fragments in their flak jackets and the backs of their legs. On several occasions Captain Breeding's men used this technique. (Shore 65)

The North Vietnamese made later attempts to take Hill 861 at sunrise, and then again at noon. With fire support from Khe Sanh Base, Echo Company was capable of repelling each attack. As the enemy withdrew during the afternoon, Marines from adjacent hilltops provided withering fire. Little information reached the American public about the confrontation, even though statistics were noteworthy: after twelve hours of fighting, the Marines had lost seven troops while the North Vietnamese left over one hundred bodies on the slopes of Hill 861. The Marines still held the tactically vital high ground above the Khe Sanh base, thereby stifling a rerun of Dien Bien Phu.

A Bad Day for Company B—In Living Color
On the morning of February 25, a fledgling Second Lieutenant was asked to take a reconnaissance patrol just outside the base

perimeter. The maps issued to ground troops in Vietnam were on a 1/50,000 scale and the lack of detail made them hard to read; the inexperienced officer strayed from his designated route and the patrol stumbled into a North Vietnamese bunker complex. The results were horrible: twenty-six Marines were not only killed, but left behind in the ambush zone; although a member of the patrol dragged the Lieutenant back to base, the young officer bled to death along the way.

A free-lance photographer, Robert Ellison, was on the scene as the patrol stumbled back into the perimeter. He captured images of reality which would be used by *Newsweek* as microcosms. In a special story entitled "The Agony of Khe Sanh," *Newsweek* printed the final moments in living color. Against the rich elephant grass, we see the wan face of the Lieutenant; a caption under the adjacent photo reads: "men had to make it back to the base the best way they could" (29). Marines have always been very sensitive about the recovery of bodies: an ignominious implication of this story was that those few Marines venturesome enough to leave the perimeter were unable to fight cohesively. The photo essay seemed to indicate that life at Khe Sanh base was hardly better organized. Selecting images to suit the issue's emphasis on passive suffering, *Newsweek* showed not a single Marine firing back at the enemy. Even the continuously busy guns went unphotographed.

A Good Day for Company B Goes Unreported

The members of Company B were anxious to repair their loss. Within a month of *Newsweek*'s feature story, the company left Khe Sanh under cover of darkness and silently assumed assault positions near the NVA bunker complex. (Marines hoped to keep casualties down by exploiting the element of surprise.) A protective fog concealed the company's movement across a road south of the base; intense artillery support kept the North Vietnamese in their holes as attackers climbed the hills. By noon, over one hundred North Vietnamese had been killed or captured (Shore 129). Success of this raid could be attributed to careful coordination between Marine infantry and supporting arms.

As a microcosm, the raid by Company B might have conveyed a number of messages about the Marines at Khe Sanh, perhaps even about the professionalism of American troops in Vietnam. Certainly, reports of the raid could have counterbalanced the unfortunate blunder so colorfully reported by *Newsweek*. More significantly, the raid could have represented the new posture of Marines as skies cleared over Khe Sanh and General Westmoreland began to approve airmobile operations. But this was not emphasis chosen. Instead television told the story of the "relief" of Khe Sanh by focusing on the arrival of air cavalry troops at the main gate: in their "stand uppers," some reporters stressed Marine embarrassment about being relieved by Army units; others reiterated their original complaints about military stupidity—why had this piece of territory been defended in the first place? The heroism and esprit of the morning raid went unnoticed and unreported.

Television's Vietnam: Conclusions

Prior to Tet, the Johnson administration was guilty of attempting to promote false optimism. Legitimate doubts about government credibility were generated by the obvious gap between official statements and media reports. How could officials claim that Tet was a victory for us when nightly news reports showed the very slow progress of our troops along the streets of Saigon and Hue? Why were we allowing the North Vietnamese to destroy ammunition dumps? If the Marines at Khe Sanh were really Marines, why were they continuously huddled in trenches and bunkers? Why weren't they firing back? Was the promised "light at the end of the tunnel" a beacon of victory or an *ignis fatuus*? A Herblock cartoon summed up the paradox: we may indeed have turned a corner in Vietnam, but rather than finding an open street, we had run headlong into a determined enemy (Editorial).

Conflicting information was plentiful. Media reports claimed that the American Embassy had been penetrated, yet U.S. officials in Saigon staunchly denied "the obvious." Why should American boys risk their lives for the Republic after Col. Loan's barbaric performance? Khe Sanh Base seemed in imminent peril, yet the commander was almost jolly in television interviews. If things were going so well at Khe Sanh, why were planes and reporters being shot down? Evidence in the form of television images and sounds simply outweighed official pronouncements.

Khe Sanh was no more clearly understood by political leaders than by the press. A battlefield mock-up in the White House was the offspring of President Johnson's obsession with Dien Bien Phu, not a tool designed to help a commander-in-chief. The Dien Bien Phu analogy drew attention to the worst news: a single plane shot down was translated to mean that supplies for Khe Sanh had been interdicted; a burning ammunition dump meant that "the North Vietnamese determine who lives and who dies at Khe Sanh"; ambushed patrols received special color coverage, while well-executed attacks and determined defenses were ignored. Tragedy and disaster were sought; as a result, tragedy and disaster were found. Because correspondents visited the valley only briefly, it is not surprising that preconceptions shaped their stories. When uninjured troops proved to be too jaunty, reporters and film crews simply strolled over to medevac. Story theme dictated what images should be gathered, and the story was Dien Bien Phu revisited.

The news of Tet turned American public opinion against the war in Vietnam. At least since the publication of Don Oberdorfer's *Tet* (1971), it has been public record that the Lunar New Year offensive was not a major victory for the insurgent forces: some 65,000 of the best Communist troops were killed in a period of two months, and none of the military objectives of the Tet attacks were achieved. What is important is that a nation was moved by misleading visual dramas. Compelling icons were implanted in the public mind, leaving the following impressions: the American Embassy, a traditional symbol of our nation, was violated by invaders who were evicted only after considerable effort; individual rights were not respected by our puppets; at Khe Sanh, our toughest troops were running like cowardly Keystone Kops. How could these dramatic images be contradicted by officials who had been selling invincibility for the previous year?

A number of critics have argued that there was collusion among broadcasters, but there are significant obstacles in the path of any conspiratorial interpretation. It is simply a fact that many effects wrought upon the public during Tet were unplanned. Embassy footage rolled on not because cameramen wished to give the impression of quagmire, but because news film arrived too late to be edited. While the resulting cinema verite showed American diplomats symbolically trapped and embarrassed, those messages were not the result of a conspiracy between news cameramen and anchormen. At the time the footage was aired, broadcasters were concerned exclusively with the informational content of the film; it was a breaking story and the public was curious for any visual report. Col. Loan's "rough justice" was simply too dramatic not to air; but, here again, it seems clear that the full implications of the images were not discerned by those who printed the photo or aired the film. Obviously, Igor Ogennessof did not plan to be wounded during his "stand upper" at Khe Sanh; nevertheless, the interruption of his report seemed to confirm gloomy predictions about the doomed base. Every breakdown in standard program format intensified the message that American control in Vietnam was crumbling.

Nor was the Khe Sanh story a product of malicious premeditation. Reporters did their homework before visiting the outpost, and required reading told the story of French defeat at a valley outpost surrounded by "angry hills." Khe Sanh was not overly supplied with troops, and all agreed that the base was surrounded by at least two North Vietnamese divisions. Among other things, Bernard Fall's *Hell in a Very Small Place* sensitized newsmen to look for likenesses between the predicament of the French and that of the exposed Marines. Taking into account the bad flying weather of early spring, many factors pointed to a second stunning military and media victory for North Vietnam's General Giap. Because Marine commanders appeared to be ignorant of history, they seemed sure to repeat it.

As the Saigon bureau chief for the *Washington Post*, Peter Braestrup had a hand in generating the false microcosms described. With the advantage of hindsight, his *Big Story* (1977) examined the major Tet stories in exhaustive detail. But Braestrup's two-volume work looked at the media problem from the perspective of a practicing journalist. Television's Vietnam(s) devote more attention to media and foreign policy; some useful lessons are offered.

Government should assure that it tells its own story effectively. In recent years, Presidents have used the visibility of their office to communicate with the nation in times of peril: during the

Cuban missile crisis, John F. Kennedy successfully exploited this opportunity; to his injury after Tet, Lyndon B. Johnson did not. In addition, something about "truth in advertising" should be gleaned from the Tet experience: in late 1967, government officials were manufacturing glowing reports about the war's progress; when the same officials attempted to be more realistic during Tet, they were not believed. Public relations by government are legitimate; public snow jobs are not.

Tet confusions prove that the American public needs to be educated in the language of the visual media. What social studies classes used to do with newspapers they now need to adapt to television news. Our citizens must learn that many nonverbal messages of news stories are shaped by such nonverbal devices as camera angles, types of shots, length of shots, editing, and many other factors peculiar to visual communication. Viewers also need to be aware that particular stories are often used as microcosms to convey broader meanings, and that this technique can be misleading when unrepresentative microcosms are selected. Certainly all the individual stones surveyed in this essay were intrinsically important, but the larger conclusions explicitly and implicitly extrapolated from them were false.

Neither those who captured images nor those who printed or screened them were fully aware of the impact of their work. Robert Northshield, Executive Producer of the *Huntley-Brinkley Report* during Tet, contends that it was not his job to consider impact. Rather, it was his professional responsibility to report what was "news": "I know that when I throw a stone in a pond there will be ripples. But that's about all I know. I don't know where the ripples are going, and I mustn't waste time worrying about that" (personal interview). Northshield is a skilled and dedicated practitioner. His observations are a clear indication that even purveyors of our microcosms are not fully conscious of the power they wield. And there may be considerable truth in Mr. Northshield's contention that attention to impact would inevitably lead to manipulation of materials. Perhaps reporters should assume that it is their job to deliver "hard news"; conversely, it is the job of a visually literate viewer to decide how she/he will be affected.

The Tet experience complicates this issue. During Tet, the Viet

Cong boldly attempted to capture the major cities of Vietnam. The result was failure: the Republic of Vietnam came out of Tet much stronger and more confident of its power to govern; General Westmoreland emerged ready to deliver a knockout blow to his staggering opponent. Yet, somehow dramatic images dominated facts. No praise for the Republic's ability to weather Tet could match the image of General Loan firing in anger. If the Republic was on such a firm footing, why was the American Embassy so unprotected? Why were the Marines at Khe Sanh running rather than fighting? During Tet, the press attempted to report individual stories along traditional journalistic lines. Crack-ups and bodies were scoop material at the Embassy; at Khe Sanh, the wreckage of airplanes provided effective mise-en-scene for stand-uppers; and no one could resist the photo of General Loan.

As humanists studying the effects of media on the perception of foreign policy issues, our concern must be for educating viewers. Without an awareness of the interpretive character of photojournalism, viewers will continue to be overly impressed by the putative "reality" of pictorial stories. Unless sensitized to techniques such as microcosms, they will be misled about major events in our national life. Means must be devised by humanists to assure that our citizens become visually literate.

Discussion of Literature

The television news reports discussed in this paper were viewed at a Chapel Hill conference. Professors Lawrence Lichty (Univ. of Wisconsin-Madison) and George Bailey (Univ. of Wisconsin-Milwaukee) provided helpful introductory remarks. For better or worse, the author claims these "readings" as his own, although insights from both oral remarks and the writings of the media scholars prodded thought. Kinescopes of these historic news programs are available to researchers at the Motion Picture Division, U.S. Archives. All quotes in this paper were culled at special Chapel Hill screenings and therefore may be guilty of errors of detail. After presenting this chapter to the 1978 meeting of the Popular Culture Association, the author has profited from a number of additional insights about the complexity of both the political and media dimensions of the subject. These refinements are reflected in *Television's Vietnam: The Real Story* and *Television's Vietnam: The Impact of Media*—a new DVD holds both programs plus a 30-minute talk by Peter Rollins along with some text materials.

This study has made extensive use of five sources. The best narrative history of the Tet Offensive is Don Oberdorfer's *Tet!*. A monumental study of media in the Indochina war can be found in Braestrup. The official Marine Cops history of the battle is Shore's *The Battle of Khe Sanh*. White House responses to Tet are best described and evaluated by Schandler. Both Oberdorfer (15) and Braestrup (86ff) stress the confusion surrounding the unexpected attacks on Saigon. At the Chapel Hill conference, Peter Braestrup and Charles Mohr (*New York Times*) added further observations about disorientation among reporters at the Embassy. Braestrup examines the Embassy events and reports in great detail (86-138). As elsewhere, the reading of visual language here is my own. For a detailed study of how this visual story was captured and disseminated, see Bailey and Lichty. Media scholar David Culbert's "Historians and Visual Analysis of Television News," is a pioneering study. As communications between reporters in Saigon and New York producers reveal, this is clearly a story which would not have been allowed out of the battle area had censorship been in force. Under existing practices, the U.S. military was guilty of collusion rather than repression: special armed convoys regularly escorted news film to the Ton San Hue airfield; military transport planes carried the precious "stuff" to Tokyo, from where it was beamed to the U.S. by satellite.

Interviews with Khe Sanh veterans have revealed that every officer above the rank of Captain was required to read Fall's study long before the Battle of Khe Sanh was joined. Even "media problems" related to parallels were discussed by staff members of RLT-26. For more on the President Johnson's requiring the Joint Chiefs to sign a written guarantee that Khe Sanh could be held, see Schandler (87-88). For speculation concerning the psychological motives behind such behavior, see Kearns (324-50).

The March 18, 1968, *Newsweek* editorial page re-enforced the impression that Khe Sanh was a microcosm. For the first time, *Newsweek* declared the war to be unwinnable and called for a speedy

U.S. withdrawal, helping to sour public opinion of the war. But in fact, the Viet Cong's capacity to wage war was destroyed at Tet. Thereafter, NVA units were needed. Soon after the event, Oberdorfer was keenly aware of the essential paradox of Tet: "The North Vietnamese and Viet Cong lost a battle. The United States Government lost something more important—the confidence of its people at home" (329). Unfortunately, President Johnson subscribed to the conspiratorial view, as did a number of other major political and military figures associated with Tet. Sometimes called "the Agnew thesis," this conspiratorial view is contradicted by too many facts. For a glimpse of Johnson's growing paranoia, see Kearns 331.

A thought-provoking examination of the connections between format and meaning in television can be found in McCray. Bailey and Lichty stressed the impact of deviation from format in Walter Cronkite's CBS special after Tet, "Report from Vietnam" (Feb. 27 1968). That Cronkite got up from his desk and went out to the field implied that an especially critical juncture had been reached. It would be impossible to exaggerate the impact of this single program on both official Washington and the American public opinion.

Works Cited

Bailey, George A., and Lawrence W. Lichty. "Rough Justice on a Saigon Street: A Gatekeeper Study of NBC's Tet Execution Film." *Big Story: How the American Press and Television Reported and Interpreted the Crisis of Tet 1968 in Vietnam and Washington.* Novato, CA: Presidio, 1994. 266-281.

Braestrup, Peter. *Big Story: How the American Press and Television Reported and Interpreted the Crisis of Tet 1968 in Vietnam and Washington.* Novato, CA: Presidio, 1994.

Culbert, David. "Historians and Visual Analysis of Television News." *Television Network News: Issues in Content Research* Eds. William Adams and Fay Schreibman. Washington, D.C.: George Washington U, 1978.

Editorial. *Newsweek.* March 18, 1968.

Kearns, Doris. *Lyndon Johnson and the American Dream.* New York: Harper and Row, 1976.

McCray, Curt. "Kaptain Kronkite: The Myth of the Eternal Frame." *Television: The Critical View.* Ed. Horace Newcomb. New York: Oxford UP, 1979.

Northshield, Robert. Personal Interview. U of North Carolina, Chapel Hill. Feb. 1978.
Oberdorfer, Don. *Tet!* New York: Doubleday, 1971.
Pike, Douglas. Personal Interview. U of North Carolina, Chapel Hill. Feb. 1978.
—. *War, Peace and the Viet Cong.* Cambridge: M.I.T. Press, 1969.
Schandler, Herbert Y. *The Unmaking of a President: Lyndon Johnson and Vietnam.* Princeton: Princeton UP, 1977.
Shore, Moyers S. *The Battle of Khe Sanh.* 1969. Washington, D.C.: U.S. Marine Corps, 1977.
Westmoreland, William, General. Personal Interview. U of North Carolina, Chapel Hill. Feb. 1978.

19
Press History Repeating Itself as Farce?: Critical Responses to *Television's Vietnam: The Real Story* (1985)

My documentary entitled *Television's Vietnam: The Real Story* (1985) caused quite a stir in journalistic circles during the winter and spring of 1985. The program was an hour-length critique of the PBS series entitled *Vietnam: A Television History* (1983; hereafter referred to as "the PBS Series"). My work on the show as researcher, writer, and producer-director took me from the bucolic rolling plain of Stillwater, Oklahoma, to the confusion and strife inside the beltway surrounding Washington, D.C., where, for two years, I did my best to withstand the slings and arrows of an outraged press. *Television's Vietnam: The Real Story* (1985) (and later, *Television's Vietnam: The Impact of Media* [1986]) found its way to the PBS stations of the country, but only after considerable debate, speculation about motivation, and dramatic fusillades of praise and blame from regional and national media spokesmen. The shows dealt with how the American press distorted the Vietnam War; my Washington experience exposed me to a repetition of that history of distortion—this time as farce.

Television's Vietnam: The Real Story (1985)

Television's Vietnam: The Real Story (1985; hereafter referred to as *The Real Story*) was basically a conference film. In the summer of 1984, Accuracy in Media, a Washington-based, media watchdog group, sponsored a conference to critique the PBS television series on Vietnam. First aired on PBS in the fall of 1983, *Vietnam: A Television*

My Controversial Documentaries

History received six Emmys and a host of prestigious awards—despite a scathing review by Richard Raack in the Organization of American Historians Newsletter and public demonstrations by citizen groups in London, Paris, Baton Rouge, Houston, and Los Angeles. Veterans groups and "boat people" living in the United States demanded—and, in Louisiana and California, were courteously provided—air time to present opposing views. Reed Irvine, Chairman of Accuracy in Media, received a number of telephone calls from Vietnamese civic leaders and decided to launch a campaign against *Vietnam: A Television History*. In the meantime, I was working on a critique of the series with two undergraduates at Oklahoma State University in preparation for the 1984 meeting of the Popular Culture Association in Toronto, Canada.

Vietnam: A History was the companion book to the PBS series. Accuracy in Media invited its author, Stanley Karnow, to participate in the conference. Both Karnow and Richard Ellison, Senior Producer, declined.

On the other hand, veterans, Vietnamese refugees, former POW, academics, and retired diplomats crowded the three-hundred-seat conference room at the downtown Hyatt in Washington for two

The Karnow Study

days of presentations. With a film crew, I interviewed speakers in a quiet setting, collecting a video database for *The Real Story*. Over the coming months, the show would be amplified with additional interviews; footage from networks and commercial archives across the world; and home movies by boat people and protesters. It did not take long to collect the materials needed for a potent critique of the PBS series.

Two of our best critical sources had been paid advisors to the PBS series. Douglas Pike (d. 2002), at the time Director of the Indochina Archive at the University of California-Berkeley, was the world's leading non-communist expert on the Viet Cong and North Vietnamese Army.

As a State Department analyst and, later, as an academic, he has been keeping Americans aware of developments in Vietnam. Pike tried to work with the Boston producers, but emerged from the experience unhappy with their combination of ignorance and bias. He believed that they had defined their approach prior to consulting him and that his participation was solicited only to qualify for funding from the National Endowment for the Humanities—which had virtually required WGBH to place Pike on its consultant list. In

Douglas Pike: A Consultant Critical of the PBS Series

The Real Story, Pike summarized his feelings; rather than providing new insights about our Vietnam heritage, the series "contributes to the misuses of history," a damning observation from one so knowledgeable.

Stephen Morris (historian), Stephen Young (former diplomat) and a few others who had consulted for the PBS series were equally critical. Vietnamese refugees living in France and the United States shared video materials related to their protests at public television stations around the world; they also provided accurate translations to statements which had been significantly misrepresented by the WGBH Vietnamese language specialist, Ngo Vinh Long. (Mr. Long's credentials were seriously compromised when a court inquiry in Cambridge, Massachusetts, exposed that his mother was a member of the party hierarchy in Hanoi.)

Since the PBS series consisted of thirteen episodes and involved almost as many producers, it should not be surprising that some episodes were better than others as history studies. (Anyone interested in an episode-by-episode analysis should consult James Banerian's book-length critique of the series, *Losers Are Pirates* [1985].)

Still, it did not take long to call many conclusions of the $6.5 million effort into question. The task of *The Real Story* was to outline the major errors and to highlight the bias of the series against the United States and our allies, the South Vietnamese. We also sought to explore the parallels between these errors and press distortions *during* the war years.

The Conclusions of Television's Vietnam: The Real Story

Here are the salient points made by *The Real Story*:

1. WGBH consistently depicted Ho Chi Minh as a Jeffersonian democrat. Ironically, Ho was one of the last dogmatically internationalist of Communists and a leading critic of Yugoslavia's nationalist leader, Josip Broz Tito. Repeatedly, the PBS series portrays Ho as an avuncular leader who used Communism as a means to advance nationalist ends.

2. WGBH portrayed the Yen Bay rebellion of 1930 as Communist led when in fact it was inspired by non-communist nationalists, people later liquidated by the Communists. (Vietnamese exiles were especially distraught about this distortion of their national history.)

Chairman Ho: PBS Protagonist

President Diem: The PBS Villain

3. WGBH portrayed South Vietnam's President Ngo Dinh Diem as an American puppet, a corrupt politician elevated to office by Americans to serve our interests.

4. WGBH glossed over the violence used by the Communists to achieve their ends, thus missing the significance of the large influx of refugees to the South during the Geneva discussions of 1954 (and avoiding obvious parallels with the post-1975 tragedy of Vietnam's boat people).

5. The National Liberation Front was depicted as representing a spontaneous upsurge of popular feeling rather that as a disciplined communist organization controlled from the North.

6. The South Vietnamese were treated with contempt while the Viet Cong and North Vietnamese were consistently portrayed as idealists.

7. The American service man and his sacrifice were cast in a negative light, perpetuating the stereotype of the Vietnam veteran as drug addict, loser, and victim.

8. WGBH, in one of the final episodes, predicts that our Vietnam errors will embroil us in Central American quagmires. Drawing such historical analogies is misleading; in fact, as Richard Nixon proved in his post-presidential book, "No more Vietnams" can have two very different meanings.

9. Misleading press reports out of Vietnam—especially during the Tet offensive in 1968—contributed to our defeat. As Robert Elegant says, "for the first time in modern history, the outcome of a war was determined not on the battlefield, but on the printed page, and—above all—on the television screens." (This final issue is briefly mentioned as part of a promise that a second program, entitled *Television's Vietnam: The Impact of Media*, will investigate press matters in depth.)

The program close for *Television's Vietnam: The Real Story* makes no attempt to hide its point of view: "We were right to resist communist aggression. We were wrong in thinking that the outcome would be decided by our military strength alone." The overall thrust of the program was to show that the PBS series perpetuated war-era arguments about Vietnam. In the light of the massive atrocities in Cambodia (over two million people slaughtered by Pol Pot) and Vietnam (over one million "boat people" fleeing Communist repression), our program took the position that anti-war arguments of the Vietnam-era would simply not hold up. AIM's summer conference had amassed an enormous amount of evidence; additional interviews had further shown weaknesses in the PBS series; finally, the publication of a book-length critique of the PBS series, a volume entitled *Losers Are Pirates: A Close Look at the PBS Series*, "Vietnam: A Television History" confirmed many of our findings.

In October, 1985, we brought the finished documentary to PBS; after some negotiating, PBS—sometime in November—scheduled the show as an experiment in viewer-response programming. The experiment seemed to be launched successfully when a posse of vigilantes from the Television Writers of America attempted to rescue WGBH from our clutches.

Reviewers To The Rescue

I have not taken a scientific survey of the members of the Television Writers Association of America, but I have before me hundreds of reviews by dues-paying members and I can say something about them as a group. Most are male and between the ages of 27 to 40; they write "personal" columns in which they try to entertain readers as much as guide them through the media maze of the week; none has served in the military, or at least none alludes to military service;

there is no evidence that any member has read a book-length work on Vietnam. A few, like the former President of the organization, Tom Jicha of *The Miami News*, like to pose for their cameo photos with a baseball cap pushed back off the brow or to otherwise clown; the TV writer for *Newsday* calls his column "The Marvin Kitman Show" and bills himself as its "Executive Producer."

Taken as a group, the young, male writers whose work I will be describing reminded me of a correspondent who interviewed me at the 1985 meeting of the Popular Culture Association in Louisville, Kentucky. The young man from a CBS affiliate wanted to reassure me that he could be objective. With obvious sincerity, he explained that he had never read a book of fiction or nonfiction about Vietnam, never seen a Vietnam-related film—not even *Green Berets* (1968) or *Apocalypse Now* (1979)—never enrolled in a course which dealt with Vietnam. After a moment's thought, he added that someone had given him the collected works of Gary Trudeau, so he had read all the *Doonesbury* cartoons for the 'sixties and 'seventies. In sum, he assured me that his reporting would be "objective."

As it turned out, the local CBS reporter with the help of his very competent cameraman, produced a pretty clear story about what the various professors at the PCA meeting had said on Vietnam; still, the combined ignorance and arrogance of the young man as he addressed his subject closely resembled the mindset revealed by the preponderant number of reviews of *The Real Story*. What is even more disturbing, the more I studied the reviews for threads of continuity, the more I saw repeated many of the errors which characterized reporting during the Vietnam era! Press history was repeating itself!

Reviews Recap Vietnam Errors
1. Lack of background on the subject of Vietnam.
In *Television's Vietnam: The Impact of Media*, journalist Robert Elegant says that one of the lessons of Vietnam was that reporters failed to prepare themselves to cover a complex story:

> You cannot send people into cover a very complicated situation unless they have some fundamental knowledge of the situation. There were too many people who came for quick

tours—particularly in television, a six-month tour—who never had the time to read and learn anything about Vietnam, about Communism, or about guerilla warfare, which was the kernel of what they were trying to cover.

The lesson applies to coverage of *The Real Story*. Few of our interviewed experts—despite their credentials as writers in the field of Vietnam, diplomatic, and military studies—were recognized by reviewers. More often than not, they were ridiculed as non-entities. For example, one reviewer said of Douglas Pike: "Douglas who?" Such a response shows no awareness of the network of Vietnamese scholars in the United States. Pike edits *Vietnam Chronology*, a quarterly sponsored, at that time, by the Indochina Archive at University of California-Berkeley, hardly an unknown institution of learning. Furthermore, such a comment overlooks information presented within *The Real Story*: Pike was one of the key historical consultants to WGBH, an important advisor who later repudiated the PBS series.

Some of the young reviewers ridiculed our "fixation" on the Yen Bay Rebellion of 1930 (point 2, above), neglecting to take into consideration that the uprising had been one of the sore points for Vietnamese viewers, a distortion of history so despicable that they took to the streets in Paris, London, Washington, New Orleans, Houston, and Los Angeles. In response to these protests, member stations in Houston and Orange County invited members of the Vietnamese community to provide corrective commentary. In labeling this concern as "esoteric" and "irrelevant," reviewers were only revealing that they shared the ethnocentric perspective of the American press during the war. They knew little about the roots of the struggle and cared not at all about distinctions vital to the Vietnamese.

None of the reviews I have surveyed reference books on Vietnam, although a few mention other TV documentaries. Stanley Karnow's *Vietnam: A History* (1983) is often mentioned; however, because the book was advertised at the end of each episode of the PBS series, it would have been hard to miss. Even in relation to Karnow there are problems: often, he is referred to as the author of the script for the series; even more regularly, the series is referred to as "the Karnow series." Such would be the common sense conclusion of a casual viewer who would see the Karnow book advertised thirteen times. However, any research at all into the production—to include reading those boring program credits—would have revealed that the "Karnow series" was actually written by a diverse group of people—some English, some French, some American. Any reader of Karnow's book would recognize immediately that there are great differences between the texts, with Karnow's book constantly drawing a more complex historical portrait than its TV counterpart. (Karnow is more willing to be critical of the Communists; in contrast, the PBS series never criticizes communist statements. In fact, the series frequently introduces communist propaganda films without warning viewers.) Not a single review by the Television Writers Association critics makes an attempt to refer to books or to give even a furtive glimpse at the hefty companion volume by Karnow.

Colonel Harry Summers (d.1999) was the author of *On Strategy*, a volume which is not only considered revolutionary in its perspective on America's way of fighting the war, but has been a bestseller. In *The Real Story*, Summers makes a number of very pointed remarks about the self-serving motives behind the PBS production. Not a single television writer seems to have noticed Summers; was it embarrassing to discuss the notion that producers may have had a personal stake in how the PBS series shaped the historical record? According to Summers:

> As time passes, as now it is no longer fashionable to say that you ran off to Canada, that you deliberately starved yourself, that you deliberately missed the draft. Christopher Buckley's piece in *Esquire* is testimony to that and James Fallows' piece in *The Washington Post* is testimony to that. These people are having second thoughts…they are going to be held up to some future criticism…the people who deliberately avoided the war have a need to freeze history in place at the 1969-70 period when they were in the moral ascendancy.

Harry who? Christopher who? James who? Surely the reference to *Esquire* could have been pursued. Even PBS included the Fallows article in a classroom text, *Vietnam: Anthology and Guide to a Television History* (1983).

Robert Elegant's criticism of Vietnam-era reporting holds true for reviews of *The Real Story*: there was little preparation by reporters. Ironically, both the Steven Cohen volume mentioned above, and the sweatshirt purchased for members of the WGBH production staff, bear a G. B. Trudeau cartoon—evidently the mark of objectivity for young writers of the Television Writers Association and their peers at WGBH.

2. Use of journalistic sources.
All early reviews of *The Real Story* emerged from the Phoenix, Arizona "press tour" for Television Writers. Staff members from PBS announced the experiment in viewer-response programming, hoping to create some interest for a show with (potentially) low viewer attractiveness. The network discovered more interest than it wanted. For most of the writers, the only information about AIM was obtained from statements by Barry Chase (Vice President for News and Public Affairs Programming) and Ned Schnurman, a veteran producer brought in to augment the AIM show with additional interviews and a panel discussion. A host of stories reveal that Schnurman described AIM as "an ultra right-wing group" which he, in his days with the National News Council, had gone "head to head" with on many occasions. The Chairman of Accuracy in Media, Reed Irvine, was described in unflattering terms as was the program—the show was criticized for low production values and a preponderance of "talking heads." Stories wired in from Phoenix and written later reflected oral and written source material acquired on the spot without *any* attempts by the young Television Writers to verify details.

The most flagrant—indeed, fake—story to emerge from Phoenix—to become part of later stories in *The New York Times*, *The Washington Post*, and *The Christian Science Monitor*—was generated by Richard Ellison, Senior Producer for the PBS series. Someone from WGBH started the ball rolling at Phoenix; through stories by Fox Butterfield, the Boston-based *Times* correspondent, and Arthur Unger, the Washington-based *Monitor* reviewer, Ellison whined about PBS "caving in to political pressure" from the Ronald Reagan (1981-1989) White House.

The Ellison story was repeated along the chain of television writers, beginning as a hazy speculation which could not be proved, but reaching the readers of *The Cleveland Plain Dealer* and other municipal dailies as Holy Writ. According to this apocryphal narrative, Bruce Christensen (President of PBS), Barry Chase, and others had succumbed to political pressure; they were airing the AIM film so that penny-pinching Republicans would put money back into the public television budget. Like all cynical interpretations of human motives, this unprovable thesis quickly found true believers. Word processors across the country clicked and clacked eloquent with defenses of public television, the first amendment, and calls for a "heat shield" to protect public broadcasting from partisan political influence.

Not a single television writer believed the executives at PBS who fruitlessly defended the integrity of their decision. Not a single television reviewer noted that Henry Becton, President of WGBH, made a public statement disassociating the station from producer Ellison's unfounded public speculations. Finally, no writer of any stripe conducted any investigative search for the facts; an important one was that Chase had decided to air the program—at least tentatively—back in the Spring of 1984 when he learned that AIM had received a $30K grant from the National Endowment for the Humanities. Even before the AIM conference, in other words, Chase saw NEH providing him with a chance to experiment at no charge with a viewer-response package. (The PBS series, *POV* [Point of View], was the offspring of this experiment.)

In February, 1985, Arthur Unger quietly withdrew his support for the "political pressure" theory in an interview with Chase and Ted Koppel on the need for viewer-response options. Not a single reviewer in my collection ever backtracked to the Ellison story; along the way, no one ever considered in public that Ellison might be creating a smokescreen to obscure his documentary series from public scrutiny. The general failure here seems to have been willful and malicious dependence on a few sources because the interpretation created a colorful conspiratorial interpretation.

My second program, *Television's Vietnam: The Impact of Media*, shows how similar quick-and-dirty use of unconfirmed information during the Tet offensive of 1968 led to misreporting in Saigon and distortions about the battle of Khe Sanh. The result of these errors was a tragic misperception by America of the meaning of Tet.

3. Reporting the dramatic: man bites dog.
One of the failures of our press in Vietnam was its willingness to be drawn to pyrotechnics and commotion rather than to explore issues in depth. *Television's Vietnam: The Impact of Media* scores television especially for this error, following analysis by Peter Braestrup who succinctly identified the problem: "TV loves fires." Controversy over *The Real Story* proved that print media can be just as guilty of stressing drama over information.

A high percentage of stories took ghoulish delight in reporting that PBS-national was giving one of its flagship stations a proverbial "slap in the face." Such stories played up the bad blood generated by the decision, down to details about the unwillingness of members of "the PBS family" to greet each other in the hallways of the Phoenix Hilton where the PBS press tour was held. The implicit assumption of these stories seemed to be that PBS and WGBH belonged to the same public broadcasting wagon train and that, when attacked by marauding bands of "conservative" Indians, they should circle their wagons for mutual protection. Instead of predictable trouble from the right wing, WGBH was clasped by the jaws of a fellow journalistic institution in a veritable man-bites-dog story.

Barry Chase and his staff were described as cowardly, lacking in foresight—because they were playing into the hands of the enemy—or simply needing discipline as naughty children. (One reviewer even suggested that "PBS needs a slap on the rear.") As a result of this fixation on the breakdown of harmony between WGBH and PBS, all forgot that there might be distinguishable responsibilities between local producers and national programmers. Very few stopped to remember that Ellison was an interested party in the conflict; none noted the comments by Henry Becton, President of WGBH, that the PBS efforts were genuine, healthy experiments toward a new format needed by broadcast television.

Why? The Ellison vs. Chase feud played too well as melodrama; it stood as a sign of the times as conservative repression ("Reaganism") seemed to close in on such bastions of objectivity as PBS, CBS, and *Time Magazine* in the form of the Westmoreland trial and the successful libel suit of Arial Sharon. It must have been tempting to be more readable than right.

It should be noted that Neil Hickey of *TV Guide*, John Corry of *The New York Times*, and a reviewer at *Variety* agreed that the real issue was the one articulated by Barry Chase: viewer-response programming. Hickey, Corry, and *Variety*—together with Martha Bayles of *The Wall Street Journal*—applauded the experiment as did many editorial writers across the country from my local paper in Stillwater, Oklahoma, to *The Boston Herald*. (However, in many cases, while editorial writers were celebrating the experiment, young television writers for the same newspapers earlier in the same week took the "political pressure" angle. Recent polls by the *Los Angeles Times* and the Roper Organization help to explain how America's dailies can be so schizoid).

4. Journalistic "objectivity" versus "ideological criticism."

A basic assumption about the journalistic community permeates almost all of the colorful reviews of *The Real Story*. On the one hand, we have the journalists. Journalists do not have a point of view; either as a result of unusual forbearance or due to total ignorance on a major issue affecting our society, they collect and report information without bias. That information is news, something which the public can then use to form opinions.

Some objective programs on television are, according to this line of reasoning, *60 Minutes*, and, of course, *Vietnam: A Television History*. Such investigative essays are never perfect, but they are the result of painstaking research and tireless attempts to be fair. In this scheme, producers like the team which set about to research and write the PBS series approach their subject with an open mind; they arrive at their point of view only after they have conducted their research and collected their footage. On the other hand, "self-appointed media critics" like Reed Irvine—in fact, anyone critical of the journalistic community—are probably "ideologically motivated."

The ideologically motivated work from preconceptions. For example, during the war years, an ideologue might study the history of Communism before being assigned to Vietnam. Such a reporter might visit a city like Hue and in the late spring of 1968 and—after seeing over 3000 bodies dug up from mass graves—come to some conclusions about Communist immorality. When the Communists took over in Cambodia in 1975, he might be shocked by the millions of murders and lose his objectivity. He might be in similar danger of losing detachment after listening to boat people describe their perilous flight. It is no easy task to be an objective journalist!

Only members of the journalist community are capable of making historical documentaries, a fascinating assertion challenged by historian Richard Raack in the *Newsletter of the Organization of American Historians*. Others introduce bias, interpretation, or perspectives which will force facts into reports lacking objectivity. This is a surprising argument to hear from journalists, for graduates of journalism schools are usually required to attend classes on the history of broadcasting. In such classes, students come into contact with writers like John Grierson (1898-1972), Joris Ivens (1898-1989), Leo Hurwitz (1909-976)—the kind of writers on documentary one finds in such anthologies as the ancient Lewis Jacobs collection entitled *The Documentary Tradition* (available since 1971). In such books, students learn that the genre from the beginning has been one of interpretation and exhortation, that the issue is never between objectivity and subjectivity—the categories thrown out in the discussion of the AIM vs. PBS controversy—but between honest persuasion and lying. (This obvious kind of discussion never surfaced in any of the reviews of *The Real Story*; fortunately, the issue has been explored in a scholarly essay by Baylor University Professor Martin Medhurst.)

Accompanying the rejection of "ideological criticism" by outsiders to the journalistic fraternity is a tendency of writers to commit what literary scholars call "the intentional fallacy." The fact that *The Real Story* was based on a public conference, that the script was written by me in conjunction with others who have studied the PBS series counted for nothing; almost all writers targeted *The Real Story* as an AIM program, moved from there to a history of AIM, and next to a personal attack on Reed Irvine. This line of reasoning permitted reviewers to ignore or dismiss the content of the show; to scratch their heads about why AIM was so exorcised about whether Ho was depicted as a Communist or a Nationalist, and then to dismiss the affair as a case of bad judgment by PBS bureaucrats fretting over budget cuts.

At issue in this debate between the press and "ideologically motivated" press bashers is the definition of ideology. To most members of the press, "ideology" means a set of consciously held, dogmatic beliefs—either very conservative or very radical—which no person of sophistication would consider adopting. From the Television Writers Association point of view, Reed Irvine is a classic ideologue. His statement during the roundtable discussion following *The Real Story* epitomizes his dogmatic perspective:

> I have a point a view. I am in favor of freedom and democracy. I want to see it preserved in Vietnam, Cambodia, and Laos. I want to see it preserved anywhere in the world where it exists.... Communism brutalizes people.

Such forthright statements of values led one member of the Television Writers Association—Nick Coleman—to label Irvine as "a mad dog of the right." The fact that the program included a number of converging perspectives was ignored in the delight which reviewers took in attacking Irvine, who was campishly described by *The Washington Post*'s critic as "a scowly TV cousin of David Letterman's famous frump, Larry (Bud) Melman" (Shales 18).

On the other hand, television writers were unwilling to see that it is possible to hold an ideology in the sense of unexamined values which guide perceptions and determine story line. In his monograph *TV News and The Dominant Culture* (1986), John Corry discusses with insight this blindness to a less obvious—but no less restricting—form of ideology:

> In theory, journalism's role is to define issues, without taking sides. To do this, it presumably stands in the center, applying neutral, non-judgmental standards to both right and left. The question, however, when journalism supposedly stands in, or hovers above, the center is, the center of what? What defines the center? When reporters and commentators identify the right and right-wing thinking, but decline to recognize a left wing and left-wing thinking, they are saying the left does not exist. At the same time, it is the

left that makes up the moral and intellectual framework of the dominant culture. The right, morally discredited, barely contributes. The center does not contribute ideas; it only absorbs them. The left becomes the only game in town this way, shaping the culture that tells journalism what news is and how it must be regarded. (22)

As Corry, himself a television critic for *The New York Times*, concludes, "Journalism fails when it allows the dominant culture to determine what it sees" (Corry, *TV News* 47).

Conclusion

Because the Television Writers knew close to nothing about Vietnam and were unwilling to conduct research of their own, they trusted a combination of interested parties and their own "gut" feelings. What resulted for most readers of metropolitan dailies were articles heavy with sarcasm about Reed Irvine, high on praise for the WGBH series for its many awards—conveyed by journalists to journalists for a series on history—and fraught with fears about Reagan repression. The critics felt responsible for drawing their own wagons around the exposed Boston affiliate; meanwhile, cowardly PBS had gone over to the enemy. The reading public in at least one hundred cities was poorly served. What frightens me in retrospect is how much the errors in reporting the AIM rebuttal experiment resembled press errors made during our Vietnam tragedy. As Karl Marx observed so presciently, history may repeat itself, but it comes back the second time as farce. Instead of Walter Cronkite during Tet, 1968, giving sententious instant analysis of our failed efforts, we had Tom Jicha, President of the Television Writers Association of America, flipping the visor of his baseball hat as he pondered the legacy of Vietnam in the same article he praised ESPN (the sports network) for re-running Miami Dolphin highlight films.

Discussion of Literature

As a critic, I tried to join the distinguished organization, the Television Writers Association of America, and to sign on for the Phoenix, Arizona "press tour" for Television Writers. When it was learned that I was associated with Accuracy in Media, my membership was cancelled and I was barred from the coveted tour—even from the PBS element of it! What interests me is the implicit comment about the other critics which such a decision reflected; was it assumed that they would succumb to the free shrimp and champagne?

The Cohen anthology, *Vietnam: Anthology and Guide to a Television History*, contains a number of useful booklists, but has been described by Douglas Pike as passing on "ignorance in the form of an undigested mass" (*Indochina Quarterly* 1[1983]: 25). My own guide to Vietnam studies is worthy of consideration (see Chapter 17). Fortunately, Douglas Pike never took the time to comment on my efforts!

The Roper Organization and the *Los Angeles Times* addressed the issue of America's dailies in polls during 1985-6. The gap of perspective between owners and editors *vs* reporters is discussed in Lichter and Rothman. The values-cluster which distinguishes the unselfconscious ideology of the press from other sectors in our society is also examined in Lichter. The Lichters and Rothman are engaged in a comprehensive sociology of knowledge, examining various American elites. Their work has not gone unchallenged.

Works Cited

Banerian, James, ed. *Losers are Pirates: A Close Look at the PBS Series Vietnam: A Television History*. San Diego, CA: Vietnamese Community Action Committee, 1984.

Bayles, Martha. "Taking AIM at Biased Documentaries." *Wall Street Journal* 24 February 1986: 10.

Cohen, Stephen, ed,. *Vietnam: Anthology and Guide to a Television History*. New York: Knopf, 1983.

Coleman, Nick. "PBS Working Hard to Avoid Offending Anybody." [Source lost]

Corry, John. *TV News and the Dominant Culture*. Washington, D.C.: The Media Institute, 1986.

—. "Television's Vietnam: The Real Story, on PBS." *New York Times* 27 June 1985: C22.

Hickey, Neil. "TV *Must* Create Rebuttal Time: Commentary." *TV Guide* 27-8 June 1985: 32-5.

Jacobs, Lewis, ed. *The Documentary Tradition*. New York: Hopkinson and Blake, 1971.

Karnow, Stanley. *Vietnam: A History*. New York: Viking, 1983.
Lichter, Robert S., Stanley Rothman, and Linda S. Lichter. *The Media Elite*. Bethesda, MD: Adler and Adler, 1986.
Medhurst, Martin. "Objectivity and Accuracy: PBS vs AIM." Unpublished. Presented to the national meeting of the Western Speech Communications Association, 1985.
Shales, Tom. "AIM's Vietnam Barrage." *Washington Post* 26 June 1985: F18.
Summers, Harry. *On Strategy: A Critical Analysis of the Vietnam War*. New York: Dell, 1984.
"Television Reviews." *Variety* 26 June 1985: 23, 82.

20
Behind the Westmoreland Trial of 1984: What Was so Wrong with the CBS Program, *The Uncounted Enemy* (1982)

Introduction

On Friday, January 21, 1982, major daily newspapers in Boston, New York, Washington, and Chicago carried a full-page advertisement for a Saturday night documentary on CBS. An artist's drawing gave the perspective of looking down from the ceiling at a discussion chaired by a two-star general. Seven members of his staff surrounded the table over which was written in capital letters, "CONSPIRACY." Viewers were promised an exposé which would reveal "a deliberate plot to fool the American public, the Congress, and perhaps even the White House into believing we were winning a war that we in fact were losing" (Benjamin, *Fair Play*, III.1). The advertisement certainly did not reach the masses; the program drew a very small audience, finishing dead last in the ratings for that week. However, *The Uncounted Enemy: A Vietnam Deception* (1982) was watched by an influential elite minority audience. Some, to include General William Westmoreland, the "heavy" of the show, were incensed by its distortions; unfortunately, many more were convinced by the program that CBS had caught people in high places betraying the public trust.[1]

Shortly after the broadcast, General Westmoreland began to receive calls from friends and family, asking him if the thesis of the program—that he suppressed information about Vietcong offensive capabilities—was really true. Even his daughter called! Within days, veterans groups were denouncing their former commander.

CBS Seeks (and Finds) Conspiracy

Quite understandably, the supreme commander in Vietnam (1964-68) decided to begin a slow, uphill battle to regain his honor. The counter-offensive would not come to a halt until February 18, 1985, when Westmoreland and his lawyer Dan Burt received a public statement from CBS attesting that, whatever the contentions of its program, the network did not believe "General Westmoreland was unpatriotic and disloyal in performing his duties as he saw them" (Brewin 345).[2]

Behind the Westmoreland Trial

In our time, memory of the "Westmoreland Trial" has waned. Most people I ask about the struggle remember that the general withdrew and therefore assume that Westmoreland was guilty of the "conspiracy" exposed by *The Uncounted Enemy*. Few remember that CBS withdrew the charge of conspiracy some eight months *prior to* the out-of-court settlement of Westmoreland's $120 million suit. Almost no one has seen the documentary which precipitated the struggle. I intend to summarize as fairly and fully as space permits the charges presented by *The Uncounted Enemy* and then to critique the program under some basic cinematic rubrics. The program's methodology was flawed by single-source dependence upon its paid consultant, Sam Adams, a man with an axe to grind. Interviews for the program were edited in such a way as to distort statements by those interviewed or to misrepresent events—in one case, giving the impression that people were on one side of the globe when they were over 18,000 miles away. Editing is perhaps the most powerful tool available to the documentary filmmaker as he interprets history; the device was grossly misused in *Uncounted Enemy* to make General Westmoreland appear guilty as charged. Mike Wallace's narration was more dramatic than journalistic and the media star was guilty of betraying the trust placed in him by his fans. Finally, there were significant factual flaws in the CBS presentation, all of them supporting a predetermined thesis. Little wonder that General Westmoreland took umbrage and began to explore ways to tell Americans—including Vietnam veterans and his

Mike Wallace Early in His Career

family—what was so wrong with *The Uncounted Enemy: A Vietnam Deception.*

The Uncounted Enemy: A Brief Synopsis

In his introduction, host Mike Wallace explains that the Tet offensive of January-February 1968 was a surprise because neither the President nor the American public was aware of the actual size of enemy forces before that climactic nation-wide attack:

> Tonight we're going to present evidence of what we have come to believe was a conscious effort—indeed a conspiracy at the highest levels of American intelligence—to suppress and alter critical intelligence on the enemy leading up to the Tet offensive.[3]

The remainder of the five-act documentary attempts to trace the manner by which the "conspiracy" was carried out by Westmoreland and his staff at the Military Assistance Command Vietnam MACV.

Act one portrays consultant Sam Adams as an unheeded CIA analyst whose prescient readings of enemy strength figures in 1966-67 were ignored. File footage highlights the kind of domestic political turmoil in the United States over an unpopular war, creating a context which made Adams' news politically explosive. According to *Uncounted Enemy*, President Lyndon Johnson wanted to see "light at the end of the tunnel"; he did not want to be confronted with high enemy strength. Westmoreland is then presented in his role as Johnson's salesman of good news about progress in Vietnam during the spring and fall of 1967.

In his 1982 interview with Mike Wallace, Westmoreland shows familiarity with the Sam Adams' figures, but the way he dismisses them on camera is less than convincing. Furthermore, apparently disillusioned members of Westmoreland's intelligence staff are given sound bites to question the way in which intelligence data was processed at (MACV) during the Westmoreland years, 1964-68. Responding to a hypothetical question, General Joseph McChristian states that, as a West Point graduate, he could not participate in the

Behind the Westmoreland Trial 459

juggling of intelligence figures during wartime; it would be a violation of the Military Academy's code of honor. (The editing makes it appear that McChristian is responding to the points previously made about MACV.) Wallace implies at the close of act one that McChristian was rotated back to the U.S. because of his opposition to Westmoreland's immoral efforts to suppress new intelligence information.

Act two traces the details of suppression. George MacArthur claims that his superiors in the MACV intelligence chain arbitrarily cut his estimates of enemy strength. George Allen, a crony of Sam Adams, states that the CIA—indeed, the entire intelligence community—was making a grave error by ignoring Sam. Next, CBS' paid consultant, Adams, describes a meeting of the CIA's Board of National Estimates at which his good friend from MACV, Colonel Gains Hawkins, argued for the Westmoreland numbers (called "the command figures") even though Hawkins' work as an analyst had led him to much higher estimates. Wallace leads Hawkins through a series of reflections on the tragic consequences. Host Wallace then puts words in Hawkins' mouth when he says "American troops are going to have to face a much larger enemy. A lot of them are going to get slaughtered" [in the Tet offensive]. Wallace's tone clearly emphasizes that the "command figures" were politically determined while the numbers arrived at by Adams, Hawkins, and McChristian were scientifically accurate.[4] McChristian ends the second act with another forceful statement of a West Point graduate's devotion to "Duty, Honor, Country" when confronted with a choice between political expediency and truth. Viewers are led to the conclusion that General Westmoreland and his cronies were acting unethically by West Point standards. Needless to say, this kind of rhetoric hurt Westmoreland, who was not only a proud graduate of the U.S. Military Academy, but had been Superintendent of the school prior to assuming responsibilities at MACV.

Act three focuses on the debate over "the Order of Battle," MACV's comprehensive estimate of the enemy's overall *military* offensive capability.[5] In September of 1967, General Westmoreland endorsed a move to shift the Vietcong's Self-Defense Forces—people in villages who could be used to carry ammunition, dig pungy pits, etc.—from the body of the Order of Battle. Instead, these irregular forces would be carried in the narrative portions of a variety of intelligence reports turned out by MACV and the Washington intelligence community. Looking very uncomfortable on camera as he defends this decision, Westmoreland argues that the Self Defense forces had no offensive capability, that "this is a non-issue." No sound bites are edited in to support the general's views, even though CBS had on the editor's shelf three hours of supporting material by Walt W. Rostow, President Johnson's National Security Advisor.

On the contrary, the issue would become, according to Wallace, "one of the most bitterly fought battles in the history of American intelligence." George Allen (CIA) and George Hamscher (Army Intelligence) are brought back to critique Westmoreland's decision. File footage from 1967 resurrects statements about good news just as the enemy is shown to be planning the nation-wide attacks which would be known as the 1968 Tet offensive. (There was another, more muted—but unsuccessful—Tet offensive some four years later.) *Uncounted Enemy* does an effective job of evoking a yawning gap between irreducible facts and the command's "cooked books."

Act four shifts the story from the Vietcong strength figures to estimates of infiltration by North Vietnamese Main Force units. The Westmoreland of 1967, appearing on NBC's *Meet the Press*, disagrees on the subject of infiltration with the Westmoreland of 1981 (6000 in 1967 vs 20,000 in 1981). Colonel Everette Parkins, we are told, was fired for defending accurate infiltration figures. On this point, Westmoreland is allowed his single ally. General Daniel Graham (d. 1995)—whose integrity will be impugned later in the program—is allowed twenty-two seconds to defend the command position. An apparently flustered and stammering Westmoreland contributes little to support Graham against a montage of criticisms by MACV and CIA lower echelon officers frustrated about the unwillingness of top commanders to accept their interpretations of data.[6] Wallace concludes act four with an apparently unavoidable conclusion:

> And so, the President of the United States, the American Army in Vietnam, and the American public back home were destined to be caught totally unprepared for the size of the attack that was coming the following month.

As the program cuts to commercials, the central thesis about the origins and results of "conspiracy" have been made. What remains is to demonstrate the tragic consequences of the dishonorable conspiracy.

Act five and the **epilogue** of *The Uncounted Enemy* spell out the CBS lessons about the *real* reason for our defeat in Vietnam. The Tet attacks surprised everyone in Vietnam and set the Joint Chiefs of Staff into a tailspin; they begged for immediate reinforcements and for President Johnson to mobilize the Reserves. During a special report evaluating the impact of the Tet offensive, Walter Cronkite—"articulating the sentiment growing in the country that Tet was a devastating setback"—called for a turnabout in policy and for immediate negotiations to make the best of a "stalemate."

Westmoreland, in his interview with Wallace, cites incorrect figures which are then examined graphically on screen to accent the obvious fallacy of the command policy. Wallace asks rhetorically: "If so many Viet Cong had been taken out of action, whom were we fighting?" As in earlier acts, lower echelon analysts then discredit Westmoreland's claims that he had made the right decision. Sam Adams makes his last appearance to assert that, after Tet, his estimates finally reached the White House where they were used to brief a gathering of Johnson's council of "wise men," Dean Acheson, George Ball, Arthur Goldberg, Maxwell Taylor, and others.[7] Realizing the magnitude of his error, Lyndon Johnson steps down from the Presidency. Less fortunate Americans in uniform cannot drop out: twenty-seven thousand Americans die before the inevitable Communist victory in 1975.

The Uncounted Enemy: A Vietnam Deception concludes on an elegiac note about the lessons of Vietnam. Truthfulness and a greater sense of "duty, honor, and country" could have averted the Vietnam tragedy. Furthermore, an informed public could have checked our war machine from continuing in an obviously futile direction. In his efforts to please Lyndon Johnson, General William C. Westmoreland betrayed his command responsibilities to his men. With such a moral reaching a "small" audience of twenty million Americans, can anyone wonder why Westmoreland felt compelled to challenge the CBS documentary?

The Initial Response—Laurels, Then Darts

Many intelligent viewers of *The Uncounted Enemy: A Vietnam Deception* did not see any problems with it. Immediately after the program, Burton Benjamin—who would later play a pivotal role at CBS in exposing the flaws of the program—turned off his television set with pride:

> I felt that I had just watched one of the most remarkable documentaries that CBS News had ever produced. That this kind of maneuvering could have happened during a war so futile and pointless—a war I had seen first-hand during two trips to Vietnam—sickened me.... I told my wife that *The Uncounted Enemy* might well rank with two of the more celebrated *CBS Reports* of the past, *Hunger in America* and *The Selling of the Pentagon*. (*Fair Play* 36)

The senior CBS producer was not alone in his high opinion for the program. In an unusual editorial, the *New York Times* lauded the TV special, uncritically accepting its conspiratorial thesis: "Those 'captured documents' of which he boasted were in truth packed with accurate information—but the summaries he received were doctored, to keep the press from 'drawing an erroneous and gloomy conclusion,' in [sic] General Westmoreland's words" (Quoted in Benjamin, *Fair Play* 14). In a review for *The Wall Street Journal*, Hodding Carter—who, like Burton Benjamin, would later make an 180° *volte-face*—recoiled from the program's revelations; like the *New York Times*, Carter hoped aloud that similar machinations were not taking place in relation to Central America. Even William F. Buckley joined the short-lived bandwagon for *The Uncounted Enemy* in a syndicated column. Buckley described *Uncounted Enemy* as a "truly extraordinary documentary" which "absolutely" proved that Westmoreland had lied about enemy strength. Lesser luminaries in the press and the Washington political scene followed suit. Westmoreland was thus placed in a situation where he not only had to answer the errant documentary, but to counteract hastily published judgments of network and syndicated commentators as well.

The following Tuesday, Westmoreland, along with others in the intelligence chain who had been attacked by the program, called a press conference at Washington's Army-Navy Club. For two hours, the press was treated to general statements about errors of concept and fact in the program. Ambassador Ellsworth Bunker defended the intelligence work of his "country team." Colonel Charles Morris, the officer to whom Colonel Gains Hawkins reported, denied that Hawkins had voiced reservations during Order of Battle debates of 1967. Westmoreland's Chief of Intelligence during the numbers debates, General Phillip Davidson, dismissed the complaints of junior officers on the basis of their not having access to all relevant information on enemy strength and intentions. (Published Order of Battle estimates never included highly sensitive electronic intelligence data about troop movements.) General Daniel Graham took over the job of critiquing a series of clips from *The Uncounted Enemy*. Finally, George Allen's supervisor at the CIA, George Carver, revealed that it was *he and not Westmoreland* who had suggested dropping the Self-Defense forces from the numerical portion of the Order of Battle.[8] (Ironically, Colonel Gains Hawkins, an important CBS source, had been the first person to make the suggestion to Carver during a Saigon visit in July 1967.)

Westmoreland's press conference received wide coverage, setting in motion a debate which would have two components: Vietnam and the American Press. Westmoreland was the dramatic player for the Vietnam veterans and officials; CBS took on the role of the press. Cynical observers like Stanley Karnow would laugh off the confrontation: "They were both losers from the beginning. CBS did a lousy program, and Westmoreland never understood what the war was about" (Benjamin, *Fair Play* 202).[9] Most Americans took an interest in the standoff because they were still trying to sort out the meaning of the Vietnam experience and the relationship of the press to our country's perception of its first "television war" (see Chapters 17, 18 for details about the program).

A Survey of Errors and Distortions

Shortly after the Westmoreland press conference, Sally Bedell and Don Kowet of *TV Guide* began an in-depth examination of *Uncounted Enemy*. Initially, CBS granted full access to interview transcripts, outtakes, and personnel. Bedell and Kowett also talked with those who had been interviewed for the program—whether their interviews had been used or not. When their article appeared on May 22, 1982, it bore the dramatic title "Anatomy of a Smear" and it came down hard on both Producer George Crile and CBS.[10] Immediately after *TV Guide* hit the checkout counters across the country, CBS called upon its senior documentary producer Burton Benjamin to conduct an internal investigation to test the validity of claims made by Westmoreland, *TV Guide*, and a host of angry voices. The remainder of this chapter is an amalgam of these findings, plus insights culled from a research base I have accumulated over the last forty years as a Vietnam veteran, media scholar, and television producer.

1. Methodology

Producer George Crile's key error was his single-source dependence on Sam Adams (d.1988), the retired CIA analyst. Even friendly students of the Westmoreland controversy agree that Adams was obsessed by the numbers debates; he went to great lengths to force his reports to the top of the government chain. When they were rejected, Adams presumed stupidity on the part of his supervisors. His next step was to find ways around bureaucratic roadblocks, always hoping that someone further up the ladder would recognize the validity of his analysis. He would later have the same kind of quarrel at CIA over Cambodian figures (Brewin 12-5; Kowett 43).

Beginning in 1965, Adams was assigned to research enemy strength and morale in Vietnam. During the late summer of 1966, he began to receive pouches containing translations of captured enemy documents. After close examination of the materials, Adams began to question existing Order of Battle figures for Dinh Binh Province and, by extrapolation, for the rest of Vietnam.[11] In Gains Hawkins, an analyst counterpart at MACV headquarters in Vietnam, Adams found a kindred spirit. When his superior, George Carver, turned a deaf ear to Adams' speculations, Hawkins listened. By May 1968, Adams was so frustrated at the insensitivity of his superiors that he filed charges with the CIA Inspector General. According to George Carver, "Sam wanted to get Richard Helms fired and Westmoreland court-martialed" (Kowett, *A Matter of Honor* 42). Adams volunteered to appear in defense of Daniel Ellsberg and Anthony Russo during their "Pentagon Papers" trial because he said it made no sense to "hang a man for leaking faked numbers" (Brewin 15). Much to Gains Hawkins' dismay, Adams also volunteered the services of the recently retired Colonel who swore under oath, contrary to Adams' expectations, that there had been no "cap" on intelligence figures at MACV. During 1975, Adams carried his crusade to Congressman Otis Pike's House Select Committee on Intelligence where he received a sympathetic hearing, but *not* on the issue of a conspiracy. Finally, with the help of an editor at *Harper's* magazine—whose name was George Crile—Adams found a national forum for his conspiracy theories (Adams). When George Crile moved to CBS as a producer of documentaries, he hired Adams to help him shout the message from the top of "black rock."

Crile was guilty of not revealing Adams' obsessive background to supervisors at CBS News, specifically Associate Producer Joe Zigman, Executive Producer, Howard Stringer, and the Vice President for Documentaries, Roger Coloff. Most critics of the process believe that any or all of these supervisors would have scrutinized the project more closely had they known about the Pike Committee Report. Unlike the unbalanced assemblage of rushes screened for the news executives, the Pike Committee hearings allowed officials like George Carver to submit the Adams thesis to withering analysis. By 1975, there were some tough statistical arguments to contradict the 1967 numbers vital to Adams. For example, when the Tet attacks came at the end of January, 1968, they revealed an enemy force of 80,000 men, not the 600,000-man juggernaut predicted by Adams (Kowett 48; Davidson 481). By mid-March of 1968, the CIA knew that both its estimates *and* the MACV numbers had been too high, not deceptively low.

Based on his work as a researcher for previous Vietnam documentaries, Howard Stringer, the Executive Producer, should have been aware of LBJ's thinking at Tet—especially Johnson's awareness that an attack was coming and that it would be all-out, nation-wide (Benjamin *FP*, 83). The manner in which Crile spoon-fed Adams' findings to executives precluded independent thinking on their part; frequent interventions by Mike Wallace as Crile's protector within the CBS power structure further interfered with normal oversight by news executives (Kowett 118). Finally, no one seemed willing to heed the warnings of the program's Editor, Ira Klein. Klein went to Associate Producer Joe Zigman on two occasions. In despair with the system, Klein finally took his concerns to *TV Guide* (Kowett and Bedell).

As General Phillip Davidson would point out at the hastily-called Army-Navy Club press conference the day after the broadcast, there were fundamental problems with research methods for the show. First, Davidson reminded CBS that it was not unusual for commanders to interpret and modify data submitted to them by intelligence advisors, sometimes as a matter of judgment and sometimes—as in Vietnam—because the commanders had access to top secret information collected by the National Security Agency (NSA) from a variety of satellite and electronic eavesdropping devices:

> During the Vietnam War the dissemination of certain very sensitive intelligence was limited to a few civilian and military leaders in key positions. This was necessary to protect the source of the intelligence...Most of the junior officers who appeared on the program had no access to this sensitive intelligence. Their superiors, who did have access, often disapproved the work of the junior analysts because the senior official knew that the analysts' views were invalid, inaccurate, or incomplete. (*Benjamin Report* 34532)

Commanders in Vietnam had electronically-supplied "sensitive" information which gave them a special edge. (At the Westmoreland trial, the NSA would be referred to as "Source X.")

Second, Davidson pointed to a clear error of approach to the entire intelligence controversy. Davidson, Carver, Westmoreland, Rostow, Taylor, and a host of government and military officials had acknowledged that there was *indeed* a debate within the intelligence community about enemy strength (*Benjamin Report* 34533). The debate was so notorious, that President Johnson chided Richard Helms, Director of the CIA, about the inability of his experts to come to a consensus. In September 1967 the solution formulated by *George Carver* (not William Westmoreland) resolved the debate. In his program proposal to CBS News in November 1980, Crile used the word "conspiracy" no less that twenty-four times (Kowett 15).

The term mirrored Sam Adams' obsession, Crile's own drive to find malefactors in high places, and the adversarial style of CBS' most popular news series, *60 Minutes*. It did not mirror the truth.

2. Interviews

The Westmoreland interview was central to the production—both as Wallace and Crile prepared for it and after they had succeeded in "rattlesnaking" the retired general. First, Westmoreland was not adequately prepared for the interview. Crile gave him a list of five topics over the telephone, but really planned to focus exclusively on the numbers debate, the fourth item on the list (Benjamin, *Fair Play* 54). After the adversarial interview, Westmoreland complained that he had not had adequate time to consult sources from the 1967-8 period; shortly after returning to Charleston, South Carolina, he sent Crile a large packet of materials and a cover letter asking the Producer to use his considered responses. (Both *TV Guide* and Benjamin later came down hard on Crile for intentionally ignoring these follow-up materials.) When Crile saw the "dailies" from the Westmoreland interview, he yelled: "I've got you! I've got you!" (Kowett 83). These are not the words of a fair-minded journalist.

Some of Westmoreland's corrections are worth pointing out.

George Crile (d. 2006)

When questioned about the relationship between the number of enemy killed to the number of wounded during Tet, Westmoreland in the New York City interview gave the standard Army textbook response of 3:1. *Uncounted Enemy* then went into a long computational sequence with graphics to show the implausibility of these figures, given the low pre-Tet estimate of "enemy strength."[12] Once back in South Carolina, Westmoreland realized that the figure actually used in 1968 was a ratio of 1.5 wounded for every 1 killed, a ratio which generated significantly different extrapolations. *In addition*, Crile had on hand MACV's post-Tet report on enemy deaths and casualties, a document which corroborated Westmoreland's letter of correction. As an advocate for the Adams thesis, Crile chose to stick with the "gotcha" footage from the New York interview.

Westmoreland realized how badly he had performed on camera. In the hope that others might be more eloquent, he urged Crile to interview leading officers in MACV's intelligence chain. Many of these experts later appeared at the Westmoreland press conference to reprehend *Uncounted Enemy*: they included Ambassadors Ellsworth Bunker, and Robert Komer, Lieutenant General Daniel Graham, General Walter Kerwin, Jr., plus CIA officers George Carver, and William Colby. Graham had been interviewed by Crile but, from two hours of material, only twenty-two seconds survived. The three-hour interview with W.W. Rostow, LBJ's National Security Chief, never saw its way to the screen, although Rostow made it clear through letters to the *New York Times* and detailed memoranda for the record that he found *Uncounted Enemy* to be poorly researched. Rostow and others would later have their day on TV when the PBS series *Inside Story* broadcast its controversial exposé of *Uncounted Enemy* with Hodding Carter as host.[13] Still, CBS guidelines concerned about fairness require producers to allow accused figures like Westmoreland the opportunity to defend themselves. The guidelines urge that producers leave up to viewers the matter of conclusions about guilt or innocence. When questioned by internal investigator Benjamin about this lapse, Crile responded: "Westmoreland was not the show." Benjamin's retort was short and to the point: "He came out as the heavy, George" (Benjamin, *Fair Play* 115). (Note that both men used a vocabulary more suited to entertainment than journalism.)

The imbalance in presentations was computed by Benjamin for

the CBS internal report: those supporting the Adams conspiratorial thesis were given nineteen minutes and nineteen seconds (19'19") to present their side (supported by narrator Mike Wallace), while the command position was barely sketched by Westmoreland for five minutes and thirty-seven seconds (5' 37") and by Daniel Graham for an additional twenty-two seconds (22"). A master of urbane understatement, Benjamin suggested that there was more room for balance in a ninety-minute program: "The premise was obviously and historically controversial. There was an imbalance in presenting the two sides of the issue. For every McChristian, there [should have been] a Davidson; for every Hawkins, a Morris; for every Allen a Carver" (*Benjamin Report* 345ll).

In developing his interview pool, Crile consistently favored friendly sources. General Westmoreland was not really alerted in advance about the true topic of his interview. On the other hand, Sam Adams was allowed to sit in for many interviews and even conducted a few himself. This "insider" privilege violated CBS guidelines. But Westmoreland was not the only witness treated harshly. Graham and Rostow were both interviewed in the prosecutorial style that has made Mike Wallace famous. In addition, the *Benjamin Report* found that supporters of the Adams thesis were given extraordinary attention. Sam Adams was rehearsed for an entire day before his interview; the Adams farmhouse in Leesburg Virginia was practically redecorated by Crile in an attempt to develop the right *mise en scene* for his key accuser. A transcript of the sessions in Northern Virginia reveals that Adams was constantly stroked by Wallace with such expressions as "you're doing fine, Sam" and "That's a great response, Sam." Veteran documentary maker Benjamin labeled such treatment as "coddling" (*Benjamin Report* 57). Adams was never identified as a *paid* consultant for CBS nor was it made clear that he participated in a number of the interviews for the show. An ordinary viewer would assume that Sam Adams was simply one of many historical sources giving spontaneous responses to Wallace's questions.

Crile chose not to interview George Carver on camera. Instead, he focused on George Allen, a somewhat timid friend of Adams with a strange admiration for paid the consultant's obsession. In violation of CBS guidelines, Crile brought Allen to the editing room where Ira Klein reluctantly screened other interviews in the "pool."

(Crile was trying to encourage Allen to be more critical of the CIA by showing him that he was not alone.) Furthermore, Allen was interviewed repeatedly over the same questions until he proved himself to be "convincing" witness (*Benjamin Report* 57; Benjamin *Fair Play* 113-4). The choice to interview Allen rather than Carver suited Crile's goals for the program. Allen would support the Adams thesis. On the other hand, Carver—not Allen, who was left behind in Washington—had been in charge of the team which travelled to Saigon to negotiate enemy strength figures with MACV. Friend or foe of the program, Carver should have been in it. Benjamin was very unhappy that Crile had shown such solicitude to one side of the controversy (*Fair Play* 114).[14]

3. Editing

CBS News under Frank Salant formulated guidelines for documentaries after a controversy surrounding its *Selling of the Pentagon* (1971) revealed a number of distorting editing tricks. Documented by Marin Mayer in *About Television*, these clever uses of cutaways, reverses, and transitional devices produced statements by Department of Defense officials which supported the thesis of the program, but did not represent what had been said (250-76). In his zeal to prove the conspiracy thesis of his program, George Crile committed some of the same tricks and with the same result—he was caught.

In the first act of the program, Colonel Hawkins and General McChristian counterpoint Westmoreland's statements. The program gives the impression that all three men are talking about the same meeting and the same report. Actually, Hawkins and McChristian are talking about two different events, at which only one was present; in addition, Westmoreland seems to be talking about one meeting, but the transcripts reveal that he is talking about two geographically and temporally different sessions, one in Saigon, the other in Hawaii. The flow of images and patter is so deft that the naive viewer—even the expert viewer—would assume that all three men are discussing a single meeting where a politically unacceptable report was submitted and then summarily suppressed.

The dramatic close of act two seems to address the moral implications of this meeting. General McChristian explains that, although the Uniform Code of Military Justice does not cover such matters, his faithfulness to the motto of West Point assures that he would never suppress intelligence figures. What viewers could not have known was that McChristian was responding to a hypothetical question. Clever editing of the response into a cluster of statements about the numbers controversy set up a familiar contrast for *Uncounted Enemy*. General McChristian appears as a saint among sinners, a lone moral man at MACV during the latter months of 1967.

Events are manipulated to create an artificial flow at a second crucial moment in the narrative. Toward the end of act three, Colonel George Hamscher appears to be talking about a meeting he had with Westmoreland during which MACV's commander ordered his intelligence staff to cut figures arbitrarily. Actually, the editing cleverly combines two unconnected events. Hamscher is describing a National Intelligence Estimate meeting in Washington in August 1967 while Westmoreland is describing a Saigon meeting in September 1967. In exasperation, Burton Benjamin described this *legerdemain* as creating a scene in which "Westmoreland was put in the context of talking about a meeting he did not attend in a colloquy with an officer, Hamscher, he had never met" (*Fair Play* 81). (Hamscher was an intelligence officer at CINCPAC, the overall Pacific command located in Hawaii.)

Editing is employed a few times to make Westmoreland appear mendacious. During the prosecutorial interview for act one, Westmoreland made at least ten attempts to defend his decision to discount the Self-Defense forces and to put them into a prose segment of his intelligence reports. Rather than use these sound bites, Crile selected portions of the responses which made the General look confused and guilty. One of the points made by the documentary was that LBJ did not like to receive bad news from the field; the implication, of course, was that Westmoreland created a cap for the enemy strength figures to please his boss. Below (with portions *actually used* in italics) are Westmoreland's responses on the topic of "bad news":

Well, Mike, you know as well as I do that people in senior positions love good news, and they don't like bad news, and after all, it's well recognized that *supreme politicians or leaders in countries are inclined to shoot the messenger that brings bad* news. Certainly he wanted bad news like a hole in the head. He welcomed good news. But he was given both good and bad, but he was inclined to accentuate the positive.

Later, in an unused sound bite, Westmoreland stated directly that Johnson was given a full and accurate picture of the enemy situation in Vietnam: "that doesn't mean we didn't give him bad news. We did give him bad news." By omitting this last quote and by cleverly cutting into the block quote, above, *Uncounted Enemy* gave the impression that Westmoreland was sycophantically playing to the moods of his Commander-in-Chief.

Keeping in mind that Westmoreland had not briefed himself on the numbers issues prior to his New York interview in May 1981, it is not surprising that he had problems with details. Toward the end of act four, Wallace apparently catches the General making a revealing slip. The segment begins with narration about the infiltration of North Vietnamese regular troops immediately prior to the Tet offensive. Colonel Russell Cooley comes on camera to state that there were as many as 25,000 moving south, a number *confirmed* by Westmoreland during the New York interview. After a narrative transition, the program cuts to a *Meet the Press* clip from 1967 in which Westmoreland says that infiltration is at a rate of 5500-6000 per month. When confronted with the disparity of his statements, Westmoreland looks confused: "Sounds to me like a misstatement. I—I don't remember making it. But certainly I could not retain all these detailed figures in my mind."

Close examination of this juxtaposition of statements reveals some problems for *Uncounted Enemy*. In his full response to the *Meet the Press* panel, Westmoreland had actually said that "*I would estimate between 5500 and 6000 a month. But they do have the capability of stepping this up.*" While screening this response to CBS executives, Crile, according to Benjamin, "went into a frenzy" when he discovered that the qualifying remark had been left in for the editor as an editing "trim." Subsequent screenings for superiors and later renderings of the quote would leave the qualifier out. In his post-interview letter to George Crile, Westmoreland documented his original response to *Meet the Press* and asked CBS not use his New York estimate. When pressed on this matter, Crile told

Benjamin that he did not see the correction because it was not in Westmoreland's cover letter; in addition, Crile said "the fact that we ambushed him a little doesn't bother me" (*Fair Play* 145). Furthermore, neither *Uncounted Enemy*'s narrator nor its interview sources explain that infiltration figures were typically "soft" until three months *after* the fact—which meant that Westmoreland would not have received precise figures for November infiltration until sometime in January.

4. Narrator: Journalist or "Cosmetics?"

It has been rumored that one of the most feared secretarial announcements in the corporate world is "Mike Wallace is here for your interview." For *Uncounted Enemy*, Wallace was employed to grill the "hostile" witnesses: Westmoreland, Rostow, and Graham. To get him into the program with CBS' paid consultant and whistle blower, Wallace was also asked to interview Sam Adams. Beyond that, Wallace did almost no original research for the exposé and was, in his own words, "mostly cosmetics." Almost all who have written about *The Uncounted Enemy* have speculated on the Mike Wallace approach to this controversial program against the backdrop of the CBS tradition of E.R. Murrow, Fred Friendly, Charles Collingwood, Douglas Edwards, Eric Sevareid, Walter Cronkite, and Richard C. Hottelet. The "old school" at CBS News was concerned with investigative journalism and the understanding of twentieth-century history. As the lead on-camera talent for *60 Minutes* since 1968, Wal-

Myron "Mike" Wallace: Hired Gun?

lace had developed an effective style of interviewing which, combined with the showmanship of Producer Don Hewitt, had made the Sunday night show one of America's favorite pastimes. George Crile counted on the audience Mike Wallace would bring to *Uncounted Enemy* and relied on the Wallace interview style to "break" the government's "star," General William C. Westmoreland.

Mike Wallace was *not* a journalist in *The Uncounted Enemy*; he was a hired gun. Just as Crile was totally dependent upon Adams for the thesis of the program, so was Wallace dependent upon Crile for his understanding of the issues. When Wallace did ask questions about the program during the production phase, he was invited to view interviews carefully pruned of information which might weaken the program's thesis. Wallace did not read the Westmoreland letter and packet of supporting information; rather, he relied on Crile's assurance that "Westmoreland doesn't bring anything to our attention that is particularly relevant. Certainly nothing that causes concern and requires a new look at anything we have been asserting" (Benjamin, *Fair Play* 115). Since it was Wallace who initially invited Westmoreland to participate in the program, common courtesy would have dictated that the media star take some time out of his busy schedule to look at the Westmoreland materials himself.

Mike Wallace was willing to take credit for the program while it was riding high. During the post-production phase, he was often brought into discussions with supervising executives to back up Crile's editing decisions. When the program became a *cause célèbre*, Wallace used his personal contacts with Abe Rosenthal, executive editor of the *New York Times*, to assure that America's "newspaper of record" would retract a favorable review of Hodding Carter's *Inside Story* (PBS) investigation of the controversy (Kowett 263). In these actions, Wallace threw his weight around as an Influential, neglecting, in the process, to consider the substance of in-house and peer criticism. When Ira Klein, the film's editor, brought up problems discussed in this paper, Wallace darted out of the room; on the other hand, when rumors began to point to Klein as a "leak" in CBS News' effort to stonewall *TV Guide*'s investigation, Wallace visited Klein's editing bay for a few memorable finger-pointing minutes. Such behavior was more in the spirit of Watergate than the tradition of Murrow.

Despite his lack of understanding of the issues and despite his lack of research, Wallace added a considerable aura of authority to the *exposé*. Viewers would naturally associate his role in the program with the countless investigations he had conducted during his fourteen years with *60 Minutes*. Crile placed the host in a library setting with books, lamps, and subdued lighting. The speaker was supposedly reflecting upon the results of intensive research. As narrator, Wallace would provide bridges between interviews; such bridges were not merely neutral. Hostile witnesses could be introduced or followed by commentary and interpretation which could negate the significance of their statements. On the other hand, friendly witnesses could be presented as authorities. The omnipresence of Wallace as on-camera host, as interviewer of the most important friendly witness, Sam Adams, and as disembodied voice of history was an essential factor in the program—both in getting it on the air and, once broadcast, making it a convincing exposure of malfeasance in high places.

Soon after *The Benjamin Report* was submitted in July 1983, Van Gordon Sauter, President of CBS News, issued a public memorandum about flaws in *The Uncounted Enemy*. While standing by the substance of the broadcast, Sauter focused on the absence of significant involvement by Mike Wallace. Sauter asserted that "The greatest asset of CBS News is its credibility" and linked that credibility to the role of its journalists in major documentaries. Sauter explained that, "on projects of a complex and controversial nature, the full involvement and collaboration of the principal correspondent is vital. Future assignments will take this essential need into consideration" (Kowett 222). Sauter's memo was a public slap on the wrist for Mike Wallace. Just prior to being called to testify at the Westmoreland trial, the despondent correspondent collapsed in his apartment from an overdose of prescribed medication (Boyer 193). Evidently, public exposure was not so easy to receive as to give. In any case, *Uncounted Enemy* should have taught CBS that the Murrow tradition of serious content was more reliable than the sophomoric approach of *60 Minutes*. The public tuned in for the entertainment provided by the latter, but would, in the long term, respect only the former.

5. Script: Factual Errors

During act three, Mike Wallace confronts General Westmoreland at the New York interview with "his cable" of August 20, 1967. According to Wallace, the General's cable addressed the numbers controversy within the context of a good news campaign: "We have been projecting an image of success over recent months." Wallace comes back to the cable at another point. Two problems of fact detract from this segment. First, Westmoreland was *not* the author of the cable; it had been written by his deputy, General Creighton Abrams. Second, Wallace's reading from the cable was selective for the cable had actually said: *"We have projected an image of success over recent months and rightfully so."* Further readings from the entire cable would have contradicted in detail the thesis that MACV felt it was losing in Vietnam. Instead of an accurate portrayal of MACV's true estimate of the situation, viewers of *Uncounted Enemy* were left with an on-camera portrait of a sweating and lip-licking General caught with his hand in the intelligence cookie jar. This was some of Crile's best "gotcha" footage.

At the end of act one, Wallace gives the impression that General McChristian was creating too many waves at MACV. The act ends with Wallace explaining that "Shortly after Westmoreland suppressed his intelligence chief's report, General Joseph McChristian was transferred out of Vietnam. It was at this point, we believe, that MACV began to suppress, and then to alter, critical intelligence reports on the strength of the enemy." Viewers are left with the impression that the last principled opponent to manipulation was out of range.

In fact, Westmoreland had asked Washington to extend McChristian's tour as intelligence chief at MACV. In keeping with Pentagon personnel practices and the officer's preference, the general was rotated out of Vietnam and assigned to a command billet at Fort Hood, Texas. As McChristian later explained, "I didn't want to remain just an intelligence specialist" (Benjamin, *Fair Play* 83). Transcripts of McChristian's interviews reveal that he repeatedly denied being pressured to manipulate figures. Even the response used in *Uncounted Enemy* was edited to ignore McChristian's qualifications. Uncited was his remark that "nobody ever asked me that [to keep figures down]." Thus, the script was wrong on a major point, the reason for McChristian's transfer, while editing other statements to support this incorrect interpretation. Facts were not allowed to interfere with the program's thesis.

If the primary thesis of *Uncounted Enemy* was that General Westmoreland suppressed true estimates of enemy strength from the public and the President, the secondary theme of the program was that Tet was such a great surprise because of inadequate information. The basic question was, "Did Lyndon Johnson know that the Tet attacks were coming?" Act five of *Uncounted Enemy* makes a number of claims. Repeating the errors of newspaper coverage in 1968, the program asserts that Westmoreland requested 206,000 troops as reinforcements: "it seemed to be an admission that half-million American soldiers already in Vietnam couldn't cope with the enemy." The whole matter of the 206,000-man troop request—and the press misunderstanding of its purport—has been treated at length by Herbert Schandler in his *Unmaking of a President*, a book published some five years prior to the broadcast of *Uncounted Enemy*. (Westmoreland would submit portions of Schandler's book as evidence during the trial.) Schandler explains that the Joint Chiefs of Staff were attempting to replenish the strategic reserve under the guise of helping Westmoreland in a time of need; the full number was not needed in Vietnam. George Crile and Sam Adams should have known that by 1982 (Schandler 105-20). Instead of clarifying a confused historical incident, *Uncounted Enemy* exploited a 1968 misunderstanding to advance its argument.

Immediately after the troop request fallacy, *Uncounted Enemy* claims that the inner-circle of "wise men," who shared Tuesday lunches with President Johnson, finally saw the light about Vietnam because Sam Adams' figures finally got through to them. As a result, the wise men urged the President to reach a negotiated solution. The wise men told Johnson "to begin to reduce the American involvement in Vietnam and to find a way out" (Schandler 262). By way of juxtapositioning footage, it is implied that Lyndon Johnson withdrew from the Democratic primary because of his shame over Tet. This assertion seemed correct in 1968, but many reports published since—by Dean Rusk, Walt Rostow, and others—have shown the tenuousness of that connection. (Johnson was having severe heart problems.)

Act five concludes with a dramatic statement from Host Mike Wallace about America's defeat in Vietnam. Footage of the April 30, 1975 invasion of Saigon by North Vietnamese troops, to include the assault on the Presidential Palace, is shown over commentary. Filmmakers know that conflict between visual and aural elements will always work in favor of the visual; this principle is important because it shows the intent to undercut Westmoreland and to draw connections between his villainy and the suffering that would inevitably follow his suppression of truth. Here are Wallace's closing judgments:

> Two months after the President's speech, General William Westmoreland was transferred back to Washington and promoted to become Chief of the Army. To this day, General Westmoreland insists that the enemy was virtually destroyed at Tet. Be that as it may, the fighting in Vietnam went on for seven more years after the Tet offensive. Twenty-seven thousand more American soldiers were killed; over a hundred thousand more were wounded and on April 30th, 1975, the same enemy entered Saigon once again, only this time it was called Ho Chi Minh City.

Writing from the vantage point of 2009, a time when most of the traditional networks and cable outlets have made documentaries *conceding* that Tet was a military defeat for the Vietcong, it is easy to see the error of *Uncounted Enemy*'s concluding statement. Still, there were significant works of journalism and scholarship in book form in 1981-2 which, had Crile performed responsibly as a journalist, would have thrown *Uncounted Enemy*'s concluding assertion into question. The producer came down to a decision about whether to print the facts or the myth; since the myth supported his conspiratorial vision, he chose the latter course.

The myth/reality dilemma leads back to the basic question posed by history and the documentary: What did the President know and when did he know it? The answer is clear. Lyndon Johnson's White House was plugged into all sources of information, to include those primary sources feeding MACV, the CIA, and Sam Adams. Walt Rostow, the National Security Chief, had been an

Order of Battle specialist during World War II and took a special delight in being the White House "whiz kid" on battlefield statistics. Rostow's enthusiasm and prescience has a special pertinence to *Uncounted Enemy*. A lower echelon CIA functionary named Joe Hovey is interviewed in act four. The program gives Hovey credit for predicting the Tet offensive as early as fall, 1967. According to the program, this insight did not move up the intelligence chain—clear evidence that the "diffuse machinery of American intelligence was breaking down." The program neglects to mention that Crile had on his editor's shelf at CBS an unused, three-hour interview in which Walt Rostow explained that Hovey had conducted his special investigation *at Walt Rostow's request*! In other words, Rostow's office in the White House had a better grasp of the likely developments than either MACV or the CIA. Naturally, such a possibility had no place in Crile's *exposé*. When questioned about this problem, Crile dismissed Rostow: "He was intellectually dishonest in the academic community, which is why he wasn't able to get any positions with Northeast universities" (Benjamin, *Fair Play* 118).

The bottom line on Presidential foreknowledge of Tet attacks can be summarized by the adage that actions speak louder than words. As early as November, 1967, Lyndon Johnson briefed the Australian cabinet on forthcoming Tet attacks. Johnson, Rostow, the Joint Chiefs, Westmoreland all saw Tet—correctly—as a Battle of the Bulge effort, a sign of desperation. The ultimate difference between the Bulge and Tet, of course, was that the Tet offensive was successful in undermining America's will to fight. What frustrated American leaders so was that despite being a massive military defeat for the Viet Cong, Tet was an enormous psychological defeat for the American efforts in South Vietnam (see Chapter 18).[15]

Many have blamed Lyndon Johnson, retrospectively, for not giving the American people his Australian briefing and for not going on television after the attacks to bring the country together for the next phase of the struggle. If there was an error committed at Tet, it was an error in public relations and leadership—not military intelligence. Certainly the war went on and, sadly, more Americans were killed and wounded, but the onus of Vietnam lies more in a combination of factors: Lyndon Johnson did not perform as a President should in a time of crisis; on the other hand, the American press misreported the Tet offensive and gave the American public melodramatic impressions which truthful, official statements could not contradict. As a result, America began a long process of disengagement from Vietnam after Tet 1968.

Conclusions

The two major accusations of *The Uncounted Enemy: A Vietnam Deception* were invalid. Not only did the Johnson White House know about the Tet offensive in advance, staff members knew about the forthcoming attacks before any other government agency. Second, the Tet show of force did not discredit Westmoreland or Johnson as liars undone by history; rather, the media impact of those attacks — especially on television — created a conventional wisdom which could not be refuted. The basic fallacy of these two pillars should remind readers of a notion which surfaces early in *Uncounted Enemy*: General Westmoreland wanted to readjust the Order of Battle because "the people in Washington were not sophisticated enough to understand and evaluate this thing and neither was the media." By mounting the Sam Adams hobby horse, by projecting that issue forward in time as a central factor in our defeat in Vietnam, George Crile's ninety-minute documentary proved not the validity of its two major assertions, but the wisdom of General Westmoreland's prediction.

More serious for CBS as an institution was the public rancor inflamed by the Westmoreland controversy. From the Left, influential writers like Tom Shales castigated CBS for assigning Burton Benjamin to conduct an internal inquiry. Many other commentators shuddered over the prospect of a "chilling effect" on future crusading documentaries. More dangerous rumblings came from the Right. In January 1985, associates of Jesse Helms filed papers with the Securities and Exchange Commission, declaring their desire to join with others to become "Dan Rather's boss." Two months later, Ted Turner began to orchestrate his "junk bond" assault on CBS. Ivan Boesky's name echoed in the upper-story halls of "black rock" where CBS executives, to defend the corporation, amassed considerable debts.[16] Finally, in desperation, the company turned to Lawrence Tisch, a tough-minded business man who promised to

CBS Gave Itself a Black Eye

protect CBS News. The news division begged for Tisch; unexpectedly, once in power, he ordered massive firings and cut the news budget by $33 million.

While there were many other factors leading to the demise of CBS, certainly the Westmoreland episode did much to strip the network of its aura of fairness, balance, and trust. An arbiter of American life became just another interested party in the marketplace of ideas. In the down-sizing of a great institution, George Crile's program was, indeed, the most dangerous "uncounted enemy" of all.

Notes

1. *The CBS Benjamin Report* contains a transcript of the verbal portion of the program (34571-98). Video copies of *The Uncounted Enemy: A Vietnam Deception* are available from the Vanderbilt Television Archive, 110 21st Ave, S., Suite 704, Nashville, TN 37203 (615-322-2927) or at http://tvnews.vanderbilt.edu. (The ninety-minute program will cost approximately $100.) The archive also contains a number of TV news stories concerning "The Westmoreland Trial," to include the Hodding Carter-hosted PBS special, *Inside Story: Conspiracy Unproven*.

2. Here are highlights of the agreement reached on February 17, 1985: "General William C. Westmoreland and CBS today jointly announced the discontinuance of the *Westmoreland* suit against CBS, Mike Wallace, George Crile and Sam Adams.... The matters treated in the broadcast—and the broadcast itself—have been extensively examined over the past two-and-a-half years both in discovery and then through documents and witnesses represented by both sides in Federal Court. Historians will long consider this and other matters related to the war in Vietnam. Both parties trust their actions have broadened the public record on this matter.... CBS respects General Westmoreland's long and faithful service to his country

and never intended to assert, and does not believe, that General Westmoreland was unpatriotic or disloyal in performing his duties as he saw them. General Westmoreland respects the long and distinguished journalistic tradition of CBS and the rights of journalists to examine the complex issue of Vietnam and to present perspectives contrary to his own" (T9743-4; Brewin 345-6). The statement bears the signatures of W.C. Westmoreland, Samuel Adams, Mike Wallace, and George Crile III.

3. *The CBS Benjamin Report* was an internal study conducted by senior producer Burton Benjamin after Westmoreland and *TV Guide* attacked the integrity of *Uncounted Enemy*. Benjamin undertook the task reluctantly, knowing that his investigation would raise hackles at CBS; unlike Crile, however, Benjamin was a loyal and dedicated professional who put the honor of CBS above his own personal career. The seventy-page report never would have reached the public had not Westmoreland filed suit against CBS; Judge Pierre Lavelle forced the network to share the findings with the plaintiff. As published by the Media Institute (3017 M St, NW, Washington, D.C. 20007; (202) 298-7512, or at www.mediainst.org), *TBR* includes bibliographical material and a full transcript of the program. Media teachers and their students could profit from this text in conjunction with a study of the program and the trial.

4. Colonel Gains Hawkins did not fare well at the Westmoreland trial where he appeared on February 12, 1985. For a devastating commentary on his lack of integrity and credibility—indeed, his inability to coherently present any position and then stick to it—see Adler (96-132). Hawkins testified that he had lied under oath at the Ellsberg "Pentagon Papers" trial, thereby severely impugning his credibility as a witness. Although he was brought into the trial to support the argument that there had been orders at MACV to keep the intelligence figures down, he could not identify anyone who had given him such orders (Adler 116-7). *Uncounted Enemy*'s prime witness withered under the cross-examination of attorney David Dorsen.

5. I stress "military" here because *Uncounted Enemy* never clarifies the true basis of the debate between MACV and the CIA. The military intelligence analysts wanted to keep the Order of Battle focused on Vietcong and North Vietnamese armed, maneuver elements. In contrast, the civilian analysts at the CIA wanted to include the "irregular" forces in the Order of Battle. Westmoreland has stated his reasons for the MACV position in his autobiography, *A Soldier Reports*: "Having taught a course on the Geneva Convention and the laws of war at the Command and General Staff College in the late 1940s, I was conscious of the responsibilities they placed on field commanders. Shortly after assuming command in South Vietnam in 1964, I called in my advocate general and instructed him to

form a study group to recommend what to do. From that study and from frequent later consultations emerged the strict MACV regulations which established the rules of engagement for the US military forces" (348). In an interview with Cubbage, Westmoreland further explained his approach: "The armed Vietcong were fair game for my forces; unarmed civilians were not fair game. I considered the unarmed Vietcong—the enemy noncombatants—to be in categories outside the order of battle" (footnote 177). Obviously, Westmoreland's goal was to avoid the kind of tragedy which occurred at My Lai toward the end of Tet. Since the My Lai Massacre was an aberration rather than the norm, it should be observed that Westmoreland's humane objective was achieved. *Uncounted Enemy* never chose to consider these goals or their significance for the Order of Battle debate.

6. The question of infiltration was explored *ad nauseam* during the trial. When it came to estimating enemy "infiltration," no one in the intelligence chain could have hid figures. The American military knew that the high numbers of infiltrators during the fall of 1967 were located around the Khe Sanh combat base. Both they and the CIA kept these numbers in a separate category tuned to what appeared to be an upcoming set-piece battle. Rather than ignoring the Khe Sanh buildup, General Westmoreland and the White House have been accused, in retrospect, of spending too much time on the subject. LBJ went so far as to have a six-by-five-foot relief map constructed for the White House situation room so that he could literally touch the terrain features surrounding the Marine combat base. Davidson believes that Hanoi was hoping for another Dien Bien Phu, but that the use of B-52 strikes and the electronic guidance of artillery missions prevented the enemy from massing forces for a climactic attack (551-71). Pisor describes the electronic sensor system employed at Khe Sanh to track enemy movements for supporting fires (105-7). Khe Sanh was America's first electronic battlefield, a gruesome—but effective—videogame in which Westmoreland could unleash American firepower without hurting civilians, all of whom had been evacuated from the battlefield in preparation for the siege.

7. This assertion has real problems because the briefing to the "wise men" was given by George Carver, Adams' boss at the CIA and one of the principal authors of the numbers "conspiracy" exposed by *Uncounted Enemy*.

8. The Westmoreland press conference was videotaped. A transcript is in the microfiche collection from the trial, JX600.

9. Karnow is the author of *Vietnam: A History*, a text advertised PBS as the companion volume for the series entitled *Vietnam: A Television History* (1983). Some people think that Karnow never understood what the war was about. His history and the television series are critiqued by James Banerian.

10. Kowet's book deepens the study begun for *TV Guide*. It would not be unfair to say that Kowet was harassed by his press colleagues for his criticism of CBS. Even Renata Adler of *The New Yorker* was threatened with suits from CBS—both at the stage of writing up the trial for her magazine, but also later when A.A Knopf was considering the collected articles for book publication. Adler discusses this systematic harassment (229-43). Brewin also deplores the campaign of harassment of Kowet, Adler, and others (196-9). In these ploys, CBS was acting more like a corporate bully than an institution inspired by the First Amendment.

11. General Phillip Davidson says that military analysts who believed "they had a war to fight" were impatient with Adams. Adams' figures were based on the experience of one province and were extrapolated from a core of a total of twenty-five documents, hardly a large data base (interview).

12. At this point, the misuse of language by CBS should be apparent. By "enemy strength," MACV meant armed troops of the enemy's maneuver elements. As used in *Uncounted Enemy*, "enemy strength" means the total enemy capability—including irregulars. To explain these subtleties would have robbed *Uncounted Enemy* of its melodrama. See endnote #5 for further discussion.

13. The Hodding Carter critique of *Uncounted Enemy* was broadcast on April 21, 1983. At the conclusion, Carter sternly criticized *Uncounted Enemy* for lack of fairness: "CBS is entitled to its opinion, but we are entitled to a more balanced presentation. Even if you are sure of guilt, there is a vast difference between a fair trial and a lynching. It's a distinction that was badly blurred when CBS made *The Uncounted Enemy: A Vietnam Deception*" (Kowett 263). Like his print colleagues, Kowett and Adler, Ned Schnurmann, senior producer for *Inside Story* received brickbats from his peers for finding fault with CBS.

14. I have tried to tell the story of the intelligence controversy of 1966-67 through George Carver's eyes in "The Uncounted Expert: George Carver's Views on Intelligence 'Deception' Reported by CBS in *The Uncounted Enemy: A Vietnam Deception* (1982), Chapter 21 of this collection. The Carver-oriented study draws heavily from an impressive microfiche collection entitled *Westmoreland v. CBS*. The fiche collection is a two-drawer set containing 80,000 pages of text, including all depositions, all courtroom testimony, and all joint exhibits from the libel suit. It is a treasure trove for scholars.

15. The books by Oberdorfer, Braestrup, and Davidson all speak to this paradox. My television program entitled *Television's Vietnam: The Impact of Media*, in focusing on specific stories during the Tet offensive, demonstrates this thesis in detail.

16. The corporate histories by Boyer and Joyce support these assertions.

Works Cited

Adams, Sam. "Vietnam Cover-Up: Playing War With Numbers – A CIA Conspiracy Against Its Own Intelligence." *Harper's* May 1975: 41+.
Adler, Renata. *Reckless Disregard: Westmoreland v. CBS, et al; Sharon v. Time.* New York: Knopf, 1986.
Banerian, James, ed. *Losers are Pirates: A Close Look at the PBS Series Vietnam: A Television History.* San Diego, CA: Vietnamese Community Action Committee, 1984.
Benjamin, Burton. *Fair Play: CBS, General Westmoreland, and How a Television Documentary Went Wrong.* New York: Harper and Row, 1988.
—. *The CBS Benjamin Report.* Washington, D.C.: The Media Institute, 1984.
Boyer, Peter J. *Who Killed CBS? The Undoing of America's Number One News Network.* Random House, 1988.
Braestrup, Peter. *Big Story: How the American Press and Television Reported and Interpreted the Crisis of Tet 1968 in Vietnam and Washington.* 2 vols. Boulder, CO: Westview Press, 1977.
Brewin, Bob and Sydney Shaw. *Vietnam on Trial: Westmoreland vs. CBS.* New York: Atheneum, 1987.
Cubbage, T.L. "Westmoreland vs. CBS: Was Intelligence Corrupted by Policy Demands?" *Leaders and Intelligence.* Ed. Michael I. Handel. London: Frank Cass, 1989. 118-80.
Davidson, Phillip. *Vietnam at War: The History, 1946-1975.* Novato, CA: Presidio Press, 1988.
—. Telephone Interviews. 15 and 20 Feb. 1990.
Johnson, Lyndon B. *The Vantage Point: Perspectives of the Presidency, 1963-1969.* New York: Holt, Rinehart, and Winston, 1971.
Joyce, Edward. *Prime Times, Bad Times.* New York: Doubleday, 1988.
Karnow, Stanley. *Vietnam: A History (A Companion to the PBS Television Series).* New York: Viking Press, 1983.
Kowet, Don. *A Matter of Honor.* New York: Macmillan, 1984.
Kowet, Don, and Sally Bedell. "Anatomy of a Smear." *TV Guide* 29 May 1982: 2-6, 9-15.
Mayer, Martin. *About Television.* New York: Harper and Row, 1972.
Oberdorfer, Don. *Tet.* Garden City: Doubleday, 1971.
Pisor, Robert. *The End of the Line: The Siege of Khe Sanh.* New York: W.W. Norton, 1982.

Rostow, Walt W. *The Diffusion of Power: An Essay in Recent History*. New York: Macmillan, 1972.
Roth, Patricia M. *The Juror and the General*. New York: William Morrow, 1986.
Schandler, Herbert Y. *The Unmaking of a President: Lyndon Johnson and Vietnam*. Princeton, NJ: Princeton UP, 1977.
Schneir, Walter, ed. *Westmoreland vs. CBS*. New York: Clearwater, 1987.
Television's Vietnam: The Impact of Media. Dir. Peter C. Rollins. Accuracy in Media and SONY Video, 1985.
"The Uncounted Enemy." Dir. George Crile. *CBS Reports*, 22 January, 1989.
Westmoreland, William C. *A Soldier Reports*. Garden City: Doubleday, 1976.

21
The Uncounted Expert: George Carver's Views on Intelligence "Deception" Reported by CBS in *The Uncounted Enemy: A Vietnam Deception* (1982)

George Carver: The Uncounted Expert

CBS Producer George Crile left George Carver out of his documentary exposé entitled *The Uncounted Enemy: A Vietnam Deception* (1982) because Carver, like Walt Rostow, would have contradicted the program's revelations.[1] The controversial *CBS Reports* special project (hereafter, *TUE*) aired the evening of January 23, 1982.[2] Host Mike Wallace revealed that CBS had discovered "a conspiracy at the highest levels of American military intelligence to suppress and alter estimates of enemy strength" prior to the 1968 Tet offensive. One result of this "conspiracy" had been the surprise—both in size and scope—of the Tet attacks in late January, 1968, when thirty-six of Vietnam's forty-four provincial capitals came under siege and U.S. marines at Khe Sanh and Hue suffered painful losses. In the long term, bad intelligence led to our ultimate defeat in 1975 when South Vietnamese forces were overwhelmed by Communist invaders from the North. According to *TUE*, government intelligence experts withheld life-saving information from decision makers and the public for fear that the truth would dampen officialdom's "good news" campaign. While two of George Carver's subordinates at the Central Intelligence Agency (CIA), Samuel Adams and George Allen, played crucial roles in supporting the conspiratorial thesis of the CBS program, Carver, the lead player in the intelligence controversies of 1966-1967, was

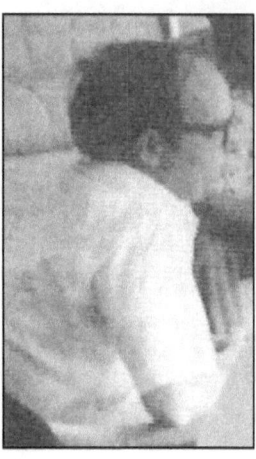

George Carver, the Key Player

ignored by producer George Crile during the pre-production and production phases of the project.

Curiously, during post-production, George Crile flew down to Washington for an off-camera interview with Carver at his office in George Washington University's Center for Strategic and International Studies. Notes from this interview for the files reflect the bias of the already-completed program: when Carver mentioned that General Westmoreland was conscious of the potential impact of new intelligence figures, Crile recorded in his notes that "Westy" had juggled figures to sell "good news"; when Carver warned Crile that Sam Adams was an enthusiast who often maligned intellectual opponents, Crile scratched a few notes portraying Carver as a threatened bureaucrat anxious to discredit a former subordinate. Should Crile's network supervisors ever inquire about Carver's absence from the program, Crile's notes would prove that the interpretation had been corroborated by a major player (JX16).[3] But the broadcast of *The Uncounted Enemy* ten days later would only mark the opening of discussions. On January 26, three days after the broadcast, General Westmoreland called a press conference at the Army-Navy Club in Washington where intelligence experts (including George Carver), diplomats and military figures rebutted the assertions of *TUE*, using clips from the program to pinpoint errors.[4] After CBS refused to televise the press conference or to allow the accused general to state his case on the air without interruption, Westmoreland filed a suit on September 13, 1982, naming George Crile, Mike Wallace, and others at *CBS News* as libelers. Depositions for the trial began in October as did the courtroom action. The following five months of legal proceedings gave George Carver ample opportunity to put into the record his version of the intelligence debates debunked by *TUE*. Initially, as part of the deposition process and then in the federal courtroom before thirteen jurors, Judge Pierre N. Lavelle, and a crowded press gallery, Carver sketched a narrative of intellectual complexity and drama—but not one of deliberate deception. Rather than the CBS tale of Cold War zeal in high places, Carver's version is a narrative about professionals with loyalties to their country, their organizations, and their methodologies striving to find a conceptual common ground so that they could effectively fight a new kind of war.[5] While this discussion occurred within a politically charged context, the results were not—as *TUE* argued—politically determined.

Origins of the Numbers Debate, 1966-67

George Carver was the logical person to ask about the debate over enemy strength. In September, 1966, Carver was appointed by the Director of the CIA, Richard Helms, to be his Special Assistant for Vietnam Affairs (SAVA). Helms told Carver to worry about Vietnam so that the CIA Director could devote his time to the rest of the globe. As SAVA, Carver recruited into his small intelligence circle a young analyst named Samuel (Sam) Adams and a long-time colleague, George Allen. Adams specialized in Vietcong organization, strength, and morale. Although Carver consistently wrote positive fitness reports for Adams while he worked at SAVA, he was quick to observe that Adams "frequently had to be reigned in" (D1312). George Allen was another matter. Carver had known Allen since the 1950s when they both spent an evening at a CIA teletype reading cables about the French debacle at Dien Bien Phu. In the SAVA informal system, Adams and Allen presented data and analysis to Carver, whose job was to brief Director Helms and other

Washington decision makers, such as Secretary of Defense Robert S. McNamara, National Security Advisor Walt W. Rostow, Chairman of the Joint Chiefs of Staff Earle Wheeler; and, at crucial moments, LBJ's famous circle of "wise old men." While Helms focused on the Soviets, the Middle East, and Africa, George Carver helped policy makers to track the Vietnam challenge.

Getting a handle on Vietnam developments was no easy chore. In the early days, when the United States was in an advisory status, data on the enemy came from dusty French and South Vietnamese sources. This information was unreliable: "we found a lot of holes and a lot of lacunae" (D79).[6] After the landing of U.S. troops in March, 1965, the intelligence community gained increasing information about enemy doctrine, organization, and strength. During the first few months of 1967, Army Combat Operations "Cedar Falls" and "Junction City" uncovered thousands of Vietcong documents, a virtual treasure trove for intelligence analysts (T1326). Close scrutiny of the resulting materials led to a revival of interest in some long-standing, but seldom used, categories for describing Vietcong Irregulars. In addition, the new information seemed to demand a recalculation of the total number of enemy. CIA figures on the types of enemy as well as their number quickly began to exceed the findings of military intelligence analysts at Westmoreland's Military Assistance Command Vietnam (hereafter, MACV). This was especially true for such irregular categories as "Self-Defense Forces" and "Secret Self-Defense Forces." As far as George Carver was concerned, this kind of disagreement was a good starting point for discussion. It was the kind of situation which had been anticipated when the National Security Act of 1947 created a new civilian intelligence agency to independently evaluate enemy capabilities (D18).

Lyndon Johnson, Walt Rostow, and Richard Helms saw potentially negative public relations ramifications in the differences over numbers. Indeed, there were explosive possibilities in a media atmosphere where the term "credibility gap" was being used with increasing stridency.[7] Someone needed to cultivate a consensus in the intelligence community. After discussing the problem with George Carver, Walt Rostow at the White House telephoned General Earle Wheeler, Chairman of the Joint Chiefs of Staff. Wheeler quickly organized a February conference in Honolulu to consider old and new reporting categories. In addition, President Johnson asked the intelligence community to formalize its findings in a report called "The National Intelligence Estimate" (NIE). Between February and the fall deadline, George Carver supervised much of the research, chaired many of the meetings, participated in some of the more heated arguments leading up to the final report, the Special National Intelligence Estimate 14.3-67, entitled "Capabilities of the Vietnamese Communist for Fighting in South Vietnam" (JX273). When *TUE* is considered as an effort to study the numbers controversy, George Carver is indeed a conspicuously uncounted expert.

For both George Crile, producer of *The Uncounted Enemy*, and George Carver of the CIA, the intelligence community's debate over the numbers reached a critical juncture during the first two weeks of September, 1967. Before that meeting, the CIA analysts and Westmoreland's intelligence staff were at loggerheads; after September 14, 1967, the gap was bridged by a temporary agreement which displeased everyone a bit—as compromises sometimes do. Carver was happy because he had subtly forced MACV to agree to a prose estimation of irregular forces. MACV, while displeased about what General Phillip Davidson has called Carver's "oblique quantification" of irregulars, at least succeeded in keeping the "hard numbers" restricted to the enemy's armed, maneuver elements.[8]

The Uncounted Enemy argues that the September agreement was a duplicitous attempt to fool the American public and Washington policymakers, including Lyndon Johnson. As a result of tainted information, *TUE* argues, the President, the Congress, and America waded further into a Vietnam quagmire. As revealed by his testimony and by 1967 cables sent during the crucial Saigon negotiations, the story George Carver told at the Westmoreland vs CBS trial was no less interesting, although it lacked the cynical, conspiratorial melodrama of the CBS exposé.

Military v. Civilian Measuring Rods

Clearly, a basic methodological difference between military and civilian analysts complicated efforts to reach agreement. The civilians in Washington were concerned with collecting information about what Carver described as the "overall strength," or "insurgency base," or "force structure" of the enemy. When examining raw information from the field, the Washington-based people applied "extrapolation techniques" to arrive at assessments which might be in error for any particular province of South Vietnam, but were accurate from a national perspective. George Carver believed that such analysis was an appropriate way to find information for policy makers attempting to make strategic decisions—such as whether to continue or suspend bombing of the North or whether or not to attack sanctuaries in Laos and Cambodia. On the other hand, Carver was wary of the numbers game. Washington experience with computer-oriented "whiz kids" in the Department of Defense had burned Carver a number of times. He was reluctant to attach specific numbers—or even ranges of numbers—to intelligence categories for which information was not solid (D235; T2816). At critical moments during the numbers debate, George Allen concurred with Carver (JX377). Sam Adams was more of a numbers man, a true believer in his calculations. In fact, Adams' fixation on numbers would later lead Carver to describe his subordinate as someone "often in error, never in doubt" (D1320). Years after the numbers debate of 1966-67, General Phillip Davidson still resents that so much credence was given to the Adams figures which were country-wide extrapolations projected from a narrow base of only twenty-eight documents.[9]

Carver did not quarrel with the need for estimates; he worried about the false sense of certitude which numbers often conveyed. He often described the intelligence picture as a triangle with main force units at the apex, supported by increasingly less armed, less organized, less formal units below (D289). Both the CIA and Westmoreland's experts at the MACV were largely in agreement about the apex figures; they argued about how to report the lower, informal echelons near the base of the triangle. Secretary of Defense Robert S. McNamara's hunger for charts and statistics often went unsatisfied at weekly one-on-one briefings by Carver (D637). It is important to note that, during the numbers debate, Carver discovered allies who shared his phobia for numbering "spongy" categories to include analysts in the military camp.

With its tactical battlefield mission in mind, analysts at MACV took a more traditional "Order of Battle" (OB) approach in counting enemy forces. As Carver knew, "MACV's position was that you should be very rigorous in including only those people who had directly military functions" (D325). The operational area defined by MACV was limited to the territory of South Vietnam. Therefore, MACV's estimates did not include Communist forces available in sanctuaries across Vietnam's borders in Laos, Cambodia, and North Vietnam. While critics of the MACV approach complained that the system was a misapplication of techniques from conventional warfare, MACV could always respond—as General Westmoreland did during the trial—that the Order of Battle approach kept American commanders focused on fighting main force troops. General Westmoreland believes that MACV's narrow definition may have prevented the kind of atrocities which we now associate with the name "My Lai." (During the shameful episode on March 16, 1968, Lt. William Calley decided to eliminate those civilians he suspected of planting land mines which had killed or wounded some of his men.) In part because it could clearly define a military enemy, in part out of habit, and in part to avoid clustering civilians with military adversaries, MACV clearly defined its role as fighting an enemy army rather than CIA-style abstractions such as "insurgency bases" or "force structures." Not all Army analysts agreed with this approach, but it was very much MACV's explicit "command position."[10]

Discussion between military analysts and their civilian counterparts was further complicated by a major difference in the way each assessed data. Military analysts based estimates on "collateral intelligence," which meant counting units and troop totals based on captured documents, prisoner interrogations, sightings or photographs by aerial observers, or reports from troops in immediate contact with the enemy (D1030-34). Carver described the military system as a "data based approach" as opposed to the CIA's "estimative projection" system. Accuracy of the Order of Battle was further inhibited by the level of security at which OBs were distributed. Anyone with a "Confidential" clearance could have access to the monthly Order of Battle reports, to include our allies from Vietnam, Thailand, Korea, the Philippines, and Australia. For this reason, information based on "signal" or "communications" intelligence from the National Security Agency (NSA) was *never* included in the published OB. Characteristically, Carver was aware of the differing approaches to numbering the enemy without denigrating the methods of his opponents in the numbers debate: "MACV was a military command fighting a war. We were synthesizing intelligence at a national level, trying to give an accurate account in the appreciation of a total political problem.... They were different approaches for difference audiences" (D1180).

The Need for an Intelligence Summit Meeting

Walt Rostow, President Johnson's National Security Advisor, was responsible for setting the "summit" process in motion.[11] The February, 1967, Order of Battle conference in Honolulu was the first chapter, a preliminary session designed to reach agreement on reporting categories (D1274). All major military and civilian intelligence institutions sent representatives. Sam Adams sat in for SAVA. Methodological differences prevented agreements. MACV and other military intelligence analysts wanted to focus upon the main force units while the civilians tried to clarify such categories for "irregulars" such as Self-Defense and Secret Self-Defense Forces, Assault Youth, etc. Given the new intelligence data acquired from Operations "Cedar Falls" and "Junction City"—and assiduously

Walt W. Rostow (d.2003)

mined by analysts—there could be an enormous impact on the (estimated) aggregate total of enemy strength.

After the Honolulu meeting in February, MACV continued to report its Order of Battle statistics to the Washington intelligence community, but everyone in the system knew there was a debate in progress and that the Order of Battle should be complemented by reports from NSA and other "sensitive" intelligence sources. In particular, President Johnson's advisor on such matters, Walt Rostow, obviously knew about the limitations of the Order of Battle. During the spring lull in the debate, some analysts at MACV developed an interest in CIA approaches. This was not strictly a civilian-military tug of war.

In August, a National Intelligence Estimate (NIE) conference was convened at CIA Headquarters in Langley, Virginia. During the course of the meeting, Robert Komer and General Creighton Abrams received feedback from their representative, General George Godding, that the draft version of NIE would press for inclusion of the "spongy" figures for Self-Defense and Secret Self-Defense forces. Godding's cables conveyed his frustration and irritation. Immediately, Komer cabled Carver that MACV simply would not go along with this approach. In addition, he shared his fears that the resulting report would create severe public relations problems. Few members of an adversary press would miss the newsworthy gap between the OB estimate of 299,000 enemy forces as opposed to a draft NIE figure (with SD and SSD included) of 420,000-431,000. Komer knew that methodological niceties would be ignored in the rush to hype a theme of doublespeak within the government: "Any explanation as to why would simply lead press to conclude that MACV was deliberately omitting SD/SSD category in order to downgrade enemy strength. This credibility gap would be further widened at very time when in fact we are moving toward much more valid estimates" (JX250).[12] The next day, General Abrams cabled General Wheeler, articulating the military's rationale for not accepting the new categories and numbers in the Order of Battle:

From the intelligence viewpoint the inclusion of SD and SSD figures in an estimate of military capabilities is highly questionable. These forces contain a sizable number of women and old people. They operate entirely in their own hamlets. They are rarely armed, have no real discipline, and almost no military capability. They are no more effective in the military sense than the dozens of other nonmilitary organizations which serve the VC cause in various roles. (JX252)

Abrams also was worried that the real successes by American ground forces during the previous year would be obscured when these kinds of figures reached the public.[13]

General Westmoreland, visiting Clark Air Force Base in the Philippines at the time, was on the distribution list for Abrams' cable. Later the same day, he wired the Joint Chiefs, concurring with Abrams and stressing that he did not approve of "inclusion of SD and SSD strength figures in the overall enemy strength. It distorts the situation and makes no sense" (JX253). Given this chorus of dissent, it is not surprising that Carver's staff came back to the SAVA suite in a depressed mood. Both sides acknowledged the impasse, promising to resume negotiations in September when representatives of the Defense Intelligence Agency (DIA), CIA, and MACV would gather in Saigon.

The Saigon NIE Summit: Was There a Real Debate?

The day after the Langley NIE meeting ended, Carver sent a cable to Saigon, outlining the challenges of the coming sessions in Vietnam. SAVA declared his belief that the "debate has produced more heat than light since the major differences lie in realm of conceptual and presentational rather than in genuine disagreement over substantive facts" (JX220). He requested that the Saigon players review the existing draft proposal of the National Intelligence Estimate, but requested that circulation of the manuscript be limited to Westmoreland, Komer, Bunker and "need-to-know" analysts at MACV. Carver did his best to underscore that, while the CIA wanted more attention given in the November NIE to "irregular militia," the CIA did "not-repeat not-advocate their inclusion in full-time military force strength figure." Discussions with Westmoreland's intelligence staff in July had shown that there might be room for compromise (JX245). Ironically, a memorandum written by Colonel Gains Hawkins—who would emerge as a major witness for CBS—had suggested a method of computation which might prove acceptable to both parties (D363; T3172).

Much effort was made to assure that the delegation arriving with Carver represented the Washington intelligence community rather than the CIA alone. The delegation also included people from the Defense Intelligence Agency (DIA), the State Department's Bureau of Intelligence and Research (INR), and the National Security Agency (NSA). As an opening position, the Washington contingent planned to defend the NIE draft proposal. Still, Carver believed that this was only a starting point, that he was open to new conceptualizations (T2843). The team arrived in Saigon on the 8th of September. Working sessions began the next morning with what proved to be a day-long briefing by MACV which Carver reported "widened rather than narrowed our differences" (JX2565) (see Table 1). The aggregate difference at this stage was considerable: MACV was offering a combined military and political OB of 298,000 in contrast with the NIE combined maximum total of 371,000.

TOWARD NIE 14.3: THE NEGOTIATIONS EVOLVE, AUG - SEPT, 1967					
Order of Battle Categories	NIE 14.3 Draft Figures 28 Aug 1967 Washington	MACV Estimate 10 Sept 1967 Briefing Saigon	MACV "Write Card" 12 Sept 1967 Saigon	Washington Delegation Compromise 12 Sept 1967	Westmoreland -Approved Synthesis 13 Sept 1967
Main and Local Forces	121,000	119,000	119,000	119,000	119,000
Administrative Services	40,000 - 60,000	29,000	25,000 - 35,000	35,000 - 45,000 NIE 14.3 to say "at least" this number in qualifying pars. 26 and 27.	35,000 - 40,000
Guerillas	60,000 - 100,000	65,000	75,000 - 95,000	75,000 - 95,000	70,000 - 90,000
MILITARY TOTAL:	221,000 - 281,000		219,000 - 249,000	229,000 - 259,000	224,000 - 249,000

Table 1: Comparative Numbers for the September Negotiations, Part 1

Carver tried to begin the second day of the summit by suggesting that the two delegations go through the categories one-by-one "without considering the ultimate total until analysis of each separate category was completed." When his MACV auditors proved uninterested, he reminded them that, in the final analysis, National Intelligence Estimates like NIE 14.3-67 were codified into the final version by the Washington intelligence community (as represented on the U.S. Intelligence Board [USIB]) and that "no one could tell the USIB chairman what his estimate had to be." During subsequent discussions, MACV participants seemed to be inventing reasons for not accepting the NIE draft figures. After these fruitless sessions, one Washington participant tartly remarked that "We did not travel 8,000 miles to be insulted." At the end of the day, Carver concluded—erroneously, he would later learn—that Westmoreland

TOWARD NIE 14.3: THE NEGOTIATIONS EVOLVE, AUG - SEPT, 1967					
Order of Battle Categories	NIE 14.3 Draft Figures 28 Aug 1967 Washington	MACV Estimate 10 Sept 1967 Briefing Saigon	MACV "Write Card" 12 Sept 1967 Saigon	Washington Delegation Compromise 12 Sept 1967	Westmoreland -Approved Synthesis 13 Sept 1967
Political Cadres	90,000	85,000	70,000 - 80,000	80,000 - 90,000	75,000 - 85,000
Self Defense and Secret Self Defense	xxxx	xxxx	No quantification	No numbers, but qualifying pars. 32-36 in NIE 14.3	As per Washington views, 12 September
EXPLICIT OVERALL TOTAL:	311,000 - 371,000	298,000	NO	No, but par. 37 of NIE 14.3 to describe in prose	As per Washington views, 12 September
IMPLICIT OVERALL TOTAL:			NO	Begin joint work on calculations of irregulars to avoid CBS-style mathematical "problems"	Same as Washington views, 12 September

Table 2: Comparative Numbers for the September Negotiations, Part 2

had told his people to place a 300,000 figure on the VC strength total and that the only way to unhinge the "straightjacket" was to speak directly to the commander himself (JX256). On the military side, feelings were strongly in favor of going a separate route with each side keeping its own computations as appropriate to its own special mission. Some MACV analysts were so irritated that General Davidson held a special meeting with his delegation to discuss the need to maintain professional decorum during debates which often descended to ad hominem exchanges (Davidson interview).

Still lacking the influence of Westmoreland, meetings went on with specialists from Washington and MACV clustering separately over topics such as Administrative Services, Guerrillas, and Political Cadre. There were discussions of the differing methodologies and some haggling for minor changes in the figures. Most important for Carver was a two-hour meeting with Robert Komer (who worked on pacification, what LBJ called "the other war"), General Phillip Davidson (the top intelligence officer at MACV), and others. Carver tried to allay concerns about numbers, hoping to encourage a better spirit of cooperation. Komer then launched into a vitriolic attack on the NIE draft. Komer was no fan of the civilian intelligence. He was particularly concerned about the NIE push to add new categories: "He was adamant...in insisting that there must not be any quantification of the irregular forces on the grounds that the press would add all figures together" (JX258). In the process, however, Komer admitted that MACV's current combined figure of 298,000 for both military and non-military was far too low and needed adjustment. Komer's concession about the need to revise MACV estimates upwards energized the heretofore dour military intelligence officers. On the way out of the meeting, General Davidson promised Carver new figures.

Early in the morning of 12 September, General Davidson handed Carver a white card on which was typed a new set of figures acceptable to MACV (see Table 1). As in the past, MACV demanded that there be no quantification of Self-Defense and Secret Self-Defense forces. On the constructive side, the figures were now presented in a highest estimate/lowest estimate spread for most categories; in addition, the total was up 31,000 from MACV's September 10 briefing. Carver was impressed that there might now be a chance for rapprochement. Carver immediately convened the entire Washington delegation—including Sam Adams—"to see if we could hammer out a position.... It took six hours, but we succeeded" (JX258).

At dinner time, Carver handed the new Washington delegation figures to Davidson. A copy was also wired back to CIA Director Richard Helms. The delegation accepted the MACV demand that the Self-Defense and Secret Self-Defense not be quantified, but asked for what eventually would become five paragraphs of prose in the NIE where the function and sizes of the various irregular forces could be explained. While acquiescing to 18,000 fewer under Administrative Services, the Washington group carefully qualified their concessions in two carefully worded paragraphs.[14] The Washington analysts also pushed for future discussions among intelligence groups to refine methods of estimating irregulars. In fact, Sam Adams was left behind in Saigon to initiate that effort.[15] Carver told Helms that the compromise unstuck MACV from its intransigent position while "the prose text adopted makes it clear that we have the three hundred thousand range in mind even though no precise figure is given" (JX258). Carver's hopes for immediate acceptance were dashed when Davidson explained that the numbers on the white card handed him prior to the morning sessions constituted a final offer, a nonnegotiable position.

Prior to visiting with General Westmoreland the next morning, Carver was told by General Davidson that the commander "would do nothing but formalize our impasse" (JX259). At the formal meeting, Davidson renewed his defense of the MACV estimates. Komer also stressed the virtues of the MACV position "but acknowledging logic in some Washington views." Carver argued that General Westmoreland's self-interest required a new "bottom line" estimate from which all parties could work. Westmoreland responded by politely recognizing the efforts of his intelligence staff under General Davidson, but agreeing with Carver that a bottom line was essential. He asked both parties to reconvene immediately to resolve differences. Westmoreland and Davidson then left the room. Seizing the opportunity provided by Westmoreland, Carver "usurped the chair" of the final negotiating session. Davidson left a subordinate behind to work with the Washington group toward an agreement which could go forward to the U.S. Intelligence Board responsible for the finished report. The resulting figures (see Table 1) show slight modifications at various points where Washington analysts were willing to concede on numbers for the opportunity to qualify in prose. For example, they were happy to cut back on the guerrilla category, but added the phrase "at least" with respect to the number of Administrative Services. Prose portions of the completed NIE report would also make it clear when figures were for in-country enemy as opposed to total enemy strengths. Carver boasted in deposition and at trial that the resulting NIE was a far better report. The prose passages made sense out of ranges of numbers and discouraged readers from adding enemy figures for groups which were often incommensurate with one another. The prose prevented novices from adding up "apples and oranges."

That afternoon, Westmoreland signed off on the agreement, promising to report the results to the Joint Chiefs. On September 14, Carver congratulated himself with the thought that "our basic mission [was] now successfully completed" (JX260). When he visited Ambassador Ellsworth Bunker, he found a man delighted that "Washington and Saigon could now speak with one voice." Carver spent two hours with MACV's Public Information Officer, General Sidle, discussing the best way to present the new estimates to the press—without making reference to the changes as part of the secret NIE effort. On the way back to Washington, Carver touched base in Hawaii with intelligence officers working for Admiral Sharp, Westmoreland's reporting senior in the chain of command. As a Ph.D. candidate at Oxford, Carver had written his dissertation on Thomas Hobbes; drawing upon a quotation from Hobbes about the accomplishment of the impossible, Carver reveled in his success. He had "squared the circle!"

MACV had kept the numbers game focused on regular troops in the field plus Administrative Services and armed Guerrillas. The Washington analysts had given the NIE—and future discussions of enemy potentials—a turn toward the "insurgency base" approach. Each party had gained a little and lost a little. In any case, these were figures and categories that could be refined over time. A heated and honest debate had resolved many differences and had provided a platform for future efforts. The American intelligence community could stop fighting itself and concentrate on the enemy.

At least in the fall of 1967, Sam Adams—who would later become the paid research consultant for CBS' *The Uncounted Enemy*—supported the compromise agreement endorsed by General Westmoreland. Subsequent events would provoke his anger and reshape his memory of the Saigon conference in early September, 1967. A MACV press briefing in October of 1967 seemed to misrepresent the agreement, arousing Adams—but also bringing Carver back for a second look (D811). The Tet offensive of 1968 seemed to Adams to be prima facie evidence that the numbers agreement was wrong—both intellectually and morally. Beginning with in-house memos and complaints and then moving to public fora, Adams, over the next decade, fashioned an elaborate hobby horse about an intelligence conspiracy. In 1982, George Crile dignified the complaints in a ninety-minute epic with General Westmoreland as the villain.[16] Although George Carver was denied a chance to appear in the CBS program, the Westmoreland gave the true author of the compromise intelligence agreement of 1967 the opportunity to stand up and be counted as an articulate enemy of the network's flawed exposé.

Notes

1. Walt Whitman Rostow served as Deputy National Security Advisor to President John F. Kennedy until 1961. Thereafter, he was Counselor to the State Department and Chairman of its Policy Planning Council. In April, 1966, he became National Security Advisor to President Lyndon B. Johnson and served in that capacity until they both left government service in 1969. Unlike Carver, Rostow was interviewed on camera by CBS for three hours, but not a second of the material was used because Rostow thoroughly contradicted the thesis of *TUE*. Through letters to the editor of the *New York Times* (7 Feb. 1982) and in memoranda for the record (see JX1232a), Rostow launched his own assault on *TUE* immediately after it was aired. Rostow's testimony at the trial and his various critiques of the program are available in the microfiche collection described in the Works Cited portion of this essay. I wish to thank Dr. Rostow for his comments on the initial draft of this study.

2. Benjamin, *The CBS Benjamin Report* contains a transcript of the audio portion of the program (34571-98). Video copies of *The Uncounted Enemy: A Vietnam Deception* are available from the Vanderbilt Television Archive, 110 21st Ave, S., Suite 704, Nashville, TN 37203 (615-322-2927).

3. See my comments under A New Source Consulted for an explanation of the citation system used in this chapter. The goal has been to simplify the reader's task by citing elements from the Westmoreland v. CBS microfiche collection in a way that will facilitate retrieval of the materials.

4. The Army-Navy Club Press Conference was videotaped. A transcript is in the microfiche collection, JX600 and a video should be available from the Vietnam Center, Texas Tech U.

5. Carver spoke to a conference in 1985 about his experiences in Vietnam and the courtroom. The talk is tape #1 in a set entitled *To Sue or Not to Sue* (see Works Cited). In his presentation, he put considerable emphasis on the compromise as the brainchild of Lt. Col. Gains Hawkins whose memo of July, 1967, suggested a prose description of irregulars (Carver D636; T3172). Carver joins such observers as Lt. Gen. Phillip Davidson, Gen. W.C. Westmoreland, and others in believing that the Tet offensive—rather than discrediting the September agreement—actually substantiated the accuracy of the estimate. Both in a recent interview and in his *Vietnam at War* (Chapter 18), General Davidson, who was MACV's chief intelligence officer at the time, stresses that "of the 6000 prisoners captured during the Tet offensive, not one belonged to the SD or SSD" (interview). Just after Tet, when Davidson asked a high-ranking prisoner about these irregular categories, the regimental commander responded that "he never heard of them" (interview). A 1968 memorandum by Halpin supports these post-Tet validations of the September figures (JX382). By March, 1968, retrospective studies of the Tet attacks placed the number of participating enemy forces at around 84,000-87,000—a far cry from Sam Adams' horde of 400,000 to 600,000 (Davidson 481). General Phillip Davidson read an early draft of this essay and generously shared his views. Presidio Press published a book by Davidson entitled *The Secrets of the Vietnam War*; it devotes three chapters to the numbers controversy.

6. All parties in the numbers debate agreed that the categories and estimates inherited from French and Vietnamese sources were inaccurate. The debate focused on how to revise the categories and the quantities within the context of a limited war which mixed traditional and counter-insurgency military characteristics. In addition, there was also a question about who would be using the numbers and for what purpose. The Army was fighting the war on a tactical level and needed figures for immediate use in the field; the CIA could sit back and take a more Olympian perspective.

7. The "credibility gap" issue within this context is discussed by Schandler (48-54) and Turner (171-81). Impartial observers will find fault with both the President and the press for this problem.

8. General Davidson, who walked out on the final proceedings, still feels that "the whole thing was trivial." He believes that MACV needed

to focus on Main and Local Forces, categories about which MACV and the CIA were in substantial agreement. As far as the "spongy" categories about irregulars were concerned, Davidson believes that "nobody knew what they did." He is still unwilling to believe that SD or SSD planted mines or booby traps which "were put in by military people." As for pungy traps, "they may have planted stakes, but the traps accounted for 1.5% of our wounds and no one ever died" (interview). (Summers agrees with this estimate.)

9. Interview. Davidson's description of Adams and others who played with the numbers has the tone of the man in the field who feels harassed, rather than assisted, by outside consultants. The disdain is implicit in the statement: "I had a war to fight."

10. General Westmoreland has made these points with me on a number of occasions over the last few years. He discusses this issue in *A Soldier Reports*: "Having taught a course on the Geneva Convention and the laws of war at the Command and General Staff College in the late 1940s, I was conscious of the responsibilities they placed on field commanders. Shortly after assuming command in South Vietnam in 1964, I called in my judge advocate general...and instructed him to form a study group to recommend what to do. From that study and from frequent later consultations emerged the strict MACV regulations which established the rules of engagement for the U.S. military forces" (348).

Cubbage focuses on this point (152-52). In footnote 177, Cubbage cites an interview with Westmoreland in which MACV's commander explained that "The armed Vietcong were fair game for my forces; unarmed civilians were not fair game. I considered the unarmed Vietcong—the enemy non-combatants—to be in categories outside the order of battle." On tape #3 of *To Sue or Not To Sue*, legal historian Stephen B. Young, Dean of the Hamline Law School, traces the details of the legal rationale for Westmoreland's decision within the guidelines of the Geneva Conventions, arguing that the General would have been subject to charges of war crimes had he acted in any other way. Westmoreland's Order of Battle and his Rules of Engagement were designed to avoid the kind of tragedy which occurred at My Lai. Since the My Lai Massacre was an aberration rather than the norm, it should be observed that Westmoreland's humane objective was achieved. In *America in Vietnam*, Guenter Lewy surveys the successes and failures of the Rules of Engagement (233-42; 324-31; 356-64).

11. This single fact deprives *The Uncounted Enemy* of its sting. Not only was the White House not fooled by MACV on the numbers games; Rostow was often ahead of the intelligence community in his analysis of enemy strength and intentions. This prescience is not totally inexplicable since Walt Rostow had worked on Order of Battle problems for the OSS

during World War II. Furthermore, it can be argued that, rather than being in the dark about the Tet offensive, Rostow was the first to see it coming. Drawing upon Rostow's intelligence summaries, Lyndon Johnson gave a briefing to the Australian cabinet on December 21st, predicting a "Battle of the Bulge" effort by the Vietcong. Unfortunately for all concerned, Johnson did not carry his message to Congress during his State of the Union Address on January 17, nor did he go on television to share his concerns with the American people. As a result, when the attacks came on January 31st, they had a decisive psychological effect in the United States which might have been averted. Braestrup and Schandler agree that the President further eroded his credibility by not going before the American people immediately after Tet to reassure them that the offensive had unexpectedly worked in our favor. Johnson publicly acknowledged his errors three years later in his autobiography, *The Vantage Point* (380-85). What matters within the context of this study is that he definitely *knew about the coming attacks* and that there is documented evidence that he shared his concerns with other political leaders. If there was a conspiracy at any level of government to suppress information about enemy intentions, it certainly was a complete failure. (Rostow was left out of *TUE* because he argued this point, treating Producer George Crile like an ignorant schoolboy in the process [JX14]).

12. Robert Komer is an important person in the numbers controversy. As a White House advisor to President Johnson, he had argued for the need to combine military and civilian efforts to win a counterinsurgency conflict. Taking him at his word, LBJ dispatched Komer to Vietnam where he was the deputy to the Commander of MACV, holding the rank of Ambassador. Once in the field, Komer organized a nation-wide program devoted to Civil Operations and Rural Development Support (CORDS). Some observers claim that Komer was LBJ's eyes and ears at MACV. In any case, Carver's depositions and testimony clearly indicate that, of all the officials with whom Carver dealt, Komer was the one most vocal—to the point of rudeness—about how the numbers debate would play in the press. More needs to be learned about his involvement in the September, 1967, agreements. In November, 1968, Komer was replaced by William Colby.

13. Virtually nothing has been written about General Creighton Abrams' part in the numbers controversy. At the time, he was deputy to Westmoreland at MACV. He evidently deplored the entire exercise. At one of the September meetings, he whispered to Westmoreland that "It all sounds like bullshit to me." General Davidson points out that, once Abrams became the Commander of MACV in July, 1968, he told his intelligence analysts to keep separate books on the enemy and to ignore

the civilian analysts. Anticipating criticism, Abrams cabled Wheeler to explain that he would not waste his time trying to build fragile bridges to the Ivory Tower (Davidson interview).

14. Paragraph 26 of the final report, NIE 14.3-67 defines the "Administrative Service Units" as headquarters personnel plus medics, ordnance, logistics specialists. Paragraph 27 estimates that "there are now at least 35,000-40,000 administrative service personnel in South Vietnam who are performing essential administrative support functions. In addition, *almost anyone under VC control can be and is impressed into service to perform specific administrative or support tasks as local conditions require*" (emphasis supplied). This hardly reads like a cover-up.

15. NIE 14.3-67 would devote a paragraph of descriptive prose to the following categories: Administrative Services (pars. 26-7), Guerrillas (pars. 28-30), Political Organization (par. 31), Self-Defense Forces (par. 33), Secret Self-Defense Forces (par. 34), Assault Youth (pars. 35-6). Looking back over its discussions, the report would conclude this way concerning combined regular and irregular strengths for the Vietcong: "In sum, the Communist military and political organization is complex, and its aggregate numerical size cannot be estimated with confidence. Moreover, any such aggregate total would be misleading since it would involve adding components that have widely different missions and degrees of skill or dedication. The VC/NVA Military Force (Main and Local forces, Administrative Service elements and Guerrillas) can be meaningfully presented in numerical totals and we estimate that this Military Force is now at least 223,000-248,000. It must be recognized, however, that this Military Force constitutes but one component of the total Communist organization. Any comprehensive judgment of Communist capabilities in South Vietnam must embrace the effectiveness of all the elements which comprise that organization, *the total size of which is of course considerably greater than the figure given for the Military Force*" (emphasis supplied.). This hardly reads like a cover-up.

16. Here is a brief chronology of Sam Adams' quest to expose the intelligence "conspiracy." In February, 1968, he left SAVA for another division within the CIA where his numbers were given more credence. In May, he filed formal charges with the CIA Inspector General, charging Richard Helms with suppression of vital intelligence information prior to the Tet offensive. When the CIA process dragged on for too long, he approached the White House where some attention was given him by the President's Foreign Intelligence Advisory Board. He also approached John Court of the National Security Council, but received little more than a polite reading of his thirty-page memo. No action was taken. In January, 1973, Adams volunteered to testify on behalf of Daniel Ellsberg and An-

thony Russo at their "Pentagon Papers" trial in Los Angeles. His rationale was that they should not be "hanged for leaking faked numbers" (Kowet 42). In 1975, Adams worked with George Crile, then an editor at *Harper's* magazine, to produce a scathing article that would become the basis for the 1982 documentary. "Vietnam Cover-up: Playing War With Numbers-A CIA Conspiracy Against Its Own Intelligence" attracted considerable attention, especially on Capitol Hill. Adams was called as a witness by Congressman Otis Pike's House Select Committee on Intelligence where his arguments were answered by Richard Helms, George Carver, and others. At that session, General Daniel Graham observed that "If you were going to assemble all Sam Adams's conspirators at the same time, in the same place, you'd have to rent a football stadium." In 1980, George Crile visited Adams to suggest that his thesis be worked up as a documentary for CBS. *The Uncounted Enemy* and the Westmoreland v. CBS trial would be the final fora for Adams. He died in 1989 without completing *Who the Hell Are We Fighting Out There?* (Norton), his book on the numbers "conspiracy," although draft versions of the work are in the microfiche collection (JX587-92). (The books by Brewin and Kowet focus on Adams and the escalation of his complaints, but no one has explored his position in real depth.)

A Invaluable Source Consulted

This chapter is an original narrative based on data in a microfiche resource entitled *Westmoreland v. CBS* (New York: Clearwater Publishing Company, Inc., 1987). The fiche collection is a two-drawer set containing over 80,000 pages of text. It includes legal arguments by both the plaintiff (General Westmoreland) and the defendants (CBS, et al.) during the various stages of the pre-trial and trial altercations. Historians will take special interest in the Depositions (alphabetical by surname) and the Trial Transcripts (indexed by surname). For this project, the Joint Exhibits section was extremely useful. The JX group contained top secret cables which provided a paper trail for reconstructing the numbers controversy in the American intelligence community during 1966-1967.

I used George Carver's depositions and trial testimony plus many of the cables introduced as exhibits in connection with Carver's appearances before and during the trial. For background and corroboration, I also spent time with the testimony of several major players in the numbers debate. A research guide to the collection (in book form) is often available separately through interlibrary loan: Walter Schneir, ed., *Westmoreland v. CBS: Guide to the Microfiche Collection* (New York: Clearwater Publishing Co., 1987). Scholars are urged to examine this text, a book which is included as part of the microfiche collection.

Readers wishing background discussion of the details of the controversy should consult Chapter 20 of *America Reflected*.

Works Cited

Adams, Sam. "Vietnam Cover-up: Playing War with the Numbers." *Harper's* May 1975: 41-44, 62-73.

Braestrup, Peter. *Big Story: How the American Press and Television Reported and Interpreted the Crisis of Tet 1968 in Vietnam and Washington.* 2 vols. Boulder, CO: Westview Press, 1977. Abridged edition available from various presses, to include the Yale UP, 1983.

Brewin, Bob, and Sydney Shaw. *Vietnam on Trial: Westmoreland vs. CBS.* New York: Atheneum, 1987.

Colby, William. *Lost Victory: A Firsthand Account of America's Sixteen-Year Involvement in Vietnam.* Chicago: Contemporary Books, 1989.

Crile, George. "The Uncounted Enemy." *CBS Reports.* CBS. KOTV, Tulsa. 23 Jan. 1982.

Cubbage, T.L. "Westmoreland vs. CBS: Was Intelligence Corrupted by Policy Demands?" *Leaders and Intelligence.* Ed. Michael I. Handle. London: Frank Cass, 1989. 118-80.

Davidson, Phillip B. *Secrets of the Vietnam War.* Novato: Presidio Press, 1988.

—. Telephone Interviews. 15 and 20 Feb. 1990.

—. *Vietnam at War: The History: 1946-1975.* Novato: Presidio Press, 1988.

Johnson, Lyndon B. *The Vantage Point: Perspectives of the Presidency, 1963-1969.* New York: Holt, Rinehart, and Winston, 1971.

Kowet, Don. *A Matter of Honor.* New York: Macmillan, 1984.

Kowet, Don, and Sally Bedell. "Anatomy of a Smear." *TV Guide* 29 May 1982: 2-6, 9-15.

Lewy, Guenter. *America in Vietnam.* New York: Oxford UP, 1978.

Rostow, Walt W. *The Diffusion of Power: An Essay in Recent History.* New York: Macmillan, 1972.

Roth, M. Patricia. *The Juror and the General.* New York: William Morrow, 1986.

Schandler, Herbert Y. *The Unmaking of a President: Lyndon Johnson and Vietnam.* Princeton, NJ: Princeton UP, 1977.

Sheehan, Neil. *A Bright Shining Lie: John Paul Vann and America in Vietnam.* New York: Random House, 1988.

Smolla, Rodney A. *Suing the Press.* New York: Oxford UP, 1986.

Summers, Harry G. *Vietnam War Almanac.* New York: Facts on File Publications, 1985. See entry for George Carver.

Turner, Kathleen J. *Lyndon Johnson's Dual War.* Chicago: U of Chicago P, 1985.

Westmoreland, William C. *A Soldier Reports.* Garden City: Doubleday, 1976.

22
Neil Sheehan's *Bright Shining Lie*: The Story of John Paul Vann or of America's New Media Elite?

During the afternoon of June 16, 1972, Neil Sheehan of the *New York Times'* Washington bureau attended the funeral of John Paul Vann at Arlington National Cemetery. For Sheehan, the event seemed ripe with symbolism. Inside the red brick chapel beside the cemetery gate were a number of key dramatis personae of the Vietnam era. In an attempt to claim him as their own, the Nixon administration had insured that major Establishment personalities were present to give John Paul Vann a proper burial. In the audience were Cold Warriors such as Major General Edward Lansdale, Lieutenant General William DePuy, and journalist Joseph Alsop, all of whom had served in some way to initiate, implement, or justify America's policies in Southeast Asia. Some Vietnam heavy-hitters were pallbearers: General William C. Westmoreland, now Chief of Staff, was the battlefield commander in Vietnam from 1964 to 1968, the period of massive buildup; General Bruce Palmer, Jr., one of the Army's most brilliant professionals, had been intelligent enough to appreciate Vann, but not bureaucratically powerful enough to assure favors for Vann's ideas; Lieutenant General Richard Stilwell was one of many establishment figures who opposed Vann initially, but eventually "realized that he had been wrong and had come to admire him" (17); William Colby of the CIA was still a Cold Warrior committed as both American and Catholic to defeating "Godless Communism" (18). Robert Komer, chief of pacification in Vietnam, seemed just the right person to be both a pallbearer and the eulogist. In July 1967, Komer was sent out to Vietnam by President Lyndon Johnson to deal directly with the problem of "hearts and

An American Epic

minds." As a result, Komer worked with John Paul Vann, whom he discovered to be both controversial and indispensable. Sheehan noticed that the pitch of Komer's voice rose as he waxed eloquently over Vann's contributions to the noble effort in Vietnam:

> I've never known a more unsparingly critical and uncompromisingly honest man. He called them as he saw them—in defeat as well as victory. For this, and for his long experience, he was more respected by the press than any other official. And he told letting the chips fall where they may. After one such episode, I was told, and not in jest, to fire John Vann. I replied that I wouldn't and couldn't; that, in fact, if I could only find three more John Vanns we could shorten the war by half. (20)

Komer's eulogy portrayed Vann as a leader who understood the Vietnamese people and devoted his life to their cause of freedom. He closed with the reflection that "his real monument will be the free and peaceful South Vietnam for which he fought so well" (21).

Neil Sheehan's *Bright Shining Lie*   511

After the funeral President Nixon was intending to award the Presidential Medal of Freedom to Mary Jane Vann for her husband's contributions, thereby presumably fixing the Establishment's imprimatur on the man and his memory.

The Arlington moment was redolent with other messages for reporter Neil Sheehan, making the ceremony more than a hollow public relations event for the Nixon Administration. The presence of Senator Edward Kennedy called attention to the breadth of Vann's influence. Although a tenacious fighter on the ground and in the air over Vietnam, Vann had shared the Massachusetts Senator's concern for the plight of the refugees in the war-torn country. For Sheehan, Ted Kennedy also symbolized the defection of the Kennedy family from the Vietnam crusade. In the early days, Jack Kennedy projected his vision of a "New Frontier" which would spread "an American-imposed order...beyond America's shores" (12). With some intellectual prodding from Daniel Ellsberg in 1968, Robert Kennedy defected from his dead brother's vision to run for the Democratic nomination on an anti-war platform, a campaign called to a tragic halt when, on live television, an assassin's bullet cut him down. Ted carried on Bobby's campaign against the war.

Daniel Ellsberg, "the turncoat knight of the crusade," upset the Establishment representatives at the funeral by sitting with the Vann family(12). Back in the winter of 1966, Ellsberg succeeded in

The Press in Vietnam: David Halberstam, Malcolm Browne, Neil Sheehan

communicating Vann's critique of America's strategy to Secretary of Defense Robert McNamara. It was an insider's success. After the Tet offensive of 1968, Ellsberg jumped ship to become a full-time peace advocate. In 1969, he began secretly duplicating the 7000-page study now known as *The Pentagon Papers*, deftly smuggling copies through security at the Rand Corporation. Finally, in 1971, as a dramatic act of conscience against Richard Nixon's Cambodian incursion, Ellsberg turned over the government study to reporter (and now narrator) Neil Sheehan, who then edited the document for serial publication in the *New York Times* and a subsequent book release. (Everyone present at the funeral knew that the Pentagon Papers trial was still ongoing.)

Many reviewers have been perplexed by the amount of space *A Bright Shining Lie* devotes to tensions within the Vann family itself, but Neil Sheehan was fascinated. Jesse Vann, age twenty-two, left half of his draft card on his father's coffin; he planned to present the other half to President Nixon during the Oval Office ceremony to follow. With some difficulty, the other children, Mrs. Vann, and Brent Scowcroft succeeded in convincing Jesse that the purpose of the day was to honor his father, not to embarrass the President of the United States. And while Jesse was angry about attempts by the American government to "deny him the freedom to live life as he wanted to live it" (26), Mary Jane Vann harbored her own bitterness because John Paul Vann would not receive the Congressional Medal of Honor.

Neil Sheehan was perfectly attuned to the many levels of tension at the Arlington cemetery. Sheehan met John Paul Vann in 1962 when, as a Lieutenant Colonel in the Army, Vann was serving as an advisor in the Mekong Delta of South Vietnam. Many details of the soldier's life mirrored aspects of the reporter's experience: an upbringing on the poor side of the tracks; a quick rise in status through education and profession (Vann through the Army and Sheehan through Harvard College and the profession of journalism); an impatience with authority; and a blind obsession with work. Also, Vann's dark side fascinated Sheehan. Vann's sexual compulsion stemmed from a deprived and abused childhood, driving Vann to exploit women in ways which repelled—yet, judged by the attention devoted to them—titillated Neil Sheehan. According to his chronicler, Vann's egotistical misuse of sexual power may have tainted his thinking on the subject of political power, especially after Tet 1968 when Vann joined Establishment figures such as Walt W. Rostow and W.C. Westmoreland, in celebrating the Pyrrhic "victory" of Tet. Whether or not such a connection is made convincingly, it is certainly true that Sheehan's detailed revelations about the seamy side of Vann's personal life discredited the hero of *BSLIE* by the time the narrative reaches Tet, 1968.

However mixed Sheehan's feelings toward John Paul Vann, the *New York Times* reporter could not elude the sense that Vann was a symbol of the entire American effort in Vietnam. From the day of the funeral in 1972 until the publication of *BSLIE* in 1989, Neil Sheehan would do apparently little else but ponder the significance of Vann as a Representative Man. Hours of interviews with family members, research trips to Norfolk, Virginia to examine the roots of the man, and months in a sterile carrel at the Library of Congress would lead to a manuscript of some 1150 pages whose sheer mass annoyed Random House editors. (With help from his wife, his editor Robert Loomis at Random House, and a brand-new word processor, Sheehan managed to whittle the text down to a mere 800 pages.) Sheehan's devotion to the project led to his being described by William Prochnau of the *Washington Post* as "The Last Prisoner of Vietnam," who monastically devoted "long nights on Klingle Street trying to figure out a war everyone else wanted to forget." The resulting work, *A Bright Shining Lie: John Paul Vann and America in Vietnam*, is certainly an exploration of the details of the man and a meditation on the roots of our Vietnam tragedy. But it is more.

The novelist Henry James would have understood Neil Sheehan's response at Arlington National Cemetery. James said on many occasions that his novels took their inspiration from such intuitive "germs" (a word James used without negative connotations, it refers to the growth center in a seed). Within *BSLIE*, the funeral of John Paul Vann is such a germinative experience. In speaking to *Publisher's Weekly* in 1989, Sheehan briefly described the revelation he would explore: "You could feel in that chapel that we were burying the mindset of what Henry Luce boastfully called 'the American century" (83). *A Bright Shining Lie* does, indeed, attempt to expose the mindset of the Cold War era through essays on American imperialism, insiders' views of the worlds of America's diplomatic and military establishments, and exposé vignettes about major historical figures such as Generals Douglas MacArthur, William C. Westmoreland, Paul Harkins, and Presidents Harry Truman, John F. Kennedy, and Lyndon B. Johnson. But Sheehan's book is less a narrative history and more a meditation on the pain inflicted on a trusting people after World War II by America's misguided military and political leaders. Quite a few of these same leaders were attending John Vann's funeral to appropriate him as a symbol for their crusade in Vietnam.

In writing his epic, Sheehan describes himself as "a newsman who got diverted into history and biography" (Steinberg 83). He is not forthcoming about the methodology which guided his work as historian and biographer, but the attentive reader can discern the outlines. In the prologue already described, a disproportionate amount of attention is given to the rebellious attitude of Vann's son Jesse. Sheehan implies that the disturbed young man has the right instincts. Like many defiant youths of the 1960s, Jesse is refusing to accept the official version of the distant war. When the coffin is escorted to the gravesite, the Army band plays Vann's favorite martial tune, "The Colonel Bogie March." Sheehan stresses that the next selection played is Mary Jane's favorite tune, "Where Have all the Flowers Gone?" — which is described by the omniscient narrator (through Mary Jane's mind) as "a song of the sadness she felt as a mother for all of the young men who had died in the war; it was the song of the ravaging of her son Jesse by the structure of authority that had made the war because he had opposed that authority and the war" (24). The images and words stray perilously close to the kind of pathos which Americans would expect to find in a "pilot" for a new television soap opera series. During the funeral, Sheehan further uses the power of an omniscient narrator to formulate some acerbic judgments—exploiting the perspective of Daniel Ellsberg. The point-of-view technique allows Sheehan, early in the narrative, to present criticism without appearing to endorse it directly.[2]

But little is said early in the epic about the new mindset, which will emerge from the fires of Vietnam. In some ways, John Paul Vann embodied the Henry Luce vision; his unquestioning support of the American Empire certainly put him in the Establishment camp. Yet Vann's lowly upbringing gave him sympathies for third world peoples. He serves Sheehan's *BSLIE* as a transitional figure who, though bound to the old politics and driven by a sexual machismo, helped younger and better educated journalists to break out of their Cold War husks. With Vann's help, Neil Sheehan, David Halberstam, Daniel Ellsberg, along with a few rare people in the Establishment—such as Victor Krulak, Frederick Weyand, and others—emerge from the Vietnam years chastened, but wiser. *A Bright Shining Lie* is more than an epic tale of ineptitude and decay; it also describes the painful birth of a new mindset and the shift of public power to a new, more socially responsible elite: our press. A close reading of *BSLIE* reveals that Neil Sheehan was not obsessed with the research project because of his fascination with Vann. Vann is only a stepping stone to a higher message, the celebration of the rise of a new class whose calling is to report on the misuses of power by America's traditional elites—the politicians and the brass hats. That Sheehan's efforts should receive the accolades of the Pulitzer Prize and the National Book Award Committees should come as no surprise. *A Bright Shining Lie* comforts American readers with the message that we emerged from the Vietnam tragedy with a new-won consciousness because the press gave the American people what it so desperately needs from its true leaders—the bright shining truth. John Paul Vann could only point his young disciples in the right direction; he could not join them in crossing over to the Promised Land.

I. The Mindset of the Old Elite

At the opening of *BSLIE*, Sheehan argues that, during the "American Century," a Northeastern elite established the dominant "standards of taste, morality, intellectual respectability for the rest of the country" (10). Theirs was the world of White, Anglo-Saxon Protestants (WASPS). Joseph Alsop, Dean Acheson, both Henry Cabot Lodges, the Woodrow Wilson who rejected Ho Chi Minh at the Versailles Conference, and the New Frontier advisors who helped John F. Kennedy and later intimidated Lyndon Johnson were all representatives of this mindset. Through its cultural hegemony, the old elite was successful in attracting the brightest scions of immigrant groups, yet often the young talent they enlisted brought with them a sense of frustration for their betrayal of their ethnic cultures. Sheehan points out that even President John F. Kennedy was willingly molded by the WASP system (297). Sheehan's colleague David Halberstam was more explicit in *The Best and the Brightest*, where he described Kennedy as carrying in him "the immigrant family's rage to get their due, but carefully concealed behind a cool and elegant facade" (98).

According to Sheehan's interpretation, the WASP elite was traditionally willing to use military power to further American interests abroad—both economic and cultural. Henry Cabot Lodge, Sr. spoke for the WASP culture as it began the "American Century" in 1898 by launching a war with Spain. Sheehan is not unpleased with the historical ironies involved when Henry Cabot Lodge, Jr. arrived at Saigon as the U.S. Ambassador to preside over the downfall of WASP hegemony (359).

WWII: *The Paradox of Victory*

After the war, America's ruling elite became complaisant and arrogant: World War II had been such a triumph of American resources, technology, and industrial and military genius, and the prosperity that the war and the postwar dominance abroad had brought had been so satisfying after the long hunger of the Depression, that American society had become a victim of its own achievement. The elite of America had become stupefied by too much money, too many material resources, too much power, and too much success (285).

The results of this success, Sheehan argues, were unhealthy, leading to intellectual inflexibility, a belief in force over intelligence, and—most tragically for Vietnam—an unwillingness to respond to the legitimate aspirations of third world nations.

At the diplomatic level, "the men who ran the American imperial system" looked for puppets who could "act as surrogates for American power" (130). Not interested in democracy or freedom, their goals were far simpler; they built an international network that would help American business. These "neocolonialists"—a group which Sheehan says included Dean Acheson, John Foster Dulles, and Harry Truman—saw Communism as a monolith in which "all

Communist movements were pawns of a centralized superstate directed from the Kremlin" (169). Ever blind to the aspirations of emerging nations, they were unable to even consider the possibility that the spirit of nationalism might be stronger than ideology: [3]

> If Tito and Ho and Mao Tse-tung were nationalists as well as communists, if differing cultures and histories might lead Communist nations to develop along distinct lines, then the world was far more complex than these American leaders imagined it to be. Their own inclinations were easier to follow in a simple Manichean world of Good and Evil. (169)

The establishment's Manichean outlook, Sheehan asserts, would prove to be disastrous in Korea and Vietnam.

Korea: A Precedent for Vietnam

Sheehan finds little to redeem America's role in the Korean War. Prior to the conflict, U.S. diplomats gave the Communists an impression that South Korea was not within America's strategic defensive perimeter. (The narrative appears to justify the North's cruel invasion of the South in June 25, 1950; his logic seems to be that military adventures are justified if they can be successful.) MacArthur's invasion of North Korea after pushing the enemy out of the South was the leadership's next error; in doing so, an egocentric commander "squandered the lives of the thousands of men who had died for the victory and the thousands more who would die in a defeat they did not deserve" (452). Some historians subscribe to a few of these criticisms, but Sheehan's contempt for MacArthur is unique. Even the landing at Inchon, a masterstroke for which even MacArthur's critics bow their heads in admiration, becomes an object of Sheehan's ridicule. Rather than a bold exploitation of the element of surprise, the amphibious assault was a "sign that MacArthur's egomania had grown beyond tolerable bounds" (454).

The overall impact of the errors in Korea set a dangerous precedent in the post-war era of rising expectations:

> The war in Korea was a prelude to the war in Vietnam. It was the first war in American history in which the leaders of the Army and the nation were so divorced from reality and

so grossly underestimated their opponent that they brought disaster to the Army and the nation. (452)

Through a frontlines narrative involving Ranger Lt. Ralph Puckett, Jr., Sheehan personalizes, in an effective microcosm, the details of suffering inflicted on ordinary men by careless leaders (453-4; 462-5). Although Puckett was proud of the fighting skills of his elite Rangers, he could do nothing to hold back the human Niagara of 300,000 Chinese troops who entered the Korean War after MacArthur foolishly advanced too close to China's borders. Vietnam would recapitulate the leadership problems—and the suffering—of Korea.

Vietnam: The Sad Fulfillment

General Paul Harkins was commander of the Military Assistance Group Vietnam (MACV) during Sheehan's first Vietnam tour, 1962-4. Harkins had been a protégé of General George Patton during World War II; he would later be advanced up the Army's chain of command, according to Sheehan, with patronage from Maxwell Taylor. (The "old boy" network helped WASPs to succeed rather than promoting those of merit.) Probably no figure other than Ngo Dinh Diem receives such vilification. First, Harkins is condemned

Gen Paul Harkins: A False Consciousness

as a pantywaist who shrinks from getting his shoes dirty in the field. Harkins "lacked curiosity about his war" and refused to be photographed with troops explaining to eager cameramen that "I'm not that kind of general" (284-5). For Sheehan, Harkins is the living embodiment of the Army's problems:

> By the second decade after World War II, the dominant characteristics of the senior leadership of the American armed forces had become professional arrogance, lack of imagination, and moral and intellectual insensitivity. These are the kinds of traits that cause otherwise intelligent men like Harkins to behave stupidly. (285)

The negative lesson of Korea reemerged in Vietnam as Harkins refused to recognize that guerilla warfare required special tactics. Harkins' successor, General William C. Westmoreland, would remake all of the same mistakes.

The American diplomats and generals—and, at the time, Neil Sheehan—did not understand the nature of the Communist Revolution in either half of Vietnam. The supposedly "diabolical" Ho Chi Minh was really only a nationalist with a long paper trail of appeals to America. During the Versailles conference after World War I, Ho took the proclamation of the Fourteen Points seriously, but was rebuffed when he attempted to visit President Wilson. In 1972, the *Pentagon Papers* revealed for the first time that Ho Chi Minh had written to President Truman after WWII, hoping the United States would live up to its reputation as "a champion of democracy" (147). In order to prove his egalitarian faith, Ho inserted quotes from Jefferson's classic state paper in his own declaration of independence. When the United States failed to recognize Ho, Sheehan explains, the desperate peasant reformer accepted assistance from the only other sources available to him, the Communists of China and the Soviet Union.[4]

The American Establishment also underestimated the intensity of Communist fervor. For centuries, the Vietnamese were forced to play the role of David against a series of Goliaths: in pre-modern eras, they fought the Chinese; later, Japanese and French invaders were defeated. In a revealing passage, Sheehan celebrates the tenacity of the little men who stand up to power:

> Ho Chi Minh and his disciples became Communists through an accident of French politics. They were mandarins, Vietnamese aristocrats, the natural leaders of a people whom foreigners have repeatedly sought and failed to conquer and pacify. There are a small number of such peoples on the earth. The Irish are one. The Vietnamese are another. The violence of their resistance forms history and legend to remind the living that they must never shame the dead. (155)[5]

Sheehan compares the Communist leaders to America's bourgeois revolutionaries (168). The overall message is that Ho is a nationalist who will fight to the last drop of blood for unification of his country. More important in terms of the forthcoming American involvement, he will not be a party to "limited war."

Meanwhile, General Paul Harkins carries on in ignorance of these Sheehanite "realities." On the political plane, the American Establishment has installed Ngo Dinh Diem, a puppet controlled by Major General Edward Lansdale to assure American policy is carried out (143). A Catholic, and therefore a member of "a tainted minority," Diem is compared to a Tory in the American Revolution; everyone knows he is a traitor to the true cause of his country (168). In his research, Sheehan came across evidence which gave rise to what might be called "the Sheehan Thesis": the second Indochina war began in the South in angry response to Diem's vicious "Denunciation of Communism" campaign in 1959. Leaders in the North instructed Southern cadres to remain inactive until Chairman Ho consolidated the gains of revolution, but, in defiance of Party instructions, Southerners rose up in wrath when America's puppet government (184-98) attacked their lives and property. In other words, the "Sheehan Thesis" asserts that it is really America which initiated the war in its blundering ignorance, proving conclusively that "the Americans knew neither the Vietnamese they were depending on to work their will, nor the Vietnamese enemy they faced" (198).

During the commands of Generals Harkins and Westmoreland,

military strategy was based on anachronistic principles. A strategy of attrition was developed during World War II with the notion that it was better to over-expend artillery and bombs than to risk the lives of America's citizen-soldiers. In a conventional war with clear boundaries for the battlefield, such a strategy made sense, but the strategy of attrition was totally inappropriate for counterinsurgency operations. Neither Harkins nor Westmoreland ever learned this lesson, despite the frequent—albeit abortive—attempts by John Paul Vann to educate them. This kind of blindness is exemplified in General Harkins' reaction to the battlefield defeat at Ap Bac. For a young reporter named Neil Sheehan, the response produced a shock of recognition:

> There was something obscene about all of this to me and the other reporters.... An American general with a swagger stick and a cigarette holder, whose four stars on his collar tabs said that he commanded the fighter-bombers and helicopters and the flow of arms and ammunition that made this battle and this war possible, but who would not deign to soil his suntans and street shoes in a rice paddy to find out what was going on, was prattling about having trapped the Viet Cong. (276)

Westmoreland was equally blind to the limits of the strategy of attrition. Since it had worked in Europe, he thought, it should work in Asia. As a man "of limited imagination," Westmoreland played "blindly to strength, no matter what its relevance to the problem" (558). An example of the logical outcome of such misuse of force in a guerilla war was the My Lai Massacre, an event which Sheehan describes as an "inevitable" outcome of a strategy obsessed with body counts (689).[6]

Ever blundering, Westmoreland would be fooled by the Vietnamese during the Tet offensive of 1968. As a ruse, Communist generals attracted American forces to the Demilitarized Zone (DMZ) in a series of bloody confrontations which played to NVA strengths while drawing allied troops away from population centers (638). Khe Sanh, where Westmoreland committed a Marine regiment plus massive supporting forces of air, artillery, and infantry, was "the biggest lure of the war" and, by Sheehan's lights, a "masterstroke of Tet" (710-11). When Vietcong attacks hit most of South Vietnam's major cities, to include Saigon and Hue, Sheehan claims that Westmoreland was totally surprised. American troops were elsewhere. The tenacity with which Westmoreland clung to his theory that Khe Sanh would be the major battle of Tet—even as the attacks on the cities continued—was a nightmarish repeat of MacArthur's rush to the Yalu in 1950, "but on a scale magnified many times by the extravagance of the failure in Vietnam" (717).

In this lumbering stupidity, Sheehan found Westmoreland to be a model of the establishment mentality:

> It has been a historic characteristic of generals like Westmoreland that whatever they are given—keen soldiers, innovative weapons, timely intelligence, discerning counsel, published primers on an opponent's strategy—they will waste. They expect their enemies to behave stupidly and they perceive their own behavior as farsighted generalship. (692)

Just as MacArthur wasted the efforts of Lieutenant Ralph Puckett, Jr. and his elite Ranger troops in Korea, so Westmoreland expended the lives of the men caught at the encircled combat base at Khe Sanh. The massive psychological victory of Tet in the minds of Americans was the result of Vietnam's "realities" finally hitting home—thanks to the efforts of a press, which had, at last, defined an adversarial stance for itself.[7]

II. The Press: A New Elite Represents the Public Interest

While *BSLIE* is explicit in its description of the establishment mindset, the manner in which Sheehan evokes a countervailing perspective is less direct. Prior to the traumatic Battle of Ap Bac in early January, 1963, members of the American press were New Frontier patriots who supported the policies of anti-Communist liberalism:

> The reporters of the period were not accustomed to thinking of their military leaders and diplomats as deluded men, and

Neil Sheehan's *Bright Shining Lie* 523

the military leaders and diplomats were not accustomed to reporters who said that they were consistently wrong. (315)

The press began to change its attitude after the allied defeat at Ap Bac. For the awakened journalists, the inept defeat of some of the South's best troops dramatized the vast disparity "between what we saw and what authority saw" (316). Mindless press support of foreign policy in the Vietnam setting was no longer in the national interest after this moment of illumination; playing along with the government and military leaders only "concealed the fact that the system was no longer rational" (315).

Many reviewers of *BSLIE* are impatient with the descriptive detail of the Ap Bac segment of the book, even though the depiction of the battle in Book III is some of Sheehan's best writing—probably because he concentrates on telling a story in a journalistic way rather than pondering heavy matters of policy and psychology. The Ap Bac segment serves some of the same functions as the battle scenes in Henry Adams' *History of the United States During the Administrations of Jefferson and Madison (1889-91)*. In an overview of war and public policy decision making, particular battles bring home the human experience of conflict—with its pain, defeat, but also its glory and heroism. (In *History*, Adams celebrates the exploits of American heroes like John Paul Jones; Sheehan's most important hero at Ap Bac is a Vietcong squad leader named Dung who "accomplished the impossible" by showing that revolutionary fervor can stop American machines from destroying the Vietnamese garden [257].) In filmmaking, the Ap Bac segment would be described as a "breakout" section which refreshes an audience before plunging back into the claustral meditation which takes up so many pages of *BSLIE*.

Within *BSLIE*, Ap Bac also functions as an empirical laboratory for the young reporters. Up until that point, Neil Sheehan, David Halberstam, and the press corps were tuned in to the Establishment message:

The American reporters shared the advisors' sense of commitment to this war. Our ideological prism and cultural biases were in no way different. We regarded the conflict as our war too. We believed in what our government said it was trying to accomplish in Vietnam, and we wanted our country to win this war just as passionately as Vann and his captains did. (271)

Ap Bac transformed everyone involved, including the Communists. In the aftermath, John Paul Vann launched his crusade to expose the errors of America's strategy; Sheehan and Halberstam realized that they must become adversaries of America's military and political leaders. On the other side of the conflict, success at Ap Bac convinced the Vietcong to wage a more aggressive war against America and its pusillanimous ally, the Republic of South Vietnam. While Ap Bac may at first be welcomed by some readers as a refreshing diversion from the passages of the book, the chapter is absolutely pivotal rhetorically. Then young members of the press corps became, in Sheehan's hindsight, adversarial journalists based on empirical fact, not as a matter of preconceived ideology. At this initial stage of their conversion process, John Paul Vann served as an unexpected guide. His spontaneous after-action analysis, filled with denunciations of the top brass, clothed each young writer in a "mental flak jacket."

David Halberstam: Vann Educates A Reporter
David Halberstam, who served in Vietnam with Sheehan, is depicted in *BSLIE* as an avatar of the new consciousness. Like Sheehan and Ellsberg, Halberstam was a Harvard graduate; more importantly, he, like his fellow journalists, did not feel entirely comfortable with the Establishment. This quality of alienation brought John Paul Vann and Halberstam together.

They were both outsiders with ambivalent yearnings to serve (318). Yet just below the surface of each man was a resentment toward the status quo, an emotion which would fuel their complaints after the Battle of Ap Bac. Vann decided to give Halberstam news leaks because the *New York Times* reached most of the power players in the Kennedy administration and because Halberstam was famous for his mental combativeness" (319). Halberstam believed that a good reporter should have "a jugular instinct" and often salted his prose with military similes and metaphors. (In 1972, his book, entitled *The Best and the Brightest*, would show the depths of his contempt for the Eastern Establishment which had educated him.) In 1962, he focused on the failure of the Diem regime to win the hearts and minds of its people.[8] Like Sheehan, Halberstam was frustrated and angry after the Battle of Ap Bac. But, while Vann used Halberstam, Halberstam used Vann to vent his rage at the stupidity of the Military Assistance Command-Vietnam (MACV).

At a French restaurant in the summer of 1963, Halberstam pounded on the dinner table and shouted, "Paul D. Harkins should be court-martialed and shot!" (351). A foreign service officer joining the correspondents for dinner worried at the time that he might be connected with the outburst. Halberstam's articles over the next year were to have a momentous influence on policy makers in Washington, but Sheehan claims that the reporters in Saigon never consciously aimed their journalistic spears in that direction. According to *BSLIE*, Halberstam and Sheehan were merely describing disturbing "realities" official Washington would never hear about through official channels.

Ap Bac had proven to them that they must speak out. Halberstam reported that intelligence figures concerning enemy casualties were being faked, and that General Harkins was too solicitous toward the Diems and not sufficiently concerned about winning the war. After Ap Bac, Sheehan, Halberstam, and Malcolm Browne (of the Associated Press) devoted their energies to "the Buddhist Crisis" of May 1963, exploiting a series of immolations and riots to dramatize the insensitivity and incompetence of the Diem family. Throughout the critical days before the overthrow of Diem in the fall of 1963, Halberstam credited John Paul Vann with opening their eyes: "it is almost impossible to kid us now...we have the mental flak jackets you gave us" (342-3). (At least at this early stage of the Vietnam War, when he agreed with Sheehan and Halberstam, Vann enjoys hero billing in *BSLIE*.)

The Halberstam exposé did not go unchallenged. Toward the end of October, President Kennedy asked A.O. Sulzberger, publisher of the *Times*, if his young reporter was not "too close to the story" in Saigon. (Halberstam was twenty-nine.) A seasoned reporter, Marguerite Higgins, flew to Saigon and reported that the crisis was in no way linked to religious persecution—as Halberstam had claimed—and that a few strategically placed reporters "would like to see us lose the war to prove they're right" (347). Joseph Alsop urged that thinking Americans ignore the "reportorial crusade" (348). Even within the *New York Times* there were concerns that the adversarial stance might backfire as it had in Cuba where *Times* reporter Herbert Matthews had mistakenly praised Fidel Castro as a nationalist seeking only to better life in his country. Sheehan, perhaps for these background reasons, strives hard in his narrative to credit the downfall of the Diems to their bizarre repressive tactics and to the negative influence of America's patrician on the scene, Ambassador Henry Cabot Lodge, Jr.

On the other hand, Sheehan acknowledges, in retrospect, that Halberstam's articles may have been influential: "We did not realize that our dispatches had been arming Averell Harriman...and Roger Hilsman in their attempt to persuade Kennedy to authorize the overthrow of Diem and his family" (359). (Unfortunately, Sheehan does not elaborate on the process of influence; for example, during critical moments in the Vietnam conflict, did members of the Kennedy and Johnson administrations—to include Roger Hilsman, Clark Clifford, and Harry McPherson—rely exclusively on the *Times* while neglecting to compare press reports with government intelligence?) Halberstam, by Sheehan's own characterization, was a "hero-villain style of journalist"; in the critical reports of 1963, Halberstam painted the Diem family and General Paul Harkins as blackguards. Sheehan's narrative, as in so many other places—follows Halberstam's lead.

The manner in which Halberstam (in 1963-5) and Sheehan (in 1988) tout the virtues of John Paul Vann reveals much about their own attitudes toward America's presence in Vietnam. In *Esquire* magazine, November 1964, Halberstam eulogized Vann as "a David who had stood up to the Goliath" of the Establishment (384). The article grew into a book entitled *The Making of a Quagmire* (1965), a work which very closely anticipates the first half of *BSLIE*. Halberstam's praise for Vann mirrored the stance which Sheehan and Browne had taken toward the Establishment. At one point in the longer work, Halberstam reflects on the criticism, which the young reporters were receiving:

One of the ironies of Vietnam was that at a time when elements unhappy with our reporting were claiming privately that the foreign correspondents in the country were a bunch of liberals who opposed Diem on ideological grounds, much of our information came from men like Vann. (164)

In many ways, this statement by Halberstam in 1965 provided a blueprint for the persuasive strategy of the first four books of *BSLIE* and reaffirms Vann's importance to Sheehan's analysis—that the press's reactions to developments in Vietnam were not the result of preconceptions brought to the story.

John Paul Vann: An Outsider Playing Insider

John Paul Vann, as presented by Neil Sheehan, is the quintessential outsider. He was the neglected baby of a narcissistic mother who supplemented her income with prostitution. John and the other children in the family saw no turkey at Thanksgiving and no tree at Christmas (406-7). Myrtle Vann frequently taunted her son about his illegitimacy. The combination of family and personal suffering was to leave permanent scars on Vann. He was aggressively ambitious: "He could not stand being relegated to Number Two. He had to be on the scramble to be Number One" (386). Vann's emotional drives were intensified by the sexual humiliation he experienced, leading him to become "a ferocious heterosexual" constantly involved

Vann: Civilian with a Military Mission

in one or more liaisons outside his marriage. In Vietnam, where opportunities were numerous, Vann sometimes enjoyed sex with three different women in a day while maintaining a breakneck pace at his job. Both Vann's ambition and his sexuality were fueled by his intense feeling of being "an outcast" (386).

Perhaps because of his sense of personal worthlessness, Paul Vann was redeemed by professional accomplishments as an Army officer: "The most important thing he had learned was that he was a different person in this uniform. When he had this uniform on he wasn't little Johnny Vann or LeGay or what's-his-name, the bastard kid of that good-timer Myrtle down at the end of the bar" (434). In Korea, he won recognition for his administrative abilities, but his aerial resupply efforts to troops at beleaguered hilltops—truly spectacular feats of personal heroism—went unnoticed by commanders in the heat of combat. Korea, his first war, taught him that he was a competent professional who could "end run" any bureaucracy. At least in memory, the airdrops became a model for what could be done by an energetic individual willing to "take on the system." In Vietnam, after the Battle of Ap Bac, Vann tried these tactics first in prolix after-action reports. Once he returned to the U.S., Vann carried on his crusade through elaborate briefings at the Pentagon to anyone who would listen. But his efforts failed in the end; the bureaucratic inertia of 1960s America won out over the insights of a feisty outsider.

David Halberstam's article and book celebrated Vann as a paladin fighting for truth. The press corps thought so highly of Vann that reporters presented him with an engraved cigarette lighter at the close of his first tour in 1963: "We decided he was deliberately sacrificing his career in order to alert the nation to the danger of defeat in this war" (323). It is difficult to stress enough the emphasis Sheehan's *BSLIE* places on Vann as an individual with the answer to America's Vietnam challenge. He is the lonely crusader in conflict with a decadent system. It is a system administered by men such as Harkins and Westmoreland. It is a system in which truth and insight are political matters to be advanced on the basis of patronage and power rather than on their correspondence to "reality." It is the system which locked up Ho Chi Minh's letters to Harry Truman in 1945, shelved Vann's revealing after-action report on the Battle of

Ap Bac, and prevented Vann, at the very last moment, from delivering his polished briefing to the Joint Chiefs of Staff (339). (Sheehan is so fascinated with the aborted JCS briefing that he reconstructs its arguments at length in a "what if..." mode [339-40].) The lesson of Vann's first attempt to take on the system would be underscored again in 1972 after the victory of Kontum: no matter what a resourceful individual might try to do to influence the action, he will be undercut, betrayed—even destroyed—by callous leaders at the top of the ladder. That was the lesson of Ralph Puckett's tragic experience in Korea when MacArthur wasted a good man and his Rangers. Ultimately, it was the lesson of John Paul Vann: although he was exhilarated with the sense that he had helped America to turn the tide after the 1972 battle of Kontum, in truth, his efforts only delayed an inevitable debacle. Far from Vietnam, Henry Kissinger and Richard Nixon would sell out the entire crusade in the 1973 Paris Accords.

Daniel Ellsberg: An Insider Forced to be an Outsider
Daniel Ellsberg was an important person in Neil Sheehan's life. During the spring of 1971, Ellsberg saw a book review by Sheehan in the *New York Times* and decided to release to the reporter the Rand Corporation's forty-seven-volume history of American involvement in Vietnam. It was a high moment in Sheehan's career and almost led to a Pulitzer Prize. (The prize for *The Pentagon Papers* coup was

Daniel Ellsberg and his Pentagon Papers

conferred to the *Times* as an institution rather than to Sheehan as an individual; characteristically, Sheehan was embittered by the prize committee's cold bureaucratic decision.) Shortly after the *Pentagon Papers* project, Sheehan attended the funeral which opens *BSLIE*. The ceremony launched his sixteen-year obsession with John Paul Vann as a microcosm of America's failure in Vietnam. It is not surprising, therefore, that Ellsberg should be a potent force in *BSLIE*; in fact, he is a role model for a moral individual in an oppressive society. After exploring every option within the system, Ellsberg broke outside to an institution which, during the 1960s, was forced to become the voice of the people.

From the beginning, Sheehan privileged Ellsberg. Many of the judgments of the Establishment personalities during Vann's funeral are through Ellsberg's eyes. Whereas John Paul Vann is eulogized as the great Vietnam hero, Ellsberg is described as a "turncoat knight of the crusade" (12). Staring at Vann's coffin, Ellsberg reflects on the evening he went to see Vann, but ended up talking to Sheehan all night about the xeroxed cache of secret studies in his possession, a collection to later become known as the Pentagon Papers (26). But before the desperation of 1971, Ellsberg had striven to be a loyal insider.

Daniel Ellsberg arrived at Harvard six years ahead of Sheehan. Unlike the journalist, he distinguished himself academically, rating a highly coveted seat among the Society of Fellows after a two-year tour as an officer in the Marine Corps. In 1959, Ellsberg went to work for the Rand Corporation, where he made the discovery that the supposed Soviet "missile gap" was really "a fable" (592), a product of what he would label the "mad dog mentality" at the Pentagon. His incisiveness—not to mention the cachet of Harvard credentials within the Kennedy administration—won him a job in Washington at what Sheehan glowingly describes as "the super-grade' rank of a GS-18" (592). In those days of the New Frontier, Ellsberg was an enthusiastic "insider" eager for power, but very distrustful of the military. During a trip to Vietnam in 1965 as part of Edward Lansdale's mission, Ellsberg met a new mentor, John Paul Vann.

Vann took time to explain to Ellsberg how America was losing the war; he also argued that pacification was the key to success.

Ellsberg was quickly won over and became yet another Vann disciple. In 1966, Ellsberg was able to preach the gospel to Robert McNamara and John McNaughton by ambushing the two DOD officials during a long flight to Vietnam. Ellsberg's two-hundred-page report emulated Vann's approach. It stressed the importance of pacification and called into question Secretary McNamara's faith in Westmoreland's attrition strategy. Once started, McNamara's doubts became an avalanche; the fact that he soon thereafter commissioned the *Pentagon Papers* was an indication of his wavering faith. McNamara would become a "haunted man" who was "ashamed of what he saw as his failure at the most important task of his life" (685). These doubts had been planted by Ellsberg, an insider who later described the 1966 flight to Vietnam aboard the "McNamara Special" as "'the height of my bureaucratic career'" (681).

In May of 1967, McNamara sent President Lyndon Johnson an official memorandum in which he told the commander-in-chief that he could not win the war and that he should negotiate a peace as soon as possible. The North Vietnamese Communists were simply not going to fight a limited war and the "cross-over point" so pivotal to Westmoreland's attrition strategy—the threshold where the allies would be killing the enemy faster than replacements could be supplied—would never be reached. Unfortunately, the only demonstrable result of the memo was the "promotion" of McNamara to the World Bank in November 1967. It was a clear case of being kicked upstairs by a President who put little credence in the advice of a man he described as an "'emotional basket case"(692). Ellsberg's bureaucratic success was thereby nullified. The war continued. Ellsberg tried every ploy within the bureaucracy to get Vann's message across, but no one was ready to listen. Westmoreland continued to stress attrition over pacification; indeed, he forced the Marine Corps in the Northern provinces to reduce pacification efforts in order to log in more "battalion days in the field" (636). Even General Victor Krulak, who eventually obtained an hour of President Johnson's time, was unable to win the government over to an acceptable mix of political and military action. While it was true that Johnson sent out Robert Komer to win "hearts and minds," the administration still thought of such activities as "the other war."

Westmoreland never made an effort to foster an effective partnership between the military and civilian elements of his command. In fact, the creation of Komer's agency was a relief to Westmoreland because it allowed him to "get on with his big-unit war and leave the [pacification] problem to Komer" (657). According to Sheehan, Ellsberg began to realize that the only option was to drop out of America's self-defeating Establishment.

When the Tet offensive erupted in late January, 1968, so did Ellsberg's moral outrage (725). *The Pentagon Papers* had convinced at least one GS-18 that "the American cause in Indochina was now and had always been wrong-headed and futile" (739). After articles, letters, and interviews proved fruitless, Ellsberg gave a copy of *The Pentagon Papers* to Senator William Fulbright. Finally, with Nixon's invasion of Cambodia, Ellsberg's frustration reached a breaking point; he turned another copy of the forty-seven volumes of material over to Neil Sheehan of *The New York Times*, hoping that the "truth that had changed me could help Americans to free themselves and other victims from a useless war" (739). His act of conscience led to painful results. Ellsberg became a lightning rod of controversy: his telephone was tapped; his former psychiatrist's files were burglarized. (Curiously, amateur psychologist Sheehan never thinks to draw back the curtain obscuring Ellsberg's notorious history of sexual excess and experimentation; if Vann's peccadilloes are relevant to an understanding of his ideas, why is Ellsberg's kinkier story left uninvestigated?) Even his mentor, John Paul Vann, betrayed him by secretly passing on information to the White House concerning defense strategies for the upcoming trial.

Not long after the publication of *The Pentagon Papers*, Ellsberg and Sheehan attended Vann's funeral. The Henry James moment was fraught with meaning. Vann was crushed by history while they survived—not only in the obvious sense of mere existence, but in terms of their collective role as guardians of American society. By publishing the *Pentagon Papers*, they felt that they had performed a heroic public service. Indeed, the lesson of *A Bright Shining Lie: John Paul Vann and America in Vietnam* is that the intellectual, now that the American century is over, has a special role—to work outside the system in order to protect the American people from inept traditional elites. During the 1940s, public service by intellectuals made sense because America was involved in a noble cause as Stalin's ally in the fight against Fascism. Later, in the Harvard of the 1950s, service in the name of power was further enhanced by the notable successes of professors on campus: "ambitious intellectuals were beginning to see scholarship as a road to high office in the new American state" (590). The two phases of Daniel Ellsberg's career were evidence of how things had changed: Ellsberg was a member of the Society of Fellows, but he had also acquired an Expert Badge with the pistol "from both right and left hand" (591). When he became a GS-18, he was very near the top of the Establishment's ladder.

Vietnam turned out to be a faulty chord in Ellsberg's perfectly orchestrated ascent because the war exposed the limitations of the post-war mindset. The values of the Northeast, perhaps most especially of Harvard, led inexorably to a condescending and manipulative stance toward the world; success in World War II led to spiritual rot. America's corrupt leadership somehow avoided detection in spite of the military debacles in Korea, but they could not escape the results of stupidity in Vietnam. In this torpid system, truth apparently could not move through channels to decisions makers; furthermore, when it did reach the appropriate leaders, their post-war complacency or their rabid anti-Communism prevented them from responding. The career of John Paul Vann had proved that gutsy, energetic, and brave men could be used by the Establishment to serve its ends; but it also proved that, in order to save the nation, intellectuals must remain outside as adversaries of the Establishment.[10]

Conclusion

Neil Sheehan's persuasive strategy in *A Bright Shining Lie* hinges on his portrayal of John Paul Vann. Vann was a paradox. He represented the best of what the Establishment mind had to offer: "He manifested the faith and the optimism of post-World War II America that any challenge could be overcome by will and by the disciplined application of intellect, technology, money, and, when necessary, armed force" (5). The first half of *BSLIE* inflates its protagonist to heroic proportions; when Vann receives his engraved cigarette lighter in 1963, he is the admired mentor of young reporters like Sheehan and Halberstam. From Book Five to the conclusion, *BSLIE* punctures Vann's image—initially on the basis of his abuse of women and then, after Tet, because he misreads the obvious lesson of the debacle. Meanwhile, reporters like Sheehan turned against their country's ruling elite—not because of their contempt for American society and its values and not due to ideological factors, and certainly not because of an overwhelming hatred of an entrenched status quo. John Paul Vann, one of the best professionals produced by the Establishment, led the journalists to their perceptions. Once Vann removed the blinders, however, the press corps would never be the same: "the generation of the 1950s was the first generation of Americans to go so naively into the world. It was destined to lose its innocence in the war and be forced to grapple with the consequences of disillusionment" (320). As a sixteen-year-long attempt at historical meditation, *A Bright Shining Lie* explores how the Vietnam experience passed the scepter of power from the traditional elite of Henry Cabot Lodge, Jr., to a now disabused meritocratic elite which includes David Halberstam, Daniel Ellsberg, and Neil Sheehan.

The reader who focuses on the story of John Paul Vann misses the message of *BSLIE*—for it is the impact of the historical experiences and the impact of Vann's story on the narrator, which matters, not the history or the biography. There are interesting parallels in this regard between the work of David Halberstam and Neil Sheehan. Halberstam's *The Making of a Quagmire* (1965) covers the same territory we found in the first four books of *BSLIE*. Sheehan's attack on the Northeastern intellectual establishment is more than matched by Halberstam's devastating sketches of McGeorge Bundy (Yale '40), Walt Whitman Rostow (Yale '36), and others in *The Best and the Brightest* (1972).[11] In fact, the only element of *BSLIE* not to be found in Halberstam's preceding volumes is the detailed portrait of Vann, the result of Sheehan's painstaking investigative research. (Vann does appear in both Halberstam volumes, but only the heroic Vann of *BSLIE*'s first four books.) Someone with more psychological insight than this historian will one day explain Sheehan's obsession with the lurid details of this underdog's personal life, especially his sex life. Focusing strictly at the ideological level, one realizes that

Vann is an important figure for Sheehan because his story proves that the American press was led to its initial alienation and then to its defiance of the Establishment by facts—clear, irreducible facts. What Sheehan does not explore is the manifest intensity of his own hatred for all hierarchies, which do not immediately reward ambitious overachievers like John Paul Vann—and Neil Sheehan.

Always a more aggressive analyst, Sheehan's friend and colleague, David Halberstam (a two-time Pulitzer Prize winner), would document in lavish detail the radical shift in power from government to the press in his book *The Powers That Be* (1979). The lessons about power in the media age are explicit in his description of the impact of Walter Cronkite's dramatic February 27, 1968 special television broadcast after the Tet offensive: "it was the first time in American history a war had been declared over by an anchorman" (514).

While *BSLIE* is a would-be meditation on history, it is also a work of denial. Neil Sheehan uses his central figure John Paul Vann as a vehicle for explaining how reluctant the American press was about turning against the post-war Establishment. Power simply had to be shifted to the press so that the true national interest could be understood and followed. Bureaucratic machines ground up good men like John Paul Vann. Fortunately, factual-minded members of the press will be on the scene to save America—especially its helpless little people-from the abuses of power by political and military elites. *A Bright Shining Lie* comes to the conclusion that the American press, with the help of a few renegade intellectuals, actually saved the United States from even worse consequences of the Vietnam fiasco. Chastened by the tragedy of their failed Indochina war, Americans will be more receptive to such adversarial voices in the future.

Notes

1. Vann's traumatic childhood fills Book Five in excruciating detail. Later, in Book Seven, Sheehan traces how Vann's will-to-power colored his appraisal of the Tet offensive. *BSLIE* takes the position—both implicit in its structure and explicitly by overt statement—that Vann is a virtuous person while he fights with Neil Sheehan and David Halberstam against a slothful Establishment; in contrast, when Vann agrees with the Pentagon and the Nixon White House, he becomes a pariah.

2. Prior to the publication of *BSLIE* in 1988, Neil Sheehan was a trusted friend of the Vann family; indeed, he was one of the executors of Vann's literary estate. In this capacity of friend and confidante in 1972, Sheehan helped Mrs. Vann to plan the richly symbolic funeral. With Mary Jane, he selected the participants to be invited, the music to be played, and other important details of the Arlington ceremony. In doing so, was Sheehan designing an evocative opening of his history?

3. *BSLIE*'s interpretation of post-war developments is clearly indebted to the work of William Appleton William, Walter LaFeber, and others of what is known as the "Wisconsin School" of diplomatic history. LaFeber is given a grateful thanks for his help (805). In this segment of *BSLIE*, as in many others, journalist Sheehan comes painfully close to plagiarizing the ideas of others. For example, this chapter is clearly indebted to book-length efforts by Williams and LaFeber, but only a minor article by LaFeber is cited. Sheehan's writing is best when it comes to piling up a series of telling details; he clearly has trouble with the big picture and falls back on historians for help. There is nothing wrong with such a strategy, but intellectual indebtedness should be clearly and accurately stated. (Criticism of the "Wisconsin School" is abundant: see articles by Unger and Schlesinger, Jr. and a book by Maddox.)

When national prize committees consider books for recognition, should they not ponder such lapses? Anyone who has spent the many hours needed to read *BSLIE* can identify patches of interpretation from a variety of sources. Within these parameters supplied by others, Sheehan paints memorable portraits of individuals and narrates compelling stories. Still, he is often dependent upon the work of others for the broad strokes of his interpretations. Throughout the text, a close reader of *BSLIE* can see Sheehan following the paper trail of his friend and colleague David Halberstam on the subjects of Vann, Vietnam, and American society. Should a powerful, but derivative, book be awarded the likes of a Pulitzer Prize or a National Book Award?

4. Phillip Davidson characterizes this portrait of Ho Chi Minh as one of seven popular "myths" of the Vietnam War (123-5). Davidson asserts

that Ho's "denial of his Communist background and concepts were designed to win American aid when only the United States could help him. His actions, his key associates, and his experience all indicate that Ho's real desire for Indochina was not just independence from France, but a Communist bastion in Southeast Asia" (125). My documentary entitled *Television's Vietnam: The Real Story* (1985) addresses this issue and shares Davidson's conclusion based on testimony by diplomats and historians. Believers in the myth conveniently forget that Ho Chi Minh was one of the most vociferous critics of Tito for the Yugoslavian's betrayal of the international Communist movement. (William Stearman of Georgetown University discusses the Ho-Tito relationship in *Television's Vietnam*.)

5. Neil Sheehan's parents emigrated to the United States from Ireland in the early 1930s. He grew up in the working class section of Holyoke, Massachusetts, and attended Harvard College on a scholarship. Interviewers report that they hear an Irish brogue when they talk with the author. Does the empathy expressed here color Sheehan's ability to evaluate the conflicting claims for legitimacy in Vietnam?

6. General William C. Westmoreland has been kind enough to read this paper in two versions, offering observations about Sheehan's argument as summarized on the latter few pages under the rubric "Vietnam: the Fulfillment." From his earliest days in country, Westmoreland had advocated that pacification be placed under military control rather than being farmed out piecemeal to AID, the CIA, and other agencies. For background lessons learned, Harkins and Westmoreland even flew to Malaysia where the British had conducted successful pacification efforts; when they returned, Westmoreland urged Ambassador Lodge to make him the "Executive Agent for Pacification." During May of 1964, Lodge went back into domestic politics, to participate in the New Hampshire primary election, before the suggested reorganization could take place. In fact, it was not until after Guam Conference in May 1967—when Robert Komer was assigned to the task—that pacification efforts were finally coordinated in a manner suggested by Westmoreland almost three years earlier. Thus, contrary to Sheehan's account, Westmoreland remembers himself to be one of the first to be sensitive to both the "hearts and minds issue and the way to address it effectively."

Westmoreland stands firm on his campaign strategy. Even after the war, he believed that the Vietcong were decimated 1966; after that time they were "merely a nuisance." Because he considered the real threat to come from regular forces—who could attack from any point of surprise along a 500-mile border with Cambodia—Westmoreland tried to keep his American troops mobile; from points of concentration, they could be flown head-to-head with conventional forces and then attrite them. Westmoreland conceded that he did not "fight for land," but prided himself on this decision given the limited number of troops available to him and the large area of responsibility. Westmoreland shrewdly points out that John Paul Vann was killed, in the end, by regular forces—and not guerrillas—after winning a conventional battle. This bald fact, according to Westmoreland, refutes Sheehan's message that Vietnam was fundamentally a counter guerrilla war. Harry Summers agreed with Westmoreland analysis, although Summers stressed that the debate should not be between the two concepts so much a complementary balance between pacification activities and conventional operations. In *BSLIE*, Sheehan presses the issue in a simplistic, either/or fashion.

In 1965, when Vann returned to Vietnam to work on pacification, he began to urge the government—his friends in the press—to consider some kind of Korean War-style takeover of command by the United States. Halberstam and Sheehan—at the time and later—liked the idea; *BSLIE* touts the wisdom of the concept. Westmoreland affirms that he opposed the idea and finally told Vann to stop talking with members of the press about it. Westmoreland felt that this French-style authoritarian leadership would be "a disaster, both practically and psychologically." The general's goal was to help the ARVN to its feet so that the final phase—America withdrawal—could take place. (As early as the fall of 1967, Westmoreland explained these goals in a speech to National Press Club.)

7. For another interpretation of the military aspects of the Tet offensive of 1968, see Phillip Davidson, *Secrets of the Vietnam War*. In his classic study of media distortion entitled *Big Story* (1983), Peter Braestrup takes argued that the putative "realities" reported during Tet were more often a combination of misinterpretation and exaggeration. Braestrup shared Davidson's conclusion that the South Vietnamese and their U.S. ally destroyed the Vietcong during Tet to the point where it never came back as a military threat. My documentary entitled *Television's Vietnam: The Impact of Media* (1986) takes a similar position. In one of the best books on Tet, Don Oberdorfer's concludes that the American press helped the Communists to win a massive psychological victory in the United States while, paradoxically, the Communists actually suffered a stunning military defeat on the battlefield. Recent books on the subject have attempted to deny these conclusions; see, for example, Daniel Hall's *Uncensored War* (1986). Sheehan ignores the controversy, maintaining that the jig was up in 1963 after Battle of Ap Bac; the only concern thereafter was getting the message of disaster across to the American people and national policy makers. In this scheme, Tet was a welcomed "streetcar" for the story of failure and disaster in Vietnam.

8. Neither Sheehan nor Halberstam speaks Vietnamese, so it must be

concluded that the young reporter relied on the talents of others concerning local public opinion. In *Flashbacks* (1990), Morley Safer reports that one "reliable source" in Vietnam, a *Time* magazine employee named Phan Xuan An, was a Colonel in the Vietcong while serving as a trusted guide for reporters: "His beat was Vietnamese politics and military affairs. He was among the best-connected journalists in the country. At *Time* he was considered a sage. It was always An who would brief new correspondents; it was An, who even the competition sought when trying to unravel the hopelessly complicated threads of Vietnamese political loyalties" (239). Lacking language competence, did young reporters Halberstam and Sheehan go to the likes of An for insight?

9. Few people would notice this detail, but—as a former Marine—it gives me pause. The Marine Corps has no such qualification with the pistol and there would be no written record of a "two-handed" qualification. Anyone who has fired the Colt .45 knows that scoring high enough to deserve an Expert Badge is sufficient accomplishment for anyone's credentials as a "man of action." Why does Sheehan include such inventions as the two-handed qualification? Is this an attempt to elevate his insider to hero status? How many such exaggerated accomplishments are there in *BSLIE*?

10. This historian comes away from *BSLIE* still curious about Sheehan's intellectual indebtedness. During his undergraduate years at Harvard, was he overly impressed by the writings of Columbia sociologist C. Wright Mills? Are these simplistic notions of a "power elite" derived from sources supplied by helpful revisionist historians like Professor LaFeber? Or is this portrait of American society part of the conventional wisdom at *New York Times* (where Sheehan worked until 1973) and *The New Yorker* (where his wife was an editor)?

11. An observer unfamiliar with the American scene might conclude that the quarrel between elites and centralists to *BSLIE* is not even a national one, but centers around the competing aspirations of two generations of Ivy Leaguers. Such an observation might lead to concerns not contemplated by Sheehan. Why is such a large country so dependent on a tight circle of talent for cultural and political leadership?

Works Cited

Braestrup, Peter. *Big Story: How the American Press and Television Reported and Interpreted the Crisis of Tet 1968 in Vietnam and Washington.* 2 vols. 1977. Rpt. of Vol 1. New Haven: Yale UP, 1983.

Davidson, Phillip. *Secrets of the Vietnam War*. Novato, CA: Presidio P, 1990.
—. *Vietnam at War: The History, 1946-1975*. Novato, CA: Presidio P, 1990.
Higgins, Marguerite. *Our Vietnam Nightmare*. New York: Harper and Row, 1965.
Lichter, Robert S., and Stanley Rothman. *The Media Elite*. Bethesda, MD: Adler and Adler, 1986.
Luce, Don. "The Search for a Final Absolution." *Commonweal* Feb. 1988: 82-3.
Maddox, Robert. *The New Left and the Origins of the Cold*. Princeton, NJ: Princeton UP, 1973.
Oberdorfer, Don. *Tet!* New York: Doubleday, 1971.
Pike, Douglas. "Vann and Vietnam as Seen through a '60s Time Warp." *The Washington Times* 3 Oct. 1988: E8.
Prochnau, William. "The Last Prisoner of Vietnam." *The Washington Post Magazine* 9 Oct. 1988: 1.
Rollins, Peter C., dir. *Television's Vietnam: The Real Story*. Sony Video, 1985.
—, dir. *Television's Vietnam: The Impact of Media*. Sony Video, 1986.
Russell, George. "Manifest Perdition." *Commentary* Feb. 1989: 78-80.
Safer, Morley. *Flashbacks: On Returning to Vietnam*. New York: St. Martins, 1990.
Schlesinger, Jr., Arthur M. "The Origins of the Cold War." *Foreign Affairs* 46.1 (1967): 22-52.
Sheehan, Neil. *A Bright Shining Lie: John Paul Vann and America in Vietnam*. New York: Random House, 1988.
Steinberg, Edward. "Neil Sheehan: An Interview." *Publisher's Weekly* 2 Sept. 1988: 83-4.
Summers, Harry. "Pacification." *Vietnam War Almanac*. New York: Facts on File Publishers, 1985.
Unger, Irwin. "The 'New Left' and American History: Some Recent Trends in U.S. Historiography." *American Historical Review* 72.4 (1967): 1237-63.

23
Dear America (HBO 1988): Oral History as Interpretation of the Vietnam Experience?

In 1981, Mayor Ed Koch appointed a special commission to create a New York Vietnam Veterans Memorial (VVM). Co-chaired by Donald Trump and Scott Higgins, the Commission raised funds for three distinguishable efforts. Immediately, a design contest was announced for a physical monument, a tribute which eventually found its place near the financial district of downtown Manhattan (55 Walter St.). While the winning design's translucent "Wall" is impressive by day, it is particularly haunting at night because of the illumination that comes from within glass bricks of the sixty-six foot by sixteen foot wall. Inscribed around the glass structure in varying fonts and in different letter sizes are quotations from letters by soldiers, sailors, airmen, and marines to their loved ones back in "the World." These poignant quotations were taken from a large pool of original materials assembled by Bernard Edelman. (Edelman was given a broader audience for the letters in an anthology entitled *Dear America: Letters Home from Vietnam* [1985]). The third effort stemming from the Memorial Commission's work was a counseling service still operating out of donated office space on Broadway. Under the leadership of Gene Gittleson, the Vietnam Veterans Leadership Program (VVLP) continues as a living memorial to those who fell in an unpopular war. One very prominent quotation on the New York "Wall" says it all: "I was a warrior when warriors weren't in season."

The Original Text

Edelman's Non-Partisan Anthology

Something needs to be said about the anthology since none of the reviews of the film adaptation reflects direct knowledge of the book's concept. (Many of the quotes in the reviews seem to have been culled from a promotion packet distributed by HBO.) Although he had not seen combat during his Vietnam service, Bernard Edelman was a Vietnam veteran who engaged in the act of collection with a sense of reverence for his materials and wariness about imposing on them his own interpretation of the war. The book is divided into seven generic sections: "Cherries" uses GI vernacular to describe first impressions of Vietnam; "Humping the Boonies" follows troops out into the field; "Beyond the Body Count" measures the human toll of combat wounds and death; "Base Camp" recalls the experiences of those who stayed 'in the rear with the gear' — in the American way of war approximately 4 out of every 5 troops in country; "World of Hurt" further recalls the pain of wounds; "We Gotta Get Out of This Place" samples the hopes of returning home after making it through the standard tour (12 months for the army; 13 months for marines); "Last Letters" take on a special poignancy because only some of the writers managed to return to their families.

As a whole, the collection throws out a broad net, using letters from different time periods, 1965-73, in each of the eight generic sections. Given the sponsorship and purpose for the volume, the anthology was very careful to include letters of substantial support of America's efforts. These "hawkish" letters are full of New Frontier rhetoric about the need to contain Communism and to defend the democratic aspirations of South Vietnam. They are more than balanced by "dovish" letters and war-weary items such as a petition circulated within the Americal Division complaining about too much time in the field. (The Americal Division was responsible for the shameful My Lai massacre and was disbanded after the war.)

Film director Bill Couturie asked the New York VVM Project for permission to combine items from the collection with other literary fragments for a compilation documentary film. The VVM people offered Couturie the collection so long as he did not mix them with other materials, fearing that the efforts to provide balance might be subverted by the filmmaker, thereby misrepresenting both the book and the city's memorializing effort.

The HBO Special: Close Ups and Medium Shots

TV Guide's Sunday "Previews" may not have been aimed at profundity, but its brief announcement about HBO's *Dear America* revealed an important intuitive insight: the forthcoming film was indeed about Vietnam, but it was clearly a reflection of a current sensibility. In her syndicated column for the Associated Press, Kathryn Baker picked up the contemporary flavor by focusing on the use of Bruce Springsteen's "Born in the USA," the popular tune which is played over credits at the end of the ninety-minute program. According to Baker, the song and the show both spoke to the "Vietnam Veterans' disillusionment and courage in the '80s" (1). Those familiar with the history of the battle for Khe Sanh and details of the war's aftermath could have read unintended ironies into the Springsteen lyrics quoted at the head of Baker's column:

> I had a brother at Khe Sanh
> > Fightin' off them Viet Cong.
> > They're still there.
> > He's all gone. ("Born in the U.S.A.")

(The Marines at Khe Sanh were fighting the North Vietnamese, not the Vietcong, some 10,000 of whom died as opposed to 354 American deaths.) That North Vietnamese troops are still in the South is a painful fact for Southerners, to include former members of the Vietcong, many of whom were sent to "re-education camps" and are now living in exile after clambering aboard fragile boats to risk their freedom. (See Trong Nhu Tang's A *Vietcong Memoir* for details on re-education.) Both brief articles linked past with present, but neither could see the connections. In Baker's case, it was a matter of pursuing misleading clues for lack of historical understanding. Granting that there were links between past and present, the reviewer for *People Magazine* asked for lessons.

Oliver Stone's *Platoon* (1986) had been in the theatres for approximately a year when *Dear America* went into distribution, inviting comparisons between the two "grunt" films. Indeed, reviewers for *The Hollywood Reporter*, *USA Today*, *The New York Post* all thought of *Platoon* as a fictional counterpart to the documentary effort. Mike Barnicle of *The Boston Globe* went so far as to describe Couturie's compilation as "what *Platoon* really wanted to be...more than a film...life and death" (29). With the advantage of hindsight, this comparison seems highly suspect for *Platoon* now stands out from so many other frontline films as a highly allegorical interpretation of the Vietnam conflict rather than as a personalized recounting of Oliver Stone's combat experience (see Chapters 17, 24).

A good number of the reviewers of *Dear America* stressed the emotional power of the production. Jeffrey Ressner of *The Hollywood Reporter* was overwhelmed (3); although she was a bit concerned about the use of Hollywood voices, Monica Collins applauded Coutourie's objective "to be...visceral rather than quietly thought provoking" (30). Don Shirley sensed the power of the "emotional arc" employed by Couturie, but recognized that this was a story limited to "an American point of view" (14). As the show progressed along in a chronological progression, David Bianculli sensed that it became "increasingly emotional" (103). *TV Guide* bordered on the tasteless by exploiting emotionalism. In a "background report," Doug Hill interviewed parents of dead veterans. In every case selected by Hill, the grieving mothers and fathers deplored the war and had difficulty understanding the significance of their young soldier's death. As an opening "grabber" for the piece, a mother tells of hearing "somebody...screaming, and the screams were so horrible they were bouncing off the walls; it was like the screams were hitting me. It was me who was doing the screaming" (37). Evidently, Hill never found a mother or father with a sense of pride in a dead son's service and sacrifice. Such selectivity reflected the mood of the program, not the demographics of the nation or the thesis of the book (see Gallop Poll results, Chapter 17).

When Samuel Freedman of *The New York Times* asked about how the filmmakers came up with a scheme for converting a book to the screen, screenwriter Richard Dewhurst explained that the "timeline" notion of a chronological progression came from the book. Dewhurst gave Freedman a paperback copy of the collected letters to prove his point, although there is no evidence in the *Times* article that Freedman—or any other reviewer—made an effort to read the book or stopped to think about alternative options for an authentic screen translation of its tone and content. Further denying interpretation, Director Couturie said that he and his staff had made "a scrapbook, a time capsule...Everything is from the period. Not us editorializing from now" (33). Further covering the production trail, Co-producer Thomas Bird hinted to *Daily News* reporter Pat Pacheco that HBO had warned the filmmakers to remain "clear of the heavy-hitting stuff" (30). How could the show be propagandist with such oversight and purity of intentions? It is conceivable that Couturie, Dewhurst, and Bird were telling the truth, that they were in such a consensus about the message of the book that they felt that they were merely liberating a story implicit in the materials.

The most trenchant response to the true spirit of HBO's *Dear America* was from Mike Barnicle of *The Boston Globe*. According to Barnicle, the American people in the time of Ronald Reagan needed an emotional jolt to awaken them to protest. A bellicose and senile President was ordering American troops to Grenada in a clear continuation of Cold War hubris. The movie *Platoon* should have gotten the anti-war message across, but theatrical distribution of *Dear America* would be "a permanent reminder of how easy the hollow arsenal of politics can steal young dreams" (29). Clearly, the program could serve as a powerful object lesson about the futility of war and a timely reminder of how much suffering has to be

absorbed by little people because of the callousness of their leaders. It is an understatement to say that the NYC Vietnam Veterans Memorial Commission would have been shocked that such a lesson could be drawn from *Dear America*, yet Barnicle's reading of the film is on target.

Long Shots

There were major matters overlooked or ignored by most reviewers, but the decision to follow a "timeline" was crucial. (There is no such evolution in the book.) Once the "timeline" concept was in place, the project tapped the NBC film archive to flesh out the narrative, ignoring the possibility that television news, the source for visual materials, was an oft-criticized misinterpreter of the conflict (see Chapter 18). Additional footage from the NBC archive plus military films from government vaults were tapped to visually cover numerous musical montage segments employing Sixties music with powerful anti-Establishment and anti-war lyrics. (See list of tunes in the HBO Press Kit.) Musical montage vignettes were often used to drive home an interpretation of letters, news clips, or to provide sidebar orientation to things like military slang. Overall, the film insistently pursued a message: America in the early days of the war was optimistic and over-confident; as the war continued, the nation (as represented by the morale of the troops at the front) sank into a quagmire of disillusionment and nihilism. While this interpretation is shared by many writers on the Vietnam experience and is one of *many* interpretations of the Vietnam years, this was most definitely *not* a theme of Bernard Edelman's book version of *Dear America*.

When the program was first aired, Robert Goldberg of the *Wall Street Journal* expressed some problems with the way in which the show had transformed a generic approach into a chronological story of spiritual devolution: "But while the historical overview is helpful, even fascinating, in the end it doesn't really work as a structure for this film. Most of the letters are about timeless feelings of war, not dates or events. When it comes to doubt and fear and pain, time lines are more or less irrelevant. (What difference does it make to the young man who writes of being bloodied by shrapnel if it happened in 1968 or 1970?)" (19). Unfortunately, Goldberg did not explore his insights about the disjuncture between book and film.

Students who have passed through journalism or film classes in universities in this country during the last thirty years should know that compilation films are not mere collections of facts and factoids; from Hitler's works of propaganda to movies like Peter Davis' *Hearts and Minds* or my own *Television's Vietnam(s)*, they have attempted to be interpretations of history aimed at moving audiences (see Chapters 17, 18, 25). Selection of "the emotional arc" approach to the program assuredly enhanced its impact as a work of art. On the other hand, the film does violence to the text from which it was drawn and clearly does so with a consistent intent to present the darkest possible picture as time passes. Two spot readings voiced by Martha Maderis provide microscopic detail on how manipulative the voice over-narration can be in two letters. Overall, 70.73% of the letters were out of chronological order. Like so many showmen in the documentary "business" before him—for example, the makers of *Victory at Sea*—Couturie went for the heart and in the process did not allow historical facts to get in the way of a powerful story assembled to promote a good cause (on *Victory at Sea*, see Chapter 15). Perhaps future students of *Dear America* will go back to Couturie's *Vietnam Requiem* and other earlier productions to trace continuities between those anti-war diatribes and his HBO project.

It is the polemical tone of *Dear America* which summoned up the connection with *Platoon* for reviewers. While Edelman strove to maintain the completeness of the soldiers' original ideas, the documentary slices and dices them to put forth its own message. Like so many predecessors in the genre of compilation, Couturie denied that he arranged into montage cinematic fragments to support his message; but the most skillful ploy was Dewhurst's disingenuous gesture of handing a copy of the anthology to a television reviewer. (Who has time to read?) Considering the enormous library of writings on compilation documentary as an interpretive medium—perhaps the most interpretive genre in film—since 1930, it is dumbfounding that he was able to maintain the pose of objectivity, or that any filmmaker would *want* to do so. The only answer that makes sense is that reviewers accepted the pose because the "reality" of the film coincided with their own paradigm for Vietnam—not only as it happened in the Sixties and Seventies, but as a meaningful message for the 1980s. Why question a "true" interpretation? The world of Reagan and Rambo needed strong medicine to calm a nation itching for new "splendid little wars."

Note on Research

This chapter owes a debt of gratitude to Tim Cremin who, while enrolled in an undergraduate class with me, conducted research in the OSU Edmon Low Library to find the multifarious sources cited back in the days when shoe leather was part of the scholarly role. His classroom report on this topic was quite stimulating and informed this chapter. As a teacher, I am proud to say that he went on to become a television producer/director in his own right.

The HBO Press Kit in the Vietnam Archive of Texas Tech University has all of the reviews quoted plus others. It is part of the 300 cubic feet of material donated to the collection by me and is available to all researchers.

Works Cited

Baker, Kathryn. Associated Press syndicated review, HBO Press Kit.

Barnicle, Mike. "Old Words, Enduring Lessons." *The Boston Globe* 20 Mar. 1988: Metro 29.

Bianculli, Daniel. "In Their Words: HBO Sheds New Light on the Vietnam War." *New York Post* 31 Mar. 1988: 103, 105.

Collins, Monica. "'Letters' Sends Home the Agony of Vietnam" *USA TODAY* 31 Mar. 1988: 3D.

Freedman, Samuel G. "Vietnam Echoes: 'We Are All Afraid to Die.'" *New York Times* 3 Apr. 1988: 33-34.

Goldberg, Robert. "Soldiers' Tribute" *The Wall Street Journal* 11 Apr. 1988: 19.

HBO Press Kit for *Dear America*. Vietnam Archive, Texas Tech University, Lubbock Texas.

Hill, Doug. "Joy and Sorrow – The Loved Ones Who Received Those Letters from Vietnam." *TV Guide* 2 Apr. 1988: 37-38.

Pacheco, Patrick. "Write Stuff: A New Vietnam Film from HBO Provides a Powerful Message from Unlikely Pair." *New York Daily News* 3 Apr. 1988: 30.

Ressner, Jeffrey. "Dear America" *Hollywood Reporter* 4 Nov. 1987: 3.

Shirley, Don. "Realism Ranks High in 'Letters Home.'" *Los Angeles Times*. 2 Apr. 1988: 1, 14.

Springsteen, Bruce. "Born in the U.S.A." *Born in the U.S.A.* Sony. 1984.

Tang, Truong Nhu, with David Chanoff and Doan Van Toai. *A Vietcong Memoir: An Inside Account of the Vietnam War and its Aftermath.* New York: Vintage, 1986.

Unger, Irwin. "The 'New Left' and American History: Some Recent Trends in U.S. Historiography." *American Historical Review* 72.4 (1967): 1237-1263.

24
Para dismentir "television's vietnam": Los motivos de un Documentarista

Introducción

Cuando supe que iba a haber una conferencia llamada "Guerra, Películas, y Sociedad" en Barcelona, me sentí muy complacido porque he querido explicar lo que me motivó a trabajar en los estudios históricos sobre la guerra de Vietnam—en artículos becados y en cine documental. Muchas veces durante mi vida, he querido hablar en español—más bien que en inglés—porque mi segunda lengua me permitiría decir cosas de una manera fresca sin el racimo de suposición que mi lengua natal tiene no solamente para mi audiencia—sino también para mí. Para mí, el español es la lengua de la juventud antes de las décadas de los 60 y 70 cuando los Estado Unidos sufría de la rebelión contra "El Establecimiento."

La Familia y La Juventud
Nací como miembro del Establecimiento. Mi abuelo era el juez del tribunal de la Ciudad de Brookline, un suburbio junto a la ciudad de Boston en el Estado de Massachussets. Daniel Ashton Rollins era un graduado orgulloso de la Universidad de Dartmouth (Hanover, New Hampshire) y de la facultad de derecho de la Universidad de Harvard (Cambridge, Massachusetts). Su héroe político era "Teddy" Roosevelt, a quien los Republicanos Progresivos le llamaban "el toro grande" durante los primeros años del siglo veinte.

En la biblioteca de su casa mi abuelo tenía libros de Theodore Roosevelt, de Herbert Spencer, y de muchos autores a quienes llamamos partidarios del "Darwinism Social." Aunque trabajaba en la ciudad como juez y abogado, durante los veranos mi abuelo navegaba por la costa del Cabo Cod, como los Peregrinos de hace tres siglos; durante el otoño, pescaba salmones en los lagos y ríos del Estado de Maine para seguir "la vida al aire libre"; durante la época de la caza, usaba algunos de sus muchos rifles para cazar venados en los bosques de la Nueva Inglaterra. Iba a comprar sus trajes de cazador a una tienda pequeña (entonces) llamada "L.L. Bean." Al mismo tiempo, mi abuelo y mi abuela asistían a los conciertos de la sinfonía famosa de Boston y asistían a la iglesia inglesa. Mi abuelo creía en el refrán latino: "Sana mens sano corpore" ("Emplee tanto la mente como el cuerpo.") Mi abuelo era el vivo retrato de la persona que llamamos un "WASP" (White Anglo-Saxon Protestant / persona de raza blanca, religión protestante, y tipo anglo-sajón) en los Estados Unidos.

Su hijo, que era mi padre, Daniel Gooding Rollins, siguió los pasos de mi abuelo. Era un jefe en los círculos Republicanos de Brookline y trabajó como el abogado de la ciudad por veinte años. Durante su carrera política los demócratas en la oposición le llamaron miembro de un "gobierno invisible." Era la verdad, pero también es verdad que su objeto era hacer las mejores leyes y políticas para el pueblo—hay muchas veces cuando el pueblo no comprende qué es mejor para ellos mismos a largo plazo. Durante la segunda guerra mundial, mi padre sirvió como Capitán en la Infantería Marinera (U. S. Marines). Creía que era un servicio necesario para un hombre libre y me contó muchas veces de sus aventuras y sus dolores en la guerra. Mi hermano, Daniel Gooding Rollins, Jr., sirvió con la Infantería Marinera en nuestra primera guerra de contención, la "acción policíaca" en Corea; mi hermano Philip Ashton Rollins, el chico más atlético de los tres hermanos, intentó servir pero las heridas que había sufrido jugando deportes lo inhabilitaron. (No es fácil vivir la vida de los WASPS.) Fue natural para mí seguir la tradición de mi familia y mi clase, pero había también razones más objetivas.

El Mundo Después De La Segunda Guerra Mundial (1945-1965)
Hoy, describimos la época después de 1948 como "la Guerra Fría." Recuerdo, cuando tenía seis años, haber visto al Presidente Harry Truman cuando anunció la "Doctrina Truman" durante la guerra

de guerrilleros en Turquía y Grecia. Era un Presidente muy resoluto que nos habló a mí y a mi madre durante un noticiario de la tarde del cine de Brookline. Un año después, recuerdo la lucha épica del bloqueo de Berlín cuando el mundo libre corrió el riesgo de otra guerra mundial para ayudar a los ciudadanos de la capital de un antiguo enemigo. (Unos doce años después, el Presidente Kennedy apoyó la doctrina de Truman con su dicho famoso: "Yo soy Berlinés!") Iba a comenzar lo que sería la "Doctrina de Contención" del comunismo. Los estudiantes en las escuelas públicas practicaban defensas contra la guerra nuclear en los refugios antiaéreos. Era un tiempo de confrontaciones y miedo de "la bomba" ("the bomb").

Como los otros niños, quise comprender los eventos contemporáneos y, como un niño WASP, tuve que definir mis responsabilidades. Desde la edad de once años, me subscribí al conocido periódico de Boston llamado *The Christian Science Monitor* (El Sereno de La Ciencia Cristiana). El periódico era muy anti-Comunista y veía la lucha internacional como entre los hijos de la luz contra los hijos de la oscuridad. Durante mis estudios universitarios, descubrí que estas también eran las creencias—con muchos requisitos—de un pensador teológico americano, Reinhold Niebuhr. Y aunque él no quería el renombre, el historiador Arthur Schlesinger, Jr. celebró su "anti-Communist liberalism" (liberalismo anti-comunista) en su libro muy influyente, *The Vital Center* (*El Centro Vital*, 1949). El derecho del hombre moral en un mundo de lucha era servir la fuerza de la libertad—mientras comprendía las debilidades de la sociedad suya. No fue mucho tiempo después de que entré en la universidad cuando el Presidente Kennedy le exigió a mi generación: "No pregunten lo que su patria puede hacer por ustedes; pregunten lo que ustedes pueden hacer por su patria." Dadas mi raíces de familia y dadas mis lecturas políticas y religiosas, parecía que a lo menos necesitaba servir lo que los americanos describimos como "nuestra obligación militar."

La presencia americana en Vietnam fue una extensión lógica de la "Doctrina de Contención." Cuando mis colegas de la Infantería Marinera y yo debarcamos en la Playa Roja cerca de Danang en marzo de 1965, podía describir con claridad a mi pelotón por qué era importante ganar lo que los comunistas como Nikita Krushchev y Mao Tse Tung llamaban las "guerras de liberación nacional." Durante los meses en Vietnam, mis soldados fueron resolutos, hábiles, y morales. En muchas ocasiones, pusieron en peligro sus propias vidas antes que herir a los civiles. Muchos de mis soldados nacieron en la clase más humilde de la sociedad, pero ellos fueron fieles, fidedignos, y tuvieron orgullo de sus posiciones en la historia del país y de la Infantería Marinera. Tenían corazones buenos y fuertes. Habían respondido a la llamada de su patria. Al final de mi contrato militar de tres años, entré en la universidad de Harvard: estaba orgulloso de mi servicio y de mi patria por su defensa del principio de la libertad.

Regreso a los Estados Unidos y veo "Television's Vietnam"

Cuando volví a Brookline y Harvard en 1966, hallé un ambiente nuevo. Los estudiantes del programa graduado no podían comprender por qué yo había servido en la Infantería Marinera. Ellos habían encontrado maneras de eludir sus obligaciones. Fue parte del clima de ideas que el Presidente John F. Kennedy había asignado al establecimiento comercial y militar o que eran ideas del tejano grosero (LBJ). La interpretación de conspiración fue un índice claro de la alienación profunda de los jóvenes, una alienación adquirida por un estudiante retirado de la Universidad de Yale llamado Oliver Stone.

Cuando terminé mis estudios, busqué trabajo en la Academia. Durante una de mis primeras entrevistas, el rector asistente de cierta universidad me dijo con indignación: "¡No queremos criminales de guerra en nuestra universidad!" No puedo olvidar su censura; al mismo tiempo que me despreciaba, me inspiraba a empezar a averiguar por qué una persona tan instruida podía haber sido tan mal aconsejada. Yo no era un criminal de guerra y lo sabía claramente; entonces, ¿De dónde le llegó su imagen falsa de Vietnam? No tuve que pensarlo mucho. Su imagen estaba en las pantallas de televisión todas las noches. He viajado al Vietnam verdadero; el rector conocía solamente "Television's Vietnam" (el Vietnam de la televisión) y sus imágenes.

Mis Tres Programas de Discurso Sobre "Television's Vietnam"

La Infantería Marinera dejó Vietnam en 1971. Todos los militares americanos se marcharon de Vietnam en 1973. Después de que el

Congreso se interpuso en política militar con "The Case-Church Amendement" (La enmienda de los Senadores Clifford Case y Frank Church); después de las negociaciones secretas de Henry Kissinger y Le Duc Tho; y después de la controversia de Watergate, Vietnam del Norte invadió al Sur en abril, 1975. A mi sorpresa, estos desastres históricos no me inspiraron mucho. Durante los últimos años de la década de los 70s, Hollywood comenzó a darle al público películas sobre Vietnam que confirmaron las mentiras de "Television's Vietnam." Estas películas me molestaron. En *Black Sunday* (*Domingo Negro*, 1977), un veterano de Vietnam ayuda a terroristas que quieren asesinar a 80,000 aficionados en el campeonato de fútbol (Super Bowl). Como víctima de su servicio en Vietnam, el anti-héroe de *Taxi Driver* (*Taxista*, 1976), realizado por Roberto De Niro, fascinó al público con su violencia y corrupción moral. La contribución de doña Jane Fonda, *Coming Home* (*Regreso a casa*, 1978), presenta a un Capitán de la Infantería de Marina que se ahoga en el mar porque no puede vivir con las memorias de sus crímenes en Vietnam. *Who'll Stop The Rain* (*¿Quién puede parar la lluvia?*, 1978) relaciona a Vietnam con los narcotraficantes. *Wolf Lake* (*El lago del lobo*, 1978) asocia a Vietnam con la violación sexual. La épica de estas películas sobre Vietnam, *Apocalypse Now* (*Apocalipsis ahora*, 1979) mezcla la consideración de Vietnam con lo que Joseph Conrad llamó "the heart of darkness" (el corazón de la oscuridad). Empezando con un malentendido, los ciudadanos de Hollywood extrapolaban un Vietnam maligno que justificaba su falta de servicio militar. Me dije a mí mismo: "Alguien necesita hablar por los veteranos que son depreciados por tantas mentiras."

Programa #1: Television's Vietnam: The Impact of Visual Images
Durante una conferencia académica en la universidad de Carolina del Norte en 1977, le pregunté al Profesor C. Townsend Ludington (quien había servido en la Infantería de Marinera, también): "Por qué nadie habla por el veterano ni trata de reformar su imagen?" Con el apoyo de su universidad y de la Fundación Rockefeller, coordinamos una conferencia en 1978 sobre la Ofensiva de Tet, 1968. La manera en que Tet fue comunicado por televisión a los Estados Unidos marcó el momento crucial de la guerra. Después del supuesto fracaso de Tet, la opinión pública se echó de cabeza. Si la

guerra de Vietnam se puede llamar—en las palabras de Michael Arlen "la guerra de la sala" a causa de la televisión, entonces Tet era un laboratorio perfecto para estudiar el poder del medio visual. Durante nuestra conferencia, entrevistamos expertos del gobierno, de las noticias, de las fuerzas armadas, y muchos historiadores. Pensábamos hacer un contra-programa para desmentir las presentaciones de "Television's Vietnam."

Dos años después de la conferencia, viajé a varios archivos de películas a través de los Estados Unidos. Coloqué descripciones de mi proyecto en revistas para veteranos; les pedí que me escribieran sobre sus experiencias durante la Ofensiva de Tet. Para responder a sus cartas, visité con muchos veteranos para hacer entrevistas filmadas. Un tercio de mi primera película es un esfuerzo de demostrar las diferencias entre la batalla de Khe Sanh así como los veteranos la recuerdan y la batalla de Khe Sanh como fue contada por la televisión. Aquí tienen un fragmento sobre la batalla según fue vista en las casas de los Estados Unidos por los que vieron "Television's Vietnam":

Murray Fromson, CBS: This is one place where the Americans cannot claim they have the initiative in Vietnam. Here, the North Vietnamese decide who lives and who dies; every day, which planes land and which ones don't, and—sooner or later—they will make the move that will seal the fate of Khe Sanh.

John Laurence, NBC: From the North Vietnamese point of view, Khe Sanh is an easy target for its mortars and rockets. A convenient place to bleed the Marines and— what may be most crucial—tie down and isolate 6000 American troops and about 20,000 reserves far from the protective coastal plain. For 20 years, General Giap has used the same tactics.

Walter Cronkite, CBS: When a plane does land, much of the activity stops, while everyone watches to see if the plane makes it. This is all that's left of a C-130 that landed, loaded with gasoline. Some inside escaped; others did not.

D.D. Duncan for ABC: When enemy fire comes in, the guys run for it. When planes come in, they try to shoot a landing so fast the enemy gunners can't knock them down with either rockets or machine gun fire. The big C-130s sometimes make it; sometimes they don't.

Un teniente que presenció batalla me escribió y me dio muchas fotos de su vida en Khe Sanh. Se llama John Kaheny—actualmente es abogado para la ciudad de San Diego (en el Estado de California). Fue de mucha ayuda para desmentir las presentaciones de la televisión. Aquí el señor Kaheny describe el artículo de la revista *Newsweek* titulada "The Agony of Khe Sanh" ("El Sufrimiento de Khe Sanh"). Su testimonio es muy interesante porque sabe la verdad; además al comienzo de la edad de televisión y de los aviones "jet", el hecho que él tenía el poder de volar a los Estados Unidos y, luego volver a la batalla demuestra la verdad de la frase "global village" (aldea mundial):

John Kaheny: During my leave I went up to Boston to visit my college roommate. As we were walking down one of the streets, we came by a news stand and I noticed a copy of *Newsweek* with a cover story on the siege of Khe Sanh. I went over and bought a copy. Most of the pictures showed either the Marines lying down in the trench line, shielding themselves from enemy fire, putting out fires, or carrying their wounded. It depressed me to see that the people with whom I had served were presented in this manner.

En vez de servir como crítico, usé las palabras de los veteranos como fundación para promover empatía entre la audiencia y los soldados. Contra las imágenes de películas como *Apocalypse Now* que demuestran soldados americanos como invasores bárbaros, quise mostrar que mis soldados eran americanos típicos con sentimientos como nostalgia, alegría, y amor para sus compañeros de batalla. En la cinta de video que sigue, contrasto un libro de fotografía sobre Khe Sanh por David Douglas Duncan con la memoria de alguien que le protegió durante su visita corta a la batalla. Tenemos aquí una gran prueba de la diferencia entre el Vietnam de los soldados y el Vietnam de los ideólogos. Primero, el punto de vista del fotógrafo David Douglas Duncan:

I left the Marines at Khe Sanh to protest. Today, defiant and surly—and self-righteous—America stands nearly alone. Johnson and Rusk stubbornly ignore many of us and much of this deeply concerned world. They conduct their anti-Communist crusade in our name—with our lives, treasure, and honor. I protest! (*I Protest!*)

Ahora, las memorias del Coronel James B. Wilkinson, quien corrió el mismo perímetro con el fotógrafo famoso. Distingan ustedes como el programa se mueve entonces a un juicio negativo de Duncan con las palabras del Colonel David Lowndes y luego, un anuncio comercial satírico:

Wilkinson: David Douglas Duncan did arrive at Khe Sanh with his cameras and film at the height of the battle. I had long admired his work. I invited him down to my command bunker. I invited him to tour the perimeter. We became familiar..I thought we'd made a great impression, but—lo and behold—a few short weeks later, he rushed into print a soft-bound book called *I Protest!*

In the book, I did not pick up one smile or the sense of humor characteristic of Marines under stress or combat. If he was looking for a "downer", he found it.

Colonel David Lowndes: (Condescendingly.) David Douglas Duncan stayed for a long time. He was a very tired man. I said: "It's time to get out of here. If you don't have what you want, come back for what you need".

Mi primer programa, *Television's Vietnam: The Impact of Visual Images* (1983) fue presentada en muchas conferencias académicas y tuvo varias respuestas mezcladas. Antes de terminarse, algunas escenas fueron exhibidas en la ciudad de Cincinnati (Estado de Ohio) en la conferencia nacional de la Organización de los Estudios de Cultura Popular (Popular Culture Association). Jóvenes que se llamaban "The Young Socialist League" (Socialistas Jóvenes) estacionaron piquetes cerca de mi presentación. Más tarde, cuando acabé, varias personas en Washington, D.C. me propusieron una presentación en los Archivos Nacionales. Se les olvidó decirme que habían invitado a dos personas del proyecto llamado *Vietnam: A Television History*, ideólogos que querían despreciar mi labor. Esa noche dramática, todos quedamos sorprendidos cuando la audiencia denunció a los críticos egoístas y aceptó mi trabajo al defender mi programa. En verdad, no fue necesario sabotear mi programa para promover una serie futura, *Vietnam: A Television History*. Al lado del libro de Stanley Karnow, *Vietnam: A History*, un trabajo de PBS (Sistema Radiodifusora Pública) y la estación WGBH-Boston gozó de un éxito grande cuando apareció en 1983—en parte debido a que confirmó en muchas formas el cuadro estereotípico de "Television's Vietnam." En claro contraste, mi programa sólo estaba disponible para ser alquilado para uso en las salas de clases universitarias. A ninguno de los programadores de televisión les gustó. Además, no se alquiló mucho porque aun mis amigos en la academia no quisieron considerar el mensaje de mi documentario—que la verdad de Vietnam no fue mostrada al público americano, especialmente durante la Ofensiva de Tet, 1968, cuando lo que fue una victoria en el campo de batalla cambió a una derrota para "Television's Vietnam." Esta tesis no era popular in 1983, aunque desde entonces, las tres cadenas han hecho documentales que lo dicen—sin comprender las inferencias para sí mismas.

Mis Dos Programas Con Accuracy in Media, Inc. (AIM) de Washington

Por lo menos una persona vio mi programa y lo copió para sus amigos en la Accuracy in Media, Inc. —una organización en Washington, D.C. Después que los oficiales de AIM la miraron, me llamaron por teléfono para ofrecerme trabajo con ellos. Es costumbre, cuando la media se ofende, que los televidentes le escriban al señor Reed Irvine, Jefe de Accuracy in Media. Durante el otoño recibió muchas cartas y llamadas telefónicas cuando la serie de PBS, *Vietnam: A Television History* fue estrenada. Veteranos, vietnameses desterrados, personas políticas y diplomáticos de las administraciones de Kennedy y Johnson les dijeron a Irvine que estaba llena de mentiras, y que alguien lo había desmentido. El señor Irvine creyó que mi programa era una fundación buena para un programa de contestación.

Le convencí que era necesario crear dos programas. Primero, habíamos hecho un programa que ataca tópicos específicos en la serie de PBS. Ese primer programa, realizado por colaboración entre Accuracy in Media y yo, se llamaba *Television's Vietnam: The Real Story* (1985). Después de tal programa, reconstruimos mi programa de 1983 que tuvo más insultos que televidentes. Con los recursos de Accuracy in Media hice una versión de sesenta minutos llamada *Television's Vietnam: The Impact of Media* (1986). Como los títulos indicaron, concebimos los programas como una pareja: el primero,

Television's Vietnam: The Real Story se enfocó sobre los detalles de un documental contemporáneo y defectuoso; el segundo, *Television's Vietnam: The Impact of Media* se dirigiría a temas más generales, especialmente el impacto de la televisión. Tuvimos suerte al principio: el señor Charlton Heston dijo que nos ayudaría porque él, también, creía que era necesario para la salud del país analizar la televisión como fuente de las noticias.

Programa de AIM #1: *Television's Vietnam: The Real Story* **(1985)**

Durante el otoño de 1984, Accuracy in Media organizó una conferencia en Washington, D.C. para analizar los trece episodios del triunfo crítico de la televisión pública, *Vietnam: A Television History*. Muchos de los veteranos y otros que habían llamado a Reed Irvine se presentaron para atestar a las mentiras de la serie. (Fue más tarde que descubrimos un libro completo y detallado sobre el asunto por James Banerian.)

Al fondo, los que hicieron *Vietnam: A Television History* quisieron llenar un vacío entre los Estados Unidos y Vietnam. Quizás su serie sería una base para acercar a los dos países.

Sus motivos eran constructivos, pero afectaron la selección de películas y así falsearon la historia. Hubo numerosos problemas. Los comunistas—especialmente Ho Chi Minh—fueron celebrados como héroes de la democracia mientras que los amigos de los Estados Unidos en el sur fueron dramatizados como políticos depravados.

En la guerra, los comunistas—enseñados en sus películas propagandistas (sin noticia por subtítulos)—fueron pintados como héroes mientras que mis soldados fueron presentados como drogadictos, cobardes, hombres sin objetivos. Para PBS—como para la prensa durante la guerra—la batalla de Khe Sanh era simbólica de toda la guerra. Entrevistas con comunistas les demuestran como sabios; al otro lado, la veracidad de diplomáticos y políticos de nuestro gobierno se niega. Mientras que PBS trabaja para hacer a los comunistas merecedores de nuestro respeto, con esperanzas de reconciliación eventual, crea un cuadro histórico que les hace muchas injusticias a los anti-comunistas de Vietnam y a los jóvenes de los Estado Unidos que combatieron según las órdenes de sus líderes—y combatieron con valor y disciplina. Repito que los motivos de los directores de PBS fueron benevolentes, pero el resultado fue una codificación de las mentiras de "Television's Vietnam" más bien que una vista nueva y global.

Mi programa de respuesta, *Television's Vietnam: The Real Story*, recibió muchas reseñas en la prensa—aun antes de su transmisión. El PBS mismo fue condenado al permitir que el programa fuera considerado. El productor de *Vietnam: A Television History* le dijo a la prensa que PBS capituló a presión política de la Casa Blanca del Presidente Ronald Reagan—quien había visto la película y le había dado mucho placer. Ver el Capítulo ? Los miembros de la Sociedad de Críticos Televidentes repitieron la mentira con mucho gusto. Por fin, el Presidente de WGBH-Boston, el señor Henry Becton negó la acusación de su empleado, el productor Richard Ellison. Después de la transmisión, muchos críticos atacaron PBS, mientras otros—como John Corry de *The New York Times* (*El tiempo* de Nueva York) dijeron que nuestro programa era verídico y que la controversia demostró que los liberales en los Estados Unidos temían que sus errores durante y después de la guerra se llevaran a la atención del público. Muchos veteranos y vietnameses me dieron premios como símbolos de su agradecimiento por *The Real Story*. (Están colgados hoy con orgullo en mi oficina.) Siento mucho orgullo porque he tenido la oportunidad de contradecir algunas de las mentiras de "Television's Vietnam." Era mi obligación como uno de los pocos intelectuales que sirvió a esa gente que no puede hablar por sí misma.

Programa de AIM #2: *Television's Vietnam: The Impact of Media* **(1986)**

Desde el principio, planeamos reconstruir mi programa sobre la Ofensiva de Tet. Otra vez, viajé a los archivos del cinema y de fotografías que se encuentran a través del país. Debido a que la red de ABC (Corporación Radiodifusora de América) había donado horas de noticias a PBS para sus programas, pedimos el mismo derecho de acceso. Estábamos agradecidos de que fue posible. En el archivo en Nueva York descubrí mucho que hizo mi argumento más persuasivo.

Para la narración, fue necesario viajar a Inglaterra porque el señor Heston estaba en una representación de *The Caine Mutiny* (*El Motín del Velero "Caine."*) Para entrevistas con miembros descontentos y desengañados del Vietcong, era necesario viajar a Francia. Allí también hallé exiliados y víctimas del régimen comunista, quienes dieron testimonio de las maldades de la guerra—especialmente en Hue durante la Ofensiva de Tet. Estudios de los programas de televisión, llevados a cabo por historiadores, han revelado que la televisión en los Estados Unidos nunca reportó el crimen en Hue; no obstante, hallé historias en los archivos de películas. Mi programa trató de explicar las razones. Nuestros reporteros estaban absortos con el masacre de My Lai (1968/69)—y trataban de reportar la tragedia cada vez que era posible—porque les servía de microcosmo de la inmoralidad de la guerra americana. Para la prensa, la masacre por las comunistas en Hue fue un hecho que quisieron dejar sobre los estantes de los archivos de la cadena. Para ellos, eran noticias que—para torcer las palabras famosas del *The New York Times*—"no es correcto imprimir." (Cuando vean ustedes la película *Full-Metal Jacket* (1987), observen, cómo Stanley Kubrick evita las implicaciones de esto aun a la orilla de un sepulcro en masa.)

Como resultado de la controversia sobre el primer programa para AIM, necesitaba documentar cada aserción de *Television's Vietnam: The Impact of Media*. Esto resultó en menos escenas poéticas e introspectivas; por esta razón, pienso hoy que hay mucho en el programa original, *Television's Vietnam: The Impact of Visual Images* (1983) que merece estudio. La diferencia es entre un tratamiento que quiere evocar la dimensión humana y un ensayo que quiere comunicar hechos y opiniones en poco tiempo para pasar rápidamente al próximo argumento. Todavía, mi segunda película para AIM no está desprovista de arte visual. Por ejemplo, como algunas otras películas sobre Vietnam, el programa comienza frente a la Estatua en Honor a los Veteranos en Washington, D.C. como una meditación sobre la historia. Durante esta parte, como en otros momentos, traté de entretejer las palabras, las filmaciones, y la música:

Charlton Heston: As the tenth anniversary of the end of the Vietnam War approached, we began to see a new attitude toward the war and America's role in it. This new mood was symbolized by the completion of the Vietnam Veterans Memorial in Washington, D.C. with the unveiling of this statue portraying the men who fought and died in that far off land as heroes.

At the same time, this country experienced a new wave of patriotic sentiment. With it came a rejection of the notion that Vietnam was an ignoble war.

Major General George B. Price, USA (Ret.): ...And we accomplished all of our missions, sir. We failed this country not one step. We never dropped the flag, nor did we ever turn our backs.

Rep. David Boniar (D-Mich.): The soldiers of the Vietnam War met our nation's highest standards of service. The house-to-house battles for Hue, the murderous shellings absorbed at Khe Sanh, tested the courage of our soldiers no less than the battles of World War II and Korea.

Como su predecesor de 1983, *Television's Vietnam: The Impact of Visual Images*, *Television's Vietnam: The Impact of Media* se enfocó en las historias principales de Tet, 1968: el incidente frente a la embajada de los Estados Unidos donde en las noticias dijeron que soldados de los Vietcong habían penetrado al edificio—que era una mentira; adicionalmente, la masacre en Hue—que para la prensa de televisión—nunca pasó; y la foto del Coronel Loan mientras mataba a un Teniente Vietcong en las calles de Saigón. La batalla de Khe Sanh ocupó un tercio del programa con John Kaheny junto con entrevistas con veteranos e historiadores de la guerra y los medios de comunicación. El señor Charlton Heston fue excelente como narrador, pero mis soldados quedan en la historia humana. (Aquí tienen una muestra de video con el humor de los soldados sobre las dificultades de la vida bajo la tensión del combate.)

Television's Vietnam: The Impact of Media concluyó con algunas lecciones del anfitrión famoso:

Charlton Heston: I've been part of the image empire since my first appearance on television in 1948. Since then I've made over 50 motion pictures. As a performer, I am reminded daily of the malleability of visual images. We used to say that "a picture is worth a thousand words." Now we know that a picture may often require a thousand words to explain what it means. The new wisdom will spread as Americans develop media literacy skills. And while we do justice to the sacrifice of our Vietnam veterans, let us also examine the specific media lessons of Vietnam; modern struggles involve words and images as well as weapons. This new challenge affects all of us: leaders have to know how to communicate in a complex media environment; responsible citizens have to become critical viewers. The press, too, has to reconsider its role as a social force, tempering its freedom with a sense of responsibility. Only by confronting this challenge can we fully pay our debt to those who died for us in Vietnam.

Conclusión

Television's Vietnam: The Impact of Media (1986) producida por PBS después de una lucha en la prensa, rápidamente iluminó muchas de los acusaciones de la primera lucha sobre *Television's Vietnam: The Real Story* (1985). Pero el segundo programa para AIM, visto por millones de televidentes cuando la función fue repetida por la estación WTBS de Ted Turner—quien me llamó por teléfono para darme las gracias. Después de la terminación de estos proyectos, volví a mis clases en la universidad. Estoy muy agradecido por haber tenido la oportunidad de grabar en la memoria histórica el Vietnam de mis soldados. Por mucho tiempo los libros y antologías ignoraron mi trabajo, pero he observado que hay discusiones en libros que salieron en la década de los 90, como las antologías *Inventing Vietnam* (*Creando Vietnam*, 1991) y *The Vietnam War and American Culture* (*La Guerra de Vietnam y la Cultura Americana*, 1991). En veinte años, cuando la Guerra Fría ya no exista, cuando la generación de los 60 (con su rabia y culpabilidad por irresponsabilidad) se haya muerto, los estudiantes de la historia presentarán una historia equilibrada. Cuando los historiadores piensen sobre el significado de Vietnam dentro del contexto de la Guerra Fría, la guerra será un momento de dolor y sacrificio en una lucha que concluyó en victoria durante el día de Navidad, 1991, cuando la bandera comunista fue bajada por última vez. Hasta luego, los escritores y los académicos no pueden ver la verdad porque viven—algunos sin querer, algunos por preferencia—en el mundo de imágenes que fue llamado "Television's Vietnam."

Nota especial en referencia a los programas y los títulos:

Mis documentales que describo aquí son fáciles de confundir porque los nombres son semejantes. En orden cronológico son:

1983. *Vietnam: A Television History*. (*Vietnam: Una historia televisiva*) (Dir. Peter C. Rollins) Durante mi discurso, menciono la serie para televisión sobre Vietnam que se llama *Vietnam: A Television History* (1983); esta serie famosa fue hecha por la estación WGBH en la ciudad de Boston. La serie trata un tema que examinaron mis programas de los próximos tres años, muchas veces como respuesta a los mensajes engañosos de la serie de PBS.

1983. *Television's Vietnam: The Impact of Visual Images*. (*El Vietnam de la televisión: El impacto de las imágenes visuales*). (Dir. Peter C. Rollins) Hecho con el apoyo de la División de Humanidades de la Fundación Rockefeller, este es un programa de 2.5 horas que incluye música popular de la época (según las listas archivadas de música que tocaron en *Armed Forces Radio [Radioemisora de las Fuerzas Armadas]*), así como los anuncios comerciales televisados que sirvieron como contrapunto fascinante a los informes de la guerra—muchas veces con el propósito de enfatizar el consumerismo de la época o para revelar recursos dramáticos que compartieron los anuncios comerciales y los noticieros durante esta época.

1985 *Television's Vietnam: The Real Story* (*El Vietnam de la televisión: La historia verdadera*) (Dir. Peter C. Rollins) Este es el primero de dos programas para AIM. Fue elaborada a base de un congreso que tuvo lugar en Washington, D.C.; reporteros, diplomáticos, y veteranos desmienten algunos de los temas engañosos de la serie de WGBH/PBS intitulada *Vietnam: Una historia televisiva* (13 episodios, 1983).

1986 *Television's Vietnam: The Impact of Media* (*El Vietnam de la televisión: El impacto de los medios de la comunicación*) (Dir. Peter C. Rollins) Este programa es una nueva versión del programa de 1983 (ver arriba), ampliado por entrevistas nuevas y fuentes nuevas; el programa enfoca la ofensiva de Tet de 1968. Para intensificar tal enfoque, se cortó gran parte del programa más largo de 1983. La versión más larga del programa será de interés para cualquiera que se interese en los tiempos y la cultura que rodearon los informes y los debates que aparecieron en los medios de comunicación.

Notas a Propósito de Television's Vietnam

1. Artículos sobre *Television's Vietnam: The Real Story* (1985):

Rollins, Peter C. "Critical Responses to My Show, *Television's Vietnam: The Real Story* (1985): Press History Repeating Itself as Farce?" Capítulo 20 de este volumen.

---. "TV's Battle of Khe Sanh: Selective Images of Defeat." *Television Coverage of International Affairs*. Ed. William C. Adams. Ablex Publishing, 1982. 200-16.

Medhurst, Martin J. "Propaganda Techniques in Documentary Film and Television: AIM vs. PBS." *Television Studies: Textual Analysis*. Eds. Gary Burns and R.J. Thompson. NY: Praeger, 1989. 183-204.

Vlastos, Stephen. "Revisionist Vietnam History." *The Vietnam War and American Culture*. Eds. John Carlos Rowe and Rick Berg. New York: Columbia UP, 1991. 52-74.

2. Artículos sobre *Television's Vietnam: The Impact of Media* (1986):

Corry, John. "'Television's Vietnam,' A Documentary on 31." *The New York Times* 1 Oct. 1986: Sec. C, 26.

Sobran, Joseph. "Now It Can Be Told." *National Review*. 29 Aug 1986: 48-9.

3. Artículos y libros sobre *Television's Vietnam*:

Slater, Tom. "Teaching a Politically Balanced Vietnam Documentary Film Course" *Inventing Vietnam: The War in Film and Television*. Ed. Michael Anderegg. Philadelphia: Temple UP, 1991. 259-79.

Braestrup, Peter. *Big Story: How the American Press and Television Reported and Interpreted the Crisis of Tet 1968 in Vietnam and Washington*. 2 vols. Boulder, CO: Westview Press, 1977.

4. Artículos sobre la serie, *Vietnam: A Television History* (1983):

Banerian, James. *Losers Are Pirates*. Phoenix, AZ: Sphinx Publishing, Inc, 1984.

Podhoretz, Norman. "Vietnam: The Revised Standard Version." *Commentary* April 1984: 35-41.

Raack, Richard. "Caveat Spectator: *Vietnam: A Television History* yet another Vietnam debacle?" *OAH Newsletter* Feb 1984: 25-7.

5. La aflicción de un veterano que pide justicia:

Adler, Renata. *Reckless Disregard: Westmoreland v. CBS, et al; Sharon v. Time*. NY: Knopf, 1986.

Cubbage, T.L. "Westmoreland vs. CBS: Was Intelligence Corrupted by Policy Demands?" *Leaders and Intelligence*. Ed. Michael I. Handel. London: Frank Cass, 1989. 118-80.

25
Teaching International Politics: What the Historian-Filmmaker Has to Offer

> In film...we have an instrument much more suited to the specific purpose of education than any other of the arts. It really can bring the outside world alive to the growing citizen. It really can extend his experience. It really can serve an interpretative function. Working as it does from the living fact, it can, if mastered and organized, provide this necessary umbilical to the community outside.
>
> John Grierson, 1936 (Hardy 139)

As far back as 1986, a Roper Poll estimated that nearly sixty-six percent (66%) of our fellow citizens knew what they knew about international events through television. Television and film are compelling visual media with the ability to combine eye-catching pictures with (apparently) natural sound, and (seemingly) authoritative narration. These compelling visual stories compete each day with the lecture/discussions of classroom teachers; little wonder that students of the 1990s quickly learned to depend on Dan Rather, Tom Brokaw, or Peter Jennings for enlightenment rather than on their own teachers; the problem of media dependency continues into the 21st century when Keith Olbermann, Glenn Beck, Stephen Colbert, and Don Imus—even *Saturday Night Live*—are cited as legitimate media sources by otherwise intelligent people. Because most viewers believe that visual media cannot lie, teachers have great difficulty competing with television for student attention—

either to inculcate new information or to contradict misinformation consumed at family entertainment centers.

Beginning in the early 1970s, there emerged a body of criticism of existing historical films and a small collection of new productions representing an alternative approach to documentary. I have called this development the "historian filmmaker movement." In articles for *Film & History* and *The History Teacher*, such spokesmen for the movement as Patrick Griffin, Richard Raack, and I have called for a repudiation of the dominant style of history and news presentation; our historian-filmmaker productions have demonstrated that there is another way—something which will enhance the teacher's role in the classroom while sharpening student visual literacy skills (4). This chapter will critique existing formats, and then suggest ways in which filmmaking and film awareness can enhance the study of international politics. Throughout, emphasis is on training citizens to be critical viewers. While I concede that today's student needs

Video Vietnam

to know the location of Mosel (Iraq) and Kabul (Afghanistan), I would suggest that it is equally important to know how to "read" the television images which are often his sole source of information about international politics (Raack *Clio's* 109-18).

Weaknesses of Existing Films

Traditionally, historians have been among the last people to be consulted about historical films. In the best cases, trained academics have been brought into consulting roles or their works purchased by producers as "properties" to be used in connection with scripting. For example, when the Project XX group at NBC set about to produce a film about the 1920s, it turned to Frederick Lewis Allen's book entitled *Only Yesterday* (1931). Filled with fiction footage presented as documentary images of a dizzy time, *The Jazz Age* confirmed existing clichés about the period rather than providing new insights based on the massive caches of authentic documentary film sources in Manhattan archives available to the network. Allen's book has been criticized for its simplification of a complex era; *The Jazz Age* by NBC further averted complexity in an eye-catching show which—unfortunately—is still a classroom staple.

The $6.5 million series from WGBH-TV in Boston entitled *Vietnam: A Television History* is a more recent example of the same kind of error (see Chapters 17, 18). The thirteen-hour survey of America's tragic loss in Vietnam was, most people assumed, based on Stanley Karnow's book *Vietnam: A History* (1983). The book/film relationship is similar to that which existed between Allen's work and the visualization by NBC: a simplification was further trivialized. Like Allen's popular tract, Karnow's book carries little weight in the historical profession. (Karnow is a journalist who "covered Vietnam," but does not even speak the language.) People constantly ask me about "Karnow's series." *Vietnam: A Television History* was *not* produced by Stanley Karnow, but by seven or eight independent producers in England, France, and the United States who were hired by WGBH. These producers had no training in history and knew little more about Vietnam than what they had experienced as college students during the 1960s or what they had read in publications such as *The New York Review of Books* or rhetorical works like

Francis Fitzgerald's *Fire in the Lake* (1972). Possessing fervor where they lacked insight, they set about rendering their vision of Vietnam, using Karnow's tome as a jumping off point rather than as a *vade mecum*. The resulting thirteen programs were shown over national television in three cycles between 1983 and 1986 and then successfully marketed to high schools and colleges. That this doggedly anti-American series fast became a revered classroom authority is a sad commentary on the state of historical filmmaking in 1983.

Since the 1970s, journals like *The History Teacher* and *Film & History* have carried articles by trained historians condemning this misuse of film and television. The essence of the historians' criticism is twofold: first, the photojournalists who actually make the documentaries which teach about the past and about international affairs are not trained in history; as a result, once focused on a project, they tend to gravitate toward the most popular interpretation of the events—a single-source dependence which historical training should help analysts to avoid. The popular interpretation inevitably reflects a distorted view: in the case of Frederick Lewis Allen's book on the Twenties, the distortion came from seeing the Depression as some form of retribution for an irresponsible decade; in the case of the WGBH series—supposedly based upon Stanley Karnow's book—gross errors were guaranteed when WGBH-TV engaged producers who wished to justify, from the vantage point of 1983, their antiwar stance of the 1960s. Most recently, the work of Ken Burns consistently embraces a single source, yielding effective television programming—but not necessarily good history.

The second criticism of existing historical programs concerns the misuse of primary sources—in this case, film. As early as the first semester of graduate school, professional historians are trained to critically evaluate sources. Often, colorful tidbits and personal anecdotes which might add flavor to historical analysis are dropped by the wayside. In addition, historians know that too many documents have been planted along history's "paper trail" because historical personalities want to leave a flattering memorial to themselves or an unflattering picture of their enemies. Historians eschew such materials.

Not so journalists and filmmakers. With an eye for the most dramatic picture or the "scoop" footage, photojournalists leap at the opportunity to use subjective items. In addition, there is the press of deadlines which tempt cinematic historians to plunder especially exciting footage—irrespective of the source. In *The Jazz Age*, NBC borrowed extensively from fiction footage of the 1920s and 1930s, introducing it as documentary material—a clear violation of the historian's respect for provenience. In *Vietnam: A Television History*, WGBH producers had a unique opportunity to interview such Communist leaders as Le Duc Tho and Vo Nguyen Giap. A trained historian would have been equally excited. When it came time to use the interviews in the series, there would be a clear parting of the ways: continuing in their excitement with a "scoop," the WGBH producers presented the self-serving statements of Communist officials as primary source data rather than as secondary sources needing careful evaluation. As a result, General Giap and a host of Communist Party Officials were allowed to spout the party line in statements which conflicted with *known* historical facts. Historians have been roundly critical of this basic violation of historical method by WGBH. Seen from the journalistic side of the fence, the opportunity was simply too good to miss because of the novelty of the footage. Drama and impact—here and elsewhere—were at the top of the journalists' list of priorities, far above veracity and insight. Historians and those concerned with using film for the classroom and general television audiences can only wring their hands with anguish, knowing that such errors are not only representative of current practice; they seem to be the stepping stones to major industry awards for excellence!

In addition to quarreling with existing methodology in filmmaking for television and the classroom, historian-filmmakers take a different approach to the role of the viewer. Current news and documentary practice presumes a passive viewer who must be constantly titillated with exciting pictures. Presumption of a passive viewer leads to excesses already mentioned, especially the temptation to use the most powerful footage available—whatever the source. Such an assumption also leads to the notion that almost anything can be done to a viewer, that there is no limit to audience credulity. In *The Jazz Age*, Hollywood studio scenes of "New Yorkers" boozing and dancing are coupled with moralistic commentary; in *Vietnam: A Television History,* Communist propaganda films are uncritically supported by narration and described as "archival films." While the films may have come from archives, to label them such is, at best, misleading and, at worst, an insult to the intelligence of the viewing audience.

The Visually Literate Viewer

One of the novelties of the historian-filmmaker movement is the presumption of the visually literate viewer. Films in this genre posit a critical and active mind at work, dissecting and evaluating the film experience as it would the experience of reading an essay or other persuasive work in print. In a trenchant, 1972 statement of the historian-filmmaker credo, Professor R. C. Raack (California State University, East Bay) called for a new approach:

Teaching films must be cinematically advanced, artistic, and historically sound. Professional historians must control conception, content, and form as well, since the last clearly determines the first. These films must be created for dual use in the instruction of mature audiences through television and public forums, and for college and secondary school audiences. For these uses they must be adult, undidactic, and informational...the products must be calculated to stimulate the viewer /the viewer's interest so that they can be exploited by instructors to encourage further historical investigation and understanding. When used alone on television, they must convey impressions of the complexity of the historical issues and of the importance of temporality as the final condition of change and existence. They should be rich enough in image and sound to reward countless viewings...Only such material-rich productions will assure the maximum long-run return from the modest funds and considerable energies which will often be invested. (Raack *Clio's* 119)

Historian-made films are designed to observe the standards of historical writing; in addition, they are primers of film language, acquainting students with the ways in which filmmakers assemble fragments of pictures and sounds to create their cinematic interpretations of the past. Students are encouraged to enjoy the film experience, but to do so in a critical way. After such experiences in the classroom, I have been told by students that I have "ruined television" for them—by which they mean that they can no longer innocently submit to the mesmeric power of the screen. They have learned to view television as a text that they are responsible for reading. In these complaints, there is probably more pride than a sense of loss: they have become aware that they control their viewing; it does not control them.

Film as Fact

Film can serve as primary historical material, revealing events and personalities distant in time and space. My experience as producer/director of Accuracy in Media's two Vietnam-related programs speaks to this issue of getting important factual material before the American audience (see Chapters 18, 19, 25). The first program, *Television's Vietnam: The Real Story,* highlighted the efforts of prominent Americans to sway public opinion. Many Americans had seen the famous still photograph of Jane Fonda seated at an anti-aircraft gun, but that very damning image is not nearly as powerful as the North Vietnamese propaganda film of the same pseudo-event. By adding a touch of interpretive music, and by editing the shots to accompany the beat of the music, I produced a sequence which

The Hue Massacre Not Reported

illuminated the forgotten image for popular memory. Testimony by Senator John McCain (R-Ariz.) sets up the scene and defined the way in which it should be construed: although a factual sequence, it was not without visual interpretation.

While working on the second AIM Vietnam film, I encountered an unusual find in the ABC television archive in New York City. We have evidence from Peter Braestrup's exhaustive study, entitled *Big Story*, that none of the three major TV networks broadcast stories about the Hue Massacre (February, 1968); many scholars who study news have assumed that the reason relates to the absence of footage. In my search for other items, I found numerous Hue massacre stories, including an on-camera report by an ABC correspondent. Going back to look at the Hue Massacre and what it meant about the Communist intentions for the future of South Vietnam, these visual records of fact proved important building blocks for our coverage: first, they helped to show the horrors of the unreported atrocity; second, they provided important evidence to contradict the false portrayal of the event by the WGBH series, *Vietnam: A Television History*. To be sure, I have edited the footage and added music; nevertheless, the very existence of such visual evidence in an archive of a major network is extremely damning. (It should be noted that WGBH had access to the same archive in 1982; as in 1968, the footage went unused.)

Administrators, teachers, and historian-filmmakers need to seek out aspects of major stories not being portrayed by our press. There is footage available and interviews in quantity to be had in such key cities as Washington, New York, and Atlanta. Unfortunately, network correspondents often deliberately ignore such sources. Someone needs to fill this void, to supply a larger spectrum of visual facts about international politics.

Film as News

The theatrical newsreel was an important documentary form prior to the television age. Considerable research has been published in the last ten years about the ways in which *The March of Time*, Frontier Films, and other newsreel producers used their reports to sway theatrical audiences. Research also has shown that the way in which Hitler's rise to power was portrayed by British newsreels influenced the public to accept Prime Minister Chamberlain's ignominious agreement at Munich in 1938. During World War II, moviemaker Frank Capra in his classic series *Why We Fight* sought to inform Americans about the threat of fascism; the result was stirring propaganda for a good cause, but Capra's films were so strident that some have not aged well (see Chapter 12).

Anyone who works in television knows that it is an interpretive medium, that time limits for stories, the availability of footage, and the political persuasion of newsmen and gatekeepers all contribute to shaping how the viewing public will perceive the news of the day. Students in our schools need case-study training tapes on how television works as a medium, addressing some of the following questions:

- How does the format of television news contribute to the message?
- How does a news division work and how do the various people in the news chain influence story selection and content?
- What are the aesthetics of television news?

Film as Documentary
John Grierson is quoted at the opening of this chapter because he established the direction for documentary filmmaking in the English speaking world through his essays, his films, and his work as an administrator of governmental film units in England and Canada, 1930s and 1940s. Grierson wanted to educate citizens with more than categorical information; he wanted to arouse feelings, to promote empathy across physical distances and social divides.

All filmmakers use an essential cinematic technique, "montage," to communicate such messages. The current problem in historical and political filmmaking is that the power of montage is in the hands of those who would "blame America first." In the short space I have to substantiate this claim, I will turn to the issue of interpreting Vietnam through montage. (Since Vietnam "lessons" are so often invoked in discussions of flash points around the world, this is a more general issue than it might appear to be at first.)

In the opening montage of the WGBH series on Vietnam, the narrator addresses issues in a neutral manner, but the pictures making up the montage are arranged in such a manner as to portray the

American involvement as hypocritical, stupid, and wasteful, especially for the poor American "boys" on the front lines. Very little of the message contained in the previous sentence is stated in the verbal portion of the montage; instead, it is wordlessly conveyed by the conjunction of images and sounds. It is the sort of video message which the visually literate viewer could detect; on the other hand, the passive viewer will absorb the pictorial message without noticing.

It was my honor to produce and direct the media-on-media documentaries about Vietnam for Accuracy in Media. One of our goals was to arouse Americans about the consequences of the Communist victory. To elicit sympathy, I edited U. S. Navy footage of boat people with commercial newsreel footage to convey the sense of pain experienced by the dispossessed. For aural support of the tragic feeling, I introduced a musical leitmotiv of reflection which runs through the first AIM show together with a poem by a boat person—first read in Vietnamese by a young boat person and then in English by Charlton Heston. The goal of this montage was to press home a realization of the suffering brought about by our hasty exit from South Vietnam. The poem's testimony was in rebuttal to the WGBH condemnation of our defense of freedom in that tragic land.

Summary

Anyone interested in educating people about the complexities of international politics must confront the challenge of visual media. Currently, our film, video, and DVD libraries are full of journalistic productions made by audiovisualists rather than historians. I have cited the example of NBC's *The Jazz Age*; it was dated when it was made because of its dependence on Frederick Lewis Allen's entertaining—but historically superficial—survey of the 1920's. The WGBH series on Vietnam would have been a far better effort if it had been based more rigorously on Stanley Karnow's *Vietnam: A History*. Karnow's popular volume has been criticized as history, but it is a marvel of balance when compared with the television series which now graces the shelves of public libraries and audiovisual centers across the country. The examples of misled history and adversary journalism could be extended *ad infinitum* and would end with a long list of programs for The History Channel—since 2008, renaming itself as simply HISTORY. (A frightening prospect since most programs on this Arts & Entertainment venue are of lesser quality than the Project XX series so strongly critiqued in this chapter and elsewhere in *America Reflected*.)

Historian-filmmakers have a clear challenge to provide better materials for the classroom. At the same time, a new kind of viewer needs to be developed in our schools. Perhaps, in the end, it will be the educated viewers themselves who will demand more of those who choose to teach them through film and television. In any case, historian-filmmakers have a special role to play in this creative pedagogical challenge. History as film is simply too important to be left to the filmmakers!

Discussion of Literature

This paper was originally presented to a 1986 Washington, D. C., conference for high school teachers sponsored by the Ethics and Public Policy Center. During the fall, 1986 controversy concerning *The Africans*, the Chairman of the National Endowment for the Humanities (NEH), Ms. Lynne Cheney, demonstrated that she was visually literate. In a scathing letter to WNET-TV, Washington, D. C., she demanded that the NEH funding credits be removed from the tendentious, nine-part series. For more, see an Associated Press syndicated story by R. P. Laurence, as well as numerous articles on the subject in major newspapers during this period. The most telling review of the WGBH series on Vietnam is Raack's, "Vietnam: A Television History" and Culbert's "Television's Vietnam." For historical contrast, see Pisor. During the fall of 1986, considerable controversy erupted over the reluctance of PBS to air an award-winning documentary concerning Stalin's bloody program to starve the millions of Soviet farmers who defied collectivization. After months of embarrassing publicity, PBS finally broadcast *Harvest of Despair* along with a panel designed "to provide balance."

The American Historical Association has supported the need for visual literacy by publishing an excellent pamphlet entitled *Teaching History with Film and Television* by O'Connor and Jackson.

For an in-depth study of Project XX objectives and practices, see Chapters 15, 16. The pre-television persuasive film efforts are surveyed in Barsam. For more on the aesthetics of the television news medium see *The Aim Report*, a bi-monthly newsletter with timely assessments of current programs, a publication distributed by Accuracy in Media (www.aim.org).

Works Cited

Barsam, R. M. *Non-fiction Film: A Critical History*. New York: Dutton Paperbacks, 1973.

Culbert, David. "*Television's Vietnam* and Historical Revisionism in the United States." *Historical Journal of Film, Radio, and Television* 8.2 (1988): 253-65.

Hardy, Forsyth. *Grierson on Documentary*. London: Faber and Faber, 1946.

Laurence, R. P. "PBS Investigates Africa's Triple Heritage, Stirs Controversy." *Washington Post* 5 Oct. 1986: 6.

O'Connor, John, and Martin Jackson. *Teaching History with Film and Television*. Washington D. C.: American Historical Association, 1987.

Pisor, Robert. *The End of the Line: The Siege of Khe Sanh*. New York: W. W. Norton, 1982.

Raack, R. C. "Clio's Dark Mirror: The Documentary Film in History." *The History Teacher* 9.2 (1972): 109-18.

—. "*Vietnam: A Television History*: Yet Another Vietnam Debate?" *Organization of American Historians Newsletter* Feb. 1984: 25-8.

Part III

American Cultural Figures, Movements, Classics

26
Uncle Tom's Cabin (1852): Harriet Beecher Stowe's Declaration of Independence from Calvinism

> The heart of a human creature is like the millstones: if corn be shaken thereon, it grindeth the corn, and maketh good meal; but if no corn be there, then it grindeth away itself.' Luther tried the latter process all the first part of his life; but he got the corn at last, and a magnificent grist he made.
> *Sunny Memories of Foreign Lands* (1854)

Plato says somewhere that the only perfect human thinker and philosopher who will ever arise will be the MAN-WOMAN, or a human being who unites perfectly the nature of the two sexes. It was Esther's misfortune to have, to a certain degree, this very conformation. From a long line of reasoning, thinking, intellectual ancestry she had inherited all the strong logical faculties, and the tastes and inclinations for purely intellectual modes of viewing things, which are supposed to be more particularly the characteristic of man. From a line of saintly and tender women, half refined to angel in their nature, she had inherited exquisite moral perceptions, and all that flattering host of tremulous half-spiritual, half-sensuous intuitions that lie in the borderland between the pure intellect and the animal nature. The consequence of all this was the internal strife of a divided nature. Her heart was always rebelling against the conclusions of her head. She was constantly being forced by one-half of her nature to movements, inquiries and reasonings which brought only torture to the other half. (*Oldtown Folks*, 1869)

H.B. Stowe's Postal Recognition

The Artist: A Dialogue for the Nineteenth Century

In 1861, when Lyman Beecher's children compiled a series of personal letters, sermons, and reflections which they called his autobiography, Henry Ward Beecher appended to a letter written by his mother during her engagement to Lyman: "Upon this letter is endorsed, in a tremulous hand, 'Roxana, beloved still; this December 5, 1854'" (Cross 5). Henry was being more than editorially correct, for the children still regretted her death as much—if not more than—their father. Roxana Foote's correspondence presents the children's side of a dialogue between two faiths within the autobiography: Lyman's letters constitute the voice of a self-scrutinizing Calvinism which his children repudiated; in Roxana's replies is the voice of the child-like faith to which they all aspired. Through the children's eyes, Roxana expressed a faith, informed by romanticism and a confidence in man, superior in its humanism to the stark sense of sin which was the taint of their father's noble, but essentially syncretic attempt to adapt the Calvinism of Jonathan Edwards (hereafter Edwardsian Calvinism) to the nineteenth century. Barbara M. Cross provides a tableau suggesting that, if there were a variety of responses, the Beecher children shared a common repulsion from their father's God:

> Henry Ward grew up hating religion, and when Charles studied theology under his father, he became a materialist and a fatalist. George was a perfectionist, Harriet dallied with Episcopalianism and spiritualism, and Catherine finally decided that salvation depended on education. James went insane and committed suicide. George could not endure religious apathy, and died by the explosion of a gun barrel he placed in his mouth. (xiii)

Lyman Beecher's (1795-1863) tragic flaw was that while his head was in the eighteenth, his heart was in the nineteenth century. Educated at Yale under arch-Federalist Timothy Dwight (1752-1815), who predicted that atheism, anarchy, and the deflowering of Connecticut virgins would follow the election of Jefferson, Beecher tried to reset Edwardsian theology in order to renew the influence of Calvinism and its clergy. In response to the disestablishment of the Church in Connecticut, and the assumption of political power by democrats and free-thinkers, Beecher attempted to inject into his theology the contemporary belief that man could redeem himself through virtuous activity. Ironically, while making this concession to the spirit of the age, Beecher continued to assume that he was, if expanding, in no way deviating from the Edwardsian doctrine of election. Beecher borrowed his definition of sin from Nathaniel Taylor, another disciple of Dwight similarly modifying Calvinism without admitting to do so. For Beecher and Taylor, sin became not a tendency of man's nature, or an imputed taint from Adam's sin, but a choice made by man to act counter to the laws of God. Rather than an unavoidable fate, it became "man's own act, consisting in a free choice of some object rather than God, as his chief good — or a free preference of the world and of worldly good, to the will and glory of God" (Foster 370). Beecher and Taylor assumed that they had not deviated from the spirit of Edwardsian theology because they believed that man would inevitably sin once capable of moral action.

By thus palliating the Edwardsian doctrine of depravity, Beecher hoped to act as a synthesizer of faith, not only rekindling the smoldering fires of orthodoxy, but mollifying the rebellious Unitarians as well. Unfortunately, his moderate success achieved in this direction, The Plan of Union of the Congregational and Presbyterian Churches in 1830 was driven asunder by Charles Grandison Finney (1792-1875), lawyer-turned revivalist. Finney gained his meteoric ascendancy as an awakener by preaching the doctrine of individual ability untrammeled by Beecher's qualifications. Finney's disruptive popularity and impolitic attacks upon those who clung to a more Edwardsian view of grace brought upon both of them (in Beecher's case it was a matter of guilt by association) the charge of heresy, and destroyed the plan of union.

The restrictions Beecher imposed on his doctrine of ability affected his children. While he exhorted his congregations to melt their hearts for a loving Jesus, in his own spiritual life Beecher retained the assumption that man was really powerless, and that an omnipotent God granted election to undeserving sinners. Finney, on the other hand, made man and not God the measure of all things, and from that assumption, claimed that a preacher could even manufacture revivals if he made proper use of the natural means, among them, the infamous "anxious seat." Applying the Jacksonian animus to his preaching, Finney campaigned for his revival with the gratifying insight that "the object of the ministry is to get all the people to feel that the devil has no right to rule this world, but that they ought all to give themselves to God, and vote in the Lord Jesus Christ as the governor on the universe" (Finney 81).

The Beecher children were more intellectually and emotionally the contemporaries of Finney than their father. Ironically, Finney's gleanings from Beecher's neo-Edwardsianism provided a prototype of their break with him. They were torn by Beecher's syncretic fusion of a higher conception of man with his retention of the implacable Edwardsian God. The attempt to reconcile these two incongruous concepts constitutes themes in the novels by Harriet Beecher Stowe.

In a second footnote to Lyman and Roxana's letters, Lyman reminisced that Roxana's Episcopal parents "thought I was making her crazy" (Cross 55). The children probably agreed with the Footes, for they idealized their saintly mother's unquestioning affection for God, in contrast with their father's insecurity, the result of his constant probing of the religious affections. In an almost archetypal passage exhibiting this baneful doubt, Beecher exposed how he suffered a sense of distance from the sustaining peace of God's love, even while an enthusiastic minister called to his first church. Although constantly traveling and preaching, he needed someone to lead him to Christ:

> Wednesday I did little but weep at my unhappy hardness of heart. Read in the Theological Magazine the experience of several eminent Christians. Perceived they had emotions that I never felt and feared I never should. Felt an earnest desire to live the life of the righteous, but saw I did not. Contemplated the Divine character as glorious to those who could see with the heart; then burst into tears, and cried, 'Lord light upon me the light of thy countenance!'…'Great God!' then I cried, 'deliver me from myself; enable me to pray from love to thee.' (52)

He warned Roxana that her love for God might be merely a natural affection. Roxana, writing from her father's farm, "Nutplains," just outside New Haven, promised that she would attempt to analyze her love for God under the microscope of reason. Roxana's complacency at the conclusion of her introspection would so inscribe itself in the anxious mind of her daughter that Harriet actually inserted it verbatim into a novel written fifty-nine years later when she, at the age of forty eight, was still aspiring to imitate Roxana's trust in God. Within Roxana's answer were Harriet's basic complaints against Calvinism: first, Roxana explained that analytical dissection of her love for God was foreign to her nature; second, she had never experienced a period in which she disavowed her faith and could not even imagine one; third, her love for God was a joyful emotion, inextricably woven into the pattern of her natural response to the beautiful; fourth, the damned who are penitent ought to resent a creator who ignored them; finally, she described one of her frequent spiritual transports, a viseo dei which mystified Lyman and the children:

You observe of the feelings I described that resting on them you should inquire whether it was the result merely of natural susceptibility. To love God because he is good to me you seem to think, is not a right kind of love, and yet every moment of my life I have experienced his goodness…When recollection brings back the past, where can I look that I see not His goodness? What moment of my life presents not instances of merciful kindness to me, as well as to every creature more and greater than I can express. Were I not an object of God's mercy and goodness, I cannot have any conception. …Imagination never yet placed me in a situation not to experience the goodness of God in some way or the other. …The disinterested love to God which you think is alone the genuine love, I see not how we can be certain we possess, when our love of happiness and our love of God are so inseparately connected…In contemplating the character of God, his mercy and goodness are most present to my mind, and as it were, swallow up his other attributes. …You complain that your heart is inclined to rise at the idea of suffering eternal punishment. I do not know as I understand what this feeling is. …Is it wickedness in me that I do not feel a willingness to be left to go on in sin: Can anyone joyfully acquiesce in being thus left? I can joyfully acquiesce that God should be a sovereign in the disposal of mercy, if he will have mercy on me; but when I pray for a new heart and a right spirit, must I be willing to be denied, and rejoice that my prayer is not heard? …I cannot now describe what have been my feelings before, but on Sunday night I experienced emotions which I can find no language to describe. I seemed carried to heaven, and though that neither height, nor depth, nor things present, nor things to come, should be able to separate me from the love of God which is in Christ Jesus. (56-7)

Like one of the spirits in Harriet's novels, Roxana influenced the lives of her children from the grave. The intensity of their devotion to her memory is not exaggerated in Henry Ward Beecher's famous tribute that, although he was only three-and-one-half-years-old at the time of her death, "My mother is to me what the Virgin Mary is to a devout Catholic" (Wagenknecht 21). The confidence with which Roxana prepared for death furthered the idealization of her memory. While riding home under a full moon after an evening's entertainment at a parishioner's house, in 1816, Roxana calmly turned to Lyman and informed him not to expect her to be with him for much longer. To his incredulous reply she explained that "I have had a vision of heaven and its blessedness" (Cross 213). Six weeks later, after committing her children to the love of God, she went to heaven: "She told them that God could do more for them than she had done or could do, and that they must trust Him...Mr. Beecher then made a prayer, in which he gave her back to God and dedicated all that they held in common to Him. She then fell into a sweet sleep, from which she awoke in heaven" (217).

A Childhood Ends at the Age of Six

Harriet never knew her mother as a living person. Roxana was an idea ever improved upon by her father and her maternal grandparents. But she always remembered her father as an emotional weathervane, unpredictably swinging from moods of self-confidence which inspired him to initiate temperance and missionary movements, to abysmal periods of depression in which he suffered from "the hypos." In *Oldtown Folks*, Harriet gave a good description of her father's temperament in her picture of the emotional needs of John Rossiter, a human shipwrecked by the tempests of Calvinist doubt:

> Was he conscious, our great man and master, of that weakness of his nature which made an audience, and an admiring one, always necessary to him? Of a soul naturally self-distrusting and melancholy, he needed to be constantly reinforced and built up in his own esteem...What seemed the most trenchant self-assertion in him was, after all, only the desperate struggles of a drowning man to keep his head above water...our good opinion, our worship and reverence, were the raft that kept him from sinking in despair. (448)

As he admitted himself, Lyman was set adrift for a least a year by the death of Roxana. Hoping to shelter young Harriet from the gloom of the Beecher household, her aunt took her for that year to live at her maternal grandparents' farm, Nutplains.

At Nutplains, away from an unstable father who frequently sighed that he wished she had been a boy, Harriet was taught "according to the old school," to act and speak as a lady. Her indulgent grandmother smothered her with affection, and kept the memory of her departed mother before her as a feminine ideal. Harriet would later recall that "our mother, lost to us, seemed to live again. We saw her paintings, her needle-work, and heard a thousand little sayings and doings of her daily life" (Cross 233). The ritual, the unrepentant Toryism, and the aestheticism of her lost mother's religion intoxicated the child's imagination. In recollecting what was so attractive about the nightly prayer services, Harriet focused upon two parts of her grandmother's Episcopal catechism: first, the definition of status openly acknowledged in the household gave her a sense of elevation above the servants whose tasks she was destined to perform when she returned to Litchfield: "a portion of the Church Catechism which always pleased me, particularly when applied to them, as it insured their calling me 'Miss Harriet,' and treating me with a degree of consideration which I never enjoyed in the more democratic circle at home" (234). A second portion which caused her delight was the opening question propounded to the catechumens. This detail reveals more about the Nutplains experience and the meaning of the theme of lost childhood in her writings than at first appears. At Litchfield, the first query of Harriet's Calvinist primer was the awesome and confusing "What is the chief end of man" which "was vastly too difficult to remember" (229). At Nutplains, the Episcopal Catechism began with the happy question "What is your name?", a question attractive to a child because it seemed to indicate God's personal concern for her, and because a child could answer so smartly.

Litchfield and the Beecher home signified oppression, even if Harriet tried to smooth the jagged edges in retrospect. This famous celebrator of childhood innocence and the joys of motherhood was wrenched out of her childhood by the loss of her mother, for when she returned to her father's house, after a year of being treated as a child, she found that the new family organization assigned her the role of mother to her two younger brothers, Henry Ward (age four), and Charles (age two). As a result of this new life of maternal responsibilities, Harriet fell into a perpetual state of mourning, clear evidence of a withdrawal from the world because of the lack of affection. Catherine, the oldest child, who acted as the woman of the house, gleefully (and unperceptively) remembered how Harriet was always the most distressed of the children at the graves of family pets, for whom she requested Catherine to compose memorials she called "epithets."

Harriet's new responsibilities and her perpetual mourning were related. She identified with dumb animals (as she would later identify with her children) and longed for death as an escape from life to love. Death for Roxana had been a peaceful transition from earth and mere love for God to His actual home of complete love. Her peaceful asylum was an enviable alternative to a home in which there was little love directed toward Harriet, but which demanded constant maternal duties from her. Life at Litchfield was also unpleasant when compared with the peace of death because of the soul-struggle imbedded within the contradictions of her father's theology. Just as for Jonathan Edwards, before his own conversion, there was always the fear inspired by Lyman, that her heart might secretly be turned against God, or that the love sensed for Him might only be a natural, rather than a truly religious affection.

Adolescence (1800-1878)

Catherine Beecher's alienation from her father's faith had a lasting impact upon the younger sister's emotional and religious development. Catherine was engaged to Henry Metcalf Fischer, a Yale graduate who, at twenty-three, was to assume a chair in mathematics at Princeton. The marriage of this eldest daughter was planned to take place upon Henry's return from a European trip taken to purchase needed books and equipment for the college. Henry was loved by the entire Beecher family, by whom it was hoped that his single flaw, unregeneracy, would be eliminated with time. Henry's ship, "The Albion," went down in a storm off Ireland. Like one of Job's messengers, the lone survivor reported that Fischer had not experienced grace during the last moments. A trunk had knocked him unconscious while he was attempting to repair the ship's compass. Catherine was prostrated by the news, not simply by the loss of this loved one, but because Henry's spiritual irresolution mirrored hers. She spent the next two years at Fischer's home, submitting his papers to the most sympathetic inspection in the hope of uncovering some evidence that he had been saved. Instead, she discovered that he had only felt an involuntary disaffection for an omnipotent God who allowed men to be damned. Searches through his diaries and letters, and talks with his parents and neighbors revealed that he had been very much like Roxana in natural goodness: "I found that, even from early childhood, he had ever been uncommonly correct and conscientious, so that his parents and family could scarcely remember of his ever doing anything wrong" (Cross 369).

Catherine finally concluded that Henry had not experienced grace because of the "appalling doctrines" of the local preacher, Nathaniel Emmons. Emmons' antediluvian fixation on the omnipotence of God relegated sentient humans to the status of "mere machines, and all our wickedness was put into us; and then we were required to be willing to be forever miserable." In the face of Emmons' preaching: "he sought to yield that homage of the heart to his Maker which was required, but he could not; like the friend who followed his footsteps [Catherine herself] he had no strength, and there was none given from above" (Cross 369). In retrospect, Harriet tried to explain away the family tragedy of Catherine's reeling from Calvinism by attributing it to the fortuitous conjunction of her deep loss with the location of Fischer's home within the confines of Emmons' parish. Nevertheless, letters exchanged between Lyman and Catherine show that it was clearly connected to the unresolved contradictions in Beecher's theology.

The effect of this tragedy upon Harriet was linked to the early death of her mother and her adjustment to her father's religion just prior to the tragedy. During a revival in the spring of her twelfth year, the lonely girl experienced what she later termed an "easy" conversion. That Sunday, her father's "theme was Jesus as a soulfriend offered to every human being" (Stowe *The Life of Harriet* 33). Lyman spoke extemporaneously from a suggestive text, a method of preaching in which he was notoriously effective in winning souls, but not so equally distinguished for his faithfulness to Edwardsian or even Taylorian theology.

Soon after her conversion, Harriet joined the staff of a girl's school in Hartford which Catherine was forming as a means of putting her bitterness to use for the good of others. Catherine convinced young Harriet that her feelings toward Jesus, her soul friend, were incompatible with the Calvinist deity who had allowed Henry Fischer to die unsaved. By this sisterly kindness, Catherine reopened the case of Harriet's adjustment to the loneliness of a loveless childhood. Convinced of her lack of faith, and unwilling to explain her problem to Lyman Beecher after he had given his sanction to her experience, Harriet was left with the counsels of the despairing Catherine. For the next three years she plunged into grueling projects of language study and painting, in addition to her normal teaching duties, which were followed by periods of hypochondria. She learned to live this painful existence by believing that it must be part of the "initiation of a great spirit" (Stowe *The Life of Harriet* 19). When her emotional condition became unsupportable, she retreated to the rural peace of Nutplains.

Searching for an answer, Harriet asked her brother Edward (a sort of father-confessor among the alienated children) if he thought her love for Christ were really an illusion: "Do you think, my brother, that there is such a thing as so realizing the presence and character of God that he can supply the place of earthly friends?" (40). Her self-defense in answer to his skeptical reply is an ungerminated seed of her most effective critique of New England Calvinism in her novels after *Uncle Tom's Cabin* (1852). Writing to her brother from Nutplains, she sounded very much like Roxana gently reproving Lyman years earlier: "Your speaking so much philosophically has a tendency to repress confidence. We never wish to have our feelings analyzed down; and very little, nothing, that we say brought to the test of mathematical demonstrations" (43). This vindication of the heart over the head, however, was not a completely satisfying resolution. In fact, the very tenuousness of this answer contributed to the anxiousness of her thirst for love. She was uneasy that she could love the Christ who had taken the place of her mother, but was incapable of making the necessary second step in the Christian ideal, the love of man through God: "He can supply the loss of all, earthly love…[but] even then I had doubts as to whether these feelings were right, because I felt love to God alone without that ardent love for my fellow creatures which Christians have often felt" (Stowe *The Life of Harriet* 39).

Harriet did not understand that her desire to be loved was woven into her love for Christ, nor that she desired to be extracted from the reality of human relations because her mother's death had proven them to be unrewarding and perilous. Hence, when she regretted the reticence which prevented her from making friends, she was describing an emotional poverty which would impede her maternal feeling for her own offspring. But while fearful of friendship, she always kept in mind an alternative to friendship, an escape to a heaven of love: "Friends may change; they must die; they are separated from me, and I ask myself why should I wish to love with all the pains and penalties of such conditions? ...Well, there is a heaven—a heaven—a world of love, and love...after all is the life blood, the existence, the all in all of mind" (Stowe *The Life of Harriet* 51).

Marriage: "Poverty and Sickness"

In 1832, after a humiliating rejection of his attempts to integrate Calvinism, Lyman Beecher seized at an offer to assume the Presidency of Lane Theological Seminary, Cincinnati, Ohio. Forging for himself a role as redeemer of the American West from the forces of Popery and atheism, he enthusiastically accepted this new start at the age of fifty-seven. Harriet and Catherine accompanied him, with the idea of establishing a female seminary to assist in bringing on the Kingdom of God. For Harriet, life in Cincinnati was a continuation of the soul-sickness which had plagued her since Catherine had jarred her from the comfortable delusion of her "easy" conversion. During this period, she read the autobiographical novel *Corrine* with a personal knowledge of the longing and frustration suffered by its authoress, Madame de Staël, who, like Harriet, was an intellectually afflicted woman searching for redemption. Harriet's response to Corinne, like that of Margaret Fuller, and Elizabeth C. Stanton is important as an index of the frustration of American women in the nineteenth century. Just as Margaret Fuller saw in it the message that "Women do not understand the life of thought; what matters to them is not the pulsations of the brain, but the beatings of the heart," (Miller xiii) so Harriet saw in it a vindication of her thirst for a loving Christ. Unlike Margaret Fuller, however, Harriet did not

Professor Calvin and Mrs. Stowe

interpret its message merely in terms of the repression of woman's intuitive wisdom. She projected it as a problem of the American mind which, shaped and molded by Edwardsian Calvinism, had perverted the longings of the heart:

> [I]n America feelings become still more deep, morbid, and impassioned by the constant habits of self-government which the rigid forms of our society demand. They are repressed, and they burn inward till they burn the very soul, leaving only dust and ashes. It seems to me the intensity with which my mind has thought and felt on every subject presented to it has had this effect. It has withered and exhausted it, and though young I have no sympathy with the feelings of youth. All that is enthusiastic, all that is impassioned with admiration of nature, or writing, or character, in devotional thought and emotion, or in the emotions of affection, I have felt with vehement and absorbing intensity—felt till my mind is exhausted and seems to be sinking into deadness. Half of my time I am glad to remain in a listless vacancy, since thought is pain, and emotion pain.
> (Stowe *The Life of Harriet* 62)

Through a local literary club, and Cincinnati's magazines, Harriet found a means of expression in fiction which helped her to escape from her emotional repression. Then, inexplicably, after the death of her best friend, she married the mourning husband, Calvin Stowe (1802-1886), out of sympathy with him for their mutual loss.

The responsibilities of motherhood made marriage just another clog to the spirit. The fiction which had previously been a means of escape from depression now became an indispensable supplement to Calvin's meager salary. The frustration of trying to write, while tending the children, and keeping an eye on the maid, widened the gap between her need for love, and the demands imposed upon her by a family. Since the emotional temperature of the Stowe house was the Beecher coldness all over again, there was nothing new to redeem the pressure except the children who made their arrival progressively less welcome by coming with an implacable biennial regularity. In the biography of his mother, Charles Stowe aptly named his chapter covering the period from 1840 to 1850, "Poverty and Sickness."

In 1843, the suicide of her brother George (who thought he was controlled by the devil) went through her heart like a spear. It took her months to recover from the birth of her fourth child that year. In 1845, after the birth of her fifth child, Harriet appealed to Calvin for sympathy (he was in the East on a fund-raising campaign for the seminary) with desolate self-pity:

> I am sick of the smell of sour milk, and sour meat, and sour everything, and then the clothes will not dry and no wet thing does, and everything smells mouldy; and altogether I feel as if I never wanted to eat again...I suffer with sensible distress of the brain...and you know that, except for this poor head, my unfortunate household has no mainspring, for nobody feels any kind or responsibility to do a thing in time, place, or manner except as I over see it. (111)

Her condition was so severe, that she fled East, first to Nutplains, and then to a Dr. Wesselhoeft's "hydropathic" treatment of douches and baths at Brattleboro, Vermont, where she remained for an entire year!

Nine months, almost to the day, after her return to Cincinnati, Charles, her sixth child, was born. Probably with her own welfare in mind as much as Calvin's, Harriet immediately dispatched her husband off to Dr. Wesselhoeft where he remained for the next fifteen months! During his absence, she nursed her family through a cholera epidemic which she said left not a single house untouched, including her own. The cholera took her youngest baby. In 1849, Calvin was offered a position at Bowdoin College in Maine, but since he was required to remain at Lane until his replacement arrived, Harriet was entrusted with the task of moving the entire family from Cincinnati to the East. Although she interpreted this to be another stone piled onto her soul, it was also, for the first time, in the forty years of her life, an escape from the influence of her mercurial father and her skeptical sister. Writing to Calvin about her sacrifices for her family, she revealed her understanding of the trials of motherhood as she, a woman with so little love or energy to exert in life, experienced then:

> [I]n kindness...and justice...I want you to reflect calmly how great a work has been imposed upon me at a time when my situation particularly calls for rest, repose, and quiet. To come alone such a distance with the whole carriage of children, accounts, and baggage; to push my way through hurrying crowds, looking for trunks, and bargaining with hackmen, has been a severe trial of my strength, to say nothing of the usual fatigue of travelling. (131)

Even during this taxing move, Harriet found it necessary to write articles to pay for the furnishing of the New Brunswick home. In "Earthly Care a Heavenly Discipline," one of these articles, she made an effort to construe her role as a mother in religious terms, in conflict with her wish for the solitary comfort of a God who would help her escape from life's oppressive responsibilities. The article commences by stating as a general problem what had been Harriet's particular problem from the time she was forced to become a mother of her two younger brothers in Litchfield, until the household move in 1850: "Nothing is more frequently felt...as a hindrance to the inward life of devotion, than the 'cares of life;' and even upon the showing of our Lord himself, the cares of the world are the thorns that choke the word and it becometh unfruitful" (Stowe

Writings of Harriet vol. XV 194). Significantly, she explains that the normal Christian can abstract himself into an unearthly sense of supplication in prayer only when "the hand of death is laid on his child, or the bolt strikes down the brother at his side." In contrast to these painful, but elevating moments, the multiplicity of duties of a parent or businessman cloud,' the perception of God, leaving the aspiring Christian confused and gloomy: "the soul shut itself within itself becomes morbid; the fine cords of the mind and nerves by constant wear become jarring and discordant; hence fretfulness, discontent, and habitual irritability steal over the sincere Christian" (199). All that is needed to consecrate this waste of despair is to recognize that every act in life has a holy meaning, and that earthly care is the preparation of the soul just as when "We learn to know God as the infant child learns to know its mother and its father, by all the helplessness and all the dependence which are incident to this commencement of our moral existence" (200). With this insight, the Christian begins to see the loving concern and design of God, in the most trivial of worldly responsibilities: "our faith seems gradually almost to change to sight...and multiplied cares and trials are only new avenues of acquaintance between us and heaven." And this must be the answer for a true Christian faith for "Not till belief in these declarations, in their most literal sense, becomes the calm and settled habit of the soul, is life ever redeemed from drudgery and dreary emptiness, and made full of interest, meaning, and divine significance" (Stowe *Writings of Harriet* vol. XV 201).

From 1850 until 1852, Calvin remained in Cincinnati, while Harriet dutifully cared for the children, furnished and renovated the newly acquired house, and paid for it all with her royalties. As early as 1850, she was writing on the Negro's potential for citizenship in the *National Era*, (which would later serialize *Uncle Tom's Cabin*) based upon her observation of free Negroes in Cincinnati. After passage of the Fugitive Slave Law as part of the Compromise of 1850, she and Henry Ward discussed the moral consequences for the North of a law which required Northern complicity in the sin of slavery. He and some of her close friends suggested she write something on the subject. On a Sunday in February, 1851, at the communion rail of the college chapel in New Brunswick, Harriet was transported by the vision of Uncle Tom's death. Returning home, she immediately committed this divine visitation to paper. In the vision of Uncle Tom's struggle with faith, she saw herself projected, and from that vision, which embodied her deepest emotions, she began to write a novel about the trials of bondage that would sear her nation's conscience.

Uncle Tom's Cabin (1852)

What was not admitted by Mrs. Stowe (she claimed that she was nothing more than God's amanuensis), nor never fully delineated by those who have written about her, is that *Uncle Tom's Cabin* is her declaration of independence from Calvinism. The public that wept over *Uncle Tom's Cabin* fully appreciated that the novel was as much about religion as slavery. Since its best-seller days, literary historians have been satisfied with the rather unpenetrating insight that Uncle Tom is a black Christ.

The critique of Calvinism within *Uncle Tom's Cabin* is more explicit in the original subtitle, "The Man That Was a Thing" than "Life Among the Lowly" which was later added. It is a protest against Calvinism's denial of the efficacy of familiar affections as a means of grace. The emotional havoc suffered by Harriet because of the damnation of the unconverted found a direct counterpart is the disruptive effects of the sale of black children upon the emotional equilibrium and the religious faith of black parents.

The two apparently contradictory accounts which Harriet gave of her inspiration for the novel suggest this interpretation. In the more famous of the two, she claimed that she learned to sympathize with slave mothers –who had no right to keep their children –when she lost Charlie during the cholera epidemic. Although she did not elaborate on the lesson, it should be added that the abnormal painfulness of the loss was in great measure caused by the child's unregeneracy according to the tenets of Calvinism,, The second account, concerned her vision of Uncle Tom in New Brunswick. Both explanations were right, for *Uncle Tom's Cabin* was a synthesis of her struggles, and an imaginative exploration of the means of resolving them. It was her cry of pain that would, in later years, be allayed when, through her New England novels, she attained a historical distance from anxieties induced by Edwardsian Calvinism.

In the characters of Uncle Tom and Little Eva, Harriet embodied the doubleness of her sense of the Pilgrim's Progress in which her long-suffering spirit was always tempted by the yearning for unity, through death, with a loving Christ: Tom's faith is the victory with the battle against the distractions of Earthly Care and Calvinist doubt; Eva's is the triumph without the battle, the peaceful passage from the imperfect love of earth to the all-sufficient love of Heaven.

Faith: Tom

Uncle Tom's story is an ennoblement of the Christian dilemma which Harriet had tried to resolve in her magazine article, "Earthly Care a Heavenly Discipline." Tom was sold down the river with the conscious intent to sacrifice himself for his family. According to the contract of sale, little Harry, child of Eliza, would be torn from the maternal bond as payment for Selby's debts. Eliza, a representative mother, planned to avert this fate by escaping to Ohio. This rebellion was an imaginative fulfillment of Harriet's attempt to wrest herself from the authority of the God who had taken her innocent child. Tom was fully aware of Eliza's plan to escape, and even helped her. He could have escaped, but he decided, instead, to sacrifice himself so that no other member of his family would be traded. Here, Harriet was projecting her resolution to sacrifice herself for her family, despite the attraction (Tom's freedom would be selfishly acquired) of being absorbed in an unearthly love of God through the peace of death.

Until his trials at Legree's viciously efficient plantation, Tom's life is a placid one, because he learns that the love of Christ as expressed in the Revelation, is a substitute for the love he had experienced in his family:

> O, Mas' r, when I was sold away from my old woman and the chit' en, I was jest a' most broke up. I felt as if there warn't nothn' left; and then the good Lord, he stood by me, and he says 'Fear not, Tom;' and he brings light and joy into a poor feller's soul—makes all peace; and I's so happy, and loves everybody, and feels willin jest to be the Lord's and have the Lord's will done, and be put jest where the Lord

wants to put me. I know it couldn't come from me, cause I's a poor complainin' cretur; it comes from the Lord. (Stowe *Uncle Tom's* 359)

This companionship with Christ is only an ad hoc solution, since his life with the St. Clare family involved no harder task than his being Eva's playmate.

Under the domination of Legree (who is from Vermont), Tom meets the real test of his faith. Early passages describing Tom's fight for faith on Legree's plantation are no more than shadow-boxing compared to the real struggle. In this transitional period, before he is spiritually shackled by the oppression of the plantation system, Tom observes that kindness awakens the womanhood of the slave women:

> Moved by the utter weariness of two women, whom he saw trying to grind their corn…he ground it for them, put together the decaying brands of the fire, and then went about getting his own supper. It was a new kind of work there,—a deed of charity, small as it was; but it woke an answering touch in their hearts,—an expression of womanly kindness came over their hard faces; they mixed his cake for him, and tended its baking. (429)

Their domestic instincts thus ignited, these women become receptive to Tom's Bible readings, but finally warn the novice that he will not find his loving Christ on Legree's property. Legree's threats and beatings do not really test Tom's faith. These direct challenges of his faith, like the high moments of tragedy in "Earthly Care A Heavenly Discipline," only fan the coals of his communion with a loving Redeemer. Like Harriet, his greatest obstacle is the consecration of the trials of hard work and brutalizing conditions:

> Have not many of us, in the weary way of life, felt, in some hours, how far easier it were to die than to live? The martyr, when faced even by death of bodily anguish and horror, finds in the very terror of his doom a strong stimulant and tonic. There is vivid excitement, a thrill and fervor, which

may carry through any crisis of suffering that is the birth-hour of eternal glory and rest.

But to live—to wear on, day after day, of mean, bitter, low, harassing servitude, every nerve dampened and depressed, every power of feeling gradually smothered,—this long and wasting martyrdom, this slow, daily bleeding away of the inward life, drop by drop, hour after hour,—this is the true searching test of what there may be in a man or woman. (478)

Just as the burden of daily living is about to drain the last of Tom's consoling faith in a Redeemer, Legree prematurely announces his victory. At this moment, Legree's taunt, "join My Church," becomes meaningful. What Harriet saw as Legree's "church," whether she was conscious of it or not (and I think not) was the continuous magnetism of Calvinism upon her belief against her emotionally strong, but conceptually vulnerable, reaction from it. Slavery treats men as things and denies the inviolability of the family. It is therefore, like Calvinism, the enemy of the emotional and moral faculties which Harriet believed could be fostered only in a family through a mother's love. Harriet could write such an

Legree's Oppression

effective picture of the mental anguish of slavery because her father's Calvinism was also like slavery, in that it demanded an admission by the regenerate, that another segment of humanity would eventually fall under the punishment of God's curse, just as the Negro, according to the clerical proponents of slavery, is under the Curse of Canaan. As a Southern minister explains earlier in the novel:

> It's undoubtedly the intention of providence that the African race should be servants—kept in a low condition...'Cursed by Canaan; a servant of servants shall he be...It pleased Providence for some inscrutable reason to doom the race to bondage, ages ago; and we must not set up our opinion against that. (152-3)

For Harriet, the Calvinist counterpart of this Curse of Canaan, the doctrine of election, was not a conception to be accepted or denied upon mere intellectual investigation, since it had behind it the full authority of the New England Puritan tradition. Like Tom's loss of the sense of an ever-present Jesus when he is under the burden of field work, Harriet's alternative to Calvinism, the role which she conceived for herself as a mother, and the religious potential with which she infused the maternal emotions, was under severe attack during the move to New Brunswick.

In answer to Legree's taunt, Tom's vision of a suffering Christ is the embodiment of Harriet's answer to her father's demand that she accept the damnation of a majority of humanity. It should be remembered that Legree intends to make Tom his overseer when Tom finally succumbs, just as the elect obtain preferential treatment from the Calvinist God once they join his inhumane church. At the lowest ebb of doubt, with the weight of life forcing him farther from God than he has ever been, Tom answers Legree, spokesman for the Calvinist God, with the mystic vision of a bleeding Christ:

> The atheistic taunts of his cruel master sank his dejected soul to the lowest ebb; and, though the hand of faith still held to the eternal rock, it was with a numb, despairing grasp... Suddenly everything around him seemed to fade, and a

vision rose before him just as Tom's vision did to Mrs. Stowe of one crowned with thorns, buffeted and bleeding. Tom gazed in awe and wonder, at the majestic patience of the face; the deep, pathetic eyes thrilled him to his inmost heart; his soul awoke, as, with floods of emotion, he stretched out his hands and fell upon his knees—-when, gradually, the vision changed; the sharp thorns became rays of glory; and, in splendor inconceivable, he saw that same face bending compassionately towards him, and a voice said, 'He that overcometh shall sit down with me on my throne, even as I also overcame, and set down with my Father on his throne.' (481)

Harriet's exaltation at Tom's visionary answer to Legree, "Ah, Legree, try all your forces now" is an expression of relief after her vicarious triumph over the emotional starvation and intellectual perplexity caused by her father's implacable God. Tom's reward for his trials is a victory over the oppression of Legree, objective-correlative of the Calvinist God whose threat of damnation fragmented man's emotional life, exhausting him of any natural capacity to love. Tom's painfully acquired love illuminates the hearts of his companion sufferers, just as Harriet saw herself in the role of a mother inspiring her children with a love which it was always a strenuous and self-conscious effort for her to furnish:

> Tom's whole soul overflowed with compassion and sympathy for the poor wretches by whom he was surrounded. To him it seemed as if his life-sorrows were not over, and as if, out of that strange treasury of peace and joy, with which he had been endowed from above, he longed to pour out something for the relief of their woes. It is true, opportunities were scanty; but on the way to the fields, and back again, and during the hours of labor, chances fell in his way of extending a helping hand to the weary...The poor, worn-down...creatures, at first, could scarce comprehend this; but, when it was continued week after week, and month after month, it began to awaken long-silent chords in their benumbed hearts. Gradually, and imperceptively the

strange, silent, patient man, who was ready to bear everyone's burden, and sought help from none...the man who, in cold nights, would give up his tattered blanket to add to the comfort of some woman who shivered with sickness...this man, at last, began to have a strange power over them. (485)

Faith: Eva
In contrast to Tom's triumph, Eva's death "is the victory without the battle—the crown without the conflict." However morbid and sentimental the portrayal of Eva may be to the modern sensibility, the child is a strangely moving amalgam of her creator's repressed religious aspirations. Eva embodies at once the unworldly tranquility of Roxana, the assurance that Charlie's death was ordained by God, and, most importantly, a projection of Harriet's inward desire to die—or to have died—as a child, with the faith of her mother. The function of Eva as an Evangel to her father is also important because it indicates the kind of love and identification which Harriet invested in her children, loving them not so much for themselves as their use as vicarious escape routes from the life assigned her by fate.

For all practical purposes, Eva, like Harriet, has no mother. Marie is so absorbed in her hypochondria that she is incapable of loving. In addition, Eva's father, Augustine St. Clare, is so paralyzed

The Death of Little Eva

by religious doubt and guilt about slavery that (like Lyman Beecher's need for Roxana, and Harriet's need for her mother's child-like faith) he stands more in need of help than his child. With this lack of parental affection, it is not surprising that Eva begins to commune with a loving Christ who fills the child's lonely heart with love.

As Tom exposes Eva to the well-marked passages of consolation in his New Testament, she gains a faith which is a simple duplication of Roxana's assurance, including a mystical recognition that she will be returning to God. Since Tom is a Negro (see below) he is not surprised when Eva tells him that she has seen "a band of spirits bright/ that taste the glories there" in the words of a Methodist hymn he sings to her. Just as Roxana announced to Lyman that she was going back to God, Eva tells Tom: "I'm going there...to the spirits bright, Tom; I'm going, before Long" (322). Harriet explains (unconvincingly, but with obvious sincerity) that Eva's death should not disturb her parents or the reader, for it is now merely the dissolution of the earthly bonds on a heavenly spirit:

> Has there ever been a child like Eva? Yes, there have been; but their names are always on grave-stones, and their smiles, their heavenly eyes...are among the buried treasures of yearning hearts. In how many families do you hear the legend that all the goodness and graces of the living are nothings-to the peculiar charms of one who is not [Roxana, Charlie] It is as if heaven had an especial band o angels, whose office it was to sojourn for a season here, and endear to them the wayward human heart, that they might bear it upward with them in their homeward flight. When you see that deep, spiritual light in the eye,—when the little soul reveals itself in words sweeter and wiser than the ordinary words of children,—hope not to retain that child; for the seal of heaven is on it, and the light of immortality looks out from its eyes. (323)

The story of Old Prue, by showing the impediments which slavery creates to prevent the expression of love, is the world's share in Eva's death. Old Prue, the local drunk, was brought to her abasement by slavery's denial of her right to love her children. As a young woman she was used like a beast to breed offspring for the slave market. When she was sold into a domestic position, she brought with her the last of her children, but even this last of her ties to the dignity of motherhood was shattered when the child's crying piqued her mistress. After the child died of hunger and exposure, Old Prue turned to rum: "I tuck to drinkin' to keep its crying out of my ears!" (268). Her story is complete when she dies from a beating administered to her for stealing the liquor which alone brought her solace. In addition to the story of Old Prue, St Clare's boasting about how he "broke" an African Negro through affection and trust convinces Eva that in a world which allows slavery, love can express its power only for perverted ends. Because Eva has no real home (i.e., loving parents) and because homes cannot exist where there is slavery, she merely detaches herself from the wounding relationships of life to go "to our Savior's home; it's so sweet and peaceful there—it is all so loving there!"(343). In Eva's death scene, the difference between her "victory without the battles longed for by Harriet, and the battle of life fought by Uncle Tom becomes evident:

> A bright, a glorious smile passed over her face, and she said, brokenly,
>   —O! love,—joy,—peace! gave one sigh, and passed from death into life!
>   Farewell, beloved child! the bright, eternal doors have closed after thee; we shall see thy sweet face no more. Oh, woe for them who watched thy entrance into heaven, when they shall wake and find only the cold grey sky of daily life, and thou gone forever! (365)

Doubt: Augustine St. Clare
When Charlie Stowe died of cholera, Harriet could only watch with her rebellious heart, powerless to give the child or herself any comfort. She wrote to her husband in Brattleboro: "I looked on his imploring face when I could not help nor soothe nor do one thing, not one, to mitigate his cruel suffering, do nothing but pray in my anguish that he might die soon" (Stowe *The Life of Harriet* 124). Augustine St. Clare, who is so like Harriet in his religious doubt, is

unlike her in that he is allowed to participate in Eva's childish faith. In St. Clare's question about what it means to be a Christian, Harriet imaginatively grants herself a colloquy with her dead mother to assure herself of the destiny of her lost child; and the validity of her own wavering faith:

> "What is being a Christian, Eva?"
> Loving Christ most of all, said Eva.
> "Do you, Eva?"
> "Certainly I do."
> "You never saw him," said St. Clare.
> "That makes no difference," said Eva, "I believe in him and in a few days I shall see him;" and the young face grew fervent, radiant with joy.
> St. Clare said no more. It was a feeling which he had seen before in his mother. (359)

With Augustine as her spokesman, Harriet examines the source of religious faith and attempts to prove that it is dependent upon maternal love. As an alternative to the Calvinist belief that grace is a visitation of what Edwards called a "divine and supernatural light," Harriet demonstrates that it is the effect of the physical presence, the mere being of an affectionate and sensitive mother which makes a man truly religious. St. Clare's father was a domineering Vermonter who became a rich planter, but his mother, to whom he gravitated, was so holy that she might have been a visiting angel. By the natural sweetness of her person, she was as inspiring as little Eva becomes through loneliness and painful sympathy:

> My mother...she was divine! Don't look at me so!—you know what I mean! She probably was of mortal birth; but, as far as ever I could observe, there was no trace of any human weakness or error about her; that mother has been all that has stood between me and utter unbelief for years. She was a direct embodiment and personification of the New Testament, a living fact, to be accounted for, and to be accounted for in no other way than by its truth. (45)

St. Clare's mother fostered in him the aesthetic appreciation of the beautiful and the good. Had she not died when he was thirteen, leaving him spiritually longing, or had he later married a woman who could have taken her place as a living embodiment of Christian love, he could have been a believer, and worked toward making the South a society of loving families by helping to outlaw slavery. Since his loveless marriage, he claims, that he has continued his empty existence only for the sake of Eva. Upon her inspiring death, he is thrown into a recollection of his own childhood faith in his mother, searching in the lost past for a means to escape from the torture of religious doubt and his guilt about vacillation in the face of slavery. Singing the "Dies Irae" from his mother's copy of Mozart's *Requiem Mass*, he absolves himself from the moral battle against slavery just as Harriet desired to escape the moral tension of denying the historically authoritative Calvinist concept of sin. Through him, Harriet consummated a communion with the peace and love of a home in Heaven with her mother. During St. Clare's last moments, the family doctor announces that the dying man's mind must be wandering, to which St. Clare answers:

> No! it is coming HOME, at last!" said St. Clare, energetically; "at last! at last!
>
> The effort of speaking exhausted him. The sinking paleness of death fell on him; but with it there fell, as if shed from the wings of some pitying spirit, a beautiful expression of peace, like that of, a wearied child who sleeps...Just before the spirit parted, he opened his eyes, with a sudden light, as of joy and recognition, and said "Mother!" and then he was gone! (391)

Doubt: George Harris and Family

Harriet's projection of her concern about the saving grace of a Christian home into her denunciation of slavery is demonstrated more transparently in George Harris' search for light. Because he aggressively defies the laws which define him as a thing rather than the man, husband, and father, Harris is the most virile male in the novel. He is equally manly in his opposition to a God which, at least as interpreted by the Establishment, justifies an institution which first prevented him from being a child in a family, and then threatens to repeat the tragedy by selling his son. George shuttles between religious doubt and faith according to his family status. Brought up as a child with "no father, no mother, no sister, not a living soul that cared for me more than a dog," (139) it was impossible for him to believe in the Christian God. After marrying the pious Eliza, his faith brightens, but he is thrown back down into the pit of despair when he hears that his wife has fled to Ohio to prevent the sale of their son.

Defending himself in terms of his perception of his inner worth, despite his being one of the damned in a slave society, George boldly rejects a God that allows him to be treated as a thing: "O, I've seen things all my life that have made me feel that there can't be a God, You Christians don't know how these things look to us. There's a God for you, but is there any for us? (144). But George's bitterness is soon melted when he has an opportunity to observe a Christian family. The Hallidays, a Quaker family who assists George, Eliza, and Harry to escape along the Underground Railroad to Canada, present, in their domestic felicity, a model which convinces him of the reality of Christian love and piety as experienced within a home:

> This, indeed, was a home—home—a word that George had never yet known a meaning for; and a belief in God, and trust in his providence, began to encircle his heart, as, with a golden cloud of protection and confidence, dark, misanthropic, pining, atheistic doubts, and fierce despair, melted away before the light of a living Gospel, breathed in living faces, preached by a thousand unconscious acts of love and good will, which, like the cup of cold water given in the name of a disciple, shall never lose their reward. (174)

Eliza fled across the Ohio with bleeding and frozen feet, spurred on with a maternal love for her son no less than that which Harriet felt in her desire to deny the Calvinism which considered her child a thing rather than a loved one. Through Eliza's eyes, the Halliday home is described in terms of the peace, love, and beauty which Eva and St. Clare found only in the escape of death. It is the home described in this passage which, in later novels, would represent Harriet's alternative world of love to the abstractness, the fruitless introspection, and emotional aridity of Calvinism:

> When she awoke, she found herself snugly tucked up on the bed, with a blanket over her, and little Ruth rubbing her hands with camphor. She opened her eyes in a state of dreamy, delicious languor, such as one who has long been bearing a heavy load, and now feels it gone, and would rest. The tension of the nerves, which had never ceased a moment since the first hour of her flight, had given way, and a strange feeling of security and rest came over her; and, and she lay, with her large, dark eyes open, she followed, as in a quiet dream, the motions of those about her. She saw the door open into the other room; saw the supper table with its snowy cloth, heard the dreamy murmur of the singing tea-kettle; saw Ruth tripping backward and forward, with plates of cake and saucers of preserves, and ever and anon stopping to put a cake into Harry's hand, or pat his head, or twine his long curls round her snowy fingers. She saw the ample, motherly form of Rachel, as she ever and anon came to the bed-side, and smoothed and arranged something about the bed-clothes, and gave a tuck here and there, by way of expressing her good-will; and was conscious of a kind of sunshine beaming down upon her from her large, clear, brown eyes. She saw Ruth's husband come in,—saw her fly up to him, and commence whispering very earnestly...She saw her with the baby in her arms, sitting down at teas; she saw then all at table, and little Harry in a high chair, under the shadow of Rachel's ample wing; there were low murmurs of talk, gentle tinkling of teaspoons, and musical clatter of cups and saucers, and all mingled in a delightful dream of rest; and Eliza slept, as she had not slept before, since the fearful midnight hour when she had taken her child and fled through the frosty star light. (172)

This long passage is included in full because Eliza's perspective of the family, like Harriet's, is that of an outsider finding life's component of death, sleep. Harriet's deepest feelings about the family are here displayed in her drawing Eliza as a child rather than a mother. Harriet's mind was perfectly attuned to the needs of a family precisely because she experienced a sense of tension between her subjective desire to be in a receptive role and the objective demands that she fill the creative role of a mother. The poetry of this vignette is the poetry of a longing imagination, not the report of one securely resting within the bosom of a family.

After the Harris family ferries to the Canadian side of Lake Erie, Harriet interjects a poem about the meaning of a freedom which guarantees the integrity of the conjugal family. In the poem, she seems to be more concerned with death as experienced by Eva and St. Clare than the joys of family life in a free nation:

> Twas something like the burst from death to life; From the grave's cerements to the robes of heaven; From sin's dominion, and from passion's strife,
>
> > To the pure freedom of a soul forgiven;
> > Where all the bonds of death and hell are riven,
> > And Mortal puts on immortality,
> > When Mercy's hand hath turned the golden key,
> > And Mercy's voice hath said, Rejoice, thy soul is free.
>
> (477)

But in fact this poem bears within it the Christian dilemma and its solution. Just as George Harris will worship God once he is a man and not a thing, so Harriet is explaining that recognition of the divine role of the family as a vehicle of religious affections will allay spiritual torment, and yield a new kind of piety, in which the natural emotions will be liberated for the good of man, rather than turned inward to torture him. It was in reaction to a world in which George Harris' could not belong to, or maintain the integrity of, their families that Eva went to her motherly Jesus, and St. Clare resigned from life to join his dead, but not forgotten mother.

After George attends college in France, he devotes himself to founding a Negro Republic in Africa. Like a fulfilled St. Clare, as a tribute to his gratefulness for a mother's love.

George is dedicating his energies to the cause of his mother's race rather than his father's. He may have been "no more than a fine dog or horse" to his father, but to his mother "I was a child; and though I never saw her, after the cruel sale that separated us...yet I know she always loved me dearly" (531).

Women

Even Simon Legree has his moments of regret for rejecting his mother's loving influence. A woman's love is a type for the bleeding Christ's love for man, and she makes the home a temple through her complete renunciation of self in her love for her children. By their love for children, the mothers of America "learned by the cradles...to love and feel for all mankind." Only women can truly comprehend the immorality of slavery which deprives slave mothers of the right to guide their children to blessedness, just as the Calvinist God deprived Harriet of her influence over Charles.

Women represent the heart. The sons of Adam who have erected the grinding machinery of commerce, politics, and organized religion are ever willing to compromise the dictates of the intuitive heart. Mrs. Bird, wife of a Senator who voted for the Compromise of 1850, vindicates her moral duty to assist the escaping Eliza with an argument for the superiority of a mother's feeling which embodies the substance of Harriet's attack on the "logic traps" of her father's Calvinism: "I hate reasoning, John,—especially reasoning on such subjects. There's a way you political folks have of coming round and round a plain right thing; and you don't believe it yourselves, when it comes to practice" (100).

The extent of the influence of a mother's love has already been illustrated. Shackled to Haley's wagon, Tom's parting homily to little George Selby begins and ends with the veneration of motherhood. Through Mrs. Selby's influence, George becomes one of the few effectual and moral males in the novel. The lesson to be learned is that slavery never could have prospered in the West had Northern mothers been faithful to their Christian duty:

> If the mothers of the free states had all felt as they should, in times past, the sons of the free states would not have been

the holders, and proverbially, the hardest masters of slaves; the sons of the free states would not have connived at the extension of slavery, in our national body; the sons of the free states would not, as they do, trade the souls and bodies of men as an equivalent to money, in their mercantile dealings. (546)

In contradiction with her apotheosis of the conjugal family, Harriet implies that a dedicated mother supported by a devoted son—rather than a husband and wife—constituted the ideal pair for proper accomplishments. This distortion is perhaps an unfortunate side effect of Harriet's experience of carrying the man's and the woman's load after her marriage, together with her tendency to see her children as extensions of her stifled self. Frequently in her novels, repressed New England women experiment with a second romance by vicarious participation in their son's rebellions from the family, or their daring voyages to enchanted lands. Within *Uncle Tom's Cabin*, Mrs. Selby is not only morally superior to her spouse; she has "a clear, energetic, practical mind, and a force of character every way superior to that of her husband." When Mr. Selby is conveniently removed from the scene by scarlet fever, she and George promptly unravel the Gordian Knot of family debts by shrewd financing. This mother-son team liberates the Selby slaves, and commences a head start program to train the Negroes to be fit citizens of the African Republic to which they will ultimately be transported.

The Negro

By attributing to the African American an emotional and aesthetic superiority over the Anglo-Saxon, Harriet was vindicating the woman's heart against the cold-blooded church which supported slavery (and infant damnation) with its chapter and verse. The Establishment has corrupted irrepressible emotions by applying masculine logic. In contrast, the intuitive wisdom of Mrs. Bird and Mrs. Selby cuts through political sophistry. The effects of not recognizing emotional needs, aspirations, and insights are clearly written in the stories of Eva and St. Clare, who must die to find their fulfillment.

Harriet's belief that the Negro is "not naturally enterprising, but home-loving and affectionate," (119) or that "the principle of reliance and unquestioning faith, which is the foundation of the Gospel is more a native element in this race than any other" (486) at first appear as well-intentioned prejudices, but both of these characteristics have a direct relationship to her argument that women are morally superior to men, and that the sex which personifies these principles, should be allowed full sway in a Christian home. Going beyond popular prejudice, Harriet calls into question the emotional vacuousness of the Christianity developed by the Anglo-Saxon spirit. As George Harris explains, an Anglo-Saxon Civilization is a cul de sac: "To the Anglo-Saxon race has been entrusted the destinies of the world, during its pioneer period of struggle and conflict. To that mission its stern, inflexible, energetic elements were well adapted but, as a Christian, I look for another era to arise" (534).

Although she tempers George's description of the new Christianity, her earlier reflection upon Tom's response to the floral luxuriance of St. Clare's mansion gives some idea of how the Negro will humanize Christianity and Christianize civilization:

> If ever Africa shall show an elevated and cultivated race,—and come it must, some time, her turn to figure in. the great drama of human improvement,—life will awake there with a gorgeousness and splendor of which our cold western tribes faintly have conceived. In that far-off mystic land of gold and gems, and spices, and waving palms...and miraculous fertility, will awake new forms of art...and the Negro race...will...show forth some of the...most magnificent revelations of human life. (222)

With his responsiveness to the beautiful in nature, his simplicity of affections, together with a past of suffering, the Negro will assure that the new Christianity will encourage a tasteful expression of emotion in religion and in the family.

At the conclusion of *Uncle Tom's Cabin*, Harriet rhetorically asks the reader: "is man ever to have wholly irresponsible power?" (544). The self-evidence of the answer was equally applicable to her father's God. Timidly and illogically in the theology of Lyman Beecher, brazenly in Charles Grandison Finney's divinity who ruled by the consent of the governed, the religious mind of nineteenth-century America steadily evolved toward an ever emphatic negation. Not until she was forty, in writing a novel about a sensitive man thwarted by oppression from communing with his loving God, could Harriet Beecher Stowe utter her own declaration of independence from the celestial absolute monarch of Calvinism.

In her later novels, Harriet made a more conscious and articulate critique of Calvinism. In *A Minister's Wooing* (1859) she essayed to reveal the emotional poverty of its concepts of grace and disinterested benevolence. In her magnum opus, *Oldtown Folks* (1869), she consummated her victory, this time with understanding and sympathy for the Calvinist tradition. "Good, grandmotherly Cotton Mather," had foreseen that the abandonment of the Half-Way Covenant would eventually destroy the Christian family. The individualism latent within the theology of her historical villain, Jonathan Edwards, not only resulted in a devaluation of the importance of the family, but ignored entirely the product of a truly Christian Home, a piety which blended the goals of the heart and the head. By viewing the evolution of New England Calvinism in this light, she could assert that she was not rebelling from her father's religion, only returning to its purest sources.

Notes

Both the research and writing of this article were mentored by Harvard Professor Kenneth S. Lynn (d. 1987); his superb "Introduction" to the Belknap Press edition of *Uncle Tom's Cabin* is a model of its kind and should be consulted by any serious student of Harriet Beecher Stowe and the 19th-century concepts of "Home." For more on Catherine Beecher, see Charles Edwards Stowe and Katharine Kish Sklar.

Works Cited

Adams, John R. *Harriet Beecher Stowe*. New York: Twayne, 1963.
Cross, Barbara M., ed. *The Autobiography of Lyman Beecher*. 2 vols. Cambridge: Belknap, 1961.
Finney, Charles Grandison. *Lectures on Revivals of Religion*. 1868. Ed. William G. McLaughlin. Cambridge: Belknap, 1960.

Foster, Charles H. *Rungless Ladder: Harriet Beecher Stowe and New England Puritanism*. Durham: Duke UP, 1954.
Foster, Frank Hugh. *A Genetic History of the New England Theology*. New York: Russell and Russell, 1963.
Miller, Perry, ed. *Margaret Fuller: American Romantic*. New York: Anchor, 1963.
—. *The Life of the Mind in America: From the Revolution to the Civil War*. New York: Harcourt, Brace, and World, 1965.
Sklar, Kathryn Kish. *Catharine Beecher: A Study in Domesticity*. W.W. Norton, 1976.
Stowe, Charles Edward. *The Life of Harriet Beecher Stowe*. New York: Houghton Mifflin, 1891.
Stowe, Harriet Beecher. *A Minister's Wooing*. New York: Derby and Jackson, 1859.
—. *Oldtown Folks*. 1869. Ed. Henry F. May. Cambridge: Belknap, 1966.
—. *Sunny Memories of Foreign Lands*. 2 vols. Boston: Philips, Samson, 1854.
—. *Uncle Tom's Cabin: or Life Among the Lowly*. 1852. New York: Heritage, 1938.
—. *Writings of Harriet Beecher Stowe*. 16 vols. Boston: Houghton Mifflin, 1896.
Wagenknecht, Edward. *Harriet Beecher Stowe: The Known and the Unknown*. New York: Oxford UP, 1965.

27
Frederick Henry Hedge: Brookline's Conservative Transcendentalist

Frederick Henry Hedge (1805-1890) of Brookline, Massachusetts has remained one of the lesser luminaries of the Transcendental Movement. Indeed, we only remember Hedge (if we think of him at all) because Emerson sometimes referred to the irregular meetings of the Boston area Transcendentalists as gatherings of the "Hedge Club." The later pastor of the First Unitarian Parish of Brookline belonged to that first generation of young Americans who went to Europe in search of education. Under the supervision of his tutor, George Bancroft, Hedge spent from 1818 to 1822 at German Gymnasia. Thus, when things German became of interest in New England, Hedge was one of the very few who did not have to depend upon translations or interpretations of the new ideas, but could plunge directly into the original sources themselves. As scholar and as sensibility, he set a precedent for some future denizens of a Boston suburb so attached to its traditions that it refused to abolish its inefficient representative town meeting form of government and resisted incorporation into the City of Boston even unto the 21st century.

At the Harvard Divinity School, Hedge met Emerson and encouraged him to study German. Emerson characteristically declined—he felt that German could not amount to much if he was not interested in it. Yet Emerson respected Hedge's somewhat different orientation and felt that he could learn from him. In 1833, shortly after Hedge published an article on Coleridge in the

The Rev. Professor Hedge

Christian Examiner, Emerson wrote: "Henry Hedge is an unfolding man who has just now written the best pieces that have appeared in the *Examiner* and one especially was a living, leaping Logos and he may help me" (Letter to Thomas Carlyle).

Indeed, it is not difficult to see that Hedge anticipated many radical notions that were to become popular among his peers, for Hedge's articles *did* leap. For example, he defended Coleridge against those critics who charged the literary philosopher with obscurity. Hedge was ready to admit that Coleridge's style was often convoluted, but he added tartly that "we are inclined...to suspect that the greater part of this alleged obscurity exists in the mind of the reader, and not in the author." Hedge felt that New Englanders were especially obtuse and wrongheaded in their reading of Coleridge's speculations because the New England intelligentsia had exhibited "no taste for hardy application, no capacity for vigorous and manly thought." In short, Hedge behaved very much as the precocious young man who accused an older generation of allowing its intellectual nerve to go slack: "A hard word scares us, a proposition which does not explain itself at first glance, troubles us; whatever is super sensual, and cannot be made plain by images addressed to the senses, is denounced as obscure, or beckoned away as mystical and extravagant. Whatever lies beyond the limits of ordinary and outward experience is regarded as the ancient geographers regarded the greater portion of the globe—as a land of shadows and chimeras" ("Biographia Literaria" 115, 117).

German scholars had proved themselves of hardier mettle. The young Hedge was presumptuous enough to claim that one could not understand the ideas of modern Germany unless one was "with it"; "In order to understand Transcendentalism we must raise ourselves at once to a Transcendental point of view, and take one's stand from the interior consciousness, a state of free intuition to be attained by a vigorous effort of the will" (121). Thus, if the stodgy Unitarian readers of the *Christian Examiner* could not comprehend the rebellion of the younger generation, they had only themselves to blame.

Hedge also shared with Emerson an inner uncertainty about the direction of his personal life and thought. Margaret Fuller sensed the gravity of this dilemma, the more so after Hedge wrote to her about wanting to found a "society" of like-minded young thinkers. In 1833, she wrote Hedge from Groton: "Could you once be brought into unison with your day and country without sacrificing your individuality all would be well. Let me once more entreat you to write to bring your opinions into collision with those generally received" (Letter of July 4, 1833).

Margaret Fuller here articulated the central *motif* underlying the Transcendental movement: the young rebels wanted to join actively with the issues and problems of their society, but they feared that participation would lead to an eclipse of individuality. They had to face the paradox that they could only act on the minds of others by bringing their opinions into collision with those generally received. This indeed was their creative contradiction: in order to link themselves to society, they were willing to constantly entertain the necessity of revolt. It may well be that Frederick Henry Hedge has remained a minor figure among them because he was thwarted, rather than stimulated, by the tensions of such a struggle. Instead of exploiting it to advantage as did Margaret Fuller and Emerson, Hedge sought to resolve the opposition with the help of German historicism.

Emerson sensed this fear of tension in his friend quite early and described Hedge in 1833 as an "unfolding man" (Letter to E.B. Emerson). Yet two years later, Emerson confided to his journal that Hedge was not really destined to unfold into a full, transcendental bloom. Instead, he saw that his friend was seeking a more conservative and modest place, "uniting strangely the old and the new" (qtd in Sack 73). The mixed reactions to Hedge's *Christian Examiner* article on Coleridge are a good case in point. Emerson may have thought of it as a potential Transcendental bombshell, yet Henry Ware, Jr., found that his fellow Unitarian ministers were equally well pleased with the piece.

Reading the Coleridge article with an understanding that it pleased *both* Transcendentalists and Unitarians, helps to define Hedge's position. First, no "true believer" would have lingered so long over Coleridge's limitations. Furthermore, the conservative in him displayed a real fear of the excesses to which a sanguine Transcendentalism might lead, especially if Transcendentalism meant celebrating the liberation of an "absolute self...incapable of being determined by anything higher than itself." (120). It seems clear that, in spite of his own Transcendental leanings, Hedge drew back from a full-fledged radicalism of the ego.

This is not to condemn Hedge for being less radical than his Transcendentalist friends. Rather, he remained a minor figure because he limited his spectrum of imaginative possibilities: his refusal to admit the validity of the radical posture made him cease to speculate about it, and in doing so to give *form* to it. Here is where Hedge and Emerson definitely parted company, as Emerson clearly understood: "I owe him gratitude for all his manifest kindness to me, though he is quite wrong to say he loves me, for I am sure he does not quite" (Letter to Fuller March 30)

Hedge not only missed the opportunity for greatness by dismissing the novel idea of his time too hastily; he shied from accepting the responsibilities of leadership at a moment when leaders were needed most. His inability to come forward at the opportune moment is best revealed in his dealings with Margaret Fuller and Emerson when the *Dial*, a much-needed venue for transcendentalist articles and poems, was being launched. As early as 1834, Hedge had suggested the idea of a periodical. Nothing had come of his proposal, but in 1840 the time seemed ripe. Margaret Fuller wrote to Hedge that she needed him: "We depend on you for the first number, and for solid bullion, too. Mr. Emerson will write every number and so will you if you are good and politic, for it is the best way to be heard from your sentry-box there in Bangor. In the journal you will write to us constantly and *of your best life*" (Letter to Hedge, 1840. Emphasis supplied.).

The Best of One's Life

The best of one's life. We should be grateful to the Transcendentalists for giving shape to this ideal of self-fulfillment through life and art. Yet at this creative moment, Hedge felt spent and prematurely old: "No one can feel a stronger interest in the new journal than myself. I conceived the plan of one and urged its execution in conversation with Ripley and others some five years since. Then, I could have been the editor. I felt equal to any amount of literary labor. But I have grown less enterprising and more diffident...I should like now, if possible, to have no other part in it than that of reader and subscriber" (Letter to Fuller, 1840). Hedge revealed more when he continued that "you frighten me with your sudden announcement," for he was mistrustful of the direction which the *Dial* was likely to take. He might contribute to the *Dial*, but he insisted that he remain anonymous and added significantly, "I wish you would all do so," for he felt that the mystery surrounding anonymity was not worth sacrificing for "the Quakerish downrightness of signatures and first persons singular." The best of one's life, then, could well do without a Transcendentalist's ego.

Emerson confided to Margaret Fuller that the *Dial* might succeed better without Hedge's involvement. As a historically minded scholar, he did not show sufficient sympathy for the fundamental Transcendentalist belief that the center of gravity had shifted from society to the individual. This was an egoistic doctrine which Hedge was unwilling to accept. Emerson was growing increasingly pessimistic about his friend's potential: "Hedge's view of the matter is to me quite worthless. The poor old public stands just where they always did; garrulous orthodox conservative whilst you say nothing; silent the instant you speak; and perfectly and universally convertible the moment the right word comes. If three or four friends undertake the book, I will answer for the world" (Letter to Fuller, 1840).

Hedge was as aware as Emerson of the differences which separated him from his friend. In reviewing Emerson's *Essays, Second Series* for the *Christian Examiner* in 1845, the German-trained scholar attempted to clarify these differences, while giving full due to Emerson's merits. He praised Emerson for placing strong emphasis on "the present momentary life "and quoted with approval from Emerson's "New England Reformers"; he admired Emerson for keeping his sanity in spite of the "ultraisms" of the day. It was true, Hedge admitted, that Emerson attached "great significance to these movements as an indication of the growing trust in the private, self-supplied powers of the individual," yet the historically-minded scholar in him especially relished Emerson's observation that reformers were "partial, they are not equal to the work they pretend" (92).

After giving Emerson his deserved praise, Hedge nevertheless felt constrained to scrutinize the arguments as a *christian* examiner, and here he found his Transcendentalist friend seriously wanting. Emerson's relation to the Christian church troubled Hedge. Although it would probably not destroy interest in Emerson as a writer, Hedge felt that the sage of Concord's rejection of "a special and miraculous revelation" would inevitably and essentially vitiate the general influence of his writings. Because Emerson regarded Christ as a "mere teacher of moral and religious truths" (94), Hedge as a believer was forced to draw a line beyond which tolerance and imaginative sympathy could not go: "We profess our inability to comprehend how a mind, with any pretensions to philosophic culture, can be satisfied with it; how so acute a thinker as the writer of these essays can overlook the violence it does to that fundamental principle in philosophy, which requires an adequate cause for every effect, or can fail to perceive that, in its anxiety to avoid a miracle, it substitutes a greater wonder for a less" (96).

Hedge generously allowed that Emerson was a direct follower of Christ in his deep sympathy for humanity and his "genuine regard for individual man." But he was unwilling to venture beyond this rather unspecific acknowledgment, for Brookline's conservative transcendentalist had his own distinctive ideas about the uses of the past, the meaning of Christ, the place of the church, and the role of the scholar.

Frederick Henry Hedge and the Brookline Sensibility (1857-1872)

In 1839 Hedge married Lucy Pierce, daughter of John Pierce, minister to the First (Unitarian) Parish from 1796 until 1849. In 1857 he returned to Brookline to fill the pulpit that had been left open by the death of his father-in-law. While Hedge had done considerable thinking and writing before his arrival in Brookline in 1857, during his fifteen years in the Boston suburb his pen flowed more freely than at any other period in his career. Indeed, he was quite busy during his Brookline years. From 1857 to 1861 he served as editor of (and regular contributor to) the Unitarian quarterly, the *Christian Examiner* in which thirty-five years earlier he had made his *debut* as a young writer. From 1859 until 1862 he served as the President of the American Unitarian Association. Also during his Brookline years, Hedge held a part-time appointment in Church History in the Harvard Divinity School in Cambridge, some five miles to the north along what is now Harvard Street. His *Ways of the Spirit* (1877) emerged from his lecture course at the Divinity School. Finally, Hedge wrote his *magnum opus, Reason in Religion* (1865) in the study of his Brookline manse on Walnut Street. Thus Brookline may well claim the mature Henry Hedge, in his most generative period, as its own and at least one observer has concluded that his historical vision was inspired as much from the stable and detached

The Walnut Street Church

environment of his parish's location in an independent suburb as from his treasured tomes of Kant and Hegel.

Hedge's special role in the Transcendental movement is defined by the value which he attached to the preservation of the past. Looking back upon the heyday of the Transcendentalist club, he mused that at that time he "seemed to discern a power and meaning in the old, which the more impassioned would not allow." Unlike his contemporaries, Hedge was partial to the historical rather than the visionary element of religion. Above all, he believed that the progress of religion must not be abandoned to the willful aberrations of individual inspiration: "such a dispensation once initiated in human society, is not left to itself to take what direction chance may impart." The inexorable movement of history had a pattern which it was the scholar's task to explain to his fellow men: "The world's history is not an aimless succession of events—a heap of facts fanned together by the flight of time, as the wind piles sand-drifts in the desert—but a process and a growth. The succession of events is rational; they follow each other by a necessary order" (*Ways of the Spirit* 19, 20, 21). As Hedge grew older, he stressed more and more that this "necessary order" could only be comprehended through imaginative sympathy. Modern rebels would not judge the past so harshly if they could be taught to realize that their own thought, like the thought of the past, was immersed in the flow of history. In short, to Transcendentalism Hedge owed his conviction that the Spirit was the motor of history, but he differed from the movement in his conviction that the Spirit used the Christian Church, rather than the individual, as its vehicle. For this reason Hedge deplored the proliferation of sects within the Christian Church; they only succeeded in downloading valid elements of the universal design into isolated, and mutually exclusive, files.

The Brookline cleric saw it as his task to sift through the past in order to find the components that would achieve an ecumenical reunion among the multitude of alienated sects within the Christian religion. In this search, the incarnation of Christ became increasingly important; the incarnation, Hedge believed, was not only historically significant *qua* doctrine. It seemed to be the only correct description of the relationship of Christ to His church. Furthermore, belief in Christ as a divine agent endowed the church with a distinctive, supernatural authority. On this point Hedge was adamant. The church was not merely a platform from which ministers dispensed a code of estimable ethics. It is "much more than a system of moral philosophy. Christianity means a great deal more than that. It means participation of the Divine nature, through faith, and through the communion of the Spirit, of which the Church is supposed to be the repository and mediator." Without divine authority, which had been imparted to the church by Christ's incarnation, the church would be unable to "carry weight with the mass of mankind" ("Conservatism and Reform" 135).

In spite of some major flaws, Hedge believed that the Church of Rome had managed to do just that. Catholicism and other "legal" religions had shown their "superiority...over liberal Christianity as a method of Church-life." Given this admiration for churchly traditions, it is not surprising that he was critical of the inability of Unitarians to organize and discipline themselves. In an address of 1851 before a ministerial conference in Boston, Hedge lamented to his Unitarian colleagues:

> We want more of the corporate spirit, a stronger sense of our denominational mission and calling, and through that of our relation with the Church Universal. I suppose there is no denomination of Christians in which there is so little of this spirit, so little concentration, so little care for their commonweal and its success. This I consider a fault in our connection, the result sometimes of a daintiness which refuses to mix with the mass in any movement and sometimes the result of an insensibility which ignores the obligation laid on every believer, in some way to cooperate for the maintenance and promotion of Christian truth. ("Ecclesiastical Christendom" 133)

This criticism of his Unitarian brethren is not dissimilar from George Ripley's strictures of Emerson when the latter decided not to participate in the experiment in cooperative living at Brook Farm (West Roxbury). Emerson's journal reflections are famous; "I do wish to remove from my present prison to a prison a little larger, I wish to break all prisons. I have not yet conquered my own house...Shall I raise the siege of this hencoop and march baffled away to a pretended siege of Babylon?" (Oct 17, 1840). But for Hedge, this Babylon was real enough. He felt that the impatience of liberal Christians with rites, forms, and scriptures was not necessarily proof of a larger spirituality. It was "often but a proof of weakness of faith—a want of power to penetrate into the soul of these things, to interpret their deeper import, and discover their latent life" ("Ecclesiastical" 128).

To many of his nineteenth-century contemporaries, the claims of faith and reason seemed to contradict each other. Hedge, however, believed that a proper sense of the past would enable man to place himself in the world, without having to rely on his unpredictable emotions as his only guide. The problem for modern man was not so much that he should assert himself, but that he should sustain himself through time by carefully modifying and modestly readjusting his institutions. In Hedge's mind, this was not a case of pouring new wine into old bottles so much as injecting the proper amount of preservative in order that the mellowness of the ages could slowly ripen into the future. For Hedge only that "reason" which demoted itself to dredging the truth out of past and present Christian ideals, could be considered authentic. Too often, other applications of intellect were destructive to the true ends of faith. They involved "mere curiosity, a thirst for mental excitement amusing itself with mental pictures, as a child turns over the leaves of his picture book, or pulls its playthings to pieces, with a scrutiny in which there is more love of marvel than of wise research" ("The Cause of Reason" 208).

For Hedge, then, the truths of religion did not exist on a transcendental plane. Religious truths would be understood only after an imaginative projection of the self into the lessons taught by history:

> Ecclesiastical continuity means that mankind does not consciously and willfully foreshape its own future; that history is not the product of human foresight, but divine ordination, education.... The individual may think he is rid of it, but his fancied emancipation is only the flight of the aeronaut, who seems to detach himself from the earth when he

cuts the rope which held his balloon; but all the while an invisible rope—we call it gravitation—has fast hold of him. The length of his tether is the quantity of gas there is in him. The gas escapes, the tether shortens; the gas all gone, ecclesiastical continuity resumes its sway. (130)

In "Anti-Supernaturalism in the Pulpit" Hedge addressed himself to what he perceived as an increase of arid intellectualism in the Harvard Divinity School. Rather than helping young men to assume their posts as ministers, the bookish training undermined their faith in the divinity of Christ, and hence their ability to speak with real authority:

The authority of a young man just entering the ministry who shall be understood to speak from no warrant but his private opinion, with only his own talent or his own conceit to back him, cannot be exactly measured, but we are safe in placing it somewhere in the neighborhood of zero. (153)

Hedge captured the impact of this dysfunctional education with a humorous, *reductio ad absurdum:* at the end of his three years of training, the divinity student discovered that his work "Brought him to accept, as his solution to the great historical and miraculous fact of Christianity, the theory thus stated by a recent critic, that 1800 years ago, in Galilee on the shores of Tiberias and round about Judea, nothing happened'" (154).

Such a powerful diatribe against the destructive use of individual reason was not allowed to go unanswered. Daniel Bowen defended the prerogatives of individual judgment in a response pamphlet aptly titled "Authority Assumed: A Review of Rev. Dr. Hedge's Address 'Anti-Supernaturalism in the Pulpit.'" Bowen and Hedge obviously disagreed on many points of doctrine, but what stands out in retrospect is the contrast of sensibilities—the younger scholar looks eagerly forward for inspiration while the older Unitarian professor looks back to the past for an anchor against the erratic potential of personal inspiration.

Bowen's pamphlet radiates a shining confidence in the authenticity of religion as a living, inward experience. While Bowen does not reject the record of history, he sees the past as a resource to be consulted rather than an inexorable caravan to be joined. Instead, Bowen encourages Unitarian contemporaries to use history according to their own lights; they should sift through it and control it, rather than submit to it. The young man's demand for religious experience is too strong, and too personally rooted for him to accept the detached, "historical" perspective which Hedge revered.

Ultimately, of course, each man had his own content for the general term, "faith." Hedge feared that if "faith" were exclusively tied to the individual temper, it was bound to degenerate into an irrational, erratic emotion. To avoid this pitfall, Hedge urged institutional and traditional boundaries understood through the prism of a reason turned to the past—not to unmask it, but to empathize with it. Bowen saw no need for such timidity: "Faith apprehends divine realities as sense perceives the outward world. The belief in traditions, be they true history or not, is not religious faith. It belongs to the secular and not the sacred part of our nature" (15). Because his idea of faith was pinned to individual inspiration, Bowen saw the source of a minister's authority to flow from personal commitment and public example rather than institutional association:

> There is...something to be said in behalf of that 'young man' who stands up in the presence of his fellow men, clothed less with priestly sanctions than with the consciousness of sincerity and something to say; who speaks, not because he has been told something as tradition, but because of the inward, irresistible prompting. There was once such a thing as men, old and young, speaking as they were moved by the Holy Spirit; and if it is no longer possible to do so, then divine authority no longer exists, and it is worse than vain to parade a show of it. (16)

Bowen's most telling criticism of Hedge grew out of his sense that supernatural authority is a matter of "facts of personal inward experience" rather than what Hedge emphasized so often, "facts dependent upon outward testimony." Hedge's mistrust of the inward experience, Bowen concluded, had led the Brookline divine to a position which was suicidal to Unitarianism as a liberal faith. Bowen warned that Unitarianism "flourished so long as it... contended for...our God-given reason," that by tipping its hat to orthodoxy, it will "forget its proper mission." If it lost its confidence in the individual, "Why should it prosper, or even survive?" (27).

The two men also disagreed in their views on Christ. Whereas Hedge held up a meek and modifying Christ who "accepted the conditions of his lot and made his life divine by perfect obedience to those conditions," Bowen presented the ideal of a man who "did not devote himself to reshaping effete creeds and forms," who "supplanted ancient maxims by the insight of a present inspiration" (20). And present inspiration is of course always "new." To Bowen, history proceeded in discontinuous leaps: "There are crises in all growths, when great and radical changes are demanded, without which the life would become extinct" (22). On the other hand, according to Hedge, history evolved by a process of slow development. Its main characteristic was continuity rather than crisis, although Bowen feared that Hedge was evincing a "blind clinging to the past" rather than a vital faith. (25).

Reason in Religion was Hedge's most eloquent plea for religion as a corporate, historically conscious experience, but again his fellow Unitarians balked. In a review of this *magnum opus*, Francis Abbott, like Daniel Bowen before him, found something to praise in the work, especially Hedge's assertion that the pieces of history, of biblical criticism, and the insights of the Bible are all useless and inert by themselves: "private experience and individual consciousness, the scriptures of creation and of literature, the facts of history, and the whole circle of the sciences become data for the soul's analysis, and *thus alone* have theological worth" (93). But the Unitarian reviewer also voiced more enthusiasm for inspired faith than could be sanctioned by the Brookline scholar.

The soul's analysis was all that one needed if one wanted to publish the best of one's life. Both Hedge's Transcendentalist and Unitarian friends rejoiced in this discovery. They admonished their Brookline friend for falling behind, for had he not been one of the first to point the way? The irony was that Frederick Henry Hedge, the class poet at Harvard in 1825, had given up the afflatus of poetry for the appealing stability of history. William H. Lyon, who became pastor to the First Church of Brookline in 1896, had left a portrait of Hedge at the end of his Brookline period. The year was 1871, just before Hedge moved to Cambridge to become professor of German Literature—and it is here that the strengths and limitations of Brookline's Transcendentalist are subtly sketched:

> It was a beautiful day in a beautiful town, and I recall a crabapple tree just outside the window that was a wonderful mass of joyous blossoms. Of the conversation, however, I recall nothing. I suspect that I was in such mortal awe before the great scholar that I understood little of what was said… He was a man of the study rather than the world, and at ease with thoughts rather than with persons. Mingled with my reverence for his profound scholarship and his lofty thought, there has been ever since the tender memory…of a heart, as it were, imprisoned in the habits of a student. (20)

Brookline has produced other such sensibilities striving to match a lively interest in present enthusiasms with an equally animated respect for historical traditions.

Special Note on Sources

Otto Van Os contributed his knowledge of Emerson and the Transcendentalist movement to an early talking paper; I provided the research on Hedge and rounded out the chapter for this publication. Bryan Le Beau was so kind as to provide input to citation of sources. The article by Hunter proved helpful in "resetting" this chapter, although what is here presented was written some twelve years prior to the publication of Hunter's excellent reconsideration of Hedge within the Transcendentalist debates

An electronic source entitled American Transcendentalism Web has some of the esoteric sources here cited plus other publications by major and minor players in the group: www.vcu.edu/engweb/transcendentalism/authors/index.html. Emerson's entire writings are on the web.

Works Cited

Abbott, Francis. "Hedge's *Reason in Religion.*" *Christian Examiner* 79.1 (1865): 84-96.

Bowen, Daniel. "Authority Assumed: A Review of Rev. Dr. Hedge's Address 'Anti-Supernaturalism in the Pulpit.'" Boston: Walker, Wise, 1864.

Emerson, Ralph Waldo. *Journals of Ralph Waldo Emerson, with Annotations.* Ed. Waldo Emerson Forbes. Boston: Houghton Mifflin, 1909-1914.

—. "Letter to Edward Bliss Emerson." Dec 22, 1833.

—. "Letter to Margaret Fuller." March 30, 1840. Letters 270.

—. "Letter to Thomas Carlyle." Nov 20, 1834.

Fuller, Margaret. Fuller Family Papers, Harvard U.

—. "Letter to Hedge," Jul 4, 1833.

—. "Letter to Hedge," Jan 1, 1840.

Hedge, Frederick Henry. "Anti-Supernaturalism in the Pulpit."*Christian Examiner* 77.3 (1864): 145-160.

—. *Atheism in Philosophy* Boston: Roberts Bros., 1865.

—. "Biographia Literaria." *Christian Examiner* 14.1 (1833): 108-130.

—. "Conservatism and Reform." *Martin Luther and Other Essays.* Ed. Frederick Henry Hedge. Boston: Roberts Bros., 1888. 129-163.

—. "Ecclesiastical Christendom." *Christian Examiner* 58.1 (1851): 112-135.

—. "Letter to Margaret Fuller." Jan 20, 1840. Fuller Family Papers. Harvard U.

—. *Martin Luther and Other Essays.* Boston: Roberts Bros., 1888.

—. *Reason in Religion.* 5th ed. Boston: American Unitarian Association, 1901.

—. "The Cause of Reason, the Cause of Faith." *Christian Examiner* 70.3 (1861): 208-215.

—. *Ways of the Spirit.* Boston: Roberts Bros., 1878.

—. "Writings of R.W. Emerson." *Christian Examiner* 38.1 (1845): 87-107.

Hunter, Doreen. "Frederick Henry Hedge: What Say You?" *American Quarterly* 32.2(1980): 186-201.

LeBeau, Bryan. *Frederick Henry Hedge: Nineteenth-Century American Transcendentalist.* Eugene, OR: Pickwick Publications, 1985.

Letters of Ralph Waldo Emerson. Eds. Leslie Rusk and E.M. Tilton. New York: Columbia UP, 1939.

Lyon, William H. *Frederick Henry Hedge: Seventh Minister of the First Parish in Brookline, 1856-1872.* Published by the Parish, 1906.

Sack, Kenneth. *Understanding Emerson: The American Scholar and his Struggle for Self-Reliance.* Princeton, NJ: Princeton UP, 2003.

28
Amy Lowell of Brookline: The Patterns of a Life

> A book which needs to be written is one dealing with the childhood of authors. It would be not only interesting, but instructive; not merely profitable in a general way, but practical in a particular way. We might hope, in reading it, to gain some sort of knowledge as to what environments and conditions are most conducive to growth of the creative faculty. We might even learn how not to strangle this rare faculty in its early years.
>
> Amy Lowell, "Introduction," *Poems by a Little Girl* (1920)

Growing Up in Brookline

Amy Lowell was truly a native of Brookline. She was born in 1874 in the home of her parents, "Sevenels" (for the seven Lowells living there). She spent her youthful springs and summers at Sevenels, (winters belonged to Boston) and when her father died in 1900, she became mistress of the family mansion at 70 Heath Street. Two years later, she dedicated herself to the art of poetry. The grounds of Sevenels may constitute the most poeticized nine and one-half acres in America; nearly half of her poems deal in some way with its natural scenes and moods.

Amy Lowell may not have won any popularity contests among her contemporaries, but her diaries and notebooks trace the growth of an aristocratic spirit. This chapter will examine her early years and give a fresh reading of some core poems in the light of personal and regional factors.

A Writer's First Explorations

One of the earliest records of Amy Lowell's childhood is her "Private Book," begun when she was eight years old. The inner flap of the volume warns sternly about the privacy of the document; written in pencil is the insistent notation: "Private...PRIVATE...Amy Lowell...Private Book, PRIVATE BOOK." All of the succeeding pages are numbered, and all are headed by the warning "PRIVATE" written in capital letters.

At the back of the volume, an index identifies the real persons who are discussed. "Jupiter" (Teddy Lyman) is one of the first children to be closely scrutinized under Amy's moral microscope:

> Jupiter's caractear
>
> J's caracter is something like that of g.d...he has a good hart. I am shure he selldom is mean or cheats and does not back out of a thing the way V. dose. He allways remains a friend to a friend and does not leave one friend for another you may trust him with anything even your most private things and places. That is all about J.

This diarist scrutinizes every companion for the slightest traces of weakness. She is very concerned about having her "private things and places," but more in search of someone who will be worthy of sharing those very same private things and places. Walter Cabot (coded as Vulcan) was closely observed:

> I do not know much about V. but from what I have heard from J. I think that he is a coward I do not think that he likes N. he does not teas girls the way N. does and is a much nicer boy he and Bessie are great friends. he is a great climber; that is all about V.

Amy Lowell's biographers often find passages like this to be excessively critical. A more sympathetic view might be that this is a child who is being conditioned to look at the world with a testing eye. Her judgments do not issue from self-confidence, but from a sensitive conscience, which is undoubtedly as brutal on itself as it, at first, appears to be toward others.

The diaries reflect the loneliness of a forgotten child, but not without some redeeming humor. For example, consider the previous description of Walter Cabot (Vulcan). The child may be quick to apply the moral labels to condemn the weak, but she is unconsciously drawn to appreciate those qualities of kindness and friendliness which a weak boy might show young girls. Humor shines through a reflection on "nurse":

Mu's Caracter

Mu is my nurse She is very funny and a big bore When she comes after me we sometimes run away then she gets mad and scolds when she gets mad it is great fun when you have somebody with you but when you get home it is not so much fun. That is all about Mu.

The index identifies Amy Lowell under the pseudonym, "Mercury." The historian hastily turns to the appropriate entry, only to discover that this eight-year-old child not only holds others to a demanding standard of personal conduct, but is too critical to attempt any flattering self-portraits:

Mercury's Character

I aought not to say much about M. for that is my self their for I think I had better not say anything for of course I should either make myself very good or very bad Therefore I will not say any more about it. That is all about M.

Toward the conclusion of the Private Book, next to pages marked "Particularly private...particularly private...Amy Lowell" are two later entries. An early note reads, "Why are children such fools?" and is dated 1890 (when she was sixteen). A later notation reads, "Are they such fools? I wonder? I am inclined to think not?" The initial scornful remark is the attempt by a troubled adolescent who wants deny her inner struggles. As later diary entries reveal (especially in 1889-1890) the word "fool" seems to mean anyone who is silly enough to expose her true and vulnerable feelings to the world.

The second reflection is the reaction of a mature adult, Amy Lowell, an unmarried woman of thirty-one who has discovered how to respond to the world, and, more importantly, as an artist, how to make that response take permanent form. It is a statement by someone who approves of the capacity to feel.

Reading and Learning

In the same period as the "Private Book" (i.e., years eight to eleven) Amy filled out a cultural catechism. This series of responses helps to limn a more complete picture of those personal qualities most admired at Sevenels. The drama of Amy Lowell's search for a wholeness begins at this moralistic pole, and may be said to be striving to both reject its condemnation of spontaneous feeling *and* to escape the narrowness of its categories—all the while fulfilling its demands of strict and uncompromising individualism. Here are some of the telling questions and responses:

> Name? Amy Lowell.
> Residence? Brookline.
> What is your favorite moral characteristic? Self-controll.
> Which one do you most dislike? deceat.
> What is your favorite extravegence?…[No answer provided.]
> Who is your favorite heroin in the history of other countries? Josephine.
> What character (female) in all history do you most dislike? Joan of Arc.
> What are your reasons for your likes and dislikes? Josephine's husband ill treated her Joan of Arc was too masculine.
> What is your idea of misery? Not to be allowed to tobbogan.
> What is your idea of happiness? To be loved.
> What quality do you like best in a man? Manliness.
> What do you most dislike? Cowardliness…

What quality do you most like in a woman? Modesty.
What do you most dislike? Immodesty"

As the catechism of the "Composition Book" reveals, the eight-to-eleven year-old Amy Lowell was an avid reader of both juvenile and adult fiction. In an essay entitled "That Bookcase," she later outlined some important characteristics of her reading. Many of the books had been the childhood reading of her parents, carefully preserved over the years. Amy's interest in them was at least partially animated by the vicarious communion they gave her with the emotionally distant adults; each volume absorbed served as a unit of hoarded affection.

Unlike her peers, the inquiring Amy did not find the stories of Jacob Abbott's *Little Rollo* overly moralistic; indeed, she was surprised to discover that her contemporaries disliked the 'Little Rollo' stories. It seems fair to conclude that Amy Lowell was evolving into a character type closer to the antebellum ideal of Connecticut author Jacob Abbott (1803-1879).

This excessive moralism without any compensating religious consolation served to isolate her even more from a satisfying relationship with herself, her peers—even those members of her family who deigned to notice her existence. Debunkers of Amy Lowell usually mention two anecdotes about her. One reports that "Amy Lowell was brought-up by the coachman, Burns." A second refers to her being allowed to "drive" the coach home from St. Paul's (Episcopal) Church (near the intersection of Harvard and St. Paul streets) all the way back to Sevenels, a distance of three miles south along Cypress Street and then north on Walnut Street—past the First Unitarian Parish of Frederick Henry Hedge (see Chapter 27).

These two anecdotes need not be negatives. They indicate that Amy, as a Lowell, was expected to adopt an aggressive posture toward the world, but as a young child with a need for affection, she had only the coachman and other servants for companions. Her mother was an invalid both before and after Amy's birth, and her father, Augustus Lowell, at the age of fifty-two, was detached and unaffectionate. As Elizabeth Ward Perkins was to recall, when the elder children were home, the atmosphere was charged with exuberance:

> To the visiting girl, fresh from two years abroad, the drama of life in Sevenels, the Lowell house in Brookline, was literally as good as a play. All the children, a dozen years older than her friend, Amy, married and unmarried, were at home; men, authorities already in government and astronomy, the women keen for civic betterment and public affairs...As they gathered for the over-abundant meals of the era, it seemed to the stranger quite possible that the art of listening might be dispensed with, having become superfluous. Any two members of the family could talk and listen simultaneously, effecting a great economy in time and patience, for conflicting opinions might be stated, registered, and answered at the same moment. New England reserve did not prevail at the large table. No Latins or Slavs could have discussed more fervently, or with more expressive gesture, the local happenings or larger questions of the day. (329)

Here is the atmosphere in which being a Lowell required one to be quick-witted and aggressive.

A second insight from Mrs. Perkins' memoir of the Sevenels of young Amy Lowell illuminates the problem of the lonely child, capable and willing to be a Lowell, but unfulfilled in those needs which would make her the full-fledged, self-controlled individualist her family expected:

> When this distinguished middle generation had gone about its engrossing interests and the house was left to the parents and the two girls (i.e., Amy and Mrs. Perkins) reserve descended like a fog carried by the local East wind. The mother's invalidism, the father's stern conventions as to time and order, ...left non-conformist youth without sun or sun-warmed air to breath. Unaccustomed terror fell upon the visitor, a spoiled only daughter, when a portfolio left on a forbidden table, or arrival late for breakfast, shadowed the hospitable spirit of the house and lowered the temperature. (329)

Under these circumstances, it is not surprising that the young Amy Lowell became a child of reverie and fantasy. Of one of her favorite New England books, *Moon-Folk,* by Jane G. Austin, she confided, "I have read so many times that I have lost count":

> A lonely little girl makes the acquaintance of a delightful person, a chimney elf, and under his guidance drifts away to sea in a rowboat over the broad glade of the full moon. But the "moon glade" takes them straight to the moon, where she meets all the persons of child literature, even to King Arthur and his knights. So deep an impression did this story leave, that even today, when I see a wide path of moonlight over the sea, I invariably think of Rhoda drifting to the moon in her dory, with the irresistible chimney-elf sitting in the bow. ("That Bookcase" 7)

Her literary interests led to Thackeray, Victor Hugo, and finally, Shelley and Keats. Indeed, exposure to the English Romantic poets: "was my Waterloo…I surrendered completely to poetry, and with that surrender the chapter of my childhood definitely closed" ("That Bookcase" 10).

Life in Literature and Photography

Amy Lowell's work was offered to the public when she was thirteen. With the help of her mother and sister, she wrote some children's stories that were collected under the title *Dream Drops or Stories from Fairyland By a Dreamer.* Given the inmost thoughts of the young girl, it is no surprise to find countless imaginary characters in these stories, nor do the rather unpleasant situations which these figures experience come as any shock. Foster Damon, the "official" biographer of Amy Lowell, concluded that these stories reflected "an imagination rejoicing in its own powers, exploring the five senses and the four elements," and that the stories are "vivid, vigorous, original…without the least trace of eccentricity" (82-3). Damon's conclusions were enthusiastic, but they may point more to his own exposure to, and acceptance of, this kind of literature than serve as an accurate analysis. For example, the following opening paragraphs of one story are quite germane to troubling aspects of young Amy Lowell's life:

> Once upon a time, a little girl named Rosa said to her mother, yawning, 'Oh! how dull it is here, I have no children to play with.'
> 'Go out and dig in your garden' her mother replied, and prepare it for the pretty flowers you expect to plant in it by and by; and think how much pleasure you will have yourself, and be able to give others. (*Dream Drops* 23)

The little girl exits, begins to dig, discovers a trap door, which opens into fairyland—which is a garden, but a garden of fantasy:

> a very large garden, the velvet turf divided by paths of brilliant colors, and bordered by trees bearing for fruits dazzling jewels, emeralds, rubies, sapphires, amethysts...the paths seemed covered with powdered gems. (*Dream Drops* 24)

Other stories in *Dream Drops* tell of lonely children who seek companions in the world of sleep. These companions are the characters from *Little Lord Fauntleroy*, *Alice in Wonderland*, *Little Rollo*, and Cooper's leather-stocking tales. In one story, "The Good Little Henry," a boy seeks "the plant of life to cure my poor sick mother, who is dying." He performs a series of Herculean efforts to purchase the valuable plant. His reward at the end of his labors is to have a mother well enough to forget her self-absorption and devote attention to him. The unstated irony of such a story as "Good Little Henry" by Amy Lowell, age thirteen, is not unlike that of the Horatio Alger tales of industry and pluck. No young hero who could perform all of these grueling tasks of self-assertion could afterward revert to the childlike passivity of the boy described at the end of the story.

Dream Drops was written when Amy was thirteen. The next record of her growth is recorded in her diaries of 1889 and 1890, when she is fifteen and sixteen. One of the first characteristic comments comes in a description of her feelings about school. A child who was ignored by parents and indulged by servants was not well disposed to accept classroom discipline:

> 2 Jan. School began, nasty old thing, I *hate* it...We are going to have gymnastics in school under Dr. Possey, a Swede, studied for 3 years to teach us how to wiggle our thumbs, *etc.*, hope he knows how by this time.

A day later, she added to this mordant condemnation of things institutional:

> 3 Jan. Everything horrid, school as stupid as death. No, not death, that would have some contentment and some pleasure in it, stupid as music lessons.

It is noteworthy that most biographers see in these passages the first glimmering of a sarcastic, masculine personality taking shape in this chunky adolescent. A different response would be more positive: coming to light is an independence and vigor of personality which, for all its built-in repressions, rebels against restrictions. Amy is most truly a Lowell in these statements of reprehension.

On 8 and 10 January are two important entries: on the eighth of January, Amy was allowed to view, during an open house event, the inner-rooms of the newly constructed Boston Athletic Club. After seeing the indoor track, the swimming pool, the exercise rooms, and the steam bath, she reflected in her diary:

> 8 Jan. wouldn't it be nice to be a man...being a man would be fun: no dependence, go where you please, do what you please. I can imagine falling in love with a woman, but not with a man, I should like to be a man, and fall in love with a woman. Ah, well! What must be must be.

The entry of 10 January concludes with an easily overlooked — but nonetheless significant — statement, "I hate effusion." Here is the beginning of a second dimension of psychic conflict. The first involved the severe standards of conduct and character of her parents. In addition, there is the issue of female identity, a crisis which is often exploited by Amy's unsympathetic biographers and critics. Yet the conflict, as it begins to develop, is very understandable. In many ways, the stern individualism inculcated by the Lowell ethic is here colliding with one of the obstacles to self-expression. "Manliness" in this setting is identified with the independence and self-reliance.

The 10 January entry, "I hate effusion," is even more touching. Even though this unloved and thwarted person suffers, she believes in the virtues of "self-control." Thus the intense conflict between a fractured self and a society unfair to demanding children and women can only be turned inward, to intensify the adolescent's sense of loneliness. Here the diaries reveal a more frequent employment of the epithet "fool."

Amy's biographers almost universally interpret this word "fool" or such reflections as "I was a fool" to mean that, because of her homeliness or lack of social grace, she could not get along with her peers. This interpretation is true only in part. "Fool" often means having talked so much, so vivaciously, so brilliantly that boys were frightened off. But "fool" also means lapsing from the Lowell ethic of self-control and self-discipline, and expressing one's deep emotions to others. Basically, the import of the word "fool" is that it is wrong in Amy's mind both to feel strongly *and* to express those feelings.

Our young Lowell was not easily convinced that she, as a woman, should immediately be relegated to a lower status. After all, she was also a Lowell: "13 Jan. What would I not give to be a poet. Well day dreams are day dreams and I shall never be a poet." Later in the month, she considers the career opportunities for her in the rising field of photography: "22 Jan. Miss Amy Lowell, the leading photographist of today! Oh dear *dreams are but dreams.*" Such aspirations are often undercut by her sense of lesser value as a female, and the problem of communicating her loneliness to others: "16 Jan. Papa is going to his club tonight—I wish I was a man... I am dying to be a boy and go to a swimming bath...19 Jan...I don't think anybody (unless they know me *very* well) would guess how sensitive I really am about things."

During this period of adolescent conflict, Amy discovered that she could withdraw from a hostile world by being sick. During her frequent illnesses and consequent absences from the small private school she was supposed to attend, she plowed into the literature that would ultimately lead her to poetry. Thackeray, all of Dickens, Scott and Victor Hugo became her companions, and reading served as her solace from a problematic world.

On 30 April each year, the Lowell family emigrated from the Boston townhouse in Back Bay to their Brookline "cottage" on Heath Street. Amy always called Brookline "home," and felt that she could express herself more unselfconsciously in the autonomous suburb. Often the diary's pages for these seasons are left without entries, except the brief words "baseball," "tennis," or "tennis tournament." As Amy reflected upon the changed atmosphere for her exuberant spirits: "30 April…How much easier it is to talk to the boys out here…"

It is also in Brookline (where boys were easier to talk to) that Amy had her first crush on a boy, Paul Hamlyn. In her description of the difficulties of expressing herself, she provided an excellent picture of inner turmoil:

> 5 Nov. …Paul talked to me, all the time [as they go out for a ramble over the countryside] but he talked to Amy Cabot all the time coming home. To Stevie…I made some remarks that were meant to be sarcastic, but he is too deadly dull, everybody may not think so though. He probably thought I was *a fool* to try to make myself out bright, and I know I was for minding who Paul talked to…I *tried* to get interested in what Stevie was saying, but couldn't for the life of me. I shall probably read this some years hence and think what a *fool* I was. Yes, I know it is true. Nobody will ever know it though, for I have given up—letting Polly…read this. It's too private.

Alas, leaving Brookline for the townhouse in Boston meant leaving Paul Hamlyn. On 18 November she reflected: "We are going to town on Wednesday. Oh Dear! ! ! !" And on arriving at the townhouse she recorded:

> 20 Nov. Fough! I hate this old hole. However I am not going to think of myself this winter; I wonder when I shall

see Paul again. Poor, Dear Boy!!!! I miss him, and the others very much. It is dreadful in here! Boo-hoo-hoo-hoo!

During the first few lonely days in Boston, Amy was sick. By 22 November, she mustered enough courage to begin attending the small private school conducted in the Cabot Town House: "22 Nov. School. I quite look forward to school now, it is so nice to see the other girls. I have no faculty for making friends. The Shattucks disgust me. Paul!" Finally, at the end of November, this sixteen year old poured out her incommunicable loneliness to her diary:

> 26 Nov. ...I am getting discouraged. It is so hard to do right. I am alone for nobody cares for me. I am a fool and a bore in school. Though often when I am most a fool, I dislike myself... When Mama says, if I am not better I shall go to boarding school, it doesn't make me feel repentant, but only mad. When Miss Folsom tells me I mean to do right, I try to make her think I don't. I'd rather lose my eye-teeth than have her know the truth.
>
> Polly might lead me but she wouldn't. Patty Storrow is fast growing to be a true and loving woman. If she only cared enough about me to take me in hand, she could do anything with me.
>
> This P.M. when I was getting a book, I sat down in Patty's chair and leaned my head on her desk and prayed God 'to make me a true, loving, and strong (morally) woman and to help me to do my duty cheerfully and to control my beastly temper and to help me to make others happy. And to give me Patty to help me and to keep me straight.
>
> And the tears came into my eyes. I stayed there a long time.
>
> At last, I came away.

Later in the year, she again regretted her inability to make friendships which would refresh her spirit:

> 26 Jan...Nobody could ever love me, I know. I am but a contemptible being. But I want love, love. I know I am making

a fool of myself, but surely there are others who have such thoughts.

Theatrical Projections of the Self

During the severe Boston winters, the theater supplied the single positive life experience for Amy. Books were a consolation for loneliness, books served as companions in times of withdrawal, but the theater featured living persons revealing the most intense emotions. While at the Commonwealth Avenue address, Amy attended as many as three plays or operas per week. It is not hard to imagine what an actress must have meant to her and countless other privileged girls: unlike them, an actress could legitimately express the strongest emotions in a socially acceptable environment. Furthermore, the actress' expressions of feeling could have a forceful impact upon an attentive and sympathetic audience. The actress was, in many ways, the consummate woman.

For the young Amy, the bonds of adolescent introspection were yet to be loosened. In her confusion, any novelty was welcomed. In the middle of December, her horse broke out of control, with thrilling speed and danger: "Bezique was so fresh that he nearly ran away. We had great fun. [Her maid was terrified.] You bet! At least I did." Later in the year, the boredom was relieved by a near destruction of the house by fire: "11 March. ...Mama upset the lamp and nearly set the house on fire. Quite exciting!"

Amy as Unlikely Debutante

Ironically, and to her great disadvantage, Amy was fundamentally unable to enjoy what pleasures were offered to her by the companionship of peers. It has been noted previously in this chapter that her taste in children's literature was a generation behind. The future flaunter of conventional modes of behavior, although yearning for the society of her Brookline neighbors, strictly refused to participate in an innocent dancing party on the Lord's day: "16 March. ...Went into Walter Cabot's house. I believe the others danced; but I don't like that sort of thing on Sunday one bit." Another revealing statement from the diary of a future liberated woman is recorded after her visit to a public gymnastics display:

> 5 April. ...Went with Katherine Crowninshield and Marie to an athletic exhibition... if I was Mrs. Schlesinger I would not let my daughter perform in loose knickerbockers, before a lot of people, many of them men.

It is during this adolescent phase that Amy discovered an anthology of English poetry called *Imagination and Fancy*. It is not difficult to imagine how this emotionally starved young girl responded to editor Leigh Hunt's description of poetry and the role of the poet:

> Poetry is imaginative passion...He who has thought, feeling, expression, imagination, action, character, and continuity, all in the largest amount and highest degree, is the greatest poet. (3)

As Amy herself explained, the discovery of Keats and Shelley marked an end to one era of her life: "There indeed was my Waterloo, I surrendered completely to poetry, and with that surrender the chapter of my childhood definitely closed" ("That Bookcase" 10). She began to give readings in her room on the third floor of Sevenels. In what she called her "sky parlor," she began to try on the role of poetess, and to find that role provided expression for her contradictory emotions.

The Mature Poetess

In 1900, after the deaths of her parents, Amy Lowell took possession of Sevenels and became mistress of her own destiny. Her health, which had been perilously close to exhaustion since her mother's death, suddenly improved. And then, a catalytic agent precipitated a new identity—Amy Lowell, poetess.

Eleanora Duse, sometime mistress of the *fin de siècle* author Gabriel D'Annunzio, visited Boston with a theater company in 1902, "doing nothing but D'Annunzio." Amy Lowell had for years been strongly attracted to both the idea and the person of visiting actresses. Plays formed a major part of her cultural education, but acting and the opportunity of the actress to express her feeling was far more important to Amy. Here is her report of the experience of watching Eleanora Duse:

> What really happened was that it revealed me to myself...I had to express the sensations that Duse's acting gave me somehow. I knew nothing whatever about the technique of poetry, I had never heard of vers libre, I had never analyzed blank verse—I was as ignorant as anyone could be. I sat down, and with infinite agitation wrote this poem. It has, I think, every cliché and every technical error which a poem can have, but it loosed a bolt in my brain and I found out where my true function lay. (Letter to Eunice Tietjens)

A Demanding Regimen

With the launch of her first volume of poems in 1912, Lowell became mistress of Sevenels, and dedicated to a poetic vocation. After Mrs. Ada Russell moved into Sevenels as Amy's companion, a rigid schedule was established for the maintenance of the household. Mrs. Russell handled all the mundane tasks of maintaining the home, answering correspondence, and insulating the working poetess from disturbances. Amy Lowell continued to live in the "sky parlor" of her youth, on the third floor. She slept on a bed made by her own hand, and strewn with sixteen pillows. The poetess would arise at three in the afternoon for breakfast, and spend the next six hours surveying typed copies of her poems. (These copies had been neatly prepared during the morning by the two secretaries working for Mrs. Russell.) If guests were invited to dinner, Amy would descend

The Distinguished Poet

to the dining room just as they were commencing dessert. Amy was a brilliant conversationalist, and enjoyed these social evenings, but the guests were reminded in no uncertain terms that their welcome would terminate at eleven promptly.

After turning the lock in the heavy front door of Sevenels, Amy would go to her library, put the fire in order, and sit down in her easy chair for five to six hours of writing. An understanding of the forces defining the "patterns of her life" illuminates much of what was written during those lonely hours of silence, reflection, and artistic creation. Lowell's work evinces a pervasive sense of being bound by convention, tradition, and role as it conflicted with the desire for flight, for active participation in those activities and feelings forbidden by the Victorian tradition of the Lowells. Four prominent works reflect this creative dilemma.

1. "New Heavens for Old" (1925)
Probably the most explicit poem in this cluster is "New Heavens for Old." Early in the poem, the persona is manacled by traditional values associated with the house and its gates. She watches her contemporaries who are (for reasons left unexplained) liberated from

her restraints. Perceiving this contention between the binding and expansive impulses of her soul, she sees no alternative, except to remain restricted while yearning for release. Only the poetess, who artistically transcends this dilemma, can break free:

> I am useless
>   What I do is nothing,
>   What I think has no savour.
>   There is an almanac between the windows: It is of the year when I was born.
>
> My fellows call to me to join them,
>   They shout for me,
>   Passing the house in a great wind of vermilion banners.
>   They are fresh and fulminant,
>   They are indecent and strut with the thought of it,
>   They laugh, and curse, and brawl,
>   And cheer, a holocaust of/Who comes first!' at the iron fronts of the houses at the two edges of the street
>   Young men with naked hearts jeering between iron house-fronts, Young men with naked bodies beneath their clothes
>   Passionately conscious of them,
>   Ready to strip off their customs, their usual routine,
>   Clamouring for the rawness of life,
>   In love with appetite,
>   Proclaiming it as a creed,
>   Worshipping youth,
>   Worshipping themselves.
>   They call for women and the women come,
>   They bare the whiteness of their lusts to the dead gaze of the old house-fronts,
>   They roar down the street like flame,
>   They explode upon the dead houses like new, sharp fire.
>
> But I—-
>   I arrange three roses in a Chinese vase: A pink one,

A red one,
A yellow one.
I fuss over their arrangement.
Then I sit in a South window
And sip pale wine with a touch of hemlock in it, And
think of Winter nights,
And field-mice crossing and re-crossing
The spot which will be my grave.

2. "*Patterns*"

A Google search of the Internet reveals Lowell's poem, "Patterns" is still taught in high schools across the country. (I remember studying it in literature class at Brookline's Runkle School in the 1950s.) The 21st century reader may at first be unconvinced by the 18th century scenes, especially by the Hollywood *mise en scene* of garden and costume. Yet it is important to remember the artistic sensibility of the poet. For Amy Lowell, these 18th century trappings were objective-correlatives: the garden at Sevenels, in its complex, orderly patternment, was in harmony with the values of her father and the period dress was an objective-correlative for her sense of entrapment within the conventional notion of womanhood.

As in "New Heavens for Old," the conflict is not resolved. The last line, "Christ, what are patterns for" falls far short of a triumph over adversity. In the end, it is a desolate, confused and pathetic cry thrown upward toward an absent God. The soul does not hope for redemption; it expects to remain defined within the fixed patterns set by society and nature.

In both "Lilacs" and "Meeting-House Hill," Lowell attempted to identify her work with the spirit of Yankee New England. Yet even these most objective of poems reflected the dynamics of the poet's inner tensions.

3. "*Lilacs*"

Much of the effectiveness of "Lilacs" derives from the tension between order and rebellion. The poet, on this occasion, appears to be content to present playfully the tang of the New England character as a combination of animal spirits subdued by generations of Yankee piety and practicality. The line "You tapped the window…"

introduces a form-breaking vitality. It is followed by a similar impulsive influence, "And ran along the road beside the boy going to school." These form-threatening impulses are followed, however, by a form-sustaining influence: "You stood by pasture-bar to give the cows good milking./ You persuaded the housewife that her dish pan was of silver/ And her husband an image of pure gold." Even in the second section, where the Eastern passion and sensuality are recalled, a controlled conclusion is effected:

> You have forgotten your
> > Eastern origin,
> > The veiled women with eyes like panthers,
> > The swollen, aggressive turbans of jeweled Pashas.

From this contrived Oriental fantasy of lust and luxuriance, the poem returns to a picture of the New England spirit as disciplined as an 18th-century garden:

> Now you are a very decent flower
> > A reticent flower,
> > A curiously clear-cut, candid flower,
> > Standing beside clean doorways.

In the final section, the poet correctly explains her emotional association with the New England lilacs. "Lilacs" is probably one of Lowell's most popular poems because it concludes on a note of optimism—alas, false optimism. While such a passionate avowal of identification with a region is laudable, it is hardly convincing for a reader who has studied the poet's Brookline roots, leaves, and flowers.

4. "Meeting-House Hill" (1920)

"Meeting-House Hill," rather than "Lilacs," is the mature Amy Lowell's most distilled statement of her spiritual affiliation with the New England past; it does so by reprising the tensions of a Brookline childhood.

The opening line, "I must be mad, or very tired," appears to be merely a device for introducing an imagist fantasy; it is the report of a poet who has, at her roots, really rejected what she believes to have been the constraints of her region's cultural heritage. Initially, she describes how the 18th century spirit was "refined to a cautious elegance." But this self-contained style is out of place in the economic hubbub of industrial America (indicated by the railroad track she must look over to see the bay). Foreign immigration and expansion of the city (indicated by the fact that the meeting house is "Pausing a moment upon a squalid hill-top") has also contributed to make the house of worship obsolescent. Still deeper than mere economic or social issues lies the problem of faith. Faith in the sense of intellect united with emotional experience was forever debarred from Amy Lowell—as it was for many in the New England tradition. (See Chapter 26 on Harriet Beecher Stowe.) The persona of the poem recognizes this dilemma as she looks at the spire of the meeting house:

> And the shot of its spire
>   Is cool, and candid,
>   Rising into an unresisting sky.
>   Strange meeting-house
>   Pausing a moment upon a squalid hilltop. I watch the spire sweeping the sky,
>   I am dizzy with the movement of the sky.

The poem terminates with a contrast between the controlling discipline, placed in contention against the thrust of a nearly deranged sensuality. This conclusion serves as a fitting resting point for my investigation of the sensibility of Brookline's Amy Lowell. On the one hand, there is here a conflict between a fixed mast and the free energy of wind: "I might be watching a mast with its royals set full/Straining before a two-reef breeze." Here is an image of energy being used for productive, social work. The following lines then define this image of 18th century industry by describing the orderly maneuvering of a vessel as it progresses against an opposing wind: "I might be sighting a tea-clipper/Tacking into the blue bay." Finally, the idea of control and delicate artistry is concentrated into a report of the contents of the vessel, returning from the mysterious Far East: "Just back from Canton/With her hold full of green and blue porcelain."

Until this point, the poem has drafted a clever mechanism of interlocking patterns. Yet at the moment of apparent control, the reader is assaulted by a form-destroying jolt from the last three lines: "And a Chinese coolie leaning over the rail/Gazing at the white spire with dull, sea-spent eyes." Here the responsive reader should be wrenched out of a nostalgic reverie about New England's nautical golden age. What the reader is left with may now be clarified by connecting this conclusion with the outcome of "Lilacs." While Amy Lowell may have been correct in "Lilacs" when she said that her roots, leaves, and flowers were in the soil of New England, we should not automatically assume that even the most privileged Brookline child could be exempt from the angst of being human. We can be grateful, however, that Amy Lowell found a creative identity to yield beauty from her unique stresses and talents—fulfilling the promise of the Sevenels tradition even as she recognized its severe limitations for the creative spirit.

Discussion of Literature

All of the diaries, notebooks and letters which are mentioned in this article can be found among the Amy Lowell papers in Harvard University's Houghton Library. The reader is encouraged to read all of the numerous poems written by Amy Lowell about the actress and woman, Eleanora Duse. While I continue to be both entertained and informed by Damon's biography, anyone truly interested in Amy Lowell as an artist will be disappointed; his was an "official" project which benefited from access, but suffered from the restraint which often goes along with such privilege. His conclusions are either over the top or condescending—despite these shortcomings, his long work is a storehouse of information in the "life and letters" genre so popular back in the days before jargon.

Works Cited

Damon, S. Foster. *Amy Lowell: A Chronicle, with Extracts from her Correspondence.* Boston: Houghton Mifflin, 1935.

Hunt, Leigh. *Imagination and Fancy.* London: Smith, Elder, 1891.

Lowell, Amy. *Dream Drops or Stories from Fairyland By a Dreamer.* Boston: 1887.
—. Letter to Eunice Tietjens, June 5, 1923. Houghton Library Collection, Harvard U.
—. "Lilacs." *Selected Poems of Amy Lowell.* Eds. Melissa Bradshaw and Adrienne Munich. Rutgers UP: 2002. 77-79.
—. "Meeting House Hill." *Selected Poems of Amy Lowell.* Eds. Melissa Bradshaw and Adrienne Munich. Rutgers UP: 2002. 80.
—. "New Heavens for Old." *Anthology of Modern American Poetry.* Ed. Cary Nelson. Oxford UP: 2003. 53.
—. "Patterns." *Selected Poems of Amy Lowell.* Eds. Melissa Bradshaw and Adrienne Munich. Rutgers UP: 2002. 58-60.
—. "That Bookcase." MS. Houghton Library Collection, Harvard U.
Perkins, Elizabeth W. "Amy Lowell of New England." *Scribner's Magazine* 82 (1927): 329-335.

29
John James Audubon: The 'American Woodsman'?

> If Napoleon by perseverance and energy rose from the ranks to be an emperor, why should not Audubon with perseverance and energy be able to leave the woods of America for a time and publish and sell a book?
>
> From Audubon's *English Journal*, 1827

Formation of a New Identity

On November 3rd, 1820, John James Audubon, earning his passage to New Orleans as a professional hunter for the crew of an Ohio flatboat, glided slowly past a deserted sawmill at Henderson, Kentucky. Ownership of that sawmill had led to imprisonment and bankruptcy and he was anxious to distance himself from this symbol of his failure. It made his "blood turn cold," for it was the most recent in a series of failures: first a trading post, then a steamboat, then a lumber project, and finally this infernal sawmill. Like a row of dominoes, they had fallen in sequence. In desperation, he was now bent upon exploiting his unique talent for drawing birds. Although beginning at an inauspicious moment, considering his age of 35 years, his ambition was to surpass the leading figure in American ornithology, Alexander Wilson (1766-1813), as an artist and scientist—and to reap a profit as well!

Considering Audubon's almost complete lack of formal training in drawing, ornithology, and, most painfully, the English language, this was an impractical objective. Even a futile attempt would

John James Audubon: A Dream of Success

entail years of study in the rudiments of his science, not to mention frequent separations from his family. It would demand renunciation of all comfort to procure specimens which—despite bad weather, lack of materials, or inexperience—would have to be conveyed to his portfolio as drawings, and to his journal as reliable scientific data. It would eventually require a consummate business sense to build a list of subscribers, supervise the publication of the prints, and write the biographies of each species while simultaneously producing new drawings to complete a survey of all the species in North America.

From the day he passed the defunct mill at Henderson, until the completion of his *Birds of America* (1827-1838), with its accompanying narrative, the *Ornithological Biography*, Audubon's life was to be a voyage toward stabilizing an identity which he fashioned in the financial and spiritual "Slough of Despond" of 1820. While advancing toward this goal, he applied a driven energy which he admitted even he could not understand: he knew he would encounter periods of depression and defeat along the route of this voyage, but he hoped that, by the tenacity of will, he could ultimately attain the kind of prominence as a naturalist which he had abysmally failed to garner as a merchant.

Childhood and Family

Captain Jean Audubon, the naturalist's father—a successful merchant, planter, and sea captain—was part of the bourgeoisie that gained ascendancy in the ferment of the French Revolution. The revolution had convinced him that education provided a fund of skills which prepared a man with potential for success which outlasted political upheavals. Since he was frequently absent on business, he placed a series of tutors over John; they were told to impress upon his son this necessary and practical learning. These teachers are always described by Audubon as dull and brutal men who—like his father—inspired fear and a grudging respect, but imparted little knowledge to the silently contemptuous student.

Young John's stepmother spoiled him. Without a husband for long periods, she was more than happy to indulge her stepson's every whim, one of which was the privilege of skipping school. In her extreme permissiveness she went so far as to allow him carte blanche at the village candy store. While his father was absent, John was allowed to roam the woods, collect nests, eggs, and rocks. When his father returned from a voyage, the boy was severely punished and sent to a new master. The residue of this conflicted parentage was Audubon's memory of his father as an icon of worldly success and discipline, while his stepmother symbolized an escape from responsibility, an emotion sublimated into a passionate love for birds.

Now, at the age of thirty-five, the indigent Audubon recognized wincingly what his biographers have often pointed out: his pursuit of birds had been at least partially the cause of his demise. By becoming absorbed in specimens when his mercantile projects needed supervision, he had been evading the responsibilities of maturity. Stripped bare by unbelievably bad luck as much as inattention, the only talent he had left to exploit after bankruptcy was his ability to draw. For immediate needs, portraits would yield a small income, but he proposed to put his compulsive enthusiasm for birds to good use, building his portfolio by "travel, and finish my collection or so nearly so that it would be a Valuable Acquisition." It is a major step toward understanding Audubon's imagination to note that he conceived of his failure in an allegory involving the objects of his art:

> A Young Man of Seventeen sent to America to Make Money (for such was my Father's Wish) brought up in France in easy Circumstance who had never thought on the Want of an article I had had at Discretion, was ill-fitted for it—I spent much Money and One Year of My life as Happy as the Young Bird; that having Left the Parents sight carols Merrily, While Hawks of All Species are Watching him for an easy prey. (Corning 45)

In this passage, Audubon deceptively focuses on extreme youth to justify failure. Actually, he was given an allowance while in America until he reached the age of twenty-three. Even after his marriage, with the patronage of his father-in-law, he entered a merchant house where he suffered the first of a series of business fiascoes which culminated in failure of his mill. The interest in the view he takes of himself as a young bird let loose too soon among the predators is that, as an ornithologist, he saw his relationship to his beloved birds to be precisely that described—with the naturalist as the predator hawk, and the birds as the victims. The source of violence in Audubon's art is thus linked to the decision of 1820 to carry his desperate ambition into the American forest.

Audubon allots considerable space in his early writings to a contemptuous view of the business mentality. His biographers are fond of dilating upon this theme to prove that he was a wholehearted son of nature. For example, at Natchez, while visiting a merchant who had helped ornithologist Alexander Wilson, Audubon ridiculed the insensitivity of a mind too bent on gain to appreciate the beauties of nature: "James Wilkins assured me that... through his mere transient observations he had discovered several New Specimens, but being a Man of Business he Never had Noted any" (Corning 93). Audubon's biographers do not understand that this flippant barb was not spoken from a position of strength, but was only an attempt to distinguish, in a defensive manner, between the apparent dignity of the wealthy trader and the true worth of the impoverished—but dedicated—naturalist. This pose becomes clear when, without a hint of irony, Audubon confides to his journal the vicissitudes of trade as they affect an acquaintance in Cincinnati: "have passed this day three flat boats belonging to William

Noble...that left that place early in August—three of six are lost" (28). When stopping at a prospering trading post managed by a beautiful French woman in partnership with her lover, he betrays his disappointment for not succeeding as a merchant when he is overpowered by one of his recurrent waves of morbid retrospection: "Felt dull this evening for every object that brings forward the Background of My Life's Picture shows too often with poignancy the difference of situation" (35).

Anyone genuinely estranged from the values of a commercial society would not have been as excited as Audubon was by the prospects for quick profits which wharf construction at New Orleans had made possible for owners of the numerous saw-mills along the river. Nor would a pure son of nature have been intent upon instructing his children never to "sell or buy without immediately paying for the same—a constant adherence of this maxim will keep your mind and person at all times free and happy" (94).

However oppressed by abject self-pity, Audubon lacerated himself throughout this period to produce the self-imposed quota of one hundred and twenty drawings he had set for the expedition. This effort included recording copious data about the habits as well as the specific measurements of every bird's exterior limbs and internal organs. In his journal, he daily noted the time of his arising to commence work. One entry, in its redundancy, shows his desire to convince himself of his industry: "Drawing this morning as soon as the Light would permit me—started early" (25). From this point forward, an iron regimen was followed: after a day's hunt, he sketched the outlines immediately, by candlelight, often until midnight. After a sleep of three or four hours, he rose before the sun and stayed at his drawing board until the picture was completed, frequently working over a period of days to the point of collapse.

Audubon's journals from 1821 to 1826 are lost, but there is a discernible pattern in the events of those years, a pattern which might be called a "premature assumption of success." The concluding entries of the 1821 diary show a sparse concern with the wonders of nature. The naturalist was busy burning his candle at both ends, for, while painting portraits and giving drawing lessons, he was also adding daily one completed drawing to his portfolio. To keep all these "mills" going, he even hired a hunter with the stipulation that at a rate of one dollar per day, for ninety-nine days, the hunter would bring a different species each day—excluding those birds which Audubon had already drawn.

Assuming that he had at last become a self-supporting artist, he wrote to his wife that she should join him. His attempt to reunite his family in New Orleans and to support it on his earnings as a portrait painter and teacher failed miserably. Lucy Audubon was again forced to support the family by teaching school while the naturalist returned to the woods, finding solace for his sense of failure by bringing new species into the portfolio.

In 1824, he entered Philadelphia to make his first bid for an audience and a publisher. While enthusiastically received by the painter, Thomas Sully (1783-1872), a jealous opposition was launched by Alexander Wilson's admirers to convince the public that Audubon's drawings were pale imitations. Many of these slanderers were members of the American Philosophic Society; they were successful in thwarting Audubon's chances of gaining official sanction and without the approval of the society, no American printer would venture to publish such an expressive project as *The Birds of America*.

Charles L. Bonaparte advised Audubon that his only hope was to bring his work to an English audience. Before making a transatlantic voyage, however, Audubon knew that he would have to augment his collection and immediately set sail for the Northwest Territory. Although his spirit may have faltered after the disappointment of Philadelphia, his will to succeed had not been subdued. Signing in at a hotel near Niagara Falls, he showed his pluck in noting after his signature: "Who like Wilson, will ramble, but never, like that great man, die under the lash of a bookseller." In bed, he went to sleep "thinking of Franklin eating his roll in the streets of Philadelphia, of Goldsmith traveling by aid of his musical powers, and of other great men who had worked their way through hardships and difficulties to fame," and fell asleep "hoping, by persevering industry, to make a name for himself among his countrymen" (Herrick 340). After completing his tour of the northern states, he became dancing master for his wife's pupils, beating time to the accumulation of dollars that would finance a portentous assault on England.

Making It

In May, 1826, Audubon sailed from New Orleans on the merchant ship *Delos* bound for Liverpool, carrying a precious portfolio of four hundred and fifty drawings. The interval between 1826 and 1829 marks a crucial period for the recognition of Audubon's work, but still more importantly, they show a transformation of the failure of 1820 into a man of destiny.

Audubon's brilliant entrance on the English cultural scene is undoubtedly the most colorful of any in American history, exceeding even Franklin's in Paris, for it must be remembered that Audubon was completely unknown when he debarked at Liverpool. Within a week, however, after a display of two hundred and fifty drawings, he was instantly proclaimed a darling prodigy from the American woods. At first, the American unconsciously lived the role which Franklin cultivated, in masquerade, but once he saw how the image of the frontiersman disarmed the English, he consciously exploited it. He quickly adopted for himself the sobriquet, "American Woodsman," a moniker which one of the English reviewers had given him, and used it throughout his later works.

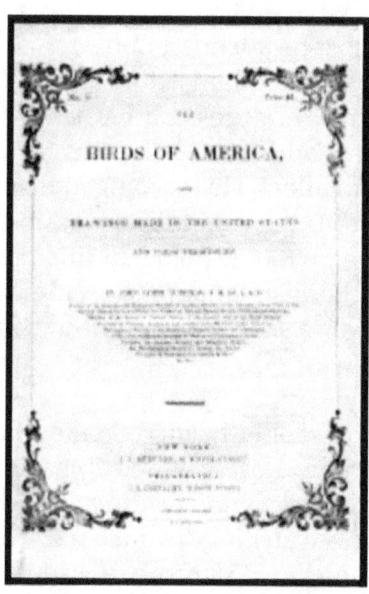

Title Page of *The Birds of America*

Looking back on the debut from the perspective of his entire career, it appears that this spontaneous acclaim by the aristocracy, along with the freshet of memberships to scientific societies, would have immediately dissipated any anxieties about success. Audubon soon learned, however, that the British were more lavish with their praise than with their pocketbooks. He set a high subscription rate, equal to one thousand American dollars, to be paid over a fourteen year period. Even the ravished aristocrats were reluctant to subscribe, and when they did, were usually tardy—if not simply negligent—in payments which were the sole support for *The Birds of America*.

Early in the tour, Audubon calculated that he could complete four hundred plates of *The Birds* with a minimum of two hundred subscribers. Having established this goal, and while still under pressure to find the proper printer, he toured the major cities of northern England, attending every dinner and society meeting to which he could gain admittance, always assiduously pressing members of the audience to sign his subscription book. Once, when he had received three invitations for the same hour on the same day, he returned acceptances to all three. When the day and the recognition came of what he had done, he was thrown into such a spell of depression that he attended none!

He constantly upbraided himself for the involuntary diffidence which prevented him from pressing harder for subscriptions. An additional torture was added when he was forced to churn out oil paintings to keep him afloat. He rearranged his schedule to shorten the hours of sleep from the usual four, until he could feel himself being stressed to the breaking point. In this period of frustration, the tameness of the English landscape seemed a cruel mockery of his sense of turmoil and struggle. Describing an English pond, he lamented that there was:

> No moccasin nor copper-headed snake...near its margin; no snowy Heron, no Rose-Colored Ibis...wild and charming...no sprightly trout, nor waiting garfish, while above hovers no Vulture watching for the spoils of the hunt, nor Eagle perched on dreary cypress in a gloomy silence. (M. Audubon 113)

London's reaction, he knew, would determine his fate. If he could win the patronage of the capital, his name would be established, and success would follow as a matter of course. The prospect of entering the city for this trial terrified him:

> London is just like the mouth of an immense monster, guarded by millions of sharp-edged teeth, from which if I escape unhurt it must be called a miracle. I have many times longed to see London, and now I am here, I feel a desire beyond worlds to be in my beloved woods. (251)

He savagely portrayed his sense of this life-and-death struggle in massive oil paintings he so vehemently detested: "English Pheasants Surprised by a Spanish Dog" especially suggests that Audubon was living out in his art the assault he himself was making on fame. "Eagle and the Lamb" and "Pheasants attacked by a Fox," portray the same aggression. Painting in oils only added to his frustration. He was aware that a trained eye would quickly discern his inexperience in this medium. (Once he had extricated himself from these financial straits, he vowed to his journal that he would never, under any conditions, use oils again.)

During this gloomy period of anticipation, when he was informed that he might never gain an audience with Sir Walter Scott, he slid into depression. That night, in his room, he reviewed his past, present, and future, as he had done so many times since his decision in 1820 to dedicate himself to his *Birds*. Worn thread-bare by exertion, and conscious that his life was filled with the promise of the highest success or the most abysmal failure in a life of failures, the very sub-conscious of his tenacious spirit welled up before him:

> I unpacked my birds and looked at them with pleasure, and yet with a considerable degree of fear that they would never be published. I felt very much alone, and many dark thoughts came across my mind; I felt one of those terrible attacks of depression to which I so often fall prey overtaking me.. I looked at..the little cherubs on the mantelpiece, the painted landscape on my right hand, and the mirror on my

left, in which I saw not only my own face, but such a strong resemblance to that of my venerated father that I almost imagined it was he that I saw. (M. Audubon 147)

Finding the Right Publisher

When the "American Woodsman" reached London, he was immediately elected to the Linnaean Society, the unanimous vote being taken in his presence. In London he also found a new printer, Robert Havell, who was more skilled and personally more compatible with Audubon than William Lizars of Edinburgh (who had printed the first six plates of *The Birds*). Audubon felt overawed by Lizars, since it had been through the printer's efforts that he had gained entrance to the right circles in the northern cities. With Havell, the relationship was reversed: Havell's establishment was about to fail when Audubon, the now-famous naturalist, arrived on the London scene. Havell's dependence gave Audubon a sense of control, inspiring him with confidence that *The Birds* would be printed to the artist's specifications.

Paralyzed by anticipation before entering London, Audubon had gained encouragement from lectures of the English phrenologist George Combe on the powers of the human mind. But for the first time, after the success of his London shows, he began to believe (not merely hope) that his future was no longer dependent upon fate, but would assume whatever proportions his dedication could give it. This new self-assurance is reflected in his extremely temperate reaction to the indifference of the great universities. On a still Sunday afternoon, in Trinity Chapel, Cambridge, he experienced a mystical moment of overwhelming communion with the author of destiny. The former agonies of self doubt and despair were replaced by a secure sense of harmony with a higher power. This power, which he called God, transcended the vicissitudes of his career, and was the source of Nature. Not long after this rapturous moment of reassurance, Audubon performed one of the rare acts of kindness to birds ever recorded by his pen. Walking through Regents Park in London, he bought "four beautiful little Redpolls from a sailor, and gave them all liberty to go. What pleasure they must have felt rising, and going off over London; and I felt pleasure too, to know they had the freedom I so earnestly desired" (M. Audubon 298).

The irony of this complex man's character was that he could never be as free as the Redpolls. The only settlement he could ever effect with the inscrutable passion which drove him was to identify with the compelling force. In surrendering to its demands, he was transformed from an ordinary individual of private ambition into an inspired recorder of God's great design. Once this identification was completed, his *Birds* was no longer primarily a source of support for his family, but a tribute to the Creator: "I only wish to enjoy more of Him by admiring His works still more than I have ever done before. He will grant me life; He will support me in my journeys, and enable me to meet thee this wife in America" (298).

Before sailing for America, the naturalist went to Paris in search of subscribers. He interpreted the tribute to him by the French Academy as no longer a credit to his personal skill, but a spontaneous response to the works of God in Nature. For the return voyage to America, he chose the "Columbia" since he sincerely believed that his work was now not only a faithful record of God's work, but an expression of a distinctive American spirit. The sense of destiny which caused him to make this choice was an unexpected prize at the end of a journey commenced in 1820 near Henderson, Kentucky when he passed the "infernal mill." Returning to America in 1829, there still remained before him a formidable enterprise which required not only the skills of science and art, but a keen attention to the details of finance and business. It demanded that he apply all his energies, often to the point of collapse. But at this juncture in his career, all these challenges were a spur to greater efforts, since behind him and supporting him was a knowledge that he had laid the foundation for an artistic monument.

Violence in Audubon's Art: The Predator Theme

Considering Audubon's choice to follow his artistic bent in 1820, it seems clear that, since he saw himself as a helpless victim in the impersonal economic world, he sought compensation, with rifle, powder, and ball, as the dominant predator of the woods. His relationship with nature is knotty because in it he fused the need to succeed—the father-principle—with his love of birds—the sublimation of his love for his stepmother. While following the father principle into nature, his conception of it was not without a memory of violence and cruelty. The fusion of these two principles yielded a dynamic identity. Drawing birds stopped being an escape from maturity and responsibility, and became an activity permeated with self-discipline and ambition. Although his art reveals that he never fully integrated these competing forces, the bankruptcy which necessitated their fusion must be considered a "fortunate fall" for posterity. It released a torrent of creative force which made Audubon capable of the intense exertion without which there would have been no *Birds of America*.

The birds, animals, and people who excite Audubon's attention are the predators of their environments. In almost every chapter on predators in the *Ornithological Biography*, there are passages which, while they have no scientific value, provide an insight into the lust to kill and capture. In the following passage, the "mortification" experience in missing a Caracara Eagle is especially revealing since Audubon identified himself with the eagle more than any other species:

> Convinced that it was unknown to me, and bent on obtaining it, I followed it nearly a mile, when I saw it sail towards the earth, making for a place where a group of Vultures were engaged in devouring a dead horse. Walking up to the horse, I observed the new bird alighted on it, and helping itself freely to the savory meat beneath its feet;...I moved circuitously until I came to a deep ditch, along which I crawled, and went as near the bird as I possibly could;...I shot, but to my great mortification missed it. However it alighted a few hundred yards off in an open savanna, on which I laid myself flat on the ground, and crawled towards it, pushing my gun before me, amid burs and mud-holes, until I reached the distance of seventy-five yards from it, when I stopped to observe its attitudes. The bird did not notice me; he stood on a lump of flesh, tearing it to pieces, in the manner of a Vulture, until he had nearly swallowed the whole.. I shot a second time, and probably touched him; for he dropped his burden, and made off with alternate sailings and flappings of a Vulture, but more gracefully. He never uttered a cry, and I followed him wistfully with my eyes until he was quite out of sight. (Audubon, *The Ornithological* 2: 350-57)

This passage continues at great length to describe two later attempts. The third attempt was made by one of Audubon's assistants, he says. There is a touch of mixed envy and self-satisfaction in this account when he reports that the assistant returned with the bird half an hour after he was dispatched—envy because the assistant succeeded where Audubon had failed, yet self-satisfaction because Audubon, the predatory naturalist, has the power to order an assistant to shoot the aviary predator.

Although some habits of the bird are superficially described in the passage, the real interest is obviously in the chase, and the difficulties and discomforts suffered by the naturalist to capture the prized eagle. At times, the intoxication of the hunt rises to a fever pitch. A casual reader might countenance an occasional sanguinary chapter in natural history, but one wonders what would have been the public reaction if anyone but a naturalist had claimed to enjoy the sadism of this bear hunt:

> We were anxious to procure as much sport as possible, and having observed one of the Bears, which from its size we conjectured to be the mother, ordered the negroes to cut down the tree on which it was perched, when it was intended the dogs should have a tug with it, while we support them, and assist in preventing the Bear from escaping by wounding it in one of the hind legs...[after the bear is down]...A cur daringly ventured to seize the Bear by the snout, and was seen hanging to it, covered with blood, whilst a dozen or more scrambled over its back. (1: 481-481)

Plate Sixteen of the *The Birds of America*, "The Great Footed Hawk," along with its narrative accompaniment, gives a shocking picture of the predator-victim relationship. In the *Ornithological Biography*, Audubon describes the drawing in a manner which shows how involved he was with his predators:

> Look at these two pirates eating their dejeuner à la fordette, as it were, congratulating each other on the savoriness of the food in their grasp. One might think them real epicures, but they are in fact true gluttons. The male has obtained

Predators and Victims

possession of a Green winged Teal, while his mate has procured a Gadwall Duck. Their appetites are equal to their reckless daring, and well deserved the name of "Pirates" which I have bestowed upon them. (1: 85)

In the original, elephant-sized edition, this print has a dimension of brutality which is not communicated by smaller reproductions. Because the birds are life-size, the viewer is forced to pull up a chair at this gory repast. The beak of the female is smeared with blood, two rosy drops of which are dripping toward the ground. The ducks lie so passively that they seem to be lost in a peaceful sleep, rather than to be victims of a violent death. Their passivity, as a contrast, accentuates the power of the hawks. A single breast feather floats in mid-air above and between the two marauders; it has been pecked out of the bleeding chest of the Gadwall duck, and intensifies the ferocity of the scene. As in many of Audubon's pictures of predators, the talons of the male on the left, while accurately drawn, are poised menacingly toward the viewer. The hawks clutch their victims so tightly that drops of blood spurt from the incisions made by their talons, as if they are warning the intruder that these ducks are their possessions, fairly won in the struggle for life. The powerful shock effect of this and other pictures of predators causes the observer to gasp at the turn of each enormous page of the elephant edition. (29 ½" by 39 ½"). It suggests that Audubon demanded that his *Birds* be printed life size not merely for the interests of science (all dimensions were faithfully transcribed from nature to paper) but also because he wished the audience to join his involvement with the sublimity of the scene.

An obvious question arises about Audubon's approach to nature: if he is so fascinated by carnivores, how does he treat the gentle, herbivorous birds?

Most often, Audubon simply provides the dimensions of these birds, with other scientific data, and wastes no print about the kill. For example, in describing the Yellow Crowned Wood Warbler, he merely indicates that "I have shot only three or four... of this species and these were all I ever met with" (3: 87). When he extends the discussion at all, he focuses upon the god-like naturalist who deigns to allow these birds to live, if he can satisfy the needs of science without killing them. The reader is always more conscious of the magnanimity of the naturalist than the delicate beauty of the bird. If the birds display rage, their impotent soarings are treated with disdain.

Audubon's treatment of smaller birds raises a deeper question than simply his relation to them as a naturalist, because he infuses them with the characteristics of monogamy, mutual co-operation, and undying maternal affection. The family of these small birds resembles the contemporary sentimental ideal which colored Audubon's thinking about his own family. After he relishes a contemplation of unflagging maternal affection, there seems to be almost a vengeance in his violation of it, a violation which he often attributes to the needs of his "gentle reader" to conceal his own involvement. This might be a perverse revenge against what, beyond his control, was his experience as a boy of seventeen, when his father precipitously exiled him from his stepmother's indulgent influence, compounded with his confused understanding of the meaning of the disruption of his own family in 1820. After missing a first shot at a mother and chick seated in their nest, Audubon observed:

> [T]o my great surprise... [the mother] gently lifted her young and sailed with it to another tree, about thirty yards distant, deposited it there. My feeling at that moment I cannot express. I wish I had not discovered the poor birds, for who could have had witnessed, without emotion so striking

an example of that affection which none but another can feel; so daring an act, performed in the midst of smoke, in the presence of a dreaded and dangerous enemy. I followed however, and brought both to the ground at one shot, so keen is the desire of possession. (2: 109)

Even in his idyllic portrait of the "House Wren," where he directly compares the harmonious relationship of the Wren and its mate to the love he shared with his wife, he cannot conclude without wondering at what he calls the "hereditary antipathy" which the bird feels toward the family cat: "it follows her and scolds her until she is out of sight" (1: 429). In his drawings of small birds, Audubon does considerable violence to the naturalness he claims to exhibit. He defended himself against frequent criticisms that these positions were outré, usually accusing critics of being closet-naturalists interested only in finding flaws in his monument.

A Wren Family

But the untutored viewer of *The Birds* is immediately impressed that many of the positions show more concern for the display of plumage from every possible angle rather than a faithfulness to nature.

Winning of the West

Because Audubon's approach to nature was impelled by his drive for success, his writings have little affinity with the doctrines of environmentalists who invoke his name. He was as drunk with the enthusiasm for material progress and westward expansion as any advocate of Manifest Destiny. The frontier was where "persevering industry" could realize the Horatio Alger myth.

In an episode of *The Ornithological Biography*, "The Ohio," he at first seems to be pleading for the preservation of the wilderness. Surveying the banks of the Ohio River, once populated by scattered bands of nomadic Indians, he reflects:

> Instead of being in a state of nature, is now more or less covered with villages, farms, and towns, where the din of hammers and machinery is constantly heard by day and the fire by night..the woods are fast disappearing under the axe. (1: 31)

Claiming that he cannot bring himself to morally judge the results of these changes, he goes on to describe what is irrevocably lost in this transition. With the popular conception of Audubon, in mind, one expects an impassioned plea for American writers to preserve Nature's wildness before it is tamed. However, what Audubon really wants art to preserve for posterity is an epic of the heroic conflicts of the first agents of civilization. Cooper and Irving should write novels to capture for future generations the spirit of "the progress of civilization in our western country. They…[should] speak of the Clarks, the Croghans, the Boons, and many other men of great and daring enterprise" (1: 32). The interest of the frontier is focused here on the war by man against nature's Native Americans, animals, and trees. The ethos of this epic of expansion and conflict is thus an extension, in its spirit of invasion and possession, of Audubon's passion for the hunt.

At the frontier, the discipline of civilization, once relaxed, leads to a Hobbesian war of all against all. In describing the informal justice of the regulators, however, it is interesting to note that—while Audubon almost delights in the tortures which the regulators substitute for court-room procedure—he also (in contradiction to his articulated doctrine) evinces a guarded admiration for the "industry in bad deeds" of a licentious renegade named Mason. Despite his empathy for the outlaw, Audubon emerges as a spokesman for law and order: "the most depraved of these emigrants are forced to retreat farther and farther from the society of the virtuous, the restraints imposed by which they find incompatible with their habits and the gratification of their unbridled passions" (1: 105).

Civilization is a desirable replacement for this moral chaos. After describing the single brush with death that he experienced in all of his expeditions, Audubon reflects approvingly that such wildness has been bred out of the frontier:

> Will you believe, reader, that not many miles from the place where this adventure happened, and where fifteen years ago no habitation belonged to civilized man was expected...large roads are now laid out, cultivation has converted the woods into fertile fields, taverns have been erected, and much of what we Americans call comfort is met with. So fast does improvement proceed in our abundant and free country. (1: 84)

Western settlement is a benefit for the urban poor who have been pushed out of the race for life in an overpopulated East. Although they enter the western lands with the most rudimentary tools of society, Audubon rhetorically asks: "Who is he of the settlers of Mississippi that cannot realize some profit?" and quickly answers, "Truly none who is industrious." Building on this statement of the protestant ethic, the former business failure swells to a vision of progress as it is exhibited at a promontory on the mighty river. The industry of a squatter family transformed this spit of land from a wood-stop for Mississippi steamboats, into a thriving river port:

Where a single cabin once stood, a neat village is now to be seen; warehouses, stores..Thus are the vast frontiers of our country peopled, and thus does civilization, year after year, extend over the western wilds. Time will no doubt be, when the great valley of the Mississippi, still covered with primeval forests, interspersed with swamps, will smile with cornfields and orchards, while crowded cities will rise at intervals along its bank, and enlightened nations will rejoice in the bounties of providence. (2: 134)

Even within civilization itself, the predatory relationship has a bewitching wickedness. While Audubon treats pirates, "Wreckers," and "Eggers" with stern condemnation, he betrays an attraction to the underlying darkness of their violence, power, and wealth. One wonders how much Audubon vicariously participated in a dying pirate's description of himself at the end of an immoral, murderous—but lucrative—life of plunder:

I am an outlaw, perhaps you will say a wretch—I have been for many years a pirate. The instructions of my parents were of no avail to me, for I have always believed that I was born to be a most cruel man. I lie here, about to die in the weeds because I long ago refused to listen to their admonitions. Do not shudder when I tell you—these now useless hands murdered the mother whom they had embraced. (2: 187)

In this pirate's self-description, is a grotesque of the savage effects of guilt in Audubon's imagination, a guilt originating from a sense of having failed to live up to his father's standards, a guilt which could be assuaged only by complete identification with the success of his project. When *The Birds of America* and the *Ornithological Biography* were brought to a close in 1839, the world-famous naturalist, together with his family, sailed back to America, where, without breaking stride, they joined forces to publish an immensely profitable octavo-size edition. Later, he commenced *The Quadrupeds of North America* which, after his death in 1851, was brought to a close by his sons.

American Woodsman and American Myth

Audubon was the first to admit that, after the completion of his *magnum opus,* all subsequent work took on the pallor of a denouement. Closing the fifth and final volume of *The Ornithological Biography*, he took considerable satisfaction in reflecting that he had more than doubled Alexander Wilson's contribution to science, and he encouraged dedicated young men to shoulder their rifles to carry the work to even further fullness. Shutting down the presses on *The Birds of America* marked the successful completion of a goal which he had established before boarding the river boat in 1820, a goal achieved in the face of what to less driven men would have been insuperable obstacles. Satisfied with the fulfillment of that mission, he said he was "like the traveler, my journeys all finished, my anxieties vanished, my mission accomplished" (5: vii).

After following him through the voyage, the spectator is constrained to join the admirers of Audubon and his achievement, if for different reasons than his votaries. It is disappointing that the popular myth of Audubon, like so many of America's myths about its great men, (for the purpose of giving unreflecting hope and confidence) has concealed the darker complexity and intensity of Audubon's doubt, pain, and thirst for immortality. Certainly, there was great poetic truth in one of John James Audubon's letters to his wife when he said: "What a curious, interesting book, a biographer, well acquainted with my life, could write; it is still more wonderful and extraordinary than that of my father" (Herrick title page).

Works Cited

Audubon, John James. *The Birds of America*. New York: Macmillan, 1937.
—. *The Ornithological Biography*. 5 vols. Edinburgh: A. Black, 1839.
—. *The Quadrupeds of North America*. 3 vols. New York: V.G. Audubon, 1854-5.
Audubon, Maria, ed. *Audubon and His Journals*. 2 vols. New York: Dover, 1988.
Burroughs, John. *John James Audubon*. Boston: Small, Maynard, 1902.
Corning, Howard, ed. *Journal of John James Audubon Made During His Trip to New Orleans in 1820-1821*. Boston: Club of Odd Volumes, 1929.
Herrick, Francis H. *Audubon the Naturalist: A History of His Life and Time*. 2 vols. 2nd ed. New York: D. Appleton-Century, 1938.
Rourke, Constance. *Audubon*. New York: Harcourt Brace, 1936.

30
Ideology and Film Rhetoric: Three Documentaries of the New Deal Era (1936-1941)

The precept of aesthetics that form and content are inextricably related also applies to the art of film. While all filmmakers are aware of this principle, very few film scholars have taken it seriously. For this reason, film scholarship could profit from more attention to a basic distinction between thematic and cinematic elements of film. The theme of a film is the central idea around which it is constructed. The themes of the Thirties documentaries here examined are readily stated: *The River* strives to show that uncoordinated industrial exploitation has so abused the ecological system of the Mississippi Valley that biennial floods have resulted; *Land of Cotton* stresses that the Old South's commitment to a single crop has led to an agricultural depression which affects both sharecropper and landlord; *Native Land* tries to convince workers and farmers to band together so that they may enjoy traditional American rights in the industrial era.

The cinematic elements of a film are the devices of film language which contribute to the distinctively filmic communication of the theme. Each cinematic factor is carefully selected by a director and then arranged by his editor to convey a unique message. In social documentaries such as *Land of Cotton, The River,* and *Native Land,* it would seem only logical that the differing political persuasions of the filmmakers would determine not only different contents for each film, but that different choices in film language would be made so that the rhetoric of each film would be consonant with the liberal Republican or New Deal or leftist persuasion of the filmmaker.

This chapter will attempt to contrast these three film rhetorics concretely. *Land of Cotton* (1938) is an episode from the famous *March of Time* newsreel series. Louis de Rochemont felt that *March of Time* was breaking new ground in the newsreel tradition because it attempted to go below the surface of events. Selected scenes from *Land of Cotton* will be analyzed to correlate *March of Time's* cinematic language with the liberal Republican world view of Time, Inc. Moving somewhat leftward on the political spectrum, portions of a government-sponsored documentary, *The River* (1937), will be examined. Pare Lorentz justified the existence of his U.S. Film Service on the grounds that it took a needed additional step beyond the documentary insight provided by *March of Time*: not only were problems exposed to public view, but the New Deal's solutions to these problems were persuasively presented. Still further to the left, Leo Hurwitz and Paul Strand worked as independent filmmakers in order to carry the contribution of social documentary films beyond the mark established by Lorentz. These makers of *Native Land* had actually worked as cameramen for Lorentz during the making of *The Plow That Broke the Plains* (1936). As that project had progressed, Hurwitz and Strand became increasingly unhappy with Lorentz's "arty" script. They drafted their own and presented it to Lorentz. As Lorentz recalled the ideological/production confrontation, "they wanted it to be all about human greed and how lousy our system was. And I couldn't see what this had to do about dust storms" (Snyder 31). The rhetoric of *Native Land* (1942) reflects its leftist orientation. This article will first describe the orientation of these three documentaries of the New Deal era, and then relate their different rhetorical styles to the political ideologies of their makers and sponsors.

The March of Time (1935-51)

During the twenties, Louis de Rochemont rose from cameraman to vice president in the newsreel business: As a professional, he was disturbed that newsreels "never get behind the news...[never explain]...what has led up to a given event. What does it portend?"

He boasted that "Someday I'm going to revolutionize the newsreel." In 1931 Time, Inc. gave him an opportunity to make good on his claims (Bluem 36).

Time, Inc. had already sponsored a thirty-minute radio program called *The March of Time,* a series which dramatized news events through reenactments. De Rochemont approached the program's producer, Roy Larsen, with a plan about adapting the program's format for the screen. Henry Luce was excited by the idea of using the powerful medium of film: he convinced his board of directors that a special corporation should be established to launch Time, Inc. into this "colossal" field (Elson 231). Over $100,000 was spent during the trial period alone. The venture was richly rewarded, for one year after its premiere in 1935, episodes of *The March of Time* were playing before an international audience of some 15,000,000.

The March of Time was controversial enough to jar the sensibilities of those in the industry who considered film to be an innocuous diversion. Martin Quigley, oracle of the Motion Picture Code and an ardent believer in wholesome entertainment, cautioned theatre owners to maintain a censorial attitude toward the newsreel series: "The exhibitors of the country ought to tell *The March of Time* that it is welcomed when it behaves itself but only then. They should tell it...that they expect it to be mindful of the proprieties of theatrical presentation—that they do not want controversial political material which is calculated to destroy the theater as the public's escape from the bitter realities, the anguishes, and the turmoil of life" (White 8). Libel suits by the Reverend Gerald K. Smith (a crony of Huey Long), diplomatic protests by dictators Rafael Trujillo and Adolph Hitler attest that this New York based newsreel series could be controversial, especially on issues related to foreign affairs and the rather antediluvian injustices of Southern society.

Probably the most obvious novelty about *The March of Time* was that it made a profit. Although many felt that *The March of Time* was slick and commercial, some hoped that the series would cultivate an audience for headier stuff. English documentarian, John Grierson, was elated: "In no sense conscious of the higher cinematic qualities, it has yet carried over from journalism some of that bright and easy tradition of free-born comment which the newspaper has won and the cinema has been too abject even to ask for" (163). Because of

March of Time's success, "The world, our world, appears suddenly and brightly as an oyster for the opening; for film people—how strangely—worth living in, fighting in and making drama about" (Grierson 163).

Unfortunately, like its literary predecessor, *Time, March of Time* lacked a coherent, self-conscious political viewpoint. As the 'Thirties depression worsened, *Time*'s policy of "unbiased, objective journalism" came under increasing attack (Elson 249). An in-house memo to Henry Luce by a *Fortune* editor attempted to highlight the limitations of *Time's* much vaunted "objectivity" in a suffering world: "*Time* is ostensibly impartial but actually (perhaps unconsciously) right wing. Because its bias is unadmitted and perhaps even unrecognized by its editors, it is unable to allow for its prejudices" (251-52). *March of Time*'s "objectivity" often led viewers to come away from the series with entirely different impressions. An especially controversial episode, "Inside Nazi Germany-1938," was so ambiguous that it was at once attacked as "a flaming pro-Nazi story," defended as "an editorial for democracy," and lauded for its impartiality.[1]

Both the opening and closing segments of *Land of Cotton* are full of similar equivocations. During the establishing shots which follow the main title, viewers become visually acquainted with a tenant shack in the middle of seemingly endless fields of cotton:

Southern Sharecropper Family

laundry hangs on the front porch; barefooted men sit and smoke on the back seat of an automobile which serves as their porch glider. Only the most callous viewers could withhold sympathy from these impoverished people.

Instead of pursuing an examination of the plight of Southern sharecroppers, *Land of Cotton* re-enacts a disturbing dialogue between a representative landlord and his tenant. As in many other scenes of this film, the visual evidence contradicts the explicit oral statements of the people photographed: visually, a gap in the status of the two men is clearly established by their contrasting dress, posture, smoking devices. The sharecropper wears overalls and sits on the front stairs of his shack. The landlord stands over him dressed in white. As the landlord speaks, he lights a cigar and throws the expended match at the feet of his tenant. The eyes of the unsmoking tenant involuntarily follow the flight of the match to the ground. What is most disturbing about this re-enactment is that it completely contradicts evidence later adduced about the intense struggle between landlords and tenants:

> LANDLORD: "I know times are hard and I know conditions are far from perfect. It's the system that's wrong. It's been handed down to us through generations. It can't be corrected over night. You don't think I'm getting rich, do you?"
> TENANT: [Abjectly] "No, seh..."

A subtle, nonverbal element of film rhetoric is at work here to support a conservative interpretation of the Southern problem. The interview described above is strategically placed. It is preceded by shots of tenant suffering. The contrived interview then verbally asserts that landlords share that suffering. The shots which then follow the interview return to images of sharecropper poverty. The resulting effect upon the audience of this shot sequence is to arouse sympathy for all classes in the region. Significantly, the only villains identified are the long-dead generations who committed the South to a single crop.

Like the opening segment of *Land of Cotton*, its closing is edited in such a way as to muffle any implication that classes are in conflict.

Words uttered again conflict with the information communicated by visual images. The narrator concludes that "only basic change can restore the one-time peace and prosperity of the Kingdom of Cotton," but the remedy suggested by cinematic language is far from radical. An establishing shot of a small rural chapel is followed by a close-up of the bell which summons the community to worship. The service inside is then quickly depicted by montage: a series of medium shots reveals that it is attended jointly by both members of the ragged sharecropper class and the white-shirted middle class. The entire society is united in song, the Episcopal hymn, "Holy, Holy, Holy." We are asked to conclude that all ranks of Southerners would be happy to continue living with their semi-feudal system if they could only obtain enough to eat. Good times will return with diversification. The rich will be less cruel; the poor whites and blacks will willingly return to their allotted places on the social ladder.

How can these conservative opening and closing scenes be reconciled with *Land of Cotton*'s revelations of evictions, beatings, and lynchings by the dominant class in its effort to repress both black and white tenants? The editing choices can be explained only by *March of Time*'s curious liberal Republican ambivalence toward reform. On the one hand, *March of Time* (like its parent company, Time, Inc.) obviously wanted to generate an awareness of social and political issues. Yet, as "objective" (and unconsciously conservative) journalists, *March of Time*'s staff could not go so far as to incite action against any sector of society. The rhetoric of *Land of Cotton* thus reflected the liberal Republican dilemma: it wished for relief, but could not agitate for the radical changes required to effect the needed reforms. Contemporaries were exasperated by *March of Time*'s reticence about solutions. One critic, George Dangerfield, voiced the irritation of many: "I wish that the editors of *March of Time*, since they have at their disposal these fictions which excite and enrage people, would use them to some purpose. I wish they would say—outright, beyond question—that somebody was right or wrong. Then we would attack them or defend them, and they would be exciting their audience honestly" (43-45).

The unwillingness to incite audiences to action was clearly reflected in *March of Time*'s lack of attention to the expressive

Ideology and Film Rhetoric 683

potential of film. Filmmakers are always aware of the difference between the informational and the compositional content of film. *March of Time* was characterized by its complete lack of attention to the compositional qualities of its footage. Shots were cut to keep up with the pace of narration rather than being arranged to suit their own natural lengths. This reliance on a narrative spine might be traced back to the radio origins of the series, but it seems more likely that *March of Time*'s lack of exploitation of film as an expressive medium can be explained by the unconscious conservatism of the series. Properly edited films might be inflammatory.

March of Time must also be faulted for its ineffective use of sound. While the series was famous—indeed, infamous—for its sepulchral "voice of doom" narration, the effect upon the viewer was often less than persuasive. All subtlety of feeling was lost. The music of the series relied more upon cliché and volume rather than the host of established commentative techniques that were utilized by Pare Lorentz and Leo Hurwitz. It seems clear that the rhetorical anemia

Depression Paradox

of both the visual and the aural tracks reflected the ideology of the filmmakers: an effective film would violate the code of objectivity.

The River (1937) as a New Deal Version

Two of the first significant social documentary films produced in America, *The Plow That Broke the Plains* (1936) and *The River* (1937), were made by a thirty-six-year-old West Virginian who had never heard of the term "documentary film." As one critic reported in 1936, Pare Lorentz "knew in general the difference between the camera's tripod and its lens [but] his information stopped a little beyond this point" (8).

By the early 1930's, Pare Lorentz had made his mark as a film reviewer who was unhappy with Hollywood's twaddle of "sin, sex, and six-shooters" (Black 38). Lorentz believed that film should be used to clarify public perception of issues. In an especially trenchant review praising the work of King Vidor (*Our Daily Bread*, 1934), Lorentz pointed out that "a social revolution was in progress and crying to be photographed while most studios ground out the same old escape stuff" (White 8). Since Lorentz believed that the movie was "America's greatest contribution to art," he hoped that Americans would be the first to explore this new potential for film (Snyder 17).

Simultaneously, the Roosevelt administration was exploring new avenues to communicate the message of the New Deal to the American people. This was an especially vexing problem because the most influential newspapers, radio, and film corporations were controlled by conservative Republicans with a bitter hatred for "That Man." As a result of this problem of media, Roosevelt and his administration experimented with alternate avenues of approach. Roosevelt himself created the now standard Presidential press conference with its intricate unwritten rules and restrictions. The President's famous "fireside chats" were an informal method of giving the American people a sense that their leader cared about their dilemma—an especially welcome relief after the silence and stolidity of Roosevelt's predecessors, Coolidge and Hoover. The Department of Agriculture, headed by Henry Wallace, made some noteworthy efforts to communicate the dilemma of the farmer to the nation as a whole. Under the leadership of Rexford Tugwell, the Resettlement Administration (later called the Farm Security Administration) sponsored an extensive photographic survey of rural poverty conditions "to educate the city dweller to the needs of the rural population" (Snyder 23). The still photography works of Dorthea Lange, Walker Evans, and Arthur Rothstein in this effort have become iconic.

Wallace and Tugwell were also interested in using motion pictures to bridge the communications gap between government and the public. They called Pare Lorentz to Washington for an interview. Lorentz quickly convinced Tugwell and Wallace that a few "films of merit" should be made rather than a host of innocuous films "about such inspired subjects as the manufacturing of paving-brick and the love-life of the honey bee. Instead, the government should produce "films...good enough technically to bear comparison with commercial films and be entertaining enough to draw an audience" (Snyder 25). Only by quality dramatization of the goals of the New Deal could government films win the minds (and the votes) of the American people.

Lorentz's films were received with great éclat by the aesthetes: among its many awards, *The River* was named as the best documentary film by the 1938 Venice International Film Festival. A man who knew something about language, James Joyce, observed for the press that the narration of *The River* contained "the most beautiful prose I have heard in ten years" (White 9).

While stating its praise humorously, the *American Magazine* was not far from a deep truth when it suggested that "Pare Lorentz has done for the United States what Hollywood has done for its glamour girls" ("Rev." 109). All of the major critics praised the film for its sensitive combination of pictures, words, and music to create an aesthetic "rhythm which is irresistible, exciting, transparent" (Van Doren 485).

The films impressed some as potent political weapons. President Roosevelt himself saw the potential of both *The Plow That Broke the Plains* (1936) and *The River* (1937) to impress the public with the need for soil conservation, relief for the South's sharecroppers, and regional planning. In the case of *Ecce Homo* (1939) and *The Fight for Life* (1941), Roosevelt was not above indicating to Lorentz that his films would soften up the public for specific New Deal measures related to public works and health (Snyder 101-2). At lower echelons, some prospective Democratic congressmen and senators found a place for *The Plow* and *The River* in their campaigns for election (Snyder 75-78). In response, a cry of pain about government propaganda issued from the Republican camp. Lorentz had a ready answer to such charges: if Henry Luce could have his popular *March of Time* film series shown in theaters around the nation, "The United States government deserves to have at least thirty minutes a month to explain in film the major problems which affect the whole country, Republicans and Democrats alike" (Snyder 144).

While Lorentz's argument may have carried the power of logic, the American people (especially after the World War I experience) were too frightened of the word "propaganda" to make subtle distinctions. As one theater manager reported, "It could be the greatest dramatic miracle of all time and I wouldn't touch it if the government made it" ("Review" *Literary* 34). A particularly irritated (perhaps even terrified) reviewer claimed that *The River* "is on the intellectual level of a voodoo ceremonial. Its aim is to win acceptance of a falsehood" (White 9). Rep. Eugene Worley of Texas went so far as to threaten to punch Tugwell in the nose for sponsoring a film that was "a libel on the greatest section of the United States." After the drought recorded on film had abated, many plains region legislators resented the image of their home areas that *The Plow* perpetuated. Rep. Karl Mundt explained in 1939 that the sovereign state of South Dakota had turned to greener pastures since the drought, and that the continued circulation of *The Plow* was an insult to his constituents. With the help of his colleagues, Mundt was able to have *The Plow* withdrawn from circulation in 1939, supposedly to have it revised in the light of "improved agricultural conditions." Funds for the revision were never appropriated, and *The Plow* did not become available to the public again until 1961.[2]

Unlike *Land of Cotton*, *The River* makes effective use of cutting to reinforce thematic messages. For example, during the section on lumbering, each shot is reduced in length to accentuate the mood of frenetic extractive activity. Later, slow pacing is used when the film returns to survey the disastrous results of exploitation. A series of long panning shots are linked together by dissolves. Because the

Taking the Valley Apart

composition of the shots matches so well, we seem to be examining an endless horizon of devastation. This matching of composition together with the slow pace from shot to shot yields a mood of involved reflection—a mood further intensified by Virgil Thomson's score.

In *The River,* Lorentz made extensive use of intellectual montage, a basic cinematic device entirely absent from *Land of Cotton.* The solution phase of *The River* contains one of the most impressive New Deal montages. The narrator explains: "We had the power to take the valley apart. We have the power to put it back together again." The following visual images were juxtaposed by Lorentz to evoke this idea:

LS: Explosion of dynamite.
MS: Steam shovel scooping tons of rock.
MS (Low Angle): Pneumatic drill operator with breathing mask.
LS (High Angle): Dam under construction from moving crane.
LS: Pouring concrete for dam.
LS: Controlled water flowing thunderously.

LS: Explosion of dynamite (as above).
MS: Pneumatic drill (as above).
LS: Explosion of dynamite (as above).
MS: Pneumatic drill (as above).
LS: Pouring concrete (as above).
LS: (With dissolve transition): Before/after shots of gorge now blocked by the Norris Dam.

Sergei Eisenstein, the early advocate of intellectual montage, spoke of ideas as new creations generated in the minds of viewers as a result of the collision of images. In this example, the images and sounds were edited by Lorentz to evoke an idea about the relationship between machines and men. Early sections of *The River* demonstrated the misuses of technology. In harmony with New Deal thinking, this intellectual montage asserts that man is essentially a tool user despite previous excesses. What the nation needs is not a rejection of technology, but the intelligent guidance of planners who can coordinate its application. The controlled consumption of resources will yield a better life for all.

The soundtrack of *The River* was also designed to arouse the viewer. A series of roll calls announce the names of trees, rivets, cities, and dates of floods. While these roll calls obviously convey factual information, their main function is to evoke poetic feeling. Even the tone in which the narrator reads the names is varied to

Putting the Valley Back Together

suit the mood of each section: for example, the roll call of trees is expansive during the scenes of exploitation, but the same words are uttered in an elegiac tone when the film returns to calculate the cost of denuding the Northern hillsides. The Whitmanesque repetition and metaphor exploited throughout the film establishes an effective verbal rhythm:

> We cut the top off the Allegheny
> and sent it down the river;
> We cut the top off Minnesota,
> and sent it down the river.

The musical component of the soundtrack subtly reinforces thematic messages. Leitmotivs are announced during the roll call sequences. Just as the narrator's voice is optimistic and dynamic during the first roll call of trees, so is the river theme which is played in the background. During the exploitation scenes, the leitmotiv turns minor and brassy, reinforcing the dolorous second narrative roll call of trees. During the early lumbering sequence described above, we watch one-hundred year old trees race down a sluiceway. An orchestra which becomes increasingly larger plays the tune "Hot Time in the Old Town Tonight." The intended contrast between the vigorous industrial activity on the screen and the orchestrated barroom song evokes an obvious reflection in the minds of viewers—this exploitative intoxication will end in a very painful hangover.

Social documentaries often follow a problem-solution formula, and *The River* is no exception. What is unusual is the curious difference between the intensity of the problem phase and the confidence of the solution section. This difference in tone can only be accounted for by reference to the New Deal orientation of the filmmaker and his sponsor. The problem phase of the film is powerfully conveyed: our indignation is aroused at those who have misused the land and resources of the Mississippi Valley. But even as we view the widespread suffering that has resulted, viewers are never thrust into the scene. We are always concerned observers of a social problem rather than involved participants. The solution portion of the film confirms this observer status. The floods, the poverty, and the backwardness of the South are being dealt with by the Roosevelt administration. Viewers need do no more than ratify the ongoing work of the New Deal. In sum, while *The River* works hard to arouse the feelings of its audience, film rhetoric does not promote a sense of participation, nor is personal action demanded.

Native Land (1942) as a Progressive Version

Native Land (1942) is generally acknowledged to be the best product of a short-lived American radical film movement in the 'Thirties. The first radical film group, the Workers Film and Photo League, worked closely with a leftist relief group known as the Workers International Relief Organization. Members of the League accompanied union representatives to textile mills in New England and coal mines in Harlan County, West Virginia, where the resistance of workers was recorded on film. Locally, the League filmed the protests by taxi drivers and tenement dwellers in New York City. The League felt a special calling for its labors because the bourgeois press simply left the labor story unreported. As one League member noted wryly: "There was no *March of Time* even to simulate

Views of Oppression

the reality of the early thirties in film" (Sweet 12). Until the midthirties, the League attempted to do little more than accumulate a visual record on celluloid. Tom Brandon's description of his own motives for participating communicates the basic spirit of the early days: "I didn't consider myself a filmmaker. I saw certain needs and I learned how to use a 35mm camera and I went and covered some important things because I knew nobody else was doing it" (Sweet 33).

By 1935, some members of the League wanted to move on to more sophisticated projects, and these men founded a production group which they called Nykino (i.e., New York "kino" or film-eye). This group experimented with *March of Time* style re-enactments in *Sunnyside* (a story of New York evictions) and *The Black Legion* (a study of an American fascist group). *Pie in the Sky* tested the possibilities of improvisation for social documentaries. As Leo Hurwitz recalled, the more committed filmmakers of the League had been struck by "the necessity of expanding our ideas from simple coverage to something like an essay form that would have ideas and events, connectives and preparations, to show what was not necessarily visible or photographable" (Klein 4).

Frontier Films, an affinity group consisting of Leo Hurwitz, Paul Strand, Ralph Steiner, Jay Leyda and others, was an outgrowth of the Nykino experiments. The filmmakers convinced such prominent intellectuals and artists as Ernest Hemingway, John Dos Passos, Archibald MacLeisch, and Lillian Hellman to contribute time, effort, or money to their cause. Some of the best films which resulted were on foreign crises: *Heart of Spain* (1937) and *Return to Life* (1937) were designed to raise funds for the Loyalist cause in the Spanish Civil War; *China Strikes Back* (1937) portrayed a unified people struggling against an imperial invader. Frontier Films also produced some excellent studies of domestic American conditions: the struggle of Detroit auto workers was intensely portrayed in *United Action* (1939); rural poverty (but also the pleasures of rural life) was explored in *People of the Cumberland* (1938). Finally, the epic of Frontier Film's seven year activities was *Native Land*, a film begun in 1938, but not issued until May, 1942.

Contemporary reviewers welcomed *Native Land* enthusiastically. *Time* called it "vitally American" even though it portrayed a bitter class struggle at work in America ("The New Pictures" 50). *The New Republic* was especially pleased that the civil rights issue had at last received filmic treatment: "a story which too long has been distorted through the mouths of congressmen and newspapers" (Farber 734-35). *Native Land* has been called "the most important U.S. independent thirties film," but it has been neglected by film scholarship (Sweet 16). The press of events worked against proper recognition of *Native Land*. Leo Hurwitz received the answer print from the laboratory the day after Pearl Harbor was bombed. With the United States at war, not even the Communist party was interested in distributing a film which could be construed as an attack on national unity (Klein 6).

Native Land attempted to use specific incidents of civil rights violations as a means to evoke a general picture of repression in America. The efforts of little men to challenge the policies of "the big shots," "the interests," "powerful corporations" are shown to be fruitless if conducted on an individual basis. Sharecroppers, workers, small merchants must learn to work cooperatively in the industrial era. Freedom is the result of vigilance, not an automatic condition. As in his other films, Hurwitz worked hard in *Native Land* to develop a maximum number of intellectual and moral implications for the particular stories told.

Native Land closely examines eight civil rights violations. While only the second incident will be analyzed, its thematic content and rhetorical style are representative. The plot of the incident is extremely simple. A young girl is washing the windows of an urban apartment building. In the course of her duties, she discovers the unconscious body of one of the tenants, a man who has been beaten for attempting to organize a union at a nearby factory.

The rich film rhetoric of this incident was organized in such a way as to thrust the viewer into the story of a participant. As the scene opens, we are swept down the street toward the girl by means of a moving camera. Involvement of the viewer builds through the use of subjective camera and reverse angles: as the girl sits in an apartment window cleaning the outside of a large lower pane, she turns to look down into the street. Through subjective camera, we see a boy below showing off his skill with a paddle ball. A reaction shot of the girl indicates that she has the same smile on her face that a responsive viewer has probably assumed. The camera angle is again reversed: we look up at the girl in the window through the boy's eyes. They are both obviously happy to be alive and active on this sunny day. Viewer attention is then humorously focused upon the girl's dog, a small mutt who frets over the safety of his mistress. Throughout the scene, a slightly operatic tune is developed.

Such an extended portrayal of persons apart from issues might at first seem irrelevant to the goals of a social documentary film. Certainly, neither *Land of Cotton* nor *The River* considers the private lives of the people whose problems are reported. Yet such a slow beginning has a very necessary place within this leftist film. In part, it is a logical result of the egalitarianism of the Frontier Film group. But this close scrutiny of simple pleasures in the lives of the working class has a second purpose more closely linked to *Native Land*'s rhetoric of involvement. The invasion of an established fabric of existence will shock us all the more if we first become acquainted with the girl as an innocent young person rather than as a special problem (*March of Time*) or as a client of the government (*The River*). The ideology and rhetoric of this introduction are inextricably related.

Once viewer identification with the girl has been established, the scene progresses. She carries her pail upstairs to the second floor. The camera at the top of the stairs follows her movements in long, slowly paced shots. As she climbs the stairs and turns the corner, she continues to hum the tune which we heard during the charming opening scene. The little dog follows dutifully behind.

The girl knocks at the union man's door, but no one answers. At this point, many different elements of film language work in concert to develop a new mood: the light operatic tune shifts from violins to sour brass; the pace of editing accelerates; close-ups of details inside the room are intercut with shots of the girl's attempts to push her way in. Throughout this quickly-paced scene, camera angles change rapidly to further charge the atmosphere. Finally, she succeeds in pushing aside the dresser which barred the door. Although we learn of the harm done to the union organizer inside, viewer attention does not remain focused on the victim. Instead, we cringe because we anticipate the traumatic effect which this incident will have on the innocent young girl.

As the girl steps inside the room, we re-enter her point of view: through a subjective camera, we survey the damage. The soundtrack goes dead. This silence is especially effective because the brass has been playing the leitmotiv with increasing volume and dissonance. We look up at the girl from a low angle. There is a delay in sound and expression as we observe the full effect of this brutal scene. Thematically, we are shown that large corporations can crush individuals who attempt to stand up for their rights. But this conceptual acknowledgment is informed by personal feeling. We have shared in the girl's painful discovery as participants in the scene rather than as concerned observers of a distant wrong.

The leftist persuasion of the filmmakers determined the conclusion of this representative incident from *Native Land*. *March of Time* would have assured viewers that a vigorous press was contributing to the eventual solution by exposing the abuses of power. *The River* would have softened the blow by pointing to President Roosevelt's growing moral and legislative support of the union movement. *Native Land* provides no such escape clause from personal responsibility. Because its creators assumed that both the press and the government of the United States too often bowed to money interests, *Native Land* requires nothing less than full participation by viewers. The narrator muses: "Again. It happened again. They say he was a union man. Nothing in the newspapers...It wasn't on the radio... Don't understand it...New York, Chicago, Cleveland..." The implication here, and at the close of the other eight incidents, is that the reader must come to conclusions on his own based upon the strength of the emotional involvement promoted by the rhetoric of the film.

Summary

The different film rhetorics of *Land of Cotton*, *The River*, and *Native Land* can be related to the liberal Republican, New Deal, and leftist persuasions of the respective filmmakers. As we move leftward on the political spectrum, there is a greater appeal to our feelings and an ever-increasing pressure upon the viewer to become involved in the action. *Land of Cotton* rests on the principle that "exposure" by an objective, free press will generate discussion and—at some future date—action. Yet a number of obstacles were placed in the path of a concerned viewer: for every exposure of a social problem, there was a contradicting note about social harmony in the Kingdom of Cotton. The film rhetoric of *Land of Cotton* was not exploited fully because of this underlying ambivalence. In its ideological and rhetorical confusion, the cinematic monthly shared the weakness of Time, Inc.'s literary weekly: by its unwillingness to take a stand, it inadvertently supported the status quo.

The rhetoric of Pare Lorentz's *The River* is of pure New Deal vintage. During the problem phase of the film, every rhetorical device in the lexicon of film is employed to force upon the viewer a realization of the folly of our industrial exploitation. Editing, music, and narration are used to their fullest to arouse our indignation about the plight of those who would later be called the "Other America." Yet the solution segment allows viewers to sit back and watch rather than encourage them to help bring about a solution. We are assured that we can surrender our responsibility to government planners who will solve our economic and ecological problems for us. We are told that we are justified in giving planners such sweeping powers because the original problems to be solved were created through ignorance and lack of foresight rather than by any inherent human tendency to misuse power.

The film rhetoric of *Native Land* is as distinctive as its radical message. Viewers are never allowed to merely observe contemporary scandals (*Land of Cotton*), nor to trust in the benevolence of public officials (*The River*). By first introducing viewers to the wholesome lives of farmers, laborers, urban merchants and then dramatizing the disruption of these lives, *Native Land* elicits a deep emotional response. The mounting emotion which we feel at the end of these eight incidents is the pain of personal tragedy.

Henry James once described the American Dream as the pervasive desire of his countrymen to make so much money that they could stop caring. By their differing lights, "objective" journalist Louis de Rochemont, New Dealer Pare Lorentz, and leftist Leo Hurwitz attempted to counter the tendency of Americans to ignore the responsibilities of citizenship. The film rhetorics of *Land of Cotton*, *The River*, and *Native Land* are consonant with their differing demands for feeling and action.

Notes

1. This confusion is documented in detail by Raymond Fielding.
2. Rep. Karl Mundt deserves the credit for suppression of *The Plow* while Orville Freeman was responsible for its re-release. See Snyder, *Pare Lorentz*, pp. 76, 89-80. The upbeat New Deal conclusion to *The Plow* was restored to official copies of the film in the 1980s.

Works Cited

Black, C.M. "He Serves America." *Colliers* Aug. 1940: 38.
Bluem, A. William. *Documentary in American Television*. New York: Hastings House, 1965.
Dangerfield, George. "Time Muddles On." *The New Republic* 19 Aug. 1936: 43-45.
Elson, Robert T. *Time Inc.: The Intimate History of a Publishing Enterprise, 1923-1941*. New York: Atheneum, 1968.
Farber, Manny. "The Naked Truth." *New Republic* 25 May 1942: 734-35.
Fielding, Raymond. "Mirror of Discontent: *The March of Time* and its Politically Controversial Film Issues." *Western Political Quarterly* 12.1 (1959): 146-53.
Grierson, John. *Grierson on Documentary*. Ed. Forsyth Hardy. Berkeley: U of California P, 1966.
Klein, Michael, and Jill Klein, "*Native Land*: An Interview with Leo Hurwitz," *Cineaste* 6.3 (1975): 4.
Quigley, Martin. *Motion Picture Herald* 5 Feb. 1938: 8.
Rev. of *The River*. Dir. Pare Lorentz. *American Magazine*. May 1938: 109.
Rev. of *The River*. Dir. Pare Lorentz. *Literary Digest*. November 20, 1937: 34.
Snyder, Robert L. *Pare Lorentz and the Documentary Film*. Norman: U of Oklahoma P, 1968.
Sweet, Fred, *et al*. "Pioneers: An Interview with Tom Brandon," *Film Quarterly* 26.5 (1973): 12.
"The New Pictures." Rev. of *Native Land*. Dirs. Leo Hurwitz and Paul Strand. *Time* 8 June 1942: 50.
Van Doren, Mark. "The Poetry of Erosion." *The Nation* 30 Oct. 1937: 485.
White, William L., "Pare Lorentz." *Scribner's* Jan. 1939: 8.

31
Tulsa (1949) as an Oil Field Film: A Study of Ecological Ambivalence

Americans have always been ambivalent about industrial progress, and the feature film *Tulsa* reflects a national mind divided between enthusiastic approval of economic development and deep-seated anxieties about despoiling a Virgin Land. This abiding ambivalence has been part of our heritage since the Romantic era when America constructed an identity that proclaimed us to be Nature's Nation. There is quite a pantheon of writers who warned about the dangers of industrialism. James Fenimore Cooper, in his *Leatherstocking Tales*, delineated the dangers of mindless exploitation in a time when national expansion was just barely beyond the Mississippi River. For example, Cooper's *The Pioneers* (1823) condemned the slaughter of wildlife—in this case, wild pigeons—in a passage often reprinted by the Audubon Society. In *The Prairie* (1828) Cooper decried the family of Ishmael Bush as crude, violent, and wasteful; at the end of the novel, the family backtrails east because it needs the checks and balances provided by developed society. In this case unchecked freedom on the frontier led to licentiousness and the misuse of both human and natural resources. Also in the antebellum era, Henry David Thoreau contributed his classic treatise on spiritual ecology, *Walden* (1854). Here the threat of the machine age was symbolized by a railroad that passed close by Walden Pond. Thoreau, more than any other Romantic writer, feared the spiritual implications of a machine-oriented society and warned about the dangers of machines for the great Garden of America. He was not alone in seeing railroads as symbolizing such a threat to rural values. Certainly, in the film *Tulsa*, the oil industry—at critical moments—represents such a disruptive force.

The Course of Empire

Probably the most dramatic portrayal of the threat of material progress in the early Romantic period was a series of paintings by Thomas Cole entitled *The Course of Empire*. These paintings have been described and interpreted too many times for me to stop and engage them again, but the trajectory of the argument needs to be summarized. These massive works toured the nation teaching a very somber lesson: America was unique because it was Nature's Nation and, as we expand cities and develop industry, we move away from what made us special. Cole believed that all great empires—to include the American Empire of his own day, which had just acquired the Republic of Texas—were doomed to rise and fall. They started close to the land, developed in harmony with Nature up to the point that engineering and nature were in balance; then, unfortunately, they moved into periods of excess and decadence. Finally, these empires were overwhelmed by people who lived more vitally connected to Nature. As early as 1836 Cole believed that America was headed toward ecological imbalance—and eventual destruction. His apocalyptic vision stirred many editorials and sermons as the five-panel *Course of Empire* series toured America's major cities. (Each painting was 20 feet by 15 feet.) In a short poem entitled "Lament of the Forest," Cole summarized his concerns:

> And thus come rushing on
> > This human hurricane, boundless as swift.
> > Our sanctuary, this secluded spot,
> > Which the stern rocks have guarded until now,
> > Our enemy has marked. (Quoted in Miller, 213)

The ruin of Nature seemed as inevitable as it was tragic.

The Era of Railroads and Trusts

After the Civil War the railroads and other industries surged forward like Cole's hurricane. The new era was symbolized in the early pages of a novel about the railroad, Frank Norris's *Octopus* (1901), in which a herd of sheep is slaughtered by a speeding freight train. Here the machine murders and mutilates; it does not merely disrupt the philosophical calm of Thoreau's Walden Pond or Cole's Catskills wilderness. The steel, railroad, and oil industries expanded undisturbed during this period, led by captains of industry who were also called "robber barons," further reflecting the nation's ambivalent feelings about triumphant industry. Indeed, industrialism ran rampant and America was covered by tracks and telegraph wires, forever unified as an industrial nation. Standard Oil Company of Ohio, led by John D. Rockefeller, became the model trust in an era of corporate empire building.

In response to these developments, Frederick Jackson Turner in 1893 delivered his famous address, "The Significance of the Frontier in American History," a statement about the dynamic relationship between civilization and the wilderness that reflected both the strong feelings of his generation as well as scholarly insight. Turner's thesis had many facets, but the most important aspect for our discussion was the concept that American character had been

Black Gold Enriches a Flourishing City, Tulsa

forged in the pioneers' conquest of nature. The existence of a frontier during the first three centuries of our national experience on the continent had continuously tested and challenged America, resulting in such national characteristics as flexibility, democracy, and equality between the sexes. With the disappearance of the frontier, it was possible that these qualities would vanish from our way of life—that, like Cole's imagined empire in the epic series of paintings, we would become decadent and weak, deserving of destruction.

Like so many other frontier enthusiasts, Turner—as well as those who made the film *Tulsa* (1949)—was caught in a logical dilemma. Conquering the frontier developed the sinews and muscles of national character, but what would happen once the frontier was gone? F. J. Turner pointed to a new spirit in state universities that he hoped would foster the same values that had developed from frontier conquests. This chapter will explore the dynamics of the film *Tulsa*, which seems caught on the horns of its own dilemma: the film celebrates the excitement and creativity of a free-enterprise system that encourages entrepreneurs to gamble for the great rewards to be gained in the marketplace; at the same time, the film chastises those who are driven by market forces alone and pleads for governmental planning by social engineers.

The film *Tulsa* reveals the pervasive ambivalence about progress that has been an integral part of American culture from Thomas Cole to Frederick Jackson Turner to 21st-century debates over offshore drilling and global warming.

1. Two Crusading Filmmakers or Two Hollywood Pros?

Walter Wanger

Not surprisingly, the career of Walter Wanger is replete with evidence of ambivalence about American capitalism. Wanger had been the producer of a highly controversial film entitled *Blockade* (1938), written by John Howard Lawson. Lawson was the leading member of the Communist Party in Hollywood, and the film was seen at the time—and later—as a defense of the Loyalist side in the Spanish Civil War. At the time of release, the New York State Council of the Knights of Columbus called the film "a red trial balloon"

(Bernstein 134). On the other hand, secular critics praised Wanger for his daring; Frank Nugent of the *New York Times* said:

> Most of us have been urging Hollywood to descend occasionally from its cloud-tipped mountain peak, look at the world beneath and make some comment on the contemporary scene. If every bold producer who does so is to be repaid by misinterpretation, threats, and abuse, it is obvious that the road from the mountain will be closed for good. (Bernstein 137)

Nugent's point, clearly, was that *Blockade* was refreshing because it showed that Hollywood could address contemporary topics and illuminate them. Later, during the investigations of the House Committee on Un-American Activities (HUAC), *Blockade* would return to haunt Wanger, as would his frequent employment of Lawson as a writer. In the case of *Blockade*, Wanger had committed the sin of being "prematurely anti-fascist," a term now used with disdain, but a label that cut like a knife in 1947.

If there is a cinematic trail of radicalism in Wanger's career, there was countervailing evidence as well. Wanger believed that he was a spokesman for American individualism, and he promoted the film *Tulsa* in the context of a series of post–World War II Eagle-Lion productions that would honor the American economic system. Subsequent films in the *Tulsa* package—which were never made—would celebrate the airline industry, the American press, and the coal-mining sector. In an expansive moment, Wanger touted the potential of his efforts: "American free enterprise…is a fancy name for our individualism… . [C]apitalism as an economic term isn't money—it is opportunity" (Bernstein 228).

Wanger's ambivalence surfaces in his hopes for the film industry: he boasted big dreams for the potential of movies to change the world; yet these visions were never matched by achievements. The *New Republic*'s Otis Ferguson in 1939 accused Wanger of "turning an A.B. degree from Dartmouth College into the biggest shell game even this industry has seen." Ezra Goodman cut closer to the truth when he criticized Wanger's tendency "to talk about the brave new world of cinema while turning out celluloid old hat" (quoted in Bernstein, xiv).

The film *Tulsa* (1949) reflects this ambivalence—at certain moments it is a stinging criticism of free enterprise; in contradictory segments it lashes out at the individualism fueling that system. Different viewers of *Tulsa* will reach differing conclusions about where Wanger and the film come down: some will see the liberal compromise of a New Deal solution in which business is allowed to operate freely within parameters established by government; others may see in the Robert Preston character (Brad Brady) the makings of a new Soviet man trained as an engineer and ready to direct a planned society for the good of all.

This chapter will focus on the ambiguity of the film's message—allowing others to reach their own conclusions about the precise social vision to be yielded from the film.

Stuart Heisler

Stuart Heisler will be remembered by film historians for his crusading work as director of *The Negro Soldier* (1944), a production that was part of the Frank Capra series of information films produced during World War II to orient service men and women before their embarkation for overseas duty (see Chapter 12). Working with a black writer named Carlton Moss, Heisler produced a breakthrough motion picture in which African Americans were celebrated as citizen–soldiers.

The Negro Soldier showed the contribution of African Americans to western settlement (as Buffalo Soldiers), followed by their work on the Panama Canal. The admirable—but overlooked—record of the 369th National Guard in World War I is underscored. As might be expected, but far more powerfully than anyone anticipated, the film destroyed the screen stereotypes that plagued Hollywood films in the 1930s and 1940s. *The Negro Soldier* showed that black Americans were decent, hard-working, and patriotic people with a proud ethnic tradition and rightful claims to the American dream.

Two leading historians of American life and cinema, David Culbert and Thomas Cripps, have concluded that *The Negro Soldier* was indeed a breakthrough production. Without the success of this informative film, Hollywood would never have made such landmarks as *Home of the Brave* (1949), *The Defiant Ones* (1958), and *Guess Who's Coming to Dinner* (1967). Thus Heisler certainly had liberal credentials—indeed, credentials more fully realized in *The Negro Soldier* than in any film by Wanger. (Yet it needs to be added that Wanger was a good friend of Walter White of the NAACP and was instrumental in convincing Hollywood moguls to pledge to create better images of African Americans during and after World War II.)

In *Tulsa* Heisler seems to have followed the direction set by Wanger without too much original input, but we can imagine that he was sympathetic to the conservationist message of the film—while at the same time trying to tell a good action story about the oil fields.

2. The Romance Technique: A Woman Chooses the Right Man

The main character of *Tulsa*—perhaps the symbol of Tulsa itself—is Cherokee Lansing, played in color by beautiful, red-headed Susan Hayward, who was 31 at the time. In the opening scene of the film, she is identified as a frisky young girl of spirit. When her father dies suddenly—this Garden man, a character linked to the land and named Nels Lansing, is killed by the debris from a machine, a gusher—she is thrust into the world to find her way. Throughout the film, everything that Cherokee does has analogic significance about progress from a frontier to an industrial society.

First, Cherokee must surrender the deed to her father's ranch, The Buffalo Horn. In making this decision, she cuts herself off from the frontier days of Oklahoma and assumes a modern identity. The film acts out this transition with the ranch foreman's departure; Cherokee shakes hands with him and bids him farewell in the lobby of the Tulsa Hotel—a place where oil business deals are made.

The plot structure of the film mixes up the sequence a bit, but the logical choices then follow quickly. In her pastoral identity, Cherokee Lansing is associated with Jim Redbird (Pedro Amendáriz), a neighboring Indian rancher who constantly hints about marriage. Jim is a person who is close to the land and shares Cherokee's father's love of the preindustrial life of the ranching West. To his own disservice he funds Cherokee's first attempt to strike oil, but he does it because he loves and believes in the lovely Cherokee. When competition to exploit the Indian lands becomes intense—and Cherokee becomes caught up in the exploitation fever—Jim Redbird is left behind. Indeed he is driven temporarily insane by the intrusion of the oil industry's frantic and unnatural pace.

As Cherokee strides into the business arena, she becomes enamored with the world of Bruce Tanner (played by Lloyd Gough). Tanner lives in the Hotel Tulsa, thrives on room service, and prides himself on being a gambler both with his wells and his money. While Tanner shows civic spirit by contributing to Tulsa's opera, building skyscrapers, and improving the city's water system, he is predominantly an old-school business tycoon. Tanner sees the land and its oil as means to an end—to make Tulsa the oil capital of the world. He has no sympathy for Redbird's views about ecological balance and rejects other pleas for conservation. At the peak of her business phase, Cherokee joins Tanner in projecting a vertical trust from the wells of Oklahoma to gas stations of America in a company probably based on Skelly Oil or Phillips Petroleum—two Tulsa businesses that accomplished that kind of vertical integration. Until the penultimate segment of the film, Cherokee is entranced by Tanner and his passion for profits.

Tulsa leads Cherokee to a third kind of man—who has both a scientific vision and respect for the land. Brad Brady (played by Robert Preston) is the son of the man who gave Cherokee her first oil leases—but this young man has studied geology at Princeton and toured the globe, learning about the oil industry, before coming

Cherokee Lansing with Two Romantic Leads: Engineer Brad Brady and Preindustrial Oklahoman, Jim Redbird

to Tulsa. Brad Brady shows that he is a man's man by defeating Cherokee's foreman in a fistfight, but he is also much more educated in what is happening underground than Tanner—who tries to dismiss the Ivy Leaguer as a bookworm. Most significantly he tells Cherokee that "oil means to me what pure-bred Herefords meant to your father." In other words, unlike the capitalist Bruce Tanner, Brad Brady has authentic feelings for the environment and its future.

Brad's plans for proper exploitation are revealed in a number of scenes in which he seems to be the spokesman for Director Heisler and Producer Wanger. Brady correctly explains that over-drilling a field reduces the pressure in the field and works against full exploitation of the natural resources; over-drilling leads to exploitation of only 30 percent of the Glennpool—the rich source of oil just south of Tulsa that made the city an oil capital. With better planning there could have been a much higher yield—more energy and less work.

Brady works with Redbird to balance ranching needs with the goals for oil extraction. They limit drilling to one derrick per ten acres and surround the derricks with fences to protect both the machines and the cattle. The plan pleases Redbird, and the land flourishes. To teach the other landowners and the other oilmen the lessons of moderation, Redbird and Brady call a meeting. They show slides of Glennpool when it was being intensively extracted, and then afterward, when all that remains is a mucky wasteland. They propose that their fellow Oklahomans limit production and control the number of wells put into service, to preserve the environment for future generations. Operating entirely in character, Tanner convinces the landowners to maximize profit in the shortest time and to forget about wimpy pleas for the health of grass, flowers, and steer.

Through a plot device Cherokee sees the errors of her ways and throws her loyalty to Brady, the engineer. Tanner's vision led to the catastrophic fire that is tamed in an exciting action portion of the film's conclusion. During this crisis Brady uses a Caterpillar tractor to save Cherokee, proving that the machine can work beneficently if used correctly and by the right people—for example, trained engineers who care about both the land and its people. As they reflect on the near-disaster, Cherokee embraces Brady and his vision.

Oklahoma will create a plan in which oil production is restricted and where state standards are enforced, thereby providing a model to the nation. According to Chill Wills in the epilogue of the film, Oklahoma has set a high standard for conservation; California and other states are emulating the Oklahoma example. The new approach, we are told, pleases "cattlemen, oilmen, and us Tulsans."

3. Classic Precedents of Montage on the Misuses of the Environment—Some Artistic Borrowing by Eagle-Lion Productions?

Tulsa was nominated for an Academy Award for Editing and, indeed, there are some very powerful and message-laden montage sequences. Their power has special resonance because there are clear allusions to at least two famous films—one documentary and one feature, both related to America's misuse of the land.

One of the classic American documentaries about the environment is *The Plow That Broke the Plains* (1936) by Pare Lorentz. The film was made about the disastrous conditions in mid-America during the 1920s and 1930s and stresses the misuses of the land, which turned many sections of Kansas, Oklahoma, and Texas into the legendary "Dust Bowl." Through such films as *The Plow That Broke the Plains* and its successor, *The River* (1937), the Farm Security Administration of the Agriculture Department hoped to bring home to urban audiences the grievous conditions affecting rural America—conditions that would otherwise be unseen, a perennial problem with rural poverty in our country (see Chapter 30).

Much of the land taken under heavy cultivation in the early 1920s proved profitable because of a devastated Europe's postwar needs for food. During this boom era, the weather was accommodating; however, in the mid-1920s, droughts began to drive farmers off the land and to send dust blowing across the region. Indeed, even Chicago suffered a severe dust storm in the late 1920s in which high winds deposited tons of silt from as far away as Iowa and Nebraska.

In a famous montage, *The Plow That Broke the Plains* likened the intensive, mechanized farming of the area to a military attack on the land. Finally the profit motive that fueled the boom is linked to the stock exchange and its disaster. The point of these intellectual montage sequences was to show that it was human greed—and not just bad weather—that put man and nature out of harmony.

Some three years later, John Ford's rendering of *The Grapes of Wrath* would revisit the issue of tractors cutting into the living flesh of the plains. John Steinbeck, in the eponymous novel, had laid out a true ecologist's vision of the land's misuse in chapter 5, called "The Cats." Drawing upon Steinbeck's lead and the precedent of the New Deal films about the environment, John Ford's film version provided a powerful montage of disruption. In the final portion of the anecdote where this montage is placed, the tractor runs over the home of Muley Graves—a representative sharecropper. This invasion of the machine into the garden of Oklahoma carries over into Wanger and Heisler's oil-patch film.

At the climax of *Tulsa*, Jim Redbird (Pedro Armendáriz) attempts to stop Cherokee Lansing from increasing the number of wells on his property. Cherokee and Bruce Tanner enforce their drilling-rights lease by asking for a hearing before Judge McKay. Redbird begs them to preserve his land, but the judge threatens to have the Indian declared *non compus mentus*—evidently a legal stratagem commonly used to deprive Indians of their rights. The hearing is the true climax of the film because it chills Cherokee's passion to exploit the land. It is also important because of the following montage in which the red man—who represents the spirit of the land before industrialism—is overwhelmed by the mechanical and legal mechanisms of white society. It is both a visual and an aural montage, featuring the derricks, machines, and sounds of industrial development that have replaced the natural sounds of country life, along with the voice of the judge and Cherokee saying "crazy Indian," and the sounds of music and pounding of machines.

The sequence reaches a powerful climax as Redbird lights a match to test the water, just as Nels Lansing had done. This time the fire gets out of hand. What we have up to this point is an industrial nightmare that ends in an apocalypse of sorts. It is the worst conceivable result of unchecked industrial development. It looks very much like the destruction in the last panel of Thomas Cole's *Course of Empire*.

This exploitation killed Nels Lansing, Cherokee's father, and now it nearly kills the Native American. Symbolically it has destroyed both the eighteenth- and nineteenth-century ways of life on the land.

Conclusion

The opening montage of *Tulsa* presents a picture of "heroic industry" in the form of oil exploration, refining, and distribution from "the oil capital of the world." As the down-home actor Chill Wills explains during this celebration of American industrial progress, "Oil is the lifeblood of civilization." This celebration of commerce and the exploitation of resources is a part of our national myth—in this case, the dream of success. In F. Scott Fitzgerald's *Great Gatsby*, this dream is epitomized in the "little green light" at the end of Daisy Buchanan's dock and is as hypnotic as it is ultimately unobtainable—a veritable *dream* of success and wealth. Within the film *Tulsa* there are oil-drilling and production sequences that pay homage to the effort and dedication that go into such achievement—success and wealth do not fall into one's lap but are *sometimes* a reward for those who devote themselves to its pursuit. The final credits of *Tulsa* recapitulate a rousing message about the oil industry, but twenty-first-century viewers will note the enormous quantity of polluting smoke belching from the coal-fired electric plants and the considerable quantity of noxious vapors being released from the refining towers of west Tulsa. Certainly the film *Tulsa* pays homage to the sublimity of industrial development and, in the opening and closing moments, it does so without second thoughts about the ineluctable changes introduced when the machine enters the American Garden.

On the other hand *Tulsa* criticizes the very sublimity it seeks to celebrate. We know that Walter Wanger wanted the film to be a paean to the oil industry, but any proponent of environmental reform could find a wonderful defense of environmentalism in the motion picture. The ambivalence is as old as America's identification of itself as Nature's Nation. In a famous essay entitled "Nature and the National Ego," the American studies scholar Perry Miller posed an insightful rhetorical question: "But how could we at one and the same time establish our superiority to artificial Europe upon our proximity to Nature, and then view with complacency the rapidity of our despoiling her?" (206)

Despite the explicit vow to celebrate industry, Producer Wanger and Director Heisler were affected by this national myth and created a film about the oil industry that is characterized not by a clear message but by ambivalence about America's relationship to the land. To point out this dilemma is not to unmask the film but to recognize a pervasive contradiction in our national myths.

Coda

Those who consider other oil films are invited to study the presence and impact of other American myths. For example, it seems clear that Elia Kazan's *Splendor in the Grass* (1961) was an exploration of how the success myth inspires and rewards the vulgar and the insensitive as often as it may the diligent and virtuous. With great poignancy, the film starring Warren Beatty and Natalie Wood showed how success destroys young people, often leaving them only fleeting and painful memories of youthful idealism. The George Stevens' film *Giant* (1956), perhaps the greatest of oil-field epics, exposed the social repression and prejudice. By showing the mistreatment of Hispanics and the relationship of the dominant

Fighting the Fires of Greed

class to other whites, the film countered Frederick Jackson Turner's celebration of the American frontier as a level playing field for those who seek to strive and succeed. The Snopes-like and bumptious Jett Rink (played by James Dean) stumbles on success by accident—indeed he becomes enormously rich through a combination of his own stubbornness and the sentimental attachment of a brutal and possessive spinster who deeds him a patch of oil-rich land. As has been asserted in this chapter, *Tulsa* examines the myth of the machine in the garden.

Viewed from the perspective of myth, oil-field films not only study the regions where the black gold is discovered and tell action stories about exploration and discovery but drill down—whether they intend to or not—to the fundamental, bedrock level of the American mind. As a result, in studying such films as Walter Wanger's *Tulsa*, we find America reflected.

Works Cited

Bernstein, Matthew. *Walter Wanger: Hollywood Independent*. Berkeley: U of California P, 1994.

Culbert, David H., and Thomas Cripps. "The Negro Soldier (1944): Film Propaganda in Black and White." *Hollywood as Historian: American Film in a Cultural Context*. 2nd ed. Ed. Peter C. Rollins. Lexington: UP of Kentucky, 1998. 109-33.

Miller, Perry. "Nature and the National Ego." *Errand into the Wilderness*. Cambridge: Harvard UP, 1956. 204-16.

Smith, Henry N. *The Virgin Land: The American West as Symbol and Myth*. 1950. New York: Random House, 1957.

Steinbeck, John. *The Grapes of Wrath*. 1939. New York: Penguin, 1992.

Tulsa. Dir. Walter Wanger. Perf. Susan Hayward and Robert Preston. Eagle-Lion, 1949.

Turner, Frederick Jackson. "The Significance of the Frontier in American History." In *America's Great Frontiers and Sections*. Ed. Wilbur Jacobs. Lincoln: U of Nebraska P, 1969. 84-93.

Photo Credits

Preface
Captain Daniel G. Rollins, 1945. Credit: Peter C. Rollins.
The Rollins Chapel: Vox Clamantis in Deserto. Credit: Peter C. Rollins.
Perry Miller. Credit: Harvard University.

Introduction
Orestes A. Brownson (1803-1876). Credit: Notre Dame University.
A Satirical Voice from America's Past. Credit: Will Rogers Memorial.
Whorf Found Patternment Even in the Monosyllabic Word.
    Credit: Benjamin Lee Whorf Legacy CD ROM.
Lt. Rollins aboard the USS Renville, 1964. Credit: Dave Winter.
Television's Vietnam: Impact of Visual Images. Credit: Accuracy in Media.
General William C. Westmoreland (1914-2005). Credit: U.S. Army.

Chapter 1
Will Rogers: America's Conscience. Credit: Will Rogers Memorial.
Urban America in the Jazz Age. Credit: U.S. Archives.
Ford Innovations "Move" America. Credit: U.S. Archives.
Will Rogers as "Relief" During the Depression Years. Credit: Will Rogers Memorial.
Rogers as Both Cowboy and Journalist. Credit: Will Rogers Memorial.
Will Rogers in *Jubilo* (1919). Credit: Will Rogers Memorial.
As Innocent Abroad in *Connecticut Yankee* (1931). Credit: Will Rogers Memorial.
Uncle Will at Work. Credit: Will Rogers Memorial.
Will Shows "Horse Sense." Credit: Will Rogers Memorial.
"All I know is what I read in the papers." Credit: Will Rogers Memorial.

Chapter 2
Lorimer Was "The Boss." Credit: U.S. Archives.
Will Rogers Brought Will, Jr., on the 1926 Trip. Credit: Will Rogers Memorial.

Will Rogers and his Pen Pal. Credit: Will Rogers Memorial.
Rogers Loved to Fly. Credits: Will Rogers Memorial.
Object Lesson. Credit: http://newman.baruch.cuny.edu/digital/redscare/images_lg/object_ lesson.jpg.
Will Rogers: A More Generous Approach. Credit: Will Rogers Memorial.
Rogers with the First Lady, 1933. Credit: Will Rogers Memorial.

Chapter 3
Will Rogers on Tour (with Newspaper). Credit: Will Rogers Memorial.
Lorimer's Own Epistolary Effort. Credit: Edmon Low Library, Oklahoma State University.
Rogers Meets Europe in a Series of Short Films. Credit: Will Rogers Memorial.

Chapter 4
Technology, Luxury, and Values. Credit: U.S. Archives
General Mitchell's Bona Fides. Credit: U.S. Archives.
Lindbergh and Friend. Credit: Will Rogers Memorial.
Frank Hawks Piloted the Mercy Flights. Credit: Will Rogers Memorial.
Hope for the Youth of America. Credit: Will Rogers Memorial.
The Concern about American Character Continues. Credit: Warner Bros, 1979.

Chapter 5
SEP and the 'Old West' of Emerson Hough, 1923. Credit: Library of Congress.
Hough's *The Covered Wagon* Adapted to Film, 1923. Credit: American Film Institute.
The Post's Racial Stereotyping. Edmon Low Library.
Uncle Will at Work. Credit: Will Rogers Memorial.
Lincoln T. Perry. Credit: Library of Congress.
Will Rogers Campaigns with FDR, 1932. Credit: Will Rogers Memorial.

Chapter 6
The Will Rogers Memorial, Claremore, Oklahoma. Credit: Will Rogers Memorial.
Rogers a Radio Presence. Credit: Will Rogers Memorial.
Rogers' Humor Tickled President Wilson. Credit: Will Rogers Memorial.
Will Rogers, Jr., and James Rogers. Credit: Will Rogers Memorial.

Chapter 7
B. L. Whorf: Engineer, Linguist, Visionary. Credit: Whorf Collection.

Whorf's Major Articles Republished and Reconsidered. Credit: MIT University Press.
Hubble Images Renew a Sense of Cosmic Beauty. Credit: NASA.
Sir Arthur Eddington, Scientist and Quaker. Credit: Cambridge University.
The Leopold and Loeb Case: Original Sin in the Jazz Age. Credit: National Archives.
New Perspectives from Ancient Cultures/Languages. Credit: New Mexico Tourism.

Chapter 8
Acoma Pueblo, New Mexico. Credit: Ridgemont Media.
Boas: Father of the American School. Credit: The Smithsonian.
Sapir: Disciple of Boas, Mentor to Whorf. Credit: Library of Congress.
Whorf Saw (Mystical) Patternment in the Permutations for a Monosyllabic Word in English. Credit: *The Benjamin Lee Whorf Legacy CD-ROM.*

Chapter 9
Müller as Gifford Lecturer: Both Linguist and Believer. Credit: University of Glasgow.
Hopi Observers, 1906. Credit: The Smithsonian.
Hopi Kachinas. Credit: New Mexico Tourism.

Chapter 10
Movement to Contact in *The Big Parade* (1925). Credit: MGM.
Tomb of the Unknown. Credit: Ridgemont Media.
The Heroic Version of WWI. Credit: Ridgemont Media.
Nightmare on the Western Front. Credit: Universal Pictures.
The Conversion of Alvin York. Credit: Warner Bros.
The Original Victory Medal, 1919. Credit: The McCormick Foundation.
Korean Patrol: "Freedom is not free." Credit: Ridgemont Media.
Memory on the National Mall. Credit: Vietnam Veterans Memorial.
A Poignant Addition to the Memory. Credit: Vietnam Veterans Memorial.

Chapter 11
Rubert Brooke, "A dust whom England bore." Credit: Library of Congress.
Charlie Sheen as Taylor in *Platoon*. Credit: Hemdale Film Corporation.
Birth of a Lost Generation. Credit: National Archives of Australia.
Tom Cruise as Ron Kovic. Credit: Universal Pictures.
Battle of the Somme. Credit: U.S. Archives.

Photo credits

The Tank Brings Technology to War. Credit: U.S. Army.
I.A. Richards Inherits the Meaninglessness of Meaning. Credit: Cambridge University.
Hair Meets the Draft. Credit: Broadway Photos.

Chapter 12
Why We Fought Taught Courage in a Darkening World. Credit: U.S. Army.
Frank Capra: American Dreamer. Credit: Library of Congress.
Hitler Arouses Masses. Credit: National Archives.
Lincoln's Message of Freedom. Credit: National Archives.
Gary Cooper and Barbara Stanwyck in *Meet John Doe*. Credit: Warner Bros.

Chapter 13
Omaha Beach Fallen. Credit: Ridgemont Media.
Assaulting Fortress Europe. Credit: U.S. Army.
A Moment to Remember. Credit: Ridgemont Media.
A Revisionist Perspective. Credit: Johns Hopkins UP.

Chapter 14
Dresden on Fire. Credit: U.S. Archives.
Dresden in Ruins. Credit: U.S. Archives.
The Inner City is the 'Target for Tonight'. Credit: U.S. Archives.

Chapter 15
History with a Cinematic Pen. Credit: NBC.
RCA Gold Seal Album. Credit: Robert Russell Bennett.
Film Rhetoric Recycled on DVD. Credit: NBC.
Marines Swarm an Objective on Tarawa. Credit: U.S. Marines.

Chapter 16
V. I. Lenin Ignites the Flame. Credit: The Film Archive.
Stalin Brings 1984. Credit: U.S. Archives.
Sergei Eisenstein's *October*: A Major Source of "Reality" Footage. Credit: The Film Archive.

Chapter 17
Danang Landing, March 8, 1965. Credit: U.S. Marines.
General William C. Westmoreland, the Ground Commander, 1964-68. Credit: U.S. Army.
A Marine Junior Officer's Personal Narrative. Credit: Henry Holt and Company.
NYC Vietnam Veterans' Memorial with Pool and Glass Wall. Credit: New York Vietnam Veterans Memorial Commission.

Photo credits 715

Rebuttal to the PBS Series and Other Journalistic "Histories." Credit: Accuracy in Media.
Mel Gibson as Lt. Col. Moore Promises to Be the First into Battle. Credit: Icon Entertainment.
Vietnam's Boat People Experience the Agony of Exodus, 1975. Credit: US Archives.

Chapter 18
Viet Cong Attack: Success or Failure? Credit: National Archives.
Col. Loan Shoots Viet Cong Lieutenant. Credit: Eddie Adams Collection.
Was Khe Sanh Hell in a Very Small Place? Credit: US Marine Corps Historical Center.
President Johnson Follows Khe Sahn Closely. Credit: LBJ Presidential Library and Museum.
Marines Take the High Ground. Credit: U.S. Marine Corps.
Khe Sanh Resupply Without Landing. Credit: U.S .Marine Corps.

Chapter 19
My Controversial Documentaries. Credit: Accuracy in Media.
The Karnow Study. Credit: Penguin Books.
Douglas Pike: A Consultant Critical of the PBS Series. Credit: Douglas Pike Collection.
Chairman Ho: PBS Protagonist. Credit: U.S. Archives.
President Diem: The PBS Villain. Credit: U.S. Archives.

Chapter 20
CBS Seeks (and Finds) Conspiracy. Credit: Vietnam Archive.
Mike Wallace, Host. Credit: Museum of Broadcasting.
George Crile (d. 2006). Credit: Television Archive.
Myron "Mike" Wallace: Hired Gun? Credit: Museum of Broadcasting.
CBS Gave Itself a Black Eye. Credit: Museum of Broadcasting.

Chapter 21
George Carver, the Key Player. Credit: Vietnam Archive.
Walt W. Rostow (d.2003). Credit: LBJ Library.

Chapter 22
An American Epic. Credit: Amazon.com.
Neil Sheehan. Credit: Vietnam Archive.
Gen Paul Harkins: A False Consciousness. Credit: Vietnam Archive.
The Press in Vietnam: David Halberstam, Malcolm Browne, Neil Sheehan. Credit: Museum of Broadcasting.

Vann: Civilian with a Military Mission. Credit: Vietnam Archive.
Daniel Ellsberg. Credit: Vietnam Archive.

Chapter 23
The Original Text. Credit: Amazon.com.
Couturie's Film. Credit: Amazon.com.

Chapter 25
Video Vietnam. Credit: Amazon.com.
The Hue Massacre Not Reported. Credit: Vietnam Center.

Chapter 26
H.B. Stowe's Postal Recognition. Credit: U.S. Government.
Professor Calvin and Mrs. Stowe. Credit: Stowe Papers.
Legree's Oppression. Credit: Stowe Papers.
The Death of Little Eva. Credit: Stowe Papers.

Chapter 27
The Rev. Professor Hedge. Credit: Harvard University.
The Walnut Street Church. Credit: First Parish Archive.

Chapter 28
Amy as Unlikely Debutante. Credit: Lowell Papers.
The Distinguished Poet. Credit: Lowell Papers.

Chapter 29
John James Audubon: A Dream of Success. Credit: Audubon Collection.
Title Page of Birds of America. Credit: Harvard University.
Predators and Victims. Credit: Bartlett Collection.
A Wren Family. Credit: Bartlett Collection.
American Woodsman and American Myth. Credit: Mill Grove Museum.

Chapter 30
Southern Sharecropper Family. Credit: WPA Photos.
Depression Paradox. Credit: WPA Photos.
Taking the Valley Apart. Credit: WPA Photos.
Putting the Valley Back Together. Credit: WPA Photos.
Views of Oppression. Credit: Frontier Films.

Chapter 31
Black Gold Enriches a Flourishing City, Tulsa. Credit: Musuem of Modern Art.
Cherokee Lansing with Two Romantic Leads: Engineer Brad Brady and Preindustrial Oklahoman Jim Redbird. Credit: Museum of Modern Art
Fighting the Fires of Greed. Credit: Museum of Modern Art.

Index

Page numbers in italics indicate illustrations.

Abbott, Francis, 629
Abbott, Jacob, 637
ABC (American Broadcasting Corporation), 561, 574; and compilation films, 373; and Tet offensive, 412, 419
Abrams, Creighton, 476, 495-96; and enemy strength, 505-506n13
Acheson, Dean, 461, 515, 516
Acoma Pueblo, *190*
Accuracy in Media (AIM), 435, 445, 559-62, 564-65; and *Vietnam: A Television History*, 387-89, 441, 446, 449, 451-52, 574, 576
Adams, Eddie, 412
Adams, Henry, 226
Adams, M. Clay, 329
Adams, Michael, 307-308
Adams, Samuel (Sam), as CBS consultant, 502; in CIA, 489; and "conspiracy theory," 506-507n16; criticism of, 484n11, 488, 504n9; and enemy strength, 492, 494, 500, 502, 503n5; and *Uncounted Enemy*, 457, 458, 459, 461, 464-66, 468-69, 473-74, 475, 477-78, 480, 487, 506-507n16; and William Westmoreland lawsuit, 481-82n2
Addams, Jane, 33, 273n12
Adler, Renata, 484n10
Air Power (CBS, 1956), 12, 294, 372
Alexander Nevsky (film, 1938), 292
Allen, Frederick Lewis, 569, 570
Allen, George, 459, 460, 469-70, 487, 489, 492
All Quiet on the Western Front (book, 1929; film, 1930), 10, 239-40, *240*, 241
Almost a Husband (film, 1919), 143
Alsop, Joseph, 509, 515, 525
American Diplomacy: 1900-1950, 333, 366
American Expeditionary Force (AEF), 256, 262
Americanism, 32; lack of, 78
American Magazine, 685
American Philosophic Society, 660
American Power and the Mandarins (book, 1969), 253
American Studies Association, 3, 311
An, Phan Xuan, 538-39n8
Anna Cross, The (film, 1954), 356, 369-70

718 Index

anti-Communism, 295, 362, 522, 553, 557; of U.S. decision-makers, 533
Ap Bac, Battle of. See under *Bright Shining Lie, A: John Paul Vann and America in Vietnam*
Apocalypse Now (film, 1979), 264, 401, 442, 555, 557; and Vietnam as evil, 390
Arlen, Michael, 555-56
Armstrong, William, 245
Army of the Republic of Vietnam (ARVN), 17, 414, 424, 537-38n6
Arnett, Peter, 16, 268
Arts & Entertainment (A&E), 398, 577
Asner, Edward, 396-97
Audubon, Jean, 657, 673
Audubon, John James, 1, 3, *656, 674*; as "American Woodsman," 661, 664; business failures, 655-56, 657, 658; childhood, 657-58; in England, 661-64; *English Journal*, 29, 655; and expansionism, 20, 672-73; journals, 659, 663; materialism of, 671-72; as naturalist, 656, 658, 664, 669-70, 673; ornithological passion of, 657-58, 659-60, 664, 665; as painter, 662, 663; "predator theme," 666-69; religious faith, 664-65; "Slough of Despair," 656; transformation of, 661
Audubon, Lucy, 670, 674
Austin, Jane G., 639
aviation, 113; endurance flights, 118-19, 120. See also under Rogers, Will

Baker, Kathryn, 543-44
Baker, Newton, 235-36
Ball, George, 461
Banerian, James, 387, 398, 402, 438, 560
Baptism of Fire (film, 1940), 341
Barnicle, Mike, 544, 545-46
Battle of Algiers, The (film, 1966), 367
Battle of the Somme, The (film, 1916), 238, 271n4
Bayles, Martha, 448
Becton, Henry, 446, 447, 561
Bedell, Sally, 463-64
Beecher, Catherine, 589, 592; religious alienation of, 583, 589-90, 591
Beecher, Charles, 589, 611; as materialist, 583
Beecher, Edward, 591
Beecher, George, as perfectionist, 583; suicide of, 594
Beecher, Henry Ward, 582, 589; devotion to his mother, 586-87; and religion, 583
Beecher, James, 583
Beecher, Lyman, Calvinism of, 582, 583, 585, 589, 590, 591, 611, 613; loss of wife, 588, 604; relocation to Cincinnati, 592; and sin, 583-84
Beecher, Roxana Foote, death of, 587, 589, 603-604; religious convictions of, 582-83, 585-86
Beesley, Stanley, 386, 399
Bell, Daniel, 266
Benjamin, Burton, 370, 373; and *Uncounted Enemy*, 390, 462, 464, 467, 468-73, 480
Bennett, Robert Russell, 327, 329, 338, 340, 351, 375
Best and Brightest, The (book, 1972), 516; and anti-establishmentarianism, 534
Best War Ever, The (book, 1994), 307-8

Big Parade, The (film, 1925), 10, 234, 234
Big Story: How the American Press and Television Reported and Interpreted the Crisis of Tet 1968 in Vietnam and Washington (2 vols., 1977/1994), 388, 429; and Hue Massacre, 574
Billingsley, Lloyd, 394
Bird, Thomas, 545
Birds of America, The (books, 1827-1838), 656, 660, 663-64, 666, 667, 668-70, 673-74; subscriptions for, 662, 663, 665
Birth of a Nation, The (film, 1914), 263, 356
Black, Max, 162, 270n2
Black Legion (film, 1937), 691
Black Sunday (film, 1977), 555
Blockade (film, 1938), 702-703
Bloomfield, Leonard, 194, 205
Blunden, Edmund, 251
Boas, Franz, 8, 183, *191*; and "American School of Anthropology," 189, 191; and Benjamin Whorf, 216; as Edward Sapir's mentor, 191; and language, 191-92, 193-94, 195, 197, 202, 209; and primitive cultures, 191; and structure of language, 217
Bonaparte, Charles L., 660
Boniar, David, 563
Boorstin, Daniel, 3, 348, 366, 375
Born on the Fourth of July (film, 1976), 257, 257-58; and American Adam, 400
Boston Herald, 448
Boston Quarterly Review, 3
Bourne, Randolph, 273n12
Bowen, Daniel, 627-29
Boys Will Be Boys (film, 1921), 143
Braestrup, Peter, 388; and false microcosms, 429; and media distortions, 447; and Tet offensive, 538n7. See also *Big Story: How the American Press and Television Reported and Interpreted the Crisis of Tet 1968 in Vietnam and Washington*
Brandon, Tom, 691
Breeding, Earl, 425
Bright Shining Lie, A: John Paul Vann and America in Vietnam (book, 1988), 16-17; alleged exaggeration in, 539n9; and America's mindset, 515, 522; Ap Bac, 521, 522-25, 528-29, 538n7; and Cold War mindset, 513-14; awards for, 515; criticism of, 533-34; derivative content of, 538n3; and elites and centralists, 539n11; and establishment mindset, 515-20, 526; germinative process of, 509-14; and John Paul Vann as outsider, 527-38, 532-33; Korean War, 517-18; and media in Vietnam, 522-27, 535; as meditation on Vietnam, 513, 514-15, 534, 535; and pacification, 530-32, 537-38n6; and "power elite," 539n10; and precedence for Vietnam, 517-18; and Tet offensive, 522, 532, 538n7; and Vann family, 512; and Vann's funeral, 526; and Vietnam War, 519-25; as work of denial, 535; and "Wisconsin School" of diplomatic history, 536n3; and World War II, 516-17
Bright Shining Lie, A (PBS, 1998), 17-18
Brindley, Thomas, 421
British National Pictures, 93
Brooke, Rupert, 252, 260

Brookline, Mass., 551, 553, 554; and Amy Lowell, 19, 633, 636, 643, 646, 651-53; and Frederick Henry Hedge, 617, 622, 623, 624, 628, 629-30; and Peter C. Rollins, 3, 19, 21

Brothers Karamazov, The (book, 1880), 358

Browne, Malcolm, *511*, 525, 526

Browne, Ray, 3

Brownson, Orestes Augustus, 1, 2, 6; career, 2-3; and cultural history, 21; as democratic spokesman, 2; epistemological pilgrimages of, 7; as philosopher, 2; social activism, 2; spiritual journey of, 21

Bryan, William Jennings, 163

Buckley, Christopher, 444

Buckley, William F., 462

Bunker, Ellsworth, 463, 468, 496, 501

Bureau of Intelligence and Research (INR), 497

Burns, Ken, Capraesque filmwork of, 296; criticism of, 570

Burt, Dan, 456

Bush, George H. W., 397

Butterfield, Fox, 445

Cabot, Walter, 634, 635, 646

Cadre Films, 11, 147-48; bias of, 322; and cinematic elements, 321; founding of, 311; and historical authenticity, 311-13; interpretations of, 272n6; and war films, 254, 255, 256, 258; and *Will Rogers' 1920s*, 148-49, 150, 152, 155. See also *Frozen War, The: America Intervenes in Russia, 1918-20*; *Goodbye Billy: America Goes to War, 1917-18*; *Storm of Fire: World War II and the Destruction of Dresden*

Caine Mutiny, The (film, 1954), 562

Calley, William, 493

Call to Freedom (film, 1957), 353, 372

Canon Films, 391

Capra, Frank, *281*, 290, 296-97, 330, 346, 704; career, 279-80; compilation filmmaking, 371; and "forgotten man," 279; and "linkage," 285; newsreels, 575; as spokesman for democracy, 281, 285; World War II films, 11-12. See also *Why We Fight*

Caputo, Philip, 258, 383-84, 399, 400

Carroll, John, 162

Carter, Hodding, 462, 468, 474, 484n13

Carver, George, 16, *488*; career of, 489-90; and enemy strength, 492, 494, 495, 497-502, 503n5; methodology of, 491-92; and Robert Komer, 505n12; and *Uncounted Enemy*, 463-66, 468, 469-70, 483n7, 484n14; as "uncounted expert," 487-88, 491; Vietnam War, 490-91

Case-Church Amendment, 554-55

Castro, Fidel, 396, 526

Casualties of War (film, 1989), as flawed, 398; and *Platoon*, 401

Catch-22 (book, 1961), 260, 261, 273n10, 337

Cathon, Charles, 306

Cavett, Dick, 373

CBS (Columbia Broadcasting System), 16, 294; and compilation films, 372-73; fairness guidelines of, 468, 469, 470; misreporting by, 465-69, 479, 484n12; and objectivity, 447; and "old school" news, 473-74; and reaction to *Uncounted Enemy*, 463-64, 475, 480-81, 484n10, 492; and Tet offensive, 415-16, 417-19, 433; and Westmoreland conspiracy theory, 457, 460, 466, 469. See also *Uncounted Enemy, The*; and under Westmoreland, William C.

CBS Benjamin Report, The (book, 1984), 481n1, 482n3. *See also* Benjamin, Burton

Central Intelligence Agency (CIA), 470, 478, 482-83, 483n6, 488, 489, 497; and enemy strength, 459-61, 463-64, 465-66, 468, 490, 492, 496, 503n6, 503-504n8, 506-507n16; methodology of, 493

Chamberlain, John, 134

Chamorro, Violeta, 397

Chaplin, Charlie, 262

Chase, Barry, 445-46, 447-48

Chetwyn, Lionel, 391

China Strikes Back (film, 1937), 691

Chomsky, Noam, 205, 253; and pseudoscientific jargon, 266, 267-68, 273n12

Christensen, Bruce, 446

Christian Examiner, 617, 619, 620, 622

Christian Science Monitor, 553

Chung Kai-shek, 292-93

Churchill, Winston, 291, 301, 315, 320

Churchill Films, 155

Cimino, Michael, 263-64

Citizen Kane (film, 1941), 289-90

Clearwater Publishing Company, 16

Clifford, Clark, 526

Clinton, Bill, 236-37, 247

Cochran's Revue, 93

Cobb, Irvin S., 70, 143; insouciance of, 38; racist writings of, 129, 131

Cohen, Octavus Roy, 142; racist writings of, 129-30

Cohen, Steven, 445, 452

Colby, William, 468, 505n12, 509

Cold War, 10, 12, 21, 489, 509, 545; and brainwashing, 246; and Eisenhower administration, 362; mindset of, 344, 514-15. See also *Nightmare in Red*; *Victory at Sea*

Cole, Thomas, 700, 702, 709

Coleman, Nick, 450

Coleridge, Samuel Taylor, 617-18, 620

Collier, Peter, 394-95

Collins, Monica, 544

Collins, Reba, 154

Coloff, Roger, 465

Columbia Pictures, 280

Combat Diary: The Marines of Lima Company (A&E, 2006), 398

Combe, George, 664

Coming Home (film, 1978), 390, 398, 555

Coming of Christ, The (film, 1961), 372

compilation genre, 285, 373-74, 547, 548; and fiction footage, 294; study of, 374; volume of, 372

Connecticut Yankee, A (film, 1931), 51

containment, 399, 553-54

Cooley, Russell, 472

Coolidge, Calvin, 73; and election of 1928, 121; and Mexico, 76; and Will Rogers, 5, 47, 72-74, 90-91, 95-97, 99, 101-103

Cooper, James Fenimore, 671; leather-stocking tales of, 640; and mindless exploitation, 699

Corrine (book, 1807), 592
Corry, John, 446, 448-49, 561
Council for International Exhibition (CINE), 6, 155
County Chairman, The (film, 1935), 153; screenplay for, 138
Course of Empire, The (paintings), 700-701
Court, John, 504-505n16
Couturie, Bill, and *Dear America*, 18, 386, 543-45; and *Vietnam Requiem*, 548
Covered Wagon, The (book, 1922), 128, 131-32, 142
Covered Wagon, The (film, 1923), 128, 131-32, 143
Cozzens, James Gould, 80, 134
Creed, George, 239, 267
Crile, George, 16, 390, 467; criticism of, 464, 465, 466-75, 476-77, 480, 481; and enemy strength, 491; and George Carver, 487-88; and Sam Adams, 506-507n16; and *Uncounted Enemy*, 502; and William Westmoreland lawsuit, 481-82n2
Cripps, Thomas, 704
Cronkite, Walter, 372, 525; and Khe Sanh, 415-16, 418, 433, 556; and Tet offensive, 451, 461
Crowninshield, Katherine, 646
Croy, Homer, 143
Cruze, James, 131, 132
Culbert, David H., 12, 704
Culver City, Calif., 117-19, 120
Cupid, the Cowpuncher (film, 1920), 143
Curtis, Cyrus, 70, 126
Cushman, R. E., 416

Daccardo, Ethel, 370, 375
Daily Worker, The, 364
Damon, Foster, 639, 653
Dangerfield, George, 682
D'Annunzio, Gabriel, 647
Darwinian theory, 172, 173, 174-75
David Harum (film, 1934), 54, 55, 55-60, 62, 66, 136, 153; and "American everyman," 138; and New Deal, 82, 137-38, 141; ruralism of, 143; screenplay of, 137-38
David Harum: A Story of American Life (book, 1898), 136-37
Davidson, Phillip, 463, 466, 484n11; and enemy strength, 492, 499-501, 503n5, 503-504n8; and George Carver, 491; and Ho Chi Minh, 538-39n4; and Sam Adams, 504n9; and Tet offensive, 538n7
Davis, Peter, 18, 253, 295, 296, 386, 398; and language of film, 402
D Day, fiftieth anniversary of, 12, 299-306, 308; legacy of, 305-306; and Normandy invasion, 301-303; planning for, 301
Dear America: Letters Home from Vietnam (book, 1985), 18, 385-86, 541, 547, 548; as non-partisan anthology, 542-43
Dear America: Letters Home from Vietnam (HBO, 1988), 18, 263, 542, 543-44; polemical tone of, 547-48; reaction to, 543-48; "time line" concept in, 546-47
Deer Hunter, The (film, 1978), 246, 263-64, 401; and Vietnam as evil, 390
Defense Intelligence Agency (DIA), 496, 497
Defiant Ones, The (film, 1958), 705
Denby, David, 391
DePalma, Brian, 398, 401

DePuy, William, 509
de Rochemont, Louis, 242; and *Land of Cotton*, 678, 695; and newsreels, 678-79
de Staël, Madame, 592
DeVoto, Bernard, 332-33, 351, 352
DeVries, Hugo, 174
Dewey, John, 273n12
Dewhurst, Richard, 545, 548
Dial (journal), 620-21
Diem, Ngo Dinh, *440*, 518-19, 520, 525, 526, 527
Dillon, Matt, 386
Dispatches (book, 1977), 381
Doctor Bull (film, 1933), 5, 66, 80-82, *81*; nativist script of, 135, 141; ruralism of, 143
Documentary Tradition, The (book, 1971), 447
Doolittle, James (Jimmy), 105
Dos Passos, John, 236; Frontier Films, 691; Tomb of Unknown Soldier, 265; *USA* trilogy, 240-41
Doubling for Romeo (film, 1921), 143
Dresden Blasted (film), 321-22
Dulles, John Foster, 516
Duncan, David Douglas, 419, 556, 557-58
Duse, Eleanora, 647, 653
Dwight, Timothy, 583

Eagle-Lion Productions, 703, 708
Ecce Homo (film, 1939), 685-86
Eddington, Arthur, 167-68, *169*; writings of, 173
Edelman, Bernard, 18, 541, 547, 548
Edwardsian Calvinism, 583-84, 591, 593, 597, 607, 614
Ehrhart, W. D., 258, 264, 383, 399, 400
Einstein, Albert, 7, 167, 168
Eisenhower, Dwight D., 301; administration of, 362; era of, 294; and D Day, 299, 301
Eisenstein, Sergei, 272-73n9, 317, 318, 369; and intellectual montage, 688
Elder, Harris J., 272n7, 323
Elegant, Robert, 440, 442-43, 445
Eliot, Charles W., 255
Ellison, Richard, 14, 561; and *Vietnam: A Television History*, 436, 445-46, 447-48
Ellison, Robert, 476
Ellsberg, Daniel, 17-18, 464-65, 506-507n16, 514, *529*, 529-30, 533; and John Paul Vann funeral, 511-12, 532; and pacification, 531-32
Elwell, Leo, 305-306
Emerson, Ralph Waldo, 166, 228, 617-18; and Christianity, 622; and cooperative living, 625; and *Essays, Second Series*, 622; and tension, 619-20. *See also under* Hedge, Frederick Henry
Emmons, Nathaniel, 590
English Journal (book, 1827), 29, 655
Erikson, Erik, 209
evolution, 174-75

Fabre d'Olivet, Antoine, 8, 183, 213; linguistic theories of, 215-16
Fahrenheit 9/11 (film, 2004), 12, 398
Fair Play: CBS, General Westmoreland, and How a Television Documentary Went Wrong (book, 1988), 389
Fall, Bernard, 415, 429
Fallows, James, 444-45
Farewell to Arms, A (book, 1926), 241, 252; "symbolic wound" in, 273n11

Index

Ferber, Edna, 71, 128
Ferguson, Otis, 703
Fetchit, Stepin (Theodore Lincoln Perry), 139, 140, *140*
Fields of Fire (film, 1978), 383, 399
Fight for Life, The (film, 1941), 685-86
Film & History (journal), 568, 569
film and television, cinematic elements of, 677; impact of, 567; language of, 401-402; misuse of, 569, 570; and montage, 575-76
film irony, 272-73n9
film rhetoric, 677-78
Finney, Charles Grandison, 584, 613
Fire in the Lake (book, 1972), 569
Fischer, Henry Metcalfe, 589-90, 591
Fitzgerald, Francis, 569
Fonda, Jane, 391, 555, 573-74
Ford, Henry, 121
Ford, John, 38, 53; *Doctor Bull*, 81, 135; *Grapes of Wrath*, 709; world view of, 5
Ford Motor Company, 150
For Vietnam Veterans (PBS), 399
Fox, Michael J., 401
Franklin, Benjamin, 660, 661
Freedman, Samuel, 545
Freeman, Orville, 696n2
Frompson, Murray, 419, 556
Frontier Films, 691; egalitarianism of, 693
Frozen War, The: America Intervenes in Russia, 1918-20 (film, 1973), 11, 148, 270, 272-73n9, 311; bias of, 322; and cinematic elements, 316, 317, 318, 319-20; and interventionism, 261-62, 264, 267, 313; loss of innocence, 259; as non-didactic, 313; Red Scare, 269-70; Vietnam War comparisons to, 256-57, 259-61, 262
Fugitive Slave Act, 596
Fulbright, William, 532
Fuller, Margaret, 592, 619. *See also under* Frederick Henry Hedge
Full-Metal Jacket (film, 1987), 562; and American Adam, 400; as anti-Vietnam, 390-91; and loss of innocence, 258
Fussell, Paul, 10, 238, 239, 251-53, 262, 263, 306-308; and dramatic irony, 261, 272-73n9. See also *Great War and Modern Meaning, The*

Galloway, Joseph L., 392
Gates, Eleanor, 143
Genius of American Politics, The (book, 1953), 348
George, Terry, 17, 18
Giant (film, 1956), 712
Giap, Vo Nguyen, 418, 429, 556, 571
Gibson, Mel, *392*, 392
Gittleson, Gene, 541
Glenn, John, 245
Godding, George, 495
Going after Cacciato (book, 1979), 269
Going to Congress (film, 1924), 51
Goldberg, Arthur, 461
Goldberg, Robert, 547
Goldwyn, Samuel, 50
Gompers, Samuel, 264, 269
Gone with the Wind (film, 1939), 356
Goodacre, Glenna, 248
Goodbye Billy: America Goes to War, 1917-18 (film, 1976), 11, 148, 270, 272n7, 311; advertising of, 269; bias of, 322; and cinematic elements, 316, 319; collision mon-

tage in, 255; and doughboy-as-victim, 273-74n13; film irony in, 261, 272-73n9; film language of, 312, 323; historical authenticity of, 312-13; lost generation, 254, 255-56, 258, 313; propaganda vs. reality in, 266-67; selective service draft, 269; "symbolic wound" in, 273n11; and wartime technology, 264
Goodman, Ellen, 19
Goodman, Ezra, 703-704
Good Morning, Vietnam (film, 1987), as anti-Vietnam, 391; and film irony, 402-403
Goodwin, Edwin, 19
Goodwin, Richard, 11
Graham, Daniel, 460, 463, 468, 469, 473; and Sam Adams, 506-507n16
Grand Illusion, The (film, 1939), 241
Grapes of Wrath, The (film, 1939), 709
Graves, Leonard, 335, 338, 339, 340, 343
Graves, Robert, 251
Great War. *See* World War I
Great War, The (NBC, 1956), 371
Great War and Modern Memory, The (book, 1975), 251-52, 253, 257; Battle of the Somme, 271n4; limitations of, 272n6; militarism, 269; moral disenfranchisement, 270; post-war language, 264-65; regimentation of society, 268; skepticism, 273n10; victims of history, 259-61, 270n1; wartime technology, 262-63
Green, Paul, 80-81, 135
Green Berets (film, 1968), 442; as World War II film, 401
Grierson, John, 285, 449, 567, 575, 679

Griffin, Patrick, 5, 147, 148, 153, 311, 321, 323; historian filmmaker movement, 568
Griffith, D. W., 263-64, 356
Guess Who's Coming to Dinner (film, 1967), 705
Gulf of Tonkin incident, 267
Gulf War, 265. *See also* Operation Desert Storm; Operation Iraqi Freedom

Hair (play, 1968; film, 1979), *268*, 269
Halberstam, David, 16, 17, *511*, 515, 516; as anti-establishment, 524-25, 534; Ap Bac, 523; criticism of, 525-26; and John Paul Vann, 526-27, 528, 534, 535-36n1; new consciousness, 524; pacification, 537-38n6; power of media, 535; as reporter in Vietnam, 538-39n8
Hamburger Hill (film, 1987), 391-92
Hamlyn, Paul, 643-44
Hamscher, George, 458, 469
Handy Andy (film, 1934), 51, 66
Hanoi Hilton (film, 1987), 391-92
Hanser, Richard, 351, 353, 354
Harding, Warren G., 72, 241, 255; and Unknown Soldier, 267; and war and peace, 235; and Will Rogers, 90
Harkins, Paul, 514, *518*, 518-19, 520, 528, 537-38n6; ineptitude of, 521, 525
Harris, Louis, and Vietnam veterans poll, 392-93, 403-404
Hart, Frederick, 247, 248
Hartz, Louis, 348, 375; and Cold War, 366
Harvest of Despair (PBS), 577
Havell, Robert, 664

Hawkins, Gains, 459, 463, 464, 465, 470, 482n4, 468, 503n5
Hawks, Frank, *114*, 115
Hawks, Howard, 242
Hawthorne, Nathaniel, 95
Hayakawa, S. I., 161
Hayward, Susan, 705
Hazard, Patrick, 365
HBO (Home Box Office), *Bright Shining Lie, A*, 17-18; and compilation genre, 373; *Dear America: Letters Home from Vietnam*, 263, 386, 542, 543-44, 545; *Taking Chance*, 398
Headless Horseman, The (film, 1922), 143
Heart of Spain (film, 1937), 691
Hearts and Minds (film, 1974), 12, 18, 295-96, 398; and film language, 402; propagandist techniques in, 386
Hedge, Frederick Henry, 1, 3, 19, 21, *618*; anti-supernaturalism, 627-28; "best of one's life," 621; Catholicism, 625; Christ, 629; Christian views of, 622-23, 624-25; early career of, 617-19; faith, 628; Harvard Divinity School, 627; Margaret Fuller, 620-21; parish of, 637; Ralph Waldo Emerson, 620-22; *Reason in Religion*, 623, 629; religious truths, 626-27; tension, 619-20; Transcendental movement, 624, 629; *Ways of the Spirit*, 623. *See also under* Brookline, Mass.
Hedge Club, 617
Heisler, Stuart, and *Tulsa*, 704, 707, 711
He Is Risen (NBC, 1962), 372
Heller, Joseph, 260
Hell in a Very Small Place (book, 1967), 415, 429
Hellman, Lillian, 396; Frontier Films, 695
Helms, Jesse, 480
Helms, Richard, 464, 489; and enemy strength, 490, 506-507n16
Hemingway, Ernest, 239, 252; Frontier Films, 691; language and style, 270-71n3; and "symbolic wound," 273n11
Herr, Michael, 381-84, 399
Hershey, Louis, 268-69
Heston, Charlton, 13-14, 560, 563-64; and Vietnam, 562-63
Hickey, Neil, 448
Higgins, Marguerite, 525-26
Hill, Doug, 544-45
Hill, George Roy, 256
Hilsman, Roger, 526
historian filmmaker movement, 568; educational challenges of, 577; film as fact, 573; and visually literate viewer, 572-73
historical filmmaking, aesthetics, 677; fiction footage, 569; misinterpretations in, 570; passive viewer, 571; use of subjective material, 571
History Channel, 576-77
History Teacher, The (journal), 312, 401, 568, 569
Hitler, Adolph, 12, 281, *282*, 315, 316, 679; and D Day, 302, 303; film depictions of, 284, 286, 291, 292, 315; propaganda of, 547; rise to power, 574
Ho Chi Minh, 396, *439*, 449, 528, 560; as committed Communist, 536-37n4; nationalism of, 515, 519, 520
Home of the Brave (film, 1949), 705
Honest Hutch (film, 1920), 143

Hoover, Herbert, 121; federal relief programs, 115
Hope, Bob, 246
Horowitz, David, 394, 395
Hough, Emerson, 71, 77-78, 128, 131, 142
House Un-American Activities Committee (HUAC), 703
Hovey, Joe, 479
How We Advertised America (book, 1920), 239, 267
Hudson, Rochelle, 38
Hue Massacre, 562, 563, 574
Hunt, Leigh, 646
Huntington, Samuel, 266
Hurwitz, Leo, 344, 345, 346, 449; Frontier Films, 691; *Native Land*, 678, 683, 692, 695
Hutton, James, 173, 175
Hyatt, Donald, 294; *Call to Freedom*, 372; cinematic eye of, 375; as Project 20 producer, 372, 374
Hynes, Samuel, 271n4

Ifshin, David, 395
I Led Three Lives (TV, 1953-1956), 367
Illiterate Digest, The (film, 1919-1920), 152
I'll Take My Stand (book, 1930), 30
Imagination and Fancy (book, 1844), 646
Immigration Act (1924), 127
industrialism, 32-33, 106, 701
Innocents Abroad (book, 1879), 72, 89, 94
Innocent Years, The (film, 1957), 371-72
In Old Kentucky (film, 1935), 5, 59, 60, 61-62, 66; nostalgic image of, 31, 63-64; racist screenplay, 138, 139-40; release of, 29
Inside Story (PBS, 1983), 484n13

Inside Story Special, 388
Inventing Vietnam (book, 1991), 564
I Protest! (book, 1968), 547-48
Irvine, Reed, 13, 436, 445, 448, 559; criticism of, 449, 450, 451
Irving, Washington, 671
isolationism, 74, 100, 242; new school of, 308. *See also under* Rogers, Will
It Happened One Night (film, 1935), 280
It's a Wonderful Life (film, 1946), 280
Ivens, Joris, 449

Jackson, Martin A., 323
Jacobs, Lewis, 449
Jacobson, George, 410
Jazz Age, The (1957), 371; historical inaccuracies in, 569, 571, 576
Jeans, James, 7, 167-68
Jes Call Me Jim (film, 1920), 53
Jessup, David, 422
JFK (film, 1991), 269
Jicha, Tom, 442, 451
Johnson, Herbert, 69
Johnson, Lyndon B., 253, 458, 514, 515, 557; administration of, 409, 427, 559; enemy strength, 471-72, 490, 491, 504-505n11, 505n12; Khe Sanh, 416, 416-17, 427-28, 432-33, 483n6; pacification, 531; use of media, 429-30; Tet offensive, 461, 465, 477, 479-80; Vietnam, 294-95, 399, 402, 509-10
Jones, Daniel, 351, 370
Joyce, James, 685
Jubilo (book, 1917), 141
Jubilo (film, 1919), 50, 50, 141; regional stereotyping in, 143
Judge Priest (film, 1934), 60, 66, 141; literary origin of, 129, 131; racist screenplay, 138, 139

Kaheny, John, 527, 563
Kant, Immanuel, 212-13
Karnow, Stanley, 17, 29, 296, 387, 483n9, 569, 570, 576; *Vietnam: A History*, 558; and *Vietnam: A Television History*, 436, 443-54. See also *Vietnam: A History*
Kauffman, Stanley, 391
Kazan, Elia, 711
Kearns, Doris, 417
Kelland, Clarence B., 128
Kennan, George, 333, 344, 348, 375; and Cold War, 366
Kennedy, Edward, 511
Kennedy, John F., 514, 515-16, 525, 554; administration of, 524, 559; Berlin, 553; use of media, 429; Vietnam, 308, 511
Kennedy, Robert, 511
Kerwin, Walter, Jr., 468
Khe Sanh, Battle of, 409, 414, 420-27, 421, 424, 431, 483n6, 521-22, 543-44, 556-58, 560, 563; and allied victory, 420; and Dien Bien Phu, 415-19, 420, 425, 427-28; media reports, 417-19, 426-29, 432; misreporting of, 447
Kitman, Marvin, 442, 529, 555
Klein, Ira, 466, 470, 474-75
Kleinerman, Isaac, 294, 338, 341
Komer, Robert, 468, 495, 496, 500; and enemy strength, 505n12; John Paul Vann funeral, 509-11; pacification, 499, 531-32, 537-38n6
Koppel, Ted, 446
Korean War, memories of, 245, 245-46, 316; Vietnam compared to, 563
Korean War Veterans Memorial, 245
Kovic, Ron, 257-58, 400

Kowet, Don, 389-90, 463-64, 484n10
Krulak, Victor, 17, 515, 531
Kubrick, Stanley, 258, 390-91, 400, 562
Ku Klux Klan, 31-32
Kyne, Peter B., 71, 128

Land of Cotton (film, 1938), and agricultural depression, 677; ambiguities in, 680-82, 695; cinematic language, 682, 686, 695; liberal Republican views of, 678, 682, 694-95; and *March of Time*, 678; reaction to, 682
Lane, Maud (Mrs. C. L.), 41-42
Langdon, Harry, 280
Langley, Samuel, 108-109, 121
Lansdale, Edward, 509, 520, 530
Larkin, Phil, 257
Larsen, Roy, 679
Last Adam, The (book, 1933), 80; nativist views of, 134-25
Late George Apley, The (book, 1937), 128
Laughing Bill Hyde (film, 1918), 49-50
Laurence, John, 556
Lawrence, D. H., 222
Lawson, John Howard, 396, 702-703
League of Nations, 52, 74, 89, 97-98, 100
Le Duc Tho, 555, 571
Lenin, Vladimir I. See *Nightmare in Red*
Leopold, Nathan, 175-76, 176
Letters of a Self-Made Diplomat to His President (book, 1926), 74
Letters of a Self-made Merchant to His Son (book, 1902), 72, 89
Leval, Pierre N., 482, 489
Levine, Irving R., 364

Lewis, Sinclair, 42
Leyda, Jay, 370, 691
Liberal Tradition in America, The: An Interpretation of American Political Thought Since the Revolution (book, 1955), 346
Life Begins at Forty (film, 1934), 38, 59, 66
Life Magazine, 106, 121
Lilienthal, David, 20-21
Lindbergh, Anne Morrow, 111, 113
Lindbergh, Charles A., 44, 94, 109, *111*, 112-13; media attention, 111-12; in Mexico, 76; transatlantic flight of, 111, 114, 119, 235; and Will Rogers, 114; and *Wings*, 235
Linnaean Society, 664
Lippmann, Walter, 239, 267
Little Rollo (book, 1835), 640
Lizars, William, 664
Loan, Nguyen Ngoc, 407, 409, 411-14, 419, 427, 429, 431, 563
Locke, John, 214-1
Lodge, Henry Cabot, 515, 516
Lodge, Henry Cabot, Jr., 515, 516, 534, 537-38n6
Loeb, Richard, 175-76, *176*
Long, Nguyen Linh, 402, 438
Look at Russia (film, 1956), 364
Lorentz, Pare, 20; as film reviewer, 684; and New Deal, 685; *The Plow That Broke the Plains*, 708; *The River*, 678, 683, 684, 687-88, 695. See also *Plow That Broke the Plains, The*; *River, The*
Lorimer, George Horace, 5, *70*; economic views of, 76; and Europe, 74; isolationism of, 74, 77, 84; nativism of, 127, 131; New Deal, 82, 83, 127; racist writings of, 129; and regional nostalgia, 131; as *Saturday Evening* Post editor, 69-70, 83, 126-27, 142; social views of, 69, 70, 71-72, 77-78, 83; and Will Rogers, 69, 75, 84, 89-90
Losers Are Pirates (book, 1985), 296, 387, 398, 438; and *Vietnam: A Television History*, 402
loss of innocence, 270n1, 271-72n5. See also under Vietnam War
Lowell, Amy, 3, 19, 21, *645*, *648*; aristocratic spirit of, 633; Brooklyn childhood of, 633-34, 637-45, 651-53; "Composition Book," 636-37; *Dream Drops*, 639-41; and effusion, 641-42; favorite writers of, 639, 640, 643; and female identity, 642-43; independence of, 641, 642; "Lilacs," 650-51; "Meeting-House Hill," 650, 651-53; *Moon-Folk*, 639; "New Heavens for Old," 648-50; "Patterns," 650; and photography, 642; as poetess, 647-50; "Private Book," 634-36; published writings of, 639; search for wholeness, 636; sensitive conscience of, 634-35; and Sevenels, 633, 636, 637-38, 647-48, 653; and theater, 645; and theme of identity, 19. See also under Brookline, Mass.
Lowell, Augustus, 633, 637, 638, 642, 647
Lowell, Katherine B. (Mrs. Augustus), 637, 638, 644, 645, 647
Lownds, David, 415-16, 419, 422, 424, 558
Luce, Henry, 679, 680, 686
Ludington, C. Townsend, 12, 555
Lyon, William H., 629

MacArthur, Douglas, 514; Korean War, 517-18, 522, 529
MacArthur, George, 459
MacLeisch, Archibald, 691
Maderis, Martha, 547
Making of a Quagmire, The (book, 1965), 526, 534
Malloch, William, 148, 150, 272n7, 311
Manly, G. B., 105
Mannes, Marya, 364-65
March of Time, The (newsreels, 1935-1951), 341, 686, 690-91, 693; compositional content, 682-83; "Inside Nazi Germany–1938," 680; and objectivity, 680, 684, 694; in style of, 690, 691; success of, 679-80; use of sound, 683-84. See also under titles of films in series
Marquand, J. P., 128
Marshall, George C., 11, 279, 284
Marshall, S. L. A., 238, 271n4
*M*A*S*H* (film, 1970), 269
mass media, 108
Matter of Honor, A (book, 1984), 390
Matthews, Shailer, 164
Maysles, Albert, 19
Maysles, David, 19
McAdoo, W. G., Jr., 118
McAuliffe, Anthony, 300
McCain, John, 573-74
McCarthy, Joseph, 365-66
McChristian, Joseph, 458-59, 469, 470-71, 476-77
McCormack, John W., 364
McCormick, Robert, 243
McGee, Frank, 412
McGovern, George, 396
McNamara, Robert S., 490, 492, 512; and pacification, 531
McNaughton, John, 531

McPherson, Harry, 526
McQuiddy, Lynn, 256-57, 259, 261-62, 267, 269, 322
Meaning of Meaning, The (book, 1923), 11, 252, 265-66
Medhurst, Marvin, 388
Medved, Michael, 395
Meet John Doe (film, 1941), 290, *290*
Meet Mr. Lincoln (film, 1959), 372
Meet the Press (TV interview series), 472
Mellon, Andrew, 96
Mencken, H. L., 8, 42, 121, 163
Middle-West fiction, 71-72
Midnight Frolic (revue), 93. See also under Rogers, Will
Milestone, Lewis, 239
Military Assistance Command Vietnam (MACV), 458-59, 468, 477, 479, 505n2, 505-506n13, 525; and enemy strength, 466n12, 490, 491, 492, 494, 497-99, 501, 502, 503-504n8, 504-505n11; and Order of Battle, 459-60, 464, 465-71, 482n4, 482-83n5, 492-93, 495-96, 504n10
Military Service Act, 268
Mission, The (film, 1986), 397
Mitchell, William (Billy), *109*, 109-10
Modern Temper, The (book, 1929), 272-73n9
Monroe, Harriet, 192
Moore, Harold C., 392
Moore, Michael, 398
Morison, Samuel Eliot, 327, 328, 329, 352
Morris, Charles, 463
Morris, Stephen, 438
Morrow, Dwight W., 76, 94
Moss, Carlton, 704
Motion Picture Code, 679

Movies Learn to Talk, The (film, 1959), 373
Mr. Deeds Goes to Town (film, 1936), 281-82
Mrs. Miniver (film, 1942), 288
Mr. Smith Goes to Washington (film, 1939), 282, 283-84, 287
Müller, F. Max, 8, 183, *214*; linguistic theories of, 215-16; *Science and Thought*, 214-15; *Theosophy: or, Psychological Religion*, 216
Mundt, Karl, 686, 696n2
Murphy, William T., 150
Mussolini, Benito, *92*, 92, 97, 101
My Lai Massacre, 493, 521, 564; as aberration, 483, 504n10; and Americal Division, 266, 543
My Son John (film, 1952), 367

National D Day Museum, 303, 308
National Endowment for the Humanities (NEH), 147, 155, 387; and *Vietnam: A Television History*, 437, 446
National Era (newspaper), 596
National Intelligence Estimate (NIE), 495, 496, 497-98, 499-501, 506nn14,15
National Liberation Front, 440
National Press Photographers Association, 407
National Review Magazine, 364
National Security Agency (NSA), 466, 493, 495, 497
Native Land (film, 1942), cinematic language, 693-94, 695; civil rights violations, 677, 694-93; as leftist film, 678, 690, 694, 695; reaction to, 691-92;
nativism, 7-8
NBC (National Broadcasting Corporation), 293, 351, 354; archives of, 548; and *Nightmare in Red*, 362, 364; Project 20, 372, 373; and Tet offensive, 410, 412-13, 420, 422; and *Victory at Sea*, 329, 330, 349, 350. *See also* Project 20 (XX)
Needham, Ed, 418
Negro Soldier, The (film, 1944), 704-705
Nessen, Ron, 418
New Deal, 82, 282-83, 684; films of, 708, 709; and historical filmmaking, 678, 685; and social documentary, 20-21. *See also under* Lorimer, George Horace; *River, The*
New Republic Magazine, The, 692
Newsletter of the Organization of American Historians, 386, 387, 436, 449
Newspaper Enterprise Association, 4-5
newsreels, as persuasion, 574-75. See also *March of Time, The*
Newsweek Magazine, 426, 432, 557
New York Review of Books, 569
New York State Vietnam Veterans Association, 385-86
New York Times, 15, 17, 448, 468, 527-28, 564; influence of, 524; and *Inside Story*, 474; and *Pentagon Papers*, 512, 529-30; and *Television's Vietnam: The Real Story*, 561; and *Uncounted Enemy*, 462
New York Vietnam Veterans Memorial (VVM), 541, 543, 546
Nightmare in Red (film, 1955), 373, 374; aesthetics and history, 368-70; anti-Communist closing in, 360-61, 362; and Cold War, 359, 365; dramatic irony in, 356; as failed history, 366-67; freedom

theme in, 353; and Josef Stalin, 358, 359, 360; new insights, 365-67; origin of, 354; post-production issues, 361-63, 370, 371 as propaganda, 370-71; reaction to, 363-65, 367; and Russian history, 355-61, 369; success of, 351-52, 371; and Vladimir Lenin, 356-57, 359, 360, 368; and World War II, 359

1919 (book, 1932), 273-74n13

Nixon, Richard M., 397, 440, 529; administration of, 509; Cambodia, 512; and John Paul Vann, 511

Noble, William, 658-59

Northshield, Robert, 430

Nugent, Frank, 702

Nykino, 691

Oberdorfer, Don, 428, 432, 538n7

O'Brian, Jack, 333, 349

O'Brien, Tim, 269

O'Connor, John E., 323

Octopus (book, 1901), 701

Ogden, C. K., 265, 270n2

Ogennessof, Igor, 418, 429

Oldtown Folks (book, 1869), 66, 582, 587, 614

One Day in 365 (film), 49

Only Yesterday (book, 1931), 569, 570

Operation Desert Storm, 397-98, 403. *See also* Gulf War

Operation Iraqi Freedom, 403. *See also* Gulf War

Orcutt, April, 386

Order for Battle Conference, 491, 494-95

Ornithological Biography, The (book, 1839), 656, 666-68, 669-70, 671, 673-74

ornithology, 555. *See also* Audubon, John James

Ortega, Daniel, 396

Others Who Should Care (PBS), 399

Owen, Wilfred, 253

Palmer, A. Mitchell, 30, 256

Palmer, Bruce, Jr., 509

Paris in the Twenties (film, 1960), 373

PBS (Public Broadcasting Service), 294, 388; *For Vietnam Veterans and Others Who Should Care*, 399; *Harvest of Despair*, 579; objectivity of, 447; *Television's Vietnam: The Real Story*, 441, 445, 446, 447-48; *Television's Vietnam: The Image of Media*, 561, 564; *Victory at Sea*, 328; *Vietnam: A Television History*, 296, 387, 558-59, 560-61, 565. *See also Vietnam: A Television History*

Pentagon Papers, The (book,1971), 512, 529-30, 531-32

Perkins, Elizabeth Ward, 637-38

Perot, Ross, 246

Perry, Theodore Lincoln. *See* Fetchit, Stepin

Peterson, Arthur, 154

Pie in the Sky (film), 691

Pike, Douglas, 439-40, *438*, 443, 452

Pike Committee Report, 467, 506-507n16

Pioneers, The (book, 1823), 699

Platoon (film, 1986), 253, 269, 397; and American Adam, 400; as anti-Vietnam, 390, 391, 392, 395; and *Dear America*, 544, 545, 548; and loss of innocence, 258; success of, 401

Plow That Broke the Plains, The (film, 1936), 20-21, 678, 684, 685; and

Index 733

environmental conditions, 708-709; suppression of, 686, 696n2
Poganuc People (book, 1878), 66
Pool, Ithiel, 266
Popular Culture Association (PCA), 3, 14, 148, 558; and Vietnam War, 442
Potemkin (film, 1925), 319, 369; and *Nightmare in Red*, 355
Pound, Ezra, 198
Powell Doctrine, 397, 398
Powers that Be, The (book, 1979), 437
Prairie, The (book, 1828), 699
Price, George B., 563
Price, Walter, 299-300, 306
Primo de Rivera, Miguel, 92, 97-98
Project 20 (XX), 294, 351, 352, 362, 370, 373, 577; and "consensus historians," 375; importance of, 372; *Jazz Age*, 371, 373, 576; objectives of, 367-68; and objectivity, 365; success of, 371-72; and theme of freedom, 353-54. *See also under individual titles in series*
Public Opinion (book, 1922), 239, 267
Puckett, Ralph, Jr., 518, 522, 529
Pushkin, Alexander, 353, 355, 361

Quadrupeds of North America, The (book, 1854-1855), 673
Quigley, Martin, 679

Raack, Richard C., 5, 147, 148, 150, 272n7, 294, 311, 321; and documentary authenticity, 296; historian filmmaker movement, 322-23, 568, 572; and journalistic objectivity, 449; *Vietnam: A Television History*, 387, 436. See also *Storm of Fire*

racism, 142
radical critic, 398697
Rambo film series, 400-401
Ramparts Magazine, 394, 395
Ramparts We Watch, The (film, 1940), 10, 242
Read, Opie, 143
Reagan, Ronald, 248, 545, 548, 561; administration of, 445
Real West, The (film, 1961), 372
Redacted (film, 2007), 398
Red Scare, 256, 269-70
regional literature, 125. *See also under* Rogers, Will
Remarque, Erich Maria, 239, 240
Remember When (HBO, 1981), 373
Renoir, Jean, 241
Ressner, Jeffrey, 544
Return to Life (film, 1937), 691
rhetorical irony, 272-73n9
Richards, I. A., 11, 265, *265*, 270n2
Riefenstahl, Leni, 284, 285
Right Stuff, The (film, 1979), 119-20
Ripley, George, 625
River, The (film, 1937), 20-21, 687, 688, 708; cinematic language of, 686-89, 695; and industrial exploitation, 677; as New Deal film, 678, 686, 687-88, 689-90, 694, 695; and propaganda, 686; reaction to, 685-86; use of sound, 688-89
Roberts, Kenneth, 142
Robinson, Bill (Bo Jangles), 139
Rockefeller, John D., 701
Rockwell, Norman, 70
Rodgers, Richard, 327, 329, 331
Rogers, Betty, 36, 94
Rogers, James (Jim), 94, *153*; and *Will Rogers' 1920s*, 153
Rogers, Mary, 94
Rogers, Will, 1, 3, *30*, 39, 43, *50*, 52,

55, 65, 71, 75, 83, 88, 111, 114, 141, 151, 200, 320; and advertising, 45, 106, 121; and airmail pilots, 113; as America's conscience, 30-31; in Asia, 76-77; and aviation, 105, 108-13, 114-19; and Benito Mussolini, 92, 97, 101; and "bunk," 105-107, 108-13, 121; Cherokee heritage of, 79; Cherokee perspective of, 7; and cowboy imagery, 112, 116-17; as cultural symbol, 6; death of, 4, 29; drought relief tour of, 115; in Europe, 73-74, 77, 87, 88, 91-102; family of, 36, 36-37, 108; film career, 5, 30, 38, 93; film persona, 4, 49-50, 52, 53-61; and film reviewers, 64-65; and film scripts, 125, 135-36, 138-39, 141; film success of, 54, 65; film travelogues of, 72, *93*; and Frank Capra, 282; and Franklin D. Roosevelt, 138; and Great Depression, 45, 48; humanitarianism of, 39-41, 45, 93-94, 114-16; and immigration, 80-82; impact of, 29-30; industrialism, 6, 106; as "Innocent Abroad," 50-52, 53, 54, 65, 72, 89-90, 94-96; internationalism of, 102-103; isolationism of, 74, 77, 97-101, 102; as journalist, 4-5, 30, 43-44, 109, 144; "Jubilo" persona of, 50, 65; lecture tours of, 87; "Letters of a Self-Made Diplomat" series, 72-73, 90-98, 100, 102; in Mexico, 76, 77, 94, 114; in *Midnight Frolic,* 90; as mock presidential candidate, 106, 121; as moralist, 43-46, 48-49; and mutual goodwill, 115-16; as national spokesman, 20, 21, 108, 152; and nativism, 79-80, 84; and New Deal, 82-83; nostalgic style of, 72, 78, 83; persona of, 35-39; "playful" journalism of, 46-49; and preparedness, 97-98; prescience of, 119-20; presidential humor of, 72, 73, 74, 90-91, 151, 152; privacy of, 41-42; and "progress," 33; as public confidant, 90; and racism, 82, 125, 135-36, 139-41, 144; radio broadcasts of, 38, 82-83, 93, *149*; regionalism in films of, 125-26, 131-40, 143; in Russia, 75-76, 77, 91, 92, 112; and *Saturday Evening Post,* 69-77, 89-92; as spokesman for times, 147; as "symbolic man," 4, 6, 65-66; and technology, 46; values of, 5, 36, 41-43, 44, 142-43; and war debts, 96; world travels of, 5; writings of, 4-5, 30, 43, 115; and *Ziegfeld Follies,* 87-88, 90. *See also under titles of his films and books*

Rogers, Will, Jr., *71,* 91, 94, 100, *153;* and *Will Rogers' 1920s,* 153

Rogers-isms: Cowboy Philosopher on the Peace Conference (book, 1919), 88

Rollins, Daniel Gooding, 552

Rollins, Daniel Gooding, Jr., 552

Rollins, Peter C., early career of, 551-52; education of, 3; influences on, 1, 21, 22; Marine Corps career of, *9,* 9-10, 12, 14, 21; and popular culture movement, 3; and Television Writers of America, 451-52; Vietnam booklist of, 452; Vietnam documentaries of, 435, 437, 449, 554-55, 558, 565, 573-74, 576; as Vietnam veteran, 9, 14, 21; *Will Rogers' 1920s,* 147, 148; and *Writings of Will Rogers,*

Index   735

4. See also *Television's Vietnam: The Impact of Media*; *Television's Vietnam: Impact of Visual Images*; *Television's Vietnam: The Real Story*; *Will Rogers' 1920s*; and under Brookline, Mass.
Rollins, Philip Ashton, 552
Roosevelt, Eleanor, 83
Roosevelt, Franklin Delano, 20, 82, 127, 137, *141*, 335, 684-85, 694; New Deal films, 685-86; internationalism of, 102-103; and invasion of Europe, 301; and preparedness, 243; and *Victory at Sea*, 329-30; and *Why We Fight*, 286, 288; and Will Rogers, 31, 90, 147
Roosevelt, Theodore, 551
Ropin' Fool, The (film, 1922), 143
Rosenthal, Abe, 474
Rostow, Walt Whitman, 460, 466, 469, 473, 478-79, *494*; and CBS, 502n1; and enemy strength, 490, 504-505n11; and Tet offensive, 487, 513
Rotha, Paul, 289
Ruler of the Universe, The (book, 1925), 8, 11, 162, 185, 186, 220; and arms race, 178-82; and defense of orthodoxy, 163-65, 168-72, 214; democratic vision of, 165-66; and evolution, 174-75; and "ineffable realities," 166-67; literary approach of, 165; and "lost generation," 175-76; and military-industrial complex, 177-78; motive for, 163; and original sin, 175-76, 225-26; publishers' rejection of, 163, 167; and quantum mechanics, 168; religiosity of, 198; and "uniformitarian" hypothesis, 172-74

Rumor of War, A (film, 1977), 253, 383; and American Adam, 400; and loss of innocence, 258
Rusk, Dean, 294, 557
Russell, Ada, 647-48
Russo, Anthony, 465, 506-507n16

Safer, Morley, 538-39n8
Salant, Frank, 470
Salomon, Henry, 293, 294, 329-30, 332, 340, 348; and freedom theme, 353; historical vision of, 375; *Nightmare in Red*, 361-62, 367, 371; Project 20, 351, 354, 367, 368, 372, 374
Sapir, Edward, 107, *193*; and "American School" of anthropology, 216; and Benjamin Whorf, 189, 194-95, 202, 203, 216, 229; and culture vs. personality, 203-204, 229; and fragmentation of culture, 33-34, 45; humanism of, 7, 8, 198-99, 201, 202, 203; and individual socialization, 204-207; influence of, 183, 216; and intellect and emotion, 200-201, 203; and language, 192, 193-94, 207-209; and language analysis, 196-97, 208-209; and linguistic form, 194-95, 217; and modernism, 199-200, 209; Native American studies of, 8; and primitive cultures, 191; and "The Status of Linguistics as a Science," 194, 196; versatility of, 192; and Whorf hypothesis, 195-98
Sapir-Whorf hypothesis, 189. *See also* Whorf hypothesis
Sarnoff, Robert W., 293, 329, 330, 352; and *Nightmare in Red*, 371; and Project 20, 374

736 Index

Sassoon, Siegfried, 251, 252, 253, 271n4
Saturday Evening Post Magazine, 5, 69, 74, 75, 79, *126*; nativism of, 127, 128-30, 136, 138; racist advertising in, 130-31; and regional literature, 80, 125, 127-29, 141, 143; social views of, 82
Sauter, Van Gordon, 475
Saving Private Ryan (film, 1998), 12
Schandler, Herbert, 477
Schenck, Joseph, 29-30
Schlesinger, Arthur, Jr., 417, 553
Schneider, Bert, 295
Schnurmann, Ned, 445, 484n13
Schwartz, Stephen, 395
Schwarzkopf, Norman, 263
Scopes, John T., 7, 32, 163
Scourby, Alexander, 355, 357, 358
Scowcroft, Brent, 511
Secrets of the Vietnam War (book, 1988), 538n7
Selznick, David O., 356
Senior Scholastic Magazine, 365
Sergeant York (film, 1941), 10, 242, 242-43
Shales, Tom, 480
Shalit, Sid, 363
Sharon, Ariel, 448
Sheehan, Neil, 16-17, *511*, 537n5; funeral of John Paul Vann, 511-13, 514, 530, 532, 536n2; and John Paul Vann, 514, 525, 534-35, 535-36n1; methodology of, 516; and military ineptitude, 521-25; pacification, 537-38n6; *Pentagon Papers*, 511, 529-30, 532; as reporter in Vietnam, 538-39n8; "Sheehan Thesis," 520; and Tet offensive, 538n7. See also *Bright Shining Lie, A: John Paul Vann and America in Vietnam*
Sheen, Charlie, 386
Sherriff, R. C., 260
Shirley, Don, 544
60 Minutes (CBS), 474, 475; adversarial style of, 467
Slaughterhouse-Five (book, 1969; film, 1972), 256, 272n8
Smith, Garret, 143
Smith, Gerald K., 679
Smith, Henry Nash, 348; and America's self-image, 3
Smith, Paul, 323
Smithsonian Institution, 108-109, 121
Sobran, Joseph, 295
Social Darwinism, 551
Society of Television Critics, 561
So This Is London (film, 1930), 51
Spanish Civil War, 704
Spencer, Herbert, 551
"Spirit of the American Doughboy, The" (1920), 237, *237-38*, 243
Splendor in the Grass (film, 1961), 711
Springsteen, Bruce, 543-44
Stalin, Joseph V., *360*, 533, 577. See also *Nightmare in Red*
Standard Oil Company, 701
Stanley, LeRoy, 300, 302, 303, 305
Stanton, Elizabeth C., 592
Stars and Stripes (newspaper), 235
Stars and Stripes and You, The (radio documentary), 272n7
State Fair (book, 1932), 132, 134
State Fair (film, 1933), 53, 66, 132, 141; and New Deal, 133-34; and racism, 82; ruralism of, 133-34, 143
Steamboat Round the Bend (film, 1935), 29, 59, 60, 66; nostalgic image, 31; racist screenplay, 138

Steiner, Ralph, 695; and *The River*, 678
Steinman, Ron, 413
Stevens, George, 712
Stilwell, Richard, 511
Stone, Oliver, 14, 258, 269, 390, 397; combat experience of, 544; *Platoon*, 400. See also Plato
Storm of Fire: World War II and the Destruction of Dresden (film, 1978), 12, 311; bias of, 322; cinematic elements, 316-19, 320; and "historical writing," 315-16
Stowe, Calvin, 593, 594, 595, 596
Stowe, Charles (Charlie), 594; death of, 597, 603, 604, 605
Stowe, Harriet Beecher, 1, 3, 21, 66, 597, 599, 603-604; African-Americans' emotional superiority, 612-13; anti-slavery, 19-20; and Calvinism, 584, 585, 591, 600-602, 611, 613-14; and Christianity, 596; in Cincinnati, 592-94; conversion of, 590-91; and *Corrine*, 592-93; and Episcopalism, 583, 588; and grace of Christian home, 607, 610; illness of, 594; lost childhood, 588-89, 604; marriage, 594-96; parents, 585-86, 587, 591; religious doubt of, 605-607, 609; and repressed women, 612; sacrifices for family, 595, 596; spiritual search of, 19; writings of, 594, 595, 596-98, 614. See also *Uncle Tom's Cabin*
Strand, Paul, 678, 691
Strange Victory (film, 1948), 344-47
Stringer, Howard, 465
Strong, Phil, 132, 134
Stuart, Mel, 373
Students for a Democratic Society (SDS), 394, 395

Sully, Thomas, 660
Sulzberger, A. O., 525
Summers, Harry, 391-92, 444, 537-38n6
Sunnyside (film), 691
Sun Yat Sen, 292
Swayze, John Cameron, 363, 370

Taking Chance (HBO, 2008), 398
Tarkington, Booth, 71, 128
Taxi Driver (film, 1976), 555
Taylor, Maxwell, 459, 466, 518
Taylor, Nathaniel, 583-84
television. See film and television
Television's Vietnam (AIM, 1985-1986), 13-14, 296, 554, 555-56. See also under individual titles
Television's Vietnam: The Impact of Media (AIM, 1986), 13-14, 388-89, 431, 435, 440, 442-43, 559-60, 561-65; Hue Massacre, 574; Khe Sanh, 419-20; and misreporting of the war, 446-47; Tet offensive, 538n7
Television's Vietnam: The Impact of Visual Images (AIM, 1983), 13, 13, 558-59, 562, 563, 565
Television's Vietnam: The Real Story (AIM, 1985), 13, 387-88, 431, 559-61, 564, 565; conclusions of, 439-42; as conference film, 435-36, 441, 449; and film as fact, 573-74; Ho Chi Minh, 536-37n4; Khe Sanh, 419-20; making of, 437; reaction to, 435, 441-47, 561
Television Writers of America, 441-42, 444, 445-46, 450, 451-52
Ten Days That Shook the World (film, 1928), 357, 370
Tet! (book, 1971), 428, 432
Tet offensive, 14, 16, 18, 80, 81, 416-

17, 440, 458-61, 465, 468, 472, 477-79, 502, 555-56, 559, 561-64, 565; and American public opinion, 428-30, 433; and enemy strength, 487, 503n5, 504-505n11; failure of, 414, 430-31; interpretations of, 538n7; misreporting of, 446-47; and television news coverage, 407, 408-15, 430-31; as victory, 513. *See also* Khe Sanh, Battle of

That War in Korea (film, 1963), 372

There's Not a Bathing Suit in Russia, & Other Bare Facts (book, 1927), 75-76, 92

They Had to See Paris (film, 1929), 37, 51, 52; ruralism of, 143

Thomas, Michael, 421

Thomson, Virgil, 687

Thoreau, Henry David, 699-700, 701

Tiede, Tom, 393

Time, Inc., 678, 679, 682; and journalistic objectivity, 680

Time Magazine, 447, 538-39n8; and *Native Land*, 691-92;

Tisch, Lawrence, 480-81

Tito, Josip Broz, 439, 536-37n4

Tolstoy, Leo, 355, 368

Tombs of the Unknown Soldiers, 235-37, *236*, 238, 240, 255, 256, 267

Transcendentalism, 620, 621

Transcendentalist Club (Hedge Club), 19

Transcendental movement, 617, 619, 629. *See also under* Hedge, Frederick Henry

Triumph of the Will (film, 1936), use of music, 320; and *Why We Fight*, 284-85

Trotsky, Leon, 101-102

Trudeau, Gary, 442

Trujillo, Rafael, 679

Truman, Harry, 514 517, 519, 528, 552-53

Truman Doctrine, 552-53

Trumbo, Dalton, 396

Tucker, Howard, 412, 413

Tugwell, Rexford, 685, 686

Tulsa (film, 1949), 699, *700*, 703, *710*; ambivalence of, 702, 704; as America reflected, 712; cinematic elements, 708, 709-10; and exploitation, 20; and industrialism, 700, 710-11; synopsis of, 705-707

Turner, Frederick Jackson, 19-20; frontier thesis of, 701-702, 712

Turner, Ted, 480, 564

TVA: Democracy in Action (book, 1944), 20-21

TV Guide Magazine, 448; and *Dear America*, 544; and *Uncounted Enemy*, 463-64, 466, 467, 474, 482n3, 484n10

TV News and the Dominant Culture (book, 1986), 450-51

Twain, Mark, 89, 94

Twentieth Century, The (CBS, 1957-1961), 294, 372-73

Twentieth Century-Fox Films, 5, 29, 39, 53, 54, 80, 131

Twisted Cross, The (film, 1956), 353, 354, 371

Two Wagons—Both Covered (film, 1923), 132

Tyler, Royall, 66

Tylor, E. B., 183

Uncle Tom's Cabin (book, 1852), 19, 591, 603-605; as critique of Calvinism, 597-603; and felicity of Christian family, 607-11; and

New Christianity, 612-14; and religious doubt, 605-607; serialization of, 596; and women, 611-12; writing of, 596-97
Uncounted Enemy: A Vietnam Deception (film, 1982), 16, 502; bias of, 488; and conspiracy theory, 457, 461-63, 465, 476-78, 482-83n5, 483n7, 487-88, 491, 506-507n16; and language of film, 402; low viewership of, 455, 457, 461; marketing of, 455, 456; methodology of, 457, 464, 484n12; reaction to, 455, 462-64, 481n3, 484n13; synopsis of, 458-61; and William Westmoreland, 382, 389-90, 467-68, 470-73
Unger, Arthur, 445, 446
Unitarianism, 620, 623, 627-29
United Action (film, 1939), 691
Unmaking of a President, The (book, 1977), 477
urbanism, 32
U.S. Film Service, 678
U.S. Intelligence Board (USIB), 498, 500-501

Vann, Jesse, 512, 514
Vann, John Paul, 17, 18, 527; as anti-establishment, 524-25; at Ap Bac, 528-29; criticism of, 533-34; and Daniel Ellsberg, 530-31, 532, 534; and David Halberstam, 525, 535-36n1; death of, 537-38n6; and errors of U.S. strategy, 521, 524; funeral of, 509-11, 512, 513, 514; as military officer, 528; and Neil Sheehan, 525, 534-35, 535-36n1; pacification, 537-38n6; personal life, 512-13, 535-36n1; as quintessential outsider, 527-29, 532-33; symbol of Vietnam, 513; transitional figure, 515
Vann, Mary Jane, 511, 512, 514, 536n2
Vann, Myrtle, 527, 528
Variety Magazine, 448
Venable Mohr, Evelyn, 153-54
Victory at Sea (documentary series), 12, 293-94, 346, 372, 373; chauvinistic tenor of, 333-35; Cold War, 329, 344; as consensus history, 334-35; emotionalism of, 547-48; errors in, 341-44; failures of, 347, 348; framing devices in, 336-37; freedom theme of, 353, 354; impact of, 328-29; making of, 329-30; and "participant-observer," 337-39; reaction to, 327-38, 330-33, 351, 352, 354; use of sound, 319, 338-40
Vidor, King, 234, 684
Vietnam: Anthology and Guide to a Television History (book, 1983), 445, 482
Vietnam: The Heartland Remembers (book, 1987), 385
Vietnam: A History (book, 1983), 436, 443-44, 483n9, 558; balance of, 576; criticism of, 387, 569, 570; and *Vietnam: A Television History*, 569-70, 576
Vietnam: A Television History (film, 1983), 13, 386, 388, 448, 558-59, 560-61, 565; awards for, 436; critique of, 435-41, 443-46, 449, 452; historical errors in, 569-70, 571; Hue Massacre, 574; and language of film, 402; and manipulation of viewer, 570-71; montage in, 477-78; reaction to, 296-97, 387, 451, 481, 571; success of, 387

Vietnam Chronology (journal), 443
Vietnam-Perkasie: A Combat Marine Memoir (book, 1983), 264, 383; and American Adam, 400; and loss of innocence, 258
Vietnam Requiem (HBO), 548
Vietnam Syndrome, 397, 403
Vietnam Veterans Against the War, 414
Vietnam Veterans Leadership Program (VVLP), 541
Vietnam Veterans Memorial, 245, 246, 246-47, 562-63
Vietnam Veterans Memorial Fund, 246, 248
Vietnam War, 256, 551, 553-64; and American Adam, 399-401; and attitudinal shifts, 393-95; and biased consensus, 383; "body counts," 263; "corruption of innocence," 383-84; and compilation technique, 294-95; and enemy strength, 503n6; and film montage, 575-76; and "freezing history," 395; and Hollywood, 555; images and realities of, 17; interpretations of, 11, 18-19; jargon of, 266; and limitations of post-war mindset, 533; lost of innocence, 253-54, 257-58, 271n5; and "lost war" premise, 398-99; media coverage of, 13-17, 442-43, 445; memories of, 246; and parallels to World War II, 267-68; and popular culture, 381-95, 401-403; "Second Thoughts" movement, 394; spectrum of perspectives of, 382-83; veterans of, 392-93; wartime technology, 263-64. *See also* Khe Sanh, Battle of; Tet offensive; *and under film titles*

Vietnam War and American Culture, The (book, 1991), 564
Vietnam Women's Memorial Project, 247, 247-48
Viquesney, Ernest, 10, 237, 238, 243
Virgin Land: The American West as Symbol and Myth (book, 1951), 3, 348
Vital Center, The (book, 1949), 553
Vonnegut, Kurt, 272n8

Walden (book, 1854), 699
Walker (film, 1988), 397
Wallace, Henry, 684, 685
Wallace, Mike, 19, 390, *473*; and George Crile, 465-66; and *Uncounted Enemy*, 15-16, 457, 459, 460, 469, 473-77, 487; William Westmoreland interview, 458, 473, 474, 476-77; William Westmoreland lawsuit, 481-82n2
Wall Street Journal, 448
Wanger, Walter, 702-704
Ward, Henry, 596
Ward, Henry, Jr., 589
Ward, John William, 3
Ware, Henry, Jr., 620
Warner Bros., 242, 243
Washington Post, 450
Wayne, John, 401
Weaver, Sylvester (Pat), 371
Webb, James, 381-84; and *Fields of Fire*, 399
Webster, Don, 417-19
Wellman, William, 234
Wescott, Edward Noyes, 136-37
Wesley, T. Perry, 238
Westmoreland, William C., 15, *389*, 416, 478, 514; in defense of, 382; and enemy strength, 466, 471-73, 488, 491, 492, 496, 498-99, 500, 501, 503n5, 504n10, 505-

506n13; and *Hearts and Minds*, 402; John Paul Vann funeral, 509; Khe Sanh, 417, 420, 427; lawsuit against CBS, 16, 448, 456-57, 466, 481-82n2, 482n4, 489, 491, 502n1, 506-507n16; military leadership of, 528; military strategy of, 17, 521-22, 531-34, 527-38n6; and Order of Battle, 459-60, 480, 482-83n5; pacification, 537-38n6; rebuttal of *Uncounted Enemy*, 488-89; Tet offensive, 417, 430-31, 513; and *Uncounted Enemy*, 16, 402, 455-56, 457-58, 459-60, 461, 462-63, 467-68, 470-73, 476, 481, 482n3; and Vietnam legacy, 14-15

We Were Soldiers (film, 2002), 392

Weyand, Frederick, 515

WGBH-Boston, 14-15, 296, 446, 561; and *Vietnam: A Television History*, 17, 398, 437-38, 439-43, 445, 447-48, 558-59, 565, 569-71, 574

Wheeler, Earle, 490-91, 495, 505-506n13

White, Walter, 705, 707, 711, 712

Whitman, Walt, 367, 370

Whittier, Paul, 118

Who'll Stop the Rain (film, 1978), 555

Whorf, Benjamin Lee, 1, 3, 159, *160*, 215; and anthropology, 216; *Collected Papers on Metalinguistics*, 161-62; criticism of, 162; and "crisis of modern physics," 220-21, 222; and cultural humility, 21; defense of orthodoxy, 163, 168-72; "Language, Mind, and Reality," 162, 228, 229; "Languages and Logic," 227, 229; and linguistic "crypotypes," 202, 217, 218, 220; and linguistic relativity, 6-7, 8-9, 160-61, 183-85, 195, 204, 205-206, 220; "Linguistics as an Exact Science," 160, 227, 229; and military-industrial complex, 177-78; and mysticism, 216; Native American studies of, 7, 8, 162, 184, 207, 217, 218, 222-25, 226-27; "Outline of the History of Linguistics," 195; and primitive cultures, 191; reification, 219-20; religiosity of, 7, 8, 21, 201-202; "Science and Linguistics," 159, 227, 229; and Standard Average European (SAE) languages, 8, 218-19, 220, 222-23, 226; supernaturalism, 164-65, 172, 174; *Technology Review*, 228, 229; *Theosophist*, 229; and Theosophy, 213-14, 224, 225, 229; and Transcendentalism, 166, 228-29; writings of, 8, 161, 183. See also *Ruler of the Universe, The*

Whorf hypothesis, 159-60, 162, 195, 196, 197-98, 202-203, 209, 227-28

Why Vietnam (film, 1965), 295, 296

Why We Fight (film series, 1942-1945), 282, 283; and American spirit, 296; and anti-Semitism, 287; appeal of, 289; and Axis aggression, 287; *The Battle of Britain* (P-4), 288, 292; *The Battle of China* (P-6), 287, 292-93; *The Battle of Russia* (P-5), 288, 292; and compilation films, 293; and democracies as reluctant warriors, 287-88; *Divide and Conquer* (P-3), 286, 288, 292; and German racial superiority, 286-87; goals of, 285; impact of, 288-89, 290-91, 293, 297; importance of, 279; and Nazi repression, 286; *The*

Nazis Strike (P-2), 285-86, 291; and Office of War Information, 286-87, 288, 296; as persuasion, 575; *Prelude to War* (P-1), 285, 286, 288, 291; as propaganda, 330; treatment of children in, 288; vitriol of, 294; *War Comes to America* (P-7), 285, 288
Wiley, Hugh, 142; racist writings of, 129-30
Wilkins, James, 658
Wilkinson, James B., 558
Williams, Ben Ames, 70, 71, 128, 141
Will Rogers Memorial and Museum, 5, 6, 147, *148*, 155; archival resources of, 149-50, 152, 153
Will Rogers' 1920s: A Cowboy's Guide to the Times (film, 1976), 5-6; awards for, 311; bias of, 322; cinematic elements, 316, 317, 318, 320; and evolution of cowboy persona, 150; historical authenticity of, 313; impact of, 154-55; making of, 147-54; music in, 150; script for, 152; as structured film, 313-14; workbook for, 154-55
Will Rogers Publication Project, 147
Will Rogers Story, The (film, 1952), 48
Wills, Chill, 708, 709
Wilson, Alexander, 655, 658, 660, 674
Wilson, Charles E., 362
Wilson, Woodrow, 72, 97, 100, 241, 515; and Ho Chi Minh, 519; and military intervention, 267; and self-determination, 99; and Will Rogers, 90, 151; World War I, 97, 243, 255, 258, 259
Wings (film, 1927), 10, 234-35
Winston Churchill: The Valiant Years (ABC, 1960), 373
Workers Film and Photo League, 690-91. See also *Native Land*
Workers International Relief Organization, 690. See also *Native Land*
Wolfe, Tom, 119-20
Wolf Lake (film, 1978), 555
Woods, Walter, 137, 138
World Court, 97, 98
World War I (Great War), and Battle of the Somme, 252, *260*, 260, 270, 271n4; as heroic crusade, 233-38, 242-43, 244; legacy of, 10-11; "lost generation," 239-41; memories of, 233; and post-war realities, 52; recriminations after, 264-65; and telluric continuities, 251, 254, 270; as traumatic nightmare, 233-34, 238-41, 244, 252; veterans of, 233, 2453-44; and wartime technology, 262. See also under film and book titles
World War II, as amoral power play, 306; images and realities of, 11-12; naval operations during, 328; Vietnam compared to, 563; as virtuous war, 299. See also D Day and under film and book titles
Worley, Eugene, 686
Wright brothers, 108-109, 121
Writings of Will Rogers, The (book series, 1973-1983), 3-4, 147
Wyler, William, 288

Yen Bay rebellion, 439, 443
Ying Lin, Maya, 246, 248
Young, Stephen, 438
Young Socialist League, 14, 558
York, Alvin, 242-43

Ziegfeld, Flo, 72, 87-88
Ziegfeld Follies, 49, 50, 52, 87-88, 93. See also under Rogers, Will
Zigman, Joe, 465, 466